An Anthology of Philosophy in Persia

Previously published volumes of *An Anthology of Philosophy in Persia:*

Volume 1: From Zoroaster to ʿUmar Khayyām
Volume 2: Ismaili Thought in the Classical Age
Volume 3: Philosophical Theology in the Middle Ages and Beyond

An Anthology of Philosophy in Persia

VOLUME 4

From the School of Illumination to Philosophical Mysticism

SEYYED HOSSEIN NASR

and

MEHDI AMINRAZAVI

I.B.Tauris *Publishers*
LONDON • NEW YORK
in association with
The Institute of Ismaili Studies
LONDON

Published in 2012 by I.B.Tauris & Co Ltd
6 Salem Rd, London W2 4BU
175 Fifth Avenue, New York NY 10010
www.ibtauris.com

in association with The Institute of Ismaili Studies
210 Euston Road, London NW1 2DA
www.iis.ac.uk

In the United States of America and in Canada distributed by
St Martin's Press, 175 Fifth Avenue, New York NY 10010

ISBN 978 1 84885 749 0

A full CIP record for this book is available from the British Library
A full CIP record for this book is available from the Library of Congress

Library of Congress catalog card: available

Typeset in Minion Tra for The Institute of Ismaili Studies
Persian poem typeset in Nastaliq designed by Mirjam Somers of DecoType
Printed and bound in Great Britain by T. J. International Ltd, Padstow, Cornwall

FSC www.fsc.org MIX Paper from responsible sources FSC® C013056

The Institute of Ismaili Studies

The Institute of Ismaili Studies was established in 1977 with the object of promoting scholarship and learning on Islam, in the historical as well as contemporary contexts, and a better understanding of its relationship with other societies and faiths.

The Institute's programmes encourage a perspective which is not confined to the theological and religious heritage of Islam, but seeks to explore the relationship of religious ideas to broader dimensions of society and culture. The programmes thus encourage an interdisciplinary approach to the materials of Islamic history and thought. Particular attention is also given to issues of modernity that arise as Muslims seek to relate their heritage to the contemporary situation.

Within the Islamic tradition, the Institute's programmes promote research on those areas which have, to date, received relatively little attention from scholars. These include the intellectual and literary expressions of Shiʿism in general, and Ismailism in particular.

In the context of Islamic societies, the Institute's programmes are informed by the full range and diversity of cultures in which Islam is practised today, from the Middle East, South and Central Asia, and Africa to the industrialized societies of the West, thus taking into consideration the variety of contexts which shape the ideals, beliefs and practices of the faith.

These objectives are realized through concrete programmes and activities organized and implemented by various departments of the Institute. The Institute also collaborates periodically, on a programme-specific basis, with other institutions of learning in the United Kingdom and abroad.

The Institute's academic publications fall into a number of interrelated categories:

1. Occasional papers or essays addressing broad themes of the relationship between religion and society, with special reference to Islam.
2. Monographs exploring specific aspects of Islamic faith and culture, or the contributions of individual Muslim thinkers or writers.
3. Editions or translations of significant primary or secondary texts.
4. Translations of poetic or literary texts which illustrate the rich heritage of spiritual, devotional and symbolic expressions in Muslim history.
5. Works on Ismaili history and thought, and the relationship of the Ismailis to other traditions, communities and schools of thought in Islam.
6. Proceedings of conferences and seminars sponsored by the Institute.
7. Bibliographical works and catalogues which document manuscripts, printed texts and other source materials.

This book falls into category two listed above.

In facilitating these and other publications, the Institute's sole aim is to encourage original research and analysis of relevant issues. While every effort is made to ensure that the publications are of a high academic standard, there is naturally bound to be a diversity of views, ideas and interpretations. As such, the opinions expressed in these publications must be understood as belonging to their authors alone.

نخست از فکر خویشم در تحیّر   چه چیز است آنکه گویندش تفکّر

تفکّر رفتن از باطل سوی حق   به جزو اندر بدیدن کلّ مطلق

رهی دور و دراز است این رها کن   چو موسی یک زمان ترک عصا کن

زهی نادان که او خورشید تابان   به نور شمع جوید در بیابان

First, I wonder about thought,
what is it that is called thinking?
Thinking is going from the false towards the true,
seeing in the particular the absolute universal.
This is a long and arduous path, let it go,
and like Moses, cast away in an instant thy staff.
Hail, many a fool there is who seeks the shining sun
with the light of a candle in the middle of the desert.

Maḥmūd Shabistarī

Contents

List of Reprinted Works

Ghazzālī, Abū Ḥāmid Muḥammad. *Mishkāt al-anwār*, tr. David Buchman as *The Niche of Lights*. Provo, UT, 1998.

Ghazzālī, Abū Ḥāmid Muḥammad. 'al-Risālat al-laduniyyah', tr. Margaret Smith, in *JRAS* (1938).

Jāmī, 'Abd al-Raḥmān. *al-Durrah al-fākhirah*, tr. Nicholar Heer, together with glosses and the commentary of 'Abd al-Ghafūr Lārī, as *The Precious Pearl*. New York, NY, 1979.

Kāshānī, Afḍal al-Dīn ('Bābā Afḍal'). *Muṣannafāt*, tr. William C. Chittick in *The Heart of Islamic Philosophy: The Quest for Self-Knowledge in the Teachings of Afḍal al-Dīn Kāshānī*. Oxford and New York, 2001.

Suhrawardī, Shihāb al-Dīn. *Ḥikmat al-ishrāq*, tr. John Walbridge and Hossein Ziai as *The Philosophy of Illumination*. Provo, UT, 1999.

Ṭūsī, Naṣīr al-Dīn. *Risālah andar qismat-i mawjūdāt*, tr. Parviz Morewedge as *The Metaphysics of Ṭūsī: On the Division of Existents*. New York, NY, 1992.

Note on Transliteration

Arabic characters	
ء	ʾ
ب	b
ت	t
ث	*th*
ج	j
ح	ḥ
خ	*kh*
د	d
ذ	*dh*
ر	r
ز	z
س	s
ش	*sh*
ص	ṣ
ض	ḍ
ط	ṭ
ظ	ẓ
ع	ʿ
غ	*gh*
ف	f
ق	q
ك	k
ل	l
م	m
ن	n
ه	h
و	w
ی	y
ة	ah; at (construct state)

long vowels	
ا	ā
و	ū
ي	ī
short vowels	
ـَ	a
ـُ	u
ـِ	i
diphthongs	
ـَو	aw
ـَی	ai (ay)
ـيّ	ayy (final form ī)
ـوّ	uww (final form ū)

Persian letters added to the Arabic alphabet	
پ	p
چ	*ch*
ژ	*zh*
گ	g

List of Contributors*

SEYYED HOSSEIN NASR received his early education in Iran and completed his studies at The Massachusetts Institute of Technology and Harvard University from which he received his doctorate. Nasr is the author of over five hundred articles and fifty books. He has taught at a number of universities, both in the Middle East, especially Tehran University, and in the United States; and he has lectured widely on Islamic philosophy, science and Sufism. Nasr is currently the University Professor of Islamic Studies at The George Washington University.

MEHDI AMINRAZAVI received his early education in Iran and completed his master's degree in philosophy at the University of Washington and his doctorate in philosophy of religion at Temple University. He is the author and editor of numerous articles and books including *Suhrawardī and the School of Illumination; Philosophy, Religion and the Question of Intolerance; The Wine of Wisdom: Life, Poetry and Philosophy of Omar Khayyām.* He is currently Professor of Philosophy and Religion, Director of the Middle Eastern Studies program and Co-Director of the Leidecker Center for Asian Studies at the University of Mary Washington.

MOHAMMAD REZA JOZI is a scholar of Islamic mysticism and philosophy. He has previously taught courses on Islamic philosophy and philosophy of art at Tehran University and the Free University of Iran and is currently affiliated to The Institute of Ismaili Studies.

WILLIAM CHITTICK completed his undergraduate degree at the College of Wooster in Ohio and his Ph.D. at Tehran University. He specializes in Islamic intellectual history, especially the philosophical and mystical theology of the twelfth and thirteenth centuries as reflected in Arabic and Persian texts. He is Professor of Religious Studies at the State University of New York at Stony Brook and has also taught at Aryamehr University and Beijing University. His numerous publications include

The Self-Disclosure of God; Principles of Ibn 'Arabī's Cosmology; Faith and Practice in Islam; and *The Sufi Path of Love: The Teachings of Rūmī.*

CARL W. ERNST studied comparative religion at Stanford University and Harvard University. He is a specialist in Islamic studies, with a focus on West and South Asia. Among his publications are *Following Muhammad: Rethinking Islam in the Contemporary World; Teachings of Sufism; Eternal Garden: Mysticism, History, and Politics at a South Asian Sufi Center*; and *Words of Ecstasy in Sufism*. He is currently William R. Kenan Jr. Distinguished Professor of Religious Studies in the Department of Religious Studies at The University of North Carolina at Chapel Hill.

MOHAMMAD H. FAGHFOORY completed his graduate work at the University of Wisconsin-Madison. He has taught at Tehran University, University of Mary Washington and The George Washington University. A specialist on Islamic intellectual history, he has published extensively on Sufism. Among his major works are *Dastūr al-mulūk* and *Kernel of the Kernel*. He is currently teaching in the Department of Religious Studies at The George Washington University.

MAJID FAKHRY studied Islamic philosophy at the American University of Beirut and the University of Edinburgh. He is the author of numerous articles and books, including *History of Islamic Philosophy*. He is currently Emeritus Professor of Philosophy from the American University of Beirut and a research scholar at Georgetown University.

ALMA GIESE completed her degrees in Islamic studies at Freiburg and Giessen Universities. She has published several works on Islamic philosophy and theology, and is an independent research scholar.

NICHOLAS HEER received his B.A. from Yale University and his Ph.D. from Princeton University. He has taught at Stanford University, Yale University and Harvard University. From 1965 until his retirement he was Professor of Arabic at the University of Washington. His publications include an Arabic edition of 'Abd al-Raḥmān al-Jāmī's *al-Durrah al-fākhirah*, and an English translation of the same work published under the title *The Precious Pearl.*

IBRAHIM KALIN studied in Turkey and Malaysia and received his Ph.D. from The George Washington University. His areas of specialization are Islamic philosophy and theology, Sufism, Islam and the West, and Islam in the modern world. Author of many books and articles including *Knowledge in Later Islamic Philosophy*, he is associate editor of Resources on Islam and Science, a web-based project of the Center for Islam and Science. Formerly a professor in the Department of Religious

Studies at Holy Cross College and Georgetown University, he is now Senior Advisor to the Prime Minister of Turkey.

JOSEPH LUMBARD studied at The George Washington University and completed his graduate work at Yale University. His areas of specialization are Sufism, philosophical Sufism and Islamic intellectual thought with a focus on the brothers Aḥmad and Abū Ḥāmid Ghazzālī. He is currently Assistant Professor of Islamic Studies at Brandeis University.

LATIMAH-PARVIN PEERWANI was educated at the American University of Beirut and Tehran University and has taught at The Institute of Ismaili Studies in London and at the Pontifical Institute of Islamic Studies in Rome. Her main areas of research and publications are Shiʿi and Ismaili philosophy and Sufism.

OMID SAFI completed his undergraduate and graduate work at Duke University. His areas of specialization and interest are Islamic mysticism, contemporary Islamic thought, Islamic mysticism and mystical poetry. Among his publications are *Progressive Muslims: On Justice, Gender, and Pluralism* and *Islam and the Politics of Knowledge: Political Loyalty and Religious Orthodoxy in Pre-modern Islam*. The author of numerous articles and recipient of many awards, he is currently Assistant Professor of Philosophy and Religion at The University of North Carolina.

*Contributors mentioned here are the editors and those who have translated new material for this volume. The names of those whose translations have already appeared elsewhere and of which we have made use appears in the List of Reprinted Works.

General Introduction

This fourth volume of *An Anthology of Philosophy in Persia* deals with one of the richest, most complex and yet least-known periods of philosophical life in Persia. It encompasses the period between the seventh/thirteenth century which saw the eclipse of the School of Khurāsān, and the tenth/sixteenth century coinciding with the rise of the Safavids. It is a period whose extensive philosophical activity proves false the still widely-held view that Islamic philosophy came to an end with Ibn Rushd. Since our treatment of the subject of philosophy in all the volumes of this *Anthology* has been according to schools as well as chronological periods, in the present volume we have sought to keep to this method, but with two major exceptions in our dealing with philosophy in Persia from the seventh/thirteenth to the tenth/sixteenth century. The first is that the *ishrāqī* tradition in this volume is treated in its wholeness as a continuous one stretching into the Qājār period. The second is that because of the already extensive nature of this volume, the School of Shiraz, which flowered during the period treated in this work, will be included in volume five rather than here, except for those of its figures who are central to the history of the School of Illumination or *ishrāq*, namely, Quṭb al-Dīn Shīrāzī and Jalāl al-Dīn Dawānī.

Unfortunately, even this compromise is not perfect because there are other members of the School of Shiraz such as Ghiyāth al-Dīn Manṣūr Dashtakī, who also wrote important *ishrāqī* works but who are treated not here but in volume five because we feel that they were central figures of the School of Shiraz and should be dealt with there rather than as part of the School of *ishrāq* where they also belong. Also, the coming together of various schools of thought in the period treated in this volume has made such omissions and/or overlaps unavoidable since a thinker often belongs to more than one school.

In any case with the coming of the Mongol invasion the history of Islamic philosophy in Persia enters a new chapter. With the great seats of learning in Khurāsān destroyed to a large extent as a result of the Invasion, the centre of philosophical activity shifts for several decades from the middle to the end of the seventh/thirteenth century to western Persia to the extent that one can speak of the School of Azarbaijan including the circle of Marāghah succeeding the School of Khurāsān as the centre of philosophical activity in Persia. It is here that such figures as Naṣīr al-Dīn Ṭūsī, Quṭb al-Dīn Shīrāzī, Dabīrān-i Kātibī, Athīr al-Dīn Abharī and many others taught or studied.

The origin of the School of Azarbaijan can in fact be traced to a century earlier and the appearance of Suhrawardī who was born and studied in the province of Azarbaijan before coming to Isfahan. Also the recent discovery of two major collections of philosophical treatises, the *Majmūʿa-yi falsafī-yi Marāghah* (The Philosophical Collection of Marāghah) and *Safīna-yi Tabrīz* (The Ship of Tabriz) which were probably used as texts in the schools of Azarbaijan wherever philosophy was taught, attest to the continued interest in Suhrawardī in that region and also to a very active philosophical life during the seventh/thirteenth century. Furthermore, philosophical treatises appear in these collections by philosophers hitherto unknown. In any case the presence of Naṣīr al-Dīn Ṭūsī in Marāghah and the establishment of a major intellectual circle in which philosophy was also taught mark a major revival of Islamic philosophy centred in Azarbaijan. Of course that does not mean that there was no philosophical activity elsewhere in Persia at that time as we see in the notable figures of Afḍal al-Dīn Kāshānī and Quṭb al-Dīn Rāzī. But the primary centre in the seventh/thirteenth century remained Azarbaijan.

It was at the end of this period that the main locus of philosophical activity shifted to Shiraz and its environs and the School of Shiraz became established. The main link between these two schools may be said to be Quṭb al-Dīn Shīrāzī who hailed from Shiraz but who was active in Marāghah. And the School of Shiraz itself was the major source and primary background for the School of Isfahan and the revival of Islamic philosophy in the hands of Mīr Dāmād and Mullā Ṣadrā.

One of the essential characteristics of philosophical activity in Persia from the later part of the seventh/thirteenth onward is the coming together and synthesis of various schools of thought that had remained completely distinct and separate in earlier Islamic history. It is true that Fārābī and Ibn Sīnā were interested in Sufism but they did not combine *mashshāʾī* philosophy and Sufism in a synthesis and a single vision of the nature of things. The fact that *mashshāʾī* philosophy itself is a synthesis of Neoplatonism, Aristotelianism and Islamic teachings is another matter and does not change the gist of our argument here. The *Fuṣūṣ al-ḥikmah* (Bezels of Wisdom) attributed to Fārābī is a gnostic work but it does not combine Peripatetic philosophy and gnosis in a new synthesis. As for Ibn Sīnā's *Kitāb al-Ishārāt wa'l-tanbīhāt* (The Book of Directives and Remarks), the last chapters deal openly with *ʿirfān*, but they are not integrated with the *mashshāʾī* teachings of the earlier chapters. If anything, Ibn Sīnā considered his 'Oriental philosophy' (*al-ḥikmah al-mashriqiyyah*), which we dealt with in the first volume of this *Anthology*, as being the philosophy for the 'elite' (*khawāṣṣ*), but he did not try to synthesize it with his Peripatetic teachings in a single work. Rather, he kept fully faithful to the general principle of the Islamic intellectual sciences of earlier Islamic history that one should respect the integrity of each science and school of philosophy, its methodology and rules and should avoid the 'sin' of 'mixing methods of discussion' (*khalṭ al-mabḥath*). One sees outstanding examples of this approach in such figures as Fārābī and Naṣīr al-Dīn Ṭūsī who were masters of several sciences and intellectual perspectives and wrote major works from the point of view of each science and perspective without seeking to combine them into a single vision. For example, Ṭūsī wrote the major work on Twelve-Imam Shiʿi *kalām*, the *Kitāb al-Tajrīd* (The Book of Catharsis), revived Peripatetic philosophy in his *Sharḥ al-ishārāt* (of Ibn Sīnā), composed major works on Ismaili philosophy discussed in the second volume of this *Anthology* as well as a beautiful treatise on Sufi ethics called *Awṣāf al-ashrāf* (Characteristics of the Noble) without mixing these various schools together. His work on Sufism does not discuss Peripatetic philosophy; nor do his works on Ismailism deal with Twelve-Imam Shiʿi *kalām*, or Ibn Sīnā.

Ṭūsī was, however, at the cusp in the arc of Islamic philosophy as far as this issue is concerned. Although he knew *ishrāqī* teachings well, and according to some scholars even taught the *Ḥikmat al-ishrāq* (The Theosophy of the Orient of Light) in Marāghah, he remained completely within the matrix of Ibn Sīnā's thought while commenting upon his *Ishārāt*. Of course Ṭūsī also commented on the last part of the *Ishārāt* dealing with *ʿirfān* as we shall see in this *Anthology*, but he did so to remain faithful to Ibn Sīnā's text. He did not seek to create a new synthesis as we see in the writings of Quṭb al-Dīn Shīrāzī, Ṣā'in al-Dīn ibn Turkah Iṣfahānī or of course Mullā Ṣadrā. But there is an exception when, in his commentary in writing of God's knowledge of His creation, Ṭūsī accepts Suhrawardī's rather than Ibn Sīnā's view and places this *ishrāqī* view in the context of his understanding of Avicennan philosophy. This exception gives an inkling of what was soon to become characteristic of the philosophical scene in Persia and through the influence of Persian philosophers in Ottoman Turkey and India, namely, an attempt to synthesize various intellectual perspectives. Already Tusī's colleague and friend in Marāghah, Quṭb al-Dīn Shīrāzī, who like Ṭūsī was an important scientist, had written the philosophical encyclopedia *Durrat al-tāj* (Pearl of the Crown) selections of which appear below, as a work which can be called an *ishrāqī* interpretation of Avicennan philosophy. Afḍal al-Dīn Kāshānī combined Peripatetic philosophy and Sufism; Dawānī, Peripatetic philosophy, the doctrine of *ishrāq* and *kalām*; and one could go on with many other examples. In fact as we shall see in volume five of the *Anthology*, the major figures of the School of Shiraz, such as Ṣadr al-Dīn Dashtakī, his son Ghiyāth al-Dīn Manṣūr Dashtakī and Shams al-Dīn Khafrī were all synthesizers of various philosophical, gnostic and theological schools and perspectives who prepared the ground for the grand synthesis of the School of Isfahan, especially in the 'transcendent theosophy' (*al-ḥikmah al-muta'āliyah*) of Ṣadr al-Dīn Shīrāzī.

The schools of thought which were very active and which are of particular importance during the period from the seventh/thirteenth to tenth/sixteenth century are, the Peripatetic (*mashshā'ī*) School, the School of *ishrāq*, the various forms of philosophical and doctorial Sufism especially the School of Ibn 'Arabī, and *kalām* in both its Sunni and Shi'i forms that we dealt with in volume three of this *Anthology*.

Let us consider briefly the state of each of these schools in or after the seventh/thirteenth century. By the seventh/thirteenth century, the *mashshā'ī* School in Spain had already become more or less defunct and that in the East was eclipsed as the result of attacks made against it by scholars of *kalām* with whom we have already dealt. But the school had not died out completely in Khurāsān and was revived in a remarkable fashion by Naṣīr al-Dīn Ṭūsī. Henceforth it continued as a living and powerful philosophical tradition over the centuries that followed although often interpreted in an *ishrāqī* manner.

The School of Illumination or *ishrāq* had been founded a century earlier by Suhrawardī who hailed from the western region of Persia although he died in Aleppo. Because of his violent death, his followers went underground for a few decades but his teachings came out fully in the open in the seventh/thirteenth century when Shams al-Dīn Muḥammad Shahrazūrī and Quṭb al-Dīn Shīrāzī wrote very influential commentaries upon the masterpiece of Shaykh al-Ishrāq, the *Ḥikmat al-ishrāq*. Henceforth the School of *ishrāq* became a powerful and widely popular philosophical perspective that attracted many major thinkers not only in Persia, but also in India and the Ottoman world. The period of the flowering of the School of *ishrāq*, is, therefore, the seventh/thirteenth century.

Doctrinal and philosophical Sufism also flowered fully in the seventh/thirteenth century with Ibn 'Arabī and the dissemination of his teachings in the East especially by his student Ṣadr al-Dīn Qūnawī. There is little doubt, however, that the beginning of philosophical and doctrinal Sufism goes back a century earlier to Abū Ḥāmid Muḥammad Ghazzālī, his brother Aḥmad and 'Ayn al-Quḍāt Hamadānī. And yet it was in the seventh/thirteenth century that the appearance of the works of Ibn 'Arabī and his school began to provide a vast and diversified source for philosophical thought. From this period onward, on the one hand many gnostics (*'urafā'*) wrote works that possessed a philosophical dimension—although *falsafah* and *'irfān* have always remained distinct disciplines—and on the other, many philosophers turned to the study of *'irfānī* or gnostic texts. In this domain the presence of the School of *ishrāq* also played a very important role. In any case this period is among the richest in the development of what one can call philosophical Sufism as well as mystical philosophy throughout many parts of the Islamic world and especially in Persia.

As for *kalām*, it is necessary to repeat briefly what was discussed more fully in volume three of our *Anthology*. In the seventh/thirteenth century there appears the seminal work of Ṭūsī on Shiʿi *kalām*, the *Kitāb al-Tajrīd*, which is itself quite philosophical and becomes later the subject of numerous philosophical commentaries. Also it is in the eighth/fourteenth and ninth/fifteenth centuries that the earlier Sunni philosophical *kalām* of men such as Ghazzālī reaches its peak with such figures as Jurjānī, Ījī, Dawānī and Taftāzānī. Although a number of these figures were against *falsafah*, some of their views nevertheless became the subject of philosophical discussion as we see in many of the philosophical texts of later schools of philosophy in Persia.

In any case to understand the philosophical life of the period treated in this volume, one must keep in mind that all these schools were very much alive at that time. Moreover, various thinkers sought to combine them to create different types of synthesis of their teachings. Some like Dawānī sought to combine Peripatetic philosophy and *kalām* while being also an *ishrāqī*; some like Āmulī sought to combine Shiʿi *kalām* with gnosis and Ibn ʿArabian doctrines in particular; and some like Ibn Turkah sought to combine *mashshāʾī, ishrāqī* and *ʿirfānī* teachings, preparing the ground, as did some of the figures of the School of Shiraz, for Mullā Ṣadrā.

A point of great interest, as far as the subject of this volume and also part of volume five dealing with the School of Shiraz is concerned, is that during the period between the seventh/thirteenth century and the tenth/sixteenth century, many of the greatest Persian philosophers, even those interested in Sufi or Illuminative doctrines or *kalām*, were also notable scientists. One need only recall the names of Naṣīr al-Dīn Ṭūsī and Quṭb al-Dīn Shīrāzī, known as two of the greatest scientists of Islamic history, but one must also remember in this context the names of Ṣadr al-Dīn and Ghiyāth al-Dīn Manṣūr Dashtakī and Shams al-Dīn Khafrī, whose scientific works have not been fully studied until now, but who were nevertheless outstanding scientists. In Persia today Khafrī is known primarily as an acute commentator upon the *Tajrīd* of Ṭūsī, but his commentary upon Ṭūsī's astronomical work the *Tadhkirah* (Treasury of Astronomy) is perhaps even more remarkable, revealing him to be a major astronomer. In fact the recent discovery of him as an outstanding astronomer by Professor George Saliba completely changes the prevailing view of the history of Islamic science during later centuries.

One needs therefore to mention that the period under consideration here is also of great importance for the history of Islamic science and the interaction between theology, metaphysics, philosophy and science in later Islamic civilization. Unfortunately this period is also one in which the least amount of scholarly work in both philosophy and science has been carried out. Many major works remain in manuscript form and need to be critically edited and published. Many others have appeared in printed form but have never been seriously analysed and studied. For this very reason the present volume cannot be any more than a depiction of the general contour of the peaks of the philosophical landscape of this period. The more detailed picture of this landscape has to await further monographic study. But even this tour of the general characteristics of the philosophical landscape reveals remarkable richness and diversity in the least-known period of the intellectual history of Persia during the Islamic era.

In this volume, three major philosophical schools, each of which we shall deal with more specifically later, are discussed in the following order: the school of *ishrāq*, the revived school of *mashshā'ī* philosophy and philosophical Sufism, as well as of necessity some of their interactions. These schools are the most important of this period in the tradition of philosophy in Persia. Furthermore, the only major arena of philosophical activity, which was deeply influenced by all three schools, is the School of Shiraz, which, as mentioned already, will be treated in the fifth volume of this *Anthology* only for practical considerations, seeing how extensive the present volume has become. Otherwise, that School could have been included here where it really belongs.

The school of *ishrāq* began in the sixth/twelfth century with Suhrawardī, but as already mentioned, because of the tragic events surrounding his death, it flowered exactly at the time when the other two schools included in this volume began to flourish. The school of *ishrāq* transformed the philosophical landscape in all of the eastern lands of the Islamic world including not only Persia, but also Muslim India and Ottoman Turkey. It found numerous followers from Ankara and Kaysari to Lucknow but the centre of its flowering and later development remained in Persia, although Suhrawardī spent the last part of his life in Syria. Although in many ways related to Sufism, Suhrawardī himself having been initiated into Sufism as a young man, the school of *ishrāq* is not simply a form of philosophical Sufism but a distinct school of philosophy which is also a 'theosophy' in the original sense of this term. As shall be seen later, it has its own distinct philosophical features and technical vocabulary and this philosophy was both a challenge to *mashshā'ī* philosophy and in certain ways its complement. In any case the School of *ishrāq* is definitely a new and distinct Islamic philosophical school that has preserved its life in Persia up to the contemporary period. It must not be confused with the School of *'irfān* or what is often called philosophical Sufism.

The flowering of *ishrāq*, as mentioned already, coincided almost exactly with the revival of Islamic *mashshā'ī* philosophy and more particularly its Avicennan interpretation at the hand of Naṣīr al-Dīn Ṭūsī. As demonstrated fully in volume three of this *Anthology*, the Ash'arite School of *kalām* set out to criticize the *mashshā'ī* School and such major figures as Ghazzālī, Fakhr al-Dīn Rāzī and Shahrastānī (who was also inspired by Ismaili philosophy) caused the eclipse of Avicennan teachings in Persia in the sixth/twelfth and early seventh/thirteenth centuries. During this period *mashshā'ī* philosophy thrived in Andalusia and one of the foremost philosophers of that land, Ibn Rushd or Averroes, set out to respond to Ghazzālī's attack upon the philosophers, especially in the latter's *Tahāfut al-falāsifah* (Incoherence of the Philosophers) by writing a rebuttal to this work entitled *Tahāfut al-tahāfut* (Incoherence of the Incoherence). In this work the specific theses of Ghazzālī were criticized point by point but strangely this work did not exercise any notable influence in Persia where Naṣīr al-Dīn Ṭūsī was to succeed in the task of responding to the attacks of the *mutakallimūn* in a different manner.

Ṭūsī achieved his goal of reviving Ibn Sīnā in several works of which the most significant and most influential is his commentary on *al-Ishārāt wa'l-tanbīhāt* of the latter. Here Ṭūsī followed a method very distinct from that of Averroes. Rather than answering the attacks of the opponents of *mashshā'ī* philosophy point by point, as Averroes had done, Ṭūsī chose the most learned commentary by any figure among the earlier *mutakallimūn* upon a *mashshā'ī* text and then set out to comment in turn upon that commentary. Among the *mutakallimūn* of the earlier centuries preceding Ṭūsī perhaps none had been as familiar with the works of Ibn Sīnā, the master of the eastern *mashshā'ī* School, as Fakhr al-Dīn Rāzī. In order to criticize Ibn Sīnā, Rāzī chose Shaykh al-Ra'īs's philosophical masterpiece written late in his life, the *Kitāb al-Ishārāt wa'l-tanbīhāt*. This work is very synthetic in nature and not easy to understand fully by beginners. Rāzī commented in detail upon the whole text line by line, clarifying the meaning of many difficult passages and then set out to refute what Ibn Sīnā had said. His work therefore contained the key for the understanding of the meaning of this seminal text as well as its refutation. In a decision that must be considered 'a stroke of genius', Ṭūsī chose this commentary, making use of Rāzī's clarifications and elucidations but then responding to Rāzī's criticisms. The result is one of the great masterpieces of Islamic philosophy, a text full of remarkable intellectual rigour and a clear structure, characteristics which reflect the fact that it was written by one of the greatest mathematicians who ever lived.

The writing of this text along with several other important treatises on *mashshā'ī* philosophy in both Arabic and Persian by Ṭūsī and also his teaching of Avicennan philosophy in Marāghah caused a major revival of this school in Persia. From the seventh/thirteenth century onward, the teaching of this philosophy became widespread, at least in centres in Persia where Islamic philosophy was taught from Marāghah, Zanjān and Tabriz to Isfahan and Shiraz. Also numerous independent *mashshā'ī* works began to appear in both Arabic and Persian, some like the *Kitāb Hidāyat al-ḥikmah* (The Book of Guidance to Philosophy) by Athīr al-Dīn Abharī and the *Ḥikmat al-'ayn* (Wisdom from the Source) by Dabīrān-i Kātibī-yi Qazwīnī becoming very popular texts for the teaching of this philosophy. Other works that are also of great value such as those of Afḍal al-Kāshānī, which mark a peak from the literary point of view as far as philosophical Persian is concerned, did not gain as much popularity but remain nevertheless very significant. In any case following Ṭūsī we see a rich development of the *mashshā'ī* School which in some cases became combined with other philosophical perspectives but which continued its own distinct life into the Safavid and Qājār periods.

Finally in this volume, a major section is devoted to philosophical or doctrinal Sufism which is associated mostly with the name of the seventh/thirteenth-century Andalusian master Muḥyī al-Dīn ibn ʿArabī but which, as already mentioned, has its origin in a certain sense somewhat earlier in the fifth/eleventh and sixth/twelfth centuries in the writings of the two Ghazzālīs and also of ʿAyn al-Quḍāt Hamadānī. Earlier Sufism did of course deal with salvific and unitary knowledge or gnosis (*maʿrifah* or *ʿirfān*) which lies at the heart of Sufism as such. But the early masters spoke of this reality mostly through allusions and rarely in a systematic manner even in such cases as Junayd, Dhu'l-Nūn al-Miṣrī and Ḥakīm Tirmidhī who were openly devoted to gnosis. Gradually with the two Ghazzālīs and ʿAyn al-Quḍāt the expression of Sufi teachings gained greater philosophical import and this quality becomes much more accentuated through the School of Ibn ʿArabī which reached Persia mostly through Ṣadr al-Dīn Qūnawī and also a number of major poets such as Fakhr al-Dīn ʿIrāqī and Awḥad al-Dīn Kirmānī. Although one of the titles of Ibn ʿArabī was 'the Plato of his day', his doctorial expression of gnosis in a more explicit and synthetic form, which we have called philosophical Sufism here, must not be confused with *falsafah* as this term is understood in traditional Islamic thought and Ibn ʿArabī himself was careful to point out this distinction. However, this School does have much philosophical significance. Not only did it produce major literary works of gnostic and mystical significance, some of which like the *Gulshan-i rāz* (Secret Garden of Divine Mysteries) of Shaykh Maḥmūd Shabistarī and the *Lawāʾiḥ* (Gleams) of Jāmī, are masterpieces of Persian literature, but it also provided a rich source for philosophical speculation on the part of many masters of other schools during later centuries. We cannot understand the philosophy of such major later figures as Mullā Ṣadrā and Sabziwārī without knowledge of what we have called philosophical Sufism in this volume. Moreover, this School is of great innate significance philosophically even today, dealing as it does with crucial metaphysical and cosmological questions that remain as pertinent today as in days of old.

Because so much of the thought of the philosophical currents and schools under consideration here is unknown to the general public, including most Persians themselves, and because of the richness of choice from which selections could be made, it has been difficult to prepare this volume in such a way that it would be completely representative of all the different currents of thought and at the same time reveal, for the first time, the most salient features of a generally unknown philosophical landscape. We have, therefore, sought to select works that were later influential within intellectual circles in Persia while at the same time presenting, as much as possible, writings of innate philosophical and literary value. Nor has our task been made any easier by the fact that many of the major works of the period do not possess a critical edition and some have not been printed even in lithograph form.

In any case this volume is the first in English to present, in the form of an anthology, several centuries of philosophical thought in Persia stretching from the seventh/thirteenth to the tenth/sixteenth centuries, a period which has remained the least known and studied of all eras in the history of Islamic philosophy. We hope that despite its shortcomings the volume will shed light on some of the riches of this period of philosophical activity in the Islamic world, which influenced nearly all later philosophical activity in Muslim India, Ottoman Turkey as well as Arab lands such as Syria and Iraq and in Persia itself, and also create greater interest in a period which produced many works of metaphysical and philosophical significance for all those concerned today with what the ancient sages, including Pythagoras, Parmenides and Plato, considered to be real philosophy.

S. H. Nasr

Introductory Analysis

The result of several years of work on the part of translators and editors, this volume brings together translations from some of the major works of Persian philosophers reflecting their contributions to the rich tradition of philosophy in Iran during the least-known period of the history of Islamic philosophy. We have presented the intellectual perspectives of twenty major philosophers and selections from twenty-four of their major texts which, together with the selection included in the first three volumes of this series, constitute a unique source for students and scholars in the field. Suffice it to say that a great number of significant philosophers could not be included out of concern for the length of this book. Our hope is that younger scholars continue our project in the future by introducing the more neglected figures among philosophers in Iran.

In his comprehensive introduction Seyyed Hossein Nasr has outlined the context within which the materials presented here constitute various dimensions of a single philosophical tradition. A detailed description of the materials is included in each chapter at the end of our biographical introductions. However, our intention here is to present their content in a more specific way.

We have begun the volume with Suhrawardī, the founder of the School of Illumination (*ishrāq*), not only because of the inherent significance of this major figure, but also because of the lasting effect of his Illuminationist thought on the later Islamic philosophical tradition. In the first chapter are selections from Suhrawardī's most important work *Ḥikmat al-ishrāq* (The Philosophy of Illumination) which is representative of his metaphysics of illumination. In the second, we have included selections from Suhrawardī's commentator, Shahrazūrī and his *Nuzhat al-arwāḥ wa rawḍat al-afrāḥ* (Excursion of Spirits and Garden of Delights). Here Shahrazūrī offers a history of philosophy that corresponds to Suhrawardī's view of that history and bears testament to the illuminationist doctrine. Accordingly, various civilizations are discussed as conduits through which *ḥikmah,* which originated from God, has flowed over the ages.

The third and fourth chapters consist of yet more commentaries on Suhrawardī. Quṭb al-Dīn Shīrāzī's *Durrat al-tāj* (Pearl of the Crown), presented in chapter three is concerned with the classification of sciences. In chapter four we have included Jalāl al-Dīn Dawānī's commentary on Suhrawardī's *Hayākil al-nūr* (Temples of Light) which discusses such topics as causality, motion, corporeality and its relationship to cosmology and the role of light in an *ishrāqī* context. Traditional metaphysical problems and Suhrawardī's technical terminologies are presented and discussed in this work. The second part of the chapter devoted to Dawānī consists of his treatise on ethics titled *Akhlāq-i jalālī* (The Jalālian Ethics) where he discusses a wide range of problems pertaining to ethics and political philosophy and in a didactic manner reminds those in a position of power of their moral responsibility.

Chapter five deals with Ibn Abī Jumhūr Aḥsā'ī. Here we have included a section of his *Kitāb al-Mujlī* (The Book of the Illuminated) where he presents the opinions of the theologians (*mutakallimūn*) and philosophers such as Rāzī and Ibn Sīnā, and discusses such problems as epistemology, the role of revelation, purification and providence. His treatment of the opinion of other Sufis and his esoteric reading of the prayers of the prophets David, Moses and Jesus are of particular significance.

In the sixth chapter we have included a section from Mullā Ṣadrā's major glosses on Suhrawardī's *Ḥikmat al-ishrāq* (Theosophy of the Orient of Light or Philosophy of Illumination) dealing with the subject of eschatology. It begins with a discussion on the difference between resurrection on the Day of Judgment and the transmigration of the soul. Following a discussion where Mullā Ṣadrā mentions the opinions of Greek and Persian sages, he offers an analysis of how the ontological status of a person in this world is related to their status and visions of light and darkness in the Hereafter. Mullā Ṣadrā offers a discussion of his controversial views on corporeal resurrection and the gradual perfection of the soul from the animal soul to the human to the angelic soul. This work represents a gnostic interpretation of Suhrawardī's illuminationist views on eschatology.

In Part Two of this volume we present the revival of the Peripatetic philosophy whose influence had been substantially curtailed in Persia for some two centuries after Ibn Sīnā. This section of the book begins with Naṣīr al-Dīn Ṭūsī's commentary on the *Sharḥ al-ishārāt* of Ibn Sīnā by Fakhr al-Dīn Rāzī where he discusses the stations of the gnostics, the philosophical allegory of Salāmān and Absāl, the relationship between asceticism and epistemology and the faculties of the soul. We have also included parts of Ṭūsī's Persian treatise, *Risālah andar qismat-i mawjūdāt* (Treatise on the Division of Existents). Discussions here are concerned with the subject of atomism and the opinions of the Muʿtazilites and the Ashʿarites on corporeality and the problem of infinite divisibility.

In the second chapter of this section, selections from Afḍal al-Dīn Kāshānī's *Muṣannafāt* (Compositions) have been included. Following a discussion on how awareness concerning the self is obtained, 'Bābā Afḍal' continues with an examination of different types of existence and existents, knowledge and self-awareness and the reality of the human being. This treatise ends with a discussion of such traditional philosophical problems as subjects and predicates, attributes, genus, species and some of the Aristotelian categories.

The third chapter focuses on Dabīrān-i Kātibī Qazwīnī, a significant but relatively unknown figure. The selection from Qazwīnī's *Ḥikmat al-ʿayn* (Wisdom from the Source) discusses the problem of existence and quiddity and their relationship to the Necessary Being. Different types of existences, abstract and real, their relation to the rational soul, revelation, prophecy, life after death and the problem of knowing the intelligibles are among the other discussions in this chapter.

In the next chapter, Athīr al-Dīn Abharī, another relatively unknown figure, has been introduced. Abharī's major work *Hidāyat al-ḥikmah* and the commentary (*Shaḥr*) of Amīr Ḥusayn Maybudī that are included here, begin with a discussion concerning the knowledge of God and continue by treating the relationship between the attribute of necessity and Divine Reality. Abharī's discussion of necessity and its relation to God's Being and Essence and such concepts as reality, existence, non-existence and essential and non-essential attributes are among the problems discussed here.

For the last chapter of Part Two we have chosen Quṭb al-Dīn Rāzī's *al-Taṣawwur wa'l-taṣdīq* (Conception and Judgment). This text deals primarily with epistemology. The author discusses the correspondence theory of truth and the affirmative and negative nature of the propositions that address the content of the mind. Rāzī, who saw Ibn Sīnā as his 'Shaykh', discusses modalities of propositions and their truth value and comments on what Ibn Sīnā and Ṭūsī have said in this regard. Knowledge, certainty, proof and verifiability are among the themes that Rāzī discusses in this treatise.

Part Three presents selections from the work of those philosophers who have dealt with the subject of philosophical Sufism beginning with Abū Ḥāmid Muḥammad Ghazzālī. The chapter devoted to Ghazzālī opens with his *Mishkāt al-anwār* (The Niche of Lights) where he relies on the Neoplatonic scheme of emanation to explain, as a commentary on the Qur'ānic 'Light Verse', the hierarchy of lights, knowledge of God, refinement of character and the problem of unity and multiplicity. In the second section, *al-Risālat al-laduniyyah* (The Wisdom from God) has been included. Here we see a brief discussion concerning different worlds (e.g. revealed, hidden, angelic). The treatise continues by examining divisions of the soul and different modes of knowledge such as the intellectual, religious and mystical, as well as various methodologies for acquiring knowledge. In the final section of this chapter, we have included some of the most esoteric writings of Ghazzālī, *Thalāth rasā'il-fi'l maʿrifah* (Three Treatises on Knowledge). Here, the knowledge of God, an inquiry concerning the nature of knowledge and knowledge of the self as three modes of knowledge, is explained. Among other topics discussed are Sufism, asceticism, the spiritual journey of the soul and its difficulties, essential and non-essential types of knowledge and different levels of knowing. Of particular interest here is Ghazzālī's esoteric interpretation of numerous verses of the Qur'ān. The three texts provide the reader with a comprehensive perspective of Ghazzālī's views on philosophical Sufism.

The next chapter is devoted to Ghazzālī's younger brother Aḥmad. We have included a section from the *Sawāniḥ al-ʿushshāq* (Auspices of Divine Lovers), a gnostic interpretation of love not as a mode of feeling but as a mode of knowledge and being. Aḥmad Ghazzālī analogizes the lover, love and the relationship to the knower, known and the epistemic mode of cognition between them. Such mystical concepts as unity, types of love, and the role of will-power in the spiritual journey and the stages of love are among topics discussed here.

An extract from ʿAyn al-Quḍāt Hamadānī's *Tamhīdāt* (Dispositions) and his *Nāmā-hā* (Letters) have been chosen for the third chapter. It begins with a discussion of the differences between acquired knowledge through sense perception and Divine knowledge and moves on to explain the role of a spiritual master in leading the seeker of the truth to the right type of knowledge. In the final parts of the chapter ʿAyn al-Quḍāt tells us how he was 'saved from falling' by studying the works of Abū Ḥāmid Ghazzālī, but in another place he supports Ibn Sīnā's views on the eternity of the world against Ghazzālī's view of creation *ex-nihilo*. The chapter ends with a selection of ʿAyn al-Quḍāt's *Letters*. This brief selection offers an esoteric interpretation of several verses of the Qur'ān and the central role of the Prophet Muḥammad as the ultimate spiritual guide.

In the fourth chapter of Part Three of this volume we have included a section of *al-Nuṣūṣ* (The Texts) by Qūnawī. This treatise, which begins with a discussion concerning knowledge and its modalities, examines the relationship between knowledge and existence, unity and plurality and that which is real. The chapter examines further the stations of gnosis, degrees of knowledge and different levels of knowing God. Identifying the Real as Being is the heart of Qūnawī's discussion throughout this work.

A major section of Āmulī's most important work, *Jāmiʿ al-asrār* (The Sum of Secrets), makes up the next chapter. Following a discussion of the concept of 'Unity' and the manifestations of Divine Unity, the complex subject of 'Divine Self-disclosure' has been examined. The relationship between existence, Reality and human faculties are discussed next, both discursively and also based on what has been transmitted by Sufi masters and gnostics. This selection ends with a discourse on the essential unity of religions and the harmony that exists between reason and revelation as well as what Āmulī calls 'Islam and its various levels'.

In the sixth chapter of Part Three, Ibn Turkah's *Tamhīd al-qawāʿid* (Establishing the Principles) has been included. This significant but much neglected philosopher begins his treatise by attempting to elucidate the laws of *tawḥīd* (unity) and offers a classification of such different epistemological means of gaining cognition as sense perception, reflection and inspiration. Ibn Turkah applies Plato's doctrine of participation to the concept of existence and argues that existence participates in existents in both meaning and concept. Different types of intelligibles, the necessity of existence and its relation to existents are among other topics treated here.

In the next chapter we present Shams al-Dīn Lāhījī's famous treatise, *Sharḥ-i gulshan-i rāz* (Commentary on the Secret Garden of Divine Mysteries). The selection from Lāhījī begins with a critique of the use of pure reason to discover the intelligibles in general and God in particular and continues by focusing on the categories of the real, the nature of pure thought and the epistemological problems that arise in conventional ways of knowing. Throughout this text Lāhījī offers philosophical and gnostic commentaries on Shabistarī's poetry and unveils the more subtle and hidden points in this exquisite example of Persian philosophical poetry.

The volume ends with ʿAbd al-Raḥmān Jāmī's *al-Durrah al-fākhirah* (The Precious Pearl). Jāmī himself describes this work in his introduction and tells us that his treatise deals with 'the verification of the doctrine of the Sufis, the theologians and the early philosophers'. The treatise examines the beliefs of Jāmī's predecessors concerning the being of God, His Names and Attributes, emanation and the problem of unity and multiplicity. Jāmī tells us that the reason for writing this work was to inquire about those subjects that are 'prompted by thought and reason'. This treatise is important both for the nature of the philosophical arguments it presents and because it provides us with a detailed account of early theologians, philosophers and schools of thought that played a role in the formative period of Islamic intellectual thought.

M. Aminrazavi

PART I

The School of Illumination

Introduction

There were several philosophical schools of old including Neoplatonism in which light and illumination have played a central role, but when in the context of Islamic philosophy we speak of the School of Illumination or *ishrāq* we have in mind a distinct school of Islamic philosophy founded in the sixth/twelfth century by Shihāb al-Dīn Suhrawardī, a Persian who was born in Suhraward near Zanjān in 549/1153, was educated in Zanjān and Isfahan, travelled in Anatolia and Syria and settled in Aleppo where he was put to death around 587/1191. Although influenced by earlier schools of Islamic philosophy, especially the thought of Ibn Sīnā, by Platonism and by certain currents of Mazdean thought as well as Sufism, the School of *ishrāq* is a distinct philosophical/theosophical school with its own vocabulary, method and doctrines. For eight hundred years it has remained a major philosophical current in the intellectual landscape of the Islamic world especially in Persia and Muslim India and to some extent in the Ottoman world.

The name *ishrāq* by which this School is known is based on the root *sh-r-q* which is related to both illumination (*ishrāq*) and the place where the light of the sun rises or the orient (*mashriq*). This philosophy is, therefore, both illuminative and oriental in the symbolic and not merely the outward sense. According to this School, the spiritual part of the cosmos is luminous, God Himself being known as *Nūr al-anwār,* the Light of lights, while the material domain in this world in which we dwell is the abode of shadows and darkness. The intelligible and luminous world, being the place from which light emanates into our world, corresponds to the Orient or the East in a metaphysical, symbolic and not a literal geographical sense, and our world of shadows to the Occident or *maghrib*. *Ishrāqī* teachings are oriental because they are illuminative and illuminative because they are oriental. A sacred and symbolic geography accompanies the whole notion of *ishrāq* and in one of his visionary narratives or recitals *Qiṣṣat al-ghurbah al-gharbiyyah* (The Tale of the Occidental Exile), Suhrawardī deals directly with this subject in relation to the human condition. He states that by virtue of the forgetfulness of our original spiritual nature, we have fallen into this Occident of the realm of existence, but since our spirit belongs to the world of light, we are not at home here but in exile. The goal of *ishrāqī* teachings is to make us aware of the fact that we are in exile, to remind us of our real home and to provide the guidance needed to traverse the labyrinths of the cosmic crypt and go beyond it in order to complete our homeward journey.

The School of *ishrāq* has its own distinct view of the history of philosophy. It considers the origin of philosophy to be prophecy and identifies some of the ancient prophets associated with the Abrahamic world as sages or philosophers and some of the ancient Greek philosophers as prophetic figures. This particular view of the history of philosophy is not only mentioned by Suhrawardī himself, but was elucidated more elaborately by later *ishrāqī* philosophers, such as Shams al-Dīn Muḥammad Shahrazūrī, who wrote histories of philosophy. This conception of the history of philosophy has been refuted by positivistic modern scholars but their criticism is irrelevant as far as the view of the tradition itself and its vision of its own past are concerned. Suhrawardī himself mentions how the earliest treasury of *ḥikmah*, that is, wisdom or *sophia* given by God to man and kneaded into the clay of Adam, became crystallized and bifurcated into two main traditions, one located in ancient Greece and the other in ancient Persia. He adds that Islamic civilization was heir to both of these branches that became reunited in him and his new *ishrāqī* School.

Suhrawardī also considered his School to be the culmination and synthesis of knowledge received through ratiocination as well as intellectual intuition. He calls the first type of knowledge discursive (*baḥthī*) and the second 'tasted' (*dhawqī*). According to Suhrawardī, the Peripatetic philosophers before him had cultivated the first and the Sufis the second kind of knowledge. Suhrawardī considered himself to be the first person in Islamic history in whom these two modes of knowledge had became synthesized. The School of *ishrāq* henceforth emphasized that the true philosopher who is 'God-like' (*muta'allih*) (a term originally specifically associated with Suhrawardī) must have mastered with perfection both discursive and intuitive or 'tasted' knowledge. For the School of *ishrāq* all knowledge is ultimately related to illumination and light is both knowledge and being.

Ishrāqī philosophy assumes the existence of the teachings of the *mashshā'ī* School upon which it builds but which it also criticizes. Suhrawardī himself criticized several aspects of Peripatetic logic including the categories, which he reduced to four, and the meaning of logical definition. He also added the concept of *iḍāfah ishrāqiyyah* (illuminative relation) where the relation between B and A constitutes B itself. This new category plays a major role in *ishrāqī* metaphysics and cosmology as well as epistemology. The metaphysics of the *ishrāqī* School is based completely on light. God is pure light, the Light of lights, and the whole universe is nothing but degrees of light which become combined with darkness to the extent that a particular light becomes distanced from the Source of all light and also higher lights in the vertical hierarchy of lights. Suhrawardī describes an elaborate scheme of vertical and horizontal orders of light constituting the angelic world, and it is especially in his angelology that he reveals clearly the integration of Mazdean doctrines and symbols into his *ishrāqī* metaphysics and cosmology that is inseparable from angelology. Even the name used by Suhrawardī for the highest angel or light below the Lights of lights is Bahman which is a modern Persian version of the Avestan Vohu-Manah. The angelology of Suhrawardī is among the most fascinating features of his teachings and angels play a central role in *ishrāqī* psychology, epistemology and soteriology as well as cosmology and physics.

In the domain of metaphysics, it is important to add that Suhrawardī considered being or existence (*wujūd*) to be simply an accident added to the quiddities (*māhiyyāt*) of things that possess reality. His was, therefore, an 'essentialist' metaphysics which was to be transformed later by Mullā Ṣadrā into an 'existential' metaphysics. Later in Islamic philosophy when the question arose as to whether *wujūd* or *māhiyyah* is principial (*aṣīl*), that is, is the source of reality of an object, Suhrawardī was always identified with the school of the principiality of *māhiyyah* and Mullā Ṣadrā with the principiality of *wujūd*. For example, the great founder of the School of Isfahan, Mīr Dāmād, defended the principiality of *māhiyyah* and was therefore automatically identified with Suhrawardī by later historians of Islamic philosophy and philosophers themselves. In reality the role that *wujūd* plays in the philosophy of Mullā Ṣadrā is played by light (*nūr*) in Suhrawardī and if one equates *nūr* and *wujūd* in the two grand metaphysical 'systems' which have dominated the Persian philosophical scene for so many centuries, then it becomes evident how close the two 'systems' are to each other and also how deeply the *ishrāqī* School has influenced the School of Isfahan and especially *al-ḥikmah al-muta'āliyah* of its most illustrious representative, Mullā Ṣadrā.

In natural philosophy Suhrawardī rejects the foundation of Aristotelian physics which is hylomorphism. For him in contrast to the Stagirite and Ibn Sīnā, physical bodies are not composed of form and matter but are a mixture of light and darkness. In fact bodies are divided into three categories on the basis of the degree to which they are transparent to light. Furthermore, the reality of various species is not determined by the Aristotelian *morpha* of various species but by the angelic presences or particular lights that dominate over that species or what in *ishrāqī* language are called *arbāb al-anwā'* or lords of the species, the lord being none other than a particular angel or light located originally in the world above in a horizontal order where are to be found the lords of all the species.

In psychology, Suhrawardī draws heavily upon Ibn Sīnā's divisions of the faculty of psychology, but here again he substitutes a particular kind of light for the soul or *nafs* understood in the Avicennan sense. In *ishrāqī* psychology angels or entities of light play a major role in every domain of human life including protection and guidance of the soul. Even the act of seeing with physical eyes is for Suhrawardī an illumination in which the seer and the seen are united in a single illumination. As for knowledge gained by the soul, at every level it has a relation to *ishrāq* and even sensible perception is related to illumination. This becomes of course even more central for intelligible knowledge that is intimately bound to illumination.

One of the major doctrines of the *ishrāqī* School is the distinction between conceptual knowledge (*al-ʿilm al-ḥuṣūlī*) which is knowledge attained through the intermediary of mental concepts, and knowledge by presence (*al-ʿilm al-ḥuḍūrī*) in which the object of knowledge is present in an immediate manner before the knower without the intermediary of concepts. This distinction is basic and was debated among many later philosophers. This idea, along with that of the unity of the knower and the known in the act of intellection, which Ibn Sīnā had refuted but which Suhrawardī had accepted, was accepted by Mullā Ṣadrā and became a cornerstone of his own 'transcendent theosophy' (*al-ḥikmah al-mutaʿāliyah*).

The writings of Suhrawardī and many later *ishrāqī*s who sought to follow his example are mostly of high literary quality using a symbolic rather than a purely discursive language. Suhrawardī's Persian treatises are in fact among the greatest masterpieces of Persian philosophical prose while his *magnum opus, Ḥikmat al-ishrāq* (The Theosophy of the Orient of Light) marks a peak of Arabic philosophical writings. *Ishrāqī* works have their own distinct vocabulary and symbolic language. They are usually more poetic and symbolic than other philosophical works and in any case form a very distinct body of philosophical writings in both Persian and Arabic as far as their literary qualities and language are concerned. This high literary quality is to be seen even in many of the didactic works of this School, the best example being the *Ḥikmat al-ishrāq* itself.

The *ishrāqī* School has had a continuous life in Persia for over eight centuries from a generation after the life of its founder. As mentioned earlier, it has also had a long history in the Indian Subcontinent and Ottoman Turkey as well as to some extent in Arab countries such as Syria and Iraq. The history of none of these branches of the tree of the *ishrāqī* School is as yet fully known. But in any case the main trunk of this tree is rooted in Persia and its most salient features have been studied. Following the tragic death of Suhrawardī in Aleppo, a generation of silence followed. Then suddenly in the seventh/thirteenth century there appears the first commentator and after Suhrawardī the greatest figure of this School, Shams al-Dīn Muḥammad Shahrazūrī, followed by Quṭb al-Dīn Shīrāzī. After these two major figures, the *ishrāqī* School becomes a main feature of the intellectual life of Persia and soon of Muslim India and Ottoman Turkey. Throughout the centuries that follow, this School manifests its presence in two ways: first, through philosophers who wrote *ishrāqī* works either in the form of commentaries on texts of Suhrawardī and other figures of this School or independent works; and second through the influence of *ishrāqī* doctrines on other philosophical schools chief among them *al-ḥikmah al-mutaʿāliyah* established by Mullā Ṣadrā, a major intellectual school with which we shall deal with in volume five of this *Anthology*.

In the pages that follow we have chosen selections from important works of *ishrāqī* character starting with Suhrawardī himself and ending with a thirteenth/nineteenth-century figure whose very existence bears testimony to the continuity in the life of the *ishrāqī* School as an independent School and not only as integrated into later philosophical currents. If we have included Mullā Ṣadrā's *Glosses* upon the commentary upon the *Ḥikmat al-ishrāq* here rather than in volume five, it is because this work is among the greatest masterpieces of the *ishrāqī* School and Mullā Ṣadrā writes here as an *ishrāqī* philosopher and not as the master of the 'transcendent theosophy', the School which he founded and into whose teachings many of Suhrawardī's theses are integrated.

We have also included Dawānī's commentary upon Suhrawardī's *Hayākil al-nūr* (Temples of Light) here rather than under the School of Shiraz where Dawānī really belongs, because of the great fame of this opus as a major *ishrāqī* work not only in Persia, but also in India and Ottoman Turkey where Dawānī was so well known. Of course, another member of the School of Shiraz, Ghiyāth al-Dīn Manṣūr Dashtakī, wrote a rebuttal to Dawānī and was himself also very knowledgeable in *ishrāqī* teachings, but his commentary on Suhrawardī did not gain the same international fame as Dawānī's. Furthermore, the main *ishrāqī* work of Ghiyāth al-Dīn Manṣūr, *Ishrāq hayākil al-nūr* (Illumination of the Temples of Light) had not been edited when the translations for this volume were completed. It has just now appeared for the first time in printed form edited by ʿAlī Awjabī. Ghiyāth al-Dīn was a towering and central figure of the School of Shiraz and will be discussed fully in the next volume where the School of Shiraz is treated. Although we have decided to include him in the next volume, we must acknowledge here that he and many other philosophers of Shiraz also wrote works of an *ishrāqī* nature which, except for Dawānī, have not been included in this volume. What are presented here are examples drawn from seven centuries of writings of the *ishrāqī* School without in any way claiming to have included all the significant texts. The works that appear below are, however, all of importance for understanding this major school of Islamic philosophy that has had such a wide influence upon philosophy in Persia during the past eight hundred years.

We cannot conclude this introduction without saying a word about the question of the revival of interest in Suhrawardī in contemporary Iran. It was Henry Corbin who began to edit critically the works of Suhrawardī for the first time while he spent the whole of the Second World War in Istanbul. His two-volume work *Opera Metaphysica et Mystica,* which include the metaphysical sections of Suhrawardī's didactic works as well as the whole of the *Ḥikmat al-ishrāq*, was followed by volume three edited by myself and including all of the master's Persian texts. These volumes along with Corbin's and my own other writings and lectures aroused considerable interest in him even among some Western-educated Iranians drawn to philosophy. Many were drawn to him because he had successfully synthesized the philosophical thought of ancient Persia and Islamic philosophy and they compared him to Firdawsī in the realm of epic poetry. Interest in Suhrawardī, however, went deeper than chauvinistic and nationalistic sentiments and began to draw a number of younger philosophers educated in traditional Islamic circles to *ishrāqī* teachings. This resulted in serious works on this school by such traditional philosophers as Sayyid Jaʿfar Sajjādī and especially Ghulām-Ḥusayn Ibrāhīmī Dīnānī, the author of a major work in Persian on Suhrawardī, *Shuʿāʾ-i andīshah wa shuhūd dar falsafa-yi Suhrawardī* (Rays of Thought and Intuition in the Philosophy of Suhrawardī), a work which is itself an *ishrāqī* philosophical work and marks the continuity of this school in contemporary Iran, a period which we hope will be treated in a separate volume after the completion of this *Anthology*. There are also Persian philosophers and scholars of philosophy abroad such as Mehdi Aminrazavi and especially the late Hossein Ziai who have made notable contributions to the study of this school, along with some of the French students of Corbin who have introduced certain aspects of *ishrāqī* teachings as living philosophy into the contemporary philosophical scene in Europe.

S. H. Nasr

1

Shihāb al-Dīn Suhrawardī

Shihāb al-Dīn Yaḥyā ibn Ḥabash ibn Amīrak Abu'l-Futūḥ Suhrawardī, also known as 'Shaykh al-ishrāq' (Master of Illumination), was born in 549/1170 in the village of Suhraward near Zanjān, a north-western Iranian city. His early education seems to have taken place in the city of Marāghah where he studied philosophy among other subjects with Majd al-Dīn Jīlī. Suhrawardī then travelled to Isfahan, where he pursued his advanced studies with Ẓahīr al-Dīn al-Fārsī in philosophy, theology and the sciences, including studying *al-Baṣā'ir* (The Observations) of 'Umar ibn Ṣalāḥ al-Ṣāwī (or Sāwajī).

Like so many other notable thinkers of the Islamic world at that time, Suhrawardī travelled to Anatolia and Syria where in Aleppo in 579/1183 he met Malik Ẓāhir, the son of the famous Ṣalāḥ al-Dīn Ayyūbī. Suhrawardī's esoteric orientation and his intellectual perspective, which were more inclusive of other traditions such as Zoroastrianism and Manichaeism, antagonized some of the exoteric jurists at Malik Ẓāhir's court. Having declared him a heretic, they asked Malik Ẓāhir to put him to death; the king however refused. The exoteric jurists then signed a petition and sent it to Ṣalāḥ al-Dīn Ayyūbī who, needing the support of the jurists amidst the Crusades, ordered his son to have him killed. While the manner in which Suhrawardī was executed is unknown, we do know that Malik Ẓāhir carried out his father's order reluctantly. Suhrawardī, who received the title 'al-Shahīd' (the Martyred) and also 'al-Maqtūl' (the Murdered), was put to death in 587/1191.

Evidence concerning Suhrawardī's life is scarce and unreliable. He lived in a somewhat monastic fashion and shied away from people; one day he would dress in the manner of a courtier and the next as a wandering dervish. He had a sharp tongue, a reddish face, was handsome and of medium height.

Suhrawardī lived at a time when respect and reverence for rationalist theology (of the Mu'tazilites) had been replaced by the more faith-based theology of the Ash'arites. Even though some degree of debate among the advocates of intellectual sciences continued, the golden era of philosophical and theological activities in the eastern part of the Islamic world had declined. Ghazzālī's defence of Ash'arite theology and of Sufism and his criticism of Avicennan philosophy had also put rationalistic activities on the defensive and philosophy was challenged both by the Ash'arites and the Sufis, although in a way Ghazzālī also opened an intellectual space for the appearance of *ishrāqī* doctrines.

Suhrawardī, in the tradition of great synthesizers, wanted to bring about a rapprochement between existing schools of thought and saw himself as the reviver of that truth which lies at the heart of all the divinely revealed religions and traditions of wisdom. Beginning with Avicenna, Suhrawardī sought to rescue him from a purely Aristotelian interpretation and bring to the surface the more gnostic elements deep within some aspects of Avicennan philosophy. Suhrawardī was sympathetic to the fact that some of the exponents of theology (*kalām*) had found Avicenna's logic and metaphysics to be a useful means to defend the tenets of Islam. Finally, there was the mystical aspect of Avicenna, which before Suhrawardī had received less attention than his rationalistic writings. In writings such as *Ḥayy ibn Yaqẓān* (Living Son of the Awake) and the final chapters of the *Ishārāt*, the esoteric and mystical aspects of Avicenna's philosophy are evident. Suhrawardī, who was well aware of such writings, uses some of the same symbols in his work *Qiṣṣāt al-ghurbah al-qharbiyyah* (A Story of the Occidental Exile).

Suhrawardī attempted to bring about a rapprochement between discursive philosophy, mysticism and intellectual intuition. This consistent and coherent philosophical paradigm, known as *al-ḥikmah al-ilāhiyyah* (literally, 'theosophy') or *ḥikmat al-ishrāq* (philosophy of illumination), bridges the differences between various intellectual schools of thought in the Islamic tradition in a new synthesis which is also a new intellectual perspective.

Suhrawardī respected logic and discursive philosophy but nevertheless acknowledged the limitations in the application of reason alone as the means of discovering the truth. According to him what is required to apprehend completely the higher truth is illuminationist wisdom. Drawing from a deep mystical intuition, Suhrawardī compared the principles of logic and discursive reasoning with his findings through mystical vision, accepting only those elements of the former that could be harmonized with the latter. For Suhrawardī, reason, mystical experience and intellectual intuition constitute a single epistemological system and are reconcilable.

Suhrawardī's writings are diverse—Peripatetic, mystical and illuminationist (*ishrāqī*). They include his four large works that are of a doctrinal nature: *al-Talwīḥāt* (The Book of Intimations), *al-Muqāwamāt* (The Book of Opposites), *al-Muṭāraḥāt* (The Book of Conversations) and finally his *magnum opus, Ḥikmat al-ishrāq* (The Philosophy of Illumination). The first three of these works are written in the tradition of the Peripatetic philosophers and yet are filled with *ishrāqī* elements and with commentaries and criticisms of certain Aristotelian concepts.

His *Ḥikmat al-ishrāq* consists of two parts: in the first he continues with the Peripatetic themes and in the second he employs a particular language known as *lisān al-ishrāq* (the language of illumination). It is here that his illuminationist doctrine is fully elaborated often in a symbolic language.

Suhrawardī composed a number of shorter works, some of them in Arabic and some in Persian. Many of these treatises which are also of a doctrinal nature should be regarded as further explanations of the larger doctrinal treatises. They include *Hayākil al-nūr* (Temples of Light), *Alwāḥ-i ʿimādī* (Tablets Dedicated to ʿImād al-Dīn), *Partaw-nāmah* (The Book of Radiance) *Fī iʿtiqād al-ḥukamāʾ* (On the Faith of the *Ḥakīms*), *al-Lamaḥāt* (The Flashes of Light), *Yazdān-shinākht* (Knowledge of the Divine), and *Bustān al-qulūb* (The Garden of Hearts).

Suhrawardī also composed a number of highly esoteric works in Persian in which he used a variety of symbols drawn from different traditions such as Zoroastrianism and Hermeticism as well, of course, as Islamic sources, especially the Qurʾān. These treatises, which are among the most beautiful examples of Persian prose, are initiatic narratives and contain highly symbolic language. They include: *ʿAql-i surkh* (Red Intellect), *Āwāz-i par-i Jibraʾīl* (Chant of the Wing of Gabriel), *Qiṣṣat al-ghurbat al-gharbiyyah* (Story of the Occidental Exile), *Lughat-i mūrān* (The Language of Ants), *al-Risālah fī ḥālat al-ṭufūliyyah* (Treatise on the State of Childhood), *Rūzī bā jamāʿat-i ṣūfiyān* (A Day among Sufis), *Ṣafīr-i sīmūrgh* (The Song of the Griffin), and *al-Risālah fiʾl-miʿrāj* (Treatise on the Nocturnal Ascent). The journey of the soul toward unity with God, the inherent yearning of man toward knowledge of the Divine and the way this knowledge can be attained constitute the salient features of these works.

Suhrawardī also wrote a number of other treatises of a philosophic and initiatory nature. These include his translation of Avicenna's *Risālat al-ṭayr* (Treatise of the Birds) and his commentary in Persian on Avicenna's *al-Ishārāt waʾl-tanbīhāt*. There is also his *al-Risālah fī ḥaqīqat al-ʿishq* (Treatise on the Reality of Love), which is an elaboration of many themes of Avicenna's *al-Risālah fiʾl-ʿishq* (Treatise on Love) and commentaries on several verses of the Qurʾān and some *ḥadīth*s. Although it is not known for certain, it is said that Suhrawardī may have written a commentary on Fārābī's *Fuṣūṣ*. Finally, there are his *al-Wāridāt waʾl-taqdīsāt* (Invocations and Prayers), which are his liturgical writings and include prayers, invocations and litanies.

In the following chapter we deal with Suhrawardī's most important work *Ḥikmat al-ishrāq* (The Philosophy of Illumination). We have included the second part of this major work which represents Suhrawardī's metaphysics of illumination. The question of hierarchy, light and darkness and their various types as well as his ontology, cosmology and angelology are discussed here.

M. Aminrazavi

THE PHILOSOPHY OF ILLUMINATION

Ḥikmat al-ishrāq

Reprinted from Suhrawardī, *Ḥikmat al-ishrāq*, tr. John Walbridge and Hossein Ziai as *The Philosophy of Illumination* (Provo, UT, 1999), pp. 77–111.

Part Two: The First Discourse

Section [three]

[On light and darkness]

(109) A thing is either light and luminosity in its own reality or is not light and luminosity in its own reality. The meanings of 'light' and 'luminosity' are the same here, for I do not use these in a metaphorical way, as when 'light' is used to mean that which is evident to the mind, though even such usages do at the last derive from this light. Light is divided into light that is a state of something else (the accidental light) and light that is not a state of something else (the incorporeal or pure light). That which is not light in its own reality is divided into that which is independent of a locus (the dusky substance) and that which is a state of something else (the dark state). The barrier is the body and may be described as a substance that can be pointed to. Some barriers are seen to be dark when light ceases to shine on them. Darkness is simply an expression for the lack of light, nothing more; and it is not one of the privatives conditioned upon possibility.[1] If the world were posited to be a vacuum or a sphere with no light in it, it would be dark. This would imply the deficiency of darkness without implying the possibility of light in it. Thus, it is established that everything that is neither a light nor illumined is dark. If a barrier is cut off from light, it does not need something else to be dark. These are like other barriers that never lose their light—the Sun, for example. These are like other barriers that may cease to have light in that they are barriers, yet they differ in having light continually. The light by which these barriers differ from the others is superadded to their being barriers and subsists in them. It is thus accidental light, and its bearer is a dusky substance. Therefore, every barrier is a dusky substance.

(110) Sensible accidental light is not independent in itself, since otherwise it would not depend on the dusky substance. Since (light) subsists in (the dusky substance), it is dependent and contingent. (The light's) existence is not from the dusky substance, since it would otherwise be its concomitant and the dusky substance

1. Quṭb al-Dīn, *Sharḥ ḥikmat al-ishrāq*, ed. A. Nourani and M. Mohaghegh (Tehran, 1980), p. 286, explains that the Peripatetics thought that only that which could be illumined could be said to be dark. Thus, they held, against Suhrawardī, that air was not dark because it was transparent and could not itself be illumined.

would never be without it. This is not so; how, indeed, could it be, considering that nothing necessitates that which is nobler than its own essence? Thus, that which gives all dusky substances their lights must be something other than their gloomy quiddities and dark states. You will learn that dark states[1] are caused by light, even though the light itself may also be accidental. The dark states, moreover, are hidden: how could they necessitate something less hidden than themselves?[2] Therefore, that which gives lights to the barriers is not a barrier, nor is it a dusky substance. Otherwise, all barriers and dusky substance would cause accidental lights. Thus, that which gives them their lights must be something other than the barriers and dusky substances.

Section [four]

[On the dependence of the body in its existence upon the incorporeal light]

(111) The dusky barriers possess dark aspects—shapes, for example—and particularities of magnitude. Although magnitude is not superadded to the barrier, nevertheless there is a certain peculiarity, boundary, and limit by which one magnitude is distinguished from another. These things by which barriers differ from each other do not belong to the barriers by essence, since otherwise all barriers would share them. Nor do the boundaries of barriers belong to them by essence, since otherwise all would be equal. Therefore, they have the accidents by virtue of another. Were the shapes and other dark states independent, their existence would not depend on the barrier. Were the reality of the barrier independent by its essence and were it necessary, its existence would not have to be actualized by particular dark states and other such entities. Were the barriers independent of magnitude and states, they could not be multiple, for there would be no separate states to distinguish them, nor could the essence of each one be particularized. It cannot be argued that the distinguishing states are concomitants of the quiddities of barriers that necessitate them, for were that so, they would not be different in different barriers—yet they do differ.

Intuition affirms that no lifeless dusky substance receives its existence from another, since with respect to the lifeless reality of the barrier no one (substance) would have priority over the others. Through another proof, you will learn that one barrier does not bring another barrier into existence. Moreover, neither the barrier nor its dark and luminous states can receive their existence in a circular manner from something else, for nothing can depend on something that depends on it. Were that the case, it would bring into existence that which brought it into existence and would so be prior to it and to itself—which is an absurdity. Since they

1. Some manuscripts read 'most dark states'.
2. In being hidden, they are the opposite of being manifest, which is the primary quality of light.

are not independent by essence, they are all dependent on something that is neither a dusky substance nor a dark or luminous state—that is to say, an incorporeal light. The substantiality of the dusky substance is intellectual[1] and its duskiness privative. Therefore, it does not exist in virtue of these. It is simply a concrete thing with particular properties.

A rule [stating that incorporeal light cannot be pointed out by sensation]

(112) Since you know that any light that can be pointed to is an accidental light, then if there is a pure light, it cannot be pointed to, nor be located in a body, nor have spatial dimensions.[2]

A rule [that anything that is light in itself is incorporeal light]

(113) Accidental light is not light in itself, since its existence is in another. Thus, it can only be light due to another. The incorporeal pure light is light in itself. Therefore, everything that is light in itself is incorporeal pure light.

A General Section [five]

[Showing that whatever perceives its own essence is an incorporeal light]

(114) Nothing that has an essence of which it is not unconscious is dusky,[3] for its essence is evident to it. It cannot be a dark state in something else, since even the luminous state is not a self-subsistent light, let alone the dark state. Therefore, it is a non-spatial pure incorporeal light.

A detailed section [on what we have just mentioned]

(115) The self-subsistent, self-conscious thing does not apprehend its essence by an image of its essence in its essence. If its knowledge is by an image and if the image of its ego is not the ego itself, the image of the ego would be an 'it' in relation to the ego. In that case, that which was apprehended would be the image. Thus, it follows that while the apprehension of its ego is precisely its apprehension of what it is itself, its apprehension of its essence would also be the apprehension of something else—which is absurd. This is not the case with externals, since the image and its object are each an 'it'. Moreover, if its apprehension of itself were by an image and it did not know that this was an image of itself; it must have already known itself without an image. How could something be conceived to know itself by something superadded to itself—something that would be an attribute of it? If it were to

1. That is, while substances are external entities, substantiality exists only in the mind.

2. That is, if there is any such thing as metaphysical light, it is something different from visible light.

3. Meaning, bodily. 'Essence' here renders *dhāt*, which means both 'self' and 'essence' in the sense of the concrete being of the thing. The two meanings are not sharply distinguished in Suhrawardī's Arabic. This translation tends to use 'essence' whenever there is any doubt.

judge that every attribute added to its essence, be it knowledge or something else, belonged to its essence, it would have to have known its essence prior to and apart from any of the attributes. It would therefore not have known its essence by the superadded attributes.

(116) You are never unconscious of your essence or your apprehension of your essence. Since this apprehension cannot be by a form or by something superadded, you need nothing to apprehend your essence save that essence, which is evident in itself and not absent from itself. Therefore, it must apprehend its essence due to what it itself is in itself, and you can never be unconscious of your essence or any part of your essence. That of which your essence can be unconscious—organs such as the heart, liver, and brain and all the dark and luminous barriers and states—do not belong to that part of you that apprehends. Therefore, that in you which apprehends is neither an organ nor anything to do with a barrier, since otherwise you would always be aware of these as you are always and unceasingly aware of your own essence. Substantiality, whether taken as the perfection of its quiddity or as an expression for the denial of a subject or a locus, is not an independent entity that could be your essence itself. If substantiality is taken to be an unknown meaning and if you apprehend your essence continually by some means other than something superadded to your essence, then this substantiality, of which you are unconscious, can be neither the whole of your essence nor any part thereof. If you examine this matter closely, you will find that that by which you are you is only a thing that apprehends its own essence—your 'ego'. All else that apprehends its own essence and ego shares with you in this. Apprehension, therefore, occurs neither by an attribute nor by something superadded, of whatever sort. It is not a part of your ego, since the other part would still remain unknown. Were there something beyond consciousness and awareness, it would be unknown and would not belong to your essence, whose awareness is not superadded to it. It is thereby apparent too that thingness is not superadded to awareness, for it is evident in itself and to itself. There is no other property with it of which being evident could be a state. It is simply the evident itself—nothing more. Therefore, it is light in itself, and it is thus pure light. Your apprehension is not something else posterior to your essence. If your essence were assumed to be an identity that apprehends its essence, it would itself be prior to its apprehension and therefore be unknown—which is absurd. Thus, the matter is as we have said.

A rule

(117) If you wish to have a rule regarding light, let it be that light is that which is evident in its own reality and by essence makes another evident. It is, thus, more evident in itself than anything to whose reality being evident is superadded. Moreover, that the accidental lights are evident is not due to something superadded to them, since if that were the case they would be hidden in themselves. Rather their

being evident is simply due to their own reality. Nor is it the case that the light occurs and its being evident is a concomitant of it, since then it would not be light in its own definition and would be made evident by something else. Rather, light is evident, and its being evident is its being light. Some incorrectly argue that our vision makes evident the light of the Sun, whereas in reality its being evident is its being light. Were there no men and nothing at all possessed of senses, it would not cease to be light.

(118) Here is another way to express this: You ought not to say, 'My ego is a thing whose concomitant is being evident, but that thing is hidden in itself.' Rather, it is nothing but being evident and being light. You already know that thingness is one of the intellectual predicates and attributes, as are a thing's being a reality and a quiddity. Lack of unawareness is something negative and cannot be your quiddity. Nothing, then, remains but being evident and being light. Thus, anything that apprehends its own essence is a pure light, and every pure light is evident to itself and apprehends its own essence. This is one of the methods of proof.

A judgment [that a thing's apprehending itself is its being evident to itself]

(119) In addition, we argue that were we to posit a flavour abstracted from barriers and matter, we would only have shown that it was a flavour in itself—nothing more. If we assume a light to be incorporeal, it is light in itself; and it then follows that it is evident to itself, which is apprehension. It does not follow that an incorporeal flavour is evident to itself, only that it is a flavour in itself. Were the fact that a thing is free from prime matter and barriers sufficient to make it aware of itself, as is the opinion of the Peripatetics, then that prime matter whose existence they assert would also be aware of itself, since it is not a state in something else but has its own quiddity and is free from any other prime matter—there being no matter of prime matter. Thus, it would not be unconscious of itself, if by 'unconsciousness' they mean awareness, then the awareness of the separate intellects cannot be attributed to lack of unconsciousness. Indeed, lack of unconsciousness is an allusion to and symbol for awareness, in this sense. According to the Peripatetics, a thing's apprehension is the fact that it is incorporeal and is not unconscious of its essence. The particularity of the matter itself, as they argue, only occurs through states. So, granting that the states are hindered from apprehending their own essences by the matter, what, then, is it that hinders the matter? They admit that prime matter has particularity only through the states that they call 'forms.' If these forms occur in us, we perceive them. If prime matter in itself is just something unconditioned, or a certain substance considered apart from magnitudes and all other states, as they claim, then there is nothing that is more perfectly simple in its own definition than prime matter—especially since its substantiality is the denial of its having a subject, as they admit. Why, then, does it not apprehend its essence by reason of this freedom from substrata

and parts? And why does it not apprehend the forms that are in it? But we have explained this substantiality and thingness and have shown that these and their likes are beings of reason.

(120) Then these people argue that the Creator of everything is nothing but pure existence. But if we examine the prime matter posited by their school, it turns out that it is simply existence, since its particularity is by means of forms and substantiality, as has been explained. There is nothing that is quiddity absolutely; but rather, when some particularity is established, it is said that it is a quiddity or an existent. Prime matter, then, must either be some quiddity or some existent. If its need for forms is due to its being some existent, then the same is true of the Necessary Existent—exalted is He above that! If the Necessary Existent intellects His Essence and the things because of such simplicity, then this must also be the case with prime matter, since it too is an existent and nothing more. The falsity of such doctrines is plain. Thus, it is established that whatever apprehends its own essence is a light in itself, and vice versa. If an accidental light were assumed to be incorporeal, it would be evident in itself and to itself. That whose reality is evident in itself to itself has the reality of the light posited to be incorporeal. The one is the other; they are one and the same.

Section [six]
[On the lights and their classes]

(121) Light is divided into light of itself and in itself and light of itself but in another.[1] You know that accidental light is light in another. Thus, it is not a light *in* itself, since its existence is not a light *in* itself although it is a light *of* itself, since its existence is in another.[2] The dusky substance is not evident of itself or to itself, according to what you know. Life is a thing's being evident to itself, and a living thing is percipient and active. You know about perception; and the attribution of activity to light is clear, since light emanates by essence. Thus, pure light is alive, and every living thing is a pure light. If a dusky thing perceived its own essence, it would be light in itself and not a dusky substance. If the barrier or some dusky substance as such necessitated life and knowledge, that would have to be the case for all other things that were also barriers or dusky substances, which is not true. If the dusky substance were posited to have life and knowledge through an added state, the same argument would apply. Moreover, a state certainly cannot be evident to itself, as we already know. Nor would it be evident to the barrier, since the barrier is dusky in itself. How could something be evident to it, when something to which something else is evident must certainly be evident to itself

1. Immaterial light and accidental light respectively.

2. According to Quṭb al-Dīn, *Sharḥ*, p. 300, a light is a light *in* itself if it is manifest, and it is a light *of* itself if it is manifest to itself—in other words, if it is self-conscious.

of itself? That which has no awareness of itself cannot be aware of another. Since neither the barrier nor the state is evident to itself, nor are they evident to each other, then nothing evident to itself may result from either of them. Since the state has existence only in another, then nothing self-subsistent may result from it and the barrier. Of these two, only the barrier is self-subsistent. If one of those two perceives its own essence, it could only be that which has its own essence: the barrier. For, the barrier and the state are two things, not one—but you know that the barrier is not evident in itself.

(122) Here is another proof: We say that a thing may make something evident to something else—as accidental light does for the locus—but its being evident to another does not imply its being evident to another, then that other thing ought to be evident to itself so that something else could be evident to it. Once this is established, we say that there cannot be an entity that makes a thing evident to that same thing in such a way that that thing becomes evident to itself. This is because there is nothing closer to itself than itself. It was hidden from itself, and its self being hidden from itself is of itself. Therefore, nothing else could ever make it evident to itself. How could it be otherwise, when the fact that something else made its self evident to itself implies the absurdity that its self was already evident to itself? The barrier is thus in itself hidden from itself and nothing can make it evident to itself.

(123) There is still another way of proving this. If anything were to make the barrier evident to itself, it would be light. Every illumined body would be evident to itself and so would be alive, which is not so. No particularity that the dark states give to the barrier can make it necessary for light to make the barrier evident to itself. It has been shown by another proof that if something is evident to itself, its being evident to itself is neither by any state nor by any dusky substance.

A principle [stating that a body cannot bring another body into existence]

(124) You know that you are in yourself an incorporeal light and that you are incapable of giving existence to a barrier. If an active, living, substantial light can be incapable of giving existence to a barrier, a lifeless barrier will certainly be unable to do so.

Section [seven]

[Showing that the intellectual, incorporeal lights differ by perfection and deficiency, not by species]

(125) Light in itself varies in its reality only by perfection and deficiency and by entities external to it. If it had two parts, neither of which was light in itself, each would be either a dusky substance or a dark state, and the whole would not be a light in itself. Were one of them light and the other not light, the latter would not

participate in the luminous reality, though it was one of the parts. You will learn in detail how the lights are distinguished.

Section [eight]

[Also on the differences among the incorporeal lights]

(126) We claim that the incorporeal lights do not differ in reality. Were their realities to differ, there would be luminosity and something else in each incorporeal light. Either that other would be a state in the incorporeal light, or the incorporeal light would be a state in it, or each would be self-subsistent. If it were a state in the incorporeal light, it would be external to its reality since a state of a thing occurs in it only after its realization as an independent quiddity in the mind. Thus, the reality does not differ by the state. Were the incorporeal light a state in that other, it would not be an incorporeal light. Instead, there would be a dusky substance with an accidental light in it. Since it was posited to be an incorporeal light—this is absurd. Were each of them self-subsistent, neither could be the locus of the other nor share in a locus with the other. Not being barriers, they could not intermingle or touch, so neither would have any attachment to the other. Therefore, the incorporeal lights do not differ in their realities.

(127) Here is another proof: It has been shown that your ego is an incorporeal light, that it is self-conscious, and that the incorporeal lights do not differ in their realities. Thus, all the incorporeal lights must apprehend their own essences, since that which is necessarily true of a thing must also be true of that which has the same reality. This is another method—though if you have understood what came before; you will have no need of these proofs.

A principle [stating that which gives existence to the barriers must apprehend its own essence]

(128) Since an incorporeal light gives all the barriers their lights and existence, that light must be alive and self-conscious, since it is a light in itself.

Section [nine]

[Proving that there is a Being necessary by essence]

(129) If an incorporeal light is dependent in its quiddity, its need is not directed toward the lifeless dusky substance, which is not worthy to give existence in any respect to that which is nobler and more perfect than it. How could the dusky emanate light? Thus, though the actualization of the incorporeal depends on a self-subsistent light, these lights ordered in ranks cannot form an infinite series, since you know by demonstration that an ordered simultaneous series must be finite. Therefore, the self-subsistent and accidental lights, the barriers, and the

states of each must end in a light beyond which there is no light. This is the Light of Lights, and All-encompassing Light, the Eternal Light, the Holy Light, the All-highest Almighty Light, the Dominating Light. It is absolutely independent, since there is nothing beyond It. The existence of two independent incorporeal lights is inconceivable. They would not differ in reality, as has been shown. One would not be distinguished from the other by something they have in common; nor would they be distinguished by something assumed to be a concomitant of their reality, since they share in this as well. They would not differ by a foreign accident, dark or luminous, since there is nothing beyond them that would cause them to become particularized. If one of them particularizes itself or the other, both would be individual before their particularization without something to particularize them—though individuality and duality are inconceivable without a particularizer. Therefore, the independent incorporeal light is one. It is the Light of Lights. Everything other than It is in need of It and has its existence from It. It has no equal, nor any peer. It rules over all things, and nothing rules it or opposes it; for all sovereignty, all power, all perfection derives from It. Nonbeing cannot overtake the Light of Lights; for were it contingently non-existent, it would be a contingent existent and there would not be sufficient reason in itself for it to come into reality, as you know, but it would require some sufficient reason. Thus, it would not be independent in truth and would need something absolutely independent—which would be the Light of Lights, since this series must end.

(130) Moreover, there is another proof: A thing does not imply its own nonbeing, or else it would never enter reality. The Light of Lights is unitary, having by Its own essence no condition, and everything else follows from It. If It has no condition and no opposite, nothing can nullify It, so It is eternal and everlasting. No state, be it luminous or dark, adheres to the Light of Lights, and It may have no attribute in any respect.

(131) The general proof is that if a dark state were in It, It would necessarily have a dark aspect, in Its own reality, necessitating It. Thus, It would be composite and not a pure light. A luminous accident may only belong to that in which light is increased. Were the Light of Lights made more luminous by a state, Its independent essence would be illuminated by an accidental dependent light that It Itself necessitated. This is because there is nothing above It to necessitate a luminous accident. Thus, this is absurd.

(132) Another general proof is this: That which illumines is more luminous than that which is illuminated in that respect in which the former gives the latter its light. Thus, its essence is more luminous than the other essence—which is, in this case, impossible.

(133) Here is a detailed proof: Were the Light of Lights of Itself to necessitate a state, It would act and receive. The aspect of activity would be different that the aspect of receptivity, every recipient would be active when it received, and every

agent would be a recipient by the activity itself when it acted—but this is not so. Then it would follow that in the Light of Lights there would be two aspects: an aspect that necessitated activity and an aspect that necessitated receptivity. Since this could not regress infinitely, the series would end in two aspects in Its essence.

(134) Of course, neither of the two aspects would be an independent light, since there are not two independent lights, as you know. Nor could one of them be an independent light and the other a dependent light, since if the dependent light were a state in the other, the argument would regress. If it were not a state, it would be independent and would not be in the independent light; but this is impossible, since the dependent light was posited to be a state in the essence of the independent light. Nor could one of them be a light and the other a dark state, since this argument, too, is regressive. Nor could one of them be a dusky substance and the other in an incorporeal light. In that case, neither would be connected to the other, and the one, moreover, would not be in the essence of the Light of Lights. Thus, it is established that the Light of Lights is abstracted from all else and nothing is part of It. Nothing is conceivably more splendorous than It! Since a thing's knowledge of itself amounts to its being evident to its essence, and since the Light of Lights is pure luminosity whose being evident is not by another, the life and self-consciousness of the Light of Lights are essential, not additional to Its essence. You have already seen the proof of this for every incorporeal light.

The Second Discourse
On the order of existence, in [fourteen] sections

Section [one]
[Showing that from the Truly One, in that respect in which It is one, only one effect is generated]

(135) A light and a darkness, whether dusky substance or dark state, cannot both occur[1] from the Light of Lights; for causing a light is not the same as causing a darkness. If this could occur, the essence of the Light of Lights would be compounded from that which necessitated the light and that which necessitated the darkness. The absurdity of this has been made plain to you. Indeed, darkness can only be engendered by It through an intermediary. Moreover, the Light as light engenders only light. Nor may two lights occur from It, for the one would not be the other and that which engendered one would not be that which engendered the other. Thus, there would be two aspects in the Light of Lights—the impossibility of which we

1. Suhrawardī seems to deliberately avoid the use of the term *fayḍ*, 'emanation', preferring more neutral terms like *ṣudūr*, 'generation', and *ḥuṣūl*, 'occurrence'.

have already made clear. This is indeed sufficient proof of the impossibility of any two things occurring from It, whatsoever they might be. In further explanation, we say that there must be something that distinguishes between two things. Thus, we must explain that which they share and that by which they are distinguished. This would imply two aspects in its essence—which is absurd.

Section [two]

[Showing that what is first generated from the Light of Lights is a single incorporeal light]

(136) If we posit the existence of a darkness (occurring directly from the Light of Lights), then no light in addition to it would come about from the Light of Lights, for otherwise the aspects of the Light of Lights would have to be multiple, as was explained before. Yet, it is obvious that there are many self-conscious incorporeal lights and accidental lights. Were a darkness to be generated from the Light of Lights, it would be alone and nothing else would exist, whether lights or darknesses. Existence itself testifies to the falsity of this. Multiplicity cannot conceivably result from the Light of Lights in Its unity, nor can any darkness be conceived to result from a dusky substance or state, nor yet two lights result from the Light of Lights in Its unity. Therefore, that which first results from the Light of Lights must be a single incorporeal light. This, then, cannot be distinguished from the Light of Lights by any dark state acquired from the Light of Lights. This would imply the multiplicity of aspects in the Light of Lights in contradiction to the demonstration that the lights, particularly the incorporeal lights, do not differ in their realities. Therefore, the Light of Lights and the first light that results from It are only to be distinguished by perfection and deficiency. Just as among the objects of sensation the acquired light is not like the radiating light in its perfection, so, too, is the case with the incorporeal lights. The accidental lights may differ in their perfection and weakness by reason of the light that illumines them, though the recipient and its capacity remain the same. A single wall may accept the light of the Sun or of a lamp or the light of the Sun's rays reflected from a glass onto the clay; but it is plain that the light the clay receives from the Sun is more perfect than that which is reflected from a glass or which comes from a lamp. The difference in perfection and deficiency between them is due only to the two givers of light. The agent may also be the same; but the perfection or deficiency of the ray may differ by reason of the recipient, as is the case with the rays of the Sun that fall upon crystal, jet, or earth. That which crystal or jet accepts, for example, is more perfect. The incorporeal light, however, has no recipient, so that all such lights other than the Light of Lights have their perfection and deficiency by reason of the rank of their agent. The perfection of the Light of Lights has no cause; rather, It is the pure light which has no admixture of dependence or deficiency.

(137) Question: Insofar as the quiddity of luminosity does not necessitate perfection, would not its particularization as the Light of Light (*sic*) be a contingent effect?[1]

Answer: the quiddity of luminosity is a mental universal, not in itself particularized in the external world. That which is concrete is a single thing, neither a basis nor a perfection. The mental thing has beings of reason inconceivable in the concrete thing.

(138) Allusion has already been made to the arbitrary assertion that the self-subsistent thing does not admit of perfection and deficiency. Indeed, the difference between the accidental lights and the incorporeal lights, to which reference has already been made, consists in two aspects: the ranks of the agent and of the recipient. It has been shown that the first emanation of the Light of Lights is single—the Proximate Light, the Mighty Light, that which some of the Pahlawīs aforetime called 'Bahman'.[2] The Proximate Light is dependent in itself but independent by virtue of the first. The existence of a light from the Light of Lights does not happen by the separation of something from It, for you know that separation and connection are specific properties of bodies. Far exalted is the Light of Lights above that! Nor can it be by something moving from It, since states do not move, and you know the absurdity of there being states in the Light of Lights. We have written for you a chapter in which it is shown that the rays of the Sun simply exist by reason of it, nothing more. So you must also understand that this is so for every accidental shining light or incorporeal light. It must not be imagined that an accident is transferred or that a body is separated from it.

Section [three]

[Concerning the determinations of these barriers]

(139) Know that in any direction you may point, there are limits. If there were no impenetrable barrier surrounding all other barriers, then movement and pointing would go on into nothingness once they passed this last sphere—though it has been clearly explained to you that ordered simultaneous classes, whether bodily or otherwise, are finite. Nonbeing cannot conceivably be pointed to. It would be the same if this all-encompassing barrier admitted of division or if it were composed of many barriers. In the latter case, each one of these barriers—even if it was assumed to be indivisible—would necessarily be composite and so would be subject to compounding and division. Thus, movement could occur toward nothing and

1. In other words, there must be some cause to explain the perfection of the Light of Lights, since other lights have the same quiddity of light and yet are not the Light of Lights.

2. 'Bahman' is the New Persian and Arabic form of the name of the Avestan Vohu Manah (Good Thought), the first of the Zoroastrian archangels (*ameša spentas*) to be created by Ahura Mazda.

in no particular direction—which is absurd. Also, heterogeneous things must necessarily occur individually first and then be compounded. The simple substance must first be made as a single body and then be divided, if it admits of that. Thus, it must necessarily be a homogeneous, single, indivisible, all-encompassing barrier in which parts cannot even be imagined to exist. Two different directions cannot occur from it alone, for it is single and homogeneous, from which in itself only one direction can occur—namely, height. All that is near to it is high. Therefore, the low is simply the extremity of distance from it—that is, the centre. This, then, is the encompassing barrier.

(140) There is evidence showing the indivisibility of that entity from which direction is derived and which was posited to be unique. If that which moves upwards were to divide it, then either it moves upwards after penetrating the nearer of the two parts (in which case 'up' refers only to the farther part) or it moves away from up (in which case 'up' refers only to the nearer part). In either case, all of that which was assumed to be the direction of a part is the direction (of the whole), and the other part would have no role in it. While we said that that which has no role in direction is not to be considered together with that from which the direction is, the same arguments do not apply to the 'down' determined by the centre of the celestial sphere.[1] When the moving thing reaches its limit, it becomes, by virtue of its portion of bulk, part of that which has essentially the extreme of lowness. Each thing is related to a place by being in it, its place being different from it and different from its parts. It is possible for its parts to move in relation to the parts of that which is posited to be its place, whether the transfer cannot be complete (as is the case with the spheres) or can be complete (as is the case with other things). Therefore, place is the interior of its proximate container, and that which is not contained has no place.

Section [four]

[Showing that the movements of the spheres are voluntary and how the many are generated from the Light of Lights]

(141) The lifeless barrier does not revolve of itself; for no lifeless thing can have a goal that it seeks, reaches, and then separates itself from. If an inanimate thing does tend, of itself and by nature, toward something, it does not then leave its goal; for it would then tend by nature toward something from which it was also repelled—which is absurd. Every point that the celestial barriers seek they also leave without anything compelling them, for the lower has no power over the higher. Nor do they vie with each other, since there is no mutual resistance between the encompassing and the encompassed, neither one of which leaves its place. How,

1. Suhrawardī is replying to the objection that the same argument could be used to prove the indivisibility of the earth.

indeed, could they, when they have differing movements while sharing the daily movement? The daily movement is not compelled, for the compelled movement would not result from another movement,[1] and the body cannot at the same time have two different movements by essence in one state. There can be no doubt that some of the movements of the spheres are accidental and some essential, as when a man walks on board a ship in a direction different from its movement so that he accepts one motion essentially and the other by virtue of what he is in. Thus, the daily motion in which all the celestial barriers participate can only be from the encompassing spheres, while each one of the spheres has another motion. The mover of each one of these barriers is alive by essence and is therefore an incorporeal light. Thus, it is also plain that the barriers are ruled by the lights. Because the spheres are preserved from corruption, desires, and anger and the movement cannot be for the sake of some desire related to barriers, it must be for some luminous goal. The seven planets are known to have many movements so they must have many barriers. None of these are independent; rather, each is in need of an incorporeal light for its realization and perfections.

(142) Now, only the Proximate Light comes to be from the Light of Lights. The Proximate Light does not contain multiple aspects, since any multiplicity in it would imply multiplicity in that which necessitated it and thus imply the absurdity of multiplicity in the Light of Lights. However, there is multiplicity in the barriers. If only a single barrier and no light come to be from the Proximate Light, existence would cease with it. But this is not so, since barriers do have multiplicity, as do their managing lights. Then, if an incorporeal light came to be from the Proximate Light, and from this light came another incorporeal light without ever leading to barriers, everything would be lights. Thus, although the Proximate light cannot bring into being a dusky substance with respect to its own luminosity, yet still a barrier and an incorporeal light must result from it, since it contains dependence in itself and independence by virtue of the First. Its intellection of its dependence is a dark state; but it beholds the Light of Lights and beholds its own essence, since there is no veil between it and the Light of Lights. There are only veils among barriers, dusky substances, and dimensions. The Light of Lights and the incorporeal lights have no direction or dimension at all. Thus, by that whereby (an incorporeal light) beholds the Light of Lights, it shadows and darkens itself in comparison to It, since the more perfect light rules the more deficient. By the manifestation to itself of its dependence and the darkening of its own essence in its contemplation of the glory of the Light of Lights in relation to itself, a shadow results from (the incorporeal light). This is the loftiest barrier, greatest of the barriers, the all-encompassing barrier of which we made mention. But with respect to its independence and its necessity by

1. Quṭb al-Dīn, *Sharḥ*, pp. 230–231, explains that the daily movement of the outermost sphere, which the other spheres follow, cannot be by compulsion, since there is no sphere beyond it to drive it and since the motion of a lower sphere cannot drive the motion of a higher sphere.

the Light of Lights and its contemplation of its glory and might, it brings into being another incorporeal light. The barrier is its shadow, and the self-subsistent light is illumination from it. Its shadow is only due to the darkness of its dependence. By 'darkness' here, we merely mean that which is not light in its own essence.

A principle [explaining how multiplicity comes to be]

(143) Since there is no veil between the lower and the higher light, the lower light beholds the higher and the higher shines upon the lower. Thus, a ray[1] from the Light of Lights shines upon the Proximate Light. If it is argued that the aspects of the Light of Lights must become multiple by Its giving existence and illuminating, one may reply that that which is impossible because it leads to multiplicity is that the Light of Lights should give existence to two things simply by virtue of Its essence. That is not the case here. The existence of the Proximate Light is solely from the essence of the Light of Lights, and the absence of any veil. There are a multiplicity of aspects here, a receptive cause, and conditions. Many different things may indeed result from the one thing by virtue of differing and multiple states of receptivity.

Section[2] [five]

[Concerning the generosity of the Light of Lights]

(144) Generosity is giving that which is appropriate without any recompense. The one who seeks praise or reward works for a wage, as does the one who seeks to be free of blame and the like. But there is nothing more generous than that which is light in its own reality. By its essence, it reveals itself to and emanates upon every receptive one. The True King is He who possesses the essence of everything but whose essence is possessed by none. He is the Light of Lights.

A principle [governing beholding]

(145) Since you know that vision is not by the imprinting of the form of its object in the eye nor by something emerging from the eye, it can only be by the illumined object being opposite a sound eye—nothing more. Imagination and images in mirrors will be explained later, for they have great importance. Being opposite amounts to the absence of a veil between that which sees and that which is seen. Extreme nearness hinders vision only because illumination or luminosity is a condition of being seen. There must be two lights: the seeing light and the light seen. When the eyelid is covered, there can be no question of its being illuminated by external lights, nor does the light of vision have the power of luminosity to illuminate it. Thus,

1. 'Ray' should be understood not as a line of light connecting the radiant existent with the thing it illumines but as an increase in illumination caused by the presence of the illumined thing before the radiant light.

2. Some manuscripts read 'Principle'.

one cannot see due to the lack of illumination. This is the case with all excessive nearness. Extreme distance acts as a veil because of the small degree to which they face each other. Thus, the nearer the illuminated object or light, the more easily it is beheld, so long as it remains a light or illuminated.

Another Illuminationist principle [explaining that beholding the light is not the same as the shining of a ray of that light upon that which beholds it]

(146) Know that your eye both beholds and is shone upon by a ray. The shining of the ray is not beholding; for the ray falls upon the eye wherever it is, but the seeing eye can only behold the Sun when it faces the Sun from a great distance, as was indicated before. Were the eyelid luminous or the Sun as near as the eyelid, both the ray and the beholding would be increased accordingly.

Section [six]

[Showing that every higher light has dominance in relation to the lower light and the lower light and that the lower light has love in relation to the higher light]

(147) The lower light cannot comprehend the higher light, for the higher light dominates it; but the lower light nevertheless beholds the higher. When the lights become many, the higher light possesses a dominance over the lower light, and the lower has a desire and passion for the higher. The Light of Lights has a dominance in relation to what is other than It. It does not Itself have a passion for another, but It does have a passion for Itself, because Its perfection is evident to It. It is the most beautiful of things, the most perfect of things. It is more evident to Itself than anything else; for nothing else is so evident, either to that thing itself or to another. Pleasure occurs only by the apprehension of the actual perfection in respect to its being perfection and actual. He who is unconscious of the acquisition of a perfection does not experience pleasure. The pleasure experienced by the one who experiences pleasure is in the measure of his perfection and his apprehension of his perfection. Since there is nothing more perfect, nothing more beautiful than the Light of Lights—nothing more evident to Itself and to another—then there is nothing more pleasurable to Itself and to another than the Light of Lights. It has a passion for Its own essence and is the object of the passion of its own essence and of everything else.

At the root of the deficient light is passion for the higher light. At the root of the higher light is dominance over the lower light. Just as the fact that the Light of Lights is evident to its essence is not something added to its essence, so too, its pleasure and passion are not additional to its essence. Just as the luminosity of another cannot be compared to it, the pleasure and passion of another cannot be compared to its pleasure in its own essence or to its passion for its own essence—nor can the passion of other things for another be compared to their passion for and pleasure in it. Thus, all existence is ordered on the basis of love and dominance. The rest of this will be explained to you. Since the incorporeal lights are multiple, they necessarily have the most perfect order.

Section [seven]

[Showing that the love of each lower light for itself is dominated by its love for the higher light]

(148) The Proximate Light beholds and is illuminated by the Light of Lights. It loves the Light of Lights and itself, but its love for itself is dominated by its love for the Light of Lights

Section [eight]

[Showing that the incorporeal light does not shine by something being separated from it]

(149) The illumination of the Light of Lights upon the incorporeal lights is not by something being separated from it, as has already been made clear to you. Rather, the illumination is a radiated light that occurs due to it in the incorporeal light. It is like the illumination caused by the Sun in that which admits of such illumination. Beholding is another matter, to which we have made an analogy for you. The light that occurs in the incorporeal lights from the Light of Lights is that which we distinguish by the name 'propitious[1] light'. It is an accidental light, for accidental light is divided into that which occurs in bodies and that which occurs in the incorporeal lights.

Section [nine]

[On how and in what order the many are generated from the truly one]

(150) From the Proximate Light a barrier and an incorporeal light result, and from this light result another incorporeal light and barrier. This continues until there are the nine spheres and the elemental world. You know that the succession of ordered lights must be finite, so the series ceases with a light from which no other incorporeal light results. Since we meet with a star in each of the ethereal barriers—and, in the sphere of fixed stars, with such stars as are beyond the power of man to number—to these must correspond individuals and aspects beyond our reckoning. Thus, it is known that the sphere of fixed stars does not result from the Proximate Light, since the causal aspects thereof do not suffice for the fixed stars.

1. The word means both a favourable omen and something that comes into the mind.

If it is from one of the higher lights, that light cannot have many aspects, especially in the view of those who consider each intellect to have only the aspects of necessity and contingency. If it is from the lower lights, how, then, may this sphere be conceived to be greater and higher than the barriers of the higher intellects when its stars are more numerous than theirs? This leads to absurdities. Let us not, then, linger over this series that the Peripatetics talk of. Each star in the sphere of fixed stars has a particularity, requiring it to be necessitated and requiring something to necessitate it, by which it is particularized.

(151) Therefore, the dominating lights—that is, the incorporeal lights free of connections with barriers—are more in number than ten, or twenty, or one hundred, or two hundred, or a thousand, or two thousand, or a hundred thousand. Some among them cause no independent barrier, for the individual independent barriers are fewer in number than the stars are ordered in rank. So a second light results from the Proximate Light, and from the second a third, and likewise a fourth and fifth, up to a great number. Each of these beholds the Light of Lights and is up to a great number. Each of these beholds the Light of Lights and is shone upon by Its rays. Moreover, light is reflected from one to another of the dominating lights. Each higher light shines upon those that are below it in rank, and the lower light receives rays from the Light of Lights by the mediacy of those that are above it, rank on rank. Thus, the second dominating light receives the propitious light from the Light of Lights twice: once from it, without intermediary, and another time with respect to the Proximate Light. The third light receives it four times: the two reflections from its master,[1] from the Light of Lights without mediacy, and from the Proximate Light. The fourth receives it eight times: the two reflections from its master, the two reflections from the second, once from the Proximate Light, and from the Light of Lights without intermediary. In this way they are doubled and redoubled to a very great number; for in the case of the higher incorporeal lights, the lower light is not veiled from the Light of Lights, veiling being a peculiarity of the dimensions and distractions of the barriers. Moreover, each dominating light beholds the Light of Lights, and beholding is not the same as being shone upon and the emanation of rays, as you know. If the propitious lights have redoubled from the Light of Lights in this way, how, then, must be the doubling by reflection of each higher light by its beholding and by its shining its light upon each lower light with, and without intermediaries!

(152) If the rays of physical light fall upon a barrier, the light on it is increased in accordance with their numbers. These may be united in a single locus in such a way that the individual rays may not be distinguished except through their causes. When the rays of several lamps fall upon a wall, for example, though one of them may be shaded, another will remain. This is not like something that becomes more

1. Meaning the light immediately above it that gives it being.

intense from one or two sources with the intensity remaining after them, nor is it like the parts of a cause of one thing, however it may be. Many illuminations may be combined in a single locus, like two desires for two things in a single locus. The barrier has no knowledge of the increase caused by each illumination, but the essence of a living thing is itself conscious of what illuminates it and of the increase in illumination from each. Thus, a great number of dominating lights result, rank on rank, one from another, in accordance with the particular beholdings and the magnitude of the complete rays. These are the fundamental and highest dominating lights. Then other individual lights result from these fundamental lights by reason of the combinations of aspects, interactions, and correspondences. For example, there is the interaction of the aspects of independence, dominance, or love with them. There is the interaction of the rays of one dominating light with another, or the rays of dominating lights with the aspects of beholding each other. There is the interaction of their substantial essences, or the interaction of one of the rays of some one of them with one of the rays of another. The fixed stars and their sphere result from the interaction of the rays of all of them, especially the lower, weak lights with the aspect of dependence. The constellations of the fixed stars correspond to the interaction of the rays of all of them, especially the lower, weak lights with the aspect of dependence. The constellations of the fixed stars correspond to the interaction of the rays of some with others. By the interaction of the rays with the aspects of independence, dominance, and love, and the extraordinary correspondences between the perfect, intense rays and the others, the dominating lights bring into being the celestial archetypes[1] of special and the talismans of the simples, the elemental compounds, and all that is beneath the sphere of the stars.

(153) The origin of each of these talismans is a dominating light that is the 'archetype of the talisman' and the luminous self-subsistent species. Insofar as the archetypes of the talismans fall under the classes of love, dominance, and moderation in accordance with their origins, the planets and other things differ in being fortunate, sinister, or intermediate. The dominating luminous species are prior to their individual—that is, prior intellectually. The most noble contingency[2] necessitates the existence of these incorporeal luminous species. The species do not occur in our world simply by chance, for there is no man save man, nor wheat save wheat. The species preserved among us are not by chance. They are not due solely to the conception of the souls moving the spheres, nor are they ends. Because the conceptions of these souls are from above them, they must have causes. We shall prove

1. Literally, 'masters of species idols', meaning the incorporeal lights that are the Platonic Forms of the various earthly species. It is synonymous with 'lords of talismans', 'talismans' being the earthy instances of the Platonic Forms: individual men or horses. Talismans and idols both are material representations of immaterial spiritual realities. This complex of terms stoutly resists being rendered by English equivalents that are both literal and clear.

2. This is a technical term for a fundamental Illuminationist principle stating that every existent must have a cause ontologically prior and superior to it. See section 164 below.

the non-existence of that which they name 'providence.' There are no such things as species forms corresponding to what is below them engraved in the dominating incorporeal lights, for these lights are not affected by what is below them. Nor do the forms occurring accidentally in some of them result from the forms occurring in another, for this would imply multiplicity in the Light of Lights. Thus, their species must be self-subsistent and fixed in the World of Light.

(154) It is inconceivable that dominating lights of equal rank come into existence simultaneously from the Light of Lights, for multiplicity is inconceivable from It. Thus, there must be intermediate lights ranked vertically. Nor can the higher-ranked dominating lights be archetypes and of equal rank. Therefore, the archetypes of equal rank must be caused by the exalted lights and their multiplicity be from the interactions of rays in the higher lights. If some excellence and some deficiency is conceivable in the archetypes of talismans due to the perfection and deficiency of the rays that necessitate them, the like must occur in the talismans,[1] so that one species rules over another species in some respect, but not in all. Were the ranks of volume among the spheres caused by the exalted ranked lights, Mars would be unconditionally more noble than the Sun and Venus. This is not so, since some have larger planets and some larger spheres while being equal in other respects. Thus, the same must also be true of their lords—which is to say, the archetypes. The fixed and everlasting excellences are not based on chance, but on the archetypes of the ranks of their sphere.[2]

(155) The incorporeal lights are divided into two classes. The first are dominating lights, those with no connection to barriers, either of imprinting or control. The dominating lights include exalted dominating lights and formal dominating lights: the archetypes. Second are the lights managing barriers. Though they are not imprinted in the barriers, they occur from each master of an idol in its barrier shadow with respect to some exalted luminous aspect. If its barrier admits of being controlled by a managing light, the barrier itself is from an aspect of dependence. The incorporeal light does not admit of connection or division; for division, though it is but the lack of connection, is only said of that in which there might be connection. The aspects of dependence in the exalted lights is made evident in the common barrier.[3] These aspects of dependence are also made evident in the talismanic archetypes as an aspect of dependence by which their luminosity is diminished. Dependence in the lower lights is greater than in the exalted lights. Since ranks must be finite, there cannot be a dominating light from every dominating light, nor multiplicity from every multiplicity, nor a ray from every ray. Deficiency ends in that which necessitates nothing at all, even though multiplicity may only

1. Some manuscripts read 'archetypes of talismans'.

2. Reading *muthul*. If it is read as *mithl*, the meaning would be 'on something like the ranks of their sphere'. Some manuscripts read, 'on the ranks of their causes'.

3. The sphere of the fixed stars, according to Quṭb al-Dīn, *Sharḥ*, 353.

be conceived to be caused by multiplicity and a dominating light by another dominating light.

(156) Since the spheres are alive and have managing lights, their managing lights are not their causes, since the luminous cause is not perfected by the dusky substance, and the dusky substance does not dominate the luminous cause by this connection. On the other hand, the managing light is dominated in a certain respect by its connection. That which manages it is an incorporeal light that we might name 'the commanding light'. From this fact, you will know that by virtue of the First it necessarily has the aspects of dominance and love; and in the dominating lights there are the two aspects of the duskiness of dependence and luminosity. Thus, the classes of effects must be ordered as follows: a light in which dominance is predominant; a light in which love is predominant; a dusky substance in which dominance is predominant, as some of the luminous planets; another dusky substance in which love is predominant, as with other luminous planets; non-luminous dusky substances in which dominance is predominant—the ethereals immune from induced corruption; and the dusky substances in which love and lowliness are predominant—the elementals obedient to and loving their vile lights when they are veiled from them. Since fire is near to the ethereals, it also necessarily has dominance over what is below it. We will explain that, if God the Exalted be willing.

(157) Know that in relation to its effect every luminous cause possesses love and dominance, and that its effect possesses a love whose concomitant is humility. Therefore, all existence occurs in pairs, being divided into luminous and dusky; love and dominance; might—the concomitant of dominance in relation to the lower—and humility—the concomitant of love in relation to the higher. As it is written, 'All things have We created in pairs, that perchance ye might take heed' (Qur'ān 51:49).

Section [ten]

[Completing the discussion of the fixed stars and the other planets]

(158) Since the arrangement of the fixed stars is not haphazard, it is the shadow of some intelligible order; but this order—nay, even the pattern of the planets among the fixed stars—is beyond the knowledge of any man. The wonders of the ethereal world, the relations among the spheres, their precise and certain enumeration—all these are very difficult. And there is nothing to prevent there being other wonders imperceptible to us in and beyond the fixed stars.[1]

(159) There is nothing lifeless in the ethereal world. The sovereignty and power of the higher managing lights reach the spheres through the mediacy of the planets. From them their faculties go forth, and the planet is like the absolute and supreme

1. Some manuscripts read 'the sphere of fixed stars'.

organ. 'Hūrakhsh', who is the talisman of 'Shahrīr',[1] is a light of great brilliance, the maker of the day, lord of the sky, to be venerated, according to the custom of the Illuminationists. It does not exceed the planets by magnitude and nearness—rather, by intensity—for the magnitude of all that which is seen from the fixed stars at night and from the rest of the planets is incomparably greater than the Sun and yet does not make the day.

Section [eleven]

[In explanation of His knowledge—exalted be He!—according to the Illuminationist principle]

(160) It is clear that vision is not conditioned on the imprinting of an image or on the emission of something: it is sufficient for there to be no veil between the seer and the object of vision. The Light of Lights is evident to Itself, as was shown before, and all else is evident to It. 'Not the weight of an atom in the heavens or in the earth escapes Him' (Qur'ān 34:3), since nothing veils It from anything. Thus, Its knowledge and vision are one, as are Its luminosity and power, since light emanates by Its essence.

(161) The Peripatetics and their followers say: 'The Necessary Existent's knowledge is not something superadded to It but is only its lack of absence from Its incorporeal essence.' They also say: 'The existence of things is from Its knowledge of them.' Against them, it may be argued that if (the Necessary Existent) knows and then the thing follows from Its knowledge, the knowledge is prior to the things and to the lack of absence from them; for lack of absence of things is posterior to their actualization. Just as (the Necessary Existent's) effect is not Its essence, so, too, Its knowledge of Its effect is not Its knowledge of Itself. Their argument that Its knowledge of Its concomitant is bound up in Its knowledge of Itself is without force, since according to this Its knowledge is negative. How can the knowledge of things be contained in a negation? Incorporeality is negative, as is lack of absence; for 'presence' cannot be taken to mean 'lack of absence', since the thing is not present to itself. That which is present is not him to whom it is present. Thus, 'presence' may only be said of two things, or 'lack of absence' is yet more general. How, then, may knowledge of another be encompassed in a negation? Moreover, risibility[2] is something other than humanity, and knowledge of it is not knowledge of humanity. For us, the knowledge of risibility is not bound up in humanity,[3] for humanity does not indicate it by correspondence or inclusion, but only externally.

1. 'Hūrakhsh' is the sun. 'Shahrīr' is the Zoroastrian angel Xshathra Vairya, 'Good Dominion', associated with the sky and metal.

2. 'Risibility' is the ability to laugh, which is a property of all human beings but is not part of the essence of humanity.

3. Some manuscripts read 'in the knowledge of humanity'.

Even if we know risibility, we also need another form[1] known to us potentially, apart from that form. They make analogies to explain the differences among the detailed knowledge of subjects, the potential knowledge of them, and the kind of knowledge man finds in himself as soon as the question is asked, but these analogies are worthless. When men find knowledge potentially in themselves when they are presented with questions, they have found in themselves an ability and power to answer such questions. This power is nearer than before the question [was asked], for potentiality has degrees. [A man] does not know the answer to each one in particular so long as he does not possess the form of each one. [But] the Necessary Existent is exalted above these things. Moreover, if C is not B, how can such a negation be knowledge of both and be the providence that knows the order best for both? And if Its knowledge of things occurs from the things, then how can you seek prior providence toward the things or prior knowledge of them?

(162) Therefore, the truth about the Necessary Existent's knowledge is given in the Illuminationist principle—that is, Its knowledge of Its essence is Its being a light in Its essence and evident to Its essence. Its knowledge of things is their being evident to It, either in themselves or in their connections, which are the locations where the higher managing lights continuously perceive them.[2] That is a relation, and the lack of veil is negative. That this in itself is sufficient is indicated by the fact that vision occurs simply by the relation of the thing's being evident to vision, along with the lack of any veil. Thus, the relation of the Necessary Existent to anything evident to It is Its vision and perception of that thing. The multiplication of intellectual relations does not imply multiplicity in Its essence. Though there is no such thing as providence, the order of the world is a concomitant of the wonderful arrangement and relations necessitated by the incorporeal lights and their reflected illuminations, as was explained before. This 'providence' is part of what they use to refute the principles of those upholding the luminous realities and the talismanic archetypes—but there is no truth to it. Once this is refuted, it follows that the order of the barriers is based on the order among the pure lights and their illuminations in the descending order of causal rank, such causality being impossible for barriers.[3]

(163) If there is black and white in a certain surface, the white will appear nearer, since it is closer to being evident in the way that near things are. The black will appear more distant for the opposite reason. Thus, in the world of pure light, which is without the dimension of distance, all that is higher in degree

1. That is, the form of humanity.

2. According to Quṭb al-Dīn, *Sharḥ*, 365, these are the past and future contingents, which are manifest in the souls of the spheres.

3. Since bodies cannot cause bodies, this hierarchical order must be based on the causal relations among the lights.

of cause is closer to that which is lowest because of the intensity of its being evident. Exalted be the Farthest and the Nearest, the Loftiest and the Lowest! If it is nearer, it is more worthy to influence and perfect each essence. Light is the very lodestone of nearness!

Section [twelve]

[On the principle of the most noble contingency]

(164) One of the Illuminationist principles is that if a baser contingent exists, a nobler contingent must already have existed. Thus, if the Light of Lights had necessitated the basest darkness through Its unitary aspect, no aspect would have remained to necessitate that which was more noble. If it were supposed to exist, it would require the absurdity of an aspect more noble than the Light of Lights to necessitate it. We have demonstrated the existence of the incorporeal managing lights in man. The dominating light—that which is entirely incorporeal—is nobler than the managing light; being further from connections with darkness, it is thus nobler. Thus, its existence must be prior. Therefore, in all things except contingency, you must believe that which is noblest and best of the Proximate Light, the dominating lights, the spheres, and the managing lights. These are beyond the world of chance, so nothing prevents them from being as perfect as they may be.

(165) There is a wondrous order occurring in the world of darknesses and barriers, but the relations among the noble lights are nobler than the relations of darkness and so must be prior to them. The followers of the Peripatetics admit that there is such a wondrous order among the barriers, yet they confine the intellects to ten. Thus, according to their principles, the world of barriers would have to be more wondrous than the world of lights, more subtle and generous in its order, and the wisdom therein greater. This is not true, since a sound mind will judge that the wisdom of the world of light and the subtle order and astonishing correspondences occurring therein are greater than that of the world of darkness, which is but a shadow of the world of light. That there are dominating lights, that the Creator of all is a light, that the archetypes are among the dominating lights—the pure souls have often beheld this to be so when they have detached themselves from their bodily temples. They then seek proof of it for others. All those possessing insight and detachment bear witness to this. Most of the allusions of the prophets and the great philosophers point to this. Plato, Socrates before him, and those before Socrates—like Hermes, Agathadaemon, and Empedocles—all held this view. Most said plainly that they had beheld it in the world of light. Plato related that he himself had stripped off the darkness and beheld it. The sages of Persia and India without exception agreed upon this. If the observation of one or two individuals is to be given weight in astronomy, how, then, may we ignore the testimony of the pillars of philosophy and prophecy as to that which they beheld in their spiritual observations?

(166) The author of these lines was once zealous in defence of the Peripatetic path in denying these things.[1] He was indeed nearly resolved upon that view, 'until he saw his Lord's demonstration' [Qur'ān 12:24]. Whoso questions the truth of this—whoever is unconvinced by the proof—let him engage in mystical disciplines and service to those visionaries, that perchance he will, as one dazzled by the thunderbolt, see the light blazing in the Kingdom of Power and will witness the heavenly essences and lights that Hermes and Plato beheld. He will see the spiritual luminaries, the wellsprings of kingly splendour[2] and wisdom that Zoroaster told of, and that which the good and blessed king Kay-Khusraw unexpectedly beheld in a flash. All the sages of Persia were agreed thereon. For them, even water possessed an archetype in the heavenly kingdom, which they named 'Khordad'. That of trees they named 'Mordad', and that of fire 'Ordibehesht'.[3] These are the lights to which Empedocles and others alluded.

(167) Do not imagine that these great men, mighty and possessed of insight, held that humanity had an intellect that was its universal form and that was existent, one and the same, in many. How could they allow there to be something unconnected to matter, yet in matter? How could one thing be in many and uncounted material individuals? It is not that they considered the human archetype, for example, to be given existence as a copy of that which is below it. No men hold more firmly that the higher does not occur because of the lower. Were this not their view, the form would have another form, and so to infinity.

(168) Nor should you imagine that they held [universal forms] to be composite, for that would have implied that they would disintegrate some day. Instead, these are luminous simple essences, though their idols[4] are only conceivable as composite. The form need not have a resemblance [to concrete things] in every respect, for even the Peripatetics admit that humanity in the mind corresponds to the many and is a form of the concrete things, though it is incorporeal and they are not, and that it is without magnitude or substance and the concrete things are otherwise. Thus, being a form is not conditioned on resemblance [to concrete things] in every respect. Moreover, they need not hold that animality has a form, and bipedality as well. Rather, each thing whose existence is independent has something holy that corresponds to it. The scent of musk does not have a form and the musk another; rather, there is a dominating light in the world of pure light with luminous states—rays and states of love, pleasure, and dominance—whose shadow falling in this world has as its idol musk with its scent, or sugar with its

1. That is, denying that there are more than ten immaterial intellects—or in other words that the Platonic Forms exist.

2. The terms in this passage translated as 'spiritual' and 'kingly splendour' are words borrowed from pre-Islamic Persian and carry strong Zoroastrian connotations.

3. These are well-known Zoroastrian angels associated with nature.

4. Meaning, their material instances, such as individual men. The Arabic expression rendered here as 'archetypes' is literally 'masters of idols'.

taste, or the human form with its various organs, according to the interaction mentioned above.

(169) There are metaphors in the words of the Ancients. They did not deny that predicates are mental and that universals are in the mind; but when they said, 'There is a universal man in the world of intellect', they meant that there is a dominating light containing different interacting rays and whose shadow among magnitudes is the form of man. It is a universal—not in the sense that it is a predicate, but in the sense that it has the same relation of emanation to these individuals. It is as though it were the totality and the principle. This universal is not that universal whose conception does not preclude being shared; for they believe that it has a particularized essence and that it knows its essence. How, then, could it be a universal idea? When they called one of the spheres a universal orb and another particular, they did not mean 'universal' in the sense used in logic. Know this well!

(170) Some men adduce in proof of the forms the argument that humanity per se is not many, and so it is one. This is not valid, for humanity as such implies neither unity nor multiplicity but may be said of both. Were unity a condition of the notion of humanity, humanity could not be said of many. To say that humanity does not imply multiplicity does not mean that its not implying multiplicity then implies unity. Though the contradictory of multiplicity is non-multiplicity, its not implying multiplicity is not an implication of non-multiplicity, and the contradictory of implying multiplicity is nothing more than not implying multiplicity. This latter may be so without implying unity. Therefore, the unitary humanity said of all is only in the mind, and its use as a predicate does not require another form. The argument that the individuals perish but the species endures does not necessitate that there be something universal and self-subsistent. One might well answer that what endures is a form in the mind and with the origins.[1] All such arguments are rhetorical.

(171) The faith of Plato and the master visionaries is not built upon such rhetorical arguments, but upon something else. Plato said: 'When freed from my body I beheld luminous spheres'. These that he mentioned are the very same highest heavens that some men will behold at their resurrection 'on the day when the earth will be changed for another earth and heavens, and will appear before God, the One, the Triumphant' [Qur'ān 14:48]. Plato and his companions showed plainly that they believed the Maker of the universe and the world of intellect to be light when they said that the pure light is the world of intellect. Of himself, Plato said that in certain of his spiritual conditions he would shed his body and become free from matter. Then he would see light and splendour within his essence. He would ascend to that all-encompassing divine cause and would seem to be located and suspended in it, beholding a mighty light in that lofty and divine place. The passage of which this is a summary ended with the words 'but thought veiled that light from me'.[2]

---

1. Meaning, among the immaterial lights; cf. Quṭb al-Dīn, *Sharḥ*, 377.
2. Pseudo-Aristotle, 'Theology of Aristotle', in *Aflūṭīn 'ind al-'Arab*, ed. 'Abd al-Raḥmān

And thus spoke he who gave the Law to Arab and Persian: 'God hath seven and seventy veils of light. Were these to be stripped from His face, the majesty of His countenance would consume all that He beheld.' And God, 'the Light of the heavens and the earth' [Qur'ān 24:35], revealed unto him, 'The throne is of My light.'

In the prophetic prayers we find: 'O Light of Light! Thou wouldst be veiled without Thy creation and no light would behold Thy Light. O Light of all light! The people of the heavens are illumined by Thy Light, and the people of earth are brightened by Thy Light. O Light of all light! O Thou Who dost extinguish every light by Thy Light.' And among the traditional prayers is this: 'I ask Thee by the light of Thy Countenance, which fills the pillars of Thy Throne.' I do not adduce these things as proofs; I only point them out. The testimonies in the holy books and the words of the ancient sages are beyond count.

Badawī (Cairo, 1955), 22.

2

Shams al-Dīn Muḥammad Shahrazūrī

Shams al-Dīn Muḥammad ibn Maḥmūd Shahrazūrī, a major figure in post-Avicennan philosophy and especially in the School of Illumination, and an illustrious biographer of philosophers, sages and thinkers in the Islamic and even pre-Islamic world, lived in the seventh/thirteenth century. Although his *Nuzhat al-arwāḥ wa rawḍat al-afrāḥ* (Excursion of Spirits and Garden of Delights) also known as *Fī tārīkh al-ḥukamā' wa'l-falāsifah*) recounts the life and thought of 122 notable figures, his own life has remained shrouded in mystery. We know that he was born in Shahrazūr but do not know the exact date of his birth or his death. By some accounts he was alive in 687/1288, whereas the contemporary scholar M. T. Dānish-Pazhūh mentions that he died in 687/1288.

If we know little of him as a person, a number of his works have survived that provide us with detailed information about his intellectual orientation. We know that he was an avid follower of Shihāb al-Dīn Suhrawardī, the master and founder of the School of Illumination (*ishrāq*) whom he referred to as '*al-Shaykh al-ilāhī*' (divine master).

Shahrazūrī's major work is a philosophical encyclopedia entitled *al-Shajarah al-ilāhiyyah* that he completed in 680/1281. According to Hossein Ziai, this work was composed 'after most, if not all of his other works'.[1] The inclusion in this work of the division of the sciences, logic, practical philosophy, physics and metaphysics together with his extensive reference to other philosophers clearly demonstrates his familiarity with and mastery of a wide range of philosophical subjects and schools.

Whereas this work remains his single most important *ishrāqī* text, it is his commentary upon the *Ḥikmat al-ishrāq* and *Talwīḥāt* of Suhrawardī that reveal most about Shahrazūrī's own intellectual perspectives. Another of his works *al-Rumūz*

1. Shams al-Dīn Shahrazūrī, *Commentary on the Philosophy of Illumination*, ed. H. Ziai (Tehran, 1993), p. xv. For a complete discussion of the intellectual orientation of Shams al-Dīn Shahrazūrī see ibid. pp. vi–xxvi.

wa'l-amthāl (Mysteries and Archetypes) pertains to an illuminative way of knowing the metaphysical modalities. As already mentioned, Shahrazūrī also composed a commentary on Suhrawardī's *Talwīḥāt,* which is a major text written in the tradition of the Peripatetics, but with certain *ishrāqī* elements.

Shahrazūrī, who trod the *ishrāqī* path and referred to it as '*al-niẓām al-atamm*' (the most complete system), saw himself not only as an illuminationist philosopher but also as the '*Qayyim*' (upholder) of illuminationist philosophy. Whether there was an established hierarchy among whom Shahrazūrī assumed the mantle of mastery or whether he was using the title '*Qayyim*' in an esoteric manner remains unknown.

While we know nothing about his teachers or students, we do know that such *ishrāqī* thinkers as Quṭb al-Dīn Shīrāzī and Ibn Kammūnah, both of whom wrote commentaries on Suhrawardī's works, were deeply influenced by him. Shahrazūrī's writings also influenced other philosophers among whom one can name several members of the School of Shiraz. Mīr Dāmād and Mullā Ṣadrā can be named among masters of the School of Isfahan—the former in his *Qabasāt* and the latter in his *Asfār* make detailed references to Shahrazūrī's treatment of philosophical issues.

In his history of philosophy, Shahrazūrī presents in methodical detail the views of other philosophers, in particular, Plato, Aristotle, Fārābī, Avicenna and Suhrawardī. Among the theologians, he uses the arguments of Fakhr al-Dīn Rāzī to present counter-arguments to Avicenna and devotes some discussion to an analysis of the perspectives of the Sufi Ḥasan al-Baṣrī and the Muʿtazilite theologian Abu'l-Hudhayl al-ʿAllāf.

Despite Shahrazūrī's illuminationist perspective, he was a philosopher who advocated reading Greek philosophy, in particular Aristotle. He neither shied away from rational argument, nor saw it as a peril to illuminationist philosophy but instead embraced rational philosophy as the preliminary stage for understanding *ishrāqī* doctrines. His defence of Greek 'rationalism' is genuine and throughout his works he comes across not just as a commentator of Aristotle or Suhrawardī but as an independent thinker who may have been reacting to Ashʿarite *kalām* and the rise of theological strictures against philosophy. Shahrazūrī, like so many other major thinkers of the fifth/eleventh and sixth/twelfth centuries, was witnessing the rise of the dogmatic theology of the Ashʿarites and defended philosophy against this movement.

In this chapter, we have included a section of Shahrazūrī's *Nuzhat al-arwāḥ wa rawḍat al-afrāḥ*. Although strictly speaking this is not an *ishrāqī* text, it is a survey of Greek philosophical thought, including both the pre-Socratics, Plato and Aristotle, seen from an *ishrāqī* perspective. Shahrazūrī goes beyond the standard intellectual biography of early philosophers and remains faithful to Suhrawardī's view of the history of philosophy by including non-Greek Persian figures. Illuminationist doctrine considers *ḥikmah* to have flowed through various channels including the philosophers of both Greek and Persian civilizations in addition to some of the prophets of the Abrahamic tradition. Whereas the Greeks and Persians were channels for the transmission of *ḥikmah*, Shahrazūrī maintained that Adam, Seth, Idrīs and Shuʿayb were also channels through whom *ishrāqī* wisdom was revealed to humanity.

This section is also of significance to historians of philosophy in that it demonstrates the extent to which medieval Islamic philosophers knew of the Greeks and were constructively engaged with their ideas. Furthermore, it reveals that Islamic philosophers were not merely transmitters of Greek philosophy but that they did philosophize independently on the basis of several traditions of *ḥikmah* that the Muslims inherited.

M. Aminrazavi

EXCURSION OF SPIRITS AND GARDEN OF DELIGHTS

Nuzhat al-arwāḥ wa rawḍat al-afrāḥ

Translated for this volume by Majid Fakhry from Shams al-Dīn Muḥammad Shahrazūrī, *Nuzhat al-arwāḥ wa rawḍat al-afrāḥ*, ed. Muḥammad ʿAlī Abū Rayyān (Alexandria, 1993), pp. 87–297.[1]

The Beginnings of the History of Philosophy

You should know that wisdom[2] is sought either for the sake of action and is then called practical wisdom, or for the sake of mere learning and is called theoretical. Some philosophers have given the practical part priority over the theoretical, while others have regarded it as subsidiary. In fact, the practical part (of philosophy) bears on good deeds; I mean, the refinement of character, whereas the theoretical part bears on the knowledge of the truth; I mean, knowing the essences of existing entities.

Those two parts may be attained through perfect reflection, but the reliance of the practical part on other disciplines is greater. Thus, the prophets have been assisted with spiritual instruction (that is, through revelation)[3] to confirm the practical part supplemented by some additions from the theoretical part. The philosophers, by contrast, have received some rational assistance in confirmation of the theoretical part, as well as some assistance from the practical part. The ultimate goal of the philosopher is the total unfolding of the whole universe to his reason and the emulation of God Almighty, as far as possible; whereas the goal of the prophet is the unfolding of the order of the universe to his reason, whereby he is able to safeguard the welfare of the masses and ensure that the world order endures and the welfare of humanity is regulated. That goal cannot be attained, except through exhortation and warning, or (simulation)[4] and representation. Hence, all that the different religious laws and creeds have prescribed is affirmed by the philosophers, in the way we have mentioned, except for those who received their wisdom from the 'niche of prophecy',[5] for they are believed to have attained the perfect rank.

Philosophers included the Brahmin philosophers of India, who denied all prophethood, the philosophers of the Arabs, who constitute a small band, most of whose wisdom consists of flights of fancy and mental rambling, and finally the

1 Topics that are scattered in the text are presented here in collated form.
2. Arabic *ḥikmah*, used interchangeably for philosophy or wisdom.
3. Added by the editor.
4. Added by the editor.
5. A reference to the Qur'ān 24:35.

philosophers of Greece and Byzantium.[1] They are divided into the ancients, who are the pillars of that wisdom and the moderns, who include the Peripatetics and the Stoics, and their modern followers, who are the philosophers of Islam.

1. *Thales*

It is said that the first philosopher of whom this title is predicated, despite the historians' differences on this point, was Thales of Miletus.[2] He was the first to philosophize in Egypt, from where he travelled to Miletus as an old man.

Thales says that the first thing God Almighty created was water, into which everything dissolves. He surmised that all things derive from humidity, supporting this claim by quoting the words of the poet Homer, to the effect that the first created entity was water, which is the first principle or source of material compounds, rather than the first principle of higher entities. However, having asserted that the first element is susceptible of every form; namely, is the source of all forms, he was led to assert the existence in the material world of a paradigm parallel to it in receiving all the forms, of which he could not find a parallel other than water. Thus, he regarded it as the first created compound, from which he held that celestial and terrestrial bodies originated.

This accords with what is stated in the Bible[3] to the effect that the origin of the world is a substance created by God Almighty, upon which he cast a divine glance which caused its parts to dissolve into water. Then vapour arose from it, similar to smoke, from which He created the heavens. There, then, appeared on the surface of the water a froth similar to the sea's froth, from which He created the earth; whereupon He held it in place by means of mountains and other props.

Thales actually received wisdom from the 'niche of prophecy'.[4] For, what he asserts with respect to the first principle which is the source of all forms is very similar to the Guarded Tablet.[5] Now water, according to the second view, is very similar to the water upon which the (divine) Throne rests: 'And His Throne was upon water.'[6]

Thales also said that the world has a Maker that human reason cannot apprehend but can know only through His effects. For His name cannot be known, let alone His Essence, except by reference to His actions and His creation i.e. by His origination of all things. Therefore, He cannot become known through a name that

1. *al-Rūm*.

2. On the western coast of Asia Minor, known as Ionia, hence the Arabic *Yūnān* for Greece. Thales is said to have predicted the eclipse of the sun in 585 BC, when he is presumed to have flourished.

3. Arabic *Tawrāt* for Torah. The reference is to the Book of Genesis, I:1–10.

4. See note above. The rest of the verse reads: 'And it is He who created the heavens and the earth in six days, and His throne was upon the water.'

5. Cf. Qur'ān 85:22.

6. Qur'ān 11:1.

denotes His Essence, but only by names that refer to His qualities. He brought forth what He brought forth without its having a form in reality; for prior to creation, the only thing that existed was He. There is no sense in which He could have existed together with anything possessing a form in any place. For His absolute unity is incompatible with such propositions.

(Thales) also said that beyond the heavens, there exist worlds of light, but human reason cannot describe their creation nor fathom their beauty by intellect soul or nature.

2. *Anaximander*

Thales was succeeded by Anaximander the Milesian, who believed that the first entity created by God Almighty was the Infinite,[1] from which the universe came into being and into which it will return.

3. *Anaximenes*

Anaximander was succeeded by *Anaximenes*[2] the Milesian, who believed that the first entity created by God Almighty was air, from which everything else came and into which it will dissolve. It is similar to breath in us, since it is air that keeps that in us. Similarly, air and spirit hold the world together. Air and spirit denote the same thing and are univocal.[3]

4. *Anaxagoras*

Anaximenes was succeeded by Anaxagoras[4] and Philharmainus,[5] who believed that the first principles of existed entities created originally by God Almighty are the objects of similar parts.[6]

Anaxagoras is one of the Milesian philosophers who were known for their wisdom and goodness. He said that God Almighty is eternal, without beginning or end. He is the source of all things, and has no origin and nothing is comparable to Him. He is the Creator, whose form was part of His primal knowledge and for whom forms are infinite. The forms are eternal and cannot be multiplied with the multiplication of knowables or change with them. Through His oneness, He created the form of the (primal) element, then the form of reason. He then arranged the varieties of forms (in reason) according to the classes of light and the types of traces in them. Then, those varieties became multiple forms at once, just as the form appears in a polished mirror without reference to time or order; but since

---

1. Called by Anaximander *to apeiron*. His dates are 611–545 BC.
2. Anaximenes is said to have died around 499 BC.
3. In Arabic, air or wind *(rīḥ)* and spirit (*rūḥ*) are homonyms.
4. Born around 500 BC, and died around 428 BC.
5. Probably Philolaus.
6. Called by Anaxagoras, *homoiomereiai*.

prime matter[1] does not bear receptivity, the lights of the forms have diminished in that matter.

He used to say that the comparative value of this world to that of the (higher) world is similar to the comparative value of a vegetable to its peel, from which it is distinct. Thus, the permanence of this world depends on the little light of that (higher) world found in it; otherwise it would not last for a single moment. In fact, it will only last so long as reason sheds the part mixed with it, and the soul likewise sheds the part mixed with it. When the two parts are shed, the remaining parts of this (lower) world would perish, while the impure souls would remain confined to the realm of darkness.

The view of Anaxagoras, the Milesian,[2] is similar to that of Thales, although he differs from him on the question of the first principles. Those parts, according to him, consist of objects of similar parts,[3] or subtle particles that are not perceived by sense or grasped by reason, but from which both the lower and higher worlds are formed. For, compounds are preceded by simple elements and non-homogeneous by homogeneous, from which compounds are made up. When animals and plants feed on homogeneous parts and their like, they become homogeneous in the stomach and, as they flow in the body, turn into non-homogeneous parts.

Anaxagoras agreed with the other philosophers that the first principle is the Active Reason,[4] but differed from them in his view that the Creator is at rest and is immovable. He says that the origin of things is a single body, which is the locus of all things and is infinite. He did not state clearly whether it was one of the elements or not, adding that all bodies, species and variety of forces emanate from it. He is the first to have spoken of latency and outer manifestation.[5] He came after Anaximenes, the Milesian. Aristotle has filled his books with his sayings, opinions and doctrines, together with refutations of what he disagreed with.

Anaxagoras led a life of frugality and bore well with hardships, exposing himself to cold, ice and snow, walking barefooted, despite his old age and debility. He was asked about it, but he answered: 'Because my soul is prone to merriment, I feel that it might stray and drive me to cling to its vile caprices. Why cannot I subject it to me rather than be subjected to it; and why cannot I force it to bear with hardships, rather than it force me to commit indecencies?'

There was some commotion and disturbance over certain incidents in his hometown, while he remained unmoved. He was asked: 'Does this matter bother you?' He answered: 'Were you to see this in your sleep, would you move while awake? That is why this matter does not bother me, because the matters of this

1. *Hayūlā.*
2. Anaxagoras originated from Clazomenae in Ionia.
3. *Homoiomereiai.*
4. *Noūs.*
5. In Arabic *al-kumūn wa'l-ẓuhūr.*

world are all like a dream and sound judgment is like waking.' He also said: 'The tongue sometimes swears falsely, but reason swears only truthfully; so see to it that they are in harmony.'

It is said that his wife quarrelled with him once and continued for a while to abuse him, while he remained silent. She became very furious and as she was washing her clothes, she got up and poured the dirty water over his head. He happened to be reading a book, he put it down, raised his head facing her and said: 'You have thundered, flashed like lightning and then rained,' adding nothing else.[1]

He once passed by a fat and hefty man, who abused him flagrantly, but he took no notice. People then said to him: 'Does not his abuse bother you?' He replied: 'I do not expect to hear from a crow the sound of pigeons or from the duck the singing of the canary.' Whenever bad people praised him, he was frightened, saying: 'Maybe I did something awful.'

5. *Arselaus*

Arselaus,[2] son of Apolodorus, who was an Athenian, believed that the first principle of existing entities created by God Almighty is the infinite,[3] which is susceptible of condensation and rarefaction, so that part of it becomes fire and part water.

Those philosophers succeeded one another and in them Greek philosophy reached its zenith. This, then, was the beginning of philosophy as it emerged in Miletus. However it appears to me that these statements attributed to them and other ancient thinkers are all allusions to their stations and states as well as their inner secrets; for some of the statements attributed to them would not be said by one with the slightest discernment, let alone by an eminent philosopher.

6. *Pythagoras*[4]

It is also said that philosophy had another origin, going back to Pythagoras, son of Mnesarchus, a citizen of Samos. It is said that he was the first person to give philosophy its name.[5] He believed that the first thing created by God was number or equations made up from numbers, which he used to call harmonies and compounds made up of their elements,[6] ratios or geometrical (proportions).

I say that his intent is not that the first principles are numbers and that number is a self-subsisting entity that is the origin of existing entities. His intent was rather that there exist in the intelligible world certain immaterial realities, that are pure,

1. A variant of this story is told about Socrates and his wife, Xantippe.
2. Archelaus.
3. *To apeiron*, already introduced by Anaximander.
4. Born around 580 BC on the island of Samos and died around 500 BC.
5. It is reported that when his disciples addressed him as *sophos* or wise, he objected, saying: 'Call me not *sophos*; for only God is *sophos*, but call me *philo-sophos*' or 'lover of wisdom'.
6. *Ustuqussāt*.

self-subsisting entities,[1] which are not in space. These are numerals or numbered (entities); for it may be said rightly of God Almighty that He is First and His second is the First Intellect and so on and so forth.

Pythagoras came after Empedocles[2] by a long stretch. He learned philosophy at the hands of the followers of Solomon in Egypt, when they entered it coming from Syria.

Before that, he had learned geometry from the Egyptians. Then, he returned to the land of the Greeks and revealed geometry to them, as well as physics and theology.[32] Thanks to his own talent, he developed music, which he subsumed under numerical proportions, claiming that he had received that (knowledge) from the 'niche of prophecy.'[4]

With respect to the world and its composition from number and its ratios, Pythagoras held strange opinions and far-fetched views. He came close to Empedocles in holding that beyond the world of nature there exists a spiritual and luminous world, but reason cannot encompass its beauty and splendour, a world which only pure souls can enter. He who sets his soul straight and cleanses it of arrogance, oppression, hypocrisy and jealousy, as well as other bodily desires, will become worthy of joining (that world) and exploring its jewels and indulging in its pleasures.

Pythagoras has written valuable works on philosophy, music and other subjects. It is said that he favoured travel and avoiding the touching of both killer and killed. He advocated the hallowing of the senses and just dealings, as well as the practice of the other virtues, refraining from sins and seeking the human gift (of reason), so as to know the nature of all things. He also advocated experimentation and learning the meaning of the higher sciences, resisting sins, exhorting the soul and mastering strife.[5] He ordered long periods of fasting, sitting upon chairs, constant reading of books and advised his followers to teach other men and women. He also called for clear speech and exhortation of kings.

He believed in the survival of the soul in the hereafter wherein it will be subject to reward and punishment, as the metaphysical philosophers have taught. He took two types of nourishment, so he would not be hungry with one, and he had accustomed himself to one regular way of life, so he would not be sick one time and healthy another, nor be obese at one time and frail another.

His temper was very mild and moderate, so he never became unduly glad or sad about something and no one ever saw him laughing or crying. He always preferred his friends over himself and was the first to say that the possessions of

1. In Arabic *inniyyāt.*

2. Empedocles' dates are 490–430 BC, which makes him a successor and not predecessor of Pythagoras.

3. Arabic, science of religion.

4. Qur'ān 24:35, a metaphor for revelation.

5. *al-Jihād.*

friends are common and undivided. He used to express his philosophical ideas in symbols to conceal them. Of his symbolic expressions is the saying: 1) 'Refrain from excess in seeking pleasure'; that is, avoid excess and 2) 'Do not stir the fire with a knife, because it was heated by it once', that is, avoid words which excite the angry and infuriated man, and 3) 'Do not settle down to a life of poverty'; that is, do not lead an idle existence, and 4) 'do not come near fierce lions'; that is, do not heed the opinions of giants, and 5) 'do not let bats dwell in your home'; that is, do not listen to the opinions of the proud, who have no control of themselves, and 6) 'do not relinquish a burden to is bearer, so he will need to be assisted in bearing it'; that is, let no one overlook his own performance of deeds of virtue and obedience, and 7) 'do not display the figures of angels on the bezels of rings'; that is, do not reveal your religion and confide the secrets of the divine sciences to the ignorant.

Porphyry (of Tyre) has given in his *History of Philosophy*[11] strange accounts of things that Pythagoras had foretold and of mysterious acts of his, reported or observed … .

When he reached Babylon, he sought the company of the Chaldean priests and studied with Zarpata, who introduced him to what the saints should do and the music of high-ranking people and the nature of the first principles of all things. That is why Pythagoras' philosophy was highly regarded and thanks to him, the path of leading the nations and guarding them against sins was discovered, due to the great number of sciences, drawn from every nation or clime that he had acquired.

Pythagoras visited Pherecydes, the Syriac philosopher[2] early in life in a Syrian city called Delon, from which Pherecydes migrated and settled in Samos. He became very sick, to the point that lice were eating his body. When his illness increased, some of his pupils took him to Ephesus, but when his condition deteriorated, he pleaded with the people of Ephesus to drive him out of their city. They took him to Megania;[3] his students served him until he died and so they buried him and wrote his epitaph on his tombstone.

Thereupon, Pythagoras returned to the city of Samos and studied with Hermodamese the philosopher, nicknamed Aphrocyleme, whose company he kept for a while. By then, the government[4] of Samos had reverted to Polycrates, the tyrant.

Pythagoras then sought the company of the Egyptian priests; so he implored Polycrates to assist him in that matter. The latter wrote to Amasis,[5] king of Egypt, informing him about Pythagoras' wish and telling him that he was a friend of his, whom he wished he would be gracious to and treat well. Amasis then received him

1. This book of Porphyry (d. 304) is lost.
2. He came from Syros, an island in the Aegean (not Syria).
3. Or Megara (?).
4. Arabic *tarānih*, Greek tyrant.
5. Egyptian pharaoh of the 18th dynasty.

well and wrote to the chief priests regarding (Pythagoras') request; and so he came to the City of the Sun, which is known in our day as ʿAyn al-Shams, carrying the letter of their king and so they received him well … .

It is reported that Pythagoras stayed in Samos sixty years, then travelled to Antioch, from whence he headed to Crotona where he stayed for eight years. When its people rose in revolt against him, he moved to Metapontum, where he stayed for five years and there he died.

It is said that Pythagoras wrote two hundred and eighty books and left a large number of disciples. The stamp of his ring read: 'An evil which does not last is better than a good which does not last either'; that is, an evil which is expected to cease is better than a good which it is feared will come to an end. On his belt was inscribed: 'Silence is a way out of likely regret …' .

7. *Heraclitus*[1] and *Athales* (?)

Then came Heraclitus and Athales, who are affiliated to Metantes. They held that the first principle of all things is fire, to which all things will ultimately return. When that fire is extinguished, the world will come into being … .

8. *Empedocles*

Empedocles son of Hethon[2] came from Phrygia.[3] He believed that the elements created by God Almighty are the well-known four,[4] whereas the principles are two: love and conquest. The first generates congregation, the second segregation. I say that this is also a metaphor, and is not the same as literalist philosophers have claimed.

Empedocles is one of the great and eminent philosophers, very perceptive in the philosophical sciences, careful in practical matters. When he acquired the principles of philosophy from David and Luqmān, peace be with them, in Syria, he returned to Greece to teach philosophy saying: 'God Almighty's essence has always been pure knowledge and pure will, generosity and majesty, power, justice, goodness and truth. I do not conceive of any other powers bearing these names, but are simply He. He is identical with all those creative attributes, not that He was created from anything else and co-existed with anything else. Instead, He created the simple elements that are the first intellectual element; I mean, the primary substance. Then simple entities, generated from that simple and unique, created entity began to multiply. Then, He created compounds out of the simple elements and He is the creator of opposites and contraries, intelligible, imaginative or sensuous … .

1. Heraclitus' dates are 544–484 BC.
2. Or rather Meton. Empedocles' dates are 490–430 BC.
3. Or rather Agrigentum.
4. That is water, fire, earth and air.

Muḥammad Ibn 'Abd Allāh Ibn Masarrah, the Esoteric,[1] who came from Cordova, was fond of Empedocles' philosophy and intent on its study. He was in general a great man, of high distinguished standing, dedicated to Sufi practices, self-divinization and frugality, who despised the world and turned to the hereafter. He excelled in the knowledge of the soul and immaterial entities, their natures and order. I saw a book of (Ibn Masarrah's) on philosophy, which reveals his mystical inclination, his powerful character and his pre-eminence in the metaphysical science and its wisdom. He was the first to preach the unity of the notions of God's attributes, and the fact that they all denote the same thing, rather than distinct notions pertaining to each of the different attributes. For, He is truly the One in whom there is no plurality whatsoever, contrary to all other existing entities. For, the higher unities[2] are susceptible of plurality, either in their parts, their connotations or their analogues. By contrast, the essence of God Almighty is entirely free of all this.

This idea is also expressed in the words of 'Alī ibn Abī Ṭālib, may God be pleased with him, al-Ḥasan al-Baṣrī, a group of the Mu'tazilites and some Muslim philosophers … .[3]

9. *Democritus*[4]

He was a contemporary of the physician Hippocrates and lived during the reign of King Bahman, son of Isfandiyār, son of Gushtāsp. Many writings (and opinions) are attributed to him and are mentioned by other philosophers in their works.

He is one of the ancient philosophers, who was once told: 'Do not blink'. So, he closed his eyes; then: 'Do not listen', so he stopped his ears. Then, he was told: 'Do not speak', so he put his hand over his mouth. When told: 'Do not seek knowledge', he replied: 'I cannot do that'.

Aristotle is said to have preferred his teaching to that of his master Plato; but on that point, he was not justified.

10. *Epicurus*[5]

Epicurus, son of Nannis, was an Athenian, who philosophized in the days of Democritus. He taught that the first principles of all things are particles, which are perceived rationally, separated by a vacuum and are colourless. God Almighty created them as eternal and indestructible entities. They cannot be broken or destroyed and their parts are not susceptible of variation or transformation. They

1. Or al-Bāṭinī, died in 931.
2. Or intelligences, existing in the intelligible world, according to Neoplatonists.
3. 'Alī ibn 'Abī Ṭālib, the fourth caliph (656–661); al-Ḥasan al-Baṣrī (p. 724), a Sufi and also forerunner of Mu'tazilism.
4. Democritus' dates are 470–361 BC. He came from Abdera and is generally recognized, with Leucippus, as the founder of ancient materialism.
5. Epicurus' dates are 341–270 BC.

are not perceived by sense[1] and they will continue to move in the vacuum and the plenum as long as God wills. The vacuum is infinite and so are bodies, which are susceptible of shape, mass and weight.

11. *Socrates*

Socrates[2] the ascetic and pious sage was a disciple of Pythagoras and Arcelaus.[3] The name Socrates in Greek means 'clinging to justice.'

He was born during the reign of Bahman and died of poison. Of philosophical subjects, he confined himself to metaphysics and ethics, shunned the pleasures of the world, retired to the mountains and lived in a cave, leading an ascetic life of self-discipline. He disagreed with the Athenians in their cult of idols and confronted their leaders with arguments and proofs. This caused the people to rebel against him and so they forced their king to kill him. He killed him by poison to avoid their wrath after a series of debates with the king which have been preserved. He left noble testaments, virtuous moral maxims, famous aphorisms, as well as views of divine attributes that are close to those of Pythagoras and Empedocles. He has certain opinions regarding resurrection which appear weak, but God knows best his secrets and symbolic allusions ... .

Socrates, the son of Sophroniscus, was born and grew up in Athens. He left three male children. When he was forced to marry, as was their custom in forcing good citizens to marry so as to continue their progeny, he asked to be married to the most shrewish woman,[4] the meanest to be found in his city, so as to grow accustomed to her stupidity and to bear with her vile manners and get used to the ignorance of both the public and the elite.

He admired wisdom to such an extent that he caused the lovers of wisdom who succeeded him a lot of harm. For, it was part of his exaltation of wisdom that he was against depositing it in journals or sheets of paper, out of reverence for it. He says: 'Wisdom is pure, incorruptible and unadulterated; therefore we should not entrust it, except to living souls, rather than the skins of dead beasts and we should guard it against rebel hearts'. That is why he never left any written works or dictated to any of his disciples that which they could commit to paper. He only instructed them orally, just as he had learned from his teacher Timaeus, who is reported to have been asked once (by Socrates) in his youth: 'Why do you not let me record the wisdom I hear from you on paper?' To this, Timaeus replied: 'How confident you are in the skins of dead beasts and neglectful of living thoughts? Imagine that someone were to meet you on the road and to ask you about some noble part of science; would you

1. The text says reason (*'aqlan*), which is absurd. The reference here is to the atoms, which are not physically perceptible by the senses.

2. Socrates' dates are 469–399 BC.

3. Archelaus.

4. That was Xantippe, renowned in antiquity for her vicious character.

prefer to tell him to return to your home and look into your books? If you do not prefer that, then keep quiet, O Socrates'. Socrates did just that.

Socrates renounced the world and was indifferent to it. It was the custom of Greek kings, when they were out on a military expedition, to get their sages to accompany them on their travels; so the king took Socrates with him on one of his travels. Socrates used then to retire to a broken tub in the king's camp to guard against the cold. When the sun was out, he used to come out, to warm himself in the sun. That is why he was called Socrates of the Tub.[1]

One day, the king passed by him in that condition and asked him: 'Why do we not see you, O Socrates, and what bars you from coming to us?' He replied: 'What work', Socrates replied: 'Seeking a livelihood?' The king then said: 'If you come to us, you will find that provided for you always'. Socrates said: 'Had I known that I could find that provision made by you, I would not have left it'.

The king then asked: 'I hear that you said idol-worship is harmful'. He replied: 'I did not say that'. The king then asked: 'What did you say?' He replied, 'Idol-worship is profitable for the king, harmful for Socrates; because the king reforms thereby the affairs of his subjects and collects his taxes. However, Socrates knows that idol-worship neither harms nor profits him; because he knows that he has a Creator, who provides for him and rewards him for whatever good he does'. So, the king asked: 'Do you need anything?' Socrates replied: 'Yes, move the rein of your mount away, for your armies have shut out the sun's light from me'. The king, then, ordered an expensive silk tunic, jewels and money for him as a favour. Socrates said to him: 'O King, you have promised life, but continued to serve the cause of death. Socrates has no need for the stones of the earth, the husk of plants or the sputum of worms.[2] Socrates is in possession of what he needs, whenever he goes … '

When his countrymen asked him about idol-worship, he barred them from it and prohibited it, forbidding people from worshipping them. He commanded them to worship the One, Everlasting God, Creator of the world and all in it, the Wise, the Holy, rather than the sculpted rock, which neither speaks, nor hears nor feels with any of the organs. He urged people to lead a life of charity and good deeds, ordered them to do right and to avoid the indecencies and vile actions, current among the rest of his contemporaries.

He did not seek the fullness of sound opinion because he knew that they would not receive that well from him. Thus, when the leading priests and statesmen of his day learned about the intent of his message, and that he believed in the destruction of idols and barring people from their worship, they testified that he must die. Those who passed the sentence of death against him were the eleven judges of

---

1. This story is told about Diogenes the Cynic in the Arabic sources, upon his encounter with Alexander the Great, referred to as 'the king' further down.

2. That is, silk.

Asles (?). He was made to drink the poison known as hemlock,[1] because the king, compelled to kill him by the judges, could not refuse. He asked him: 'Choose the death you want', Socrates said: 'By poison', and the king agreed.

What caused months of delay in the execution of Socrates,[2] once it was approved, was the fact that the boat that used to be sent to the temple of Apollo every year, carrying its load, was delayed by the wind for months. It was their custom not to spill any blood or the like until the boat returned to Selas.[3]

Socrates' friends used to visit him in prison during that whole period. One day as they came in, one of their number, Crito, said to him: 'The boat is coming back tomorrow or the day after. We have tried to pay some money to those people,[4] so that you may come out in secret and then you might head to Rome[5] and stay there, and then they will not be able to touch you'. Socrates replied: 'You know that my property does not exceed four hundred drachmas'. Crito then said to him: 'I did not mean that you will incur any cost; for we know that you cannot afford what the judges[6] ordered. However, our finances exceed the double of this sum and we would be delighted to pay it for your release, so that we will not be grieved at your loss'. Socrates said to him, 'O Crito; this city in which we have been treated so well is my city and the city of my people. I have been accused in it, as you can see, without having done any misdeed to deserve it; but simply because I opposed injustice and criticized unjust actions and those who commit them, by reason of their infidelity to God Almighty and their worship of idols. The causes of my incurring the judgment of death is with me wherever I go and I will never stop supporting right and attacking wrong and those who perpetrate it, wherever I go. Moreover, the people of Rome[7] are more removed from me in kinship than the people of my own city. Therefore, this outcome, if occasioned by a just verdict, will follow me wherever I go, so that I will never be safer than I am here'.[8] Crito then said to him: 'Remember your children and your wife and the loss they will incur'. Socrates replied: 'What they will encounter in Rome[9] will be the same as this; but you are all here with them, so they will not be lost'.

On the third day, his disciples came to him as early as usual. The jailor came and opened the door. Then, the eleven judges came, they entered, stayed for a while, then left, having removed the iron shackles from Socrates' feet. The jailer then went out to meet the disciples and greeted them. They sat with him, then Socrates came

1. Arabic *klone*, probably for Greek *kukewn*, or mixed drink.
2. Actually one month, according to Plato's *Phaedo*.
3. Delos.
4. Meaning the jailers, according to Plato's *Crito*.
5. Actually, Thessaly, in Plato's *Crito*, 45.
6. Arabic, 'those people'.
7. Or rather, Thessaly.
8. Meaning the prison in which he was held.
9. Thessaly. See note above.

down from his bed and sat on the floor. He uncovered his legs, touched them and scratched them, saying: 'How strange is this divine providence, which has brought contraries together; so that there is no pleasure, but is followed by pain and no pain, but is followed by pleasure'. This discourse led to their engaging in conversation and so Simmias and Philon[1] asked about some of the psychological acts. The conversation among them developed to such an extent that it covered the discussion of the soul, ably and exhaustively, while Socrates remained unmoved, in that state of pleasure, joy and even playfulness they used to witness in him, so much so that they wondered at his composure and his contempt for death. He never tired of seeking the truth, wherever it could be found and did not display any change in those states of his soul they witnessed, at a time when he was immune from death. They were overwhelmed with grief at the thought of his departure, and so Simmias addressed him thus: 'Questioning you while in this state is a great burden to us and an offence against good company, while refraining from questioning is a source of great sorrow. For, we know how remote are the prospects of the outcome we desire'. Socrates answered: 'Do not give up searching for whatever you desire; for your searching is something I delight in. For me, there is no difference between the present condition I am in and its opposite, as far as the pursuit of truth is concerned. For, if we believe with certainty the tales which we continue to hear, to the effect that we are going to join other virtuous, noble and praiseworthy people (after death), such as Ipselaus (?), Amares (?), Heracles and all those predecessors who possessed psychic virtues, we need not grieve'.[2]

When the discussion of the subject of the soul was concluded and the goal they sought was reached, the disciples asked him about the shape of the world, the motions of the spheres and the composition of the elements. He answered them about all that and told them many tales concerning the divine sciences and higher secrets. When he finished, he said: 'Now the time has come for us to bathe and to pray as much as we can. We should not require anybody to perform the funeral washing; for the hour calls and we are going to Zeus. As for you, you will return to your own folk'. Then, he got up, entered a bathroom, where he bathed and prayed. He was absent for a long time, while the disciples were pondering their great disaster and how they will lose in him a great sage and learned father and remain after he is gone like orphans.[3]

Socrates then went out and called for his wives[4] and children (he had a grown son and two smaller ones). He bade them farewell and gave them his instructions. Crito then said to him: 'What is it you order us to do with your wife and children

1. Arabic, Chilon (?).

2. The heroes mentioned in *Apology*, 41, that Socrates looked forward to meeting, are Orpheus, Musaeus, Hesiod, Homer and others.

3. See Plato, *Phaedo*, 112 ff.

4. Socrates had only one wife, Xantippe.

and your other affairs?' He replied: 'I order you nothing more than what I used to order you concerning reforming yourselves. If you do that, you would please me most'. Then he fell silent and so did the rest of the company.

Then, the servant of the eleven judges came and said: 'O Socrates, you are very brave in the face of what is in store for you. You should know that I am not responsible for your death, but the eleven judges are. I only obey orders. You are indeed the finest person who has been to this spot; so drink the poison graciously and bear with the consequent depression'.[1] Then, his eyes blinked and he left.

Socrates said: 'It shall be done!' He was silent for a moment, then said to Crito: 'Call the man who has the death potion for me'. That man went in with the potion, which Socrates took from him and drank it. When the disciples saw that he drank it, they were overwhelmed with crying and grief, to the point that they could not control themselves. When their crying became louder, Socrates turned to them, reprimanding and sermonizing them, saying: 'Here, we have sent away the women, so that they will not do this'. Thereupon, they felt ashamed and stopped out of obedience for him, although they were sorely tried at his loss.

Then, Socrates started walking back and forth and said to the jailer: 'My legs feel heavy now'. The jailer replied: 'Lie down'; so he did. The jailer then started pinching his feet and asking: 'Do you feel my pinching?' Socrates replied: 'No!' Then, he pinched his legs hourly, while he said: 'No'. He was getting numb and feeling colder, until the cold reached his loins. The jailer then said: 'The cold has reached his heart', and left. Crito then said to him: 'O master of wisdom, we see our minds being distanced from yours. So, tell us what you wish'. Socrates answered: 'Do what I told you earlier'. Then, he reached out with his hand to Crito's and touched his face and said to him: 'Tell me what you want'. He did not answer, then his eyes were fixed and he said: 'I offer my soul to Him who receives the souls of the philosophers'. Crito then closed his eyes and pulled his beard. Plato was not present with the other disciples because he was sick.

12. *Plato*

Then followed Plato, whose opinion on all points is identical with that of Socrates. They both believed in three first principles: God Almighty, the created matter and form.

Plato[2] was the son of Ariston, son of Aristopheles of Athens. He is the last of the Seven Ancient Sages and is known for his monotheism and wisdom. He studied with Socrates, Timaeus, the Athenian Stranger[3] and the Cretan Stranger.[4]

When Socrates died, Plato succeeded him and occupied his chair, adding to

1. Cf. *Phaedo*, 116.
2. Born in 428, Plato died in 348 BC.
3. One of the three speakers in Plato's *Laws*. The second is the Cretan, the third the Spartan.
4. The Arabic reads Alcrates (?).

his[1] curriculum the physical and mathematical sciences. His disciples, Aristotle, Timaeus (?) and Theophrastos,[2] reported that he believed that the world has an eternal Creator, necessary in Himself and conversant with all the data peculiar to universal causes. He existed in eternity, when there was nothing in existence, whether an image, a relic or model, other than the Almighty Creator. Plato seems to call these Prime Matter[3] or the element, in reference probably to the forms of intelligibles known to Him. He, therefore, created the first intellect and through its agency the universal soul, which emanates from the first intellect as a picture emanates from a mirror. Then, through the agency of the universal soul, He created the elements and prime matter, pertaining to sensible forms and other entities.[4] He incorporated time, I mean eternal time[5] in this scheme of principles and asserted that every existing entity in the sensible world has an impersonal archetype in the intelligible world. The first principles, as well as the archetypes, are simple, whereas individuals are compound. Thus, the sensible man is a particular representation of the simple and intelligible man. The same is true of all species of animals, plants, minerals and other entities in this sensible world, which are effects of entities existing in that (intelligible) world and every such effect must have an agent, who resembles it in some way.

Human reason, which emanates from the intelligible world, is able to conceive, for every sensible entity, an intelligible archetype abstracted from matter, which corresponds fully to the ideal in the intelligible world, but only partially to the existing entity in the world of sense in its particularity. Otherwise, reason would not grasp it as corresponding to the ideal, and then it will not grasp anything as corresponding to the reality of the object grasped. Moreover, sensible forms will only last if they have intelligible forms that they aspire to attain, but dread failure to catch up with them. In fact, if we were able to perceive through the senses all sensible things, which are limited in space and time, we would see that they all correspond to their intelligible archetypes.

Aristotle disagrees with Plato regarding this concept of a universal intelligible. However, he admits that it is a notion in the mind, existing in thought, but not outside it; for the same person does not correspond to both Zayd and ʿAmr, who in his essence is one. Plato, however, holds that that notion in the mind must have something corresponding to it outside it and this is the intelligible archetype or paradigm, which is the essence of the mind's conception of the thing's existence in no subject. This paradigm is prior to particular entities, just as reason is prior to sense. That is both

---

1. Socrates'.
2. He was Aristotle's commentator and successor as head of the Lyceum.
3. *Hayūlā*.
4. This emanationist account is due to Plotinus (d. 270) and Neoplatonism in general. (Here, p. 267 appears to be misplaced and is omitted.)
5. *al-Dahr*.

a rational priority and a priority in rank. The archetypes are the first principles of sensible entities, from which they came and to which they will return. From this, it follows that the human souls have existed prior to the bodies, in some mode of intelligible existence, through which reason apprehends abstract forms.

It is said that Plato joined Socrates in learning from Pythagoras, but he did not shine or become famous as a philosopher, except after the death of Socrates. He covered all the branches of philosophy and wrote many famous books on the different branches of philosophy, in which he inclined towards allegory and mystification. He graduated a group of students, whom he taught while he walked. For this reason, they were called Peripatetics.[1] He delegated teaching to the more skilful among his students towards the end of his life, when he retired from the company of people and devoted himself to the worship of his Lord. His books include *Phaedo*, or the Soul, the *Spiritual Timaeus*[2] dealing with the worlds of the soul, reason and divinity and the *Physical Timaeus* dealing with the order of the physical world.

The name Plato in their language[3] means vast and broad; his father's name was Ariston. Both his parents belonged to the Greek nobility and were descended from Ascelepius. His mother[4] in particular was descended from Solon, the Lawgiver. Early in his life, he studied poetry and language and attained a high standing in those fields till one day he attended a lecture of Socrates in which the latter was criticizing poetry. He liked what he heard, and so he gave up his own previous interests and kept the company of Socrates, listening to him, for five years. Then Socrates died.

He once heard that there was a group of Pythagoreans in Egypt, and he went there to learn from them. Before joining the company of Socrates, Plato used to incline to the views of Cratylus in philosophy, but when he joined Socrates, he lost interest in the philosophy of Cratylus, whom he used to follow in prohibited matters (?), while he followed Pythagoras in rational matters and Socrates in matters of management.[5]

Later, he went back from Egypt to Athens, where he had built a House of Wisdom,[6] where he taught the people. Then, he travelled to Sicily, where he had an encounter with Dionysius the tyrant, who was its ruler and with whom he had a trying experience. Eventually, Plato was able to leave him[7] and to go back to Athens. There, he led an exemplary life, doing good and helping the weak. The people

---

1. From Greek *peripatein* or to walk; but this practice and the consequent adjective were really Aristotle's and his followers'.

2. A reference to a late Neoplatonic collection by this title.

3. That is, Greek.

4. Perictione.

5. Meaning ethics.

6. The Academy.

7. Dionysius, the Tyrant of Sicily, actually ended by selling Plato into slavery. He was freed in Corinth, when a friend paid his ransom.

of Athens wanted him to assume the management of their affairs, but he refused because he felt that their management was different from that management he considered just, but which they had become so accustomed to, that it had taken hold of their minds. He understood that he could not prevail on them to change their ways and that, were he to force them to do so, he would perish as his master Socrates had perished, although Socrates had not sought the perfection of right management.

He was eighty-one years old when he died,[1] a man of fine character, doer of noble deeds, munificent in dealing with his kin as well as strangers, self-assured, gracious and forbearing. He had many disciples and was followed by two men, who continued his teaching, one in Athens in the place known as Akademeia, who was named Xenocrates, the other in the Lyceum[2] in Athens, who was named Aristotle. He used to express his philosophical ideas in allegories to keep them secret and to speak in enigmas so that his meaning will not be understood, except by masters of philosophy.

Plato wrote many books, of which the titles of fifty-six[3] have reached us. Some of those writings are large books containing four articles, and are divided into quatrains, each having a common theme. Each had a particular theme, subsumed under that general theme and called therefore a quatrain, each of which related to the quatrain preceding it. [Here a collection of 'aphorisms' and 'sermons' of Plato follows]

13. *Aristotle*

[Aristotle] was a citizen of Stagira, who held that the first principles are four: form, matter, privation and the four elements, plus a fifth element which is indestructible ether.

Arista[4] (in Greek) means good, *tā* that and *līs* he says. Hence, the name means 'the good who says' … Aristotle is the leading famous First Teacher and the Absolute Sage (*ḥakīm*), according to the Greeks. He was called the First Teacher because he laid down the principles of logical instruction and brought them out from potentiality to actuality. His case in this respect is similar to that of the founders of grammar and prosody; since the relation of logic to mental concepts is similar to the relation of grammar to words and prosody to verse.

Aristotle is the founder of logic, not in the sense that concepts were not already systematized before him, but rather in the sense that he distinguished

1. In 348 BC.
2. Or Leukeion, the school founded by Aristotle after Plato's death.
3. Actually, no more than 32 dialogues and 13 letters.
4. Aristotle's name in Arabic is given here as Arisṭāṭālīs. This etymology is far-fetched. *Ariston* in Greek means good or noble, *telos*, purpose or end.

the instrument[1] from the matter of discourse and rendered it more accessible to learners, whereby it could serve as a scale to which they could refer, whenever truth is confused with error and right with wrong. However, he compressed his discourse in the way writers of introductory works tend to do, while later authors expanded it in the manner of commentators. To him belongs the honour of forerunners and the merit of preface writers.

Aristotle's books on logic, physics, metaphysics and ethics are well known, and there are many commentaries, such as the commentaries of Theophrastus, Porphyry, Alexander of Aphrodisias, Basileus and others. However, most of those who succeeded the First Teacher followed his lead and adopted his views in the manner of imitators; but the matter is different from what they believed. For, Aristotle and most of his followers have erred with respect to many questions in the field of philosophical discourses and their narrow straits. The rectification of their errors should be sought in our books.[2]

Aristotle has stated that the Necessary Being is the same as the Unmoved Mover and that substance is used in three senses: two physical (or movable) and one immovable. For, every movable object must have a mover; but if that mover is movable, the process would go on *ad infinitum*, without end. Therefore, movement must depend in the end on an Immovable Mover. Aristotle in their language means 'the perfectly noble';[3] Nicomachus,[4] 'the valiant conqueror.' For his father was proficient in medicine and Aristotle was born to him in a city called Stagira, which is part of Macedonia and of the province of Thrace. His mother's name was Phaestis[5] and his father served as the physician of Amyntas II, father of Philip, father of Alexander the Great. Aristotle's pedigree went back to Ascelapius,[6] a noble pedigree for the Greeks, just as his mother's pedigree did. When he was eight years old, his father took him to the city of Athens, known as the City of the Philosophers. He settled in Qodimus[7] and so his father made him join the rhetoricians, the poets and the grammarians. He continued to study with them for nine years. The name of that science (which he studied) was called encyclopaedic,[8] I mean, linguistics, because everybody needed it as a tool for advancing to the acquisition of all wisdom and virtue and it is the expository discipline through which every science is known.

Some of the philosophers had despised the sciences of the rhetoricians, the linguists and the grammarians and reprimanded those who studied them. Those

1. Hence, the classical name of Aristotle's logical collection or corpus is *Organon*, meaning instrument or tool.
2. He means in his Ishrāqī works, which were critical of Aristotle.
3. However, compare note above.
4. Aristotle's father.
5. Given in Arabic as Aphystia.
6. The god of medicine.
7. That is Akademus Park, where Plato's Academy was built.
8. *al-Muḥīṭ*.

critics included Pythagoras and Epicurus, who claimed that no philosophy is needed for learning them, because the grammarians are the teachers of children, the poets are masters of falsehoods and lying and the rhetoricians masters of trickery, favouritism and hypocrisy.

When those charges reached Aristotle, he was furious and strove to defend the grammarians, the rhetoricians and the poets. He stood up for them saying: 'It is impossible for philosophy to dispense with their sciences; for logic is a tool[1] of their sciences'. He also added: 'Man's superiority to animals is bound up with logic. The most proficient in languages are the most competent in logic, the ablest in expressing their thoughts by themselves and placing their words in their right places. They are also the most qualified to choose the shortest and clearest types (of expressions). Moreover, wisdom, being the noblest of pursuits, ought to be expressed in the soundest logical form, the most eloquent style and the fewest words, so as to be farthest removed from error or oddity, distasteful reasoning, bad accent or perversion. For all this is bound to dim the light of wisdom, hamper communication, fall short of the writer's goal, confuse the listener, falsify the senses and generate suspicion'.

When he had mastered the sciences of the poets, the grammarians and the rhetoricians and grasped them all, Aristotle turned to the ethical, political, mathematical, physical, and metaphysical sciences. Thereupon, he kept the company of Plato and became his student, willing to learn from him while he was seventeen years of age, in a place called 'Akademeia' in the City of the Philosophers, Athens. He remained a student of Plato for twenty years, learning from him orally. Plato did not entrust him to his student Xenocrates,[2] as he did with other students, because he valued him greatly. When Plato went to Sicily for the second time, he entrusted to Aristotle the care of the city of learning called the Academy, but when Plato died, Aristotle went out to a place in Athens called Leukeion, where he founded an institution dedicated to teaching the philosophy attributed to the Peripatetics.

Plato believed that physical exercise, intended to a moderate extent to dissolve unnecessary (bodily) accretions, is similar to exercising the soul[3] by recourse to wisdom, so that both goals will be achieved in training both the soul and the body.

It has already been mentioned that both Aristotle and Xenocrates used to teach students philosophy while they 'ambled around'. That is why they were called, together with their followers, Peripatetics.[4] Xenocrates remained in the Academy to teach Plato's curriculum; whereas all Aristotle's philosophy and the books he wrote on logic and the other parts of philosophy were transferred to the place Aristotle

1. Or instrument, Greek. *Organon*, a term applied to Aristotle's logical collection, as already mentioned above.

2. The successor of Spensippus, Plato's nephew, as head of the Academy.

3. Meaning, the wind.

4. From Greek, *peripatein*, 'to amble', but see note above.

had moved to, called Leukeion and deposited there. His philosophy and his books used to be called at the time the science of learning the truth and hearing it.[1]

When Plato died, Aristotle joined Aramis, the assistant of Governor Paulus. When that assistant died, Aristotle went back to Athens. Then Philip sent from him, and so he moved to Macedonia, where he continued to teach philosophy, until Alexander (the Great) marched on the Asiatic provinces. Thereupon, he appointed a successor of Aristotle in Macedonia, and so he went back to Athens to teach for fourteen years at the Leukeion. At that time, a soothsayer called Engaden (?) started attacking him for his religious opinions and the fact that he did not prostrate to the idols that were worshipped at that time and did not honour them. He did that out of jealousy and a hidden rancour against him. When Aristotle heard this, he left Athens and went to his country, Chalcis,[2] for fear that the Athenians might do to him what they did to Socrates, the Ascetic. He came to that place, which we have mentioned in order to watch the tide in the islands of Orpheus, which lay in Euboia and its neighbourhoods, and write a book on the subject. He died and was buried there, at the age of sixty-eight.[3]

When Philip died and was succeeded by Alexander, his son, who left Macedonia to fight the foreign nations and conquer the Asiatic provinces, Aristotle chose to lead a life of piety and relinquished royal contacts. He now concentrated on attending to the welfare of the common people, assisting the weak, marrying off orphans and widows and helping those who sought learning and education, whomever they may be and whatever type of science and education they were seeking. He gave to the poor in charity and attended to the welfare of people in the cities. He renewed the building of Stagira,[4] having been the one who codified its laws. Thus, he was highly regarded by its people and received great gifts from the kings and enjoyed an exalted position.

Aristotle's withered bones were exhumed by the people of Stagira and placed in a vessel of copper, which they buried in a place called Aristoteliana, which they used as a lodge where they met to discuss serious and melancholy subjects, so they could find rest in the vicinity of his grave and be close to his buried bones. Every time they faced a difficult philosophical problem, they were in the habit of coming to that spot, to sit around it and debate that problem till they lighted on its solution and their differences were settled. They believed that repairing to that spot where Aristotle's bones were buried would enliven their minds, and rectify their thoughts and refine their intellects, let alone satisfying their desire to honour him after his death and mourn his departure. Many of Aristotle's pupils were drawn from the ranks of kings, princes

---

1. A reference to the so-called *acroamatic* (*samāʿī*) part of Aristotle's instruction in advanced subjects, as distinct from the *exoteric* or popular part.
2. His mother's home in Euboia in the Aegean.
3. Or rather sixty-three, between 384 and 322 BC.
4. Aristotle's birthplace.

and others. They included Theophrastus, Eudemus, Alexander the King, Ammonius, Antichilius and similar distinguished characters, who were famous for their learning, eminent in philosophy and reputed for noble descent.

His cousin Theophrastus, assisted by two scholars, succeeded him as teacher of the philosophy he had codified and as inheritor of his rank and occupant of his chair. The two scholars were Eudemus and Aschuares (?), who wrote a number of books on logic and philosophy.

Aristotle left a lot of money and a number of slaves both male and female and other forms of property. He left a will with Antipater[1] and some of his friends to assist him, Theophrastus being asked to assist in the will and the management of his affairs, if they found it too onerous.

He wrote a large number of books amounting to approximately one hundred. It is said that he wrote books other than the hundred, eight on logic, eight on physics, ethics, politics and a large book on metaphysics, known as *Uthūlūjiyā*,[2] which means 'divine discourse' and a treatise on mechanics. In addition, there are epistles and contracts, the titles of which have reached us, but which we have not seen. They amount to a large number.

1. The Macedonian general.

2. *Uthūlūjiyā* or Book of Divinity (*Kitāb al-Rubūbiyyah*) was a compilation of the last three chapters of Plotinus' *Enneads*, which was erroneously attributed to Aristotle in the Arabic sources. It was translated into Arabic by ʿAbd al-Masīḥ ibn Nāʿimah al-Ḥimṣī (d. 835).

3

Quṭb al-Dīn Shīrāzī

Quṭb al-Dīn Abu'l-Thanā' Maḥmūd ibn Mas'ūd ibn al-Muṣliḥ al-Shīrāzī was born in 634/1236 in Shiraz to a family of physicians and Sufis. His brother Kamāl al-Dīn Abu'l-Khayr was also a physician and the famous poet Sa'dī may have been his brother-in-law. Quṭb al-Dīn's early education took place under the guidance of his father Ḍiyā' al-Dīn Mas'ūd with whom he studied the 'General Principles' of Ibn Sīnā's major work on medicine, *The Canon*, and he continued his studies with his uncle and two other physicians by the names of Shams al-Dīn Muḥammad ibn Aḥmad Kabashī and Sharaf al-Dīn Bushkānī. The latter two figures were also teachers of Sufism and the rational sciences and Quṭb al-Dīn Shīrāzī may have learned Sufism and some philosophy from them. His father, who had studied Sufism in Baghdad with Shihāb al-Dīn 'Umar al-Suhrawardī, was without doubt the person who first exposed the young Quṭb al-Dīn to Sufism.

Ibn al-Fuwāṭī, Quṭb al-Dīn's childhood friend, said of him that he had an enormous amount of energy and stamina, a sharp tongue and treated his opponents in a cynical and sarcastic manner. John Walbridge in his work on Quṭb al-Dīn entitled *The Science of Mystic Lights: Quṭb al-Dīn Shīrāzī and the Illuminationist Tradition in Islamic Philosophy* states, 'He played chess brilliantly and often. He played the violin well. He liked wine, some said. He was an amateur magician. He was full of stories, jokes and bits of poetry in Arabic and Persian. He … gave large portions of his income to his students, to the poor, and to orphans.'[1]

Like Ibn Sīnā, at the age of sixteen Quṭb al-Dīn was recognized as a physician and ophthalmologist at the Muẓaffarī hospital in Shiraz. He left his position at the hospital when he was twenty-four in order to devote himself fully to the pursuit of knowledge. He studied Ibn Sīnā's writings and followed his interests in medicine, philosophy and Sufism with a number of masters. Like so many other great Muslim sages, he travelled extensively and met with the learned scholars of

1. John Walbridge, *The Science of Mystic Lights: Quṭb al-Dīn Shīrāzī and the Illuminationist Tradition in Islamic Philosophy* (Cambridge, MA, 1992), pp. 18–19.

Khurāsān, Iraq and Anatolia. Even though Quṭb al-Dīn Shīrāzī had been given a Sufi cloak of blessing, or *khirqah*, at the age of ten by his father and had benefited from the presence of Najīb al-Dīn ʿAlī ibn Buzghūsh al-Shīrāzī, the most prominent Sufi in Shiraz, it was during one of his journeys that he was formally initiated into the Sufi path through Muḥyī al-Dīn Aḥmad ibn ʿAlī, a disciple of Najm al-Dīn Kubrā.

Around 658/1259, Quṭb al-Dīn Shīrāzī joined Naṣīr al-Dīn Ṭūsī and his staff at the Marāghah observatory and soon became the most important associate of Ṭūsī, with whom he also studied Ibn Sīnā's *al-Ishārāt wa'l-tanbīhāt* (Book of Directives and Remarks). After a long period of association with Ṭūsī, Quṭb al-Dīn Shīrāzī left for Khurāsān, a major centre of learning, and studied *Ḥikmat al-ʿayn* with its author Dabīrān-i Kātibī Qazwīnī. Quṭb al-Dīn later wrote a commentary on this work. Quṭb al-Dīn continued his journey to Qazwīn and Baghdad, where he may have taught at the Niẓāmiyyah university. Later his spiritual quest took him to Qunya (Konya) where he studied with Ṣadr al-Dīn Qunāwī, a major proponent of Ibn ʿArabī's school of gnosis. After the death of Ṣadr al-Dīn, Quṭb al-Dīn Shīrāzī left Qunya and became a judge in Sivas and later in Malatya and then moved back to Tabriz. His fame and stature were noticed by Aḥmad Takūdār, the son of Hülagü Khān, who sent him as an ambassador to the Mamlūk court in Egypt. Quṭb al-Dīn's presence in Egypt allowed him much-needed access to the available commentaries on Ibn Sīnā in the libraries of that city, but the Persian delegation, which had not been received warmly, did not remain long in Egypt.

Quṭb al-Dīn Shīrāzī returned to Tabriz and in 679/1280 he finally began to write the texts and the major commentaries that preoccupied him for the rest of his life. In 689/1290 he wrote his second commentary on Ibn Sīnā's *Canon* and later in the same year he completed his commentary on Suhrawardī's *Ḥikmat al-ishrāq*, which he dedicated to Jamāl al-Dīn Dastjirdānī. While in Tabriz, he met Rashīd al-Dīn Tabrīzī, the powerful minister with whom Quṭb al-Dīn Shīrāzī had an uneasy relationship. He therefore soon left Tabriz and went to the court of Amīr Dabbāj, who ruled over an independent area in western Gīlān, and dedicated his philosophical encyclopaedia *Durrat al-tāj* (Pearl of the Crown) to him. While in Gīlān, Quṭb al-Dīn wrote several works, among which it is said was a forty-volume commentary on the Qur'ān as well as a work on difficult passages in the Qur'ān and glosses on Zamakhsharī's commentary on the Qur'ān.

Having spent fourteen years of research and writing in the capital of the Īl-Khānids, Quṭb al-Dīn Shīrāzī died in 709/1309, only ten weeks after completing a third version of his commentary on Ibn Sīnā's *Canon.* He is buried in Charandāb cemetery in Tabriz close to his fellow student Bayḍāwī.

Nothing is known of his family, or even whether he had any. While it would have been unusual for him not to be married, in one of his later books he passionately defends celibacy. We know that at the time of his death Quṭb al-Dīn had no family to bury him and his funeral was arranged by one of his students, Khwājah 'Izz al-Dīn Ṭībī.

Among notable students of Quṭb al-Dīn Shīrāzī we can name Quṭb al-Dīn al-Taḥtānī and Kamāl al-Dīn al-Fārsī, who were both learned in philosophy and optics. The latter wrote *The Book of Judgment*, a critical evaluation of Ṭūsī and Rāzī and a notable commentary on Ibn al-Haytham's *Optics*.

Quṭb al-Dīn Shīrāzī has been referred to as '*al-Mutafann*' (master of many sciences), and "Allāmah' (great scholar) and his passion for learning is legendary among Persians. To date, twenty-six of his books and treatises have been catalogued, most of which remain unpublished and a number of his works are no longer extant.

In terms of philosophy, Quṭb al-Dīn Shīrāzī should be viewed as a link between the earlier Peripatetic philosophy of Ibn Sīnā, Suhrawardī's School of Illumination and Mullā Ṣadrā's *al-ḥikmah al-muta'āliyah*. Between Suhrawardī and Mullā Ṣadrā, there are about four centuries when philosophical activities in Persia were concentrated first in Azarbaijan and then Shiraz. Quṭb al-Dīn Shīrāzī is considered as the first major philosopher of the School of Shiraz and he played a major role not only in keeping the flame of discursive thought alive but also in continuing the illuminationist (*ishrāqī*) tradition of Suhrawardī. His major work, *Durrat al-tāj* (The Pearl of the Crown) is a Persian encyclopedia of Peripatetic philosophy that closely follows Ibn Sīnā's *Shifā'* but with an *ishrāqī* interpretation. One of the salient features of eighth/fourteenth century intellectual ambiance in Persia was a gradual rapprochement between four schools of thought. Each of these schools, seen as the flowering of a particular tradition of wisdom, possessed its own epistemological paradigm. They include theology (*kalām*), Peripatetic philosophy (*mashshā'ī*), illuminationist philosophy (*ishrāqī*) and gnosis (*'irfān*). Quṭb al-Dīn's synthesis of the different branches of wisdom was a precursor to the later School of Shiraz and especially the School of Isfahan where such a synthesis became the *modus operandi* culminating in Mullā Ṣadrā.

In addition to philosophy, Quṭb al-Dīn Shīrāzī wrote on mathematics, optics, astronomy, geography, physics and medicine and was very interested in the classification of the sciences, a subject we have included in this chapter. Here, we have included a section from Shīrāzī's *Durrat al-tāj* which deals with the classification of the sciences, their division into the practical and the theoretical and their subdivisions.

M. Aminrazavi

PEARL OF THE CROWN

Durrat al-tāj

Translated for this volume by Mehdi Aminrazavi from Quṭb al-Dīn Shīrāzī, *Durrat al-tāj, li-ghurrat al-dībāj*, ed. Muḥammad Mishkāt (Tehran, 1899–1906), pp. 22–23; 45–49; 60–62; 71–76; 79–81.

On the Virtues of the Sciences

Know that [intellectual] matters [sciences] can be classified into four categories:

First is that which rationality and wisdom approve, while the carnal soul (*nafs*) and bodily desires do not, such as sickness, poverty, and failure in worldly affairs. The soul dislikes such things but the rational faculty is in agreement with them. Through the rules of demonstration and Qur'ānic evidence, it has become apparent that every man who is of some closeness and proximity to God, Most High, will be protected from worldly [dangers] just as a child is protected from water and fire [by his parents]. Many of the worldly desires that are not granted are God's way of protecting His subjects from being engaged with anything other than Him and it is for this reason that the rational faculty agrees with it but the carnal soul (*nafs*) does not.

Second are those that the *nafs* favours but the intellect does not, such as the physical pleasures that are contradictory to the *sharīʿah* (Divine law). Although the *nafs* favours such things for the attainment of temporary pleasure, the rational faculty knows that for a moment of pleasure, the permanent salvation of the other world will be lost; so it does not agree with it.

Third are those that both the rational faculty and the *nafs* favour and that is science [knowledge].

Fourth is that which neither the rational/intellectual faculty nor the *nafs* favour and that is ignorance. It is for this reason that the wise men have said, 'If a learned man would be called ignorant, he becomes heart-broken, though he knows they have lied. Similarly, if they call an ignorant man learned, he becomes happy though he knows that they have lied.' Since knowledge is a virtue of character and ignorance is a vice of character, both [the ignorant and the learned] are dismayed by being called ignorant although it may be a lie and become happy by having been called learned although it may be untrue.

Now that this has become clear, know the following:

There are numerous arguments on the virtue of attaining knowledge through rational proofs (*al-adillah al-ʿaqliyyah*) and traditional proofs (*al-adillah al-*

naqliyyah).[1] From each we shall offer a few examples. Traditional proofs, due to their sacred and sanctified nature over rational proofs, are discussed first, although rational proofs have [discursive] priority over the transmitted ones. This is because the truths of transmitted statements are proven by discursive reasoning.

For traditional proofs, we begin first with that from the Qur'ān, second the Torah, third the Bible, fourth the *Zabūr* (Psalms),[2] fifth *Ḥadīth* and sixth the works of past scholars. Although much can be said about that matter from the Qur'ān, we shall only mention ten reasons.

The intellectual reasons for the virtue (*faḍīlah*) of knowing the sciences are also many, however, I will mention only four of them:

First Reason

The virtue of everything lies in its perfection. The virtue of the eyes lies in the perfection of the faculty of sight, and the virtue of the ears is in the perfection of hearing and the virtue of the hand lies in the perfection of the power of striking. Now that this is understood, know that man is made up of two parts, spirit (*rūḥ*) and body (*jasad*). As Sanā'ī, peace be upon him, has said:

> Man is a unique mixture,
> Higher than any high and non-existent in between.

The perfection of the body is due to the presence of the spirit therein, and the perfection of the spirit is due to the presence of science and *ḥikmah* [in it]. It is for this reason that God Almighty in the Qur'ān calls science 'spirit' and states:

> And the spirit came to Him by our Command.[3]

Since the perfection of man is in having a spirit [or soul] and the perfection of the soul [is in pursuing] science and divine wisdom (*ḥikmat*), therefore, the perfection of man is in possessing science and divine wisdom.

Second Reason

The superiority of animals to solid bodies is in their consciousness, since animals and objects are similar with respect to corporeality but different in terms of life which indicates the presence of knowledge and consciousness. Since animals gain knowledge through their senses and inanimate objects do not have consciousness, then necessarily animals possess more virtue than inanimate objects. Amongst

1. Any proof that is based either on the authority of the Divine Scripture or on the authentic tradition of the Prophet i.e. *sunnah*.
2. The book revealed to the Prophet David.
3. Qur'ān 42:52

animals, those whose sensory perceptions are fuller and stronger are superior to those whose senses are weaker. For example, an animal that has the sense of sight is more virtuous than one who does not have it, such as the scorpion.

Although men and animals have in common the understanding of 'particulars', man is superior because of his understanding of the universals. Man has knowledge of both particulars and universals and possesses the means of understanding all of them and from this point of view, he is more virtuous than all animals. This is firm evidence that knowledge is the most virtuous of all things.

Third Reason

The virtue of adults in comparison to children is in the former's superior consciousness and not their faculty of perception. Unlike the virtue of sight which is in seeing [physical] beauty, intellectual understanding is more complete and more noble than sense perception. Therefore, whoever has a more complete intellectual faculty is more virtuous.

There are several reasons for saying that intellectual understanding is more complete than sense perception:

1) The senses cannot perceive themselves while the intellectual faculty can perceive itself and has consciousness of itself. Therefore, the intellectual faculty is more complete.

2) Sense perception can only understand the appearance of things, whereas the intellectual faculty sees the appearance of things, reflects [on them] and then understands their [inner] reality. The inner reality (*bāṭin*) in relation to intellectual understanding is comparable to appearance in relation to the senses and therefore it [intellectual understanding] is more complete.

3) Sensory perception is often mistaken. For example, people on a moving vessel consider the vessel to be motionless but think that the seashore is moving, whereas it is obvious that the ship is moving and the seashore is not. On a cloudy night the clouds move towards the moon but it appears that the moon is following the clouds. [Sensory perception] sees small things as large such as fire at night, and large things as small as from a distance. There are many such examples, for instance, the seeds of a black grape appear in water as black plums and a curve (appears in water) as straight and a sphere as flat. Such are the examples of the deceptions of sensory perception.

Since the critical faculty of sensory perception is flawed, a judge is needed to distinguish correct from false and it is the intellectual faculty that distinguishes between true sensory data and the false ones. It is apparent that since the judge is superior to that which is judged, then the intellectual faculty is more complete than [and superior to] sense perception.

4) The power of intellectual understanding is more permanent than the power of sense perception in that intellectual power does not decay with the corruption

of the body while the power of sense perception deteriorates with the decaying of the body. There is no doubt that a permanent consciousness is more perfect than a transient one.

5) The objects of rational understanding are greater than the object of sensory perception for the objects of rational understanding are limitless while the objects of sensory perception are limited. Thus a limitless understanding is more perfect than a limited one.

6) The intellectual comprehension separates the entities from what is added to them and understands them in their pure form, contrary to sense perception that can understand things only with the attributes added to them. For example, (sense perception) cannot perceive a colour unless it is in association with something that has length, width, distance and proximity. It is apparent, therefore, that intellectual power is more complete than sense perception.

Fourth Reason

First know that virtuosity comes from virtue which is a relational quality. If two things have something in common and one has an added character, as in the saying 'his knowledge is his distinction', and as it is said, 'a horse is more virtuous than a camel', this is the case since they are common in carrying weight and different in power, glory, fighting ability, beauty and sublimity of appearance.

Therefore, it is clear that knowledge is virtue, and when attributed to animals it signifies qualitative differences. The fighting ability of a horse is a virtue, but not in and of itself (whereas knowledge is intrinsically virtuous) and is not an added attribute. Knowledge (*'ilm*) is the highest Attribute of God and it is for this reason that the wise have agreed that this attribute is divine and accounts for the dignity of the angels and prophets. Even a clever horse is better than an unintelligent child. Therefore, knowledge is virtuous in and of itself without being an attribute of anything else.

On the Reality of Knowledge and Whether Concepts are Axiomatic or Acquired and other Related Discussions:

Are some concepts self-evident, without any mental exertion, such as light and darkness, or are they acquired like concepts such as *jinns* and angels that are known through definition and description? This discourse includes three principles:

First Principle: On the reality of knowledge and to which of the ten categories does it belong?

Scholars have disagreed strongly on this subject. Some have said that knowledge belongs to the category of 'relation' since it is relative to the knower and the known. Others have said it belongs to the category of 'passion' since it is an action that occurs in the soul. There are those who say that it belongs to the category of 'quality' for it is one of the qualities of the essence of the soul such as health and sickness, strength and will power. This is the right idea.

Avicenna, may God reward him well, has adopted this view although inconsistently: in one place he says that this category is non-existent and has interpreted it as something detached from matter. While somewhere else he has said that it is an existential attribute meaning that it is an embedded form in the substance of the rational soul that corresponds to the essence of what is understood. Somewhere else, he has defined this [category] as an attribute that is 'relational', and in yet a different place he has argued that it is pure relation. However, in my opinion, knowledge belongs to the category of quality.

Second Principle of the Second Chapter: On whether the concept of knowledge is axiomatic or acquired? if acquired, is it possible to define it?

Question: Some say that a concept is axiomatic since a particular knowledge is necessary if we are to say anything such as 'that writer'. Since this knowledge is necessary, then absolute knowledge which includes it is also necessary. It is impossible to conceive of the whole without conceiving of its parts. If a part depends on something, then the whole necessarily depends upon it. What is inclusive of a thing is inclusive of the whole thing.

Answer: Any existing being must have the knowledge of the particular. However, is it the attainment of the knowledge of the particulars that is necessary, or is it the notion in the mind (*taṣawwur*) of this particular knowledge that is necessary? If you seek certitude through attainment of acquiring something, its conception, or notion, is not necessarily obtained, just as from the knowledge [of the concept] of hunger and thirst, one does not necessarily have knowledge [gained through experience] of [hunger and thirst]. Thus, from the knowledge of what is necessary, [the conception] of a particular is not obtained.

Second Principle of the Third Chapter: On the division of sciences into the philosophical and non-philosophical and dividing of the non-philosophical into religious and non-religious

We say that knowledge that requires theoretical reflection can be divided into two types: first is that whose relation to all ages and nations remains the same and like astronomy, arithmetic and ethics, it does not change with the changing of place, time, nation and government.

The second is that whose relation to different ages and nations does not remain the same, such as the science of the jurisprudence of a religion which remains unchanged during a particular period with regard to particular individuals, but then it changes [when another religion is considered]. Also, [the same is true of] the grammar of a language since that is a science in relation to the speakers of that language and no one else. The first type of knowledge is called *ḥikmah* (philosophical) while the second type is not. *Ḥikmah* is the highest of all the sciences and the evidence for that is the saying of God, most High, who states, 'And I bestowed *ḥikmah* and therein lies abundant good.' It is because of this that *ḥikmah* has been considered to be equivalent to scripture and as the Qur'ān says: The book and *ḥikmah*.

As for non-philosophical science, if it is in accordance with the views of religion, it is religious; otherwise it is non-religious. We, however, are concerned with the philosophical and religious type, [and] philosophical science in particular because this book is based upon it.[1]

The Third Principle of the Third Chapter: On the division of the philosophical and religious sciences into different types

On the Divisions of Philosophy:

First know that philosophy in the tradition of the gnostics is knowing of things as they really are and the undertaking of tasks as one ought to in accordance with one's ability so that the human soul may attain perfection for which it yearns. Since this is the case, philosophy is divided into two parts: intellectual and practical.

Intellection is the study of the realities of beings, and judging their qualities and properties insofar as they are axiomatic, in accordance with human ability. *Praxis* is affiliated with action and the creating of objects (industry) is to actualize what is in the domain of potentiality, provided it leads from imperfection to perfection.

He in whose being these two forms of knowledge are unified is a perfect *ḥakīm* and a learned man and his status is the highest among mankind. As it has been said: 'Wisdom comes from Him and in that bestowed wisdom lies great good.'[2]

Since the science of *ḥikmah* is in knowing all things as they really are, then division within it has to be in accordance with the division among beings.

All beings are of two types: first are those whose existence is not contingent upon the will of human beings and second are those whose existence is dependent upon the disposal and ministration of man. Therefore, the knowledge of beings is also of two types: first, knowledge of the first type and they call that 'theoretical philosophy' (*ḥikmat-i naẓarī*). The second type of knowledge is 'practical philosophy' (*ḥikmat-i 'amalī*). Theoretical philosophy in turn can be divided into two types. First is knowledge of those beings in which matter plays no part in their existence such as God, intellects, souls, unity, multiplicity, etc. Second is knowledge of those things that unless they are materially oriented, cannot exist [by themselves] and this itself can be divided into two categories:

1) Being materially oriented is not necessary for them to be conceived or imagined, such as, even, odd, square, triangle, sphere, circle, etc.

1. The long paragraph which follows is a perfunctory passage about the King of Māzandarān whose translation has been omitted.

2. Qur'ān 2:268.

2) They are known through being materially oriented such as minerals, plants, and animals.

Therefore, theoretical philosophy is of three types: first metaphysics, second, mathematics, and third the natural sciences. The first one is the 'highest science', the second 'middle science' and third, the 'lower science'. Each of these [categories] includes several sub-sections, some of which possess major principles and some minor ones.

The principles of the first science (metaphysics) are two: one is the knowledge of God Almighty and those who are close to Him and by His Command have become the instruments of creation such as intellects, souls and the rules pertaining to the subsistence of their operation. These they call Divine Knowledge.

Second is knowledge of the universals since the existent beings attain their identity through them. Unity, multiplicity, necessity, contingency, createdness or eternity and the like are among them and [knowledge of them] is called metaphysics. The minor principles are knowledge of prophecy, the Imams, and life after death, etc.

The principles of the science of mathematics are of four types: first, knowledge of quantities and the principles therein and they call that geometry. Second, is the knowledge of numbers and their characteristics and they call that the science of numbers (arithmetic). Third is the knowledge of the relationship between the position of celestial objects to each other as well as their relationship to the terrestrial objects, the measure of their movements and their size and this they call the science of astronomy. The principles of astronomy, however, fall outside of this category. Fourth is the knowledge of composition and its intricacies and they call that the science of those realities that are composed. If applied in sung harmonies, then because of their relationship with each other and the duration of silence between the [phrases of] singing, they call that the science of music.

The minor [branches] in the science of mathematics are of several kinds such as optics, algebra, the measurement of mass and area, etc. Also among the minor [branches] are addition and subtraction in Indian numbers, the science of time measurement, astronomical tables, calendars and the science of irrigation.

The principles of the natural sciences are of eight types: First is the knowledge of the principles of changeable phenomena such as time, place, motion, rest, limit, infinity, etc. They call that 'natural philosophy' (*samāʿ-i ṭabīʿī*). Second, is the knowledge of the simple and compound substances and principles of the worlds above and below and they call that nature and the world. Third is knowledge of the principles and substances and changing of patterns in matter and they call that the science of generation and corruption. Fourth is the knowledge of the causes of events and their occurrence in the air and on the earth such as: thunder, lightning, rain, snow, earthquakes, etc., and those they call the effects of the upper realm. The fifth is the knowledge of the compound substances and the order of their mixture and they call that the science of minerals. Sixth is the science of the vegetal objects and their essence and powers and that they call the science of plants. Seventh, is the knowledge of those objects that move through their will and the principles of their movements and their soul and the powers therein and that they call the science of zoology. Eighth is the knowledge of the human soul and how it rules the body and other mysteries and that they call the science of the soul.

The minor [categories] of the natural sciences are many, such as the science of medicine, the principles of astronomy, agriculture, physiognomy, which makes inferences from people's bodily characteristics as to their temperament and moral qualities; also, the science of dream interpretation, alchemy, the mysteries (*ṭalismān*), which studies the mixing of heavenly powers with earthly substances in order to enrich them, and so can initiate many strange events in this world; [then] the science of magic which is the mixing of earthly substances with each other to generate power which initiates the occurrence of extraordinary events.

The science of logic, composed by Aristotle, deals with the ways of knowing things and the method of acquiring knowledge about that which is unknown. Logic is knowledge about knowing and serves as a means for attaining other sciences and it is divided into nine parts:

First is the *Isagoge* which is the principle of logic that consists of discussion of types of terms and five universal categories, genus, species, specific difference (*differentia*), property and accident.
Second, the ten categories.
Third, on interpretation (*Peri Hermeneias*) which is an expression that consists of a discussion with many propositions.
Fourth, Syllogism
Fifth: Demonstration.
Sixth: Dialectics
Seventh: Sophistry
Eighth: Rhetoric
Ninth: Poetry

The reason why the categories are nine is because those analogies through which unknowns can be attained consist of 'the five created' ones; they are: demonstration, dialectic, rhetoric, poetry and sophistry.

Now, such a deduction results either in assent or in imagination and the assent in turn is either definitive or non-definitive and the definitive assent is either adequate to reality or not. Thus the deduction which results in definitive assent adequate to reality is called demonstration and if not adequate to reality but accepted by general public; it is called dialectic, otherwise it is called sophistry. Again, if a deduction results in non-definitive assent, it is called rhetoric and if it results in imagination it is called poetry.

Practical wisdom is knowing the prudence of intentional acts of the human being, that are aimed at the attainment of man's material well-being in this world as well as in the Hereafter. [They] necessitate the attainment of perfection since they are aimed towards it [perfection]. That too is divided into two types: First is that which concerns each individual; second that which concerns society collectively. The second part, too, is of two different types: First that which concerns a group among whom there is partnership at home; second is that which is of concern to a group among whom there is collaboration in the city, the province and the state.

Practical wisdom is of three types: First is the refinement of character [and the self], second, the regulation of the household and third the government of cities. The benefits of the wisdom of the self is that it recognizes the virtues and the value of abstinence so that purity of the self may be obtained. The vices are also recognized and restlessness [of the soul] is [calmed] and cleansed from the soul. The benefit of the regulation of the household is that one learns that cooperation is necessary between members of the household (between husband and wife, son and daughter, owner and tenant) so the well-being of the members of the home is achieved. The benefit of civic wisdom is in knowing how the participation between groups and individuals needs to take place in order to be mutually beneficial so that humankind can survive.

Know that some have divided civic wisdom into two types: One is that which belongs to the government and they call that politics. Second is that which addresses the domain of prophecy and religious law and they call it 'the science of divine laws' (*'ilm-i nawāmīs*). There are those who have divided practical wisdom into four types; this does not contradict those who have divided them into three since two divisions can be included in one.

Some have divided the types of theoretical wisdom into four in accordance with different types of what is known. A 'known' is either contingent upon corporeal matter in its external existence or not. In the first case if its conception in the mind in inseparable from association with matter, then it is a natural entity and belongs to the region of natural philosophy. But if it can be conceived as detached from matter, then it is a mathematical entity and belongs to the area of mathematical philosophy. However if its existence has no affiliation with matter, then it is the Essence of God, Most Exalted, intellects, or souls or it is concepts such as quiddity, unity, multiplicity, cause and effect, and the like which belong to general metaphysics and philosophy. The latter type of the knowledge of things is sometimes predicated upon immaterial entities and sometimes upon material things but their predication on material things is always accidental and not essential, for if it is predicated on material things in essence, then that means it is not separable from matter and so it cannot be applicable to immaterial realities.

4

Jalāl al-Dīn Dawānī

Jalāl al-Dīn Muḥammad ibn As'ad Dawānī is one of the best-known figures of the period under consideration in this volume. Born in the town of Dawān in the province of Fārs in 830/1427, he studied in Shiraz where he soon became known as an accomplished scholar and was chosen as *mudarris* or professor at the al-Aytam *madrasah*. He was highly respected by the political authorities of the day. He was chosen as judge (*qāḍī*) at the court of Uzun Ḥasan and Sulṭān Ya'qūb and even reached the rank of minister. At the end of an active intellectual and social life, he returned to his town of Dawān where he died and was buried in 908/1502.

Dawānī was known as an authority in Sunni *kalām* as well as philosophy and his writings were highly respected during his own lifetime at the Ottoman court in Istanbul. But in a late work entitled *Nūr al-hidāyah* (Light of Guidance) he declared his attachment to Twelve-Imam Shi'ism. In any case he was an influential figure in both the Sunni and the Shi'i worlds. In addition to Persia and the Ottoman world, he was also well known in Muslim India where his writings have remained popular over the centuries to this day.

Some seventy of Dawānī's works have survived. They include works on both *kalām* and *falsafah*. His most famous work is the Persian treatise *Lawāmi' al-ishrāq fī makārim al-akhlāq* (Flashes of Illumination on Praiseworthy Ethics) better known as *Akhlāq-i jalālī* (Jalālian Ethics). This work is based on Ṭūsī's *Naṣīrian Ethics* but it intermingles the content of this work with *ishrāqī* elements and also embellishes it with verses from the Qur'ān, *ḥadīth* and sayings of Sufi masters. He identifies the moral ideal with the religious one, emphasizing that man's ideal should be to become 'the vice-gerent of God on earth' (*khalīfat Allāh fi'l-arḍ*) mentioned in the Qur'ān. His political philosophy is based on ideal kingship and he includes a section in this work on advice to kings. His metaphysics and cosmology remain, however, essentially that of Ibn Sīnā based on ontology and the emanation of the First Intellect from the Necessary Being and the other nine intellects from each other.

The second most famous work of Dawānī is his commentary upon the *Hayākil al-nūr* of Suhrawardī entitled *Shawākil al-ḥūr* (Forms of the Houris of Paradise). This work became especially popular in India where it helped in the spread of the School of *ishrāq*. In Persia itself Dawānī carried out extensive debates with Ṣadr al-Dīn Dashtakī on philosophical questions, especially *ishrāqī* doctrines. The *Ishrāq hayākil al-nūr* (Illumination upon 'The Temples of Light') of Ṣadr al-Dīn's son, Ghiyāth al-Dīn Manṣūr Dashtakī, is a trenchant rebuttal to Dawānī's commentary on the *Hayākil al-nūr.* Ghiyāth al-Dīn was in fact in many ways opposed to Dawānī's thinking and wrote several criticisms of his writings.

Dawānī also wrote a number of treatises on *kalām* issues including glosses upon the *Sharḥ al-tajrīd*. He is also the author of treatises on logic and *mashshā'ī* philosophy. In addition he was interested in the natural sciences. In his *Unmūdhaj al-ʿulūm* (Samples of the Sciences) he speaks of magnetism and why a magnet attracts iron filings and he also wrote a commentary upon the astronomical work of Chaghmīnī.

Dawānī wrote in both Arabic and Persian and even composed poems in both languages. He was also interested in Sufism and wrote a commentary upon one of the *ghazal*s of Ḥāfiẓ.

In this chapter we have included two treatises of Dawānī, first his commentary upon Suhrawardī's *Hayākil al-nūr* (Temples of Light), and second his famous treatise on ethics titled *Akhlāq-i jalālī* (Jalālian Ethics). The first treatise discusses such topics as causality, motion, corporeality and its relationship to cosmology and the role of light in this context. What makes this treatise particularly interesting is that many of the traditional metaphysical issues are presented and discussed within the context of the *ishrāqī* tradition. Many of Suhrawardī's technical terms are used here to elucidate a whole range of philosophical problems.

The second section deals with politics and ethics. Dawānī begins by discussing the moral responsibility that rests on the shoulders of the rulers and the consequences of misusing political power. In doing so, he offers examples of the political conduct of previous caliphs and sultans and draws conclusions pertaining to justice, laws and desirable virtues in a ruler. This treatise should be regarded as a work of didactic literature in which a philosopher offers moral and political advice to those in power.

S. H. Nasr

COMMENTARY ON SUHRAWARDĪ'S 'TEMPLES OF LIGHT'

Sharḥ hayākil al-nūr

Translated for this volume by Carl W. Ernst from Jalāl al-Dīn Muḥammad ibn Sa'd al-Dīn As'ad al-Ṣiddīqī al-Dawānī, *Shawākil al-ḥūr fī sharḥ hayākil al-nūr,* ed. Muḥammad 'Abd al-Ḥaqq and Muḥammad Yūsuf Kūkan (Madras, 1373/1953), pp. 147–193.[1]

The Fifth Temple

Demonstrating that the Chain of Events is Infinite, and that they Depend on a Continuous, Perpetual Motion

Chapter One: On the proof of the circular motion of the heavens, and that their motion is voluntary, not natural

1. *Know that every contingent being* is temporal, i.e., it is what comes into existence after it was not; [*it*] *requires a cause,* or something that sustains its existence, whether as a condition, an instrument, or an invalidating prohibition, [*that is*] *contingent.* This is necessary, because if all that sustains it were eternal, it would be eternal, because of the impossibility of the lack of an effect for a complete cause.[2] *This reasoning applies to the contingent cause,* because it also requires a contingent cause, and so on ad infinitum. *It is sufficient,* or rather required, *that the chain of contingent causes extended infinitely, inasmuch as it will not have an origin; for the* postulated *contingent origin is covered by this reasoning,* just as was established. Thus it is not an origin, since this would be a contradiction of the postulate.

2. It is established that in existence there are contingent beings that are subsequently renewed without interruption. *This certainly leads to that which requires*

1. Paragraphs follow this edition, though I have added the numbering for convenience. In this translation Suhrawardī's text is indicated by italicized print. I did not have access to the original Arabic text of Suhrawardī, *Hayākil al-nūr,* Muḥyī al-Dīn Ṣabrī Kurdī (Cairo, 1335/1916–17). For a Persian translation of the base text, see Shihāb al-Dīn Yaḥyā Suhrawardī, *Majmū'a-i muṣannafāt-i Shaykh-i Ishrāq/Oeuvres philosophies et mystiques,* vol. 3, ed. Seyyed Hossein Nasr (2nd ed., Tehran, 1355 Sh./1977; repr. Tehran, 1372 Sh./1994), pp. 83–108, and the introductory remarks of Henry Corbin, 'Prolégomènes III,' ibid., 25–45. For a French translation of the base text, see Shihâboddîn Yahyâ Sohravardî Shaykh al-Ishrâq, *L'archange empourpré, Quinze traits et récits mystiques,* tr. Henry Corbin (Paris, 1976), pp. 33–66; several longer extracts from the commentaries of Dawānī and Ghiyāth al-Dīn Shīrāzī are translated there also (67–73), and a few more translations from these commentaries are found in the notes (74–89).

2. A 'complete cause' (*'illah tamāmah*) is defined as 'that which requires the existence of the effect; it is said that the complete cause is the totality upon which the existence of a thing depends.' Cf. 'Alī ibn Muḥammad al-Sarīf al-Jurjānī, *Kitāb al-Ta'rīfāt,* ed. Gustavus Fluegel (Leipzig, 1845; repr. Beirut, 1978), p. 160.

renewal and continuity with its own essence. The thing that requires renewal for its essence is motion. Now time, even if it requires renewal, renewal is not essential to it; rather, it is so for its locus, which is motion, for time is the quantity of motion inasmuch as its parts are not unified. *The property of the heavens is to be correctly described in terms of uninterrupted circular continuous motions, and to be appropriately the cause of contingent beings without ceasing.* Thus it is in the text that we have seen.

Suhrawardī's saying, 'to be correctly described' is the subject of the predicate 'the property of the heavens', and 'circular' is the adjective of 'motions'. It is possible that 'circular' is a predicate after the predicate. The meaning of this sentence is that linear motions undoubtedly end, if the existence of an infinite extent is precluded in logical proofs regarding limited distance. But linear motions are not continuous in terms of retrograde motion and curvature. Logical proof does not explain both kinds of linear motion in terms of rest. The author does not completely believe this, as is mentioned in *The [Book of Encounters and] Conversations,*[1] and Plato and other philosophers deny it. This is because linear motion is either natural, by compulsion, or voluntary. If it is natural, it must cease when it reaches its natural goal. If it is by compulsion, it is only possible in terms of the [four] elements, since, as they maintain, there is no influence in the heavens.

3. Their argument implies either that the compulsion is from a compeller or his volition. If the first, [the motion] must cease when the compeller reaches his natural goal, and if the second, it must cease also. Sub-lunar entities capable of voluntary motion (i.e., the species of animals) cannot sustain [motion] perpetually, because their actions depend upon bodies, nor are their bodies perpetual, since their elemental compounds must dissolve. Thus [it is stated] in [*The Wisdom of*] *Illumination* and in its commentary.[2] I say that this is only achieved if the compeller is a moving body that moves the compelled object with a motion that is in principle not concomitant. But a necessity is concomitant with the void, compelling bodies in their motions, as in the case of the urine specimen bottle when it is filled and then poured out in water, or also a man who casts a stone upwards and follows through with his hand, and the stone keeps moving. Would that I knew why its cessation is necessarily connected to impossibility in the world of the elements and to dissolution in compounds.

4. There is no individual body in the elements that is perpetual so that it could undergo perpetual linear motion and continue in the same state. It is not conceivable that linear motion should reach successive individuals. This is common to both perspectives, and it only refutes what some philosophers have said, that time is a single thing joined to another. But it must be connected to something similar in the

1. Suhawardī, *Kitāb al-Mashāriʿ wa'l-muṭāraḥāt,* in *Oeuvres,* ed. Corbin (Tehran, 1952), I, pp. 375–376.

2. Suhawardī, *Ḥikmat al-ishrāq,* in *Oeuvres,* ed. Corbin (Tehran, 1952), II, 173.

single connection. From these introductory remarks it is demonstrated that linear motion is not appropriately called perpetual or continuous; rather, it is appropriate that the latter be circular, but the elements do not sustain perpetuity, while celestial order does. It is established that the proper motion that is perpetual and continual is this circular motion of the heavens, but the argument to establish this point is long, and space does not permit it.

5. *This,* i.e., the circular motion of the heavens, *is the cause of the events in our world,* the world of the elements, and that is by the preparation of matter for receptivity to temporal form. The likeness for that is that the sun rises over water, gradually warming it until cold is completely eliminated. It becomes subtle and the form of water is deprived of its matter, becoming air by its separate radiation on the airy form that is upon it. Then the air is heated further until it becomes subtler, and the form of water is deprived of its matter, as it radiates upon it the form of fire. Let it not be thought that its preparation is only through the cause of the perceptible natural qualities belonging to its rays. Rather, these are hidden connections, the depth and detail of which are unknown except to the Upholder of the heavens and the earths. If you wish, then follow the influences experienced in conjunctions and other astrological matters. The years will see wonders that dazzle minds.

6. He confirms the foregoing by saying, *since the First Cause does not change,* because it is impossible for it to undergo change, and it has been demonstrated that it is not subject to an attribute that changes it. *So it is not a cause for contingent motions.* The eternity of these motions is dictated by the eternity of their complete cause. *Were it not for the motions of the heavens, the origination of the contingent would not occur,* because of the impossibility of contingent beings ever depending on the eternal, as you have learned. There is no doubt that by the addition of a renewed thing [i.e., motion] the complete cause produces these contingent beings.

7. Thus he demonstrated that their motions are voluntary, saying, *The motions of the heavens are not natural, for the heaven departs from every point which it sought* by the essence of the motion with which it tended. *That which is moved by nature stops when it reaches the position it seeks, since it does not flee by nature from that which was its desire.* [1] [He says] 'by nature', for it is not possible that it be compelled; were it compelled, it would be in accord with the compeller, and the motions would be uniform in direction, speed, and delay, but that is not the case, as astronomical observations attest. [2] It is said that it has been proved that what lacks a source of natural inclination does not accept compulsory motion, and it is proved also that the heavens lack a source of natural inclination because they are not subject to linear inclination, and natural domain, by the nearest of paths, which is the straight line. [3] It is also said [that heavenly motion is not compelled] because compulsion is evil, and there is no evil in the heavens, only pure good.

8. Are you aware that the substance of these three points is open to objection? [1] Regarding the first point, it is as just described [i.e., that heavenly motion is

incompatible with compulsion].[1] [2] Regarding the second point, it is [open to objection] because the proof of the first premise is as they have mentioned. After its premises are accepted, it only demonstrates that what lacks in its essence the source of a certain natural inclination is not subject to compelled motion. Then that which is proven demonstrates that in the heavens there is no linear inclination. This does not require that they contain no source of any inclination whatever, because of the possibility that they contain the source of another, circular inclination; so it was said. I say that it is possible to reply that there is impeding inclination. If on the one hand it is linear, he has shown its impossibility, in that linear inclination does not in principle impede the circular, as appears in the sphere rotating around its centre [while] descending from above. If on the other hand it is another circular [inclination], this is also absurd, because it is already established that nature does not require circular inclination. But the likelihood remains that the impeding circular inclination is voluntary, and that there is perceptible circular motion [of the planetary sphere] to the extent that there is an excess of compelled inclination over it. [3] Regarding the third point, it has two unproven premises that are not evident [i.e., the evil of compulsion and absence of evil in the heavens]. I say that if its motion is compelled, if the compulsion is perpetual, this would require cessation of nature from its activity. If it is completely suspended, it requires the cessation of the motion that preserves time. But it has been shown that time has a unitary essence and is connected and single. Its preserving motion must be thus. Since it was established that the motions of the heavens are neither natural nor compelled, *its motion can only be voluntary.* In some manuscripts after these words, one finds the phrase, 'thus they are living and intelligent.'[2]

Chapter Two. On the proximate contact belonging to celestial motion

9. *The source emanating the motion of heaven is its sphere,* because of the proof that its motion is voluntary. There is no doubt that voluntary motion is connected to the moving soul, and because contact belongs to the motion of the body, it is not possible that it be an intellect, since the meaning of intellect is the essence completely separated from matter and its relationships. *And so its motive action belongs to the motion of the body of the heaven.* This is loose in expression, and it means the body of the moved heaven. *[It] is a voluntary motive action, and the motion of the body of heaven by its motive action is compelled motion,* because the moving object, which is the separate soul, is not the essence of the body, nor is it a part of it, since it is external. *If we consider the body of heaven and its soul as things isolated from one another, then their motion is by the motive action of its soul* which

1. A marginal note adds, 'This is only complete if the compeller (reading *al-qāsir* for *al-qasr*) is a body.'

2. This phrase also occurs in the Persian translation.

is external to it. *So their motion is compelled in relation to the soul,* as mentioned; the feminine subjects ['their'] refer to the heavens or to heaven. *And if we consider them together as a single thing, its motion is voluntary.* This is because its origin is not something external to the totality.

10. I say that this is something that we do not run across in the theory of anyone else. It does not derive from a philosophical reality, since the like of this expression borders on natural motions. This is because it is said, when referring to the body of the earth in a comparison, that it is a thing separate from its special form; its motion is compelled, since its source is external to that which is moved. This is particularly so in terms of what the author maintains regarding the existence of special forms as causal conditions for the body, which is, on first consideration, the extended known substance. For the essence of the body is then established without it [the soul]. It [the body] is only produced from the fact that it contains the species of bodies from earth, water, etc. Regarding what he mentions, the former argument will be compulsion eternally, and the latter argument will be compelled motion without impeding inclination. Both of them are contrary to the agreement of philosophers. If that is admitted, then because it is not possible that there be another compeller than the soul, it is not voluntary. But since its motion is voluntary, *it is living and intelligent* by necessity, since volition is not experienced without these characteristics.

11. *And the heavens need no sustenance*, since nothing is digested by them; otherwise, they would be subject to rectilinear motion [from desire]. Regarding this proposition, and its ancillary definite propositions, however, the proof is based upon it. But all the heavens [may be considered to] share in these [propositions] by way of intuition. [*Nor do they need*] *growth,* since it is a kind of nourishment, but that depends on rectilinear motion, which is impossible for it. *[Nor do they need] to beget,* since it also is a kind of nourishment, and because the object of generation is the preservation of the species through a succession of individuals. Rather, it [does not?] need it insomuch as it does not undergo continual individuation, for the individuals of the heavens are perpetual, not undergoing corruption. Thus they do not need to beget their like. *Nor do they have a desire*, since the object of that is preservation of the individual or the species from corruption, and they are safe from that. *Nor do they have a rival* in space or nearby, *nor anything to resist them* in existence, so *they have no anger,* since the object of anger is guarding against the rival or that which resists one's desire in general. Anger is appropriate either to the body that is acted upon and changes from a suitable condition to an unsuitable one, then returns to the suitable condition and enjoys it, or to that which conceives of a situation that requires it to depart from a suitable condition, so that it longs to reject it. *Their motion does not tend to that which is low, since it has no power over them.* The noblest is not moved by the lowest; otherwise the lowest would have influence upon the noblest by its position as agent. For the final cause is an efficient cause for the activity of the agent.

12. *Thus when we purify ourselves from the preoccupations of the body* with the aid of subtle disciplines tempered for the soul that is incited toward submersion in the desires of the world of lies and darkness, *we consider the might of the Real, and the Glory.* 'Glory' (*kharrah*) is a Persian word, the meaning of which, according to *The Commentary on [the Wisdom of] Illumination* [by Quṭb al-Dīn al-Shīrāzī], is transmitted 'from Zarathustra of Azarbaijan, the author of the Book of Zand, the perfect prophet, the excellent sage: it is the light that dawns from the essence of God the transcendent. By this one person rules over another; by its aid everyone has power over an action or product. That which is restricted to the wise kings is called "the glory of kings (*kayān kharrah*)."[1] As he says in the *The Tablets of 'Imād,* 'The conquering and blessed king Kay Khusraw established sanctification and worship, and he received[2] the ability to speak with the holy spirit; the hidden world spoke to him, and he ascended in his soul to the highest world, inscribed with the wisdom of God. The lights of God confronted him directly, and from them he realized the meaning known as 'the kings of glory', which is God himself. All necks were humbled to him.'[3] Nonetheless, they call it that because *khawar* [i.e., *kharrah*] in their language is light, and they connect it to the *kayān*, who are the emperors in their language, with the genitive object preceding the subject, as is customary in this language. He describes glory as *expansive*, because that implies expansiveness of the soul and the vast breadth of its comprehension in terms of knowledge and influence.

13. *[It is] the light emanating from his presence*, that is, from the presence of the Real, either from his essence, or from his lights that are separate from existent things, and by that light every existent being is guided to the perfection appropriate to it. *We find in our souls shining flashes of light, and dawning illumination; we witness lights, and we obtain our desires*, or fulfil our needs for information about hidden things, and control over the world of images and the elements. In one manuscript, it says [*we obtain our*] *states*, but this appears to be a mistake.[4] *And what is your opinion of the persons* who are spherical bodies, these [*that are*] *noble of form*, on account of being in the natural shape that is the best of shapes. In one manuscript it says [instead of 'of form'] 'divine', meaning sanctified beyond the opposing qualities that are the source of defects, or [sanctified] in or in love with the divine lights. That fits what he says later about the divine lovers.[5] [*Having*] *perpetual*

1. A marginal note adds, 'That is, Kay Khusraw, Kayqubād, Kay Luhrāsp, and Kayūmarth, from the kings of Persia.'

2. Following Corbin's reading *fa-atat-hu* for the erroneous *fā'ita.*

3. Suhrawardī, *Ḥikmat al-ishrāq*, in *Oeuvres*, ed. Corbin, II, p. 157; cf. Suhrawardī, *al-Alwāḥ al-'Imādī*, in *Oeuvres*, ed. Nasr, III, 186–187, with slight differences in the Persian text. This comment by Dawānī is translated by Corbin, *L'archange*, p. 71, while Suhrawardī's Persian text is translated by Corbin in ibid., p. 112.

4. The mistake is *aṭwār*, 'states', for *awṭār*, 'desires'.

5. Reading 'divine lovers' (*'ushshāq ilāhiyyīn*, cf. Corbin's reading *'ushshāq ilāhiyya* [*L'archange*, p. 80, n. 54] instead of 'lovers of goddesses' (*'ushshāq ilāhatīn*).

forms or eternal forms, *with fixed bodies* that do not move from their places, that are *safe from corruption* from the corruption of these eternal forms *because of their distance from the world or opposition*— this is a cause for [all of these] three or four propositions. *Since nothing distracts them* from the world of light, *the transcendental dawning of the lights of the transcendent God*[1] *are not interrupted for them, nor* [*are*] *the benefits of divine graces.* This means that the motions do not belong to a concupiscent or irascible cause, but to the attainment of a holy and delightful thing, which is the dawning of lights from their sources above. These most resemble the motions issuing from the soul stripped of the connections of nature, on account of the holy gleams and intimate dawnings, as the masters of ecstasy and witnessing attest. *If the object of their desire were not incessant, their movements would cease.* Inevitably, the cessation of their motion would be necessitated by their attaining the desired goal. If these motions ceased even once, this would require that no event come into existence from it at all, because the first event that takes place from it undoubtedly will be an unlimited event, and there is no event at all between cessation and its occurrence, by law. The chain of interrupted events is not a required cause, for otherwise it would be connected, so understand that.

14. *So each* of the heavens *has a beloved in the higher world.* One beloved differs from another, and that is due to the difference in their motions in terms of quantity and direction. *It is the victorious light, and it is its cause and the one that extends its light;* that is, it is the lord of its limited species in its individual. [*The beloved is*] *the intermediary between it [the heaven] and the first light that is transcendent; by its presence it witnesses his glory and attains his blessings and his lights. From every illumination arises a motion* related to that illumination. Even if the reality of that relationship is unknown to us, and we are in the world of alienation, still the soul within us is overjoyed, to the point of dancing and clapping. *For each motion another illumination stands ready.* Just as man stands ready with the prescribed legal motions of worship for the holy dawnings, so the realizers of truth among the people of transcendence may witness in their souls a holy simulating delight, being moved to dance, clap, and turn. By this motion they stand ready for the dawning of other lights until that state ceases in them from some cause, as is indicated by the experiences of the wayfarers. That is the secret of listening to music (*samāʿ*) and, for the divine [sages], its principle leading to its establishment, so that one of the leaders of this group [the Sufis] said, "The wayfarer in the assembly of listening to music is opened up to things that are not found in forty-day retreats'. It is related of Plato that whenever he wanted to pray, he moved the power of his soul by listening to appropriate voices, when he wanted to be moved by the power of wrath or love.[2]

1. Corbin's text (*L'archange*, p. 55) reads 'lord of lords' (*rabb al-arbāb*) instead of 'the transcendent God' (*Allāh taʿālā*).

2. This passage is translated by Corbin (*L'archange*), 71–72, who cites a marginal note identifying the author of the Sufi saying as Rūzbihān Baqlī.

One of the great Sufis said that the relationship of music to the power of the soul is the relationship of the flint and steel to fire; therefore they have prohibited music to beginners and those engrossed in bodily pleasures, since it incites in them the desires hidden within. *The renewal of illuminations is perpetuated by the renewal of [celestial] motions, and the renewal of motions is perpetuated by the renewal of illuminations.* But there is alternation in this [process], for the motion produced by illumination is not the motion prepared for it.[1]

15. I say that the proof of this is that they [the celestial motions] have a unitary continuously renewed illumination from which a single unitary continuous motion is produced. But here there are two motions, one belonging to the soul of the heavens in the illuminative qualities, and the other belonging to the body in its position. Each of these motions presupposes [that the two motions are] parts. If the parts are proportional to each other, the situation is as he described.[2] But if the two motions are considered as being unitary, then the first is the cause for the existence of the second, and the second is the cause for the subsistence of the first. There is no difficulty here, inasmuch as the acquired intellect is a condition for the production of the intellect in act, and that is a condition for the subsistence of the acquired intellect. *By this double chain, the production of contingent beings is perpetuated in the sublunar world.* Their motion prepares matter for the reception of contingent beings, as indicated previously and subsequently. *Were it not for their illuminations and their motions, only limited amounts of the generosity of God most high would be produced.* These are the lights and bodies that are the fixed entities.[3] *Emanation would be interrupted* since at that time there would be no production of the contingent beings that are unlimited in terms of their origin and that do not comprehend either their goal or the victorious lights. If the proofs do not demonstrate the absurdity of the chaining as an impossibility, neither do they affirm it, due to the possibility that they [the contingent beings] proceed with unordered accidental distinctions, because illuminative intuition indicates that light does not proceed from every light. This is because descent through the levels of light makes the light defective, to the degree that it ends as a weakened victorious light near the level of souls, lacking the power to give existence to another light.

16. I say that here is a discussion known to some, namely the accidental temperaments containing unlimited levels between the extremes of neglect and excess. Perhaps it will be objected that the levels of the lights are combined in existence, but that is not possible, nor does this affirm it, due to their hierarchy of strength

---

1. Following the alternate reading *al-ḥarakah* rather than *al-muḥarrakah*.

2. A marginal note adds, 'That is, one of them would be a cause prepared for the other. But it is not the case that one thing is adapted to another, but is not related to the other, in some [medium] supported by them both.'

3. The phrase 'fixed entities' (*umūr thābitah*) appears to be modelled on the 'fixed essences' (*a'yān thābitah*) of the Sufi thinker Ibn 'Arabī.

and weakness. Gradation occurs among them in a manner contrary to the levels of accidental temperament; their combinations in existence are unlimited entities.

17. I say that for this reason it is necessary to affirm the separate souls as the essence of what he maintains, based on limiting the distinction between the lights in terms of strength and weakness. It necessarily follows that the difference between lights is not absolute, nor is it limited to them at certain times. It is possible that they proceed from the transcendent, distinguished by its accidental relationship with its effects. Unlimited lights may differ in terms other than strength and weakness, but in principle lights will not be on [the same] level. That proof is not complete though it does answer the question, explaining that the distinction between the lights is only in terms of strength and weakness.

18. The most likely argument here is that the difference between the lights utterly separated from matter and its connection is limited to [the lights] themselves. Or the difference between lights joined to matter, regardless of whether it is a condition in them or connected to them like souls, is nonetheless a quality not limited to them. Spontaneity, despite its accidental character, decrees that the difference between levels of light perceived by the individual lies in strength and weakness, as with bodies equal in receiving light with a unified relationship to luminosity. Lights having obstacles then differ individually because of the difference in their locations, despite their lack of difference in strength and weakness. It is possible that he means that only a limited quantity is then produced from the forms of bodies. *Since there is no change in the essence of the first transcendent that would require change,* and change in the effect when the cause remains in a fixed condition is impossible, *thus, by generosity of the Real, the production of contingent beings persists, by the ecstasy of divine lovers.* The commentary on generosity will follow below [37]. 'Divine lovers' refers to those stripped of material connections to the extent possible for them, as is said of the divine solitaries seeking perfection, or the lovers of the divine lights, which are the intellects that resemble them. *The empyrean heaven's motions necessarily benefit the lower ones* as the secondary intention and accidentally, not as the primary intention and essentially. The supreme does not act upon the lowly, since it has no power to do so in itself, as was mentioned. That is similar to the intercourse between a male and a female caused by concupiscent love, the purpose of which is the production of offspring, despite its not being intended by them.

19. *This is not to say that the motions of the heavens give existence to things.* For then they would vanish when their effects came into existence. So how could an impermanent entity give existence to a permanent entity such as human souls and elemental forms? *But they do produce potentialities,* not in the sense that they give existence to these potentialities, for they are also things, but rather in the sense that they are a condition for their production.

20. *The first reality gives to each thing that which is appropriate to its potentiality,* since the transcendent is not miserly about that, rather, it is the eternal

absolute whose emanation does not cease except according to the capacity of the recipient.

21. If you said that the potentialities are also from its existence and its emanation, as I indicated, and there is no miserliness in the transcendent, then there is no cause for their differentiation.

22. I replied that the difference in potentialities is from the [heavens], on account of the difference in the preceding potentialities, and so on without end; the chain continues throughout contingent beings. This is not a problem, due to the lack of combination of their individual instances as they [the heavens] settle it in its place.

23. I say that the proof is that elemental matter has a motion in the potential quality, just as the heavens have a directional motion in their bodies, and an illuminative, qualitative motion in their souls. The elemental, potential motion is dependent on directional heavenly motion, and it is dependent on the motion of the soul, mentioned in connection with that which precedes its settling. Each of these three motions is a continuous unitary motion, as we have indicated previously. If their unitary character is distinct [from one another], their order is as mentioned. If they must have parts, every subsequent part is dependent on the preceding one.

24. If that is agreed, then we say that if the question concerned the cause of the partial potentialities, the reply is what was mentioned at first [22]. If it concerns the cause of potential unitary motion related to matter, the reply is that the quiddity of this matter is restricted to this motion; that is why one of the philosophers among the masters of unveiling and vision said that existent partial potentialities are created dependent on uncreated universal potentialities. You will intuit from a kind of summary the secret of the difference occurring between individuals in terms of defect and perfection. Further discussion on the subject will come later on.

25. *Since the agent does not change, its effect is renewed by the renewal of the potentiality of [the agent's] recipient. It is possible that a single thing renews its influence, but there is a difference according the conditions of the recipient, though the difference [of conditions] is not due to the different condition of [the agent].* By joining the conditions of the recipient to the agent, diverse causes are produced that require diverse effects. Then he alluded to some points to bring it closer to the mind of the students and gave some examples in such a way that the imagination would follow the command of the intellect and in this way he prevented the intrusion of illusion, as was his method of teaching, because his discourse is intended for the seekers of knowledge whose aim is to beautify the soul by spiritual perfection, not by following polemical discussions and disputation.

26. *Let this man consider as a hypothesis a person who is unmoved and unchanging, and, to continue the simile, opposite him are mirrors differing in terms of greater*

or lesser size and greater clarity or turbidity. In them there appear from him, i.e., from that person, *forms differing in terms of lesser or greater size, and perfect appearance of colour or lack of it. The person whose form it is does not change, and the difference is only in the receptacles* that are different. The person is in the position of the cause, and the mirrors are in the position of the material bases. Their difference is in characteristics, like the difference in potentialities. The difference in forms is difference in forms and accidents. *The Real (glory be to His Greatness) has connected fixity,* that is, fixed entities with fixed entities, *and contingency with contingency* or contingent beings with contingent beings. When divine grace decrees the production of contingent beings, the chain of existentiation is limited to the entity fixed in essence, necessitating difference in connections and subsequent relations. That is perpetual circular motion; from the perspective of its perpetuity, it depends upon an eternal cause, and from the perspective of its contingency, contingent beings depend upon it.

27. In detail, that which comes into existence from motion is a continuous unitary entity, which is the intermediary between the demonstrated or assumed origin, and the goal, in one of two aspects. This is a single person who is compelled by a difference in relationships in terms of the limits assumed in distance, until, when it is considered in terms of one of these limits, it becomes the above-mentioned intermediary, which is existence in the middle term. Considering that this accident exists in that limit from the middle term, which is perpetual entity, considering that its essence is contingent, and considering that this accidental relationship is in accordance with necessity, then from the perspective of the fixed essence it depends upon the fixed intellect, while from the perspective of relationships subsequent to it, contingent beings depend upon it.

28. This is the summary of their argument, and it will not surprise you that the argument persists in the chain of these subsequent relationships to the eternal essence and that it is of no use at all. It is said that they are assumed entities that do not presuppose an external cause, but there is no doubt that they are not pure assumptions, like the evenness of three. How shall the like of that become probable for an external existent? Rather, they have a kind of existence, regardless of whether it is in act in the entity itself, or in one of the levels of potency, or call it what you will. But we know that the mover at the time of reaching an assumed limit of distance has a condition that he did not have prior to this time, and which he will not have afterward. Similarly, there is no doubt that an existent thing, whether in act or in a level of potency, derives from something like what has just been said. The point of the proof of this position is that it is said that the source for every one of these relationships is the relationships prior to it. Thus, if unitary continuous motion is considered in its unity, it is fixed and dependent on fixed causes. If subsequent relationships are considered, they assume parts, to the degree that every one of these relationships is dependent on the one preceding.

29. It is said [by Ibn Kammūnah],[1] 'It is as though this motion is continuous and connected, having no parts in fact; rather, in accordance with the assumption, the chain of contingent beings is thus unitary and connected. The sound intellect decrees that the continuity and connection of the effect follow upon the continuity and connection of the cause. From this it appears that non-existence of the contingent is not real non-existence in the sense of external elimination of the quiddity. Rather, it is relative [non-existence] which is something being devoid of something else, as in the transference of the quality from the qualified thing. So it is said, 'this is devoid of that.' Or, just as the thing seen is distanced from the seeing person, it is said of that thing, 'it does not exist in the perception'. This is in reality change and transference even if it is said to him, 'it is devoid by way of metaphor', and the concepts of these ideas are subtle.'

30. I say that we have already stated something similar in discussing the dependence of elemental potentialities on heavenly motions, and I have seen the like of that in the Plato's writings. You are aware of what he mentioned regarding the connection of contingent beings and that they lack actual parts and cannot be understood by the human mind according to the postulate of their contingency. For it is not conceivable to take them as supposed parts of a unitary entity, but this theorist [Ibn Kammūnah] asserts the eternity of the soul, as he explains in his books, and this is also reported of Plato.

31. *And it,* the transcendent, *is the source and the goal in this connection.* That is, inasmuch as the transcendent is the efficient cause for the system of the world and the order of existence, it also is its goal, and the goal is commonly known to be that for which action is taking place as an essential consequence. If it is attributed to the actor in terms of effecting the act, it is called purpose with respect to the actor, and an efficient cause in relation to the action. But goal is more common, for it sometimes refers to that which is not attributed [to the actor], and it differs in this sense from purpose.

32. The actions of God the Transcendent are not caused by purposes, because of the preceding [argument], in that the final cause is the efficient cause for the activity of the actor. This is what makes the actor an actor. If this were the case [i.e., if God had purposes], the necessary [being] would be defective in its essence, seeking perfection through another, which would be the final cause. Surely there are goals, in the sense of uncounted wisdoms and advantages known to God, but they do not have influence over His Essence by making Him an actor. These goals refer to completing existent beings with their primary perfections, and to perfecting them afterward with secondary perfections, so that they resemble their highest origin to the extent conceivable and appropriate for them. That is only set in order by a love demanding the protection of existent perfection, and longing for absent

1. A marginal gloss.

perfection, whether voluntary or natural. Love produces in every existent being the state in which its perfection exists, and at the same time the state in which it is lacking. Longing is restricted to the lack of [perfection]. Therefore you see that Ibn Sīnā and other great philosophers have established that love is diffused in all beings, and beings in their totality seek similarity to their origin as much as possible, for they love it. Love is the inclination toward unification with something, not for some reason, but because the Transcendent in its essential perfection is the goal of goals. It is that which is pursued by all and which all seek, i.e., they seek similarity to it and proximity to it. It is said that love requires the consciousness of the difference in levels. This demonstrates that all existent beings have a certain consciousness differing in level according to the difference in the levels of love. So know and intuit this.

33. Here 'goal' is employed in the well-known sense mentioned previously, requiring some effort, since it means that God most High is a goal in that one becomes assimilated to it as we indicated. You should posit the goal here in the sense of the final cause; and the meaning of being the final cause is that the essence of the transcendent is sufficient in its own existence of its attributes. So consider both aspects [i.e., efficient cause and final cause], and choose for yourself that which is agreeable. *So that the good is perpetuated*—the entity that produces something else, considering it as being an influence upon it, or more appropriate and more proper for it, is called a good; considering that the production of a thing requires a certain detachment from potency, [it is called] a perfection.

34. From *al-Ishārāt* (The Book of Indications) [by Ibn Sīnā] and its commentary, it is understood that perfection is that which is actually extant, and the good relative to a thing is the perfection that this thing seeks by its primary potentiality. By the primary [potentiality], it guards against acquiring the vices that man seeks by his secondary potentiality, which is an extraneous factor to the primary potentiality that one has according to one's nature. But it [i.e., perfection] will not be a good in relation to the essence of the man, rather it will be in relation to the essence along with that extraneous factor, not without it. In this manner perfection is absolutely more common. Their previous position [33] is that the thing that produces something else, considered as being an influence, is called a good, and considered as detached from potency, [it is called] a perfection. This does not deny that perfection is more common, and it does not require that the two [perfections] be equal, nor is this concealed. Thus the good here is existence and the perfections that follow from it. *And so that emanation is established.* This is the act of an actor who acts perpetually without variation or purpose. *So that His mercy does not reach a limit* among the fixed entities, nor cross over them to the subsequent entities or by a limit among contingent beings. *Its existence is neither imperfect, defective, nor is it interrupted at either extreme.*[1]

1. A variant reads 'its generosity'.

35. It is possible that his statement, 'so that the good is perpetuated' [33], indicates the perpetual entities, and this is a result that connects fixity with fixity. His statement, 'so the emanation is established' [34], indicates the contingent beings. The perpetuity of the act only appears in its bringing them into existence. His saying, 'so that its mercy does not reach a limit [at either extreme],' indicates a denial that its mercy has a beginning and an end. Then his statement, 'its existence is not imperfect,' is not confined to contingent beings. His statement, 'nor defective,' is not confined to the fixed entities. His statement, 'nor is it interrupted at either extreme,' means that contingent beings have no beginning point nor end point.

36. But it is apparent that he did not intend that. He and those belonging to the rank of the great philosophers do not refrain from repetition to emphasize the point. Their purpose is to shorten the journey to the good and to perfection. Anything that is easier as a path to its attainment, and which sets the student upon it, is approved by them. A certain scholar has explained something similar to what we have mentioned in glosses to *The Commentary on the Indications*. Anyone who follows the sources and origins of the initiates has witnessed what we have mentioned, and has condemned the painstaking efforts studied by the moderns from the commentaries on philosophy of [the initiates]; they write down their meaning only in terms of what they know and according to what they prefer, though they [the moderns] lack the experience that is proper to the faculties of [the initiates], and they consider unlawful the dawns kindled from the emanation of their illumination.[1]

37. Then he begins to explain generosity, after repeating his reference to it [in 18], saying, '*Generosity is to give that which is sought,* or that which deserves to be given. The failure to mention by whom it is sought is caused by the passive verb which does not need it.'[2] The omission of its being one of the relative entities is only in relation to the one by whom this is sought.[3] *[It is] not for compensation* as an existing thing, that is, even if one acquired something praiseworthy or rejected its opposite. He fails to mention the postulated subject because he does not need to, since the compensation is not all property or even anything else, including praise, eulogy, and freedom from blame, as Ibn Sīnā says in 'The Indications'. *One who acts for compensation, though he achieve it, is yet poor,* because he seeks to produce by that act compensation, the existence of which precedes its non-existence, so he

1. This passage uses terms with a strong mystical flavour to bring out the difference between earlier intuitive philosophers and the later rationalistic thinkers who Dawānī wishes to criticize. The term translated here as 'initiates' is *al-qawm*, literally 'the folk', often used in Sufi writings to indicate the true mystics. The term translated as 'experience' is *dhawq*, literally 'taste', a common synonym for mystical experience.

2. A marginal note adds, '[In the case of] one who gives to someone who does not seek, this gift is not 'a gift of what was sought'.

3. A marginal note adds, 'One who mentions it [the relationship] intends to distinguish those who are related.'

needs the compensation for his perfection. *The rich one does not need anything other than himself in his essence and his perfection,* that is, his real attributes beyond the relative ones, and the pure relationships by which and without which he is connected. They have no distinction in essence, nor is he related to them, though they have perfection. In that matter it may suffice you to consider the transformation of the relationship between Zayd and what is external to him, it being left or right according to its external transfer while Zayd remains in the same state. This describes one who is rich in the absolute sense. One who does not need any specific thing in his essence and his perfection is rich in relationship to himself, though he may be poor in relation to another. *The one who is absolutely rich*, that is, rich in relation to everything except himself, who is not sullied at all by even a particle of poverty, *is the one whose existence is from his essence.* Then his perfections are also from his essence, but his very essence as described. *He is the manifest light of lights* in his essence, which manifests to what is other than him, that is everything except him. That is a spark from his light, or a spark from a spark of his light, etc. *He has no purpose in his creation,* that is, no entity is ascribed to him in action. *Rather, his essence possesses the emanative source for mercy* by his essence, by awareness and will. These two [attributes] are the very essence in connection with what has proceeded from it and the benefits of wisdom that order it, unlike the action of nature which is unaware of what proceeds from it. *He is the absolute king; to him belongs the essence of everything, though his essence does not belong to anything.* 'The light of lights' is such because everything is either from him or from that which is from him. The goal of the act regarding him is his being an actor for [the goal]. The causation of all things is rightly his, by the fact that the being of things is from him. So it is stated in The Commentary on *al-Ishārāt.*[1]

38. It is possible that this is stated because the essence of all things is from Him, and He is their existentiating cause. They depend upon Him, they are His possession, with or without intermediary. Nothing else but Him has access to Him. The slave and what belongs to him belong to his master. You may have learned from one of the principles of *[The Wisdom of] Illumination* that the stronger light cannot possibly be influenced by the weaker light, or else it is clear in the second introduction [to that work].[2]

39. *It is inconceivable that an existent is more perfect than that which has existence as its special property. The essence of the Real does not need the lower nor does it abandon the nobler,* because it would extend to ignorance, impotence, or greed in him who transcends that. *Rather, his essence requires the nobler, and he is the noblest.*

---

1. The first phrase commented on in this paragraph, 'Generosity is the gift of what is sought without compensation,' is quoted by Suhrawardī from Abū 'Alī ibn Sīnā, *al-Ishārāt wa'l-tanbīhāt ma'a sharḥ Naṣīr al-Dīn al-Ṭūsī*, ed. Sulaymān Dunyā, Dhakhā'ir al-'Arab, no. 22 (Cairo, 1957), III, 555.

2. See e.g., Suhrawardī, *Ḥikmat al-ishrāq*, in *Oeuvres*, ed. Corbin, II, 133.

40. This indicates the principle of the nobler possibility, which we have indicated previously. Its exposition is according to what the master [Suhrawardī] mentioned in his other books,[1] that when the lowest possible being comes into existence, it requires that the noblest possible being have come into existence prior to it. Otherwise, either the existence of the lower is by an intermediary, which contradicts the postulate, because this intermediary can only be nobler in that the cause is nobler than the effect or it is without intermediary. Then, if it is possible for the nobler to proceed from the necessary, that requires the possibility of the many issuing from the one, by necessity. The nobler cannot possibly proceed by the intermediary of that which is lower. It could be without intermediary, or with intermediary that is not lower. If it is not possible for the nobler to proceed from the necessary, then it is possible from its effect, that the cause is lower than the effect, by necessity. Restricting the intermediary to the lower is based on the principle that 'from the one only one proceeds,' and that it is not possible for the nobler to proceed either from the necessary or from its effect, despite the fact that this possibility was assumed. The possible does not require the existence of an assumption which is impossible. If it is required, it is only required of another thing that is not its essence, otherwise it will not be possible. This contradicts the postulate. The assumption is existent, but it does not proceed from the necessary existence nor from its effects, because the discussion postulates the impossibility of its issuing from either one. So its existence demands an aspect of necessity required in the essence of the necessary that is nobler than that which has existence as a special property, and that is impossible. This is its exposition according to the contents of The Commentary on *al-Ishārāt,* with additional notes and glosses.

41. I say that the refutation of the last difficulty is only complete if the possibility of the effect is a requirement for the possibility of the cause, but this is disproved, because the disappearance of the first effect is possible despite [the existence of] its cause, and the disappearance of the necessary is absurd. The proof is that the possibility of the effect requires the possibility of the cause, seeing the effect in such a sense that when one sees the effect, nothing exists in it that would necessitate its absurdity. The disappearance of that [cause] is denied in the form of the disputed [effect] as it is in the form of the affirmed [one].

42. It is possible that he means this: that which is not an existent being prior to a possible being is not possible [but is] nobler than it. This is converted to the converse of our statement: that which is possible is nobler, for it is a prior existent being.

43. The demonstration of the first point is that if it were possible, it would be nobler to the degree that it exists. Either it exists from the necessary without intermediary, though it is assumed that the existence of the lower is from it without

1. Suhrawardī, *Ḥikmat al-ishrāq*, in *Oeuvres*, II, 154.

intermediary, which requires the procession of the many from the one; or it exists by an intermediary, and it is restricted to the lower, which requires that the cause be lower than the effect. Both requirements are impossible. That which requires it [to exist] to the degree that it is impossible is itself impossible. Even its possibility requires that it is impossible. Here is something like the previous view; the truth is that if I mean by denial of the nobler that which includes the denial of the other, then that is the case. But if I mean the denial of the essence, then what he said is incomplete.

44. These points are not affirmed or needed after it was established that the effect in its existence and its non-existence is connected to a cause that requires it. This is because we say that the purpose of [the effect] is an absurdity, regardless of the will and volition of the actor. What was established is the necessity of the effect, as existence or non-existence, with regard to the cause. This does not prevent the will and volition of the actor from being part of this cause. To this extent, the purpose is not produced upon which was based the negation of the three imperfections from the first source, that transcends that. Persisting in the necessity of any one of these imperfections in the origin is sufficient in this subject, as we have indicated. One of the great masters of Sufism[1] relates that from the imam and proof of Islam, Abū Ḥāmid al-Ghazzālī, and he approved of it completely. *Just as the reflection of the light is nobler than the reflection of its reflection,* and so on to the end, to that which is the lowest of all, which is the isthmus between it and the darkness, by which I mean the levels of light that are connected to the darkness. The equivalent in this discussion, by way of example, is the level of bodies. *Anything more perfect than that which has existence as its special property is absurd* because of what was mentioned. This is a repetition of the preceding [39]. It is as though he returns to it to make it a preparation for the account of good and evil.

45. He states that if that is the case, 'Because some people will be excluded from that which is nobler. We see that most people are excluded from their perfections, the production of which is most important for them'.[2]

46. It is replied in *The Commentary on [the Wisdom of] Illumination,* from *The [Book of Encounters and] Conversations,* 'This principle is only rejected in the case of the continually existing fixed possible beings [i.e., the heavens], because of their perpetual fixed causes, which are uninfluenced by heavenly motions, in distinction from those taking place beneath them, [which are influenced by them], such as [the elementals of] the three kinds, etc. It is denied because of external causes. The possible belongs to them essentially, as does the nobler and more perfect. Therefore it is possible for something to be given at one time something noble and at another

---

1. A marginal gloss identifies this figure (literally 'one of the masters of unveiling and realization') as Muḥyī al-Dīn ibn 'Arabī, author of *al-Futūḥāt al-makkiyyah.*

2. Suhrawardī, *Ḥikmat al-ishrāq,* in *Oeuvres,* ed. Corbin, II, 154 (the commentary of Quṭb al-Dīn Shīrazī).

time something low, not to its essence but to its potentiality, by unlimited causes among contingent beings.

47. 'Now the entities that are above the motions, among the heavenly intelligences, souls, and bodies, and the concomitants of universal natures, are not excluded from that which is nobler than they or from the most perfect of the external entities. This is because they are either causes or effects, or neither the one nor the other. The last two are both false, because its causality of a thing is not admissible if its non-existence does not entail the non-existence of the thing. The difference between their nobility and their lowliness is not due to the difference in contingent potentialities. They have it from the motions because they precede them, and their causality is because of fixed causes, which is the difference in actors and the difference in their aspects. So the nobler is affected by the nobler and the lower by the lower.'[1]

48. I say in summarizing the reply that the sublime entities that have lofty motions are not prevented from attaining their possible perfections. They have a strange property, contrary to the entities occurring below them, because of their conjunctions with motions. The causes of these perfections in the fixed entities are not foreign to their existent essence. They are either the essence of the actor or a necessary entity to which belongs the activity of their perfections. They are, in their essence, the cause of the essence, or that which necessitates it, contrary to contingent beings. The causes of their occurrence are special in one respect. The causes of their perfections may be other than the causes of their existence or that which requires their existence. If a comparison is made, they are not nobler than their states. They are not given existence in their essences. There are no causes in their existence, nor is anything that renders them impossible found in their necessities. The difference between the two lies in their occurrence in the nobler respect. But regarding the matter of their impossibility, the nobler individuals of the ordered chain preceded the others in the vertical and horizontal hierarchies, with no basic difference, so let them govern [their sphere of activity].

49. Now, here is another reply, and that is that divine grace is connected with governance of the universal insofar as it is universal primarily and in essence, and with governance of the particular secondarily and by accident. It is not possible that the order of the universal can be more beautiful than the actual order. If it were possible for every individual, its greatest perfection would be separate with regard to its special characteristic, but that would be disruptive to the beauty of universal order, even if the particular aspect is concealed from us. This can be likened to the architect submitting a building plan. It may be more beautiful for this building from the total perspective if one side in particular is an outhouse, another is a sitting room, and another is a bedroom. This is because if there were a different

1. Suhrawardī, *Ḥikmat al-ishrāq*, in *Oeuvres*, ed. Corbin, II, 154 (the commentary of Quṭb al-Dīn; cf. Suhrawardī, *Kitāb al-Mashāriʿ wa'l-muṭāraḥāt*, in *Oeuvres*, ed. Corbin, I, 434–445).

arrangement, it would be defective for the beauty of the entire building, even if it is more beautiful, considering the special characteristic of each part, for [each] to be a sitting room, for example. This is instructive regarding the present subject, in that the universal, insofar as it is qualified by the most beautiful order, is related to the complete origin in every respect. This relationship merits the emanation of existence from [the origin], and it undoubtedly comes into existence from this perspective and no other, though from these [other] perspectives it [the universal] is farther from the relationship with the origin. Perhaps the explanations of the quality of that [universal] beauty and its imperfection are caused by the change in condition of an individual apart from that which conditions it. This is the secret of destiny, which God possesses exclusively by his knowledge, and of which no one else is aware, or of which one after another of the prophets and philosophers is aware; but God knows best the reality of the situation.

50. *And the absurd does not come under the power of anyone who is powerful.* From this it does not follow that there is a basic defect in the one who is powerful, rather the defect is in the absurdity, inasmuch as it is not properly related to the power. Since it is known that anything more perfect than the actual order is impossible, then this order is the best of possible orders. That which opposes it is evil, and that which proceeds from the first transcendent can only be good. This [discussion] encompasses the problems relating to the procession of evils from it, and it does not need to be prolonged.

51. *This only extends the discussion of good and evil,* by intending the problems of establishing their quiddity, and the quality of their procession from the origin or from another, as mentioned in the books of the moderns, particularly the theologians. Some of them deny that there are evils that proceed by the existentiating power of God the transcendent, and they are the Muʿtazilah; they are the ones referred to by the Prophet (God bless him and grant him peace), when he said, 'The Qadariyyah [or advocates of unrestricted free will] are the Magians [i.e., the dualists] of this community.' They maintain that there are influences upon God the transcendent, which by volition overpower the volition of God the transcendent, but this is pure ignorance and manifest heresy. *One who thinks that the sublime has consideration for the base*—meaning that the sublime origins by their essence bring about the existentiation of the base—*[such a person] imagines that God has no other world beyond this darkened piece of dirt,* that is, the world of elements, *and that God does not have beyond these diversions,* meaning animals both rational and otherwise, *some creatures* nobler than them, such as the intelligences and the heavenly souls. One who knows that would have no consideration for this lower world. There is [no] proof of their conditions except from the perspective that they proceed from the sublime realities. He does not prolong the likes of this discussion; only one who does not know that does so. *He does not know that if it were to happen otherwise than it is, evils would necessarily result, and a destruction of order*

on a scale unrelated to that which one now imagines. Consider burning fire; if it did not exist, many beneficial necessities would be destroyed for humanity and others. But with its existence, it is only necessary to distinguish some parts of elemental compounds, with the possibility of avoiding others. Or you may imagine that the existence of fire is possible in this world to cook and to burn that which it is useful to burn, and not to burn what damages it, and thus it would be, according to its nature. But this is a vain fancy.

52. *And this,* that is, this visible order fixed in place refers to a subject assumed by his words; And when he says, *is the ultimate possible order*, it refers to his predicate, that is, 'if it were to happen, etc.,' 'he does not know that' (51) this visible order is the ultimate possibility. It is not possible for the world of elements to comprehend oppositions and disasters. *And the world that is untouched by goals is another world.*[1] This is the world of images, the world of the heavens, and the superior world of souls and intelligences. It is *the resort of the pure ones* from the supposed and created vices, it is *[other than] our world,* the companion of humanity. If pure human souls are tightly connected to the use of natural faculties and long for them greatly, after serving the connection with the elemental body they are translated to an internal imaginal body. They enjoy the witnessing of the forms of that world, such as sensuous food and magnificent sexual intercourse. When they are connected to the heavenly bodies they become themselves a locus for imaginalization of these forms that they have, but here in the forms of the elements their benefits are realized without their evils. Other things that are conceivable, if they exist in this world, are more beautiful. If they are stripped of the connection with nature, which strongly attracts them to their origins, then they become linked with the heavenly spirits and intelligences, and are ranked differently according to their different degrees in separation.

53. *It is not* the situation *that the sublime holy ones are only occupied with ripping off veils, turning orphans from their nurse's embrace, tormenting those who are free* from bodies, and *planting false religions,* for their manifestation and growth is similar to the planting of trees, *the seducing of souls, the coddling of fools, the punishing of the wise,* and other disasters occurring in our world. This is because if the activity of these holy substances was limited to [this description], there would be an obvious defect in their activity, and this is impossible. *Their only occupation is the witnessing of the lights of God the transcendent from every place where they may be witnessed.* They witness the lights of God the transcendent in themselves, in their causes, in their effects, and in the other intelligences proceeding by accidental[2] considerations. *Their motions require necessary requirements* that inflict certain

1. Here the text of Dawānī has 'goals' (*ghāyāt*) in place of the 'maladies and afflictions' (*āfāt wa balliyāt*) of the Persian translation (III, 102), rendered by Corbin as 'les malheurs et les épreuves' (*L'archange*, 57–58).

2. An alternate reading is 'postulated' (*farḍiyyah*) rather than 'accidental' (*'araḍiyyah*).

evils on some lower entities. *If they returned to a position that benefited those people, they would thereby injure other worlds.* Either they are parts of the world, such as in the case of fire or torrential rain that may sometimes cause damage, but without which, there would be harm to crops and trees, and animals; or, they are in the sublime worlds, in that no similarity to their objects of love is produced, although these contingent beings have no primary object, for they occur in the most perfect possible aspect that they have. This he indicates by saying, *Nevertheless, they do not move for the sake of lower entities,* as was established. Lower entities are not an intention for them in essence, such that if a defect occurred in them relative to one of the parts, it would require that the defect be in these sublime ones. This is because there is no defect in their essences, nor in their actions, nor in that which is basically an intention for them in essence. That which appears, that is, the defect, although it is not a defect in actuality, is rather the most perfect thing possible, as you know. Only that which is included in the necessary is the intention in essence, not that which is in something. *But when eternal radiances and divine lights shower upon them*—it is possible that by 'external radiance' he means that which emanates upon them from the first origin, and by 'divine lights' that which emanates from the intelligences—*they are overcome by awe in the divine stations, by the power* of an overwhelming force attached to awe *of the holy rays, which does not allow them to see their essences, let alone anything else.* They are absorbed in the witnessing of the origins, inasmuch as it is not possible for them to consider anything else at all. *Despite that* overpowering force and the total absorption that is necessary to it, *they know all, whether open or concealed,* since knowledge is not limited to consideration. Thus, all things are known to them without their having to consider them. This is like our knowledge of ourselves and our characteristics by presence, at the time of total absorption in something, such as in the state of extreme anger, or complete concentration on an intellectual or imaginative matter, or the presence of a beloved. *Nothing escapes their knowledge or the knowledge of their creator,* since it would then have to cross their existence as pure lights. *This demonstrates the perpetuity of the heavenly bodies, and the fact that they are not compounded of the elements, and are free from corruption.* That is, the [lack of] corruption of their forms is attached to their not being compounds; these two points are in the position of commentary on 'the perpetuity of the heavenly bodies', as though he had said, 'the fact that they are not of the genus of the elements', as the text demonstrates. So they are not elemental at all, as will be shown below. *That which was stated* in the Fifth Temple (*al-haykal al-khāmis*) *concerned the necessity that their motions be perpetual. If they were compounds of the elementals, they would be dissolved,* because elemental parts are by their nature prone to fall apart and to incline toward their natural limits. The nature of the compound is that they are essentially these parts. The power of universal nature continues to abate, on account of the powers of the particular natures, gradually, until it is altogether abated. The power of these natures overpower it so that it is dissolved. *And as long as their motions continue,* which is attached to the phrase 'they would be dissolved', *they are not elemental at all.* That is, they are not compounded of the elements, nor are they of their genus. This is a conclusion for the syllogism mentioned in the course of this argument. The syllogism is thus: If the heavens were compounded of the elements, they would not be perpetually in motion, but they are perpetually in motion. The conclusion is that the heavens are not compounded of the elements. He neglects to mention the conclusive syllogism for their freedom from corruption, leaving it to the understanding of the student. Its form is thus: If the heavens were susceptible of corruption, their motion would not be perpetual, but they are perpetually in motion, therefore they are not susceptible of generation and corruption.

54. *Because heat is light, it only moves* by nature *upwards,* absolutely or relatively. *Cold is heavy, and it only moves downwards,* because of the preceding commentary. *Wet easily accepts form or the lack of it, conjunction or disjunction, and dry accepts them,* that is, form and conjunction in existence and cessation, *with difficulty. The heavens cannot be pierced* either easily or with difficulty. *They do not move in a straight line, nor toward the centre, nor away from it,* that is, neither upwards nor downwards, according to what precedes. This demonstrates the impossibility of piercing, because that is by motion in a straight line. I say regarding piercing, that inasmuch as an aperture occurs, it only exists in a straight line. Either it is pierced absolutely, in which case it may be that part of it is moved with a circular motion and the remaining part is at rest, or it is moved circularly in a different direction. That is also impossible for the heavens, because it is impossible for them to be at rest or to change their movements. Otherwise time would depart from continual unity, because of the preceding. You realize that this and similar matters to this are only established by demonstration in that which is limited in time and place; it applies to the rest of the heavens by intuition. *Their motions circulate around the middle,* that is, around the centre; *they are not heavy or light,* because weight is the inclination downwards, and lightness is the inclination upwards, *nor are they hot or cold,* because that would require the two inclinations just mentioned, *nor are they wet or dry,* because these require the possibility of accepting form or the lack of it, and conjunction or the lack of it, either easily or with difficulty, as mentioned. *For they are a fifth nature [i.e., quinta essentia],* that is, differing from the natures of the four elements, *and they encompass the earth* from all sides. *If heaven did not encompass the earth, the sun would not return to the east after setting except by doubling the length of the day.* That is, a day would be produced by two sequences, one travelling from east to west and the other the reverse. The conclusion is evidently absurd. Because this situation occurs among all the planets that rise and set in all regions, there is no doubts [about this proposition], and that it encompasses the earth from all directions.

55. *The heavens are all spherical,* because of their circular motions. After the establishment of circular motion, the argument that the heavens lack spherical

shape would require the establishment of division within them, which is contrary to that which is proper to these noble bodies, as confirmed by Ptolemy in many discussions in the *Almagest.* Understand that, for it is a marvellous method. *Some of them encompass others,* because all of them encompass the earth, viewing the sight of the rising of all the planets from two opposite points, in reality or in love, in all regions, intuition being added to that. *[They are] living,* because their motion is voluntary, and volition without life is impossible. *[They are] rational,* that is, they comprehend universals, and that is because voluntary motion undoubtedly has a goal of which the seeker is conscious. This is not motion itself, because its reality is a first perfection,[1] for that which is potential qua potential. This means it is a perfection regarding which matter is not separated from potency. That can only be conceived in that it exists essentially as a means for perfection, and whatever is essentially a means is not in essence a goal. I say,[2] this is prior to what was stated, because it is not possible for an essentially established mover to necessitate them [i.e., motions] according to its nature, volition, or anything else, because that which necessitates a thing persists by the perpetuity of its essence; and it necessitates them not by its essence but by something else [i.e., its goal]. That is because the fact that it does not necessitate the essentially established mover according to its nature, volition, or anything else, does not require that it be an intention in essence. This is because of the possibility that the mover necessitates them, by the addition of something that is not established, which is a part of the cause required by them and not desired by anything else. The meaning of one thing being desired by another is that the other [the goal] should be a final cause for it, and that is not required by the fact that it does not necessitate the essence of the mover by its nature, volition, or anything else. So after hinting at that, we shall shift the discussion to that other thing [the goal]. If it is an established entity, it is not possible that it proceeds from that which is moved by the addition of motion. If it is not established, it is not possible that it proceeds from that which is moved by its [own] nature, volition, or anything else, as stated in the deduction. Since it is proved that motion necessarily has a goal, and its goal is either a place, a position, a quality, or a quantity, as motion only occurs in these categories, and that the heavens can only have positional motions, so their goal is the positional. It is not a particular position, otherwise something would happen to it, so it is consequently a universal position, and it is something that apprehends the universals. Now, that does not suffice for the procession of the particular motion. A particular longing does not originate from the universal tendency. There is no doubt that the heavenly bodies have a faculty impressed upon their nature by reason of the apprehension of the particular motions and particular positions desired by them. The relation of this faculty to the

1. 'First perfection' (*kamāl-i awwal*) in Ibn Sīnā's Persian vocabulary means postulated created existence (*āfarīnash-i āfarīdah,* cf. Afnan, 259).

2. A gloss refers this discussion to *Sharḥ al-ishārāt*, the end of the third part.

heavenly souls is the relation of the sensory faculties to our souls; this is repeated by the followers of the Peripatetics.[1]

56. I say that in this subject there is no need for motion to be unintended in its essence, rather it will suffice them if they say that the object of desire is not the particular motion, otherwise it will be interrupted after its completion.

57. It may be asked why it is not possible that the object of desire is the particular unitary motion that is continuous from pre-eternity to post-eternity, not requiring interruption?

58. I would say that the corporeal faculty does not apprehend the unlimited, hence the analogy of that prohibition applies to position, which is intended essentially in their opinion. But if we follow the method of illumination, then we say that you already know that the purpose of their motions is the illuminations that unfold to them from their origins, that they may resemble them by these illuminations, as indicated by his phrase, *They love the radiance of holiness,* that is, the lights which are their origins.[2] They seek to resemble them, with all the noble luminous relationships they have. This only occurs by the outflow of the lights from the origins, so the heavenly souls undoubtedly conceive of the origins and their noble luminous attributes. However, they are separate, and the material does not apprehend the immaterial. They are immaterial souls and every immaterial being apprehends the universals (as was established) although among them it is established that whatever apprehends something apprehends itself. The Master [Suhrawardī] has explained in other books that whatever apprehends itself is an immaterial substance, so it also apprehends the universals. Whatever apprehends itself is a light to its own essence since its manifestation to itself is not an entity added to its essence. Now, the Master in *The [Wisdom of] Illumination* maintains that the victorious relationships that may be repeated are limited, although the victorious relationships are not absolutely limited.[3] This is because not every relationship that may be repeated is limited. If repetition occurs to them in that which may be repeated during cycles and eons, the resurrection will occur; then the repetition will start over again. So

1. A marginal gloss adds, 'The Peripatetics hold that the heaven has a soul that is impressed upon it, and Ibn Sīnā holds that it has a separate soul. Imam Rāzī holds that it has two souls, one impressed upon it and one separate. The philosopher Ṭūsī says that this is something that no one believed before him [Rāzī], for the single body cannot possibly have two souls, i.e., two essences, it being an instrument for both of them. The truth is that it has a separate soul and an imaginative faculty, and this is what is meant by Rāzī, as a kind of goal in this topic. Amīr Ḥusayn refers to the imaginative faculty as the impressed soul in his glosses to his commentary on *al-Hidāya al-athīriyya*.'

2. Corbin, 'Prolégomènes II', in *Oeuvres*, 39, identifies these illuminations (*ishrāqāt*) as the victorious lights or archangels.

3. Suhrawardī, *Ḥikmat al-ishrāq*, in *Oeuvres,* 176; this is a discussion of the repetition of the cosmic cycle through a return of the planets to their original positions, in a kind of 'eternal recurrence'. 'Victorious relationships' appears to mean the celestial configurations of the planetary spheres as loci of the angel-intelligences.

consider the matter in this way. Were it not for fear of prolixity, we would adduce that which proves the position. It may be that we will return to it in another book, with the aid of the Exalted Benefactor.

59. *They obey their originator* because the purpose of their motions is to attain similarity with it and to approximate it, as explained. In *The Salvation (al-Najāt)* Ibn Sīnā says that heaven is a living being that obeys God the mighty and glorious. *There is no death in the world of ether* because, he explained, all of them possess a separate soul, and it is doubtful that he intended that [they should die] after clarifying that they are living [55]. The reference is to the fact that every body among the heavenly beings possesses an individual soul, as many philosophers maintain, so that they establish that the planets have circular motion in their locations. In *The Healing* Ibn Sīnā inclines to this theory and prefers it. He explains it in *The Indications* and that is because what applies to the planets applies to the heavens, in terms of the necessity of removing possible positions from potency to action.

60. He says in his *Commentary*[1] that this thing is not perceptible in that which is above the lunar region. The black spots of the moon, even if imaginary, appear in it by reflection, as with mirages and the rainbow, or there are stable existent bodies opposite it [the moon], or something is existent in it and fixed at all times in a single condition lacking circular motion. But there is a difficulty in the decisive point. It is evident that there is no existent thing in it [the moon], because of the necessity that it be simple and the impossibility of it changing from its natural position. The position taken in *The Memoir*[2] was that the black spots are small dark planets embedded with the moon in its orbit. I say that as the moon is simple, so is its orbit. If simplicity requires that there not be an existent thing in the moon; that requires that there not be an existent thing in its orbit either. Although the position was taken in *The Memoir* that the black spots of the moon are small dark things embedded in the body of the moon that is contrary to what he maintains here. Now, the previous demonstration, that is, the necessity of its simplicity, does not demonstrate the point since simplicity does not deny that there could be another simple body embedded in its body, as in the heaven and the very same planets. This is not a demonstration of the impossibility of the planets encompassing another planet with a discrete body. What he says regarding the impossibility of it changing from its natural position is not conducive to the point and it is obvious that he speaks of its natural shape. Perhaps by position he means part of the category, that is, the relationship of the parts to each other, as change in this requires change in the shape. After this concern, which is under examination, as you know, unless indeed the most appropriate thing is said regarding these noble bodies, then there is no

1. A marginal gloss locates this remark at the end of the sixth part of the *Sharḥ al-ishārāt,* presumably the commentary of Ṭūsī.

2. Possibly the *Tadhkira-i naṣīriyya* of Naṣīr al-Dīn Ṭūsī; cf. Muḥammad Mudarrisī (Zanjānī), *Sar-gudhasht wa ʿaqāʾid-i falsafi-yi Naṣīr al-Dīn Ṭusī* (Tehran, 1335 Sh./1956), 114.

opposition established in them requiring their natures by necessity, and there is no necessity in that, despite the support of sound possibilities. So the theory remains in the soundness of these possibilities.

The Conclusion of the Temple

On the Distinction of Existent Beings in General, and the Indication of their Ranks.

61. *The first fixed relationship in existence is the relationship of the existent subsisting substance* (al-jawhar al-qā'im al-mawjūd), that is, the first effect, *to the first eternally subsistent being* (al-awwal al-qayyūm), which is existent by its essence and gives existence to others. *It,* that is, this relationship, *is the source (lit. 'mother') of all relationships* because it contains them all, *even the noblest of them,* since it is the origin of all and because it also contains them. *It is the lover of the First.* For every effect is the lover of its cause, longing to be similar to it, as just mentioned, especially the noblest possibility, which has no veil whatsoever between it and the transcendent first. *The First is victorious over it,* overwhelming it *by the light of its eternal subsistence, with a vanquishing that cannot be encompassed or even named as its light,* just as the light of the sun is victorious over the lights of vision with a vanquishing that cannot be beheld. *This relationship contains a lover* from the side of the effect *and a vanquishing* from the side of the cause.[1] According to what the Master says in his books, love encompasses both the aspects of cause and effect except that the love of the cause follows upon vanquishing, while the love of the effect follows from submitting. This is the real, as the illuminationist experience attests.

62. *The one side,* which is from the cause, *is nobler than the other*, which is from the effect. *The condition of this relationship becomes effective* by containing both sides, the active and the passive, which are referred to as vanquishing and submitting *in all the worlds.* The authority of the principles becomes effective in the ramifications, as is established among the possessors of unveiling and vision. *Thus divisions take place [in existence] in pairs* on every level of existent beings. *Substance is divided into the embodied,* which is vanquished and influenced by the origins above it, *and the bodiless,* which vanquish the latter, as indicated.

63. *The bodiless dominates it,* that is, the body, *and it,* the bodiless, *it is beloved and its cause* as was shown previously. *One of the two sides,* namely, the side of the embodied, *is inferior and in this way the substance that is separate* from matter *is divided in two parts*: a part that is *lofty and victorious,* which is the intelligences, and a part that is *descending, passive and vanquished, into the degrees [of existence],*

1. The terms translated here as 'vanquishing' (*qahr*) and 'victorious' (*qāhir*) have the general sense of force, conquest, overpowering, and they recall the Qur'ānic name of God as *al-qahhār*, the all-powerful. Corbin translates *qahr* as 'domination d'amour', while he renders the term 'love' (*maḥabbah*) as 'obédience d'amour'.

which are the souls. *Likewise, bodies are divided into the ethereal and the elemental.* The former is active and victorious, and the latter is passive and vanquished. Then he turns away from that discussion to establish that those divisions exist in some of the parts of each of the two divisions, i.e., the ethereal. He says, *Rather, some of the ethereal bodies,* namely, the planets, *are divided into those that sustain felicity,* called the auspicious celestial bodies, such as Jupiter and Venus, *and those that sustain vanquishing,* called the unlucky ones by the masses, such as Saturn, Mars, etc. Then he turns away from that, advancing to establish division among some of the parts of each part, that is, some of the planets. So he says, *Rather, there are two luminosities [i.e., the sun and the moon],* referring to the preceding divisions, assuming the meaning as though he had said, 'Rather, from this division two luminosities are produced'. Otherwise, it is obvious from the phrase, 'Rather, there are two luminosities', since it is a reference to the object of the preposition ['into', i.e., the planets]. It is possible that it is a reference to some of the ethereal bodies, as is evident even if these two [luminosities] are included among some of the ethereal bodies, still their division is of a higher degree than the division of all the planets. This division [of luminous bodies] occurs in two, contrary to the division of all the planets, which is common to a large group. *One of the two,* which is the sun, *is like the intellect,* since it is an active source of emanation, *and the other,* which is the moon, is like the soul, since it is a passive recipient of emanation. Then he indicates the outflow of that division into bodies in a general way that encompasses everything he says, by saying, *there is the high and the low, the right and the left.* This division flows into all bodies, high and low, then its outflow enters the heavens particularly, as he says, *there is east and west.* Then its outflow enters some of the genera of elementals, which are most conspicuous of all. He says, *there is the male and the female among animals.* Then he summaries all that by saying, *a perfect side is joined with an imperfect one,* that is, in all the divisions mentioned, there is *in imitation of the relationship with the First. He understands that* the secret just mentioned regarding the effectiveness of pairing in all existent beings, which is true because sex is called 'effective in all species', *if he understands the saying of God the transcendent, 'For everything we have created in pairs; perhaps you shall remember'* [Qur'ān 51:49]. They understand that it remains the first relationship, which is 'the source [mother] of all relationships' [61], and they learn from the unity of the source, which is the origin of this duality.

64. *Since light is the noblest of existent beings* by the testimony of sound nature, so that dumb animals love and adore it, sometimes risking their lives to approach it, like the moth, *so the noblest of bodies is the most luminous of them. It is the most sacred,* ['most sacred' (*qiddīs*)' being] the emphatic form of 'the sacred' (*al-quds*), or purity. *It is the father,* so called because it is the one who brings forth the three kinds [of elemental matter], which are the fountainhead of the emanation of life. *It is the king,* because it was given kingship, as was established by the possessors

of experience and unveiling, who penetrated the commands of the stars and the secrets of theurgy, among the sages of Babylon and the masters of the sciences who preceded them and followed them. *It is Hūrakhsh,* the name of the sun in Persian, *it is mighty* since it overwhelms and is not overwhelmed, *the one who is victorious over the twilight* or the darkness by its lights, *the chief* of heaven; how could it be otherwise? It is the greatest of the luminous bodies in it, rather, it holds for it the position of the heart. *It is the maker of day* by its rising, *the perfecter of potencies, the master of marvels,* as was shown to the masters of the secrets of the stars, theurgy, and talismans. *It is might of form;* it is divine, and its radiance suffices for all the lights, and for the disappearance of them all is in its victorious rays, it is the disappearance of all the lights in the sublimities of the glory of the light of lights. *It is the one who gives all the bodies their radiance, not taking anything from them.* This indicates its outward form, in that the lights of all the planets are borrowed from it, as some of the pillars among the philosophers maintain. *It is the image of God, the transcendent, the almighty,* in emanating light on all receptacles and the vanquishing of all the lights. In general, the light of lights, which is the sun of the world, is the intellect. *It is the greatest aim* and therefore it [the sun] was the prayer-direction of devotions in the ancient religions. By its nature, fire became a prayer-direction, for they called it daughter of the sun; it was as though it took the place of [the sun] in that [role], by existing and appearing in all times and places, unlike the sun. *After it,* that is, after Hūrakhsh in nobility and excellence, *are the mighty lords of dominion*, or the individual stars, both fixed stars and planets, *and in particular the master of felicity, the lord of goodness and blessings,* that is, the lesser light, which is the moon. An indication of this is that the Master, in his *Hymns* addressed to the planets, describes the moon in similar terms.[1] *Glory be to its originator.* The subject is the 'most sacred' described above, or each one of the entities mentioned above. Origination here is in its literal sense, as giving existence without imitating a model; it is not in its technical sense, which is giving existence without any intermediary. *He transcends* what the heretics say regarding its attributes, and what the abstractionists say regarding its attributes, and what the abstractionists say regarding its essence, [*transcending*] *him to whom it gave form* with the best of forms. *Blessed be God,* that is, may He increase well, for his Essence is transcendent, *the best of creators*—the plural, in popular fashion, is metaphorical, since in reality there is no source of influence except Him, as in the preceding.

1. For these hymns (*tasbīḥāt*), see Corbin's translation, *L'archange,* 483 ff.

FLASHES OF ILLUMINATION ON PRAISEWORTHY ETHICS, OR, THE JALĀLIAN ETHICS

Akhlāq-i jalālī

Translated for this volume by Carl W. Ernst from Jalāl al-Dīn Dawānī, *Akhlāq-i jalālī* (Lahore, n.d.), pp. 259–288.

The Fourth Flash: On the Politics of Kingship and the Manners of Kings

First, let it be said by way of preface that the rank of the sultanate is one of the glories of the divine bounty from the limitless treasury of graces, of which certain great individual servants of God become worthy. What rank reaches this level? For here the divine King of Kings, having placed one of His chosen servants on the throne of elect vicegerency, shines a spark from the lights of real majesty on his condition and makes the specification of the ranks and rights of all humanity subject to his decree, so that all, according to their different ranks, turn the face of need in the direction of the heaven-like court. And it has come down in a saying of the Prophet, that the emperor is the shadow of God on earth, for everyone oppressed by the calamity of the raging events of time goes to him for refuge. Gratitude for this supreme bounty and great gift is what regulates justice among both the noble and the common folk. Just so the noble meaning, 'David, we have made you a vicegerent on the earth, so judge between the people with truth' (Qur'ān 38:26), can refer to that.

Now that the preface to this introduction is complete, just as the city is divided in conformity with prior fate into the virtuous and the non-virtuous, the politics of kingship is also divided into two types. The first is the virtuous government, which is called imamate, and that is the ordering of the occupations of the servants in worldly and otherworldly affairs, so that each attains the perfection that is appropriate to him, and real happiness can undoubtedly become his perquisite. The ruler of this government is the vicegerent of God in reality, and is the shadow of God. In the perfection of government, the one who imitates the master of the religious law [i.e., Muḥammad] necessarily will attain the prosperous influences and luminous rays of that unique servant of all the lands. As the poem says,

> Take what you can see, and leave what you've only heard;
> the rising sun will brighten you more than Saturn.

An example of this type that is more splendid than the world-illuminating sun is the reign of the master of the age, who holds the station of Solomon [i.e., Uzun Ḥasan]. The great masters of unveiling and realization have mostly expressed the good news, in this time of happy influence, that the truthful day, 'the day when consciences will be examined' (Qur'ān 86:9), is the appearance of the manifestation of all things in existence. In just a little while, the joy and splendour of the kingdom and the faith will have increased to perfection, and the groups of people will be protected from the calamities of time in the enclosure of security, the wolf and the sheep will drink from the same place, and the falcon and the partridge will sleep in the same nest. May God most high keep the sun of his justice, which casts sparks of beneficence to the east and west of the world, in the day-increasing degrees of ascension, and keep him safe and preserved from the evil eye, downfall, disgrace, fall, and fault!

The second is the defective government, which is called tyrannical, and the goal of its masters is the suborning of the servants of God and the destruction of the lands of God. They do not endure long; in a little while, they are afflicted with worldly calamity joined with eternal misery. A tyrannical emperor is like a lofty structure placed on snow; necessarily, when its foundation melts in the sunshine of divine justice, the structure is destroyed. The wise know that one cannot preserve the treasure of Chosroes with a bread crust seized from a tired old woman, nor set the table of Solomon with a locust's leg stolen from the hand of a poor ant. Playing a lute made from wood taken from the property of the poor and unfortunate yields no result but groaning lament, and the wine filled from the heart's blood of the helpless produces only the gurgle of bloody weeping, and it gives birth only to the hangover of pains and illnesses. One cannot make the armour of David with a plundered beggar's garment, nor produce the pillow for a royal throne from an old quilt pillaged from the needy. A shield woven from the property of poor orphans will not ward off the arrow of fate, nor will the mail made from the substance of naked beggars repel the arrow of suffering.

Rather, the master of good fortune finds security from the arrows of time's calamities, for he entrusts his heart to the perfect minds of pure dervishes, and he succeeds in attaining the goal of the intentions and desire of those with high concentration. For at the time of commencing journeys and undertaking dangers and risks, having requested a portable shield from the thought of the residents of mosques and dwellers in Sufi hospices, the crown of empire sits on the head of the man who seeks direction from the thought of the crown-bestowing headless and footless ones. The throne of vicegerency is the residence of the emperor who begs for grace from the thought of the beggars of the heart.

At tavern's door sit rogues and rascals
Who give and take away the crown of empire.
When a brick is your pillow, you find the seven stars over your head—
Behold the hand of power and the rank of nobility.

The riders of the lead-horse of eternal happiness, in place of the proud-stepping bay horse and the fleet-footed dark horse, have joined the dun horse of dawn and the black horse of night to the stable of the emperor, for the departure of the swift steed of his intention is toward the security and contentment of those whose state is shattered. Unending grace, instead of the fleet-footed red horse and the world-striding cream horse, has led the piebald horse of the sun and the silvery horse of the moon with the halter of subjugation and the reins of proof of the world ruler. On the field of justice and compassion he has stolen the prize from worthy rulers, he has imitated the states of emperors, and he has become the just witness contemplating the daily increasing fortune of the revered Master of Time, the Divine Shadow.

In the experience of this claimant and the verification of his claim, if someone opens the eyes of significance and polishes the verdigris of heedlessness from the mirror of insight, and the master of virtuous government holds fast to the just law, he holds the people in the position of children and friends. Greed and love of wealth is abhorred by the intellectual faculty, but the master of defective government is attached to the principles of tyranny; he holds the people, in relation to himself, in the position of slaves, rather, he thinks of them as beasts of burden, while he himself is the slave of greed and desire. According to the saying, 'People in their time resemble most their parents, and people in religion follow their kings', men imitate the character of the rulers of the age. When the bridle of time comes into the hand of a just emperor, everyone seeks justice and acquires excellence. If the situation is the opposite of this, men are inclined to lying, greed, and all other vile things. It is for this reason that it has come down in the sayings of the Prophet, that if a sultan is just, he has a portion of every good deed done by his subjects; if he is a tyrant, he shares in every evil deed done by them.

The philosophers have said that the emperor should have seven qualities: first, high concentration, which is attained by purifying one's morals; second, correct knowledge and thought, which is obtained by natural quickness and much experience; third, powerful resolve, which is attained by correct opinion and the power of firmness—this is called the resolution of kings, and the resolution of men, and this very thing is basic for acquiring every benefit and excellence.

The story is told that the caliph Ma'mūn had a desire to eat roses, and on this account a great corruption affected his constitution. As much as the skilled physicians attempted to eliminate that by prescribing medical remedies, they did not attain success until a day when all the physicians were gathered to examine their books. While they conferred on this subject, one of the private boon-companions came in. When he observed what was going on, he said, 'Commander of the Faithful! Where is the resolution of kings?' Ma'mūn told the physicians, 'There is no need for any remedy, after this, I shall not be eager for this again.'

Fourth, patience in enduring afflictions, for patience is the key to the doors of purpose and security—it is said in a saying of the Prophet, 'He who knocks on a door and persists gains entry';[1] fifth, prosperity, so that he is not disturbed by covetousness for men's wealth; sixth, obedient soldiers; seventh, rank, which will necessarily cause the attraction of hearts, awe, and authority—this quality is not essential, but is preferred. Military prosperity can be attained by means of those four qualities, i.e., high concentration, knowledge, patience, and resolve, so these four are very important. Praise be to God that the revered emperor, the protector of religion (i.e., Uzun Ḥasan), has attained all these four qualities, and his noble essence has reached the limit of the ascensions of magnificence and majesty.

Since the preceding introduction discovered that the emperor is the physician of the world, and the physician cannot do without the knowledge of sickness, the causes of pain, and the nature of the cure, thus in any case it is necessary for the sultan that he know the disease of the kingdom and the way to cure it. Since civilization is an expression for a common society among various groups, as long as each of these groups stays at its level and engages in the occupation that is its task and attains the portion that is appropriate to it of riches and favours, that is, pomp and glory, then the temperament of the city will always be on the path of balance and its affairs characterized by the way of order. But if it turns away from this rule, then it will always be the cause of dissension, which is the source of the loosening of the bond of affection and the cause of corruption and confusion. For it is decreed that the origin of every state is the agreement of the opinions of society, which are related in mutual aid as the limbs of a single body. This being the case, it will also be true that a person has come into existence in the world who has the power of all these individuals, and none of these individuals can resist it. Even many people, if they are divided in their opinions, all cannot overcome it, except in the case that mutual affection is attained among them in the same fashion, so that they are related as a single person, for its power will be greater than the power of this society.

Since the situation of any multitude that lacks unity will not become a harmonious order, and that unity is justice, as was just mentioned, as long as the sultan follows the rule of justice and keeps each class of men in its own place, and prevents them from aggression, transgression, and seeking excess, the kingdom is always in order. If it is to the contrary of this, every group is overcome by the demand for its own benefit, and it rises up to harm others, and by way of excess and negligence the bond of affection is loosened. It is known from experience that every society increases, as long as there is concord among its members, and they follow the path of justice. But when injustice and enmity is predominant among them, it heads toward destruction, since in consequence of the preceding arguments, the people of the day are on the path of the sultans. Thus, when the emperor and his following strive for injustice, the demand of injustice that is

1. Furūzānfar, *Aḥādīth-i mathnawī*, p. 29, no. 71.

concealed in human nature is activated in everyone and inclines toward aggression. As it is said, unity never joins with aggression, for then it always becomes the cause of the corruption of the world's temperament. Therefore it is said, 'Government can endure with unbelief, but it does not endure with injustice'.[1]

The philosophers have said that one can protect a regime with two things. One is affection and unity among those who are in accord, and the other is contention and discord between enemies, for whenever enemies are busy with each other, they are unable to attain other aims. For this reason, when Alexander conquered the kingdom of Darius, the Persian army was vast in numbers. He considered that if he ignored them and (God forbid) they joined in alliance, it would be hard to prevent them, and if he eliminated them, it would be far from the basis of religion and virtue. He consulted with the philosopher Aristotle, and the philosopher said, 'Separate them, and return to them government and rule of a district, so that they may be occupied with each other, and you may be safe from their wickedness.' Alexander made them rulers of provinces, and from that time to the age of Ardashīr Bābak, the alliance by reason of which they could become dominant was no longer easy to attain.

The classes of people should be equal with one another, so that civil justice is attained. Just as the moderation of temperament is attained by marriage of the four elements and equality among them, moderation of the civil temperament is also conceived by equality of the four classes. (1) The first class is the scholars, such as religious scholars, jurists, judges, scribes, clerks, engineers, astronomers, physicians, and poets, for the maintenance of religion and this world is bound to and dependent on the efforts of their bold pens and elegant proclamations. They are in the position of water among the elements, and even so, the relationship that is between knowledge and water, according to insightful assayers, can be clearer than water, or rather more luminous than the sun. (2) The second class is the soldiers, such as bold men, warriors, and governors of forts and frontiers, for the organized welfare of humanity does not take form without constant care for the sword of the onslaught of their avenging standard, and the matters of the corruption of rebels are not unbound and destroyed without the fire of their thunderous wrath. They are in the position of fire, and the aspect of their relationship with that is more obvious than the requirement of proof—seeking fire by lamplight is not the task of 'those who have vision'. (3) The third class is business people, such as traders, merchants, and masters of trades and crafts. Through them the sources of trade goods and other occupations are arranged, and distant regions enjoy and delight in each other's special commodities and provisions. Their relationship is like air, which is the supplier of growth to plants and the provider of spirit to animals. By its mediation, oscillation, and motion, every kind of gift and rarity arrives by the

1. This saying is often attributed to 'Alī ibn Abī Ṭālib.

path of hearing to the realm of vicegerency, the human clarifier [i.e., the intelligence] and it becomes extremely clear. (4) The fourth class is the farmers, such as ploughmen, landlords, and cultivators, who care for plants and prepare foods. Without the means of their efforts, the survival of humanity would be in the realm of impossibility. In reality, they are the producers of that which does not exist, for other groups do not add to the existence of anything, they rather convey an existing thing from one person to another, or from one place to another, or from one form to another. Their proximity to the earth, which is the place of adoration of the planets, the locus of rays of the lights of the world of purity, the manifestation of the rarities of creation, and the origin of hidden wonders, is extremely clear.

Just as in compounds, excess of one of the elements beyond the necessary share causes immoderation, corruption, and dissolution, in civil society also the predominance of one of these classes over the other three classes makes the order of unity vain and confused. After instituting equality between the four classes, one needs to observe the conditions of every individual and assign the rank of each according to what they deserve.

From another point of view, the divisions of humanity are five. (1) The first is those people who are of a good nature, who convey their goodness to others, such as scholars of the religious law, masters of the spiritual path, and knowers of the divine reality. This group is the goal of existence and the elite of worshippers of God. They are the descent of eternal grace and the vision of unending fortune. In reality, the other divisions have entered into the inn of existence on their coat-tails.

Come, for at the table of grace of the lord of the world
you are the guest, and the world is uninvited.

The philosophers have said that the emperor should hold this group closer to himself than any other and place them in authority over the other divisions. It is said that whenever the masters of learning and sagacity are the resort of his majesty the emperor, this is a sign of the advance of fortune and the increase of dignity.

The story is told that Ḥasan Būyah in his own time was the ruler of the country of Rayy, and from his love of philosophers and scholars, he was chosen from the sultans of the age to take the drum of warfare against Rome. At the beginning of battle, victory fell to the army of Islam and they achieved complete domination over the infidels. Afterwards, the Romans underwent a general transformation, and having collected an army from all directions, they set off against the army of Iraq. The latter were defeated, and some fell into captivity. The Roman king sat and called the prisoners near to him. Among them was a man called Abū Naṣr, a native of Rayy. When he made it known that he was from Rayy, the king said, 'Shall I give you a message to convey to your emperor?' He replied, 'Yes, I am at your service'. The king said, 'Tell Ḥasan Būyah the following: I have come from Constantinople with the intention of laying waste to Iraq, but now that I have investigated your character and condition, it is clear to me that the sun of your fortune is still aimed at the zenith of perfection and is on the ascendant in the degrees of felicity. The person for whom the sun of fortune faces the nadir of decline and the twilight of sunset and extinction does not have royal associates who are great philosophers and famous scholars, such as Ibn ʿAmīd, Abū Jaʿfar Khāzin, ʿAlī ibn Qāsim, and Abū ʿAlī Batāʾī. The gathering of this group in your forecourt is a proof of your continuing felicity and increasing pomp and glory. For this reason I am not going to interfere with your country.'

(2) The second division is the people who are good by nature, but who do not convey their goodness to others. The rank of this division is lower than the first division, for the perfect beauty of the latter is adorned by the mole of guidance and perfecting, and they are honoured by the robe of 'taking on the divine qualities'.[1] But this division, although they are graced by the ornament of perfection, yet they fall short of the degree of perfecting others. This group should be revered, and their welfare and provisions should be supplied in sufficiency.

(3) The third division is the people who are neither good nor bad by nature. One should keep this division hidden in the shade of security and clip the wings of pity for them, so they remain protected from the corruption of their ability and are deserving of perfection as much as possible.

(4) The fourth division is the people who are bad, but who do not convey their evil to others. One should humble this crowd, treat them with contempt, and prevent them from crimes by prohibitions that preach and deter.

(5) The fifth division is those who from essential malice convey their evil to others. This group is the vilest of humanity, and the opposite of the first group. Those from this division for whom there is some hope of reform should be given corrective instruction. Those for whom there is no hope of reform, if their evil is not extensive, the emperor should treat kindly, in accordance with sound opinion. But if their evil is general in effect, its removal is necessary according to both religious law and reason, by the method that is soundest and most fitting.

One method of averting evil is imprisonment, and that prevents someone from mixing with the people of the city. A second method is incarceration, which prevents someone from having political influence. A third method is banning, and that prevents someone from entering the city. If the person is not expelled by these measures, the philosophers are divided over the permissibility of killing him. Their clearest saying is that the limb which is the tool of evil be amputated, such as the hand, foot, or tongue, or else the elimination of one of the senses would suffice. The truth of the matter is that one should follow the true religious law, and the legal punishments (*ḥudūd*) of amputation and execution should be preferred

1. For this Sufi saying see William Chittick, *The Sufi Path of Knowledge*, pp. 283–286.

in applicable cases. Anything beyond that should be avoided, for God has said: 'Whoso goes beyond the limits (*ḥudūd*) of God has wronged his soul' (Qur'ān 65:1). And there should be no execution of madmen. If someone deserves it according to religious law, he should not be pitied, as God says: 'And let pity for the two not hold you back from serving God' (Qur'ān 24:2). Just as a physician knows that it is permissible, or rather necessary, that he cut off a limb for the salvation of the remaining limbs, the emperor, who is the world's physician by the decree of the First Regulator (whose dignity is exalted), at times may execute an individual for the sake of the general welfare of humanity.

After establishing equality and specifying the ranks among the people according to justice, the emperor should apportion goods, favouring each one according to his deserts. Goods are of three kinds: health, wealth, and honours. Everyone is deserving of a portion of these affairs, and reducing it is oppression for that person, while increasing it is oppression for the citizens. If there is one person who lacks the food that he deserves, then to increase someone else's sufficiency is injustice for them. At times reduction may be oppression for the citizens. Whenever a deserving person is made to halt at a station lower than that which is his right, it necessarily humiliates him. Others become worthy, and this is the cause of dissension in the order of society.

After distribution of goods to the people according to their deserts, he should protect that for them, not permitting that goods rightfully belonging to anyone should be lost. In case someone has a loss, he conveys to him compensation to the degree that is deserved, in such a manner that society is not injured. He should prevent oppression by punishments for those who commit it; for every oppression there is a punishment appropriate to it. If in recompense to a little oppression he gives much punishment, it is tyranny for the oppressor, and if in response to much oppression he gives little punishment, it is tyranny for the other citizens. Some of the philosophers hold that oppression for any one of the people is oppression for all the citizens. Therefore punishment is not annulled by the forgiveness of the oppressed person, and in spite of his forgiveness, it is permissible for the sultan, who is the universal ruler and regulator, to give punishment. Some others hold the contrary of this, but since this discussion refers to the judgment of the just arbitrator of the religious law, the leader of humanity [Muḥammad] (blessings and peace be upon him and on his family), the decision is found in this manner: everything that is in the class of punishments of God, such as theft, adultery, and highway robbery, is not annulled by forgiveness, rather, it is necessary for the sultan to uphold the punishment.

But that which pertains to the class of rights of the people, if it is the law of retaliation or the punishment of false accusation of adultery, is annulled by merited forgiveness. If it is discretionary punishment, even in the form of beating, inconvenience, or contempt, most of the leading experts of the teaching of Shāfiʿī

(God have mercy on him) agree that in spite of merited forgiveness, discretionary punishment is incumbent on the sultan in terms of correction. In the same way, there is wisdom in these decrees, for some evils are of that type that is the cause of injury against the people of the region, such as adultery, theft, and the like. Lenience for such as that causes dissension in the public order, so necessarily forgiveness can have no influence on that. Some evils are restricted to a single person and from him will not infect another, such as false accusation of adultery, so punishment always depends on the desire and forgiveness of that person. Those evils for which suspicion of infection of society and the lack thereof are both supported can be dependent on the view and opinion of the sultan, so that he commands implementation of what he thinks is preferable and soundest, in accordance with correct opinion. Therefore if a victim of murder has no private inheritance, but inherits from the public treasury, the decision in that case is dependent on the judgment of the sultan. If he wishes, he can demand retaliation, and if he wishes, he can forgive.

The regulation of temporal justice is so ordered that the sultan himself diligently looks into the affairs of his subjects and helps each one attain their rightful resources and honours. This is demonstrated by the fact that subjects and oppressed people seek the way to the sultan in time of need. If this is not convenient all the time, they hold audience on a specific day for petitioners, so that they may present their needs and describe their circumstances to his majesty the sultan without intermediary. The kings of Persia had a specific time when a public audience was held for the different groups of people. The revered Messenger (God bless him and his family and grant them peace) said, 'Everyone whom God most high has entrusted with authority over the affairs of Muslims, and who closes his door in the face of the needy and oppressed, God most high will close the door of mercy to him in time of need and poverty, and will exclude him from the divine grace and favour.'[1] The commander of the faithful 'Umar ibn al-Khaṭṭāb (God be pleased with him) said, 'When you have entrusted someone with authority, you have advised him that he is not to be secluded from the needy or to close the door in their faces.' The revered chief of the Messengers (the most excellent prayers of the Muslims upon him), prayed, 'God! Whoever has authority over my community in any thing and is kind to them, be kind to him. And whoever has authority over my community in any thing and oppresses them, oppress him.'[2]

Tradition has it that Pharaoh, with all his rebellion and ingratitude, had two excellent qualities. One was that he was easy of access, and the needy could imagine meeting him without difficulty. The other was that he was adorned with liberality and generosity, and he extended good fortune to the different groups of humanity from the tables of general beneficence. His extreme generosity was to such an

1. This *ḥadīth* is quoted in Persian translation.
2. Wensinck, *Concordance*, II, 283b.

extent, that it is related that an Israelite woman became pregnant, but the foods appropriate to this condition were not available in the kitchen. When he discovered this, the fire of his wrath blazed up, and he overwhelmed the cooks with the oven of his fiery intention's anger. After that, he ordered that every day, the most pleasing kinds of food that are suitable for the different classes of people should be prepared, and that everyone should be supplied with that which is appropriate.

When the hurricane winds of divine majesty began to blow from the vents of unlimited wrath, and the commanding eternal will became concerned with his ruin and humiliation, then according to the verse, 'God does not change the situation of a people until they change that which is within them' (Qur'ān 13:11), both those two qualities were changed into their opposites. His inaccessibility reached such an extent that on a clear day when the dark night remained concealed in a veil, and when the western phoenix was in the occident of hiding and concealment, rather, when the unlucky bat took refuge in the storehouse of calamity and destruction, and no one but Satan and his armies had permission to speak with him—even so, when the revered Moses (peace be upon him) was given the honour of having speech with him, on that very night, by divine command he came to the door of the castle and stayed at that gateway for one year. But he did not obtain the opportunity of an interview until one day, when one of the boon-companions of Pharaoh's assembly jestingly remarked, 'A strange figure has appeared; someone of such-and-such a character is standing at the door, saying, 'I am the messenger of God, and I have messages.' Pharaoh said, 'Let him be summoned, so we may laugh and mock him.' When they summoned him, after the dispute and discussion that the truth-revealing scripture relates, as much as Moses applied the polish of evident miracles with the white hand, the verdigris of polytheism was not removed from Pharaoh's iron heart.

Despite the 'manifest serpent' (Qur'ān 7:107) that he used to indicate the treasure of faith, Pharaoh did not follow their path, rather, every time that a snake put its head out of a hole in order to lead him to an unwholesome punishment, he came to an evil end. His avarice reached such a degree that no one but the recording angels knew about his food, and no one but flies came to sit at the head of his table. The situation was such that trustworthy companions have recorded on the tablet of traditions that the day when Moses (peace be upon him) departed from Egypt with the Israelites by divine command, Pharaoh charged close behind them. In all his kitchens nothing had been slaughtered but a single mangy goat, and having breakfasted on its liver, he had its meat prepared for a banquet, so that after returning he could feast with his intimates. But the very king of hell had prepared infernal food, the devilish tree, and juice of corpses for the entertainment of him and his soldiers.

The philosophers have said that it is necessary for the emperor to take care of three things. The first is preservation of the treasury and the dominions. The second is tenderness and mercy toward subjects. The third is that he not entrust great matters to incompetent men. One of the Sasanians was asked what was the cause of the downfall of his family's four-thousand-year-old empire. He said, 'It is that we turned over great matters worthy of the wise and discerning to base little men.' It is said that the foundation of the edifice of justice rests on ten pillars:

First, that in every case the emperor assumes that he is the subject, and the emperor is another, so that whatever he thinks improper for himself he does not permit for his subject.

Second, that he does not permit the needy to wait, and that he beware of the danger of that. Aristotle said to Alexander, 'If you desire the assistance of God most high, hasten to rescue petitioners.'

Third, that he does not spend his time absorbed in physical desires and pleasures, for this is the most powerful cause of the corruption of the realm. Rather, during his hours of rest and leisure he should do something for the expense of the kingdom and the welfare of the subjects. A philosopher advised an emperor, saying, 'Do not sleep in heedlessness, lest the destroyers of your kingdom arise, and they take their complaint of you to the court of God. Do not sleep so long that you destroy your life, for empire and life are like sunlight, which in the morning is on one wall, but in the evening is on another wall. Act so that you consume the world and the world does not consume you.'

Fourth, that he makes the basis of his actions to be kindness and courtesy, not violence and anger.

Fifth, that in pleasing the people he seeks to please God.

Sixth, that in seeking to please the people he does not oppose God.

Seventh, that when he is asked for a judgment, he gives justice, and when he is asked for mercy, he forgives, for mercy to the people is the cause of the mercy of God most high. It is even so in the correct *ḥadīth*: 'Those who are merciful receive the mercy of the Merciful; be merciful to those on earth, and you will receive mercy from the one who is in heaven.'[1]

Eighth, that he inclines to the company of men of God, and that he does shrink from their preaching and advice.

Ninth, that he treats everyone as they deserve.

Tenth, that he is unsatisfied with merely avoiding oppression himself, but he orders the government of the kingdom in such a way that the bureaucrats, soldiers, and peasants give each other no opportunity for oppression. As the saying goes, 'You are all shepherds, and all of you are responsible for a flock.' On the day of the Resurrection, he will be questioned about whatever happens in the kingdom by reason of which his government becomes defective. It is recorded in tradition that the commander of the faithful ʿUmar ibn ʿAbd al-ʿAzīz, who possessed perfect justice and extraordinary piety and purity, so that he was called 'the fifth of the Caliphs,' was seen in a dream

1. Wensinck, *Concordance*, II, 236a.

after his death. When asked about his condition, he replied, 'For a year I was veiled on a precipice. The reason was that a hole had developed in a bridge, and a goat got his foot stuck in that hole and was injured. They reproached me, saying, "Why should this be? For the welfare of creatures was entrusted to your care, and you are neglecting the preservation and control of these affairs."'

So one should look after the people by following the decrees of justice and the acquisition of excellence. For just as the body depends on nature, nature depends on the soul, and the soul depends on the intellect, so the city depends on the kingdom, the kingdom depends on government, and government depends on wisdom, which is the essence of the religious law. To keep the affairs of the state on the path of the religious law, social order can be attained, but when one turns away from that firm path, it robs the kingdom of joy and splendour. Plato said, 'Preserve the law (*nāmūs*), and it will preserve you.' That is, watch over the religious law (*sharīʿah*) so that the religious law watches over you.

When one has finished with establishing welfare and justice, one pulls the reins of concentration toward excellence and beneficence, for no quality is nobler than excellence and beneficence, as has been clearly set forth. In beneficence, one ought to claim also considerable responsibility, so that beneficence is on a par with awe and magnificence. If awe declines, beneficence is the cause of cheering the defeated, and it increases their hope. It is as in the case of land tax; if all kingdoms were given to one person [as his responsibility], he would still not be satisfied. Aristotle gave this testament to Alexander: 'The oppressed should not have too much awe of you, lest they be unable to state their needs. Soldiers and wanderers should have considerable awe, lest they enter into tyranny and injustice.'

The revered chief of the Messengers (upon whom be prayers and peace), by reason of being the locus for the manifestation of the majestic and beautiful lights, and the revealer of the effects of divine greatness and unlimited glory, possessed awe to such a degree that Abū Sufyān, in the time when he was still a non-Muslim, came near the Prophet to make a treaty. When he returned, he said, 'By God! I have seen many kings and leaders, and none of them inspired this fear and awe in my heart.' His grace and friendliness were to such an extent that one day a woman came before the Prophet, wishing to present a request. Indeed, because of the sparks of holy lights from the windows of the holy soul of the revered Prophet, he was reflected on the four walls of that purified house. As her obvious astonishment became ever more complete, when the Prophet became aware of this, he said, 'Do not fear; I am the son of an Arab woman who used to eat dried meat.' The intention of the Prophet was to pacify the fear and awe from the heart of that woman, so that she could make her request known. Showing pride to the proud and humility to the poor and oppressed is part of the ethics of generosity.

It is one of the usages of kings that they keep their secrets concealed, so that they may have the ability fully to consider and examine them and remain safe from the plotting of enemies. The revered Prophet (God pray for him and his family and grant them peace), when setting out on a raid, would give men the impression that they were going to a different place. Although the sacred courtyard of the Prophet was free of the dust of suspicion of lying, still he travelled in this fashion: if, for instance, he was interested in going in a certain direction, he asked men about the way-stations in a different direction, and made inquiries about the conditions there, so that men fell into doubts, thinking that perhaps he intended to go there.

The philosophers have said that the way to keep secrets that require counsel is to take counsel with those who are intelligent and discerning, but to keep them hidden from those of weak intellect. After determining on a course of action, one mixes it with actions that are not externally opposed to it, or rather with actions that are conducive to that very aim. One appoints an official to inquire into the affairs of others, and by their external conditions one discovers their internal conditions. In learning their intentions, questioning followers who are known for being scatter-brained is a sound principle. The best way to engage anyone in conversation is to be friendly with them, in order to get to know them. One reveals one's own secrets, and inevitably during conversation one can learn the hidden thoughts of everyone. If someone is reluctant to understand, in order to make it easier one tries flattery to remove suspicion, so that it may not end in opposition and resistance.

If it does not become easier by flattery, one should not be eager for war, so that one can overcome by skill and trickery. To overcome enemies, trickery and writing letters full of lies is not reprehensible, but to speak with lies and excuses is not permissible in every circumstance. If there is need of war, there are only two possibilities: one is either the attacker in war or the defender. If one is the attacker, his goal should be wholly good, that is, for religion or seeking retaliation or a right that forces them to war. It should not be for conquest or to attain supremacy, for the conqueror attacks the conquered; one makes war for religion or to seek a right. As long as the army is not in verbal agreement, it will not go to war, for to go in between two enemies is very dangerous. In order to make it easy, it is not appropriate for the emperor to make war in person, for if he is defeated, the situation is incurable. If he is victorious, he cannot avoid appearing frivolous, and this is not appropriate to the awe and gravity of imperial office. If war occurs, and he has the power to resist, he should struggle and attack the enemy by way of ambush or night assault, for most emperors who are at war on their own territories are conquered. If he does not have the power to resist, he should watch with great care over the organization of forts and trenches, but not rely upon them. The philosophers have said, 'Those who are in a fortress can be seized.' Rather, to knock on the door of peace, one should employ liberal gifts and the use of tricks.

To govern the affairs of the army, one should choose a person who has three qualities. First, conspicuous bravery; second, excellent administration and discernment; third, experience in letters and management. The most important of the conditions for war is alertness and awareness of the condition of the enemy through expert spies, and maintaining morale and sparing no expense on it. Without oversight of external resources, armies and supplies have no benefit of rational evaluation at the time of destruction and ruin. The philosophers have said that one should not rely upon forts and trenches except when one is forced into a siege. The like of this is conducive to weakness and encourages boldness on the part of the enemy. When someone is distinguished for bravery in war, he should be rewarded, honoured, and praised. His high degree of compensation should consist of splendid gifts and great honours. One should not ridicule a humbled enemy. 'How many a small group has conquered a large group by God's permission (Qur'ān 2:249).' After victory, one should not give up administration [of the army].

As long as it is possible to take a prisoner alive, he should not be killed, for one can conceive of many uses for captives, such as enslavement, gift, or ransom, which can console the hearts of enemies. A Qur'ānic text proclaims this, and after victory, killing enemies is not permitted, except when security may not be attained without killing them. After achieving domination, one should not give expression to enmity and fanaticism, for in this situation enemies are property and subjects, and making war on one's own slaves and subjects is contrary to the principle of justice. It is recorded in the writings of the philosophers that when Alexander, after a victory, did not spare the inhabitants of a city from the sword, Aristotle hastily wrote him a letter to this effect, that if you are excused for killing your enemies before attaining victory, after victory what excuse do you have for killing those who are in your power?

Exercising forgiveness is one of the qualities of the great kings; it brings about a tightly knotted realm and solidifies the principles of pomp and magnificence. No matter how great power grows, extending forgiveness makes it more impressive and secure, for it is the means to ensure succession and the binding of glorious order. Someone said, 'If criminals knew what pleasure I take in forgiving, they would present their crimes to me as gifts.' In reality, human perfection lies in 'taking on the qualities' of the divine attributes, and by reason of the saying 'therefore We created them' (Qur'ān 11:119), the primordial purpose for the creation of the world and humanity is the manifestation of the real existence. Divine mercy and forgiveness induce the splendour of manifestation in the loci of human weakness and defect. It is thus in the *ḥadīth*, that if you do not commit sin, God most high will create another group that will commit sin, so that His spontaneous mercy can manifest in the mirror of forgiveness. Therefore divine manifestation in the ornament of forgiveness can be similar to the real Origin, which is the source of all good things.

Since the decisive and darkness-banishing opinion of his imperial majesty, the second builder of the foundation of world rule, the revered master of the fortunate conjunction, the architect of the principles of ruling the land, has attained the subtle methods of empire, the realities of the manners of kingdom and dominion, the secret mysteries of wisdom, and the extraordinary commands of religion, by holy inspired instruction and grace of excellent gift, without intermediary of acquired learning or human efforts, thus his sacred soul has attained to the lofty rank of 'And We taught him a knowledge from Us' (Qur'ān 18:65).

The discourse on this subject from this humble poor man without possessions, who can be the fool of the assembly of the eloquent and the reporter of the words of the masters of excellence, remains far from the canon of justice and the way of manners. While Solomon could teach the language of the birds, and Luqmān could demonstrate the canon of wisdom, I request reproach from the intellectuals and rebuke from the intelligent. If, for example, to seek help one wishes to summon a subtlety, a glance at the noble life of his imperial majesty, the master of time, the second Alexander, is quite sufficient. So without any admixture of effort or digression, since fate has bound the book of being and existence, it is filling out the pages of the tablets of human nature with the writing of the perfections of the soul.

That temperament, which with its combination of rare graces of divine favour, its manifestation of the wonders of unlimited assistance, and its essence of divine attributes and angelic qualities, can be counted among the mighty Chosroes and famous Caesars, has not previously come into existence from the pen of creation and selection and the reed of existentiation and origination. Since King Sun was seated on the four-pillowed fourth heaven, however much the travellers of the heavenly bodies have turned about the world with such a lamp, they have not seen world empire with such grandeur and awe, nor have they heard the fame of majesty and greatness of the master of the fortunate conjunction with this much glory and splendour. May God most high preserve from rise, fall, and precipitous decline the two lights of the heaven of succession and the Venus and Jupiter of the sphere of justice and mercy, which by his very overseeing care and the grace of his luminous wisdom have made time and space radiant and turned the world's expanse into a garden, in the zenith of felicity and the nobility of magnificence. May God keep his messengers of happiness and armies of fortune, like the chain of the latter times, joined to the first times, and connected to 'God by God and His words, and to the gnostics by His Essence and His Attributes'.

5

Ibn Abī Jumhūr Aḥsā'ī

Ibn Abī Jumhūr Aḥsā'ī, a major Shiʿi theologian, philosopher and Sufi, whose works in many ways complement those of Sayyid Ḥaydar Āmulī in integrating intellectual currents of his day into the Shiʿi world, was born in Aḥsā' in Baḥrayn in 838/1435. It was there that he carried out his earliest studies in Shiʿi circles of learning, his city of birth having been a centre of Twelver Shiʿism for a long time. After completing his early studies, he set out for Najaf in Iraq which was then, as in later centuries, one of the main, if not the main, centres of Shiʿi learning. Upon completion of his formal studies, Ibn Abī Jumhūr travelled to Syria and then to Mecca to perform the pilgrimage. Upon completion of the *Ḥajj*, he travelled north to Jabal ʿĀmil, another major Shiʿi centre, where he spent some time at the feet of a number of the notable teachers of that land. Then he returned to Iraq.

The second part of the life of Abī Jumhūr was spent in Persia. He first set out from Iraq for Khurāsān to visit the mausoleum of Imam Riḍā and while on this journey composed the treatise *Zād al-musāfirīn fī uṣūl al-dīn* (Provision of Travellers concerning the Principles of Religion). The rest of his life was spent journeying to various Persian cities where he would often carry out debates with Sunni *ʿulamā'*. Of these debates the most famous was the one with Fāḍil-i Hirawī in 878/1483 which has become a landmark in Sunni–Shiʿi debates over the centuries. The date of death of Ibn ʿAbī Jumhūr is not known with certainty but it is known that he was still alive in 904/1499.

Ibn Abī Jumhūr wrote a number of works on the Shiʿi sciences of *ḥadīth*, *fiqh* and *kalām* and he has been always famous among Shiʿi *ʿulamā'*, some of whom have criticized his religious studies, especially his study of *ḥadīth*, while others have held him in the highest esteem. But his most important work, from the philosophical point of view, and the reason that he has been included in this volume, is his *Kitāb al-Mujlī mir'āt al-munjī* (The Book of the Illuminated, Mirror of the Saviour) usually known as *Kitāb al-Mujlī*, which holds a position of eminence in the *ishrāqī* tradition. This book is in fact a commentary that Ibn Abī Jumhūr wrote on his own earlier work, *Kitāb al-Nūr al-munjī min al-ẓalām* (The Book of Light that Saves from Obscurity) which in turn was a commentary upon Ibn Abī Jumhūr's earlier opus, *Maslak al-ifhām fī 'ilm al-kalām* (The Path for Making Understood the Science of *Kalām*). The *Kitāb al-Mujlī* is not, however, a work of *kalām*. Completed in 895/1490, this book is one of the major texts of Islamic philosophy written at that time, a work concerned primarily with *ishrāqī* and *'irfānī* ideas and themes while he remains for the most part silent on issues pertaining to *kalām*. One can see in this work the clear influence of Shahrazūrī, whose *al-Shajarah al-ilāhiyyah* Ibn Abī Jumhūr quotes often without mentioning Shahrazūrī's name. Ibn Abī Jumhūr is both an important figure in the *ishrāqī* tradition as it developed in a Shi'i context and one of the figures who, in bringing together the various schools of philosophy, theology and gnosis, prepared the ground for the synthesis of these perspectives in the Safavid period by Mīr Dāmād and especially Mullā Ṣadrā.

In this chapter, a section of Aḥsā'ī's work *Kitāb al-Mujlī* is presented to a Western audience for the first time. Following a brief discussion of the opinions of the theologians (*mutakallamūn*), Aḥsā'ī offers a thorough and detailed discussion of problems in the field of epistemology. In doing so, he refers to the opinions of Rāzī and Ibn Sīnā and the role of revelation, purification and providence as the components needed for obtaining knowledge. Aḥsā'ī's philosophical discussions, written in the *ishrāqī* tradition, take a gnostic turn when he treats the subject of the 'secrets of the heart'. Referring to a number of Sufi masters such as Basṭāmī and Junayd, he offers an esoteric reading of the prayers of the prophets David, Moses and Jesus. This section concludes with the author's testament to the readers of *al-Mujlī*.

S. H. Nasr

THE BOOK OF THE ILLUMINATED, MIRROR OF THE SAVIOUR

Kitāb al-Mujlī mir'āt al-munjī

Translated for this volume by Majid Fakhry from Muḥammad Abu'l-Ḥasan ʿAlī ibn Ḥusām al-Dīn ibn Abī Jumhūr al-Baḥrī al-Aḥsā'ī, *Kitāb al-Mujlī,* based on Aḥmad Shīrāzī's lithograph edition (Tehran, 1329/1911).

Part 1
Exposition of the Divisions of Knowledge

Since the human species is distinguished by the attribute of knowledge (the author)[1] refers to the knowledge of its divisions, without dwelling on its definition, which is intuitively conceived, as we will show.

The human soul is characterized by the scientific faculty, which understands what is not subject to aptitude and is called the rational, logical or angelic faculty. For, the soul understands both universal and particular intelligibles, whether they derive from sensibles or not, by means of this faculty, whereby the forms of intelligibles are imprinted on it, just as the forms of visible objects are imprinted on mirrors facing them. The rational faculty is thus similar to a polished mirror, so that when the intelligibles happen to face it, their forms are imprinted on it. Its understanding, then, arises as a result of that impression, while the act of facing arises as a result of the rational faculty's disposition to receive ideas which are the causes of the rational faculty's reception of the emanation of those forms from the superabundant principle, which is the Active Intellect, as the philosopher[2] has explained.

Thinking, according to (the philosophers) prepares the rational faculty and disposes it to receive (the forms) from it.[3] According to al-Ashʿarī,[4] the creator of the forms in it is God Almighty, who has imposed the rules of custom. He thus repudiates (secondary) causes and refers all determinations to this without any intermediaries. The Muʿtazilites, by contrast, hold that ideas are actually the causes of the impressions of these forms, without reference to any other agent, insofar as causes determine their effects, as will be shown later. However, consensus exists with respect to the forms of intelligibles being imprinted on the rational faculty in whatever way in a manner analogous to the visible images imprinted on sensible mirrors; except that, what is imprinted on the rational faculty is stronger, more perfect and fuller, since it is not removed from it. It enables it, in addition, to arrive

1. Parentheses indicate that the terms enclosed are understood or required for clarity.
2. *al-Ḥakīm* usually refers to Ibn Sīnā.
3. That is, the Active Intellect.
4. Abu'l Ḥasan al-Ashʿarī who died in 939.

by virtue of that impression at the knowledge of its essential and existential features, whether separate or intrinsic, as well as the part that which is imprinted on it and the forms of visible objects or other objects of the five senses, as distinguished from the non-sensible intelligibles which correspond to them externally and are known as the first intelligibles. The same is true of the secondary intelligibles, the non-existing entities and even impossibles which differ from sensible objects. We thus have three things: (a) the form itself, (b) the soul's reception thereof and its affection by it and (c) the relation to it in point of state and plane; I mean attribution. Thus, one wonders whether the term knowledge applies to the form itself or to the receptivity, passivity, relation or pure predication.

Each of these positions was upheld by a group of scholars. The authoritative philosophers and most of the theologians (*mutakallimūn*) and the logicians have opted for the first opinion. The true knowledge, according to them, refers to the form itself. This is, why they hold that knowledge is a form other than the object itself but is derived from it, because it is a replica thereof in the soul of the human, which, were it to emerge outwardly, it would be identical with the object known. They have entertained, with respect to the manner of the inherence of those forms in the rational faculty, while turned towards universal intelligibles, inhering in a particular locus, a theory mentioned in their books, which I would have touched on, but for fear of prolixity.

I say this is a noble and venerable discourse that contains important insights into the mode of man's acquisition of knowledge. But before we explain it we wish to give a prelude concerning the mode of man's knowledge of himself, followed by the manner of his knowledge of other objects.

We hold that whoever turns to himself, having the barest measure of perception, will understand that he knows himself, because he is never absent therefrom. Thus his knowledge of himself is possible through himself, rather than anything else, as has been shown with respect to the immateriality of the rational soul; since whatever perceives the immaterial must be immaterial, for that which does understand itself or the other is the immaterial as such, rather than what does not understand itself. Then with respect to that which does not understood itself or anything else, called the soul, it will hypothetically be inquired whether it perceives itself by itself or not and so on ad infinitum. This will entail infinite regression which is absurd. It follows that the soul must be able to conceive itself by itself, and not through something else. Therefore, the rational soul, whatever it is, must conceive itself by itself, because it is the essence of manifestation and luminosity. Its self-manifestation, therefore, cannot be concealed. For how can that whose essence is manifestation and luminosity, be absent to itself? The soul is, then, reason, the object and subject of reason and therefore it is evident that it conceives itself without a form or a paradigm and conceives other things in the same way, by sheer presence. Thus it conceives its body and disposes of it in a variety of ways, but not through an impression in it, since that is a particular act, whereas the impressed form is universal. It also apprehends all its faculties, including imagination and estimation,[1] as well as its bodily faculties so as to use and dispose of them. None of the faculties, however, apprehends itself, so much so that the estimative faculty repudiates itself as well as the remaining faculties too. In fact, the soul is the agent which apprehends all the faculties in a particular way, rather than through an image impressed on it, as you have learned. Moreover, the soul is able to apprehend particulars, since it constructs definitions and premises, and it abstracts universals from particulars. This shows that it apprehends particulars in a particular way. In fact the soul apprehends itself in itself and apprehends its own body and the rest of its faculties and what is revealed through those faculties, not though a form or paradigm, but through the illuminationist present apprehension. For the soul experiences an illumination[2] of presence concerning the object and then it apprehends it without a form or paradigm. Thus the man of virtue ought to acknowledge the illuminationist knowledge of presence of the parts of the souls which are divested of matter. Even the distracted can be absent to his own self. For the apprehension of every abstract entity, by the knower endures so long as his self endures; and his constant apprehension of himself will endure so long as his apprehension of other things endures, as happens in the case of apprehending rational principles and selves. Thus, so long as the condition of immateriality is constant and strong, apprehension is more perfect and stronger. That is why the same immaterial reason is then that of the soul, its apprehension is stronger and firmer than that of the soul. Thus the apprehension of the souls differs according to their immateriality and their degree of inclining towards the corporeal faculties, inherence in them, the force of their association with the body, or rising above it and turning towards the stronger side. Therefore, according to the measure of its clinging to its weak understanding, and the measure of its dissociation from another, (the soul's) apprehension of itself increases and to the extent other things are present to it and are revealed to it, its apprehension of other things increases too.

Thus, if the thing is absent to the soul, the precondition of its being apprehended is that it should be present to it, either in itself or through its form or paradigm. If it happens to be present in itself, (the soul) will apprehend it through the illuminationist presence. If through its form, then what is apprehended through the form will either be particular or universal. If particular, then it is apprehended through the presence of its form in certain corporeal faculties pertaining to the apprehending soul, such as apprehending Zayd, who is absent to us, by means of his form. If the apprehended object is universal in form, it will not be possible to apprehend it through the presence of its form in some corporeal faculty, insofar as universals cannot be impressed on bodies or their powers. It follows, that universal forms

1. *al-Wahm*, also known as *al-wāhimah*, or estimative faculty.
2. *Ishrāq*.

ought to occur to the rational soul itself or the apprehended object ought to be the present form, regardless of whether it is in the soul or in the corporeal faculties; and then the apprehended object will not be external to the conception corresponding to the given form. For what it external to conception cannot be apprehended as a first intention but only as second.

The rational soul, then, is able to apprehend by means of all three methods a multitude of apprehended objects: (a) apprehending itself by itself and its own faculties as the object present to it by means of pure illuminationist presence, (b) by contrast, it apprehends particulars which are absent to it by means of particular forms, inherent in its particular faculties, and (c) it apprehends rational universals by means of the universal forms inherent in it.

If you look closely at this you will find that apprehension through the forms, whether universal or particular, is reducible to the illuminationist apprehension by presence. For the apprehended object in truth is the imaginative forms which are present in the particular faculties, not what emerges in conception. Similarly, what is apprehended is the same as the universal forms, not what corresponds to them in the form of rational abstractions.

It follows that apprehension is the presence of the object to the self stripped of matter; and since apprehending the object in itself differs according to the strength or weakness of its abstractness, its apprehension of something other than itself will differ according to the measure of its presence and the strength of its revelation and clarity. Moreover, the greater the abstraction, the greater the apprehension and the extent of the soul's domination of the body and the degree of its controlling it. Then, its apprehension of itself and other things will be greater or stronger; for apprehension differs according to the intensity of presence and the degree of its revelation and clarity. This is the truth of the matter in the science of psychology.

If you look carefully at what I told you in these discourses, you will know what he[1] meant by saying that the particular forms of the individual soul can be universal, and will also know that its universality depends on the immateriality of the soul; the problem existing only in the case of those who regard the soul as something corporeal. However, he who admits its immateriality and that the matter is as we explained and grasps it fully, will be worthy of learning the truth about the modality of the Necessary Being's knowledge of things, according to the theory of illumination.

So wayward philosophers have opted for the second view, applying the term knowledge to that very passivity and receptivity, and therefore have defined knowledge as the act of the rational faculty receiving the known object, its being affected by it and being united to it in some sense. To this the Shaykh[2] has inclined

1. Ibn Sīnā.
2. Ibn Sīnā.

in his book 'Beginning and Resurrection'.[1] Some theologians (*mutakallimūn*) have inclined to the third view, applying the term knowledge to the relation and abstract attribution itself. That is why they have defined knowledge as the relation of the knower to the known or a proportion between them which is not possible without the proportionality of the two.

On the first (view), knowledge falls under the category of modality, due to the accidentality of the form and its dependence on the rational (faculty), in which it is then a mode subsistent in it. My response is that, if the form is related to the accident, it is necessarily an accident; for the form of an accident is an accident necessarily. But if it is related to a substance, then controversy turns on this point. Most (philosophers) have said that (the soul) is an accident too, despite the fact that, even if it is a paradigm of substance and corresponds to it, it still needs a subject for its constitution, seeing that it seems to exist upon (the body's) cessation, and whatever is in need of a subject cannot be a subject.

Others have asserted (the soul's) substantiality on the grounds that the form and the bearer of the form are identical in reality. The form of the substance, then, can only be a substance, due to the necessary correlation of forms and their concomitants. Still others have held that it is both substance and accident in two respects; its substantiality being reducible to its being equal to the substance of which it is a paradigm and is similar to it; whereas its accidentality is reducible to the fact that it requires a subject. Thus there is no objection to its having both characters.

This is the case regarding the particular forms, but with respect to universal forms the difficulty is more acute; insofar as they are both universal and immaterial. Thus applying the term accidentality to them is most complicated. Some have posited the existence of spiritual accidents and accordingly have allowed their attribution to spiritual entities, so that those universal forms could be regarded as spiritual accidents, subsisting in an immaterial soul. Then their immateriality would depend on the immateriality of their substratum, rather than their very structure. This account is close to the preceding principles regarding the modalities of psychology.

(As regards) the second view, it belongs to the category of passivity, because it is in itself, while the third belongs to the category of relation, since it refers exclusively to the relation between the knower and the known. However, each party has a series of proofs which are mentioned in the extensive treatises of the various parties.

If this is granted, then we hold that absolute science, whatever its type, is divisible rationally and exclusively into conception and assent.[2] It is generally recognized by the learned that knowledge is divisible into the above-mentioned two categories. Some authoritative scholars have said that we should not apply this division to absolute knowledge. For absolute knowledge is not susceptible

1. *al-Mabda' wa'l-ma'ād.*
2. Or judgment, Arabic *taṣdīq*.

of this division, because some of its parts do not fall within this division, such as the Necessary Being's knowledge of Himself and of other things: According to the generality of illuminationists[1] and most authoritative scholars, it does not fall under either category, for even knowledge of each one of us of oneself is not divisible into conception and assent. For that knowledge in both cases, by way of illumination of presence, does not fall under either of the two categories, because it does not depend on the presence of the form or is conditioned by it. That which is divisible into conception and assent is that part of our knowledge which bears on the knowledge of what is other than ourselves and is part of absolute science. Thus the division of absolute science into these two categories is not sound according to them, but is sound according to those who regard science in general as impossible without the intermediary of the form, as is the case with the knowledge of the Necessary Being or other things. (You should take note of this!) However, the apprehension of entities inhering in the rational faculty alone, by summoning its forms only, is tantamount to naïve conception, not accompanied by judgment; whereas apprehension accompanying the judgment positively is the act of asserting the judgmental relation positively or negatively, which consists in abstracting it. This is assent, which has no further subdivision, according to the process of real disjunction made up of two parts and is known rationally.

There is no objection to this division on either of the two views mentioned above, due to the difference of the principle of division and its parts. For the first principle of division according to the first view is passivity and according to the second relation, each one of which is different from both parts necessarily. The only objection bears on the first view, which is the best known and consists in showing that knowledge, according to them, is identical with the form and that conception consists in the acquisition of the forms. It follows that each part of the division will entail the other, despite the fact that that conception is the counterpart of assent and consists in the acquisition of the form, which is identical with the principle of division, as you see. This is obviously false, since the principle of division must differ for each of its parts. The only way out of this difficulty is to show that conception does not consist in acquiring the forms, which is the first part of division, but rather is the counterpart of assent. It consists in acquiring the forms conditioned by the absence of judgment; whereas assent consists in its acquisition, as conditioned by judgment, the principle of division being the absolute form which is independent of both counterparts. Then that principle will not be part of either part. In other words, the principle will be shown to be the essence of absolute knowledge; I mean the essence taken unconditionally. The two parts would then be, first the essence without any judgment, which is naïve conception, or the essence of knowledge conditioned by the absence of judgment; the second being the essence conditioned

1. *Ishrāqī* sages.

by something which is assent, which is the essence of knowledge conditioned by judgment. (This should not be difficult to follow.)

Accordingly, assent would involve four factors: (a) the object of judgment which is the form, (b) what is judged by it, which is the description involved in it, (c) the relation between the two and the judgment itself. None of the three enters into the essence of assent, but neither is identical with judgment, while the three conceptions constitute three conditions on which its acquisition depends in a conditional way. Then, it would be simple and would have no part. This is the view of the authoritative *mutakallimūn*, the philosophers and the logicians. Rāzī[1] and his followers held that (the essence of assent) consists in the four factors on which it depends conditionally. Therefore, it will consist of all of these, as will be explained in logic.

He says that reflection (*fikr*) consists in passing from certain matters already present in the mind to another matter sought. The first are called principles, the second enquiries. (The author) says this is the definition chosen by Khwājah Naṣīr al-Dīn[2] in his critique of *al-Muḥaṣṣal*[3] in connection with the definition of speculation (*naẓar*), with additional rectification. For (Rāzī) states in it that reflection is the transition from certain matters present in the mind to matters sought out, which are the intended matters. Ṭūsī objects that what is present (in the mind) is a simple matter, which is the conclusion and therefore it is not multiple. That is why he has rejected it, substituting for it 'a matter sought out'. From the preferred view of the author it is apparent that the conclusion of speculation is a simple thing, in accordance with the view of the authorities, who hold that assent is simple, and that conceptions are its constituents. According to what Ṭūsī[4] has said, the conclusion is a series of multiple matters which accords with the view that assent is a composite of which conceptions are a part, just as Rāzī and his followers have held.

It follows that what Ṭūsī[5] has maintained is sound and is not open to objections. However it is not known that he subscribed to Rāzī's view of assent. It may be said, however, that if this is the definition he chose in criticizing *al-Muḥaṣṣal*, he was subscribing to the view of its author. For, since most scholars have disagreed with Rāzī, his successors have chosen the common view, holding that the conclusion is a simple matter. (You should ponder this!)

In any case, it is better than the definition attributed to the ancient philosophers, to the effect that assent consists in the arrangement of certain matters in order to attain something unknown, insofar as it is more specific than speculation. For it is a definition of speculation involving a simple movement; I mean the transition

1. Fakhr al-Dīn Rāzī (d. 1209) author of *al-Muḥaṣṣal* referred to later.
2. Ṭūsī (d. 1274).
3. A work of Fakhr al-Dīn Rāzī.
4. Original al-Khwājah.
5. Ibid.

from principles to objects sought, without conceiving those objects. This is far less common in considering speculations; for it is more common to pass from the objects sought to the principles than from this principle to those principles. None of this, however, is involved in the above divisions, contrary to what we have chosen, which involves both movements simultaneously, one of which is indicated by the definition, which is the second transition, as is clear. As for the first transition, I mean, passing from the objects sought to the principles, as the definition necessarily implies, where he says 'a matter acquired', in reference to seeking. The intent, then, is that he has passed to a matter which he sought which is possible only after conceiving it, since it is impossible to seek the absolutely unknown. Ṭūsī[1] has responded to Rāzī's[2] objections to the ancients that argument is too general to be preceded by the conception of objects sought first. Otherwise the definition would include both parts; that is both the least and the most. This rests on the notion that what comprises the one movement is part of the two divisions of speculation, otherwise the definition would not be all-inclusive. The words of Rāzī imply clearly that the lesser (of the two parts) is not involved in it. That is why he confines definition to the more general, since what belongs to the one movement is a matter of intuition, and is therefore restricted to people of holy faculties.

I say that confirming the superiority of either of the two definitions rests on the question whether speculating about the one movement may be truly designated as reflection or is a species thereof, on one hand; or rather that it is excluded by reason of the fact that it is designated by a specific name, which is intuition, on the other. Thus, if the term speculation or reflection is applied to it, that would be purely figurative. For, on the first supposition, the definition of the ancients would be sounder and better, because it comprises both parts and species of speculation; while on the second supposition, it would be false since it would then be more general than the defined, on the supposition that we understood it in the sense of the absolute which comprises both parts. If, however, we understand it in the more specific sense, it would define that which is not speculation and then the definition of Rāzī and the second explanation would be better and sounder than that of the ancients, insofar as it excluded what is not speculation, and is then fully comprehensive, whereas on the first assumption, it would not be sound. For it would be then more specific than speculation, considering that definition on the basis of the more specific is not acceptable, according to the well-informed. Moreover, we say that on the first definition its essence would be arrangement or transition, regardless of whether it is plural or singular; and then on the view of Rāzī,[3] its essence would be transition and arrangement.

He has also stated that knowledge is necessary due to the necessity of gratitude to the Gracious Giver, since warding off fear cannot be achieved without it, and

1. Original 'Allāmah.
2. Original al-Muḥaqqiq.
3. al-Muḥaqqiq.

since it is not necessary, due to the fact that (knowledge) is not necessary and doesn't arise at the inception of nature and is attended by controversy, so that it would then be necessary by virtue of the fact that the absolutely necessary is not possible without it.

The (author) says that by absolute, he means that whose necessity entails the necessity of a condition, which he excluded from the conditioned, by which we mean that whose necessity does not entail the acquisition of its condition. For the condition would then be a restriction of its necessity, contrary to the absolute, whose condition is not a restriction of its necessity, since it is absolutely necessary and thus its necessity does not require the acquisition of that on which it depends. Moreover, knowledge contingent on speculation is not restricted by its occurrence, so that its necessity would be dependent on its occurrence, but rather its necessity entails that necessity and the obligation to acquire it. Otherwise, it would entail that the obligation to do the impossible or denying that it is absolutely necessary, assuming that the obligation to seek it without presupposing the acquisition of its premises, is granted.

(Rāzī's) statement that it is the cause of its being achieved just as is the case with other causes may be countered by saying that, although speculation is a condition of knowledge, it is in fact one of the causes leading to it. For, the condition could be a cause or not, speculation in relation to knowledge being both condition and cause. The reason is that speculation generates knowledge, just as other causes generate their effects. Thus knowledge results from it by way of generation. It is therefore the cause of its coming to be, according to the Muʿtazilī view, just as the movement of the key is generated by the motion of the hand, and as the concept of causes determining their effect presupposes. Al-Ashʿarī[1] by contrast held that knowledge is created by God as a sequel of (speculation) in accordance with the principles of habituation, just as is the case with respect to other habits. He bases this view on the negation of the fact that causes determine their effects and that God has established the habit that effects are created whenever what we suppose is their cause comes to pass. For instance, burning is the sequel of contact with fire, satiety the sequel of drinking water, and so on. For according to them,[2] there is no determinant in the world other than God Almighty.

By contrast, the philosophers have held that speculation is a cause which disposes the mind to receive the emanations for the Active Intellect.[3] Therefore, knowledge ensuing upon speculation is not generated by it, according to them; it simply disposes the mind to receive those emanations. Knowledge is then emanated to the mind once it is disposed to turn towards the Active Principles. The difference between their view and that of the Ashʿarites is that (knowledge)

1. Abu'l-Ḥasan al-Ashʿarī (d. 935) founder of the Ashʿarī theological movement.
2. i.e. the Ashʿarites.
3. This was the view of Ibn Sīnā (d. 1037) and his followers.

is necessary according to the philosophers and contingent, according to the Ash'arites.

(Rāzī) also states that 'proof is that, knowledge of which necessitates knowledge of some other matter'. (The author) comments that he says a 'matter', rather than a thing, as is generally assumed so as to include both the non-existent and the existent. For the object of proof could be either existent or non-existent, whereas a thing can only be existent due to the congruence of existence and thingness, and then the definition would not be all-inclusive. But when he said a matter, he included everything.

I say this holds on the view of those who say that the non-existent is not a thing; but for those who say that the non-existent is a thing,[1] the definition is all-inclusive, or it might be said that the non-existent, once it is an object of thought, must be conceived by the mind and then it will be a thing existing in the mind and accordingly will be included in the definition,[2] which is general.

The above definition has also been objected to on the grounds that, if he meant by it the clear definition, then the three modes of proof[3] would be excluded, but if he meant the unclear, then the first would be excluded and if the common mode, then common terms will have to be used in the definition, which is not allowed.

It may be objected that exclusivity is not allowed, because it rests on the notion that the necessary is a term common to both what is clear and what is not. The truth is that the matter is different, because (the definition) is applied in reality for the element common to both. Therefore, it is not necessary to exclude one to the two terms, nor use what is common to both.

Ṭūsī also says that (the definition) could be purely rational or purely transmitted.

(The author) comments that one instance thereof is that the wine-drinker commits a grave sin. Now everyone who commits a grave sin deserves punishment, on the grounds that deserving punishment is a matter of oral transmission.[4] As for his adding 'or made up of both', it may be illustrated by reference to marrying two sisters, which the Prophet has prohibited, and whatever the Prophet has prohibited is prohibited.[5] Here, the major premise is rational, since it depends on the truthfulness of the Prophet, which is rationally known.

As for his inferring from a cause the effect thereof or vice versa, and from either of two effects its counterpart; the first being of the type *why* and the other *that* ...[6] (The author) says an instance of the first is inferring the incidence of burning

---

1. That is, the Mu'tazilites.
2. That is the definition Rāzī rejected as above.
3. The three modes of proof in Aristotelian logic.
4. *Samī'ī*, that is, based on what is reported on the authority of the Qur'ān.
5. *Ḥarām*.
6. This corresponds to the distinction in Aristotelian logic between proof by reference to the fact (that) and by the reason of the fact (*li-mā*).

from contact with fire, which is called proving by reason of the fact, since it implies recourse to inference and existence at the same time on the part of the one who reasons. An instance of the second is inferring contact with fire from the fact of burning and is called factual, because it implies that the judgment is made by the speaker, but not in the thing itself; for it is caused in reality by what is its cause in the act of inferences. An instance of the third is inferring from the light the existence of the day, since they are both caused by a simple cause, which is the rising of the sun. It is called factual also, by reason of the fact that it is merely a cause of inference. From this it can be asserted that from the non-existence of the effect, the non-existence of the cause may be inferred. For even if it is not the non-existence of the cause objectively, it could still be regarded as its cause conceptually, insofar as the non-existence of the effect is clearer to reason than the non-existence of the cause. Hence we infer from the non-existence of the effect the non-existence of the cause. For inferring the non-existence of the cause from the non-existence of the effect is a factual proof; whereas, conversely, inferring the non-existence of the effect from the non-existence of the cause is proof by reason of the fact, insofar that the middle term in the demonstration must be the cause of the assent to the judgment, which is the desired point. Otherwise it would not be a demonstration of that point, even if it be also a cause for confirming that judgment externally. That demonstration is then by reason of the fact; otherwise it is factual regardless of whether the middle term is the effect of the confirming of the judgment externally or not. The first is called proof,[1] but whether the second is so called is denied, although the authorities hold that it is a proof.

The reason why they are called factual and by reason of the fact is that by reason of the fact is equivalent to causality; whereas factuality is a matter of actuality. Thus the demonstration 'by reason of the fact' denotes the causality of judgment, mentally and externally. It was designated as the reason *why*,[2] which denotes causality; whereas demonstration by reference to *that*[3] denotes the causality of judgment mentally, but not externally; since it denotes the certainty of judgment in the mind, but not outside the mind. As to what its cause might be is not indicated. That is why it has been given the name that[4] which denotes positive actuality. The Shaykh[5] says in *al-Shifā'* that certain knowledge of whatever has a cause is possible to the extent its cause is known. He surmised from this that factual knowledge cannot be a demonstration, because the knowledge of the conclusion as certain is considered a part of the demonstration. Therefore, according to his claim, certainty is not possible unless the inference is drawn by means of the cause. This is a weak surmise,

1. Arabic *dalīl*.
2. *li-mā*.
3. *anna*.
4. Ibid.
5. Ibn Sīnā (d. 1037) author of *al-Shifā'*.

for he has confirmed judgment to what has a cause; but with respect to that which has no cause he allowed factual demonstration only. For he says that if the larger belongs to the smaller for no reason but merely for itself, but its existence is not self-evident and the intermediate is similar, although its existence is not self-evident either. Moreover, the existence of the larger is self-evident as far as the intermediate is concerned. Thus, we will have an apodictic demonstration of the factual type and not by reason of the fact.

From (Ibn Sīnā's) words, that if there is no cause for the certainty of the judgment externally, which can be demonstrated factually by recourse to the cause of the judgment or something else (which the Shaykh [Ibn Sīnā] in fact does not deny but rather affirms), the conclusion would be that factual demonstration does not yield certainty in some cases. However, with respect to what has a cause, it does not yield certainty always, but only with respect to what has no cause. (So consider his words!) He also says that it is possible for an existent to denote its like or non-existent as well; while a non-existent may denote a non-existent like it or an existent, too. (1) An instance of the first is inferring from the existence of life the existence of knowledge. (2) An instance of the second is inferring from the existence of one of two opposites, the non-existences of the other. (3) An instance of the third is inferring from the non-existence of life the non-existence of knowledge. (4) Finally, an instance of the fourth is inferring from the non-existence of one of two opposites the existence of the other.

He then says that from purely reported statements no demonstration is possible, because (demonstration) must be formed from certain propositions; although some have said it can be so formed, despite the fact that it must terminate in rational premises, just as the speculative (proof) which terminates in the necessary.

(The author) says it has been questioned whether proof by report can be regarded as demonstration conducive to certainty or not. Fakhr al-Dīn Rāzī has denied this, saying that it does not, holding that it rests on premises which are all conjectural, and whatever rests on conjecture is conjectural. The proof of this is that its validity rests on the infallibility of the reporters. Guarding against error in grammar, conjugation and language and the absence of abrogation, implication, allegory, specification, community, rational and oral protest, advancing and retarding—all these are conjectural matters, which do not yield certainty.

Rāzī,[1] has objected that we know absolutely that it yields (certainty), as in the words of the Almighty, 'Say, He is God the only One'[2] due to the certainty of divine oneness, and we also know the absence of all those things mentioned absolutely, most of the sound[3] verses in the Qur'ān being of this type.

1. Original al-Muḥaqqiq.

2. Qur'ān 112:1.

3. In Qur'ān 3:7, Qur'ānic verses are divided into 'precise' or 'sound' (*muḥkamāt*) or 'ambiguous' (*mutashābihāt*). Only the former are regarded as certain or indisputable.

I say it will be seen from his words that decisive knowledge is based on sound expression that it negates all other things in it and they are ascertained upon the acquisition of that knowledge. For knowing that they are negated is drawn from the certainty of their soundness, not that their certainty is drawn from the knowledge of their negation so as to depend on it, so that the knowledge would be conjectural, as Rāzī imagined. In fact, the truth is the reverse, because the assertion in most cases is well determined. Yet, had he said that this invalidates some forms of knowledge by hearsay, his case would be strong.

It is also said that such (reported knowledge) does not yield certainty unless it finally reaches reason, because it depends on the truthfulness of the reporter, which is a rational proposition. Now, once it reaches reason, it ceases to be purely reported knowledge and is said by some to actually yield certainty, although it is stipulated that it must reach reason and although the necessity of reaching it does not change its status as reported knowledge. For theoretical knowledge conducing to necessity does not cause its reaching (reason) from being theoretical. The same is true of reported knowledge; otherwise it would not be possible to construct a demonstration from purely theoretical data, since it must terminate in necessity.

Now, were its termination in necessary knowledge to entail that it is not theoretical, then the term demonstration would not apply except to that which is made up of two necessary premises. But convention rejects this and therefore this one principle would apply to reported knowledge too. Moreover, were it necessitated by its being purely non-theoretical, then it would have to be negated. But just as the term theoretical is not negated from it, the purely reported would not be negated of that which is made up of two reported premises, due to the necessity of its terminating in what is purely rational, while being reported without any difference.

(Rāzī's) statement that knowledge is not acquired by imitation, because it circulates among people without gaining any probability, and because two contradictory propositions will result from granting it, add to this that the Messenger[1] is commanded to know. It follows that others are so commanded by way of example; the first obligation, it is said, being knowledge. However, it is also said to consist in speculation, without which knowledge is not possible; or to consist in seeking it, since speculation is a voluntary act without which knowledge is not possible.

(The author) says there has been some disagreement as to what is the primary obligation of the responsible believer. Most theologians (*mutakallimūn*) have stated that the first obligation is knowledge, because everything else is contingent on it, so that the necessarily obligatory is really knowledge. It is this that 'Alī,[2] peace on him, intended in his saying that 'the beginning of religion is knowledge'. Others have said that the first obligation is speculation, because knowledge depends on it, so that it should be antecedent to it. A third scholar has said that it begins with the

1. Or the Prophet Muḥammad.
2. That is, Imam 'Alī ibn 'Abī Ṭālib.

intention to speculate, which is a voluntary act, any voluntary act being preceded by intention. Therefore, speculation should be preceded by intention and is therefore obligatory prior to it. Should you say that it follows from the universal first premise that intention should be preceded by intention, since it is a voluntary act too and should depend on it too, which would lead to an infinite regression, I would answer that the minor premise is excluded. For intention is not one of the voluntary acts, since the will cannot be willed, and therefore it does not follow that intention should be preceded by intention. The juridical traditionalists[1] have held that all obligations depend on intention, except will and speculation, which defines the necessity of knowledge, for fear of (infinite) regression. Some have said that the first obligation is absolute because what is sought in speculation cannot be something known, due to the impossibility of proving the obvious; nor unknown, due to the absurdity of the soul seeking what is does not feel. Therefore it is necessary that the (object of speculation) should be known in some respect, while its acquisition and perfect conception or the affirmation and negation of judgment are open to doubt, and then speculation would be preceded by doubt. (Rāzī) has objected to this on the grounds that the above-mentioned doubt, which may precede speculation, is not intended but takes place without the choice of the religiously responsible. Therefore it is not feasible and cannot be the object of obligation.

I say that this objection applies to those who speak of intention. For, although it precedes speculation, it does not entail its necessity, because it is not a voluntary act. Otherwise intention would depend on it, as already mentioned, and then it would not be one of the obligations, unless we say that it is a voluntary act and then it will be what it is.

Rāzī has spoken well in detail here; for he says that if by primary obligations is meant what is necessary in itself and by virtue of the first intention, it would then consist in the knowledge of God necessarily, because it is intended essentially and everything else, whether speculation or intention, would be intended accidentally. If the obligatory haphazardly is meant, then it undoubtedly refers to intended speculation, because it precedes everything; and then the dispute would be solved.

He also states that being and not-being are indefinable, because they are known intuitively and therefore are simple and have no genus or differentia. Judging their contradiction intuitively therefore depends on the knowledge of their essence, assent being always preceded by conception.

(The author) says that he[2] started to investigate being and not-being and to show that they are necessary and do not require acquisition. However, controversy has raged over this question, the ancient philosophers and the *mutakallimūn* holding that they are known by acquisition and can be defined and described like any other essences, giving some weak definitions thereof which will be mentioned later.

1. al-Uṣūliyyūn.
2. Rāzī.

As to authoritative scholars, they have maintained that they do not require definition because they are known intuitively and so do not need to be acquired, while differing on whether their intuitiveness is known intuitively or requires acquisition. Rāzī and his followers have chosen the second view, saying that (being and not-being) are intuitive, knowledge of their intuitiveness being dependent on acquisition, which implies that the conception of being and not-being, as described externally by intuition, does not require knowledge of what intuition is, so as to demonstrate it and ensure that knowledge is gained by it. The majority of scholars, however, subscribe to the first view, the author inclining to this view in his statement that they are intuitively known, etc. For every reasonable person observes by himself the knowledge thereof;[1] since nothing is more obvious to him than the fact that he exists and that he is not divested of knowledge of absolute being and not-being, except insofar as they are the source of that judgment. For judgment depends on the conception of its components; but having been established that assent does not presuppose the knowledge of the object or the subject of judgment in reality, it does not follow from the affirmation of their judgment that conception of being and not-being in reality is possible. Admittedly, they are conceived in some sense of the term, but this is not the problem. It may also be answered that these disputations affect the seeker of proof, not the one drawing attention to it, whose procedure here is the second and therefore he need not be questioned. Now (being and not-being) being intuitive concepts whose intuitiveness is known intuitively, they do not need a formal or methodical definition and are instead simple essences, in so for as they are among the most general knowable concepts. In fact, nothing is higher than they so as to be subsumed under it, as the genus thereof; and then each one of them is distinguished by some differentia or other, so as to define or describe them. The fact is that they have no genus, because they are not included in any category, and since they have no genus, they will have no differentia, and whatever has no genus or differentia belongs to the category of simple knowables conceived by reason.

1. That is, being and non-being.

6

Mullā Ṣadrā

Ṣadrā al-Dīn Muḥammad ibn Ibrāhīm Shīrāzī known as Mullā Ṣadrā is one of the greatest of Islamic philosophers and the reviver of Islamic philosophy in Persia in the eleventh/seventeenth century. Because of his eminence, he was given the title of Ṣadrā *al-muta'allihīn* or 'foremost among the God-like philosophers'. Mullā Ṣadrā was born into an aristocratic family in Shiraz *c.*979/1571–1572 and received the best education possible in his city of birth, developing into a serious seeker of the truth while still very young. He exhibited great intellectual acumen and at the same time piety and strong love of God from his early days, characteristics that were to remain with him throughout his life. Having mastered Arabic and Persian, Qur'ānic studies and to the extent possible the 'intellectual sciences' (*al-'ulūm al-'aqliyyah*) in Shiraz, he set out for Isfahan which was then the great centre of intellectual activity and Islamic philosophy.

In Isfahan Mullā Ṣadrā studied for years with the founder of the School of Isfahan, Mīr Dāmād, and also with Bahā' al-Dīn 'Āmilī. It is not certain whether he also studied with Mīr Findiriskī, the third great intellectual figure of the day in Isfahan, or not. Soon Mullā Ṣadrā became a well-known philosopher himself and since he spoke and wrote plainly of philosophical subjects with a gnostic bent, he incurred the opposition of some of the more exoteric *'ulamā'*. Finding himself in a difficult political position and not wanting to repeat the events that befell Suhrawardī, he left Isfahan travelling to different cities and finally settling in the small village of Kahak near Qum where he spent some seven years—eleven years according to some—in contemplation, meditation and study.

It was at the invitation of the governor of Fārs, Allāhwirdī Khān, that Mullā Ṣadrā returned from Kahak to the city of his birth, Shiraz, where he was to spend the last decades of his life. There, a beautiful school called Madrasa-yi Khān, which still stands, was built for him, and students from all over Persia and even outside of Persia from as far away as Tibet, came to study with him. These years in Shiraz were the most productive period of his life as a writer when he wrote most of his books. Being the devout person that he was, Mullā Ṣadrā made the pilgrimage to Mecca on foot seven times and while on the seventh pilgrimage in 1050/1640 he died in Basra where he was buried.

Mullā Ṣadrā founded a school of Islamic philosophy called *al-ḥikmah al-muta'āliyah* (Transcendent Theosophy) and wrote over forty important works in both philosophy and the religious sciences including Qur'ānic commentaries. Except for one treatise, a few letters and some poems, all of his writings are in Arabic. His *magnum opus* is *al-Asfār al-arba'ah* (The Four Journeys) which is considered in Persia to this day the most advanced text for the study of Islamic philosophy. Mullā Ṣadrā also wrote a number of commentaries on earlier *mashshā'ī* and *ishrāqī* works. Among these, his glosses upon the commentary of Quṭb al-Shīrāzī on Suhrawardī's *Ḥikmat al-ishrāq* is particularly significant as an independent *ishrāqī* work and is therefore included in this section.

We shall deal fully with Mullā Ṣadrā and his *al-ḥikmah al-muta'āliyah* in the next volume of this *Anthology* where we hope to discuss the School of Isfahan. But even in the short introduction here, it is necessary to point out his vast influence in Persia and Muslim India although, strangely, not in the Ottoman world as was the case with such earlier figures as Suhrawardī and Dawānī. Mullā Ṣadrā trained a number of important students, such as Mullā Muḥsin Fayḍ Kāshānī and 'Abd al-Razzāq Lāhījī, students who, along with his numerous works, made possible the propagation of the teachings of the master. Mullā Ṣadrā's immediate students sometimes veiled his teachings because of unfavourable political circumstances, but nevertheless it is through them that the chain of teachers connects so many great masters of Islamic philosophy in Qajar, Pahlavi and contemporary Persia to the founder of *al-ḥikmah al-muta'āliyah.*

Fifty years ago Mullā Ṣadrā was hardly known in the West. Now, not only is there a veritable revival of his thought, and in fact of Islamic philosophy itself around his teachings in Persia, but he is also becoming well known both in other Islamic counties and in the West. Major international conferences on him have catalyzed activity in editing, analysing and translating his works into European languages, especially English and French. There is now even a journal published in English, entitled *Transcendent Philosophy,* that is dedicated primarily to the philosophy of Mullā Ṣadrā and its later development and interaction with other schools of thought including Western ones. The full significance of Mullā Ṣadrā in the philosophical scene in Persia during the past four centuries will, we hope, become clearer in the next volume of this work.

In this chapter we have included Mullā Ṣadrā's glosses upon the commentary of Suhrawardī's *Ḥikmat al-ishrāq*, these glosses being one of the most important works of the *ishrāqī* tradition.

S. H. Nasr

GLOSSES UPON THE COMMENTARY OF THE PHILOSOPHY OF ILLUMINATION

Taʿlīqāt ʿalā sharḥ ḥikmat al-ishrāq

Translated for this volume by Majid Fakhry from Mullā Ṣadrā', *Taʿlīqāt ʿalā sharḥ ḥikmat al-ishrāq*, ed. Muḥammad Mūsawī (Tehran, 1315 Sh./1936), pp. 37–48.

Exposition of the Conditions of Human Souls upon Departing their Bodies

1. He[1] says, may God sanctify his secret: 'As for the domination by the higher world, it is not corruptive (of the soul).'

Having said that the souls, upon contact with dominant lights, will experience pleasure and passion, he sensed that a question may arise here; namely how can they experience pleasure, while dominated and obliterated by the dominant arms of pride? He removed this difficulty by asserting that the dominance of the higher world is not corruptive of what lies beneath it. This is true of every world bound to it in point of perfection, completeness and unity, rather than in point of multiplicity, otherness and jealousy. For, it is characteristic of the vegetative and animal (souls), which are subordinated in man to the dominance of the rational faculty, that they are not corrupted by it, but are rather perfected and completed by the rational (faculty), insofar as they are bound to it by way of causality. The conjunctive bond of an entity consists in strengthening or perfecting it, unlike the vegetative and animal bonds that exist outside the human community. For the former two could be corrupted or nullified by virtue of difference and contrariety in relation to some of their faculties. The same is true of the forms of the elements that are subject to some natural power that perfects or completes them, as well as those which exist as distinct from or contrary to them or that which lies beneath them. In short, the dominance of the lower by the higher in this world could be either corrupting or perfecting thereof; whereas the dominance found in the higher world appears to be a cause of either reform or completion, but never of corruption except by accident. However, the discussion of (this subject) requires a lot of analysis and exposition conducive to prolixity.

2. His statement, 'sanctified by God's holiness' refers to what we mentioned regarding the total annihilation of souls and the repudiation of duality, since he does not say 'sanctioned by God's sanctification?'

3. He says, may his secret be sanctified: 'The cause of their manifestation conflicts in some higher isthmus.'[2]

---

1. That is, the author of *Ḥikmat al-ishrāq*, Shihāb al-Dīn al-Suhrawardī (d. 1191).
2. *Barzakh*, plural *barāzikh*. Suhrawardī regards material bodies as isthmuses or compounds

Those ideal and suspended forms do not need a receptive bearer, but only an agent. If that agent happens to be a psychic faculty attached to matter, it would need, in order to arise, a determinant, such as an instrument or the like. If it happens to be a faculty independent of matter, such as pure reason, or one attached to the world of shadows beneath the world of matter, it would need, in order to arise, a determinant or cause of manifestation drawn from this world, due to its independent being. For an independent being is externally independent in point of origination and invention (as he has explained), according to his desire and wish. However, we have refuted elsewhere the view of some scholars, which the Shaykh (Ibn Sīnā) has described in *al-Shifā'* as apparently true, and described its upholder as one who is not careless in speech, in the context of his assertion that souls which are perfect in knowledge might cling to some heavenly bodies and become subjects of their imaginations. True, there is no objection to saying that some human souls might have the same status as souls which manage some of the spheres, while others have the same status as that soul, whose sphere is higher than that sphere or lower than it; so that one might say 'Īsā (peace on him) occupies the fourth sphere while Mūsā (peace on him) occupies the sixth.

4. He says: 'And it belongs to it to originate the ideal entities and the power at the same time.'

You should know that those who have fully ascertained this position are able to assert corporal resurrection without undue hardship or toil. The proof is that the soul, just as it is able by virtue of its rational faculty to acquire intelligibles and to possess them actually without the assistance of the body, does not require any corporal matter, thanks to its imaginative faculty and its imaginative activities, as you have learned from us earlier. For, if the soul, upon departing the lower world, still retains its estimative[1] faculty which apprehends particular notions and corporal forms, by means of the imagination and the imaginative faculty; then it is able to apprehend by itself or by means of that faculty certain corporal matters whose cognitive and imaginative apprehension is identical with its essential existence. The reason is the conjunction of its faculties in a single faculty which is the imagination and its lack of diversification or concern for what the senses receive from various sources, as well as the absence of its obsession with the management of the physical body and what distracts it of the accidents of that physical and material mode of existence, which is constantly in renewal and flux. For, once all its faculties have been reduced[2] to a single faculty which is the faculty of picture-forming or representation, its imaginative activity will become identical with sensation and its imaginative perception identical with its sensuous perception.

---

of both light and darkness, or (objects separating them).

1. *al-Wāhimah.*
2. Upon death.

Similarly its hearing, smelling, and tasting and imaginative touch, which are all sensuous and amount to five in appearance occupying different positions, are all in reality a single common sense internally. This is confirmed by what the Master Shaykh (Ibn Sīnā) has stated in *al-Taʿlīqāt* (The Appendices, or Glosses) to the effect that 'the souls of plants influence our souls, but our souls do not influence them, because they do not have multiple faculties, whereas our faculties are multiple, some of those faculties barring other faculties from performing their work in full, as they bar the imaginative faculty from performing its work in full. When they are not so barred, their work is performed in full, as happens in the case of a sleeper. The faculties of the planets, by contrast, are not barred by each other; that is why their action emanates from them in full, their faculties not being multiple; but are rather like a single faculty. The visual faculty in them is the same as the hearing and is identical with the picturing faculty. That is why those faculties amount to a single faculty which is able to influence us, while we cannot influence it.' (This is where his words end and their support of what we are holding is clear.)

As for his words 'as in the case of the sleeper', no one should understand by them that the action of the imagination is fully perfect in the sense conceived with reference to them, without the impact of the other faculties. For that does not take place except after death, insofar as the sleeper is not entirely free of actions occupying the imagination, such as digestion, attraction, physical and psychic motions and the like. Otherwise sleep would be a form of other-worldly waking, to which the Commander of the Faithful,[1] (peace on him), refers in these words: 'People while they live are asleep; when they die they shall awake.'

If this is established, we will assent, as some eminent scholars have done, confirming what the Master Shaykh has reported in *al-Risālah al-adhawiyyah* (Epistle of Daybreak) on the authority of some learned scholars that, when a man dies, his soul departs fully conscious of itself, accompanied with the imaginative faculty, which apprehends particulars, but not by way of impression or receptivity, but rather by way of invention and activity (as we have ascertained), then it imagines itself departing the lower world and imagines its body as identical with the buried dead person in form, and apprehends the pains which affect it in the form of sensuous punishments, according to what the religious laws have described. This in fact is the 'torture of the grave'. If, however, that soul happens to be felicitous, it will imagine itself in a convenient way and encounter the promised states in accordance with what it used to believe in life, with respect to such things as gardens, rivers, groves, boys, children, wide-eyed beauties[2] and the full cup. This is the 'reward of the grave'. That is why (the Prophet) has said: 'The grave is either one of the gardens of paradise or one of the ditches of fire.' The real grave is one of those states and the punishment and reward of the grave are as we mentioned;

1. ʿAlī ibn Abī Ṭālib (d. 661).
2. Houris.

the second genesis consisting in the soul's emergence from these conditions, just as the embryo emerges from the solid abode,[1] as the Almighty has said: 'Say: "He who originated them the first time will bring them back to life and He has knowledge of every creation".' (Qur'ān 36:79)

5. He says: 'The various types of food will be brought forward.'

Everything which man relishes and desires in the Abode of Paradise will be brought forward and will be available to him, according to what you have learned with respect to the fact that their imaginative existence is identical with their sensuous existence. The difference between the two modes of existence consists in the fact that, so long as the soul, occupied with the body, continues to cling to it in one of two ways, the first being that sensation is dependent on encountering the matter of sensation as something external to it, while, imagination consists in the mere production by the imaginative faculty of a form which does not exist outside the faculty of apprehension. The second is that the sensible object is more potent and more obvious than the imagined object and has a greater impact in terms of pleasure or pain. In the Hereafter those two differences are removed; in fact in the Hereafter matters are stronger in their existence and more easily acquired, due to their simplicity. They are also less liable to diffusion in material substrates, being similar to the core, while the latter are similar to dust and crust. It is true that the material existence of entities in this world is different from their concepts and therefore its conception does not entail the same thing as its actual existence; whereas the actual existence of entities in the Hereafter is identical with their formal and intellectual existence. That is why the pleasure experienced in connection with the pleasurable thereof and the pain experienced in connection with the painful thereof is greater.

6. He says (may his secret be sanctified): 'And those forms are more perfect than what we have (in this world).'

Some metaphysical experts have said that man's enjoyment of pleasant pictures arises from their impressions on the imagination and sensation, rather than from their existence outside. For were they to exist outside, but did not exist in one's senses by impression, there would be no pleasure; whereas were the impression to remain in the sense faculty, while it has ceased outside, his pleasure would endure. As for the imaginative faculty, it has the power to invent forms in this world, but its invented forms are imagined and not sensed or imprinted on the visual faculty. That is why if one were to invent the most beautiful pictures and imagined them as present or observed, his pleasure would not increase; for he would not be actually observing them, as happens in sleep. Were the imagination capable of picturing them in the sensitive faculty, as it is in the imaginative, his pleasure would be great and the pictures would be equivalent to those that exist outside. His experience

1. The womb of the mother.

then would not be different from that of the Hereafter in this sense, except with respect to the power of representing the picture in question in the visual faculties; and then everything he desires will be present to him at once. His desire could then be due to his imagination and his imagination to the visual faculty; that is, due to its impression in that faculty. Then, nothing desirable occurs to him but will come to be present at once; that is exist before him so that he can see it. To this (the Prophet), may God bless him and his folk, refers in his saying: 'There is in Paradise a market where pictures are sold'; the market here being a reference to divine grace which is the source of the power to create pictures at will, wherein the impression in the visual faculty would be permanent so long as it is desired and is not subject to cessation involuntarily, as happens in sleep in this world. That power is vaster and fuller than the power of production of what exists outside the senses; for that which exists outside the senses does not exist in two places. That is why when it is observed by one viewer, it becomes hidden from another, while the (other-worldly) type continues to expand without limit or obstruction. The occurrence of other-worldly matters is vaster in scope and more satisfying.

These are his[1] words, which we find to be the closest of the words of learned and eminent scholars to ascertaining corporal resurrection. However, they do not attain the level of true perfection or the desired goal; for they still require some further completing and perfecting, based on certain premises which neither he nor anybody else has grasped. We will show you shortly that neither he not his peers have been able, in point of affirmative demonstration, to prove corporal resurrection and the realization of the promised other-worldly forms, except to the extent they are attached to some heavenly body or material appearance, or are interpreted in pure rational terms.

The (above-mentioned) premises and principles are actually numerous and we have discussed each one of them in the right place. These include:

1. *That the existence of every reality is that which exists externally; essence is consequent on it and is united to it in some form of union.*

2. *Existence is susceptible of intensity or debility in itself.*

3. *Essential existence is capable of intensity and perfectibility, as well as procession from a natural mode of generation to a higher one.*

4. *The form of every compound is equivalent to its fundamental reality or essence.* Matter, by contrast, is the substratum of its possibility and the power to exist, but has nothing to do with its substantive reality. The same is true of the ultimate differentia of everything which has a variety of genera[2] and differentiae, such as man for instance, and which amounts to its fundamental identity and essence. As for other things called differentiae or genera, they are simply its external accessories or

---

1. That is, Suhrawardī's.

2. In Aristotelian logic the genus (plural genera) is the class to which an entity such as man belongs, whereas the differentia is what sets him apart from other entities.

accretions that it requires as far as its external and material generation is concerned. If speculation is trained on that form in itself it will be found to constitute the source of the existence of those accessories and the essence of aggregation, as far as the essence is concerned, its essence is what confirms all its connotations.

5. *The essence of the body and its individuation are due to the soul.* If its parts change as happens in the course of the individual's life; and if this body is replaced by a risen body at the Resurrection, while the soul remains the same, (the individual) remains the same in point of his psychic form: and thus this individual is not the same as the other in point of matter, both statements being true.[1]

6. *What we have asserted and proved to the effect that the imaginative faculty is an entity distinct from the matter of the body.*

7. *Imaginative forms are not impressed on the imagination, but rather subsist in it in the same way a thing subsists in its agent rather than its patient.*

8. *The form perceived in itself exists without being impressed on an external matter or a visual organ, in accordance with what was mentioned to the effect that vision is not a matter of radiation travelling towards an external object or making an impression on the eye.* Nor its it a relation of the soul to what lies outside, but is rather the emergence of form within the soul, emanating from the worldly illumination of reason when the organ is sound and the right conditions are fulfilled. This illuminative relation extends from the soul to that apprehensive and luminous form, rather than the external and material form which is dark in itself, as the author contends. In this world, there is no difference between vision or imagination, except insofar as the former necessarily requires a corporal organ, as well as the corporal matter of vision, which is not required in the act of imagining. However, when the soul departs this world and the body is separated from it, the imaginative faculty; I mean, the guardian of common sense, having been deprived of the element of potentiality, imperfection or deficiency and has actually become perfect in point of retention and action—it would have become in itself the principle of vision, hearing, taste, smell and touch, without requiring a multitude of different, external organs. At that point apprehending desirable objects and the power to find them would become one thing, emanating from a single faculty, which is the essence of the animal, imaginative soul. The proof that Shaykh al-Ghazzālī[2] and other adepts of official wisdom have not grasped the nature of corporal resurrection and the proof that quantitative forms exist perceptibly in no substratum or associated with any phenomenon of this world, is that he has stated in his work of *al-Maḍnūn bihi ʿalā ghayr ahlihi* (What Should be Withheld from the Unworthy) to the effect: 'You might possibly say that those sensuous and imaginative pleasures which are promised in paradise, cannot be apprehended except by means of the corporal and

1. The meaning appears to be that although identical with respect to his soul, the individual would be different with respect to this changed body.

2. Abū Ḥamīd Ghazzālī (d.1111).

imaginative faculty. Now those corporal faculties cannot be imagined as generated except by the body. The same is true of the "tortures of the grave" and of hellfire which cannot be apprehended except through corporal faculties; but when the spirit leaves the body, its parts dissolve and the sensitive and imaginative faculty ceases. How then can that be demonstrated?'

You should know that this is rejected by those who repudiate corporal resurrection and assert the impossibility of the soul's reunion with the body. However, there is no real proof of its impossibility; and in fact it is not too far-fetched to assume that some heavenly bodies may be provided for the soul's imagination and sensation following death and resurrection. What the ancients have advanced in support of its impossibility does not constitute a real proof, since the holy law[1] has mentioned it, so that it ought to be believed.

The proof that this has not been demonstrated by the philosophers is that the foremost modern philosopher, Abū ʿAlī ibn Sīnā, has demonstrated this in both *al-Najāt* (Salvation) and *al-Shifā'* (Healing) where he says: 'It is not excluded that some heavenly bodies might have been created in order to enable the soul to partake of imagination after death.' He reports this on the authority of one whom he has praised highly and described as 'no risk-taker',[2] asserting that that this is not impossible. This shows that he is skeptical in this matter and has no proof in support of it; but were it really impossible, he would not have described its expositor as 'no risk-taker'. For what greater risk is there than asserting the impossible!

I say you should know regarding his position and that of the two masters, Abū ʿAlī (Ibn Sīnā) and Abū Naṣr (al-Fārābī), who is described as 'no risk-taker', that they did not proceed in their attempt to prove corporal resurrection beyond the possibility that some of the (heavenly) bodies of this world may be assigned to the imaginings of the promised forms of those imperfect souls only. The view of the author[3] also resembles what he[4] says and turns on, especially in *al-Talwīḥāt* (Allusions), where he has asserted that it is right; although what is mentioned on this point in this book[5] is closer to the truth. We praise God who has guided us to this, which we would not have been led to but for His guidance. To Him our thanks are due for His generosity and fullness of grace.

7. He says, may his secret be sanctified: 'They will be immortal therein, because of their enduring relation to the isthmuses.'

The Shaykh[6] has interpreted the immortality of the souls of the blessed who are intermediate in their blessedness, by stating that the subjects to which they

1. *al-Sharʿ* could also be translated as scripture.
2. The reference is to Abū Naṣr al-Fārābī (d. 950), as appears in the sequel.
3. That is, Suhrawardī.
4. Ibn Sīnā.
5. *Ḥikmat al-ishrāq*.
6. Suhrawardī.

cling, namely the heavenly bodies, are incorruptible. This is open to the following criticisms:

First, the clinging of the souls after departing the body to a heavenly body is wrong, as we have explained in our book, *al-Mabdaʾ waʾl-maʿād* (Beginning and Resurrection) and have referred to it earlier.

Second, you have learned that the forms accorded to the soul in the other world do not subsist in any of the external bodies, and the soul does not need, in order to contemplate forms brought before it, any object external to it, such as the mirror or its like in this world. For the need for a positive external instrument, such as the mirror, depends on the need for a corporal and physical organ, such as eyesight, and if not then not.

Third, bodies in this world, whether heavenly or elemental, do not endure by themselves for two moments, but only in relation to the species, due to the recurrence of material forms or their flux in accordance with the recurrence of similar types of succession for states and shapes. As for other worldly forms, by contrast, they are preserved in being by means of their preservation by those active principles which are free of potentiality and disposition, unlike material (forms) which depend on the occurrence of the passive motions of matter and the succession of their possibilities, as we have shown in the treatise which deals with the generation of the universe as a whole. If this is the case, there is no reason for interpreting the eternity of what exists in the other world or its permanence, by reference to the permanence of this world which is constantly renewed and is perishable and vain.

8. *He says: 'As for the heirs of misery who are...'*

You should know that God Almighty has made the substances of the souls different in essence, either with respect to the origin of nature or the acquisition of virtues or vices. Thus, some are good, luminous and noble, inclined to divine things, mightily desirous of contact with spiritual and rational entities, on which their resurrection depends; while others are base, dark and evil, inclined towards dense corporal entities. Still others are intermediate between goodness and wickedness, falling halfway between the rational and sensuous entities. The first group consists of the favoured and are the people of sanctity, their world being the world of reason and intelligibles; the second consists of the party of the left, the criminals and lowered chins, whose rank is that of inferior natures. The intermediate group consists of various classes diverging in subtlety or density, as the commentator has indicated, their world being the world of measurable forms that are absent to worldly senses, but not other worldly senses. They include, however, the felicitous and the 'people of the right'!

If this is established, you should know that some, like the author of the *Brethren of Purity*, and others, have held that Hell actually denotes the word of generation and corruption, while fire refers to that nature which destroys the bodies which dominate the figures and skins, by means of dissolution, alteration or dissention in the shortest time. However, sometimes the nutritive faculty replaces those bodies, as the Almighty says: 'Every time their skins are burnt, we will replace them by other skins, so that they might taste the punishment.' (Qur'ān 4:56); and as He also says: 'Then guard yourselves against the Fire whose fuel is men and stones, prepared for the unbelievers' (Qur'ān 2:24) and as He says: 'You and what you worship besides God are the fuel of Hell' (Qur'ān 21:98). Those elemental bodies have a nature that disposes of them through roasting and transformation. Therefore, they have assumed that the fire mentioned in the Qur'ān is that nature flowing through sensuous bodies, especially those beneath the lowest heaven. What confirms that assumption, which is false according to us as you have learnt, is the fact that all natural entities are transient and perishable and thus are subject to corruption due to their being dominated by nature, through management, alteration and dissolution. The same is true of the soul, so long as it clings to this (earthly) body and is united to it, being influenced by nature, both in itself and its sensuous faculties. It is actually affected by the impact of the fires of that nature which are latent in the body, in the form of dissipation, dissolution and the drying up of the good humidity which it receives from nutrition step by step continuously until death. The same applies to their view of the soul being affected by the heat of lust and the fire of anger and the like; as well as its suffering due to the incidence of pains, snakes (?) and hurts, whose origin is destructive nature. This nature was created by God for the sake of repelling corruptive elements, although the advantage in the original existence of nature and its stoking the instinctive head is actually the fulfilment of the rational soul of man, so long as it dwells in the body, and that by means of those changes and transformations, that he might return to his own people joyfully.

If man is lifted from this world to the world of conception and reasoning, he will be rid of the torment of the fires, since nature exists only in this world. What confirms their conjecture also is that the number of the demons and porters of Hell is the same as the number of the subservient faculties that manage animal bodies. The same is true of the fact that (Hell's) gates are seven, just as the gates of the natural faculties which open unto the hell of the body from the world of the soul are seven. For the origin of the faculties stems from their world and they are actually accessible to the people of Hell, whether humans or jinn; whereas the gate of the heart is closed in the face of those whose hearts God has marked. That is why they are described in the Qur'ān as the lowest of the low, elemented nature being the same; for Hell is nature.

He[1] has said in chapter ninety-one of *al-Futūḥāt* (Revelations): 'You should know that Hell is one of the greatest creations; for it is God's prison in the hereafter.' It was called Gehenna, because of its deep bottom. (We say *jahannam*[2] for deep bottom,

1. That is, Muḥyī al-Dīn ibn 'Arabī (d. 1240), author of *al-Futūḥāt al-Makkiyyah* (Meccan Revelations).

2. In Persian.

since it was deep-bottomed and contained hot and cold regions, both its cold and hot climates reaching their highest degree. Between its highest and lowest points seventy-five hundred years pass, as the Almighty's words indicate: 'And whenever it abates We shall rekindle its flames.' (Qur'ān 17:97). However, fire is sensuous and the fiery form is not described as more or less except insofar as it inheres in corporal matter. For the fiery reality does not conform to this description in itself, but only the body burning in fire which is subject to the fiery (power). It is said that the above verse means that whenever it abates, meaning the fire that affects their bodies (it is abated) through the cessation of desire or anger at the weakening of the faculties due to disease. 'We increased them', refers to those who suffer, since (the verse) does not say 'We increased it', in reference to torture, affecting their inner parts by being infected by habits or illnesses in their souls, which are worse than sensuous torture. For God incites in their inner parts reflection on what they used to neglect of God's commands. Thus their inner torture would be stronger than torture associated with sensuous fire burning their bodies. The source of the former torture is the fire of the 'soul commanding evil', which affects the hearts. To this the Almighty refers in these words: 'There is not one of you but will go down to it (i.e. the Fire). That is for your Lord a decree which must be accomplished. Then We shall deliver the righteous, and leave the wrongdoers therein on their knees.' (Qur'ān 19:71–72)

(Ibn 'Arabī) says in *al-Futūḥāt al-Makkiyyah*: 'Whoever understands the meaning of these words would understand the position of Hellfire. Had the Prophet said anything when he was asked, I would have said something myself, but having remained silent, saying later that only God knows, our silence in this case is the right thing.' Moreover, Fire is not well-received by any monotheist who knows his soul as it has attained the level of reason in act and has transcended the level of sense-perception and instinct, as one of the Imams (peace on them), has said upon being asked about the whole of the Almighty's statement: 'There is not one of you but will go down to it': 'We crossed it when it was not burning.' Add to this other statements which indicate that (Hell) lies in the lowest world, and those statements which indicate that it lies in the lowest heaven, as reported in reference to the account of the Prophet's ascent (*mi'rāj*) to heaven. For, he saw in the lowest heaven, Malik, the treasurer of Hell, who opened for him one of the paths of fire to look at, and so there reached him puffs of its smoke and flames to his left from the gate. It was also reported that Ibn 'Abbās has said: 'This fire (of Hell) lies beneath seven closed seas.'

Further evidence that the fire of Hell lies in the sea is what is reported about the Commander of the Faithful (peace on him) that he asked a Jew: 'Where does Fire lie according to your scripture?' The latter answered: 'In the sea', whereupon (the Commander of the Faithful)[1] said: 'I think that is right', for (the Qur'ān) says: By 'the roaring sea' (52:6). It is also reported in the commentaries (of the Qur'ān) that the 'roaring sea' is the fire; as is reported that the Messenger of God (may God bless him and his folk) has said: 'No one can ply the sea except as a raider or a pilgrim, because there is a fire beneath the sea.' Al-Tha'labī has reported in his commentary in reference to the Messenger of God that he said: 'There is in the sea fire upon fire.' It is also reported that some of the ancestors have said in reference to the Almighty's words: 'They urge you to hasten the punishment, Hell shall surely encompass the unbelievers (Qur'ān 29:54)', that Hell is the sea, that encompasses them within the planets, and spreads so it catches fire, becoming Hell thereby.

It is also reported that al-Dahhāk has said in reference to the Almighty's words: 'They were drowned and were hurled into the Fire (Qur'ān 71:25)': 'They are in a sad condition in the world and will the drowned on the one hand, and confounded on the other!'

There are many other interpretations of this condition which is also reported equally in the sayings of the ancients. Thus Socrates says: 'As for those who committed grave sins, they will be cast into Tartaros and will never come out if it. But those who repent from their sins throughout their life will only be cast into Tartaros to suffer for a whole year, then the waves will carry them to a place from which they will call their enemies, asking them to be content with punishment, so that they might be spared the other evils. If they are excused they will be saved; otherwise they will be returned to Tartaros and this will continue to be their lot until their enemies are willing to forgive them. As for those who have led a virtuous life, they will be rescued from those places in that land and will be spared life in those prisons and will inhabit the pure lands.'[2]

Other accounts imply that parts of Hell are located in this earth. It is reported that Jābir ibn 'Abd Allāh said: 'I have seen smoke coming out of the land of Dirar', and it is also said that he attended part of it. This is similar to the account of Barhūt valley reported on the authority of the Commander of the Faithful[3] who said: 'The most hateful region in the sight of God is Barhūt valley, where the spirits of the infidels are found, and also a well whose water is black and in which the spirits of the infidels are dispatched.' Al-Asmā'ī relates that a man from Hadramaut states that 'we smell from the direction of Barhūt a very terrible stink, and then we receive the news of the death of one of the leaders of the infidels.' It is also reported that the Messenger of God as part of the Eclipse Tradition, during the Eclipse prayer used to protect his face from the Fire by his hand and his robe, and was held up

1. 'Alī ibn Abī Ṭālib.

2. Quoted from Plato's *Phaedo*, 108a by al-Bīrūnī (d. 848) in his book *Taḥqīq mā li'l-Hind*. Tartaros is the Greek equivalent of Hell.

3. 'Alī ibn Abī Ṭālib.

from reaching his destination, while he prayed to God. There are other reports that indicate that (Hell) exists in this world.

The response to all those reports and indices is that both Paradise and Hell have an essential origin in the other world and a partial origin and multiple cosmic manifestations in this world; whereas the foundation of Hell, that is, its reality is the perishable world, but it has certain manifestations and hideouts in this world. What was mentioned as part of rational aspects does not prove more than that it has a partial mode of being and a specific appearance in this world. The same is true of the various accounts which do not indicate more than that it has certain manifestations in this world. As for the real Fire, its location and manifestation are such that the whole creation cannot ascertain, its mighty power being in the other life, where its mansions surround it. As (the Almighty) says: 'And Hell shall be exhibited to whoever can see' (Qur'ān 79:36) and: 'No, if only you knew with certainty; you would surely have perceived Hell. Then you will have perceived it with visual certainty.' (Qur'ān 5:7) It was therefore hidden, neither visible nor exposed, but rather concealed, except to people of disclosure[1] and certainty. This sensible part of Fire is not burning in reality; but what causes burning and disintegration in truth and in reality is a divine Fire hidden to the senses and inaccessible to thought and reasoning, although it is related to the sensible (fire) in some way. The focus of its real fiery nature is the perishable world, not the world of real existence. May God protect us, with all the people of certainty, against its evil and injury on the Day of Judgment.

9. *He says: 'Regardless of whether transition, that is, transmigration, is true or false.'*

It appears from these words that he was in doubt regarding this matter and is not certain with respect to the falsity of transmigration, but you have seen its falsity on our part. It is strange also that al-Ghazzālī has allowed for the reality of transmigration, because it is not clear for him that transmigration and resuscitation are different. This shows that he[2] has not grasped correctly the meaning of corporal resurrection yet and did not appreciate fully the meaning of the second generation of both soul and body. The reason is that, after mentioning in his epistle that the greatest of the philosophers, Abū 'Alī (Ibn Sīnā) had allowed for corporal resurrection, on the ground that it is not too far-fetched to hold that some heavenly bodies may be assigned for the soul's imagination and sensation. He related this on the authority of one whom he held in great esteem[3] in these words.

However, one might comment that he mentioned that by way of civility and dissimulation,[4] having already admitted the impossibility of transmigration of bodies

1. *al-Kashf*, or mystical discovery.
2. Suhrawardī.
3. That is, al-Farābī.
4. *Taqiyyah*.

in the case of a simple soul, which amounts in fact to proving the impossibility of corporal transmigration. Our position is that what he said does not constitute a real proof. For he has said that, were the body to return and be disposed to receptivity, a soul would emanate from the 'Giver of Forms'[1] and be joined to it, since that which is so disposed is deserving in itself of receiving the forms, which would lead then to the emanation of a soul for it. Thereupon, the transmigrant soul would attach to it and we would then have two souls pertaining to one body, which is absurd.

Now, what he mentions may be used in asserting the transmigration of bodies, but is a weak proof, for it is possible that dispositions may vary, so that some will correspond to the pre-existing immateriality (of the body), which (the Giver of Forms) would manage, without having to impart a new soul to it. For, assuming that two sperms in the womb were disposed to receive the soul in one state, two souls would be imparted to them, each one of them having its own soul, without any reason for its inhering in it, except for the community of their corresponding attributes. If this appropriateness is possible with respect to two similar souls, why will it not be possible with respect to immaterial souls? Thus, if the disposed subject is deserving of its corresponding immaterial soul, why cannot a new soul be imparted to it by way of emanation? You should know, then, that whoever denies corporal resurrection has no decisive proof. (Here his words end.)

I say that you have already learnt demonstratively the absurdity of transmigration, in light of what we showed regarding the material origination of the soul and that it inheres in the body, with some of its faculties, its union with (the body) being according to nature. You have also learnt that there is a vast difference between transmigration and resurrection and that it is not necessary in that respect to allow for transmigration in principle. Therefore, you should thank God and sing His praise for teaching you what you did not know, God's grace bestowed on you being so vast.

10. *He says, may his secret be sanctified: 'The suspended forms are different from Plato's ideas.'*

You should know that human forms, including modes of understanding and feelings, are God's greater proof of His creation and the first evidence for the existence of the three worlds: the world of sense and the lower world, that of mystery and the hereafter, and that of reason and matter, which contains the three outlets of perception; I mean sensation, imagination and reason. Each one of these is a conduit to another world. We have ourselves proved the existence of the intermediate world and its distinctness from this lower world, by affirming the abstractness of the imaginative faculty and its objects. Estimation does not have its own world, insofar as there is no original form corresponding to it, because it is actually reason relative to particulars and relation is not one of the original entities. Therefore, it follows that the worlds are three.

1. That is, the Active Intellect, according to Ibn Sīnā.

The gnostic Shaykh, Muḥyī al-Dīn (ibn) ʿArabī states in the sixty-third chapter of his book,[1] in reference to knowledge of the survival of the soul in the isthmus,[2] separating the lower world and (the world) of resurrection, that the isthmus is a rational barrier between two adjoining objects which does not impinge on either of them, but has the power of each one of them, like the line which separates the shade from the sun, and is merely the work of the imagination, just as man becomes aware of the fact that he has perceived his own figure in one sense, but not in another sense, due to what he sees as very small, corresponding to the small size of the mirror, or very large corresponding to its large size. He cannot deny in either case that he has perceived his own image and that his image is not in the mirror or between him and mirror, and then he is neither truthful nor lying in saying that he saw his image or did not see it. For, what in fact is that image and where is it located? And what is its status? For, it is actually negated and asserted as existing and non-existing, known and well-known, and God Almighty has revealed this truth to mankind by recourse to an illustration so that (man) may know with certainty that, if he is unable or is in doubt regarding this matter while he is of the world, he is surely more ignorant of its creator, more impotent and more confused. [Ibn ʿArabī] wanted to draw attention here to the fact that the manifestations of God[3] are more minute and subtler in meaning than that which the confused intellects have been unable to understand, to the point of wondering: 'Has it gotten an essence or not?' For the intellects do not consign it to the realm of pure nothingness, while sight has perceived something (corresponding to it), nor to the realm of pure being. Thus you know that He is neither nothing nor pure possibility.

It is this reality that man is reduced to in his sleep and after his death, whereby he sees accidents as self-subsisting forms, which he addresses while they address him as bodies bearing their own spirits, without doubting any of this. For the gnostic by contrast is able to perceive in his waking state what the sleeper perceives in his sleep and the dead man after he dies, just as he sees in the other world the forms of actions being judged, although they are no more than accidents. Some people perceive this imagined object by means of the eye of sense, although others perceive it by means of the eye of the imagination also; I mean, while awake, but in their sleep by means of the eye of the imagination only..."[4] Then, if (those spirits) depart their material bodies, some of our followers say that the spirits, together with their forms, are stripped of their matters completely and they return to their original condition, just as the rays of the sun, reflected by an opaque object, return to the sun. However, they differed in two ways; one group of them said that the spirits

1. *al-Futūḥāt al-Makkiyyah.*
2. *Barzakh.*
3. The text has 'the Truth'.
4. This section consists almost exclusively of quotations from Ibn ʿArabī's *Futūḥāt*. We have therefore omitted it.

do not differ after departing (their bodies), just as the water contained in vessels does not differ if they happen to break and the water returns to the river. Another group said that they rather acquire ugly or beautiful shapes by association with the body, by which they are distinguished upon departing it; just as that water, if the vessels happen to contain certain elements which cause it to change in colour, taste or smell, will regain upon leaving the vessels those properties it had already acquired. For God will preserve those attributes (the spirits) had acquired. This group is in agreement with some philosophers in that respect.

Still another group held that spirits managing (the body) will continue to be managing it in the lower world, but once transferred to the isthmus they will manage bodies pertaining to the isthmus, which are those forms in which man sees himself in sleep or after death, which it symbolizes. He is then made to rise from the dead on the day of resurrection in the form of a physical body, as in the lower world. (Here ends the disagreement of our followers with respect to the spirits after departing [the body].)

You should know, my brother (may God keep you in His mercy), that Paradise attained by those who are worthy of it in the hereafter, is present to you today, as far as its site is concerned, but not its form. In it, you will change into your present condition, but you will not know that you are in it. For the form in which it is revealed to you will conceal it from you. However, people of disclosure,[1] who are able to apprehend what is absent to them will perceive that site and will perceive those in a green garden. If (that site) happens to be part of Hell, they will perceive it in accordance with the trials of its severe cold or heat and what God has prepared in it. Most of the people of disclosure are able to see that at the outset. The Lawgiver[2] itself has drawn attention to this in these words: 'Between my grave and my pulpit lies one of the gardens of Paradise.' (There end his noble words.) My aim in reporting (those opinions) is to acquaint you with the different views pertaining to the return of the spirits to that regeneration which follows death and how the forms pertaining to the isthmus look, what is their proper world, whether it is identical with the world of Paradise or that of Hell, in point of the essence or difference of its certain or doubtful being, or whether they are two different worlds.

The true opinion (for us) is the first. For the proportion of the forms pertaining to the isthmus, which appear upon resurrection, is equivalent to the proportion of the imperfection to the perfection of being or that of the age of the child to that of the adult. To it the Prophet refers in these words: 'The grave is either one of the gardens of Paradise or one of the ditches of Hell.' The state of the soul, so long as it is in the grave, is similar to that of the child in the cradle, as Firdawsī has said in these verses:

1. *al-Kashf*, or mystics.
2. *al-Shāriʿ*, or the Prophet.

Passing through the grave is not a choice,
The place of punishment is the grave not cradle.

And so long as the soul is in the body, its state is similar to that of the sperm or the embryo in a secure place. As for his words, 'then it will be resurrected on the Day of Judgment in physical bodies,' it may be said that, if what is meant by them is such bodies as the dense, worldly bodies, which are constantly changing and perishing, and are not stable, then they are not true; since they lead to many fallacies, such as transmigration and the like, which cannot be dealt with in this context. If, however, by the bodies in question is meant other bodies, contrived and acquired by the soul and fashioned according to its habits and deeds (then they are true).[1] It is said, however, that every such body is the same as the body that it had in this world, the unity of the soul being what matters, since it is what gives the body its identity. Thus, the body of Zayd in Paradise, for instance, is the same as his body in this world, as lead might turn in Hell into pure gold through the elixir. If then you are talking about the essence of the gold and its genuine substance, you would say that is that; but if you are talking about subtlety, brilliance and luminosity, then you would say that is not that. Therefore, the essence of this person is the same in this world and the next, and it is his spirit that finds the good or bad he had done waiting for him.

The proof of the fact that the condition of the spirit in the isthmus, and the form accompanying it, are similar to the relation of imperfection to perfection, is this saying of the Greatest Master[2] in the three hundred and fifty-fifth chapter of *al-Futūḥāt*: 'Death during the two modes of generation is an isthmus-type of condition in which the spirits dwell in imaginary isthmus-types of bodies, similar to those they dwelt in in sleep. They are accordingly bodies generated by these terrestrial bodies. For, imagination is one of their faculties, so that our spirits have not left them or what they have produced.' (You should know this.) He also says: 'If you understand the particular resurrection of this given person, you are able to understand the general resurrection of every dying person. For the isthmus of every other-worldly generation is similar to a woman bearing in her womb an embryo, whom God generates bit by bit, so that the stages of his generation would vary until he is born on the Day of Resurrection. That is why it has been said of the dying person that 'when he dies his resurrection has come'; that is, the appearance of this second generation in the isthmus has started up to the day of his rising from the isthmus; just as he rises from the womb to the earth upon his birth.' (The end.)

11. *He says: 'And it has no locus'.*

Some people have held that ideal forms are accidents inhering in the imaginative faculty, just as rational forms are accidents inhering in the rational. However,

1. This apodosis appears to be missing here.
2. Ibn 'Arabī.

both parties are off the mark, with respect to the union of reason with the object of reason. The truth is that substantial truths exist in the sensible, imaginative and rational worlds and they have corresponding forms in each of the three worlds. They are immaterial in the last two, material in the first. It is characteristic of the material (forms) to change, be subject to transition, cessation and dissolution, being part of the world of transience, death and destruction; whereas it is characteristic of the immaterial (forms) to endure and last, because they belong to the world of permanence, as it is said. If you grasp the reality of the unity of the imaginative forms belonging to the universal soul, which encompasses everything other imaginative faculties encompass, you will find that it is the locus of that world, of which those faculties are the manifestations. What we believe is that those forms have no locus, regardless of whether they are related to heavenly power or to our own power, because they are measurable and immaterial. They inhere in those psychic immaterial faculties in some other sense of inherence. In fact, every human entity will constitute in the hereafter a full world of its own, like the totality of the present world, without any competition from one world or the other. Then every man in Paradise would constitute a full world in himself, who is not aligned with anybody else of his own species in the same place, although there shows up before him whatever he desires or wishes to keep him company, be it a man, a horse, food, drink, houris, children, palaces, gardens, rivers and the like. All this will take place in the twinkle of an eye, the flash of a thought and the throb of a heart. This is the state of everyone of the blessed, but not the damned, whose hearts are 'shielded against what they are called unto'.[1] For the worlds there are infinite, because of the absence of positional arrangement, so that the scalar proof in it or the like may be in effect, demonstrating the negation of the finitude of those spaces. For each one of them is equal to the breadth of the heavens and the earths, without interference, competition or contact, but in a way that the gnostics know and is confirmed by the favoured.

It should be understood from this that he is the lord of the knowers. For every lordly knower is perfect and does not need anything nor desires anything outside himself, his kingdom and his dominion, since he lacks nothing. It is related in speaking of the condition of the people of Paradise that the angel approaches them, often seeking their permission, and if allowed, he will deliver to them a letter from God, after greeting them on behalf of God. They will then find in the letter addressed by the Living, Self-subsisting and Undying: 'Greetings, I say to a thing: "Be and it comes to be." I have authorized you today to say to the thing: "Be and it comes to be"'. The Prophet, peace on him, has said: 'No one in Paradise shall say to a thing: "Be", but it will come to be.' The finest words of the truthful people we have found in this respect are those of the Greatest Master in *al-Fuṣūṣ*[2] to the effect that 'every

1. Cf. Qur'ān 41:5.
2. *Fuṣūṣ al-ḥikam* (Bezels of Wisdom) by Ibn 'Arabī.

man is able to create by the power of the imagination that which does not exist except in it. This is the common situation; but the gnostic is able to create by his own energy what exists outside in lieu of the energy, but continues to be preserved by that energy, so long as that energy perseveres and wishes it to continue to exist. But as soon as he is oblivious of that preservation, that created object will cease to exist, unless that gnostic has control of all the presences (of that creation) and he is not oblivious at all. It is necessary, however, that he should observe a present actuality constantly. Then if the gnostic creates by his own energy what he creates and is fully in control, that creation will appear in his own image in every case and the forms will then be able to preserve each other.' He also says: 'I have made clear here a secret whose likeness the people of God continue to desire. This is a matter which nobody has embodied in a book, neither I, nor anybody else, prior to this book. It is a unique gem of the times.' He also says in chapter three hundred and sixty-one, after referring to that already mentioned Tradition which states that he came up with something: 'It is one of the foulest facts, the intent of nature being the formation of bodies and what they bear and endowing them with what they never lack or seek by nature, but not generally. For the purpose of the soul is the generation of particular spirits in their natural condition, generality has not been given except to the perfect Man, the bearer of the divine secret, everything other than God being part of the Perfect Man. So reason and look at everything other than God and how the Qur'ān[1] has described Him in these words: "There is nothing which does not celebrate His praise" (Qur'ān 17:44). It has also described all men as prostrate and does not grant any of them the power of command, prohibition, succession or general origination in the world, but has granted that to the perfect Man alone. Thus, whoever wishes to know his own perfection, let him look into himself, his command, prohibition and origination, without recourse to any tongue, organ or creature other than himself. If he succeeds in that, then he is assured by his Lord of his perfection, since he has a witness from Him. Should he then command, prohibit or start to generate anything by means of one of his organs, yet nothing emerges or emerges in one form rather than another, while he is unable to produce the means, he would have achieved perfection. It will not derogate from his perfection that some things did not come into being by his command immediately. For the divine form was manifested thereby in the world, since He has commanded His servants, according to the ordinances of His messengers and in His books. Then some obeyed, others disobeyed, since in the absence of the means, obedience is not especially possible. That is why, if man were unified in himself so as to become a single entity, then his intention will be fulfilled in whatever he wishes. This indeed is the experience of the totality of God's people; for God's hand is supportive of the community and His power is unfailing.' (The end.)

1. Original, *al-ḥaqq*, the Truth.

(Ibn ʿArabī) has also said in chapter forty-seven (of *al-Futūḥāt*): 'The Hereafter will be in constant generation. For in Paradise people will only have to say to a thing that they desire: "Be" and it will come to be, and they will not intend that anything come to be but it will come to be in front of them. The same is true of the inhabitants of Hell; for as soon as the thought of a greater torture flashes through their mind, then that torture will hit them. For, it is all a matter of thought; since in the other world the generation of things is consequent perceptibly on the occurrence of the thought, the determination, the will, the intention and the desire. All this is fully perceptible, while in this world, there is nothing higher than action by dint of determination on the part of each agent. This is accorded in this world to whoever is not a saint, such as he who acts by invoking the evil eye (?) and is motivated by strange desires (?)'[1]

1. The editor himself is uncertain of this last phrase that he marks by (*kadhā* or *sic*).

Part II

The Revival of Peripatetic Philosophy

Introduction

Had the *mashshā'ī* philosophy of Ibn Sīnā and other early masters of this School not been revived in the seventh/thirteenth century, it is possible that philosophy as a distinct discipline would have had the same destiny in Persia and in other lands of the eastern Islamic world as it did in most of the Arabic world, that is, it would have become absorbed into the schools of philosophical theology and theosophical and philosophical Sufism. Even the flowering of the School of *ishrāq*, which opposed so many *mashshā'ī* theses, benefited from the presence of the *mashshā'ī* School in order to survive as a distinct philosophical current. Moreover, the revival of Peripatetic philosophy has helped preserve the long Islamic tradition of the intellectual sciences into the contemporary period. In contrast to what certain modern Arab philosophers claim, that real Islamic philosophy came to an end with Ibn Rushd and later Islamic philosophy in Persia or for that matter in India or Ottoman Turkey, is not rigorous philosophy but mystical speculation, the revived tradition of Islamic Peripatetic philosophy in Persia, not to speak of other later philosophical schools, demonstrates how rational and logical philosophy continued in the Islamic world long after the death of Ibn Rushd at the end of the sixth/twelfth century. This later School of *mashshā'ī* philosophy in Persia was rigorously rational without being rationalistic in the modern sense and produced numerous works on logic, natural philosophy and metaphysics which are no less *'aqlī* (intellectual/ rational) than were the works of the earlier Peripatetics including Ibn Rushd.

As already mentioned, the revival of *mashshā'ī* philosophy in Persia took place on the basis of the philosophical syntheses of Ibn Sīnā and not Ibn Rushd and the latter's criticism of the Ash'arite theologians especially Ghazzālī. This latter criticism is widely known and studied in the West and the contemporary Islamic world, especially in its Arabic sector; but it had little influence on the Persian philosophical scene although Ibn Rushd was known to Persian philosophers and in neighbouring Ottoman Turkey where some rebuttals were even written against his criticism of Ghazzālī. It seems that the later life of *mashshā'ī* philosophy in Persia and adjacent lands was destined to be based on Ibn Sīnā rather than Ibn Rushd, who influenced Europe much more than the Islamic world, even if we consider his possible influence on Ibn Taymiyyah in the question of the nature of God's creation of the world.

In any case the most important figure in the revival of Peripatetic philosophy in Persia and also in Muslim India and Ottoman Turkey is without doubt Naṣīr al-Dīn Ṭūsī, who wrote a number of works defending and/or summarizing *mashshā'ī* teachings, and not Ibn Rushd. One of the treatises of Ṭūsī, dealing with the division of existents according to the *mashshā'ī* School appears in this section. But as already mentioned in the general introduction to this volume, Ṭūsī's most important opus, as far as the revival of Peripatetic philosophy is concerned, and one of the major masterpieces of Islamic philosophy, is his commentary upon Ibn Sīnā's *Ishārāt*. In reality, Ṭūsī's work is a commentary upon Fakhr al-Dīn Rāzī's critical commentary upon the same seminal text. In this long work the great theologian Rāzī is in a sense 'buried' between two of the colossal figures of Islamic philosophy, Ṭūsī and Ibn Sīnā. Ṭūsī's commentary covers the whole of the *Ishārāt* and deals with the main subjects of *mashshā'ī* philosophy discussed to some extent in the first volume of this *Anthology*. These subjects include various aspects of logic, natural philosophy and metaphysics. Such questions as the substantiality of bodies, form and matter, quantity and quality as they pertain to bodies, the possibility of the existence of a vacuum in the physical world, motion and rest and the four elements are discussed thoroughly and Ash'arite objections to Avicennan views on these and other matters discussed in detail and refuted. Then the text turns to the soul, both human and celestial, the Active Intellect and how it emanates intelligibles that are received by the soul, the relation between the 'intellector' (*al-'āqil*) and the intelligibles (*al-ma'qūl*) and similar issues. There is also an extensive discussion of the faculty of psychology of Ibn Sīnā and the various faculties of the vegetative, animal and human souls as well as the souls of the sphere which Ibn Rushd rejected but which play a very important role in Avicennan cosmology.

What is significant throughout the first part of Ṭūsī's commentary is how he refutes Rāzī's criticisms and with his remarkable intellectual rigour undoes the effect of Ash'arite attacks on *mashshā'ī* thought, thereby giving a new life to this philosophy. But the actual philosophical content of this part of his commentary is essentially Ibn Sīnā's own well-known theses. Therefore, in this *Anthology* we decided to make available in translation Ṭūsī's commentary upon the last part of the *Ishārāt* which contains the strongest intellectual defence provided by a major Islamic Peripatetic philosopher of Sufism and gnosis. The last part of the *Ishārāt* constitutes in our view a part of what Ibn Sīnā conceived as his 'Oriental philosophy' which marked a higher step of philosophical understanding meant, by his own words, 'for the elite' (*al-khawāṣṣ*). The translation of this section reveals both the amplitude of Ibn Sīnā's total philosophical vision and Ṭūsī's own mastery of that with which Ibn Sīnā was dealing in the last part of his final philosophical masterpiece. It also demonstrates the climate in which Peripatetic philosophical was revived, one in which rigorous rational philosophy and standard *mashshāʾī* theses, such as those discussed in the other selection from Ṭūsī presented in this section, were studied and defended in an intellectual universe in which there was also an opening to contemplative and illuminative knowledge and gnosis.

The other selections in this section trace the history of this revived *mashshāʾī* School in Persia through certain major figures. The selections are also chosen in such a way as to elucidate different aspects of the teachings of this School and different approaches by *mashshāʾī* philosophers of various intellectual bent lest one should think that these Peripatetic philosophers were simply repeating the same subjects. The selections from Afḍal al-Dīn Kāshānī include an exposition of his views on knowledge of the self, or what I have called the autology of Kāshānī, a discussion of *wujūd* from the *mashshāʾī* perspective as well as a discourse on substance and accidents which goes back through Ibn Sīnā to Aristotle.

The work of Dabīrān-i Kātibī-yi Qazwīnī, the *Ḥikmat al-ʿayn*, became a popular text for the teaching of *mashshāʾī* philosophy and many generations of students up to our own day have learned *mashshāʾī* philosophy through this readily accessible text. Some of the major Peripatetic theses including *wujūd* and *māhiyyah*, the relation between them, necessity and contingency of *wujūd*, human knowledge and its relation to revelation and the complex issue of causality have been chosen and translated from this treatise. There is also a section in which the author speaks of *jaʿl* or instauration, which later became a major subject in the *ḥikmat al-mutaʿāliyah* of Mullā Ṣadrā but was not discussed in the same way by Ibn Sīnā.

We have also included a selection from another popular *mashshāʾī* work, the *Kitāb Hidāyat al-ḥikmah* of Athīr al-Dīn Abharī. This work became one of the most popular in the teaching of *mashshāʾī* philosophy especially with the commentary of Qāḍī Amīr Ḥusayn Kamāl al-Dīn Maybudī and later on Mullā Ṣadrā. It is still used widely in Persia today. As for India, Mullā Ṣadrā's commentary on this text became so popular that those who studied it were given the title of 'learned in Ṣadrā'. There is hardly a major Islamic manuscript library in the Subcontinent of India without one or more hand-written copies of this work. Since we shall be dealing extensively with Mullā Ṣadrā in the next volume, here we decided to include a section from the Maybudī rather than the Mullā Ṣadrā commentary along with the original text of Abharī. The selection deals with proofs for the existence of God with which Ibn Sīnā as well as Jewish and Christian Aristotelian philosophers such as Maimonides and St Thomas were also deeply concerned. Some modern scholars have considered this issue to be a part of theology rather than philosophy and have even spoken of the 'theology of Avicenna' when discussing his views on this matter. But from the view of the Islamic *falāsifah*, this subject is definitely a part of philosophy and nearly every major Islamic philosopher has dealt with it in one way or another.

The earlier attack of the *mutakallimūn* upon *mashshā'ī* philosophy left its mark upon the revival of this philosophy as we see so clearly in Ṭūsī's commentary upon the *Ishārāt*. This concern is also to be seen in later figures especially Quṭb al-Dīn Rāzī who, in his *Muḥākamāt* (Trials), sought to judge between the criticisms of Ibn Sīnā by Fakhr al-Dīn Rāzī and the refutation of these criticisms by Ṭūsī. Quṭb al-Dīn Rāzī's work is therefore one more link in the long chain of debates between the *falāsifah* and the *mutakallimūn*. Although predominantly a *mashshā'ī* philosopher, Quṭb al-Dīn Rāzī, like many other philosophers of that era, was also well acquainted with the views of Suhrawardī. This fact is evident in his treatise on ascent and judgment, an issue that is central to both logic and epistemology and with which so many Islamic philosophers of different periods have been concerned and have treated in so many different ways.

Needless to say, there are many other important *mashshā'ī* treatises of this period such as works by Sirāj al-Dīn Urmawī and Ibn Salhan Sāwajī that have not been included in this volume because of the limitation of space. This omission here is especially true of the School of Shiraz many of whose members were masters of the *mashshā'ī* School and in fact added a distinct new chapter to its history. We hope, however, to deal with them in the next volume. The reader may also ask why we have included the whole of the *ishrāqī* School in this volume but not the whole of the *mashshā'ī* School of the later centuries up to our times. There are several reasons for this choice. First of all the history of the *mashshā'ī* School dealing with the first period of its development was covered in Volume One of this *Anthology* while a later volume dealt extensively precisely with *kalām* which curtailed the life of the *mashshā'ī* School in Persia, albeit temporarily, in the fifth/eleventh and sixth/twelfth centuries. Consequently, there was no possibility, within the general structure of these volumes to include the whole of the *mashshā'ī* tradition in one place, unless we were to devote each volume to a particular School (as we have done in the case of Ismaili philosophy and *kalām* where we felt such a treatment was needed), and forgo the possibility of the full treatment of any distinct historical period, a choice which we had decided against, from the beginning, for reasons of scholarship and also because of the need of the contemporary reader for a historical treatment of particular periods wherever possible. Moreover, there was the need to present the interactions of various schools in particular periods within such a vast work.

In addition to all these considerations there was another issue to consider. In the West the *ishrāqī* School is less known than the *mashshā'ī* and we felt that dealing with the whole of the *ishrāqī* School through selections in one place in this volume would provide a better view of its long development in historical perspective. In contrast early *mashshā'ī* philosophy is much better known and also its history in Persia is broken by its eclipse in the fifth/eleventh and sixth/twelfth centuries so that one cannot present it as a continuous tradition in the same way as the *ishrāqī*

School without stretching the historical evidence during that period despite the appearance of Khayyām and a few other Avicennan philosophers who lived during this hiatus, many of whom are known only by name and not by any extensive writings.

Finally, the destiny of *mashshā'ī* and *ishrāqī* Schools is not exactly the same after the tenth/sixteenth century. While *mashshā'ī* philosophy survived, it became often, although not always, combined with other schools, perhaps more so than the *ishrāqī*. Even Avicennan philosophers of the Safavid period such as Mīr Dāmād were also *ishrāqīs* although as we shall see in Volume Five, there were also some philosophers who were predominantly *mashshā'ī*. This fact of becoming combined with other schools is to some extent also true of the *ishrāqī* School but we believe not to the same degree. In any case on the basis of all these considerations, we have decided to divide the *mashshā'ī* School between the first, fourth and fifth volumes considering not only the early break in its earlier history but also the fact that its history is longer and more chequered than that of the *ishrāqī* School.

S. H. Nasr

1

Naṣīr al-Dīn Ṭūsī

Abū Ja'far Muḥammad ibn al-Ḥasan Naṣīr al-Dīn Ṭūsī is one of the most prominent Islamic philosophers and scientists, as well as a leading Shi'i theologian. His family hailed from Kāshān but he was born in Ṭūs in Khurāsān 597/1200 and died in 672/1273 in Kāẓimayn near Baghdad. Although Ṭūsī is primarily known as a philosopher, he contributed immensely to such fields as *kalām*, mathematics, astronomy, ethics and to some extent Sufism.

Ṭūsī's first teacher was his father, a prominent jurist in the Twelver school of Shi'ism with whom he may have studied logic, jurisprudence and natural philosophy. Ṭūsī also studied metaphysics with his uncle and different branches of mathematics with other teachers in Ṭūs. Having mastered the sciences available to him in his home town, he left for Nayshāpūr, at the time a great centre of learning where the legacy of such philosophers and mathematicians as 'Umār Khayyām was still present.

In Nayshāpūr, Ṭūsī studied metaphysics and Peripatetic philosophy with Farīd al-Dīn Dāmād, who was a student of Ibn Sīnā through four intermediaries. He also studied medicine with Quṭb al-Dīn Miṣrī, himself a distinguished student of Fakhr al-Dīn Rāzī, and finally became a student of Kamāl al-Dīn Yūnus with whom he studied mathematics.

Some time before 628/1230 Ṭūsī accepted the invitation of Naṣīr al-Dīn Muḥtashim, the Ismaili ruler, and moved to Quhistān and later to other fortresses of the Ismailis where he lived from 623/1226 to 652/1254. Ṭūsī's relationship with the Ismailis is subject to debate. There are those who have argued that Ṭūsī genuinely converted to Ismailism while others see his conversion as a move to enjoy the protection of the Ismailis in a turbulent time. Ṭūsī's life coincided with the Mongol invasion of Persia, which caused much death and destruction, especially in the province of Khurāsān where he resided. The only islands of peace and stability were the strongholds of the Ismailis where Ṭūsī could have been safe. Still others have argued that his collaboration with the Ismailis and his stay at the fortress of

Alamūt were forced upon him. In either case, it was the security and respect he enjoyed during these years that provided him with the opportunity to compose a great number of works, including works on Ismailism, some of which have been included and discussed in the second volume of this *Anthology*.

In 652/1254, Hülagü, the Mongol emperor known for his interest in astrology, sacked the Ismaili establishments in Khurāsān and welcomed Ṭūsī to his court because of his fame as an astronomer. Ṭūsī remained the scientific advisor, court astronomer and even minister to Hülagü and according to some sources accompanied him in his conquest of Baghdad in 654/1256. A year later, under the patronage of Hülagü, Ṭūsī began the construction of a major astronomical observatory at Marāghah that was completed in 668/1269. Much of the *Ilkhānīd Astronomical Tables* and new astronomical observations and calculations were the result of the efforts of Ṭūsī and the circle of scientists who had gathered around him in Marāghah. In 670/1271, while in Baghdad, Ṭūsī fell ill and died. He is buried near the tomb of the seventh Shi'i Imam Mūsā al-Kāẓim adjacent to that city.

Today, nearly a hundred and fifty works of Ṭūsī are known to have survived, of which twenty-five are in Persian, the rest in Arabic and one partially in Turkish. Ṭūsī wrote five works on logic the most important of which is *Asās al-iqtibās* (Foundations of Inference), written in Persian. On mathematics, Ṭūsī wrote a number of commentaries on the works of Greek mathematicians plus many independent texts. In these works he went far beyond being a transmitter of Greek sciences to the Islamic world and himself became a major contributor to the mathematical sciences. Ṭūsī commented on the works of such figure as Autolycus, Aristarchus, Apollonius, Archimedes, Euclid, Hypsicles, Menelaus, Ptolomy, and Theodosius. Ṭūsī's commentaries on Euclid's *Elements* and Ptolomy's *Almagest* and the corpus of texts between them known as the 'intermediate works' (*mutawassaṭāt*) were standard texts for teaching mathematics and astronomy in the Islamic world for centuries to come.

Among his original contributions to arithmetic, geometry, and trigonometry are *Jawāmi' al-ḥisāb bi'l-takht wa'l-turāb* (The Comprehensive Work on Computation with Board and Dust), *al-Risālah al-shāfi'iyyah* (The Satisfying Treatise), and *Kashf al-qinā' fī asrār shakl al-qiṭā'* (known as the Book of the Principle of [the] Transversal). The latter was translated into Latin and influenced Regiomontanus, one of the foremost mathematicians of fifteenth-century Germany. The most significant works of Ṭūsī in astronomy are *Zīj-i īlkhānī* (The Ilkhānīd Tables) and the *Tadhkirat al-nujūm* (Memorial of Astronomy). Written originally in Persian, these works were later translated into Arabic and the *Tables* was partially translated into Latin by John Greaves as *Astronomia quaedam ex traditione Shah Cholgii Persae una cum hypothesibus planetarum*. Ṭūsī also wrote treatises on particular astronomical subjects such as the astrolabe and translated a work on astronomy by 'Abd al-Raḥmān al-Ṣūfī entitled *Ṣuwar al-kawākib* (Figures of the Fixed Stars) from Arabic into Persian. In other areas of science, Ṭūsī produced significant works such as the *Tansūkh-nāmah* (The Book of Precious Materials).

During the Ismaili phase of his life, Ṭūsī composed a major work entitled *Taṣawwurāt* (Conceptions), also known as *Rawḍat al-taslīm* (The Paradise of Submission), on Ismaili theology and philosophy. *Taṣawwurāt* discusses ontology, epistemology, cosmology, eschatology, imamology and soteriology in twenty-eight sections called 'Conceptions'. Despite his importance as an Ismaili thinker, theologically Ṭūsī was a Twelver Shīʿa. His theological and metaphysical views are reflected in his work *al-Fuṣūl* (Chapters), written in Persian, and in *Kitāb al-Tajrīd* (The Book of Catharsis), written in Arabic. *Kitāb al-Tajrīd* is considered to be the most important work on Shiʿi theology and over four hundred commentaries and glosses have been written on it.

Of course Ṭūsī also composed many important philosophical works, chief among them a commentary on Ibn Sīnā's *al-Ishārāt wa'l-tanbīhāt* (The Book of Directives and Remarks). In this work Ṭūsī begins with Fakhr al-Dīn Rāzī's criticism of the *Ishārāt* and then responds to every criticism of Rāzī with great skill and in detail. Under the influence of Miskawayh, Ṭūsī wrote one of the most important works in the Persian language on philosophical ethics in Islam entitled *Akhlāq-i nāṣirī* (Naṣīrian Ethics).

Ṭūsī is one of the few Peripatetic philosophers who was also sympathetic to Sufism, and may have even practised it for a while. He wrote on Sufism and gnosis (*ʿirfān*), as is evident in his Persian work *Awṣāf al-ashrāf* (Descriptions of the Nobles). He also expressed his reverence for the Sufi masters such as Manṣūr al-Ḥallāj and corresponded with Jalāl al-Dīn Rūmī and Ṣadr al-Dīn Qūnawī. In jurisprudence, he wrote *Kitāb al-Raml* in which he explicated a variety of legal matters, particularly the laws of inheritance. In the tradition of so many philosophers, Ṭūsī also composed a number of poems, mostly in Persian.

Like many other Muslim philosophers, Ṭūsī relied on the Neoplatonic scheme of emanation to comment on a wide variety of philosophical issues, among them the doctrine of resurrection (*qiyāmah*) and the inner meaning (*bāṭin*) of religion. Ṭūsī divides human beings into three groups: the exoteric type he calls 'the people of contradiction' (*ahl al-taḍādd*), those of an esoteric nature he calls 'the people of gradation' (*ahl al-tarattub*) and those he regards as people of union (*ahl al-waḥdah*). The latter group are the spiritual elite who have achieved unity with the Truth (*ḥaqīqah*).

Perhaps more than anyone else, Ṭūsī is responsible for the revival in Persia of science and rational philosophy in the seventh/thirteenth century. He not only brought together different scientists, mathematicians and philosophers, but he also clarified and defended Avicennan philosophy against his opponents. Outside Persia, the mathematical and astronomical works of Ṭūsī were influential in the West, in the Ottoman world and among Indian scientists, as evidenced by the observatory of Jai Singh II.

Among Twelver Shiʿa, Ṭūsī is regarded as a philosopher, a scientist and, above all, a theologian whose work *Tajrīd al-qawāʿid* is a systematic treatment of Shiʿi *kalām*. In the annals of Islamic intellectual thought, there has been no other figure who is simultaneously an astronomer, mathematician, philosopher, and theologian of the highest stature.

In this chapter we have included two selections. In the first, Ṭūsī's commentary on the *Ishārāt* of Ibn Sīnā is presented. The selection begins with a discussion concerning the stations of the gnostics. The meaning of the philosophical narrative or recital of *Salāmān and Absāl* and its symbolism is also treated and, then, the relationship between asceticism and epistemology and the faculties of the soul. Ṭūsī then launches into a long and detailed discourse on psychology. Some of his discussions, which bear resemblance to Aristotle's *De Anima,* treat the specific powers of the faculties of the soul. This section ends with the virtues that a gnostic should embrace.

In the second selection, parts of Ṭūsī's Persian treatise, *Risālah andar qismat-i mawjūdāt* (Treatise on the Division of Existents), have been included. Ṭūsī begins this treatise with a discussion of atomism, which was a subject of great concern among both the philosophers and the theologians. Mentioning the views of the Muʿtazilites and the Ashʿarites on corporeality, and the problem of infinite divisibility, he goes on to consider different types of corporeality among minerals, plants and animals. His treatment of different types of corporeality then becomes more specific and includes topics such as finitude and infinity, dimension, quality, quantity and time. In a general sense, Ṭūsī's discussion in this treatise is the application of the Aristotelian categories to the subject of atomism and its philosophical consequences.

M. Aminrazavi

COMMENTARY ON IBN SĪNĀ'S REMARKS AND ADMONITIONS

Sharḥ al-ishārāt wa'l-tanbīhāt

Translated for this volume by Majid Fakhry from Naṣīr al-Dīn Ṭūsī, *Sharḥ al-ishārāt wa'l-tanbīhāt*, ed. Sulaymān Dunyā (Cairo, 1968), pp. 47–82.

On the Stations of the Gnostics[1]

Chapter 1—Ninth Section
Admonition: 'The Gnostics have certain stations and ranks by which they are favoured in their earthly life.'[2]

Having referred in the previous section to the pleasure existing entities derive from their proper perfections, whatever their ranks, he[3] wished to refer in this section to the conditions of those members of the human race who have achieved perfection and show the manner in which they have scaled the rungs of their own happiness. He has also referred to those accidental matters which they encounter in their ascent.

The eminent commentator[4] has stated that this section embodied the finest part of the subject-matter of the book.[5] For he[6] has classified in it the sciences of the Sufis in a manner which no predecessor of his has done and no successor has attained.

I say:[7] (Arabic) *jilbāb* means a cloak or whatever covers one, whether a robe or suchlike. To shed (*nada*) a robe is to drop it.

By his[8] statement: 'It is as though, while in the cloaks of their bodies, they (i.e. the gnostics)[9] have shed them and were freed from them on their way to the World of Holiness'.[10] the author means that it is as if their perfect souls, though outwardly are covered with the cloaks of their bodies, they have actually shed them. It is as though their souls shed those cloaks, were stripped of all material accretions and attained the World of Holiness, achieving thereby contact with those perfect entities which are free of imperfection and evil. They have in addition certain hidden

1. *'Ārifīn*, plural of *'ārif*, used by Ibn Sīnā to denote those who have partaken of mystical cognitive experience, Arabic, *'irfān*.

2. Opening line of the chapter in *al-Ishārāt wa'l-tanbīhāt*. Cf. Engl. tr. in *An Anthology of Philosophy in Persia*, London, 2008, vol. 1, pp. 303–311.

3. Ibn Sīnā.

4. That is, Naṣīr al-Dīn Ṭūsī.

5. That is, *al-Ishārāt wa'l-tanbīhāt*.

6. Ibn Sīnā.

7. This expression usually prefaces Ṭūsī's comments.

8. Ibn Sīnā's.

9. Or Sufis.

10. Cf. English translation, *An Anthology of Philosophy in Persia*, vol. 1, p. 303.

properties, which include their observations of what human thought cannot grasp and human tongues cannot utter, and their jubilation at what no eye has seen and no ear has heard. This is the sense of what the Almighty has said: 'No soul knows what was laid up for them secretly of joyful relief.'[1]

There are certain visible signs they exhibit, which are the effects of perfection and consummation, which appear in their words and deeds; as well as signs peculiar to them, which include what is known as miracles or divine favours. These are matters which are regarded as strange by those who doubt them; that is, are such that the heart of whoever does not know them or come close to them does not feel at ease where they are concerned; whereas he who knows them will admire them; that is, whoever knows them and comes close to them will admire them.

I say: To relate (*sarada*) a story means to recount it faithfully. We say so and so relates a story if he recounts it well.

(Here the commentator gives an account of Salāmān and Absāl mentioned in the text in a manner entirely irrelevant to Ibn Sīna's purpose. Therefore, we have omitted it) .... .

The second account is the one that reached me twenty years after completing this commentary. It is attributed to the Shaykh (Ibn Sīnā) and appears to be the one which he refers to here. In fact, Abū 'Ubayd al-Juzjānī[2] has given in the list of the Shaykh's writings the story of Salāmān and Absāl by his pen.

The gist of the story is that Salāmān and Absāl were two brothers, Absāl being the younger of the two. He was brought up in the company of his brother and was handsome, reasonable, polite, learned, temperate and brave.

Salāmān's wife fell in love with him; so she said to Salāmān: 'Let him mix with your children, so that your children may learn from him.' Salāmān gave him that advice, but Absāl refused to associate with women. Salāmān then said to him: 'My wife is like a mother to you.' So he entered her house, whereupon she welcomed him. Shortly after, she revealed to him in private her love for him; but Absāl was taken aback and she understood that he would not listen to her. She then said to Salāmān: 'Let your brother marry my sister', so she could possess him through her. Therefore, she said to her sister: 'I did not arrange Absāl's marriage to you, so that he can be yours alone; but rather that I may share him with you.' Then she said to Absāl: 'My sister is a shy virgin; so do not enter in on her during the day and do not speak to her until she is well acquainted with you.'

On the wedding night, Salāmān's wife slept in her sister's bed; but she could not control herself and so she proceeded to press her breast against his; whereupon, Absāl became suspicious and said to himself: 'Shy virgins do not do this.' At that

1. Qur'ān 32:17.

2. The editor gives al-Jurjānī, which is wrong. In fact, Salāmān and Absāl is not given in the modern edition of al-Jurjānī's list, but has been published in a collection of treatises, *Tis'u rasā'il*, Istanbul, 1298/1881.

point, the sky was covered with dark clouds in which lightning flashed, at which point he saw her face and so he rebuked her and went out, determined to part company with her.

He then said to Salāmān: 'I would like to conquer the lands for you and I am capable thereof.' So, he led an army, fought many nations and conquered the countries, on land and at sea, east and west, for his brother, without grudging him all that. He was in fact the first Two-horned[1] to conquer the vast expanse of the land.

When (Absāl) returned home, imagining that she (i.e. Salāmān's wife) had forgotten him, she returned to her old way of flirtation. When she tried to embrace him, he refused and reprimanded her.

Then an enemy appeared on the scene; so Salāmān sent Absāl to face him at the head of his army. However, his wife[2] paid the leader of the army a sum of money so that he may abandon him in battle. He did and so the enemy captured him and his own men left him to bleed, assuming that he was dead. However, an animal nursing its young took pity on him and gave him her breast to suck on, and so he was nourished, revived and recovered his health.

Absāl then returned to Salāmān, who was besieged and humiliated by the enemy. He was distraught at the alleged loss of his brother, and thus Absāl caught up with him, took hold of the army and its equipment, charged the enemy formations, dispersed them, captured their leader and restored the kingdom to his brother.

The woman[3] conspired with his cook and food purveyor and gave them money, and so they poisoned him.[4] Alas! He was upright, noble in point of lineage, knowledge and good deeds. His brother was deeply distressed at his death and so he abandoned his throne and delegated the authority to some of his associates. He then prayed to his Lord, who revealed to him a clear course of action. Accordingly, he gave his wife, the cook and the food purveyor, all three of them, the same poison they gave his brother and so they were all gone!

This is the gist of the story, whose interpretation is as follows: Salāmān is a simile for the rational soul, Absāl for theoretical reason, which rises upward until it reaches the level of acquired reason, which marks the soul's level of gnosis, as it rises towards perfection.

As for the wife of Salāmān, she is the symbol of the corporal faculty, that inclines towards lust and anger, which combined to the soul, becomes a human person.

Her love for Absāl is an instance of her tendency to render reason subservient, as she rendered the other faculties so that they may comply with her orders and

1. A reference to Alexander the Great, who is usually referred to in the Arabic sources, including the Qur'ān, as the 'Two-horned', or ruler of East and West.

2. Original: the woman.

3. Salāmān's wife.

4. i.e. Absāl.

achieve her perishable goals. Absāl's refusal is an instance of reason being drawn to its own world. Her sister, whom she dominated, symbolizes the practical faculty, known as practical reason, which is subservient to theoretical reason and is called the 'quiescent soul'.[1] Her appearing in the guise of her sister symbolizes the 'commanding soul',[2] insinuating its base desires and presenting them as genuine benefits.

The flashing lightning in the dark clouds is a symbol for the divine flash which occurs as one is preoccupied with perishable matters and it is one of the moments of gravitation towards the Truth. Absāl's reprimanding of the woman symbolizes reason's turning away from desire; whereas conquering the lands for his brother symbolizes the acquaintance of the soul, through the theoretical faculty, with the order of might and royalty and its ascent to the divine order. It also symbolizes its ability by means of the practical faculty to manage its bodily affairs well and to order the affairs of households and cities.

That is why he[3] nicknamed him the first Two-horned, which applies to one who ruled both East and West. His rejection by the army refers to the turning away of the sensuous, imaginative and estimative faculties from it,[4] as it ascends towards the higher world, while those faculties decline due to their refusal to turn towards it.

Its feeding on the milk of beasts denotes imparting perfection to him from those entities which are separate from this world and lie above it. As for Salāmān's distress at the loss of Absāl, it denotes the disturbance of the soul when it neglects the care of what lies beneath it. His going back to his brother denotes reason's attention to its interests in tending the body.

The cook denotes the irascible faculty which flares up at the time of seeking revenge. The feeder denotes the concupiscent faculty, which draws whatever is necessary for the body. Their conspiring to destroy Absāl is an indication of the mind's degeneration during the worst years of life, while the 'commanding soul' uses them both, due to their increased needs on account of weakness and impotence.

As for Salāmān destroying them, it denotes the soul's relinquishing the use of bodily faculties, towards the end of life and the cessation of the outbursts of anger and lust and the cessation of their feeding faculty. His abdicating the royal office and delegating it to another denotes the cessation of his management of the body and passing on to the care of someone else.

This interpretation is in conformity with what the Shaykh has said. In support of the fact that this is the story he intended is his allusion in the *Epistle on the Decree and Destiny* (*Fi'l-Qaḍā' wa'l-qadar*) to the story of Salāmān and Absāl. He mentioned in both the flash of lightning from the dark cloud which revealed to him

1. Cf. Qur'ān 89:27.
2. Cf. Qur'ān 12:53.
3. Ibn Sīnā.
4. The theoretical faculty.

the face of Salāmān's wife, so he turned away from her. This is what appeared to me clearly in connection with this story; but I did not give the story in the Shaykh's words for fear of adding to the length of the book.

Chapter 2
Admonition: 'He who shuns the goods of this world and its delectable things is called an ascetic'

I say: The seeker of an object begins by turning away from whatever he believes will keep him away from this object of desire. Then he turns to whatever he believes will bring him closer to it and he ends up by finding the desired object.

Thus, the seeker of truth ought to begin by turning away from anything other than the Truth, especially whatever deters him from seeking it, I mean, worldly possessions and pleasures. He will then turn to whatever he believes will bring him closer to the Truth, which, according to the general public, consists in performing certain acts, known as ritual observances. The two (which bring him closer) are asceticism and worship up to a point and relinquishing and allegiance up to a point. When he finds the truth, he will realize that the first step in the process of finding it is cognition. Therefore, the states of the seekers of truth are those three.[1] That is why the Shaykh began by defining them.

Now, those states may be found in persons in isolation, or alternatively in conjunction, depending on the variety of circumstances and modes of conjunction. Thus, the two become three and the three become one. This is what the Shaykh meant by saying 'Some of the above-mentioned (states) may be conjoined with each other.'

Chapter 3
Admonition: 'Asceticism for the non-Gnostic is a form of trading'

I say: Having referred to the conjunction of the three states, he intended to draw attention to the goal of the Gnostic and the non-Gnostic, in point of asceticism and worship, so that the two actions may be distinguished accordingly. Thus, he mentioned that asceticism and worship on the part of the non-Gnostic takes two forms: The ascetic non-Gnostic resembles a merchant who trades one commodity for another and the non-Gnostic worshipper resembles an employee who works day and night for the sake of receiving a wage, and although the two actions are different, the goal is the same.

The Gnostic's asceticism, in that state in which he is turned towards the Truth and away from everything else, is a form of shunning everything that diverts him

1. As given by Ibn Sīnā, the three states are that of the ascetic, the worshipper and the Gnostic (*ʿārif*).

from the Truth, out of preference for his own intended object. But in that state in which he may be looking to what is other than the Truth, he will feel bigger than anything other than the Truth, out of contempt for what is beneath it. His worship is then a form of exercising his energies which are the sources of his will, his concupiscent and irascible inclinations and suchlike, as well as the imaginative and estimative faculties of his soul, so that he may draw them all away from inclining towards the corporal world and preoccupation with it, and seeking instead the real world. They will then be bidding him goodbye as he turns towards that world, so that those faculties will become accustomed to that bidding and will not challenge reason or compete with the Secret, during the state of contemplation. Then reason will freely join that (real) world and all the auxiliaries and faculties beneath it will enlist with him in that process of turning that way.

Chapter 4
Remark: 'Since man is unable to cope indefinitely with the condition of his soul ...'

I say: Having mentioned in the preceding chapter that asceticism and worship are practised by the non-Gnostic in order to earn the wages and rewards of the hereafter, he[1] intended to refer to the wages and rewards in question. He, thus, affirmed prophethood and the Holy Law (*Sharīʿah*) and what pertains to them in the manner of the philosophers, because it is a subsidiary of them. Demonstrating this rests on a series of principles, which we can affirm by stating that man is not alone in the management of his means of livelihood, because he is in need of food, clothing, habitation and arms, either for himself or those who depend on him, be they his small children or others. All these things are artificial matters, which cannot be managed by a single agent, except in the course of a long spell, during which he will not survive if he is deprived of those means or will find it hard to do so, if at all. However, that is manageable for a group who assist and cooperate with one another in the pursuit of those ends, especially if each one of them delegates to one of his companions part of the work. The task will then be accomplished, either by reciprocity, whereby each one will act like the other will act; or by fair exchange, whereby everyone will give the other a part of his work equivalent to what he receives.

Accordingly, man by nature needs in his livelihood that association which is conducive to his well-being. This is what they mean by saying, Man by nature is a political animal;[2] political in their usage referring to this kind of association. This, then, is the first maxim.

---

1. Ibn Sīnā.
2. Arabic *madanī*. It is Aristotle, who states that man is a *zoon politikon*. The term 'political' derives from the Greek word for a city, *polis* (Arabic, *madīnah*).

We say further that men's association for the purpose of cooperation is not possible unless exchange and justice reign in their midst. For, everyone will desire what he needs and resent whoever competes with him in its acquisition. His desire and his anger will then lead him to be unjust towards others. Confusion will follow and the political association will break down.

If, however, cooperation and justice are mutually agreed upon, that will not happen. That is why they are both necessary. Such cooperation and justice will not apply to indefinite particulars, unless they are subject to universal rules, which constitute the Law (*Sharʿ*), and thus a *Holy Law* (*Sharīʿah*) is necessary. This term is, linguistically speaking, the source from which the thirsty draw (water to drink). It was applied to the above-mentioned process (of lawmaking), because of the equal profit society draws from it. This is the second principle.

We also say that the Law requires a person who lays down those rules and affirms them in the manner required. He is the Lawgiver.[1] Now were people to quarrel among themselves in laying down the Law, anarchy will ensue. Therefore, the Lawgiver must exceed them in being worthy of obedience, so that the others might obey him in accepting the Holy Law. To be worthy of obedience is confirmed by those rules[2] which indicate that the Holy Law comes from his Lord and these verses are these miracles, which are either verbal or performative. The particular characteristics of the verbal (signs) are more manageable; whereas the *general* characteristics of the performative are more manageable. The performative cannot be accomplished without the verbal, because prophethood and miracle-making cannot be achieved without calling for the good. Therefore, it is necessary that a lawgiver who is both prophet and miracle-maker should exist. This is a third principle.

Moreover, the general public and the weak-minded despise the disturbance of the balance of justice, which is conducive to the pursuit of their livelihood generically, whenever craving for what they need personally takes hold of them; and so they proceed to violate the law. That is why there exists reward and punishment in the life-to-come; so that hope and fear might compel them to obey and to shun disobedience. For the Holy Law cannot be secured without this as well as it should in accordance with it. Therefore, doers of good or bad deeds ought to receive a reward from God, who is able to reward them, and is conversant with what they reveal and conceal, whether in form of thought, words or deeds.

The knowledge of the author of reward and of the lawgiver ought also to be incumbent on those who obey the Holy Law from within that Holy Law. However, general knowledge is rarely certain and therefore is not fixed; therefore there must exist alongside it an agent retaining it, which is memory attended by repetition. That which comprises them both is a form of worship reminding the worshipper

1. That is, a prophet in Muslim usage.
2. Of the Qur'ān.

of the Object of Worship and repeated at successive remnants, such as prayer and the like.

Therefore, the prophet ought to be a caller to belief in: 1) the existence of a Creator, who is omnipotent and all-knowing; 2) as well as belief in a truthful lawgiver sent by Him; 3) confession of promise and threat in the world-to-come; 4) performing certain rituals in which the name of the Creator is mentioned, together with the attributes of His majesty; and 5) conforming to certain legal rules which mankind need in their transactions, so that the call to that justice which ensures the survival of the species might continue.

This is a fourth principle. Add to this that all this is predetermined by the First Providence, because of mankind's need for it. Hence, it exists in all places and at all times. This is all that is required, which is again no more general than which can be conceived. Those who obey the law are accorded, in addition to this great worldly gain the great other-worldly gain, according to what they have been promised. To the Gnostics among them has been added, above and beyond the early and late gain, the true above-mentioned perfection.

Look then at the Wisdom, which consists in the endurance of order in this fashion; then at the mercy which ensures the great reward, together with the great gain; and finally at the grace, which is the true jubilation superadded to them both. Then, you will perceive the presence of Him who provides all these goods, as One whose wonders will dazzle you; that is, will overcome and surprise you. Apply then the Law and head rightly towards that holy presence.

Here the eminent commentator objected saying: 'If by necessity in your statement, "since mankind needed a lawgiver, his existence became necessary", you mean essential necessity, then that is absurd. If, on the other hand, you mean by it is necessary where God Almighty is concerned, just at the Mu'tazilites assert, then this is different from your own view.[1] If, finally, you mean that that (necessity) is the cause of that order which is a certain good, who is God Almighty, source of every good, then it follows that it must flow necessarily from Him. However, this is also false; since it is not necessary that the best must always exist, or else all people would be naturally good, this being the best'.

'Similarly, to say that miracles do not prove that the lawgiver is sent by God is not worthy of you. For, the cause of miracles, according to you, is a psychological condition of which the prophets partake, as do their counterparts, the magicians, as will appear in the Fourth Section.'[2]

'Now, the prophet differs from his counterpart insofar as he calls for goodness, rather than evil, the distinction between good and evil being a rational proposition. It follows that miracles do not prove that their workers are prophets.

1. Ṭūsī appears to be engaging in a debate with Ibn Sīnā on the question of the good as independent of the divine decree, first raised by the Mu'tazilites.

2. *al-Namaṭ al-'āshir* of the *Ishārāt*.

Similarly, to say that miracles prove the veracity of their workers rests on belief in a free agent, who knows temporal particulars, to which you[1] do not subscribe. Finally, to assert that punishment is a corollary of acts of disobedience does not conform to your principles for the punishment of the sinner, according to you, consists in his soul yearning for this world, once it has left it. You also hold that the sinner's forgetting of his sin entails the cessation of the punishment to which he is liable.'

The answer, according to their[2] principles, is to say, as for the first point, the dependence of natural operations upon their necessary purposes, if we concede the existence of the divine providence in the above-mentioned manner, is sufficient to prove the reality of those (natural) operations. That is why they justify the existence of actions by reference to their purposes, such as broadening some teeth, for instance, which contributes to the efficiency of digestion, which is their purpose.

Now, but for the fact that that purpose entails the existence of the action, it would not be possible to use it as justification. As for his statement: 'The best is not necessary', we distinguish between the best for all and the best for some. The first is necessary, but not the second. That the people are good by nature is not of this type, as already mentioned. As for the second (statement), we comment that strange occurrences, which include miracles, are either verbal or performative, as we have seen. The miracles attributed to the prophet are not purely performative. Therefore, the correlation of the operative with the verbal is peculiar to them and is indicative of their truthfulness.

As for the third (statement), we comment that, in addition to what has been said already with respect to knowledge and power, the observation of the miracles, which are signs of the souls of the prophets, indicates the perfection of those souls and should entail believing their words.

As for the fourth (statement), we comment that committing acts of disobedience entails the existence of an ingrained habit in the soul, which necessitates its punishment. Forgetting an action does not nullify that habit, so as to necessitate the cancellation of punishment.

You should know that all that the Shaykh has mentioned, regarding the Holy Law and prophethood is not such that one cannot live without it. They are rather matters without which the order conducive to the well-being of the public, with respect to livelihood and resurrection, cannot be achieved. To be able to survive, men only need a type of political system conducive to preserving their necessary association, even if that kind (of association) were dependent on conquest or suchlike. The proof of this is the fact that the inhabitants of the inhabited world manage to live according to necessary systems of government.

1. Addressing Ibn Sīnā.
2. He appears to mean the philosophers in general.

Chapter 5
Remark: 'The Gnostic seeks the First Truth for no other reason'

I say: Having mentioned the goals of the Gnostic and the non-Gnostic, with respect to asceticism and worship, and having established the principles of the goals of others than he; I mean, reward and punishment, he proceeded to refer in this chapter to the goals of the Gnostic in what he intends.

We say: The Gnostic has in point of real perfection two states relative to him; the first is peculiar to his soul alone, and that is his love of that perfection; the second is peculiar to both his soul and body and that is his motion for the purpose of coming closer to it. The Shaykh has designated the first as will, the second as worship. He has also mentioned that the will of the worshipper and his worship are linked to the First Truth, may He be glorified for Himself and not to anyone else by virtue of His Essence. If they are linked to anything other than the Truth, that would be for the sake of the Truth also.

His statement: 'Nothing can be preferred to knowing Him' means that nothing other than the Truth can be preferred to knowing Him. For the Truth as such is to be preferred to the knowledge thereof, because knowledge is not preferred by the known for its own sake, as he indicated in what follows: I mean his statement: 'That whoever prefers knowledge for the sake of knowledge is subscribing to the second (view).' For all that is preferred, but not for its own sake, is necessarily preferred for the sake of another. Thus, knowledge is preferred for the sake of another, who is the Truth and nothing else. For the Truth is preferable to knowledge. The Gnostic is said to prefer nothing other than the Truth over His knowledge, because the non-Gnostic prefers to earn the reward and guard against punishment, rather than knowledge. For he seeks knowledge for the sake of the two only; whereas, the Gnostic does not prefer anything else to Him, except that Truth, which is preferred for itself, in relation to Him. His[1] statement: 'And worshipping it only', indicates that the worship of the Gnostic depends also only on the Truth.

Should it be objected that this contradicts what he[2] has said already, to the effect that the Gnostic's worship is an exercise of his faculties, in order to draw them closer to the presence of the Truth, which is other than Himself; since drawing our faculties closer to the presence of the Truth is not the same as the Truth Himself, we would say that his intent is not that the Gnostic does not aim in his worship at anything other than the Truth absolutely, but rather that the Gnostic does not aim at anything other than the Truth in Himself. Indeed, He seeks the Truth in Himself, and were he to aim at something else, would seek it accidentally and for the sake of the Truth, as already mentioned.

---

1. Ibn Sīnā.
2. Ibn Sīnā.

This is a sound judgment, insofar as the Gnostic observes himself in relation to the First Truth, who is his object of desire for Himself. Then, if each one of these, the Truth and worship, is observed, in relation to each other, it will be found that predicating worship on the First Truth is necessary in the two senses. As for observing the Truth in relation to worship, it is by virtue of what he[1] mentioned in his statement: 'Because He is deserving of worship', but as for observing worship in relation to the Truth, it is by virtue of what he intended in his statement: 'And because it is a noble relation to Him'.

The Eminent Commentator has mentioned in this context that the worship of the Gnostics is either for the sake of the Truth Himself, or of an attribute of His; or for the sake of perfecting themselves. These are three classes set apart. The Shaykh referred to the first in these words: 'And worshipping Him alone'; to the second in these words: 'And because He is worthy of worship'; and to the third in these words: 'And because it is a noble relation to Him'.

I say that there is in this interpretation an admission that the Gnostic may have another object of worship as such other than the Truth; whereas the rest of this chapter indicates the opposite.

Moreover, the Shaykh has referred to the fact that the object of the Gnostic is different from the objects of other people in these words: Not for the sake of any desire or out of any fear'; that is, neither for a desire for rewards, or fear of punishment.

He has also shown the falsity of the view that it is an object in relation to the Gnostic in these words: 'And they were'. That is, if the desire and fear, already mentioned, were two goals of worship, then the desired reward and the despised punishment are the motive for worshipping the Truth, and therein lies the object of desire of the Worshipper of the Truth. Thus, the Truth will not be the end, but rather the means to earning the reward and avoiding the punishment, which is the goal and this is the object. Then, that would be the object of worship in itself, rather than the Truth. (This is the explanation of this chapter.)

The Eminent Commentator says: Some people have regarded the claim that God Almighty can be an object of desire in Himself as absurd and have contended that will is a faculty which bears on contingents only, because it entails choosing one aspect of the object desired rather than the other and that cannot be conceived except in the realm of contingents. He also says: 'The Shaykh has also demonstrated at the beginning of the sixth section[2] that whoever desires a thing must feel that acquiring the desired object is preferable to not acquiring it.' By the first object of desire should be meant the first intention which is the acquisition.

He also based on it his statement, that every desirer is perfectable. Therefore,

1. Ibn Sīnā.
2. *al-Ishārāt*, vol. 3, p. 122.

whoever intends God Almighty, his intention is not God Almighty, but rather his own self-perfection.

His[1] response to both is that they are a petition of principle, because they rest on the proposition that will cannot attach except to the possible or what perfects the desirer, which is the point of the objection.

We say: The Will attaches to God and nothing other than Him also. For, the point in showing that the will, which attaches to what the desirer does, entails the possibility of the object desired and the perfectibility of the desirer; not due to the will attaching itself to him, but rather because it is an action, or is accessible to the desirer by his will. Here, however, the object willed is different. Therefore, the objections fall to the ground.

Chapter 6
Remark: 'He who regards the Truth as intermediary deserves mercy in one sense ...'[2]

The Shaykh has noted in both cases the Tradition of the Prophet, may blessing and prayer be on him: 'Whoever's tongue (*laqlaq*), belly (*qahqab*) and male organ (*dhabdhab*) are guarded is well-guarded.' (Other lexical points.)

The aim of this chapter is to excuse whoever allows the Truth to be a means of winning another over; namely, one who despises the world and worships the Truth, either out of a desire for reward or out of fear of punishment. The true aspect of the pardon consists in showing its imperfections as such.

There are in the words of the Shaykh many subtleties, which are revealed to their observer. One of them is his description of sensuous pleasures as deformities, or an imperfection that cannot disappear. The other is his comparing one who cannot envisage true jubilation to a blind man who seeks something which he has missed. For, he reaches out with his hand to what is close to him, regardless of whether it is the object he is seeking or not.

Another subtle point is his calling attention to the fact that the asceticism of the non-Gnostic is a compulsory form of asceticism. For, although he looks like real ascetics, he is, of all people, the most attached to sensuous pleasures. For, whoever relinquishes one thing so as to receive its double in the future is much closer to greed than contentedness.

Another subtlety is his attributing the non-Gnostic's industry to meanness and weakness. For his (Ibn Sīnā's) words, 'There is no scope to his vision', implies that he is too mean to deserve those sensuous pleasures. Add to this (subtlety) his eloquent expressions in singling out the pleasures of the belly and the private parts.

1. The Commentator's.
2. The commentary opens with a series of Arabic lexical points.

He (the Shaykh) has also mentioned at the end of this chapter that this imperfect pitiable fellow will receive what he expects and seeks assiduously of sensuous pleasures, in accordance with what the blessed prophets have promised. He has referred to the modality of that in the Eighth Section, where he mentions the possibility of the souls of imbeciles attaching to bodies which are the creation of their imaginations. He has designated that happiness as the happiness they deserve.

Chapter 7
Remark: 'The first grade of the motions of Gnostics is what they themselves call the will ...'

I say: *Iʿtarāh* means occurred to him, and clinging to the 'Strongest Bond'[1] is taking refuge therein.

You should know that the Shaykh, having mentioned the objectives of the Gnostics and others, wanted to mention their consequent states as they followed the path of Truth, from the beginning of their motion to its end, which is attaining God Almighty.

He also wanted to explain what occurs to them in the mansions they attain; so he gave them in eleven consecutive chapters. The first is this one, which contains the mention of the principles of their motions. Thus, he mentioned that will is the first of their grades, which are ranged according to their motions and is the proximate principle of movement. Its starting point is conceiving the essential perfection proper to the First Principle, whose effects flow upon those of His creation who are prepared, according to the measure of their preparedness. This is followed by assenting to His existence in a definite way, accompanied by the soul's quietude, regardless of whether that (assent) is apodictic, resting on a demonstrative syllogism, or an act of faith derived from assenting to the words of the masters, who guide to God Almighty. For each one of these two (modes of assent) is a form of belief entailing the instigation of its subject to pursue that emanation. Now, insofar as the will is dependent on that assent, he (*i.e.* Ibn Sīna) has defined it as a state which ensues upon investigation or the above-mentioned loss. Then, he declared that it consists in the desire to cling to the Strongest Bond, which neither changes nor perishes, and is therefore the starting point of progress towards the Sacred World. Its aim is to acquire the spirit of conjunction (*ittiṣāl*), with that world.

You should know that the Shaykh has mentioned in the Third Section[2] that voluntary animal motion has four consecutive principles: 1) understanding, then 2) yearning, called concupiscence or anger, 3) then determination, which is called decisive will and 4) the consenting faculty disseminated in the different organs.

1. Qur'ān 2:256 and 31:22.
2. Cf. *al-Ishārāt*, vol. 2, pp. 435 f.

This last faculty is voluntary, but not animal, and possesses the first of the above-mentioned principles. This corresponds to what he has termed investigation or the stage corresponding to the quiescence of the soul. It also has the second and the third, which he has designated as will. They are allied here, because they do not differ, except as a result of differing motives or deterrents; but that difference cannot be conceived in conjunction with the quiescence of the soul, which he proposed here as a condition. The fourth principle is left out, because that motion is not corporal.

(The Eminent Commentator has given in explaining this chapter the types of seekers of Truth and the training appropriate to each type; but this is not relevant to its subject-matter.)

Chapter 8
Remark: 'Moreover, he will require training ... .'

The aim of this chapter is the discussion of the disciple's[1] need for training and the aims of that training. I will mention, before engaging in the discussion, the nature of training or exercise. Now, the aim of the training of beasts consists in barring them from certain movements which the trainer does not approve and forcing them to perform what he likes, so that they will get used to obeying him.

As for the animal faculty which is the root of perceptions, as well as animal operations in man, whenever they do not possess the habit of obeying the rational faculty, they are really similar to an untrained beast. That faculty is actuated at times by its lust and at others times by its anger, both of which are stimulated by the imaginative and estimative (faculties), on account of what they resemble at times, or receive from the external senses at other times. They would then concur with them, and move in various animal ways due to those motives. The animal faculty sometimes uses the rational faculty in seeking its objectives, and thus it corresponds to the 'commanding soul,'[2] from which actions of various types arise.

The animal[3] (faculty) is submissive by force and is disturbed, but if it is trained by the rational faculty, by preventing it from imaginings, estimations, sensations and those actions which stimulate lust or anger, on the one hand, and forcing it to submit to what practical reason stipulates, to the point of becoming well-disposed to obey it and is willing to serve it, submit to its orders and desist its prohibitions, on the other hand, then the rational (faculty) will be 'quiescent'[4] and no essentially different action will emanate from it. Then all the remaining faculties will be obedient and submissive to it.

1. Or novice (*murīd*), a technical Sufi term.
2. The soul 'commanding' evil, as in Qur'ān 12:53.
3. The text says rational (?).
4. Cf. Qur'ān 89:27.

There are other intermediate conditions, depending on the degree of one or the other being in control, whereby the animal (faculty) will follow its own fancy and resist the rational. It will subsequently regret and then it will become 'reproachful.'[1] These faculties have been designated as 'commanding,' 'reproachful' and 'quiescent' in conformity with these attributes ascribed to it in the divine revelation.[2]

Accordingly, training the soul denotes prohibiting it from following its whims and commanding it to obey its master. But since the rational objectives are diverse, the forms of training are diverse. Some are forms of rational exercise, referred to in (books of) practical wisdom; others are auditory exercises, called legal observances, the most delicate observances; of which being the exercises of the Gnostics; for they only seek the Face of God, everything else being a distraction for them. Their training consists in barring the soul from turning towards anything other than the First Truth and forcing it to turn towards Him, so that turning towards Him and desisting from anything else will become an ingrained habit for it.

It is clear that every exercise is part of this training in reality, but not its converse. However, they differ to the extent their ranks differ in their conduct, beginning from the highest variety and ending with the most delicate.

This is what I wished to say on the subject of training. I will now return to the main subject and state that the highest aim of training is one thing; namely, achieving true perfection. But that is dependent on the attainment of an existential condition, which is disposition. Achieving that condition, however, depends on removing the obstacles, which are either external or internal. It follows that training in this sense is directed towards three goals: 1) The first is removing whatever is beneath the Truth from gaining favour and this is the meaning of removing external obstacles. 2) The second is forcing the 'commanding soul' to submit to 'the quiescent,' so that the imagination and estimation are drawn to the sacred presence and away from the inferior presence. Then the remaining faculties will follow suit necessarily by removing the intellectual obstacles; I mean the already mentioned animal desires. 3) The third is the subtilization of the Secret for the sake of attention, which consists in acquiring the disposition for achieving perfection. For the correspondence of the Secret to the subtle object is not possible without its subtilization.

Now, the subtlety of the Secret consists in its readiness, so that rational forms may be represented in it quickly and are affected by divine matters which easily delight the yearning and passion.

Moreover, when the Shaykh concluded the discussion of the aims of exercise, he proceeded to mention whatever is helpful in attaining each of those aims.

As for the first, he mentioned that the one thing which helps in attaining it

1. Cf. Qur'ān 75:2.
2. i.e. the Qur'ān.

is that true asceticism pertaining to the Gnostics, which consists in shunning whatever directs the Secret from the Truth, as already mentioned, and this is obvious.

As for the second, he gave three things which help in attaining it. The first is worship attended by thought, meaning that which belongs to the Gnostics. The advantage of its conjunction with thought is that worship causes the body as a whole to follow the soul. Thus, if the soul were nevertheless directed towards the presence of the Truth by means of thought, then man would become wholly turned towards the Truth; otherwise worship would become a source of unhappiness, as the Almighty has said: "Woe unto those who pray, but are oblivious of their prayer."[1] The way in which this prayer helps to attain the second aim is that it is also a kind of exercise of the worshipper's and Gnostic's powers, and the faculties of his soul, aimed at diverting them by means of habituation from the presence of illusion to the presence of the Truth, as already mentioned.

The second is melodies, which help both essentially and accidentally. The way they help essentially is that the rational soul welcomes them, due to its admiration of coordinated harmonies and regulated ratios, manifested in the voice which is the matter of reason. It then forgets the use of animal faculties for its particular aims and then these faculties are made to follow it, and the melodies will be subservient to it also.

As for its help accidentally, that will consist in finding the words corresponding to (the melodies), by way of reception on the part of the imagination, insofar as it includes simulation, to which the soul naturally inclines. Then if the words are declamatory, calling for seeking perfection, the soul becomes attentive to what ought to be done and then it will overcome the faculties distracting it and subjugates them.

The third consists in the declamatory speech itself; I mean, that which is conducive to assenting to what ought to be done by way of persuasion and the soul's quiescence. For it exhorts the soul and causes it to subdue the other faculties, especially if it is attended by four things. The first refers to the speaker, or his being intelligent. For this is an attestation of his truthfulness; the sermonization of one who does not accept advice will not succeed, because his actions belie his words.

The remaining three refer to speech. 1) One relates to the utterance, which consists in being expressed in eloquent words; that is, which are pleasant and of clear intent of all that the speaker means, without increase or decrease, as if it is a mould into which the meaning was cast. 2) Another relates to the form of the utterance, whereby it is given in a musical voice; since the soft voice indicates the form of the soul, contributing thereby to ready acceptance. Its harshness contributes, by

1. Qur'ān 107:4–5.

contrast, to a form preparing it to refusal of acceptance. Musical tones also have different effects on the soul, each of which corresponds to a different kind of form. Physicians and orators use these in treating psychic illnesses or effecting the desired kinds of persuasion, according to those modes of correspondence. 3) Another relates to meaning, which should follow a sensible course; namely, conducive to that assent which profits the disciple quickly.

You should know that the same sermonizing speech is called in the art of rhetoric the 'pillar;' whereas the aforementioned matters attached to it and conducive to persuasion are called 'drawings out.'

As for the third, he[1] has mentioned two things which facilitate it. The first is refined thought, which consists in its being moderate in quality and quantity and at times during which bodily functions, such as over-eating or vomiting and the like, do not bar the soul from rational understanding. For, excessive preoccupation with such thoughts will give the soul a property which enables it to apprehend matters easily. The second is pure love. For, you should know that human love is divisible into real, already discussed, and figurative. The latter is divisible into spiritual and beastly. The spiritual is the one whose principle is the resemblance of the soul of the lover to that of the loved one in essence, whereby he admires the fine traits of the beloved, because they are effects emanating from his soul. The beastly is the one whose principle is beastly lust and the desire for beastly pleasure, whereby the lover admires the shape of the beloved, his looks, colour, and the delineation of his organs, which are bodily matters.

The Shaykh intended by the expression 'pure love' the first of the two figures, because the second is consequent upon the 'commanding' soul's control and assists it to subserve the rational faculty. It is often attended by debauchery and clinging to it; whereas the first is different, since it causes the soul to be mellow, compassionate, characterized by yearning and tenderness, disinterested in worldly cares, repelling anything other than the beloved and reducing all its cares to a single care. That is why it is easier for the lover to cling to the real beloved than anybody else because he does not need to turn away from many things. This is what is meant by the saying: 'Whoever loves and remains pure keeps his secret, then dies, will die as a martyr'.

Chapter 9
Remark: 'Then if will and exercise have reached a certain pitch ...' (Arabic lexical points)

The Shaykh has referred in this chapter to the lower degrees of passion and conjunction which only occur after a certain measure of readiness, acquired through

1. Ibn Sīnā.

will and exercise, is achieved, and then goes on increasing with increased preparedness. Its designation as 'moment' has been observed in the saying of the Prophet, may God bless him and his family: 'I have with God a moment which no favoured angel or a sent prophet can dispense with'. The two passions attendant upon the time are not equal, because the first is a form of sorrow at the tardiness of the passion, the other regret for missing it.

TREATISE ON THE DIVISION OF EXISTENTS

Risālah andar qismat-i mawjūdāt

Reprinted from Naṣīr al-Dīn Ṭūsī, *Risālah andar qismat-i mawjūdāt,* ed. M. T. Mudarris Raḍawī, tr. Parviz Morewedge as *The Metaphysics of Tusi: Treatise on the Division of Existents* (New York, 1992), pp. 1–58.

In the Name of God, the Merciful, the Compassionate.

So states [The Learned Mawlānā], The King of the wise, the ally of the nation [of the faithful] and of religion—may he be protected by God, with His blessing and His benedictions:

(1) [Let us reflect] on the division of Existents. Among the theologians their division is of two kinds: either they do or do not have an initiator. The first are generated; the second are eternal. Eternal, however, is the essence of God the Exalted and His Attributes. The followers of Ash'arī [the theologians who are occasionalists] hold that eight attributes are co-eternal with It: power, knowledge, life, comprehension, will, [the faculty of] hearing, sight, and logos [lit. language]. The ancient [theological school of] Mu'tazilah [the upholders of free will] hold the view that Divine attributes are neither existent nor deprived [of existence]. There is a controversy between them on this topic. The true position is that the essence of the Divine Truth and The Exalted is a unity from any perspective; no existing attribute [need be] added to It.

(2) The generated is either [situated] in a [spatio-temporal] subject, or is a state in a subject, or neither is in a subject nor is a state in a subject. The majority of the theologians deny the [existence of the] third kind, and call the second kind 'an accident'.

(3) The first kind is either divisible or indivisible. If it is indivisible, it is called 'a substance'. If it is divisible, it is so from either one, two, or three dimensions. The first is called 'a line', the second 'a surface', the third 'a body'. A body is either dense or light, dense being like water and earth, light being like the angels, jinn, and air.

(4) That which is a state in a subject [i.e., the second kind] and is called 'an accident' is of two kinds. Either it cannot or [it] can be in a subject without that existent [in which it resides]. The first [divided into three groups] is called a[n actual] being and this is realized in a subject. Thus, realization in a subject comes about either due to realization by another entity, or due to the realization in [the subject] itself, or due to privation. The first is called 'motion', the second 'rest', the third 'the primary [actual] being'.

(5) The second division is of two kinds with regard to extension, [either] it is in need of, or it is not in need of, a substance [for it to be instantiated].[1] The first are the sensibles [received] by the five senses and are of five kinds. The first, being sensed by sight, is [the set of] colours. Some hold that the principal colours are white and black. Muʿtazilah hold the fundamental colours to be five: white, black, red, yellow, and green. Others hold that all [colours] are fundamental. The second kind of sensible, which is sound, is sensed by the auditory faculty. Notes are qualities found in sounds by means of instruments. The third kind are the sensibles to the sense of taste, the gustatory [sensations] such as the sharpness [of spices], bitterness, saltiness, sweetness, fattiness, acidity, astringency, briskness, and blandness, and all combinations of these [sensations]. The fourth are the sensibles to the olfactory [organ], odours, such as pleasant smells called perfumes and unpleasant odours called stenches, as well as [those which are] neither pleasant nor unpleasant. The fifth are those sensed by the sensation of touch, which are of two kinds: first sensations of pressure, which are weight and lightness; the second are these four: hot, cold, wet, and dry.

(6) The [members of the] second group which with respect to extension are in need of a place are of two kinds: one [i] which is not and the second [ii] which is in need or privation [of a subject]. The first [i] is in an aggregate [state] while the second [ii] is of two kinds.[2] Of the second, the first type [ii–a] is such that others cannot exist without it, and such is life. The other type [ii–b] is such that others exist without it, and of this there are two further types, one [ii–b1] which can exist in proportion in all parts, e.g., pain; the other [ii–b2] which cannot be in all parts but only in a specific part, and of this in turn there are two types, [ii–b21] and [ii–b22]. The first [ii–b21] is not peculiar to a unique organ and is [called] a power, the other [ii–b22] is peculiar to a unique organ, e.g., to the heart [of the entity], and of this again there are two types, [ii–b221 and ii–b222]. The first [ii–b221] pertains to attraction towards or repulsion away from an entity, while the second [ii–b222] does not pertain to attraction or repulsion. The first [ii–b221] is of two kinds, one [ii–b2211] being related to the acquisition or privation of an entity, and that is will or repulsion; or, it is not such, and that [ii–b2212] is lust and hatred.[3] That which does not pertain to attraction and repulsion [ii–b222] is of two kinds: it [ii–b2221]

1. Ṭūsī's use of the expression *buʿd* which we translate as 'extension' [and it could also be translated as 'distance'] is ambiguous here. The text specifies the classification as follows: first it belongs to those entities which are not in need of extension, or which consist of sensibles, which in the Peripatetic tradition are explained by discrete measure; and second those which are in need of an extended substance. The latter are intentional, mental, and psychological entities and predicates, such as pain, grief, and life. In order for these accidents to be realized, they have to reside in an extended entity.

2. For example, a musical duet is formed without anything perishing.

3. In the case of lust, the self is the beneficiary of the desire, whereas in the case of will the object with which one is concerned may have no effect on the subject.

is either a command about existents either in a positive or a negative [manner], or a desire [ii–b2222] for that command.

(7) A command is either [c1] decisive or [c2] indecisive. The first [c1] is called belief and is of two kinds: either it is in accord with [deliberated consent] [c11] or not [c12], in which case it is absolute ignorance.[1] If it [c11] is in accord with consent, then either it is due to a cause [c111] which is similar or dissimilar to that belief [itself]. Or, if it is due to a cause, then that cause is either [c1111] obtained or [c1112] not obtained. If it is obtained [c1111], then it is theoretical, whereas if it [c1112] is due to an inner condition such as the states of hunger or satiety it is called subjective. If it [c112] is not due to a cause that is similar to that belief, then it is imitation. If it [c2] is insufficient [to initiate the action in question], it is called conjecture [about opinions]. If one side dominates the other [it is called] a prehension.[2] If both sides are equal, it is called doubt.

(8) The second, which is a desire for a decision [ii–b2222], is called a consideration. This is the summation of the division of entities according to the theologians. Whatever is not among these is not considered an existent. Others consider annihilation, death, weakness, will, repulsion, which are [inapplicable to God], as accidents. This is far from the truth. Thus, ephemeral-created genera are in these twenty-two groups: first substance and the remainder as accident: places, colours, sounds, tastes, odours, lightness or heaviness (lit. reliance), heat, cold, wetness, dryness, completion, life, pain, power, will, repulsion, lust, aversion, belief, conjecture, and consideration. Ten of these genera depend on the five functions of the bodily parts: [experiences of] beings, sounds, lightness and heaviness, compulsion, and pain; five are actions of the heart: will, repulsion, belief, conjecture, and [scientific] speculation.

(9) The second species of division of existent according to the position of the philosophers [is twofold]: necessary or contingent. Only God the Exalted is necessary. Contingent existents, however, are of two kinds: those in need of a subject and those that are not in a subject.[3] The difference between the subject and the place is this: the subject does not depend on what is imbedded in it and [may] persist [by itself], while what is embedded in it cannot persist without it. That which is in a subject is an accident. Thus, a substance is [logically] either [i] in a place, [ii] itself is a place, [iii] composed of state and a place, or [iv] is neither a place, nor a state, nor a composite of these. The first is called a form, the second, matter; the third, body, and the fourth, the separate entities. The form is either such that all bodies

---

1. See the position of the *Theatetus* (201C-210B) that knowledge is belief plus an explanation.

2. The term *wahm* here is translated as 'prehension', see, P. Morewedge, 'The Internal Sense of Prehension (*Wahm*) in Islamic Philosophy', in James T. H. Martin, ed., *Philosophies of Being and Mind: Ancient and Medieval* (New York, 1991), pp. 182–216.

3. This is not a logical division.

in it are equivalent and is called a form of super-lunary bodies, or it is unlike this and would be a form of a [sub-lunary] species. Matter of the form of a species may be alterable or not; the former is called the matter of the elements or of the world of generation and corruption, the latter is the matter of the heavens.

(10) Bodies are of two kinds [j1 and j2]: first [j1] are noble bodies called the heavenly bodies subdivided into two, luminary [j11] and dark [j12]. The first are called the stars, the second the heavens. The second type of bodies [j2] are those of the world of generation and corruption, which are sub-lunary and are of two kinds, the simple [bodies] [j21] and the composites [j22]. Simples [j21] are of four kinds: fire, air, water, and earth. Composites [j22] are of three kinds, which are called [three] kinds [of mixtures]; first, minerals; second, plants; third, animals. Minerals are of two kinds: [solid] bodies and [non-solid] [lit. immaterial] entities. Solid minerals [which are capable of being melted] are of seven kinds: gold, silver, copper, iron, tin, lead, and *kharsiyānī* [a yellow gold-like metal]. Non-solid [minerals] are spirits and souls and the like. [Mineral] spirits are quicksilver, and active principles [lit. souls] of arsenic and sulphur, and the like. Either they are aromatic roots, such as salty mixtures, vitriol, sodium nitrate, and the like; or they are bodies like stones and the like [which do not go through a meltdown process].

(11) Plants are of two types: either they have a stem and are called trees, or they have no stem and are called bushes [lit. *najm*]. Each of them may or may not have a fruit.

(12) An animal may be rational and non-rational, rational like human beings, or non-rational like [non-human] animals. These are beasts, members of the lion family, wild animals of the deserts, birds, reptiles, insects, and alike.

(13) But the separated entities are, or are not, governors of and processors of bodies. The first kind is called soul, and it consists of two kinds: angelic and human. The second kind is called intelligence. The first intelligence is called the universal intelligence, and the last is the active intelligence and the bestower of forms. Some [philosophers] maintain that these [forms bestowed] are accidents in the souls and the intelligences and call them spiritual accidents.

(14) Accidents are of two kinds: either capable of being divided into parts or capable of being related. A third kind is neither capable of division nor relation.[1] The first are called quantities, the second relations, and the third qualities. Quantities are of two kinds: either they have or do not have a limit shared [by their constituents]. The first is called a continuous quantity, the second a discrete quantity. [Concerning a continuous quantity], the entity may be one of two kinds: either *qār al-dhāt*, a continuum [such as water] whose constituents exist simultaneously, or a non-*qār al-dhāt* continuum [such as time] whose constituents do not exist simultaneously. A continuous entity not capable of division in any dimension is called a point; if

1. Ṭūsī presupposes but does not mention this third class.

it is divisible from the dimension of length, it is called a line, of which there are two kinds: straight and curved. If it is divisible from the dimension of length and width, it is called a surface, of which there are two kinds, simple and convex. If it is divisible in three aspects, it is called a body. Such a body is an analytical [concept of a] body, while an [empirically grounded one] is a natural body. That whose parts do not persist together [i.e., non-*qār al-dhāt*] is called time, which is the measure of motion. The discrete quantitative kind is called a number.

(15) But qualities are of four [general] kinds. First [there are] the five sensible qualities [of the five senses]. The sensibles with respect to sight are of two kinds: colour and light. The sensibles with respect to the auditory sense are of two kinds: notes and sounds; the sensibles with respect to taste, food; with respect to the olfactory sense, odours; with respect to the sense of touch, the four qualities, pressure and lightness and others. The second [general] type of qualities of the soul [are psychological and are] of two kinds: either quick to depart and that is called [a psychological] state, like happiness, sadness, sorrow, shame, grief, anger, lust, and others. Or, they are slow to depart and are called agreeable and disagreeable dispositions, such as purity, resignation, avarice, jealousy, and the like. The third [general] kind is [preparing] the defensive [system] which consists of the elimination of a [malady] and is called power, such as [adopting a regime] for the cure, or acceptance of an effect, which is called lack of power, such as sickness. The fourth [general] kind is a quality specific to quantities. In continuous entities, in the case of the line, straightness and curvature; in the case of figures, four-sidedness and three-sidedness; among the discrete entities, in the case of numbers, evenness and oddness; and in conclusion, qualities capable of being increased and decreased and other classes [of qualities] with similar features.

(16) [Consider] the relational accidents; they are of seven kinds: first, relations which relate two entities [the members of the range and the domain of relations], such as fatherhood and being a son, being higher and being lower, being sister and being brother, and others. Second is 'place', which is the relation between that which resides in its [location] and [the location] itself; the third is time, and that is the link among bodies with a temporal duration, or with that aspect of time called 'a moment'; fourth is posture, the relation among parts, such as sitting and rising, and others. Fifth is possession, the relationship of a body with what is included in it and is transported with its transferral, such as the wearing of clothes, the putting on of shoes, or the placing of a ring on the finger. Sixth is action, the affecting of an existent, such as cutting and breaking. Seventh is passion, accepting the effect, such as being broken and being cut, and the like. Thus, [according to philosophers] the highest genera which apply to all contingent being are ten: substance, quantity, quality, relation, place, time, posture, state, action, passion; these are called the ten categories. In this poem there are examples of each of the ten:

A tall man, good and nobler [than any other] in town,
With his wealth, he rests on his domain today.

(17) Some say that unity and a point are two existents which are not included in the categories. According to the *mutakallimūn,* many of these divisions do not exist. For the analytical [philosophers], however, they all exist, some in the mind, and some in the [external] world of determined entities.

(18) On the differentia. On [the subject of] motion and rest the theologians hold that these are of two [distinct] genera. Among the philosophers, however, motion [is described to be] the gradual coming out [of a state]. It happens in four modes: in the category of quantity there are two kinds: first, expansion of volume, a body being augmented in its own natural place—for example, when water is heated, it cannot be confined to its place—and compression, the opposite of [expansion]; second, growth, and its opposite, withering. Among the animals it applies to being obese and being thin, which are becoming fat and lean [correspondingly]. In the same manner in the category of quality, such as leaving [the state] of blackness to [receive the property] of whiteness, from power to weakness, from health to sickness which are called modification of one's state. That which is the vapour [lit. wind] of water is not considered a motion; from one perspective it is called a corruption with respect to that vapour, and a generation with respect to the wind. With respect to the category of place, [there is] departure from a place, and that is called locomotion. Straight motion belongs to this genius. [However, if such a motion should take place] in the category of position [lit. posture], then it is called circular motion, in which case, while positions are altered, [the entity] as a whole is not transported [from its place].

(19) Types of changes which involve two things which together cannot [co-exist in their present state], are of four [types]: negation and affirmation, such as 'Zayd is a human' and 'Zayd is not human'; secondly due to disposition and privation and such as 'Zayd sees' and 'Zayd is blind'; thirdly, due to relation, such as 'Zayd is the father of Amr'; fourthly, by way of contrariety, such as 'Zayd is white' and 'Zayd is black'. The difference between contrary and contradictory is that the contraries cannot be added, but remain distinct from one another. The contradictories are neither added nor can they be taken away from one another. The distinction between contraries, privations, and dispositions is that in the pair of contraries, privations, and dispositions cannot both exist simultaneously, but at any given time one must exist. The distinction between relations and other species is such that the latter apply only to one existent, while the former apply to two [existents]. The difference between negation and affirmation, one the one hand, and contradictories, on the other, is that the former are more common than the latter, because contradictories differ with respect to negation and affirmation, and not all things distinct with respect to negation and affirmation are [necessarily] contradictories.

(20) Priority is [of] six [kinds]: First, priority with respect to order, such as priority of yesterday to today; the philosophers have proven this type of priority. Second, priority with respect to [inner] essence, such as the priority of cause to effect; the ancients did not provide proof for this [type of priority]. Third, priority with respect to time, such as the priority with respect to father and son; fourth, priority with respect to place, such as the priority between the leader [for example, Imam in the prayer] and the followers. Fifth, priority with respect to nobility, such as the priority of Muḥammad [may God bless him and his descendants] to Abū Bakr [the first caliph]. Sixth, priority with respect to nature, such as priority of one to two. Posteriority and concurrence follow the same argument. [Let us consider the following] problem.

(21) The atomic substance of a simple body is continuous for sense perception, [and] it is divisible. Thus it must be in one of two states: it [i] may be composed of parts that cannot be divided [themselves]; [in the context of perception, this] connection is a constitution among parts; discreteness, however, is privation of a constitution. Or, [ii] [the simple body] may not be a composite. In that case, the reality of the body is this very continuousness and connection that appears to the sense. If it is divided, it is either so [ii.1] due to a given cause that necessitates its division, such as cutting or diminishing; or, due to the distinction of its accidents, such as whiteness and blackness; or, due to the different oppositions; or, in conjecture. [Let us turn our attention to] the conceptual analysis of division. It is a consequence of a distinction between two or more bodies. In each of these two we are presented with two sub-cases: either there is or is not a finite [magnitude] in each part or division. Thus, concerning this issue there are four possible positions. The first concerns a body composed of parts, the parts being finite, such that largeness or smallness of the body is due to the number of the parts being many or few. Each part is called an atom[ic substance], parts being indivisible. Most theologians hold this doctrine. The second doctrine, following the first, similarly holds that a body is composed of parts, except that the parts are infinite.[1] This is the doctrine of [the theologian] Naẓẓām and some of the Ancients. The third view is that a body is not a composite, but is infinitely divisible; ultimately, however, one arrives at a point where further division is impossible, indicating the falsity of this position. The fourth school states that a body is not a composite but is receptive to division into parts that are infinite, and the meaning of infinite parts [unlike the third thesis] is that division never results in a state in which further division is impossible. [This is the case,] even though such dividing is only imaginable or thought. However, the parts realized [from this operation] are finite [in number], since one [may at any point] identify a first and a last [part]. Notwithstanding that what has been

1. The text is not clear about whether (a) each part is infinitely divisible, or (b) there is an infinite number of indivisible elements. Logically, there is a third possibility, combining (a) and (b), that a body is made up of an infinite number of infinitely divisible parts.

realized [at any stage] is finite, division will never result in a state in which the quantity is incapable of further division. This is the meaning of infinitude in this context. This is the doctrine of the philosophers, and some of the recent theologians adhere to this thesis.[1]

(22) The theologians offer many proofs of the first position [listed above], and we shall cite a few of them which we recall. The first proof states that the motion of whatever moves from one place to another must be finite [e.g., it cuts a surface or a line]. Since motion is not instantaneous [lit. *qār al-dhāt*] no two parts of it can exist at the same time. Thus, while the motion is in progress [lit. when it is between the initial and the terminal point], some part of it persists, while another part has passed away, and what had passed away and has not remained has no existence, since whatever has passed is gone and whatever has remained [to come] has not yet been realized. Therefore, in all cases there exists a part not receptive to division, because, if that existing part would be receptive to division, [then] some [constituent of the existing part] would be prior to other [of its constituents]. Now, whatever is prior belongs to the past and is deprived of existence. Whatever is posterior would not yet have been realized, since one cannot find two of its parts to be co-present. It follows then that some of the parts which had been assumed to exist, would, [in this line of reasoning,] be established not to exist; [but] this is contradictory and refutable. Consequently, what exist of a motion cannot be divided. And when this motion passes, whatever becomes realized, the same rule applies to it. Thus, uninterrupted succession is a necessary feature of motions; it means that motion is composed of indivisible parts, each [existing] part dividing the distance covered [by the motion]. Otherwise [the following situation holds: (i)] some of the sectors of motion do not dissect [a sector of the spatial span], and other cases follow this principle; [(ii)] thus, no part of the distance is covered during the entire motion. This is, of course, impossible. [Thus, according to this first proof, it follows that] the measure in question which is dissected by the part in question itself is not receptive to division, because what is receptive to being divided into two [halves] would remain divisible prior to the motion until the last [state of division, as illustrated in the case of Zeno's paradox.] Thus, the motion which we had supposed to have been indivisible turned out to be in fact divisible. Hence, a sector of this [distance] would be indivisible; that is the magnitude of the atom[ic substance].

(23) The second proof [is as follows]. Time exists, i.e., a temporal [unit] either has passed, or is expected to come, or it is in the present [state]; and the past and

1. Ṭūsī makes a distinction between an analytic, or a syntactical division, which may be infinite due to a postulated definition, and an ontic sense of divisibility as that an actual entity. The latter is never infinite, since each state of its division consists of a finite number of divided parts. Therefore, there are two realms of being, a mathematical, analytical realm, and the realm of actual entities, which, following Aristotle's rejection of an actual infinite, must be finite.

what is expected to come do not exist. Therefore, if [the present] state does not exist, time does not exist.[1] If it were divisible, some [sector of] the past, future, or present would also be divisible. the [present] state, however, is not divisible, and a portion of the body whose state the moving [agent] affects must not be divisible. If it were divisible, then what happens to its [first] half, would also happen to its terminal half. Hence, some part of the present happens to the first half [of the body], and another part happens to the second [half of the body]. Thus, the present is divisible. This, however, has been refuted. Consequently, it has been proven that a portion of the body exists without being divisible—that being the atom[ic substance]. This proof is very much like the first proof.

(24) The third proof states that if the existence of an atom were an impossibility, a body would be receptive to having infinite parts.[2] Thus, if a mover passes the body in question [the following paradox appears]. It passes the first part prior to passing the second. Since the first part is divisible, it also passes *its* first part before it passes the succeeding parts [of the first part]. And one can reason similarly regarding every part, each happening in a [distinct] temporal [duration]. Thus, this mode of passage is applicable to all sectors of the body [as shown by Zeno's paradox]. Each is realized in a given [duration of] time. Thus it necessitates infinite time to traverse the infinite parts before the mover of the body in question [can act]. Such temporal series can never be dissected. Thus any mover traversing a body can never reach the end of the body. In fact, it can never traverse even one-tenth [lit. a hundred-thousandths] of that body. This is an impossibility. Thus, body is not capable of having an infinite number of parts. Thus, atom[ic substance] is a reality.[3]

(25) The fourth proof considers the possibility of a thing being capable of having infinite parts. Each instant each of its elements has an equal measure, and any two measures would have to be larger than either of the individual measures [constituting the pair]. Therefore, one measure would correspond to infinitely many measures, [since different measures can be imposed on the same extension]. It means that the measure applied to the body in question would grow in multitude [which means that the same extension can have an indefinite number of measurements applied to it] in such a manner that it will be infinite. However, it is impossible that a single measure would include infinite measures. Therefore, it is impossible that a body be comprised of infinite parts.[4]

---

1. In actuality, to be concrete is to contain, in addition to a mere temporal passage, a non-temporal state or condition.

2. The text is ambiguous here, for infinity may refer either to (a) the number of parts of the body, or (b) to the parts themselves being infinitely divisible, or (c) to both (a) and (b). But the subsequent passage clarifies that Ṭūsī means interpretation (a).

3. Ṭūsī's main discussion applies not only to atomic 'physical' substances, but any 'atomism', including an occasionalism which might have been held by the theologians by whom reality is seen to consist of 'occasions' caused by God, without any natural causation.

4. Ṭūsī's argument is ambiguous here. It may be based on the incorrect assumption that there

(26) The fifth proof focuses on [another implication] of a body's being capable of having infinite parts. [Let us suppose also that] infinity does not increase [in this case]. Whatever would be less [in magnitude] would not have been infinite.[1] Since being a quantity does not apply to the atom [i.e., to substances which are qualitative concepts], [the mathematical mapping of] a 'larger' [domain] is not more extensive than [the measure of] 'the lesser' [actual domain]. Thus it is possible to divide, [conceptually, even] a mustard [seed in the same number of parts] as the earth. The [number of the] parts of the former would be of [equivalent] measure to the [number of] the parts of the latter. Thus [another] hideous argument is also refutable. Consider [the following analysis]. Either in the division of the earth the measure of the mustard [seed] is encompassed or it is not. The consideration that it is not so [i.e., it is not its subset] is an impossibility, because it is impossible to divide an entity without reducing its size. If it applies to a measure of a mustard seed, such a measure is divisible, since the mustard seed itself is divisible. Thus, the number of divisions which applies to the earth is greater than the division applied to the mustard seed. Otherwise, existence and non-existence of those parts would be identical. Thus [it follows] again that both are finite, and this [option] is refuted by the fourth reasoning. Therefore it is refuted that body is divisible into an infinite number of parts.

(27) The sixth proof: If body is in itself a composition of parts, then its composition is due either to its essence, or an addition to its essence. If it were due to the essence itself [that the body has this composition], then, when [this composition] is destroyed, the body also would be destroyed. If [its composition] is an addition to its essence, then [the composition] is a [feature] either necessary or accidental to the essence. If it is a necessary feature, then the body could never be divided, for it is impossible that a necessary feature be destroyed while its inner essence exists. If, however, [the composition] is an accident, then the body would not be composed in an essential manner; instead, its composition would be an accidental feature. Since it would not be homogeneous [lit. connected], then, as a divisible entity, a measure [could be applied to it]. Thus, the body itself will have many different parts, separated from one another, and this [finding] is what we desire.

(28) The seventh proof [focuses on the case of] a point exiting due to chance, when a line dissects [another line or a surface], defining a point. Moreover, a

---

cannot be an aggregate of infinite simples. Ṭūsī is correct if he holds that different infinite measure, such as the number of odd and even numbers equal the number of natural numbers. However, it is not correct to say that the natural numbers do not have infinite subsets. His mistake is that he applies the law which holds for finite arithmetic (that the sum of two positive numbers is greater than each of them) to the realm of transfinite numbers, for which the aforementioned law does not hold.

1. Ṭūsī considers the minimal infinite quantity such that if a unit of it is removed the quantity is no longer infinite. This is based on the mistaken view that an aggregate of finites leads to an infinite extension. Ṭūsī does not explicitly state this view, but it is implied in his reasoning that the supporters of the doctrine of atomic substance may have held such a view.

point is not divisible, for were it divisible, then it would not be a point. Thus it is not void of being either a substance or an accident. If it is a substance, then the desired result has been proven. If it is an accident, indeed it would have a place [p]. This place [p] would be either divisible or indivisible. If it is divisible, then the state of each of its parts would differ from [the state] of any other part. Thus the divisibility of the place necessarily implies the divisibility of the state of the body. Hence it would be divisible. We assumed, however, that it would be indivisible. Thus, a contradiction [arises]. Thus, if place were indivisible, the place would be either a substance or an accident. If it were an accident, one could make an argument about it along the lines of the argument concerning the point. [If however,] it reaches the state which is a substance and is indivisible, this is the conclusion sought.

(29) The eighth proof focuses on the case of the sphere. An actual sphere necessarily cuts an actual surface. Some [part] of the [spherical] body itself dissects a surface. That part of the body which dissects a surface is either divisible or indivisible. If divisible, then the circular surface is mapped onto the flat surface. This condition, however, is necessarily impossible, because it implies that a sphere is not a sphere, and a flat surface is not a flat surface. If it is indivisible, then the body is indivisible, which we can designate as the atomic substance. Suppose it is asserted that a sphere dissects a latitude, meaning a point. Then we say that the same argument can be made concerning this point as was made in the seventh proof. Thus it follows from all the proofs that atomic substance exists.

(30) The ninth proof considers the case of the sun shining on a flat surface and a body casting a shadow on that surface. That which cuts the boundary between the shadow and the sun light, forcing a distance between the sun[light] and the shadow, [this distance] is divisible or indivisible. If it is divisible, then part of the body would be neither illuminated nor shaded, and that is an impossibility, since what is shaded is what is not contiguous with the sun, while what is illuminated is contiguous with it. Thus the distance between the light and the shadow is indivisible. Moreover, that subject in which the distance between the sun[light] and the shadow exists is also indivisible, since the divisible limit is, as stated, either an impossibility or [in fact] not divisible. Thus the atomic substance is of the same measure, and that is what we sought to show.

(31) The tenth proof [is as follows]: when a sphere dissects a flat surface, an angle results from the perspective of the point of its dissection; such an angle is a [solid] body, as it has a length, width, and depth. No more is required for constructing a body in this situation. It has been established in geometry that it is impossible to divide this angle by another surface or a line. Hence, the existence of an indivisible body has been established by geometric deductions. All of the above are the arguments of the theologians. Beside these, other reasons are offered which at present we need not discuss. Those given are the strongest arguments; philosophers object

to these reasonings, while the theologians rebut their objections. Criticism of these rebuttals is extensive and quite satisfactory. The most distinguished of modern [scholars] has written a text on this subject. The philosophers have proofs for their position, and we enumerate ten arguments which they present.

(32) The first proof is by Shaykh Abū ʿAlī Sīnā [Avicenna] who argues on this topic in the following way: [Let us suppose the following]. If atomic substance were a possibility, ordinary bodies would be composed of them. If a substance fell between two other substances, either [i] it would not prevent them from being connected together, such that they touch each other and from the concatenation of many [atomic] substances with each other, a [single] body cannot result because its volume does not exceed the volume of a single one; or, [ii] the [substance] between [the other two] prevents their contiguity. Thus, whatever causes the contiguity of one is different that which causes the contiguity of the other; [consequently], this causes divisibility [within the substances].

(33) That second [proof, points to] a millstone, rotating a substance which is next to a stone. When it makes one revolution, the substance proximate to the spindle of a millstone also rotates once. Thus, the extent of the motion of the substance on the periphery would be the same as the substance proximate to the spindle. And that is an impossibility.

(34) However, if it [the substance proximate to the spindle] does not move at all, then the stone mill must be torn apart. A thousand times each instant it is both separated and then reconnected. This [situation] too is an impossibility. Thus, indeed, its motion parallels the peripheral motion, until the substance at the periphery of the connected body moves a distance equivalent to one substance. [Accordingly, then,] the substance proximate to the spindle dissects a lesser amount, and itself becomes divisible.

(35) The third proof: as the sun rises over the earth's surface, the shadow cast by a body becomes shorter. When the sun increases in the measure of one substance, the shade moves likewise. Thus, it must be that as the sun moves from east to west, the shadow is also reduced [leaves the sky] by half; this, [however,] is impossible. Also, if it does not move, it is impossible, since shadow prevents reflection, as has been stated. Thus, it is impossible that the sun rises and reflects on another element. If it moves less than the motion of the sunlight, less is taken away from a substance [in this context of motion]. Thus the [so-called] atomic substance [in fact is divisible].[1]

(36) The fourth proof [maintains] that, if a surface is composed of dense atomic substances, and sun falls on one of its sides, necessarily [this side] is illuminated. The other side however, is not lit. Thus, what is lit is different from that which is

---

1. In all of the arguments offered by the philosopher, there is an incompatibility between a discrete measure of one whole supposedly indivisible substance and numerous mappings of its segments onto what is shown to be a continuum.

not lit. Thus surfaces are divided in depth, making necessary division of the body. This [reasoning] approximates the first argument, which we have mentioned.

(37) The fifth proof [states] that in geometry it has been established that from any point in the circumference a line may be drawn to the centre of the circle. Thus if from both sides of an atomic substance that was in the circumference of the circle, two lines be drawn to the centre, necessarily the distance between the two lines decreases as they move towards the centre. Since the atomic substance has some measure and the distance between the two lines drawn to the centre becomes less than that measure, the substance supposed to be atomic is in fact not indivisible. The second and third arguments given above are derived from the same principle.

(38) The sixth proof has established in geometry that if we suppose any line, it can be divided into halves. Thus if [i] a line consists of an odd number of atomic substances, and [ii] this line is divided into two halves, then if [iii] the place of dissection falls on the middle of two substances, it would not be a [proper] dissection [into two halves]. If it falls in the middle of a substance, then that substance becomes divisible.

(39) The seventh proof [considers the following hypotheses]: [i] a line is constructed from atomic substances, the number of [these substances] being even; [ii] two atomic substances are connected with this line, one from below, the other from above. Each of these two substances moves until it comes to the other side, one from one direction, the other from the other direction. If they move in the same manner such that the measure of the motion of each is the same, they will necessarily pass each other. [At some point] they are parallel to one another. Both cannot be both below and above a substance, for, if it were so, then it would be necessary that the distance traversed by one substance would be shorter than the distance traversed by the other substance. Thus each of these substances is divisible from below and above due to running together and being contiguous to the two substances on the line. If the number of the substances be odd, and those two substances be directed towards a line, they move with equal motions until they touch one another. They cannot be parallel to two corresponding substances on the original line; otherwise, the motions [defined by the path of the atomic substances] are not equal. Thus there is equality among the substances; hence, both are divisible.

(40) The eighth proof states that, if we suppose a square made of sixteen atomic substances, each side would consist of four substances. The diagonal also consists of four substances. The measure of the side, however, is less than the measure of the diagonal. Thus, the four [substances] would be less than four substances. Thus the substances of the diagonal could be divided as much as the substances of the side.

(41) The ninth proof [is found] in the book of Euclid, and has been established by argument. [Consider] a right angle and its diagonal. The square of each side which surrounds the right angle would be a measure of the square of the diagonal.

For example, if we consider one side to be of three [units, lit. *gaz*], the other being of four [units], the diagonal would be five [units]. I.e., [it would be] in this form /1. Thus, if a specific measure is assigned to each side, such that both are equal, necessarily, the substance falling on the diagonal would not be an indivisible unit. This argument, in fact, approximates the eighth proof.

(42) The tenth proof indicates that in the book of Euclid [the following] has been established. In two squares of equal dimensions established between two parallel lines; according to this pattern … both of these squares are equal to one another. Thus, we consider a square consisting of sixteen atomic substances, such that from each of its two sides two equal lines are drawn from east to west, on which one will count sixteen substances. Necessarily, each substance which is broken off from its length will be added to its width. These are proofs concerning the existence of atomic substance. Numerous objections, however, can be raised to these [arguments].

(43) When [the celebrated theologian] Naẓẓām reviews both sides of the argument, both appear strong. He adopts a position composed [of both theories]. He asserts that a body is composed of atomic substances, but their number [i.e., atomic constituents of substances] is not finite; the number of bodies, however, is finite. [This theory is refuted by the following objections]. Suppose a body is composed of atomic substances, but the number of atomic substances is not finite. But the body itself is finite in measure. Assume a given finite number [which comprises the number of elements in a given substance w], such that for any infinite number, finite numbers are necessarily included in it, because a whole number is composed of units. Then let us order these finite numbers. Quantitatively, either this sum [i.e., the number of the units] is greater or is not greater in its measure than the measure of a single substance. If it is not greater, then the composed body is not one of these substances; if it is greater, then it results in being a body [that has become a composite]; moreover, the relation between that supposed body [x] and this supposed body [y] corresponds to the relationship between the constituents of that body [x] and the constituents of this body [y], because there is a correlation between the bodies and their parts. However, [it turns out that] the correlation between [this] body and another body is a relation between a finite and an infinite [set of magnitudes], whereas the corresponding relationship between the constituents is a relationship between a finite and [another] finite [magnitude]. It is impossible, however, that the relation between [an ordered pair of <finite, infinite>] be [isomorphic] with a relation between [a pair of <finite, finite>]. This [counter instance] has been evaded. But since it is held that in a body there are infinite constituents, how can there be a mover of this body in a finite [duration]? To avoid these implications they hedge and necessarily a hedge which avoids possible solutions is an unacceptable ploy. These are the canons asserted [by the philosophers] on atomic substance. A group of contemporaries such as Abu'l Ḥasan al-Baṣrī stands between this [set of]

position[s] and the doctrines mentioned previously. There is, however, no need to reflect about the refutation of Naẓẓām's position.

(44) [Consider the following] point. Whatever is infinite, must be one of the following two types. Either it has a position and an ordered structure or it lacks these. Each of these two options is not without the following [two further subdivisions]. Their constituents either exist or do not exist at once as a unit. Consequently, the group is subdivided into four kinds. First [kind applies to] [i] whatever has a position, an ordered structure and that all of its constituents exist at once. According to the insights of the followers of the intellectuals, this is called [a vicious infinite] regress; all the philosophers and theologians agree that the [existence] of such an [actual] infinite is an impossibility. Muʿammar of the Muʿtazilite [theologians] accepted this doctrine in some form. The second division [ii] is the infinite in which members all have a position and are in an ordered structure, not all of the constituents of which co-exist simultaneously. If there be an infinite in the direction of the past this is the case of events not having a first member. This interpretation exists among philosophers who assert that, prior to any generated event, there was another event without there being an initial member [of the series]. The theologians say, however, that this is an impossibility, asserting that there is a generated event prior to which there was no other event. On [the doctrine] of an infinite in the direction of the future—perchance the two [types of series] are not only possible but actual. It is so, because of the case of the inhabitants of heaven and hell for the theologians and events in the world among the philosophers. Some theologians whose names I do not remember have asserted that even this [doctrine] is an impossibility, and assert that all things in the end are annihilated. The third subdivision [iii] is that for which there is in the [infinite] neither position nor an ordered structure, all of its constituents existing at once, such as intelligent souls according to philosophers; while among the theologians this is refuted and is considered impossible.

(45) The fourth position [iv] is that for which [the infinite] has no position nor ordered structure, and not all of whose constituents exist at once. Philosophers consider this option a contingency, while the theologians consider it to be an impossibility.

(46) [Consider the following] problem. According to both philosophers and theologians, it is not possible that there be an infinite dimension, either in the vacuum, or in the plenum. Indian [thinkers] assert that bodies in the universe are infinite. For the refutation of their position and the correctness of the opposing view some arguments have been stated.

(47) The first argument [deals] with contiguity [lit. directionality] and isomorphism as follows. If there were an infinite dimension, then it would be impossible for any motion to occur in it. However, [we suppose that any dimension] allows motion. Thus, [the notion of] an infinite dimension is an impossibility. The

statement of the initial premises of the argument is that, if an infinite dimension were a contingency, then we can also assume [the following constructions: [i] an infinite line AB, [ii] a circle JZD with a centre at H. If motion in it were possible, then necessarily the [line which is the] diameter of this circle and is parallel to the [aforementioned] infinite line, such as diameter JHD, by being parallel either will or will not meet [the line]. If it does not meet the line, then the sphere is not rotating. Hence, when it rotates, the diameter also does; thus it will meet [the line]. Whenever the diameter by being parallel to the infinite line is situated to meet the line, there must be the first connection between them—because there was no connection and then there was a connection. [Consider] any point as the beginning of the line of the points of intersection; prior to that intersection there is another point. For example, before D touches the line, Z does. Thus that connection which we conjectured was not the first connection. Since there would be no first connection and at first the line [of diameter] is parallel [to the infinite] line, there cannot be any connection. This implies that the circular motion is an impossibility. But the second option is evident. Thus the conclusion is true.

(48) The second argument notes that, if infinite dimension were a possibility, two lines can be supposed surrounding an angle, so that, for example, a unit [of *gaz*] is separated from each side of a line with an inclination. Moreover, between these two lines there is another unit [of *gaz*]. On the lines AB and AJ, which are sides of the angle JAB, the distance between J and A, A and B, and J and B would be the same. If the distance from H to Z is two units [of *gaz*], from Z to H also would be two units [of *gaz*], and in the manner previously stated.[1] Consider these two lines as infinite, in the direction of H and Z. Thus if it is possible that those two lines are infinite, then the distance between them also would be infinite. However, it is enclosed between them, since whatever is enclosed between two entities has a first and a last [member]. Thus it is not infinite. Consequently, what we thought to be infinite turned out to be finite, and our original assumption is shown to be false. Thus, infinite dimension is impossible.

(49) Shaykh Abū ʿAlī Sīnā has expressed this argument in another manner. He states that, if infinite dimensions are possible, let us conjecture two lines which initiate from a given point and become infinite in one direction such that, as they continue, the distance between them increases [continuously]. As we assumed, each increase of one unit [of *gaz*] in the sides corresponds to an increase of one unit in the distance between the sides, and increase of two units in the sides corresponds to an increase of two units in the distance between them. Thus the first distance is embedded in the second and will be an addition to it. [Likewise,] the second distance exists in the third as well as an addition to it. If we assume the same logic for any further increase, the totality of distances subsumed under it exists, and the

1. The last phrase of the Persian text is mistakenly repeated.

additions exist as well. Thus if we consider the two infinite lines, the increments in the dimension on the first distance are infinite. Also from the increments which result due to [a continuous series of dimensions] from the first dimension both are infinite in their measure. If we consider the increments which exists in a distance, the infinite increments do not exist in a dimension. If the infinite increments do not exist in any dimension, then the corresponding constructed lines are finite as they increase with [the corresponding dimension], as we assume that the increments are subsumed in a dimension. We assumed them, however, to be both not standing alone as well as to be infinite, and this is a contradiction. Thus, there are dimensions in which the infinite increments exist, and this is surrounded between two supposed lines; but this is impossible. Thus, infinite dimension is impossible.

(50) The third argument: suppose there is an infinite dimension, and let us assume an infinite line ABJ, this line being infinite in both directions. Thus, let us assume a point A on the line and another point lower than that, such as B, such that between these two there is a measure AB, and this measure is finite. Since ABJ in the direction of J is infinite, and BJ in the direction of J is not infinite, either one can or cannot make these two lines congruent. If one cannot, then they are not capable of being either equivalent or not equivalent. Hence, they do not belong to the category of a quantity. Since the essence of a quantity is to be receptive of equality or inequality, necessarily it follows that it is not a line. However, we supposed it to be a line. Thus, their congruence is a possibility. When they are [made] congruent, A falls on B, and line on line. Thus, in the direction of J, they are either equal or unequal. It is impossible that they be equal, since AJ, the measure of AB, exists, but it is not in the line BJ. Thus, the existence and absence of AB are equivalent [with respect to line BJ]. Since they are not equal, AJ is either larger or smaller than BJ. It is impossible that AJ be smaller than BJ, since with respect to the direction of J they are indifferent, while in the direction of AJ, there is AB, which is not included in BJ; thus the [quantity with an] added [increment] would be less than the [one with the] lesser [increment]. Thus AJ is greater, and thus BJ is the lesser [of the two]. In this direction, it initiates from a single point. Thus, in the direction of J [the line] is dissected. Hence it is finite. AJ, which is bigger [that BJ] by the measure of AB is also finite; and this is impossible. Thus, infinite dimension is an impossibility. It should be noted that this argument could be used to refute circular arguments; instead of being applied to 'line', it could applied to 'numbers'. To this aforementioned argument numerous objections have been raised, many responses being given, [an account of] which is time-consuming.

(51) [Let us consider the following] problem. Philosophers assert that any body which has neither weight nor lightness, but is inclined towards a direction, is incapable of partaking of motion. For, we suppose that a body without a propensity traverses a distance—indeed, that motion happens in time. Thus, the body for which there is an inclination towards another direction, traverses the same distance

in another temporal duration; indeed, the latter temporal duration is longer because the inclination stagnates the motion of a body when it is in opposition to the direction towards which it is inclined. Thus, the motion without an obstacle is lighter than motion that has an obstacle. Any body which has less propensity than the body in question necessarily will have a relatively lighter motion and traverse the aforementioned distance in a shorter time. Thus, if we suppose: the relationship between the propensity of one body and that of a second body corresponds to the relationship between the time for the two bodies to move; for example, if the first duration is a quarter of the second temporal span, that propensity is also a quarter of this propensity, since that body traverses the same distance. It traverses it in a time proportional to the time which it takes the other body to traverse the same distance, the proportion being the same as the proportion between the intensities of propensity of the first and the second. Or, that time is equal to the time it takes a body to traverse the distance without the body having a propensity to do so. Thus, the body without a propensity and the body with a propensity traverse the distance in the same time. Hence, a motion without impediment would be the same as a motion with impediment. And this is impossible. Thus, the body without a propensity cannot move.

(52) It should be known that there is a mistake in this principle. Suppose we postulate a time for a body which lacks a propensity. The totality of the time of the motion of a body with propensity is not a direct proportion to the time of the motion of a body without propensity. If it were so, then, as an inclination decreased, [time would also decrease]. Instead, [the time it takes two bodies to traverse the same distance is in inverse proportion to their relative propensities.] According to this view, a body without propensity is not different from a body with propensity. [Then the following state would be true if the proportion were not inverse.] For example, suppose a body without a propensity traverses [a distance] in two [units of] time. What is attributable to the propensity is no more than eight [units] of time. If we consider a body whose propensity is one-fifth that of the first, why should it traverse the distance in two [units] of time, since it itself with respect to body per se [without a propensity] traverses the distance in two units of time? for one-fifth of that propensity [implies] five-eighths of time, added to two units of measure—and this [assessment] would be correct [and this, of course, is absurd].[1]

(53) [Consider] the problem of the proof of the Necessary Existent in the context of this debate. If there were no necessity, then there would be no existent. There is an existent. Thus, there is a necessary [entity]. [The presumed] option is that an existent [x] is either a necessity or a contingency. It is not a contingency unless its

1. Evidently, the manuscript is corrupt in this paragraph. It begins by describing an absurdity and terminates with an elliptical passage that makes an unsound argument. Our editorial suggestions accord with the fact that a body with propensity travels faster than a body without propensity.

negation is [also a contingency].[1] If that negation would be a necessity, then the first option would apply, [so the negation of the negation, the entity itself, would not be possible]. However, if it [*x] were a contingency, then it would be either the primary contingency [i] or another contingency [ii]. The first option [i] implies a circularity—which is an impossibility—because it would be necessary for each to precede the other; thus it would precede itself. The second [option [ii]] implies a continuous [regress,] and that is also an impossibility. As its [x's] contingency has been established, the conclusion has been derived, since the aggregate of infinite contingencies [by themselves] cannot exist unless each of its members exists—each being different from the aggregate. The aggregate exists only if each of its units exists, each being different from the aggregate. Whatever cannot be unless its negation also is not [a contingent entity], is a contingency, and cannot exist unless its negation also exists as a contingency. The contrary is either embedded in it, or is external to it. The first option implies that the contrary is not unless [its own] contrary does not exist. However, since it is the cause of the aggregate, it is also the cause of the unit[s of that aggregate]; and if so, then it would be the cause of itself, which is an impossibility. Hence, the second option is correct, which states that the aggregate of contingencies cannot be [realized] unless there is a necessity. If there were no necessity, there would be neither a necessary nor a contingent [entity]. Thus [even if] whatever exists is either necessary or contingent, it is necessary that, unless there is a necessity, there is no existent. Since the exception to this is a necessity, the result is correct—which is the conclusion we sought.

(54) The objection to this logic is as follows. First, this argument is based on the negation of its conclusion, so that a proof of the conclusion implies its invalidity. It asserts that if there is a necessary [entity], then there is no necessary entity. It is so, because, if there were a necessary [entity], the realm of necessary existent[s] would be divided into existents which are necessary and contingent. Otherwise, the division of existents into necessary and contingent would be like the division between animal to man and inert entities.[2] Since existence is common to necessary and contingent [beings], these consequences follow. If in a necessary existent there were nothing except for the reality of existence, and, reality of existence also applies to contingent [existents,] then a contingency would be a necessity. If something is necessary, it would be composed of existence and that factor; a composite is in need of its constituents and is other than them. Thus the necessary [entity] would be in need of another entity; thus it will not

1. For instance, a two-eared human being is a contingency because there could have been a world in which a person would have three ears. However, there is no possible world in which the number of a person's ears would be both odd and even.

2. The division of animals to men and inert entities is not correct. Either Ṭūsī wishes to point out that existents should not be divided into necessary and contingent or the text is corrupt in this passage.

be a necessity. Thus if there be a[n entity called a] necessity, [in fact,] it would not be a necessity. This argument is refuted from the view that the premise begs [the question that there be] a necessity, which is the conclusion of the argument. Thus its conclusion is the cause of the unsoundness of this argument. If we pass through this phase, we inquire on the meaning of 'necessity' used in the argument, forming the basis of the argument. We assert that a necessity is called that to which annihilation does not apply, while a contingency that to which existence and privation relate equally [in the logical sense]. Or, the necessary is that whose existence is due to itself, while contingency that whose existence is due to another. Or, [it is possible to give other descriptions of those two[modalities].

(55) In the first interpretation of existence, the division of existents into necessary and contingent is [not comprehensive,] [lit. empty of limit]. External to this division there is an existent for which existence is a nobler [state than non-existence], even though annihilation is applicable to it. If [all] existents were also of this kind, why should there be a necessity such that to that nobility existence is applied to it by an intervening factor without there being a need of an external entity [to realize this necessity]?[1]

(56) In the second division of existents, their existence is either due to itself or due to a different entity. The latter case is true when the entity is acquired from that different entity. Either it is due to its own essence or due to the essence of another entity. It is understood 'when one entity is due to another entity', the former is derived from the latter. If it is derived, then it is due to itself or due to another. If it were due to itself, it must be prior to itself; if it were due to another, it would be derived by privation. This is so, because the contrary of existence is privation. From this perspective, in principle, the proof becomes invalid. Since existence is not acquired, one cannot say that it is either due to itself or something different. If there be another interpretation, those two terms [existence, privation] must be expressed in a manner allowing us to discuss them [in a clear fashion].

(57) [Consider the following] inquiry. Let us consider another point and inquire why you asserted that a contingency cannot exist without another [entity]. If you state that, since existence and privation are identical [options] for it, preference for one option [must be due] to a [determining] factor, we can reply that existence is a preferable [option], as we have stated; [hence] there is no need [for a determining factor.] We know that existence or privation has the same weight for [contingencies]; the endorsement of one option [concerning whether or not the entity should

1. It appears that Ṭūsī makes a distinction between an entity external to a substance, such as another substance, and a law or principle which is applied to substance. The distinction could be formulated as follows: while a substantial entity may persist without being related to any another substance, the complete description of a law is reducible to the set of all possible arrangements of substances to which the law applies. Thus, a law extensionally is a mere logical construct of other primary metaphysical entities.

be realized] must be either due or not due to a determining factor. A group of Mu'tazilite theologians say that a preference without a cause of endorsement is not an impossibility, proving this doctrine by formulating [the celebrated examples] of two jugs, two morsels of bread, and the like. [In these cases, the principle that] 'whenever there is a preference, there must be an endorsement' becomes difficult [to prove]. Thus, since in the issuance of the created from the creator, the latter is temporally prior to the former in an infinite duration of time—[this priority] being established in the context of a determined set of events—there is a need to refer to a cause of preference for an option. Otherwise, from a temporal perspective an ephemeral [entity] becomes eternal. Thus the arguments on these two topics are contradictory. If the contradiction is to be avoided, either we must accept the eternity of the ephemerals or reject The Eternal Cause. Otherwise, since it is permitted in one context that there be a preference without a cause of preference, why cannot this also be permitted here, since in another context one of the options of existence or privation is preferred without an endorsement. We definitely established that the contingent needs another entity. However, there is [also] an initial entity for it, or is has no initial entity. The first is evident; the second is impossible. Why is it not permissible that the contingent be eternal and be the cause of events such as [it is stated in the] foundations, books, and the like? Thus contingencies are in need of a cause. If you say that existence is more worthy for a [contingency, i.e., it is better to be than not to be], whereas we took existence and privation to be [ontically] equivalent, we answer that, if its existence is noble, its privation is [even] nobler. The necessary [factors] are necessary at all options; [thus] we consider the relations [of] both [options to the contingency in question] to be equal, even though neither of the two options is empty of nobility. So, if its annihilation is not harmful, neither is its realization. We know for certain that a contingent [entity] cannot be without another [entity]. Why do you say that circular [reasoning] is impossible [and applies to this case]?[1] As we have stated, each is prior to the other. By this priority, do you mean priority with respect to essence, or with respect to time? It is definite that two entities cannot be prior to one another with respect to time.

(58) And why would you say that, if any two entities were to affect one another, that [they would also] be prior to one another? The effect, however, has been realized and cannot be united [as one entity with both the cause and the agent responsible for the cause]. Since effect is in the [category of] relation and obtains between two existents, it cannot obtain between an existent and an entity deprived of existence. Thus, the [entity which is an] agent [of a cause] cannot be [considered] a cause prior to [the realization of] the effect. With respect to the state of an effect, unless there be a cause, the effect is not realized. If there is an effect, there cannot

1. Ṭūsī seems to say that, if one says a contingency has an intermediate cause, then an infinite regress follows. His solution is syntactical. The meaning of 'contingency' implies that it depends on a different entity.

be priority. Subsequently, it will be shown why an effect cannot [originate] from both directions.

(59) If you wish to [consider] priority with respect to essence, its meaning of priority to essence is that the initial [and the eternal] is the cause of the later. Thus, saying that, if each affects the other, each is prior to the other, and this means that they affect one another—each is the cause of the other. Indeed, [any entity] is such [that its constituents are interdependent]. Thus, what difficulty [lit. corruption] is implied by [this sense of] priority? If you wish to consider another [sense of] priority, it must be clarified so we can discuss it. [Lest we be misunderstood, we should say that] we do not doubt that circular [reasoning is invalid]. Why do you assert that [infinite] regress is also an impossibility? If we wish to show regress, we say we reason by way of omission; we say that there is no way out of deducing [some type of] regress. It is so, since there must be a cause for events, this cause being either generated or eternal. If [this cause] would apply to it, implying that there is a regress until an eternal is reached. That is the second division which implies that the cause is eternal. Thus its effect either depends or does not depend on a condition. If it is not dependent, the generated-ephemerals are eternal. The posteriority of the events to the eternal cause is invariant either in eternity or in a specific time—it implies an endorsement without there being a (cause of) a preference, and that is an impossibility. But if it is dependent [on a condition], and that dependency is conditioned on an eternal (factor), then the same implications occur. If it is generated, then the discourse about what is generated would apply to it. [In fact, our case has been proven.] In the light of these considerations, why do you say that with respect to contingencies [your conclusion has been reached?] You say that the aggregate of contingencies is infinite, but how can we call the infinite an aggregate? Though aggregate can be ascribed only to the finite, this condition which is peculiar to it is here ascribed to the infinite. This reason begs the question.

(60) We hold indubitably that there could be an aggregate in an infinity; [there are two possibilities], either an absolute [i.e., actual] infinite, or when each [of the elements, potentially] exists. The first option is impossible; the second is necessary. In this case it is necessary that not all of the contingencies are realized. On the contrary, it is impossible that all contingent [entities] exist. And why is this type of regress prohibited? In this case each entity has a cause prior [to it], so that when an effect is realized in it [i.e., the cause] is annihilated. This [reasoning,] however, is absolute ignorance, since it equates [lit., sums up] the annihilated with the existent. We are certain that it is definitely meaningful to talk about aggregates. An aggregate, however, is in need of another entity when the aggregate either is or is not due to a condition additional to a mere unity. The first is certain; the second is prohibited. For, if it were an additional [factor], then it would not have been in need of another entity. When a factor is additional, then [its state persists] either [according to the mode of being a] unity, or without [being a] unity. The first [option]

is certain; the second is prohibited. It is so, because when unity is realized, and the cause of the aggregate has disappeared, it would be necessary that the constituents be realized fully while the aggregate [itself] would not exist; this [condition] is an impossibility. But from the factor that it is in need of unity, no more is required [of the aggregate] than that it [does not persists along] with each one of its members. Whence, circular [reasoning] is implied [either in the position] that there be only one [static state] of the aggregate, or that it be the cause of its [own] existence. Between these two options, the difference is apparent: the first dependency is due to the totality itself, while the second dependency is due to the dependency of the effect on a cause. ... And it is not implied from another entity that there be a cause for the aggregate outside of unity.[1] We are certain that this reasoning [by itself] establishes the necessity [of a being]. We argue, however, based on another reasoning which negates the necessity [argued for above.] We say that if there be a necessary existent, its existence is either identical to it, or a factor additional to it. If it is identical to it, then we say that there is no difference between saying that 'an existent is necessary' and 'a necessity is necessary'. It follows necessarily that the first does not need a proof, because the second does not. For instance, it is sufficient to assert that, if a necessity is necessary, then that necessity exists, since the meaning of [being] a necessity is that it exists. If there were an additional [factor], then between them there is or is not a dependency. The former option is impossible, for if the necessity were required for existence, then all existents would be necessary, and the ephemeral [contingent events] would also have been necessary. If existence needed necessity, then it would depend on it and necessity would be a property of existence and thus would depend on it. Thus circularity would result. The second option is not possible, because, since there is no necessity, the necessity of the existence of the necessary [entity] would be an accident as it can [conceivably] exist without being a necessity. Thus that which in reality is a contingency, and necessity is its property, is [itself] a contingency. Thus what we supposed to be necessary becomes a contingency. Since all [modal] categories become void, we proved that no necessity is a contingency. And we are victorious [in our arguments] due to God. The answer to what you said is that the argument itself is self-contradictory and implies its own refutation. We say that this argument is informative for the premises of the conclusion of our proof, which is clarified after the reply. You say that, if there is a necessary [entity], then it is required that there be no necessary [entity]. We say that this requirement is impossible. You say that it [i.e., the realm of existents] includes [all beings]. We say that the true position is that [the realm of] existents does not include all [logically possible entities], but the existence of each entity is the reality of its inner essence.

(61) You say that the [logical] division implies a common factor. We say that a mental common [factor] is sufficient. Even if the division of beings into substance

1. The Persian text seems to be missing a sentence at this point. No space is allowed before the sentence; the sentence also begins with 'and' [*wa*].

and accident is correct, [the realm of] being does share a common factor by mere chance. We are sure from the disputation that existence is common. It is not, however, necessary that whatever is correct for the necessary existent is also correct for the contingent. Thus, the basis of distinction between the necessary and the contingent types of existence is that [the actuality of the] necessary existent is established by proof by way of negation. And that proof is that accident is not a being, and a contingent existent is an accident of being. Thus, whatever you say of absolute existence holds for both divisions [of being].

(62) Absolute existence, however, is mind-dependent and is not in the external [world]. Whatever you say about the necessary existent, it is a condition [or a mode] relating to necessity. There is no need for it also to apply to contingent being, since necessary existence is contrary to contingent existence, even though it shares its principles.

(63) You say if there be another entity with existence, then the necessity would be a composite, and thus a contingency. We say that we hold definitely in disputation that necessity has a being external to existence. But, why should this imply that it is a contingency? In the description of their being, necessity and its existence are in need of one another. But neither is a contingency. It is so, since existence is a necessity, and it is not correct to describe being without either a contingency of existence or necessity. Thus there is but one entity, while compositeness is mental and from it contingencies are not realized. If one refers to the mental [realm], but has no correspondence to the external world, then it is false. We assert [that it is so,] either in concepts or deductions. The first is prohibited [by logic], the second is correct. The mistake itself is in the divisions of deductions, according to which, unless there is a factor, there is no path [of validity of the argument related to it.] The differences in the understanding of the realities of mind cannot be the cause of the [corresponding designation] in the external [realm], and is not ignorance.

(64) You say that we inquire about the meaning of necessity and contingency. We say that necessity is an existence which does not depend on another [entity] for its existence. This division is refuted.

(65) You say that the existence of the contingencies is nobler, and, consequently, privation [i.e. not being an existent] does not intervene in it. We say that this is impossible, since with the worthiness of existence the unanticipated [application] of existence either is or is not contingent. If it is, then that preference is insufficient; but what has been endorsed [must have been] preferred; thus [this reasoning implies] an impossibility. If it is not a contingency, that existent is a necessity, not a contingency.

(66) You say that existence is due to itself or some other entity; [the latter can be stated] when [its actuality] has been acquired. We say that the aim of saying that existence is due to itself is to indicate that something exists due to itself without the support from another [being,] as mentioned above.

(67) But the reason that you stated that existence is not acquired from another being, if it is proven, confirms our discourse. And from that perspective necessity and being are divisions of existence.

(68) You say, why cannot the contingent exist without [the support] of another? We say because it is included in the meaning of the contingent being [to be supported by another]. You say existence is superior and is not in need of [postulating] a preferring [agent]. We have given our position on this before.

(69) You say that the Muʿtazilah endorse [the position that there can be] a preference without a preferring [agent]. We say they have asserted that the free agent is present, and free will for one of the options is necessary. It is not the case that in principle existence and privation are equivalent without a cause, and between these two forms there is an apparent difference. For this discourse is about the inner [reality] of the cause, and there is equivalence between [the choice of] existence or privation; existence [per se] does not [cause realization] of an existent. If the maker does choose one (option), then the other option is not necessary.

(70) You say that what is difficult for you is the generation of the ephemeral from the generated in the established temporal order; we say that it [i.e., this proposal] is easier for us [to accept].

(71) You say that [postulating] the posteriority of one span of time to another span of time involves preference without a preferring [agent]. We assert that precedence [of the existence of the preferring agent to the realization of the preference] is necessary and simultaneity [among them is] an impossibility, since the action of the free agent cannot be eternal. It is so, because it obeys the initiator, and the initiator can function only if there be a privation [factor]. However, the superiority of one time to another time, that the establishment and proof of preference with a cause of preference are all derived from [empty] imagination [lit., prehension]; and there is no basis for such [theses] as that there be absolute negation [in order that] an existent be realized.

(72) You say that this creates a contradiction. We say that preference without a preferring [agent] is an impossibility among us, and that no contradiction occurs in [our argument]. With the assistance of God, we are not in need of resorting to a contradiction [to establish our proof].

(73) You say that the contingent is in need of another, when there is or there is or there is no initiator for it. We say that both options could be established.

(74) You say that the cause of dependence is the status of being generated. We say that the cause of dependence is contingency, not generated entities, since being generated is the quality of existence of the generated entities. Thus, it is posterior to the existence of the generated entities, since the attribute is posterior to the entity [to which the attribute applies]. The existence of a generated [entity] is posterior to the effect of its maker. The effect of the generated entities from the perspective of the contingent is posterior to [such an] effect. The dependency of the contingent is

posterior to its cause. Thus, if the generated entities were the cause of dependency, they would be posterior to themselves on several levels, and that is impossible. Thus, the cause of dependency is contingency, and whatever is a contingency, in the totality of its existence, is in need of a causal agent until it is realized [in an initial] state, and other times [it can persist despite] the negation of the existence [of its cause].

(75) You say that those requirements are necessary, so you can consider equivalent the relationship between [being an] existent and [having] privation with respect to the contingent [type of entity], which is always one of these [alternatives]. We say that the relation of existence or privation to the essence of [a] contingent entity from the perspective that establishes it apart from the consideration of any other entity is equivalent. However, the [positive] consideration of the realization of existence is [a] superior [choice] and, since it is a contingency, the [positive] consideration of a privation of the cause of privation is [also a] superior [choice].

(76) You ask why [we] say that this circularity is impossible. We say because the priority of its elements to one another is impossible. You ask what 'priority' we are considering. We say we are considering the priority of some of the parts of time to others, and the priority of agent to patient.

(77) You say that the agent and the patient are together. We say, [consider the possibility] that the effect either follows or does not follow the agent. The first is prohibited [by logic]; the second is required. The existence of an agent of the second kind is not required in the [realm] external to [the mind]. According to the correct position, [any] patient, among the [various] existents in the universe, is [itself] either free or determined. [Nevertheless] each patient follows its [cause, lit. agent].

(78) You say that the effect is an additional factor. We say that additional factors do not exist in [the realm] external [to the mind]. If an effect had an existence, then in it there would be another effect and this leads to a[n infinite] regress. You ask, why can it not be that the effect is due to both options, since priority from both perspectives has been found to be impossible?

(79) You say that the meaning of the priority due to essence is causality. We say that the meaning of priority due to essence is that the existence of the patient is due to the existence of the agent, while the existence of the cause is not due to the existence of the effect. If it were so, a circularity would arise. You say that regress is an impossibility; we say it is due to a reason and this reason is well known. Due to the fact that it is well known, we will not present it.

(80) You say that our reasons are [in fact] evasion. But, [we say that] doubts cannot be raised [concerning the correctness of our position].[1]

1. The text is ambiguous here, for 'doubts cannot be raised' could refer either to the position of Ṭūsī or that of his critics. We interpret the text as follows: Ṭūsī's argument is syntactical; for him 'contingency' implies the existence of a predecessor. Since the reasoning is an analytical and purely syntactical one, no legitimate doubt can be raised about its validity.

(81) You say that there must be a cause for the generated entity, which is either eternal or generated. We say that it is eternal.

(82) You say that its effects either depend or do not depend on a condition. We say that the dependence is on the producer and it is impossible that it [the effect] be simultaneous with the producer.

(83) You say that the [doctrine that first generated, lit. posterior] events are simultaneous with [eternal] time [implies the occurrence of] preference without a preferring [agent].[1] We say that time is a generated entity and that there are no temporal [sectors] in eternity. The discourse focuses on preference; thus regress is implied by all descriptions. We say that regress is one account, while [the doctrine of postulating] generated [entities] without the first [initiator] is a different account. You argue for the case of regress. Our aim in this chapter is to [point out] that from these considerations a doubt results about [the doctrine of] the generated entities.

(84) You ask how one can call the infinite an aggregate? We say that, since it has number, [this number] must be finite or infinite. It [also] has an aggregate, this being the number of all of its units. If the aggregate were finite, then an infinite aggregate would be a contradiction. The finite collection [is not the same as an infinite aggregate].[2] If we wish to avoid using the term 'aggregate', and say [instead] that [the notion of] an 'infinite series of contingencies' is not a [legitimate] possibility [lit. a contingency], then our reasoning is not syntactical but due to meaning.

(85) You say that in this case it is not necessary that these members exist simultaneously. We say that it is necessary, since the cause of dependency is a contingency, so the contingent has an existent cause. Discourses on cause [follow the dual division of being, lit. the second case];[3] either it leads to a necessity or to the infinite contingents which exist simultaneously.

(86) You say that each [generated event] has a cause anterior [to it]. We say that this discourse depends on the view that the cause of dependency is generated—and this is what we have refuted. You say that the collection would be dependent on another entity whenever there either is or is not a factor additional to unity.[4] We say it is [dependent] when it [being a factor additional to unity], holds [to be true, lit. exists].

(87) You say that it [i.e., posterior contingency] is in need of units or non-units. We reply [that it depends] on the sum of units.

(88) You say that contingency is not necessitated either by dependency on a contingent unit, or upon the contingency of dependency on a cause.

---

1. The text is ambiguous here, as it does not clarify Ṭūsī's temporal reference. Our interpretation is supported by the following sentence which makes clear that for Ṭūsī time is generated.

2. The text must be corrupt because it reads literally 'does not repeat and is not as such.'

3. The reference to the second case is unclear because no cases have been enumerated. Perhaps the text is corrupt.

4. An alternative reading is: 'whenever a factor additional to unity or it [the collection] does not exist.' There is no basis in the text for deciding between these two translations.

(89) You say that our argument depend on reasoning that negates [the significance or legitimacy] of necessity. We concur that [this reasoning] cannot be done.

(90) You say that the necessary determinate either exists or it is an additional [factor to existence]. We say that when it [is,] it is either in a negative or affirmative [mode]. The first is prohibited [by logic], the second is correct. But negative necessity relates to the prevention of privation. If it is an existent, it is only mental, and that is [merely the verbal] confirmation of the existence [of an entity].

(91) You say that the distinction between [the constituents of] necessity is necessary, as well as that distinction between [the previous statement and the fact that] necessity is a unity. [We say] that unity is not an additional [factor].[1]

(92) You say that if necessity were required for existence, then [all] existents would be necessary. We say that necessarily existence is either absolute or determined. The first is definitely the case; the second is prohibited [by logic]. But the absolute existent does not reside external [to the mind] and only is in the mind. If there were necessity for a determinate existent, it would not be that necessity [which will realize it as an existent]; what is necessary [instead] is another entity. You say if necessity would not be required, then necessity would be accidental. We say that it is additional only when existence and necessity exist as realities external [to the mind], necessary due to it and a composite from that perspective [i.e., mental perspective]. And this argument [of yours] has been refuted, as we have indicated.

(93) You say that, since all distinctions have been refuted, it is proven that the necessity does not exist. We reply that distinctions [of existents] are not limited. For if existents [could be derived by] the negation [of modalities], then [they would be external] to these divisions. This [requirement to accept] limits due to privation is not necessary [in our account of existents]. And Virtue is with God, and Victory.

1. It is not clear whether the position that unity is not an additional factor to existence and modality should be attributed to Ṭūsī or to his opponent. The argument turns on possible syntactical metaphysical and ontic aspects of 'necessary existent': the modality of necessity, the mode of being realized as an existent, and the postulation that it is a unity.

2

Afḍal al-Dīn Kāshānī

Very little is known about the life of Afḍal al-Dīn Muḥammad ibn Ḥasan Kāshānī, commonly known as 'Bābā Afḍal'. In the Persianate world the term 'Bābā', which literally means 'father', is often used to refer to a Sufi master. We know that he was a contemporary of such figures as Shihāb al-Dīn Suhrawardī, Ibn Rushd, and Ibn ʿArabī. Bābā Afḍal died around 610/1213 and is buried in Maraq, a mountain village north of Kāshān. While the date of his birth is not known, in one of his letters he mentions that he has been on an intellectual journey for sixty years; so it is safe to assume that he was born in the earlier part of the sixth/twelfth century.

It is said that he was related to Ṭūsī, who refers to Bābā Afḍal in his commentary on the *Ishārāt* in a matter pertaining to logic. Given the date of Bābā Afḍal's death, such a relationship is unlikely unless he was a relative but belonging to an earlier generation. It is also said that he may have been an Ismaili, but there is no evidence to support this and Bābā Afḍal himself tells us that Sunni Islam is the best of ways.

Not much is known about his students, but he refers to them as his 'religious brothers' (*barādarān-i dīnī*) and 'true companions' (*yārān-i ḥaqīqī*). Such a description implies more than students; so perhaps they were his spiritual companions or a group of initiated Sufis. What strengthens this view is that he was asked by Muḥammad Dizwākush, a fellow companion, to compose a book on the principles of spirituality which he wrote in Arabic and entitled *Madārij al-kamāl* (The Rungs of Perfection). In the conclusion to this work Bābā Afḍal tells us that another companion, Asʿad Nasāʾī, asked him to translate this work into Persian so others might comprehend the meanings of this book. This is a clear indication that these companions were not learned scholars, for if they were they would have surely known Arabic. It appears that this group did not have much formal training in philosophy and that leaves us with the strong possibility that the companions may have been a group of practising Sufis.

Bābā Afḍal was part of the emerging intellectual endeavour, in the sixth/twelfth century, to bring about a rapprochement between philosophy and Sufism. Like

Suhrawardī, ʿAyn al-Quḍāt Hamadānī and Quṭb al-Dīn Shīrāzī, Bābā Afḍal also used philosophical and logical terminologies to comment on such Sufi themes as the nature of self-knowledge and consciousness. Ironically, Bābā Afḍal does not mention the works of other Islamic philosophers. In fact, with the exception of Aristotle and Hermes, he does not mention any other philosopher. Furthermore, he does not discuss many of the traditional philosophical questions, such as the Necessary Being and the proofs concerning its existence. Nor does he write about other branches of science such as astronomy, mathematics, and medicine. Although he does write about logic and political philosophy, he is singularly interested in analysing one problem above all else and that is the nature of the self. What constitutes the identity of a human being is intelligence, which Bābā Afḍal refers to both as *khirad,* Persian for intellect, and *ʿaql,* the Arabic for the same concept. The salient feature of Afḍal al-Dīn Kāshānī's thought is his emphasis upon the science of the soul and spirit, or pneumatology, which one could also understand as autology, not to be mistaken for Aristotle's *De Anima,* the psychology of Islamic Peripatetics, or the modern discipline of psychology. Although his analyses are at times Peripatetic, such analyses take place within the context of a Sufi perspective. In its journey, the soul moves towards perfection, whereby it experiences states and stations of wisdom leading to the annihilation of the self in God (*fanāʾ fi'Llāh*).

Bābā Afḍal develops an epistemology that becomes central in the School of Isfahan; that is, knowing implies a unity between knowledge, the knower, the known and an epistemic unity between the subject and the object. Knowing therefore necessitates becoming one with the object of knowledge. In the case of knowing God and the realities of the spiritual world, a mode of knowledge becomes a mode of being. The doctrine of the unity between the intellect and the intelligible (*ittiḥād al-ʿāqil wa'l-maʿqūl*) is an epistemological doctrine that became fully developed later by the masters of the School of Isfahan, finally reaching its zenith in the teachings of Mullā Ṣadrā.

According to Bābā Afḍal, there are three types of knowledge: that of this world (*dunyā*), that of the other world (*ākhirah*), and finally the world of thought (*andīshah*), which bridges the two. Each branch of knowledge is subsequently subdivided. The knowledge of this world rests upon the primary functions of the human being, such functions as speech and communication, which relate man to this world. The world of pure thought is an intermediary between the corporeal and the incorporeal world. Logic is emphasized as a tool to make clear the intricacies of the spiritual and the intellectual world within the matrix of his thought. Knowledge of the other world, which Bābā Afḍal calls 'horizons and souls' (*āfāq wa anfus*), can be obtained even in this world and leaves imprints upon the soul which survive the death of the body.

Bābā Afḍal posits the existence of a relationship between ontology and autology (self-knowledge). Intelligence, he argues, is a manifestation of Divine Light, so that knowledge participates in the Divine, while logic and other means of cognition are reflections of the Divine Intellect upon the human mind.

Like the three types of knowledge, Afḍal al-Dīn Kāshānī considers there to be three separate worlds: the Divine world (*rubūbiyyaḥ*), the intermediate world (*malakūt*), and the world of nature, whose realities are reflections of the other two worlds. What is interesting is that Bābā Afḍal's hierarchy involves not only a purely ontological hierarchical scheme of 'space', but also concerns time. In this regard he distinguishes between *zamān, dahr, wujūd* and *huwiyyah,* the latter being the underlying principle of all things.

Philosophy, for Bābā Afḍal, is not an abstract intellectual exercise, but a spiritual practice aimed at awakening people from forgetfulness. The central goal of philosophy is to aid one to know oneself, as the Prophetic *ḥadīth* says, 'He who knows himself knows his Lord'. Bābā Afḍal not only wrote on the soul, but also translated into Persian four texts dealing with the concept of the soul. The first two are by Aristotle, dealing directly with the study of the soul, while the other two, the Neoplatonic *Liber de pomo* and *De Castigatione animae,* also pertain to the nature of the soul. In his exhaustive reflections on the soul, Bābā Afḍal uses various sources such as Aristotle, Plato, Neoplatonism and Hermetic writings as well as Islamic sources.

One of the more unique aspects of Bābā Afḍal's work is the fact that he wrote almost entirely in Persian and not Arabic, the traditional scholarly language in which Persians wrote most of their philosophical texts. In this regard, he followed Nāṣir Khusraw and Suhrawardī, both of whom have a substantial body of philosophical works in Persian. This fact necessitated that Bābā Afḍal further develop a technical philosophical vocabulary in Persian, in particular in logic where he made some original contributions. Bābā Afḍal's views on *qiyās-i khulf* or syllogism *per impossible,* were significant enough that Nāṣir al-Dīn Ṭūsī in his *Sharḥ al-ishārāt,* Quṭb al-Dīn Shīrāzī in his *Sharḥ ḥikmat al-ishrāq,* and finally Mullā Sadrā in his *Ḥāshiyah* upon Quṭb al-Dīn's commentary on *Ḥikmat al-ishrāq,* have discussed it.

Finally, something has to be said about Bābā Afḍal's poetry, since to most people in Iran he is known as a poet. He is unquestionably one of the great masters of Persian poetry especially among philosophers and his quatrains rank with those of such poets as Abū Sa'īd and Khayyām. These highly philosophical poems speak of certainty and contain many metaphysical doctrines within them. It is said that the following poetic exchange took place between Naṣīr al-Dīn Ṭusī and Bābā Afḍal with regard to the problem of theodicy. Ṭūsī wrote:

A cup whose parts have been moulded together,
Even a drunkard would not consider it right to break.

Those lovely hands, feet and wrists,
Why were they created and why destroyed?[1]

Bābā Afḍal responded:

When the pearl of the soul became united with the shell of the body
Through the water of life it gained human form.
When the pearl became formed, it broke the shell
And came to embellish the corner of the headwear of the king.[2]

In this chapter we have included a section of Bābā Afḍal's collected works, *Muṣannafāt* (Compositions). It begins with a discussion concerning how awareness concerning the self is obtained and continues with a thorough examination of different types of existence and existents. The discussion continues with such topics as knowledge and self-awareness, reminiscent of Suhrawardī's theory of 'knowledge by presence', culminating with a consideration of what constitutes the reality of a human being. The chapter ends with a discussion concerning an array of such traditional philosophical problems as subjects and predicates, attributes, genus, species, and some of the Aristotelian categories.

M. Aminrazavi

1. This quatrain is also attributed to 'Umār Khayyām.
2. Translation by Seyyed Hossein Nasr, in his *The Islamic Intellectual Tradition in Persia,* ed. M. Aminrazavi (London, 1996), p. 202.

COMPOSITIONS

Muṣannafāt

Reprinted from Afḍal al-Dīn Kāshānī, *Muṣannafāt,* tr. William C. Chittick, in his *The Heart of Islamic Philosophy: The Quest for Self-Knowledge in the Teachings of Afḍal al-Dīn Kāshānī* (Oxford-New York, 2001), pp. 272–306 and Selected Poems.

The Book of the Road's End

To God belongs praise—He who is worthy of praise, its patron, its utmost end, and its beginning—a praise that parallels His blessings and beneficence and makes manifest His generous giving and favour. And upon His prophet Muḥammad be prayers and peace, and upon his household and his noble companions.

Thus says the author of these words and the clarifier and stipulator of these meanings of the sciences:

A group of true companions and religious brothers requested that I write a book, the reading and the understanding of the meanings of which would allow them to become aware of three things: [1] the existence of self and the attributes of the existence of self. [2] They would become aware of what is the reality of awareness and knowledge. [3] They would become aware of the profit and benefit of awareness and knowledge.

I did not see myself without a share of the answers to these three questions, so I recognized that it was obligatory to render gratitude for this blessing. I saw that the best gratitude would be to give a share of this virtue to worthy wanters and suitable seekers. I made a covenant with myself that I would clarify these three chapters for the seekers through an explication that is proper for my own seeing and knowledge and that fits within my potency and ability. For, the person most worthy for this knowledge is he who knows to ask of it. This is because this knowledge is the final goal of all knowledges and the quintessence of the animas that have found perfection. It is the sought and the objective of the saints and the provision of the nobility of the prophets.

Since this request was made in three levels—one lower, one higher, and one still higher than the two—I have divided this book into three talks:

The first talk: On giving awareness of the existence of the self and the attributes of the self's existence.

The second talk: On giving awareness of what knowledge and awareness are.

The third talk: On giving awareness of the profit and benefit of awareness and knowledge.

The First Talk

On Giving Awareness of Self, the Existence of Self, and the Attributes of the Self's Existence

It is ten doors of speech:
The first door: On how to give awareness of the existence of self
The second door: On how many divisions existence has
The third door: On dividing existence in another way
The fourth door: On the divisions of the particular existents
The fifth door: On the divisions of the universal existents
The sixth door: On the causes of the particular existents
The seventh door: On the occasions and causes of the universal existents
The eighth door: On the meaning of self and soul
The ninth door: On the being of the soul
The tenth door: On the attributes of the existence of self

The First Door. On how one can give awareness of the existence of self

Making something clear is of two sorts. One sort is such that awareness is given of its reality through detailing its attributes. Thus, awareness of the reality of the animal is given by detailing its attributes, such as, a body with life-breath, finding with sensation, and moving through want.

The other sort is that the thing should have divisions, and you enumerate the divisions so that the questioner will grasp the reality through the mention of the divisions, since it is the same in all the divisions. Thus, the divisions of animal are numbered—flyers, crawlers, and goers—so that the questioner becomes aware of the thing that is one in all three divisions, such as sensation and motion through desire.

However, giving awareness of 'existence' cannot be through mentioning the detailed attributes of existence, because the meaning of the word *existence* is not compounded of many meanings—such as the meaning of 'animal', which is compounded of the meaning of body, the meaning of anima, the meaning of finding with sensation, and the meaning of moving through want. Each of these meanings is one of the attributes of the animal. Rather, existence has no parts from which it comes together, since the parts of the compound thing are before the compound thing, but there is nothing whose existence was before existence. Moreover, the parts of a thing are other than the thing, but there is nothing other than existence except non-existence, and existence is not compounded of non-existence. Therefore, one cannot give awareness of existence through detailing its attributes, but rather, through mentioning its divisions.

The difference between 'attributes' and 'divisions' is that the attribute of a thing may be more general than the thing, like measure, which is the attribute of weight.

Every weight has measure, but not every measure is weight. The attribute may also be equal to the thing in generality, and it may be more specific. The equal is like 'moving through desire', since every animal moves through want, and everything that moves through want is an animal. The more specific is like 'scribe', which is more specific than animal. Every scribe is an animal, but not every animal is a scribe.

As for the divisions of the thing, they are not equal with the thing in generality, nor greater in generality. Rather, they are more specific than it. Thus the divisions of body are 'animal' and 'inanimate', and both are more specific than body.

The Second Door of this Talk: On how many are the divisions of existence

Existence has two divisions—one division is 'being', the other 'finding'. The difference between being and finding is that there may be being without finding, like the being of the elemental and mineral bodies, which are without finding. But there is no finding without being.

Each of these two divisions is again divided into two—one potential being, the other actual being, then potential finding and actual finding.

Potential being is the lowest level in being. It is the existence of material things in the matter, such as the existence of the tree in the seed and the existence of the animal in the sperm-drop. Actual being without finding is like the existence of elemental bodies and others.

As for potential finding, it belongs to the soul. The meaning of the word *soul* and the meaning of *self* is one.

Actual finding belongs to the intellect. What is potential in the soul becomes actual through the intellect.

The matter of a body that is potential body reaches act through bodily nature, like the animal's sperm-drop that is potentially alive; if it comes to life actually, it becomes actual through the anima. For the body, nature is like the anima for the animal, and through it the body is a locus and receptacle for measure.

As for the potential finding that belongs to the soul, when it becomes actual, it becomes actual though intellect. The soul is a finder with intellect. Just as potential being is the meanest level in existence, so actual finding is the highest level of existence, because being is correct through finding. Whenever the being of any existent has no finding, its being and nonbeing are equal in relation to itself, even though, in relation to its finder, they are disparate.

The Third Door. On dividing existence in another way

Existence is divided in another way, though there is no great disagreement in meaning between this division and the former division. However, we will mention these words also so that this may be cause of an increase in explication.

We say: Existence is divided into two—soulish and non-soulish. 'Soulish' is said in the case of knowing: the known thing is the soulish existent. The existent is either the 'come-to-be' [*būda*], which was mentioned; or it is the 'found' [*yāfta*], which is the soulish.

In another respect, the existent is either universal or particular. The existent in the meaning of come-to-be is only particular. The existent in the meaning of 'found' is divided into two—the found with sensation and imagination, which is particular, and the found with the intellect, which is universal.

The universal can be both the attribute of the universal and the object described by the universal. The particular cannot be the attribute, or else it will not be the described object. The universal is the root of the particular, while the particular is among the divisions of the universal.

An example of the universal is the meaning 'human', and of the particular the individual humans, such as Zayd, Bakr, ʿAmr, and so on, for the root of Zayd and ʿAmr is the human. Humanness belongs to each of them equally; it is not more in one and less in another. One is not more human and another weaker in humanness.

The universal cannot be found with that with which the particular [is found]. The finder grasps the particulars with the potency of sensation and the potency of imagination, such as this human and that human, this colour and that colour, this flavour and that flavour. Then, through a light that is the radiance of the Universal Intelligence, he finds in self that a thing which is the attribute of many particulars is equal for all, such as the meaning of colour. When the knower sees this colour as white, that colour as black, and the other colour as green, then he knows and finds that, although the many colours are different from each other in some particular states, they are one in the meaning of colour, which is universal and is the attribute of all colours.

The particular can be found with the particular tool, and the universal with the universal potency. The existence of the particular can be diverse and undergoing alteration, but the universal is far from alteration and corruption.

Let us now enumerate the divisions of the particular existents, and then we will mention the universal existents, for we have taken the two as the divisions of the existent. After that, we will also mention the occasion and cause of both existents, through the success-giving and guidance of the Success-giver and Road-shower—high indeed is His loftiness and holy are His names!

The Fourth Door of this Talk: On the divisions of the particular existents

The particular existents are of two sorts—root and branch. The root is the cosmos, and the branch is its progeny. By the word *cosmos*, we mean those existents whose beginning is the remotest sphere and whose end is the orb of the earth, along with all the states and potencies of this totality, including the spheres and stars and their mover, and the four elements and their natures.

As for the branch, it is the progeny of the cosmos, like the kinds and classes of minerals, the varieties of growing things including plants and trees, and the various sorts of animals, all of which can be found with sensation or imagination.

The difference between perception by the senses and perception by imagination—though the perceptibles of both are particular—is that with sensation, one can find a thing that is present, and its form is imprinted in sensation's tools. In other words, the form of the sensible is depicted in the substance of sensation's tool so that the possessor of the senses may become aware of its being depicted. Imagination perceives everything that is depicted in the senses when the sensible is present, but, when the thing becomes absent, imagination can be aware of it in its absence just as it was aware of it in its presence. The perception of imagination is 'fancy' [*pindār*].

The specificity of the 'individual' existent is that it has no multiplicity, whether in imagination or in outside existence. Thus the individual *Zayd* cannot be many things. One cannot bring many things into the imagination, all of which will be the indicated Zayd.

Although the universal is one meaning and one reality in itself, outside of itself it may be many, all equal in that reality. Even if it is not many in outside existence, a multiplicity described by the one meaning can be brought into imagination. For example, by 'sun' is not meant this sun that is a particular. Although it is one in individual existence, many suns all sharing the meaning of sun can be brought into imagination.

Now, this cosmos and every root and branch within it are all particular in existence, for one cannot bring into imagination many cosmoses nor are there in existence many cosmoses that are all *this* cosmos.

Every particular has existence through a universal, through which it comes to stand. Thus, every particular human and every particular animal that can be indicated is *that* human and *that* animal through the universal human and the universal animal in which all share. But the universal human is not human through the particular human, for if the particular individual should be nullified the universal will not be nullified. In the same way, if the branches and progeny of the cosmos should be nullified the cosmos, which is the root, will not be nullified. The relation of universal existents to particular existents is the same as the relation of roots to branches, for the existence of the branch is from the root.

The Fifth Door of this Talk: On the divisions of the universal existents

The universal existents are not outside of two divisions: either they are the supreme level, which does not belong to any universal's division, while all the universals are among its divisions; or they are not the level of the supreme side, though these also have divisions and branches.

The first division of universal that we mentioned is the meaning of *thing* and *existent*, for the meaning of thing and existent is not the branch and division of any other universal that is more general than thing and existent. Among the branches and divisions of thing and existent are 'substance' and 'accident', and we have mentioned the divisions of accidents and substances in the book *The Clarifying Method*. But the purpose of this book and this talk is that awareness be given of the existence of the self and the attributes of the self's existence. The divisions of the universal were mentioned because the perception of universal meanings is an attribute of the self's existence, and everything that is more universal and more general is closer to the self and brighter in perception.

The universal existents belong to the division of existence in the meaning of finding, not in the meaning of being without finding. Hence being without finding is particular and is found with sensation and imagination. Everything more universal is more found.

The divisions and branches of the universal come to an end with the particular, for an individual and a part does not accept dividing, neither in the form of sensory existence, nor in the imagining potency. By these words we do not mean that the individual existent that can be indicated does not have parts. Rather, we mean that it cannot be divided such that every division should be like it—like 'animal', which is divided into human, beast, flyer, and crawler, and each division is animal. So also is 'human', which is divided into Zayd, 'Amr, and Bakr, and each of these three is human: 'colour', which is divided into black, white, red, and green, and each of these divisions is colour. This is not like the sensory Zayd who has parts, like hand, foot, and head. Zayd's hand is not Zayd, nor is his head, nor is his foot.

The beginning of the soulish existents, which are the perceptibles and knowns, is the meaning of 'thing' and 'existent'. The end of the perceptibles is the meaning of the sensible individual, and [the end of] the universals is either 'genera', 'species', 'differentiae', 'specificities', or 'general accidents'. We have spoken of the meanings of these names in *The Clarifying Method*.

The Sixth Door of this Talk: On the causes of the particular existents

Awareness was given before that the particular existents are divided into two—root and branch. The existence of the branch comes from the root, and the root in the particular existents is the celestial sphere and the elemental bodies. The branch of this root is the mineral, vegetal, and animal bodies.

Hence, the cosmos, which is the root, is one of the causes of the progeny, which are the branch. The cosmos and its progeny are compound, and everything compound must have several causes in existence according to its compoundedness.

Particular existents must have four causes in existence. One is matter, from which things can be compounded. One is form, through which they can come to be compounded. One is the actor, which does the compounding. And one is the final goal and the completeness, since the actor compounds for the sake of the final goal.

Since the cosmos and the existent things are compound, they must have matter, form, actor, and final goal. The existence of all four causes is clear. The lowest of the causes and occasions is the thing's matter. Higher than it is form, for the existence of matter reaches act through form. Higher than both is actor. And more eminent by essence than all three is completeness and final goal, since the final goal makes the actor into an actor so that it may depict the form in the matter.

In the progeny, these causes are compound, because the branches have more parts of compoundedness than the roots. For example, the form of humans is compounded from the form of animals and plants and from bodily form. Their matter is also compounded from the matter of animals, plants, and bodies. The matter of the progeny's bodies is from the elemental bodies, and the matter of the elemental bodies is unconditioned body. The matter of [unconditioned] body is substance. Hence the matter of the cosmos is simple. And since the parts of its compoundedness have become fewer, a cause has also been subtracted. This is the material cause, for the first matter has no matter. So also, the first actor has no active cause, and the final goal and completeness has no final goal and completeness.

We indicated what the final goal of existence is before, when we mentioned the divisions of existence, which are being and finding. Being is either potential or actual, and so also, finding is either potential or actual. Just as potential being is the lowest level in existence, actual finding is the most eminent level in existence, for being becomes correct through finding. Hence, the final goal and completeness of existence is actual finding. Afterwards, this will become clearer.

The Seventh Door of this Talk: On the occasions and causes of soulish existence, which we have called 'finding'

It has come to be known that the known things and the perceptibles are of two sorts—universal and particular. The particular is that which is perceived with the potency of sensation and imagination. The universal is that which is perceived with intellect and essence.

Now we say: Perceptibles are of two sorts—either compound or simple. The particular perceptibles are compound only. Different things can be perceived with different means of perception. Thus colours and shapes are perceived with the sense of eyesight, sounds and letters are perceived with hearing, flavour is perceived with the sense of taste, aroma is perceived with smell, and other qualities—such as heat and cold, wetness and dryness, roughness and smoothness, softness and hardness—are perceived with the sense of touch.

The material cause of sensory perception is the tools of sensation. The formal cause is the sensory form, by which the tool of sensation becomes impressed and formed. The active cause is the sensory and animal soul. The completing and final cause is for the particular existent to become bright and correct. In other words, the 'come-to-be' turns into the 'found', and its bodily existence becomes soulish.

As for the universal perceptibles, which we called 'known things' and 'intelligibles', they are of two sorts—simple and compound. The compound knowns have, in reality, no material cause, but rather something like a material cause. Inasmuch as the knowns are acquired from the sensibles, they are sensibles and imaginables. The active cause is the reflecting soul. The completing and final cause is for potential finding to become actual.

These knowns have no formal cause, because they themselves are forms belonging to the soul. That which is like the formal cause is their permanence and fixity.

The causes of the simple knowns are two—the active cause, which is the intellect that makes actual, and the completing cause, which is the conjunction of the known things with the knower. There is neither material nor formal cause, since the simple has neither matter nor form. This is because matter belongs to the compound things, not to the simple things, and also the utmost end of the simple forms is in the knower. When he knows his essence, all the causes become one. The actor, form, and matter of the known turn into the final goal.

The Eighth Door of this Talk: On the meaning of self

We use the word *soul* and the word *self* in one meaning. When we say that any of the existent things without perception—whether potentially or actually—is not among the possessors of soul, we mean that it has no self. When it is said about an ill person who swoons or becomes unconscious, 'He went from himself', or 'He became without self', this is said because he fails to perceive and have awareness.

The vegetal substance is called a 'possessor of soul' because it has found the first level of life, which is the movement of configuration and growth. The movement of configuration and growth is life's first level, and sensation and desire are the second level. Whatever has neither the life of movement nor the life of sensation is not called 'possessor of soul', because the soul's first trace in the body is movement. If no trace appears, one cannot affirm that which leaves traces.

The 'soul' of each thing is its root and reality, through which the thing is the thing. The growing soul is the root and reality of the vegetal substance, and through it the growing thing grows. The animal soul is the root and reality of the animal, and through it the animal is an animal, not through the bodily form. When the traces of the soul become non-apparent and nullified in these bodies, the animality of the animal and the humanness of the human come not to be, even though the body keeps its own guise and shape. Thus, one cannot judge that the dead bodies of animals and humans have humanness or animality. So also is the vegetal body that has been cut off from the vegetal soul.

The Ninth Door of this Talk: On the existence of the soul

At the first stage of the work and the beginning of the search for knowledge, the human comes to know and find everything that cannot be found with the senses by way of inference from the sensible. In other words, he uses what he has found with the senses as an intermediary and he makes it show the road to the non-sensible. Thus, from finding motion with the senses, he finds the motion-inducer. From the sensible casket he knows the carpenter.

When he becomes more complete and nears the utmost end and perfection, he reaches the effect from the cause and the occasioned from the occasioner. From knowing the root, he grasps the branch. As long as he can recognize the root only by recognizing the branch, he is still a pupil and has the level of learning. When he knows the effects from the knowledge of the causes, he is the knower, not the pupil.

Now, knowing self, which is the soul, is in this respect. When he is heedless of self and finds other than self, he is a pupil and a searcher. Knowing the traces of self in a sensible individual shows him the road to knowledge of the soul's existence, by the path of which we are talking. When we want to affirm the existence of the growing soul from its traces that we find in trees and plants—like increase, leaves, blossoms, bearing produce, and arriving at seeds and fruit—we seek out with *theoria* whether this state that we have seen from them, which is the increase of the growing body, has risen up from the body inasmuch as it is the body, or from something other than the body. If the first sort—that it has risen up from its bodiment—is null and false, then the second sort is true and truthful—that it comes from something other than its bodiment. There is no other sort than these two—that motion is from it or from other than it.

The nullification of the first sort can be by this path: We think over the fact that if the motion, the increase, and the bringing forth of seeds and fruit were from the body of the tree and the plant, then, as long as that tree is a body, this state would be with it. But there is no doubt that this body will remain in its bodiment while this state will become separate from it. Thus we know that the motion and increase rise up through that thing. So, this is the root that incites its growth, for the existence of the growing thing is through the growth-inciter.

This path, which is to know the trace and, from knowing the trace, to know the trace-inducer, is called 'inference' [*istidlāl*], that is, searching out the road-shower to and 'evidence' [*dalīl*] for something.

By this same path by which we became aware of the existence of the growth-inciting soul, we can also become aware of the animal soul. The life that is sensation and movement through desire and that becomes manifest in the body of the animal is either a state essential to the body, or a trace of something that is other than the animal's body. If it were the state of the body, so long as its body had its own bodiment, the animal would be alive. But there is no doubt that the body is sometimes alive and sometimes dead, and the body has its own bodiment in both states. Hence, the life of the living body is from something other than its body, through which the animal is alive. So, it is this thing that is the root of the living thing, not the body.

By this same path, one can find awareness of the human soul by knowing the traces of the human soul. However, there is a difference between inferring the trace-inducer from the traces of the human soul and inferring the trace-inducer from the traces of the growing soul and the animal soul. This is because the traces of the growth-inciting soul and the animal soul become manifest only in bodies, but the traces of the human soul are in the animal soul, and they reach the body from the animal soul. Also, the seeker and pursuer of the animal soul and the growing soul is not the animal soul and the growing soul, but rather, the human soul, while the seeker and pursuer of the human soul is also the human soul. By knowing them through self's essence, he knows self's essence, so this appears more surprising. After all, when searching for other than self shows the road to self, this is truly a marvellous work. Its explanation will come in the Tenth Door, God willing—high indeed is He!

The Tenth Door of this Talk: On giving awareness of the attribute of the self's existence

When many existents are made known, each comes with a specific name. The difference in names is because of the difference of specificities. The specificity of each thing is its reality. The meaning of 'reality' is to be fit for being. For example, if a body is long, and it is known that the 'long' is something with length, then the thing is self, but the length is not self. This is because first there must be the thing, which is the locus of length so that length can be. Thus the thing is fit for being, not its length, and the length has being through the thing's being.

In the same way, the name *human* is given to humans because of the human specificity, and the human specificity is the human reality. So, what is 'suitable for being' is the human soul. It is clear that humans are not human through the body, since the inanimate body can be established through shape, guise, and the conjunction of the parts and not be a human—just as we said about animals and growing things. Moreover, they are not human through the specificity of the growing soul or the animal soul. Otherwise, all animals would be human, for all animals have that specificity.

Hence, the reality and selfhood of the human through which the animal is human is not the reality and selfhood of the plant and the animal. The springhead of knowing that reality is searching, and the springhead of searching to find that reality is the human soul. Hence the searcher is self, and the object of search is also self. To search for self is to go back to self, and to know self is to reach self.

There will be searching and asking when someone's existence is potential finding, for in one respect the object of search is, and in another respect it is not. One cannot search for that which *is* in every respect, nor can one search for that which *is not* in every respect.

Potential finding is called 'desire', that is, one has found and one does not know that one has found. Actual finding is called 'knowing', that is, one has found and one knows that one has found.

When the soul seeks self, it is potentially found and finder. When it finds self, it is actually finder and found. As long as it is knower of self potentially, it is the soul. But when it is knower and finder of self actually, it is not the soul. Rather, it is the 'intellect', for, when the specificity turns into something else, the name also turns into something else.

The Second Talk

On Giving Awareness of what Awareness and Knowledge are.
This is one chapter.

Awareness and knowledge are finding things in self. Whatever is not cannot be found. It is possible for humans to know all things. Hence, if a human finds all things in self, and if what is not cannot be found, then all things are in self. Hence the human soul is general and encompasses all things, for they are within it.

Let us now recount how all things are in the human.

Know that we said before that the existents are either universal or particular. The universal is the root and reality of the particular, since the particular is among the divisions, limbs, and branches of the universal. The branch and shoot endure by the root.

The universal is intelligible, and the particular is sensible or imaginable. This cosmos—of which one extremity is the remotest sphere and one extremity the centre of the earth—and everything that belongs to it are particular.

The universal and particular share in reality, thingness, and existence, but the two are incompatible in universality and particularity. Take, for example, the human species and the human individual. In humanness, there is no difference and no twoness between them. But inasmuch as one of them is the species that is universal, intelligible, and the root, while the other is the individual that is sensible, particular, and the branch, they become two.

The cosmos, which belongs to the division of particular existents, is the celestial-sphere with all its layers and the elemental bodies and their progeny, which are the bodies compounded of the elements. Some of the things compounded of their elements are inanimate and some animate. Of those that have anima, some are sensate and some without the senses. Of those that are sensate, some are intelligent and some without intelligence.

When the human perceives the body of the cosmos, that is, the spheres and the solitary elements, while his body is one with the body of the cosmos in the reality of bodiment, then the bodiment that he has found is the come-to-be for him. When he knows the compound bodies, while his body is one with the compound bodies in combination and compoundedness, then the compound body that he has found is the come-to-be for him. When he knows the animals, while humans in respect of sensation and movement are animals, then what he has found is the come-to-be for him. And when the human knows the whole human species, while the finder is also the human, then he has found self, and the self that he has found is the come-to-be.

We said before that the come-to-be without finding has two levels. One is the potentially come-to-be, which is the existence of the body's matter. When it reaches act from the level of potency, it has an occasion and a cause that has made its potency reach act, and this is the higher level.

The body's matter, which is a potential body, is actual body through nature. Nature is the lowest branch and shoot of the soulish branches and shoots. Since body's nature is one sort, all bodies are one in the meaning of bodiment and in receiving measure and dimensions. Since the form of the bodily in all bodies is one, and this one has no diversity of parts and is simple, the shape and guise of this simple body is a simple shape and guise, in which there is no diversity of surfaces and sides. This is the spherical shape, the measure of whose thickness, length, and breadth is equal in every direction. So, the first body takes the spherical guise and form, and it is the body of the cosmos. Hence, the body of the cosmos can have come to rest in this shape through the bodily nature.

Once the come-to-be is found, it is more complete. Through the nature of bodiment the body cannot reach the act of completeness, which is finding, from the potency of receiving completeness, because perfection cannot be reached from deficiency unless through movement from potency to act, and the body's nature cannot be the cause of the body's movement. Hence the body moves through a motion-inducing potency, and the motion-inducing potency is another branch and shoot of the soul, more eminent than nature.

The first movement in the first body was revolving movement, for a circular body can only move in a circle. This is called 'turning'. From the turning of the spherical body, which is the body of the cosmos, the centre and circumference of the cosmos appear. The springhead of opposition in the cosmos's body is this movement, for when the circular body turns, a centre is designated around which it turns. The centre does not turn, but is still. Heat arises from movement, and cold from rest. Hence, the part that is nearer to the moving is warm, and that which is nearer to the still is cold. From heat lightness arises, and from cold heaviness. The heat of the cosmos is fire, and its cold earth. The part that is nearer to the earth is cold and heavy like the earth, but not to that limit; it is water. What is nearer to fire is warm and light like fire, but not like fire, and this is air. Water and air are between fire and earth.

Although these elements all agree in the bodily form, which is the reception of measures, each has another form outside the bodily form, and that form demands another nature. The plurality of the natures of these bodies is born from the celestial-sphere, for it is the trace of something else that is not bodily. The utmost end of the magnitude and measure of each element is at another element. What is between any two elements is not apart or empty, as between water and air, for the utmost end of one is joined with the beginning of the other.

By means of the revolving movement, the mover of the celestial orbs makes its trace reach the elemental bodies all the way to the centre of the earth. That trace is the mixing together of their natures' forms so that the compound body comes into existence. Through compoundedness, the potency of the mutual opposition is broken. The first compoundedness is the existence of the minerals, which is the body's first level and way-station [in moving] from the existent in the sense of the 'come-to-be' to the existent that is 'found'.

From there the body sets out until it reaches the level of vegetal compoundedness, in which the potency of seeking and movement appears from the self. For the body of the plant pulls other bodies toward its own body through attraction so that they may be like it and it may increase. It must always have those other bodies. This potency of attraction and seeking is another of the shoots, branches, and traces of the tree of the soul, in a level higher than the nature of the compoundedness and intermixing of the elements.

Another level of existence in the sense of 'finding' is sensory finding, which belongs to the animal along with the potency of vegetal seeking. The tools of sensation are many, because the states of elemental bodies increase through compoundedness, and qualities become plentiful—such as colours, flavours, scents, guises, and shapes. Each of them has finding with a specific tool. Thus, the finding animal finds out each state and quality with a tool. It finds out colours with the tool of eyesight; it finds out sounds, guises, and letters with hearing, aromas with the sense of smell, flavour with the sense of taste, and the other qualities with the sense of touch, so that all the states of the bodies may be found.

Once compoundedness in the compositional virtues and in the mixing and balance of the opposites increases, sensory finding turns intellective, the sensible becomes the known, the plural existents come to be unified, and the altering, bodily existence and generation become the fixed, spiritual thing that is known.

The divisions of existence are bodies and spirits; and the divisions of the spirits are nature, the growing soul, the animal soul, and the human soul. Once the states, guises, and qualities of these substances are all found, the human soul, in finding whatever it finds of these existents, also finds self. This is such that—as we mentioned before—humans share in the reality of whatever of this found thing they find. Hence, when they find it, they also find self. When they grasp the come-to-be, the found, and the finder, and when the self is also the come-to-be, the found, and the finder, then they have found self. The profit of being aware of and knowing this is existence. In the next talk, this will be explained further, God willing—high indeed is He!

The Third Talk

On Giving Awareness of the Profit and Benefit of Awareness and Knowledge. It is three doors of speech.

The First Door. On what profit is

'Profit' is one of the causes. In the previous discussion it was indicated that the causes are four—matter, form, actor, and final goal. The most eminent cause is the final goal, since the other causes become causes through it, because the actor depicts matter with form for the sake of the final goal. Hence, that which causes the active, material, and formal causes to be causes in the final goal.

The final goal is before all the causes in essence and after them all in existence. In other words, existence has its utmost end in it. The four causes are in compositional and compounded existence. If the existent thing is not compound, there are no causes of compoundedness. The particular existent is compound only, so it must have all four causes.

It may be that the active cause is a compound particular that has another active cause, and that the particular matter has another matter. For example, the artisan who does goldsmithery, ironworking, or carpentry must also have an artisan and actor, a matter, and a form in order to be an existent. Or, take the matter of a house, which is bricks, clay, and mortar; bricks, clay, and mortar also have a matter.

In the same way, the final goal of a thing may have another final goal, like the simple, elemental body, which is for the sake of the compound body. The compound body is the final goal of the simple, elemental body.

Compoundedness is for the sake of the equilibrium of the natures, which are mutually opposed and do not get along. The equilibrium of the natures is for the sake of worthiness to receive the soulish, spiritual potency. Worthiness to accept the soulish potency is for the sake of knowledge and intelligence. Knowledge and intelligence are for the sake of unconditioned existence. Unconditioned, general existence is for the sake of the Ipseity and Essence.

This order, harmony of occasions, and multiplicity of causes happens in the compound things. The utmost end of the causes is at the final goal, and the utmost end of the final goals is at the Essence, Ipseity, and Reality. By the word *profit* we mean the most eminent cause, which is the final goal and perfection.

Now we will indicate what 'act' is and which, among these bodily and spiritual existents, is the 'actor'. Then we will explain the cause of completeness, perfection, and act, and that of the actor, God willing—high indeed is He!

The Second Door of this Talk. On act and doing

Doing is a state that becomes manifest little by little from a substance in a substance, such that no two states of this trace exist together. Rather, one comes not to be and the other finds being. For example, the substance fire makes the trace of warmth appear little by little in the substance water; and the vegetal soul makes manifest the trace of the vegetal body's increase little by little in the substance of the plant's body. In no period of that increase and the water's warmth do two states occur together. Rather, one state comes not to be and another occurs. This state is called 'movement' and 'alteration'.

In this discussion, by the word *substance* we mean something whose existence does not require a dwelling-place that would be there before it so that it would come to exist within it. Rather, it is the dwelling-place of other things that cannot come to exist except in it—such as length, breadth, shape, colour, heaviness, and lightness—since the likes of these states exist only in a dwelling-place.

Things are of two sorts—either dwelling-place or dweller. The dwelling-place is the substance, and it is one. Plurality and multiplicity are because of the states that dwell within it. The first states are nine things and quantity is one of these states that dwell in the substance. In the book *The Clarifying Method,* we have enumerated all the states and shown how each has existence through priority and posteriority along with the divisions of each. One of them is act. Because of it, substance is another substance, for the active substance is one thing, and the acted-upon substance something else. Act is the state that keeps coming from the active substance and keeps reaching the acted upon substance, though the two are one in that they are substance.

Substance and what dwells within it share in what is understood from the word *existence.* However, they become disparate through priority and posteriority, since the dwelling-place exists before the dweller. The dwelling-place of act is called the 'actor', and the dwelling-place of being acted upon the 'acted upon'. The substance through which acts come by essence is the soul, and its first act is movement. The substance that is the first thing acted upon is the body.

When it is said that bodies are 'active' and that a trace becomes manifest from them in another body, this is not said on the basis of the reality, because bodies do not act by essence, but rather by accident. Thus the body of the fire warms the body of water, and warmth is the act of the body of fire. However, this is not by essence, inasmuch as fire is a body, but rather by accident, insasmuch as fire has a specific potency and nature—from among the potencies of the soul and beyond the form and nature of bodiment—that warms. Hence the body of fire is the doer of the warming through that potency.

Such doers are many, since each of the simple bodies and the compound bodies—the minerals, plants, animals, and their classes—has a doing that is attributed to its particular individuals. However, this is not by essence. Rather, the doing of each is through a potency that is one of the potencies and branches of soul. This is because the root of acts is movement-giving. We said before that movement does not come from the body and the bodily nature. So, it is better that what can come to be by the intermediary of movement not be from a body.

Hence, the first actor is soul. The meaning of 'soul' is root and reality, and soul's acts are of many sorts, because of the multiplicity of acted-upon things and bodies. We showed that the plurality and diversity of bodies arises from the revolving movement, which separated the centre from the circumference through stillness and movement. Two became four, and the number of bodies became as many as can be numbered.

We said that the first actor is soul, and the first acted-upon thing is body. The first act is depicting matter with body's form, which is conjunction and measure, so that body's matter may become the matter of another body through body's form. After bodily form come shape and guise, which pertain to 'quality'. After this, unconditioned body becomes the matter of the diverse bodies, such that some of them receive the form of movement from soul, like the celestial orbs, and some the diverse qualities, like the elements. The elements become the matter of the compound bodies, the compound things the matter of growing bodies, and growing bodies the matter of animate bodies.

The meaning of this discussion is not that every compound thing becomes a plant, nor that all plants become animals, but rather that every matter, in keeping with the form's worthiness, has a specific limit and utmost end beyond which it does not pass. A compound thing that has no more preparedness than for compoundedness and mixing does not pass beyond this limit and does not become a plant. What we mean is that body receives life only when it has first received the potency of growth; it receives human life, in the sense of the intellective potency, only when it has first received the sensory and animal potency. So also is the case with every other matter in relation to every form.

So, every matter belonging to the compound things has a simpler matter, and every accidental actor has an actor, until this reaches the matter of matters, which is the first matter, and the actor of actors, which is the first actor.

Act has a nature and a substance. Every state that does not belong to something's root belongs to the root of something else. The actorness of soul is by nature, and its life is by essence. Its life is from its reality and root, which is intellect. Intellect is to soul as soul is to nature, and as nature is to body. Hence, soul has no matter and no actor; as for matter, this is because the first matter has existence from soul; and as for actor, this is because act is movement-giving, and soul is movement-giver. The vegetal forms that come to bodily matter are also from soul's act and trace.

The first form in the bodies is the bodily form, within which it is possible to posit length, breadth, and depth. After the form of the body is the form of the body's shape—round or polygonal. After the form is movement—revolving or straight. After this is the form of intermixture and combination, which is generation and transformation. After this, movement increases or decreases, and this is in body's quantity. After this is animal movement. Hence all the material and active causes reach the utmost end at the soul, and it has no material or active cause.

The Third Door. On the formal and final occasion and cause of soul

Know that soul is a substance living by essence, doing by nature, and potentially knowing.

It is a substance because act exists through it and in it, and it is the dwelling-place of the act, but it is not within any dwelling-place; this is the state and attribute of a substance.

Its doerness by nature is obvious from the previous discussion, for actorness in it belongs to the root, but in other than it, it is accidental and alien.

The livingness is because all bodies are animate and living through it, but dead by their own nature.

It is potentially knowing because in knowing things it is kept distracted and heedless of self and knowing self. This is potential knowing—that it knows but does not know that it knows. It knows something and fancies that the known is something outside of self. It does not know that it is finding that thing in self.

In this respect, soul is not without deficiency, even though 'existence' in the sense of fixity and obtainment is actual in soul, and 'existence' in the sense of that which is intelligible and known is also actual in soul, for soul's substance is neither sensory and imaginal nor sense-intuitive, since sensation, imagination, and sense-intuition are each among the potencies of the human soul. Rather, soul's substance is intelligible.

The intelligible is of two sorts—either an intelligible that is not an intellecter, like the genera and species of the meanings known to soul; or an intelligible which, along with intelligibility, is also an intellecter and knower.

Soul is actually known, because soul's existence and substance came to be known through the aforementioned proofs; thus it came to be known actually. However, the knowing of soul is potential. When its potency reaches act, it is knower of self and known of self. This is the form of the intellect, by which soul has been depicted. Its potency ended up in act, and with this form, it is not soul. Just as body's matter was potentially body, and when the form of bodiment joined to it, it was body, not matter, so also soul is potentially knower, and knowing is the intellect. When soul reaches it, it is intellect, not soul.

The intellect has no cause other than the final cause, which is the possessor of intellect, because the final goal of self's knowing is to know and be aware of self through self. Knowing is universal, general existence. All the divisions of existence—substantial and accidental, bodily and spiritual, species-specific and individual, natural and soulish—come under its compass and generality. When it knows self through knowing, then it has reached self. Self is the final goal of final goals. This knowing is existence, subsistence, completeness, and perfection. This is the profit of awareness, and the benefit of knowledge. Unaware, natural, particular, deficient, and corruptible existence turns into aware, intellective, universal, subsistent, complete, and endless existence.

Awareness of this level has been given by the discussion, so we end the talk. May we, our companions, and our brothers be kept occupied, for ever and ever, with gratitude for being given success to know and to give awareness of the known.

And praise belongs to God, Lord of the world [37:182]. And blessings be upon His prophet, Muḥammad the chosen, the seal of the prophets and envoys, and upon his pure household and companions; and may He give abundant peace!

Selected poems of Kāshānī

O you who search to find the encounter,
another time beyond the heavens.
God is with you. His great throne is your heart—
If you don't find Him in self, where will you find Him?

Put to work this intellect come for work,
let it put right this mixed-up business.
Imagination has painted a house of idols in your heart—
break the idols and make the house the Ka'ba.

Don't think that I fear that world,
that I fear dying and the soul's extraction.
Death is true, so why should I fear?
I fear that I have not lived well.

Work no wrong at anyone's word,
speak with virtue and torment none.

Tomorrow you'll say, 'Why do you blame me? He told me to do it.'
They won't accept that from you—be careful, don't do it.

Afḍal, you've seen that all you've seen is nothing.
You've run from horizon to horizon—nothing.
Whatever you've said and heard is nothing,
whatever you've hidden in corners is nothing.

O You whose pure Essence is rid of existence,
all spirits fall flat on the dirt at Your door.
Whatever has come into being by non-being's road
is a drop of dew on the face of a rose.

No one will know from the surface
how form and meaning came to be joined.
All will see plainly the mysteries
only when form is broken.

O Entity of subsistence, is there any subsistence that You are not?
O You with no place, is there any place where You are not?
You whose Essence is free of all directions,
where are You after all? And where are You not?

Every impression that appears on the tablet of being
is the form of Him who made the impression.
When the old ocean sends up new waves,
they call them 'waves' but in fact they're the ocean.

Whether you see kernel as all or shell as all,
don't look crooked, for He is all.
You've no eye with which to see Him:
from your head to your feet—He is all.

First among beings are intellect and soul,
then the nine spheres that turn in their tracks.
Pass these by and come to the pillars,
then minerals, then plants, then animals.

3

Dabīrān-i Kātibī-yi Qazwīnī

Najm al-Dīn ʿAlī ibn ʿUmar ibn ʿAlī Qazwīnī known as Dabīrān-i Kātibī was one of the foremost philosophers and scientists of his day, celebrated for his expertise in logic and philosophy as well as mathematics and astronomy. A student of Athīr al-Dīn Abharī, he was already a famous philosopher/scientist when Hülagü conquered Qazwīn. At that time Naṣīr al-Dīn Ṭūsī invited him to cooperate with him in the construction and scientific work at Marāghah which he accepted. He spent some time at Marāghah and assisted Ṭūsī in the composition of the new astronomical tables (*zīj*) associated with Ṭūsī's name. It is also said that Dabīrān-i Kātibī trained a number of students, among them Quṭb al-Dīn Shīrāzī, and died after an active intellectual life *c.*657/1276.

Dabīrān-i Kātibī was Shāfiʿī, but his works gained the attention of both Sunni and Shiʿi philosophers and even theologians. He wrote a number of commentaries such as those upon the *Muḥaṣṣal* (The Collected Work) and *Mulakhkhaṣ* (The Summing Up) of Fakhr al-Dīn Rāzī and the *Kashf al-asrār* (The Unveiling of Secrets) of Afḍal al-Dīn Khunjī as well as independent works on philosophy and logic. Among the works of Dabīrān-i Kātibī the most famous are *al-Risālah al-shamsiyyah* (The Solar Treatise) dedicated to the prime minister Shams al-Dīn Juwaynī and *Ḥikmat al-ʿayn* (Wisdom from the Source). *Al-Risālah al-shamsiyyah* has remained over the centuries among the most popular texts for the teaching of formal logic and was translated into English in the nineteenth century by A. Sprenger. Many commentaries have been written upon it including those by Saʿd al-Dīn Taftāzānī and Quṭb al-Dīn Rāzī. The text is still taught in traditional centres for the study of Islamic philosophy in Persia today.

The philosophical fame of Dabīrān-i Kātibī resides, however, in his *Ḥikmat al-ʿayn* which deals with a complete cycle of *mashshāʾī* philosophy, selections from which appear in this section. This work has remained among the most popular for the teaching of *mashshāʾī* philosophy over the centuries and many commentaries have been written upon it including those by Mīrak Bukhārī, Quṭb al-Dīn Shīrāzī and ʿAllāmah Ḥillī. Dabīrān-i Kātibī also exchanged a number of letters with Naṣīr al-Dīn Ṭūsī which are of both historical and philosophical interest.

Dabīrān-i Kātibī did not simply repeat the *mashshāʾī* theses of old but in certain places was critical of some arguments given and provided his own solutions. For example, in his treatise *Ithbāt al-wājib* (Proof of the Necessary Being), while accepting the conclusion of the proofs offered, he criticizes some of those proofs especially the proof for the existence of God based on the impossibility of infinite regress for which he substitutes other proofs. His arguments about proofs for the existence of God became known as *shubahāt* or doubts associated with his name. The doubts were discussed by later philosophers and one of them Kamāl al-Dīn Fasāʾī even wrote a book entitled *Ḥall shubahāt al-Kātibī* (Solution to the Doubts of al-Kātibī).

Altogether, Dabīrān-i Kātibī must be considered one of the major *mashshāʾī* philosophers of the seventh/thirteenth century, that is, the period when this philsophical school was being revived mainly by Ṭūsī. The influence of Dabīrān-i Kātibī is not to be seen only in the circle of Marāghah, but has continued over the ages and his *Ḥikmat al-ʿayn* is still studied by many students of Islamic philosophy as a clear and comprehensive introduction to the Avicennan interpretation of Islamic philosophy.

In this chapter we have included a section from Qazwīnī's *Ḥikmat al-ʿayn* that addresses one of the most difficult of philosophical questions, namely the problem of being, quiddity and their relationship with the Necessary Being. Different types of existence, mental and objective, and their relation to the rational soul as well as revelation, prophethood, life after death and the problem of knowing the intelligibles constitute the rest of the discussions in this chapter.

S. H. Nasr

WISDOM FROM THE SOURCE

Ḥikmat al-ʿayn

Translated by Ibrahim Kalin from Dabīrān-i Kātibī-yi Qazwīnī, *Ḥikmat al-ʿayn* (with commentary by Shams al-Dīn Muḥammad al-Bukhārī), edited with an introduction by Jaʿfar Zāhidī (Mashhad, 1353/1934), pp. 49–56; 71–76; 305–321.

The Addition of Being to Contingent Quiddity

It [being] is not identical with contingent quiddity. Nor is it included in it otherwise the intellection of every contingent quiddity would be the same as the intellection of its being, or it would necessitate it. The conclusion is false because we can think of a triangle while doubting its existence [in the external world]. When being is added to the contingent quiddity, it becomes impossible to affirm of it what has already been affirmed of it. The conclusion is false because we can affirm of blackness that it is receptive of existence whereas this cannot be affirmed of non-existence and blackness with being.[1] This is so because if being was included in contingent quiddity, it would be the most comprehensive of the common essences. This would also make it a genus [but] the differentiation of species included in it from one another is through actually existing differentia and distinct from other species through other actually existing differentia. And this goes on *ad infinitum*.[2] This would further make the differentiation of the Necessary from the contingent based on a differentia that subsists by itself, in which case the Necessary would become composite, which is impossible.

That Being is Identical with the Reality of the Necessary Being

Being is identical with the reality of the Necessary Being;[3] otherwise it would be either included in it or excluded from it.[4] The former calls for compositeness [in

1. Qazwīnī's objection is based on the idea that being cannot be added to quiddities otherwise we would have to accept that quiddities exist before existence is added to them. 'Blackness with existence' added to it and non-existence illustrates this point: when 'existence as added to blackness' is removed from it, blackness (or any black object) must cease to exist rather than becoming 'blackness without existence added to it.' This is another way of stating the logical impossibility of existence as an accident.

2. Being is a common term (*mafhūm mushtarak*) among actually existing substances but not a genus or species because whereas a genus or species by definition applies only to a definite number of objects, being, as the all-inclusive reality of all things, cannot include certain things and leave out others. Such logical terms as genus and species apply to the order of thought, not the order of being.

3. The commentator Shams al-Dīn Muḥammad ibn Mubārak-Shāh al-Bukhārī notes that this is 'in contrast to the Muʿtazilites and the majority of the Ashʿarites.'

4. God is identical with His Essence because there is no distinction between His Essence and

the Necessary Being] whereas the latter for its contingency due to its need for a quiddity. Every contingent must have a cause that acts upon it. If this [cause] were to be quiddity, then this would require the precedence of quiddity over it with being because the precedence of cause over effect is a necessity. [In this case], quiddity would be existent twice. If the cause was other than quiddity, the Necessary Being would then need a separate cause in its being. And whatever is like this cannot be necessary by itself. If we reject the necessity of quiddity's precedence over being through being, then it would be permissible to say that quiddity-qua-quiddity becomes a cause for being when we do not take into consideration its existence and non-existence as it is the case in receptive (*al-qābil*) [beings].

Thus we say that the knowledge of what we have mentioned above is necessary because that which completes[1] being must have a being of its own, and it completes things other than being. There is a point to consider here. In contrast to that which is receptive of being, we cannot say that being-qua-being requires non-disembodiment (*alla-tajarrud*) otherwise it would necessitate disembodiment or it would not require anything of the two of them [i.e., the necessity of disembodiment]. The first [premise] requires that the existence of contingent beings be disembodied, viz., not occurring [to anything]. But in your view the existence of contingent beings is not disembodied. This is a contradiction.

The second [premise] assumes that in its disembodiment the Necessary Being needs a separate cause. Since its existence is intelligible (*ma'qūl*) and its reality is not intelligible, then its being is other than its reality. [It is further assumed that] if its being were to be identical with its reality, it would be then necessary because the 'necessary' is a relational state that can be conceived only between two things.

Existence. We can explain this as follows. Essence or quiddity, which I use to translate *māhiyyah*, is that which makes a thing what it is. Now, no finite and contingent being is completely identical with its quiddity because quiddities are by definition shared by other individual beings. Zayd's quiddity, for instance, is 'being human' or simply humanity. But other individuals share the quiddity of humanity just like Zayd. Furthermore, Zayd as a human being has many accidents such as walking and laughing, which are not part of his quiddity. In other words, Zayd has certain attributes besides his quiddity. Therefore Zayd is less than his quiddity (humanity), on the one hand, because others partake of it but more than his quiddity, on the other hand, because he always co-exists with accidents outside his quiddity. While this holds true for all contingent beings, it does not for God because nothing other than God can share His quiddity. In other words, God is the only instance of His kind. Furthermore, God has no accidents because He subsists by Himself. In other words, He is necessary-by-itself (*wājib bi-dhātihi*). In this sense, God cannot have accidents because accidents may exist in different substances. Accidents may or may not depend for their existence on their substratum whereas in the case of God, nothing is caused by anything other than Himself. This somewhat difficult yet central doctrine of Islamic philosophy is shared by medieval Western philosophy. Thomas Aquinas advances similar proofs for the identification of God with His Essence. See his *Summa Theologica*, Part I, Question 3, Articles 3–6.

1. Literally 'benefits' (*al-mufīd*). Like the grammatical expression in Arabic 'complete sentence' (*jumlah mufīdah*), that which completes being (*al-mufīd li'l-wujūd*) expresses the idea of the completion of actually existing substances.

Thus we respond to the first [premise] that disembodiment is a negative term (*amr ʿadamī*) and therefore the Necessary Being does not need a cause. As for the second, we do not accept that its existence is an intelligible. Rather the being-qua-being is the intelligible. As for the third, we do not accept the attribution (*ʿuruḍ*) of necessity to it. Rather, as we shall demonstrate, necessity is its own very essence. It is necessary to know that the word 'being' is predicated of the reality of the Necessary Being and other contingent beings equivocally (*bi'l-tashkīk*). This [principle] will surely erase many of your doubts.[1]

On Proving Mental Existence

Know that we can conceive of things that do not exist in the external world, and pass judgments on them through demonstrative judgments. That which is judged upon as having the attribute of being must exist since the affirmation of an attribute for something is posterior to the affirmation of that thing. Since it is not in the external world, it exists in the mind, and this proves the reality of mental existence.

In fact, the universal truths do not exist except in the mind. Consequently, every existent in the external world is a particular being. One cannot say that when the two universals of hotness and coldness exist in the mind, this leads to the concurrence of two opposites, and the mind itself becomes hot or cold. This is so because we say that we do not accept the concurrence of opposites between the universals. Nor do we accept the necessity of the form of the mind becoming hot or cold, and the mind receiving them [as particular states of hotness or coldness]. One may object [to this] by saying that we do not accept that it does not have an existence in the external world.

In fact, whatever we conceive has an actually existing form that subsists by itself or in the beings that are invisible to us (*al-mawjūdāt al-ghā'ibah*). How could it be otherwise? Indeed, this is what the sages have accepted as they have agreed upon the view that all things are inscribed (*murtasimah*) in the Active Intellect. Yet, the

---

1. Despite the difficulty of Qazwīnī's text, the issue at hand is clear enough: if God's Being is identical with His Quiddity and He is the Necessary Being, then how can we *attribute* this and other qualities *to* Him? If we follow the logic of predication, this will certainly lead us to two independent terms: that which is the predicate (necessary, disembodied, one, absolute, etc.) and that which is the subject of predication, i.e., God himself. Unless we affirm, as Qazwīnī does here, that necessity, like oneness, is identical with the Necessary Being and not a quality added to it, we cannot secure the unity of God. To address this issue, Qazwīnī introduces predication-by-equivocality (*ḥaml bi'l-tashkīk*), which states that such terms as being and oneness are common terms and predicated of things equivocally rather than univocally. In other words, substances that have these predicates have them at different levels of ontological realization in tandem with their place in the hierarchy of beings. Thus both God and the sun exist but God exists at a higher level of being than the sun.

essences such as man, tree, and stone can sometimes be found subsisting by themselves and sometimes in the soul. The former is called external existence whereas the latter is called mental existence even if both of them have external existence.

[The second investigation on the quiddity]

Everything has its own reality by which it is what it is.[1] The reality of a thing is therefore different from all other things whether it is a necessary [component] of it or different from it. Horseness-qua-horseness is thus neither one nor non-one because each one or both of them are either included in their concept, or they are their own concept. In fact, oneness [as applied to horse-ness] is an attribute added to it. Thus horse-ness becomes one with it [oneness]. By the same token, when non-oneness is added to it, it becomes no-one with it. Hence horseness-qua-horseness is nothing but horse-ness itself.[2]

Quiddity without the condition of something (*la bi-sharṭ shay'*) [i.e., as 'natural universal'] exists in the external world because it is one of its particular qualities that exist in the external world. With the condition of no-thing (*bi-sharṭ la-shay'*) [i.e., as a quiddity not conditioned by any concrete object in the external world] it has no existence in the external world for that which exists in the external world is bound up with delimitation and thus cannot be fully disengaged (*mujarrad*). Thus the agent (*al-fāʿil*) [that acts upon concrete objects through change, qualification, delimitation, etc.] has no effect on the quiddity since, if 'humanity' was instaured (*majʿūl*) by an instaurer (*jāʿil*), the doubt about the instaurer's actual existence would of necessity lead to doubt about humanity's being humanity. But the instaurer's effect applies only to the quiddity's existence.[3]

---

1. This sentence and the rest of the paragraph is obviously a tautology, and philosophical inquiry cannot thrive on tautologies. Yet, despite our common tendency to write off tautologies as empty propositions incapable of saying anything about the actual state of things in the world, they do serve an important purpose in logic: they define a concept in and of itself without reference to any of its particular members. This is what quiddities as universals are all about, and this is what Qazwīnī is trying to articulate here.

2. Keeping in mind the Platonic context of this paragraph, it is clear that quiddities do exist in and of themselves without the limitations of their particular members. Therefore, such attributes as oneness, being, unity and equivocality apply to quiddities and particular objects in different ways. All horses, irrespective of their particular attributes such as size, colour, and species, partake of the quiddity of horse-ness. The differences in their particular attributes do not bar them from possessing the quiddity of horse-ness. Similarly, horse-ness as horse-ness and nothing else is not effected by any of the contingencies we may find in particular horses in the external world.

3. Following Corbin's French translation and S. H. Nasr's adaptation of it in English, I translated *jaʿl* as 'instauration' to distinguish it from causation (*taʿlīl*). In the vocabulary of later Islamic philosophy, it refers to a special form of causality, and denotes the generation of the essential attributes of a quiddity. It can also be defined as a mode of 'existential causation' whereby quiddities either as 'natural universals' or concrete objects receive their essential as opposed to secondary attributes from an agent (*jāʿil*). The question can be formulated as follows: in the definition of

There is a point to consider there. Some hold the view that the simple is not instaured because if it was instaured, it would be contingent since that which is in need of a cause is contingency. If it [i.e., contingency] was to come about before existence, the quality of the relationship of existence to quiddity would precede it [which is false]. If it was to come about after existence, then the contingency of something would be after its existence [which is also false]. The response to this is to deny any such restraint [i.e., reject both conclusions] because we can say that a non-existent attribute [such as contingency] does not need a locus by which it subsists.[1]

Those who think this way argue that the simple is instaured on the basis that the composite (*al-murakkab*) is composed of simples, and that if the simple was not instaured, the composite would not be instaured either because every realization of a composite requires the realization of a simple. Thus the whole idea of instauration should be rejected. Now, it is to be remarked that the composite can be instaured because the establishment of its existence for its quiddity is instaured and the addition of simples to other simples is also through instauration.

The Fifth Article Concerning the Rational Soul

If the soul were eternal, then it would exist before the body. If it were one, then the soul of Zayd would be the same as that of ʿAmr. If [we assume that] there is only one soul, then whatever one knows, the other would know it too after they are related. Otherwise the soul would be capable of individuation (*tajziyah*) and thus would not be a disengaged [substance].

If the soul were more than one, then the differentiation among them would not be through quiddity and their concomitants. Otherwise that by which they

---

man as rational animal (*ḥayawān nāṭiq*), are the terms 'rational' and 'animal' an essential part of the definition of man-qua-man or are they occasioned by attributes that are outside the essential definition of man? Insofar as the actual existence of quiddities is concerned, the debate is similar to the one between those who uphold the primacy of quiddity (*aṣālat al-māhiyyah*) and those who uphold the primacy of being (*aṣālat al-wujūd*). For Ṣadrā's defence of being as 'instaured-by-itself' (*majʿūl bi'l-dhāt*), see *Kitāb al-Mashāʿir*, 7th *mashʿar*, 37–44 in *Le livre des pénétrations métaphysiques*, tr. Henry Corbin (Tehran-Paris: Institut Français d'Iranologie de Téhéran, 1982, 2nd ed.); for Corbin's commentary, see, 157–169. See also Ṣadrā's treatise *Aṣālat jaʿl al-wujūd* in *Majmūʿa-yi rasāʾil-i falsafī-yi Ṣadr al-Mutaʾallihīn*, ed. Ḥamīd Nājī Iṣfahānī (Tehran, 1996), pp. 181–191.

1. Contingency has two major applications in Islamic philosophy. The first refers to absolute contingency and characterizes all non-necessary beings, i.e., all contingent beings other than God. The contingent beings do not exist by themselves because they derive their existence from another source. The second refers to contingency as possibility and ability (*al-imkān al-istiʿdādī*), viz., the ability of contingent beings to receive effects from other agents, assume new attributes, etc. Vis-à-vis their own quiddities, contingent beings exist with a degree of necessity otherwise we would not be able to attribute any qualities to them. It is the first sense of contingency to which Qazwīnī is referring here.

are distinguished from one another would be the concomitant itself because all of them partake of the same quiddity. [The differentiation among them] cannot be through the accidents because if the attribution of these accidents to them were to be through the quiddity or another agent, then [the accidents] would be necessary. If the differentiation were because of the body, it would be attached to the body before the actual existence of the body, and this is absurd.

One may reject the participation of souls in the quiddity and the concomitant [attributes]. This rejection applies to the soul's attachment to a body before it is attached to this particular body because, as the defenders of the transmigration of souls uphold, the soul can be attached to another body before and after this particular body *ad infinitum*.

One cannot argue that if the soul had existed before this body, it would not need the body for its particularization and would have no relation to it since we do not accept that it would not need the body because of its attachment to it because the soul can be independent of the body, and its attachment to the body is required only for its [temporal] origination (*ḥudūth*). In fact, the soul subsists after the demise of the body otherwise its destruction would be due to the destruction of its form. Since the destruction of the substance is not possible without the destruction of the form, there is something in the soul that is destroyed in actuality and something that accepts this destruction, and the two are different from one another. This makes the soul composite [of matter and form]. In this case, it would have the capacity of both destruction and permanence. But one single thing [i.e., a simple substance such as the soul] cannot have both of these capacities [at the same time]. This would necessitate the soul to be a composite.

The opponent can reject the idea that the destruction of substance without the destruction of form is not intelligible because substance can be destroyed with the disappearance[1] of form from the external world. A single thing cannot have the capacities of permanence and destruction in the sense of disappearance in the external world. It has been said concerning transmigration that the soul is originated with the origination of the body in the sense that whenever a body is originated, a soul is also originated because, as explained before, the soul itself is [temporally] originated. Therefore the origination of the soul from its cause depends on the receptivity of matter, and the matter of the soul is the body. In its origination, the perfect cause depends on the origination of a perfect body for the reception of the soul in the sense that the soul ceases to exist with the body's non-existence and realized [in the external world] with its realization. Otherwise we would have to accept its existence before the body or its non-existence with the body's origination. Both of these options are impossible. Thus a single soul emanates from the active cause in its origination. If [we assume that] another soul is attached to the

1. Translating *irtifāʿ*, literally 'elevation'.

body by way of transmigration as if one single body had two commanding souls, this would be false because each one finds the commander of its body as only one. And this is based on the temporal origination of the soul, which is, in turn, based on the impossibility of transmigration.

[Revelation and prophethood]

Let's end this chapter with two investigations. The first pertains to the possibility of revelation and prophethood. Since man has the faculty of imagination (*al-mutakhayyilah*) and the faculty of common sense (*al-ḥiss al-mushtarak*), it is not unlikely for the being of a strong soul to have conjunction with the angelic intellects and souls and to perceive what both have from among the invisibles (*al-mutaghayyibāt*) in a universal way. The faculty of imagination then relates these [invisibles] through particular forms appropriate for it. Then it descends from this [state of cognition] to the common sense and becomes a sensate observation (*mushāhadah maḥsūsah*) because of the purity of the common sense for the faculty of the soul [and] because of its disentanglement from the attachments of external senses as this may happen in a state of sleep or wakefulness.

This is revelation (*waḥy*).[1] Yet, because of this reason some of the states of sleep are true [insofar as revelation is concerned] and others not. [There are three reasons why some states of sleep cannot be true for revelation. First of all,] when the soul has a sensation of particular forms, these forms are inscribed in the common sense during sleep. [Secondly,] when the soul becomes closely familiar with a form, it is represented in it [i.e., the common sense] during sleep. And [thirdly] when the temperament of the brain changes, the actions of the faculty of imagination also change. As for revelation, it can only be true.

As for the possibility of prophethood, [it is a reality] because the ideation of the soul itself can be a cause for [various] events as when the soul can command over the body by itself, the elemental primary matter (*al-hayūlā al-ʿunṣuriyyah*) obeys the ideation of the soul. We can therefore say that the relation of the existence of a strong soul to the world of generation and corruption is like the relation of the soul to the body so much so that its ideations can cause the breaking of ordinary rules. Thus wondrous things emanate from it, and these are miracles.

[Survival of the soul after death]

The second issue pertains to the states of the soul after the separation [of the soul from the body]. Some uphold that the soul ceases to exist and returns with the body

---

1. Qazwīnī's commentator Mubārak Shāh al-Bukhārī hastens to add that '[this is revelation] when the person in question is a prophet and inspiration (*ilhām*) when the person is a saint.' See al-Bukhārī's *Sharḥ ḥikmat al-ʿayn*, p. 379.

and becomes attached to it. Others say that its existence depends on a particular body, and when the soul is with it, the non-existence of the body requires the non-existence of the soul. Some others believe in its eternity and the impossibility of its subsisting by itself. When the body disappears, the soul becomes attached to another body as it was attached to yet another one before this. Still others believe in the temporal origination and subsistence of the soul after the body.

The soul subsists by itself. It attains happiness whose cause is the perception of what is appropriate [for it] insofar as it is appropriate, and misfortune whose cause is the perception of what is inappropriate [for it] insofar as it is inappropriate. What is appropriate for the soul is the perception of beings whereby it becomes capable of perceiving what it can of the First Truth, and It is the Necessary-by-Itself which is immune from all imperfections and the source of the emanation of goodness. The soul then perceives what emanates from it [i.e., the First Truth] in an actual order [of descent] in existence.

After this, the soul becomes free of the base forms of the body, which obliges the soul to become engrossed in the necessities of material faculties [such as pleasure and anger], and turn negligent of the world of the intellect. [After this], it gains the consciousness of the possibility of perfections and coming to know the unknowns from the knowns, and thus feels a strong desire towards it [i.e., this state of consciousness]. The false beliefs that cancel out the truth and the ethics that is condemned, rejected and based on the body [are all removed from the soul at this state of disengagement].

When the soul is attached to the body, it can attain neither happiness nor misfortune owing to the engrossment of the soul in the affairs of the body. When they are separate, the impediment disappears. Happiness and misfortune come about [for the soul], and the degrees of the souls vary in accordance with the happiness and misfortune [that they have]. All of this depends on the temporal origination of the soul and the impossibility of transmigration, and you have already learnt what the Master,[1] who is the slave of truth and religion, may God soothe his lying place, said concerning these two issues.

Now we say: when the soul is attached to the body, its perfections stand upon itself. When it is perfected by means of the body and becomes disengaged from the unwanted forms of the body, there remains no desire on its part for the body. It does not become attached to another body after the destruction of the body [that it has]. Instead, the perfection pulls it towards the world of the sacred (*quds*) and it enters the world of the dominion (*jabarūt*). If the soul is perfected but has not become disengaged from the forms mentioned above, it still does not have a need for the body. In this case, it does not become attached to another body but rather remains [in the body] because of the remaining forms of the body as a punishment

1. Probably a reference to Ibn Sīnā.

[or constraint for the soul] until they disappear since they are not necessary for it. They [the forms of the body] do appear owing to the directness of the affairs of the body. When they eventually disappear, the soul attains a perfect happiness. Even if it is not perfected [and thus has not attained happiness], it still needs the body. In fact, had it not been for unwanted forms [of the body], the soul could subsist all by itself after the [destruction of the] body whereby it could be completely immune from pain. It is also possible that the soul's need for perfection may attract it to having an attachment with another human body. If it has unwanted forms, then it is likely that it will always remain constrained and pained by these forms. Still, it is possible that these forms will pull the soul towards another animal body. None of these, however, can be fully ascertained, and God knows the mysteries the best.

[On knowledge]

Knowledge is the occurrence of the quiddity of something in the intellect without external attachments. It is either detailed or concise as when someone knows an issue, then becomes negligent of it, and then when he is asked about it, he attains a state of simplicity [i.e., simple knowledge].[1] This is the source of the details of these particulars that were described in a detailed manner. The Imam [Ibn Sīnā?] said: if these particulars are not known, then your claim to know the particulars before the knowledge of the quiddity would become invalid; if they are known, then some of them become distinct from others in a detailed manner. The answer to him is that we do not allow the second condition because the knowledge of something does not lead to the knowledge of what distinguishes it from others. Otherwise the knowledge of what distinguishes [something from others] would lead to the knowledge of what distinguishes that which distinguishes it from others *ad infinitum*.[2]

Intellection can be potential, and this is the absence of intellection from what it can intellect, which is called the hylic [i.e., potential] intellect. It can also be actual either through the self-evident truths together with the capacity of the soul to attain theoretical truths, and this is called the habitual intellect. Or it can be through the theoretical truths whereby they [the theoretical truths] are stored in

1. *Avicenna's De Anima Being the Psychological Part of Kitāb al-Shifā'*, ed. F. Rahman (London, 1959), pp. 241–242. This is part of a larger discussion in Islamic philosophy as to whether the intellect knows things through their essences and universal qualities, i.e., as simple knowledge or through their particular attributes, i.e., as composite and detailed knowledge. It is obvious that both kinds of knowledge inform the way we know ourselves and the world. Yet, as part of their Neoplatonic intellectualism, the Muslim philosophers tend to regard the first kind of knowledge superior to the second.

2. Qazwīnī's point can further be explained as follows: our knowledge of what distinguishes A from B does not give us the knowledge of what distinguishes A from C, D, E, and so on. It is not enough to know what A and B are to ascertain in what ways A is different from C and D without knowing what C and D are.

the soul. [In this kind of intellection], the soul is capable of reiterating theoretical truths when it wants to without trying hard to attain them anew, and this is called the actual intellect. In the case of intellection through theoretical truths, they are never absent from the soul, and the soul knows that it intellects them. This is called the acquired intellect.[1]

One cannot say that when the soul perceives, the intellector and the intellected become one.[2] Thus intellection cannot consist of what has been mentioned since we say that both of the precedents are impossible. As for the first [precedent], the intellected is a universal form and the intellector is a particular self. Each one is different from one another. As for the second [precedent], the occurrence of the quiddity of something is more general than the presence of the quiddity of another thing. A more particular falsehood [i.e., the presence of the quiddity of something different] does not lead to a more general falsehood [i.e., the presence of the quiddity of the thing in question].

Knowledge is active (*fiʿlī*) if our [mental] construction of something comes after its conception [in the mind], and passive (*infiʿālī*) if it is the opposite. The soul does not posses any of the intelligibles in its initial stages of disposition. But it is capable of them otherwise it would never attain this ability since that which subsists by itself cannot be destroyed. [This] comes about for the soul when certain conditions are met and obstacles removed. And this occurs through sensing the particulars many times. Otherwise all knowledge would come about at the beginning of the disposition [of the soul and] all intelligibles would become actual. If the second [i.e., passive] conception were not enough in the decision of the mind insofar as the relation between the two is concerned, it would then depend on the deduction of the middle term through which the relation of the one to the other comes about.

Degrees of souls vary in their deduction of the middle term. They can have a correct understanding of the middle terms and their order without any hardship. This is called the sacred power (*al-quwwwah al-qudsiyyah*)[3] and it stands

1. It is to be noted that Qazwīnī defines the acquired intellect as the self-reflective intellect, namely having the knowledge and consciousness of its knowledge of itself and other things.

2. The unification of intellect, intelligible, and intellection is a notorious debate in Islamic philosophy. While the majority of Muslim philosophers have rejected the unification argument in relation to human knowledge as philosophical sophistry and mystical illusion, they have allowed it in the case of God's knowledge. Mullā Ṣadrā, however, presents a rather staunch defence of the unification argument for both human and divine knowledge. For Ṣadrā's views on the subject see his *Risālah fī ittiḥād al-ʿāqil waʾl-maʿqūl* in Iṣfahānī, *Majmūʿah*, pp. 63–103; for a brief historical survey of the debate, see my 'Knowledge as the Unity of the Intellect and the Object of Intellection in Islamic Philosophy: A Historical Survey from Plato to Mullā Ṣadrā', *Transcendent Philosophy: An International Journal for Comparative Philosophy and Mysticism*, vol. 1, 1 (2000), 73–91.

3. The terms 'sacred power' and 'sacred intellect' go back to Ibn Sīnā who defines them as a 'kind of prophecy' (*ḍarb min al-nubuwwah*) and thus as 'the highest human capacity.' See Avicenna's *De Anima*, pp. 239 and 250. See also Ibn Sīnā, *Kitāb al-Najāt*, ed. M. Fakhry (Beirut, 1985), pp. 205–206.

in exact opposition to the idiot who cannot understand anything from the sciences. Then there are those that are in the middle depending on their degree [of understanding]. If by thought (*al-fikr*) we mean the various movements of the faculty of imagination, it does not comprehend knowledge (*al-ʿilm*) for they are preceded by other material [such as sensation]. If by thought we mean the types of knowledge with a definite order in the mind that requires the occurrence of another [kind of] knowledge, then thought must be united with it [knowledge] for thought is necessary for knowledge to come about. And whenever there is an effect, its necessary cause must be there too. Knowledge of the cause does not lead to knowledge of its immediate effect[1] otherwise the knowledge of the immediate effect would require the knowledge of the immediate effect of the immediate effect *ad infinitum*.

Now, the conception of quiddity with the conception of its immediate effect requires its relationship to the quiddity itself. In the first case, there is a point to consider because [this relationship] can terminate in that which does not have immediate effect or come to an end with that whose immediate effects are some of its concomitants. Thus we can have the knowledge of that which has a cause only after we have the knowledge of the existence of that cause because it is a contingent being. Its existence cannot be preferred [to be brought into actual existence] except through its cause, and whatever is known through its cause is known universally.

This is so because when we know that A is what necessitates B, we also know B and its derivation from A. Now, both of them are universals. By the same token, when we know that the A that is linked to universal attributes is what necessitates the B that is linked to universal attributes, we also know from this that the form that comes about in the mind from a particular thing in the external world is a universal because it is composed of a universal quiddity and universal accidents. Even if that which corresponds to such a quiddity is only one single thing, [the principle still holds true].[2]

Change in knowledge requires change in that which is known because knowledge is dependent upon the known and also because knowledge cannot correspond to two different things. Since universal natures cannot change, their knowledge does not change either. The only exception to this is the particulars because their knowledge changes as they themselves change.[3] The kinds of concomitant

1. Translating *lāzim* as effect rather than as 'necessary component' or 'concomitant.' Qazwīnī is employing here a slightly different terminology for causality.

2. As Ibn Sīnā points out, 'all [sensate] perception is particular and by means of a corporeal instrument.' Cf. *Najāt*, p. 210. In contrast, all intellectual perception is universal and by means of an incorporeal instrument, i.e., the intellect.

3. Knowledge of Zayd as 'man' does not change regardless of the particular changes that may occur in his being an individual human being when, for instance, he walks, learns something new, or sleeps.

theoretical knowledge[1] that are necessary do not become necessary [by themselves] for necessity is a quality of concomitance, not a quality of the concomitant.

Every disengaged being must be able to intellect all intelligibles because it cannot intellect [things by itself] and whatever can intellect itself can intellect through other things. Furthermore, the forms of the intelligibilia in the mind can be associated with whatever can intellect through other things. By the same token, the forms of the intelligibilia in the external world can be combined with whatever the forms of the intelligibilia in the mind can be associated with.

The forms of the intelligibilia can thus be associated with all disengaged beings, and whatever is possible for the disengaged agent does in fact come about for it by necessity. Otherwise, it would be dependent upon the ability of its matter to receive the emanation from the First Principle, and it would have relation with matter. All of these precedents are strictly forbidden. The necessary being by itself is disengaged and cannot be intellected [by others]. The knowledge about it [or its knowledge] prevents it from intellecting through others [as contingent beings intellect]. The possibility of the disengaged being's intellection through others in the mind does not lead to the possibility that the forms of the intelligibilia in the mind come to reside in it so that this would allow for the First Principle to have association with the forms of the intelligibilia that are in the mind.

The possibility of the association of the forms of the intelligibilia in the mind does not necessitate the possibility of their association in the external world. The former consists of their incarnation in it [i.e., the First Principle] just as they are found in the intellect, and the latter consists of their incarnation in it just as they are found in the external world. Thus what they have mentioned concerning the second premise is also prohibited.

1. Translating *al-ʿulūm al-naẓariyyah* as kinds of theoretical knowledge rather than as necessary 'sciences' or 'knowledges.' In philosophical Arabic, it is common to use *ʿilm* in the plural to mean different types of knowledge rather than 'sciences' (*ʿulūm*).

4

Athīr al-Dīn Abharī and Amīr Ḥusayn Maybudī

In the tradition of the history of Islamic philosophy in Persia as well as in India Athīr al-Dīn Abharī has become known primarily as the author of the *Kitāb Hidāyat al-ḥikmah* (The Book of Guidance for Philosophy) which is a text summarizing later *mashshāʾī* philosophy. Many commentaries were written on this text the most famous being those of Maybudī and Mullā Ṣadrā both of which became among the most important books of *mashshāʾī* philosophy taught to this day in traditional circles.

Athīr al-Dīn Mufaḍḍal ibn ʿUmar Abharī was born in Abhar and was one of the most important students of Fakhr al-Dīn Rāzī. He also studied mathematics and astronomy with Kamāl al-Dīn Mawṣilī. He was a friend of Naṣir al-Dīn Ṭūsī with whom he exchanged letters. When the Mongol invasion occurred, he went to Damascus and then Anatolia where he taught for some time. He died in 663/1264 after having written a number of important works and having trained several famous figures among them the philosopher Dabīrān-i Kātibī and the scientist ʿImād al-Dīn Zakariyyāʾ Qazwīnī, the author of the famous *ʿAjāʾib al-makhlūqāt* (Wonders of Creatures).

Abharī was not only a philosopher but also an outstanding mathematician and an accomplished poet. His works include several texts on logic, a response to the works of Ibn Sīnā and Bahmanyār, a number of treatises on astronomy and a treatise on the attempt to prove the fifth postulate of Euclid concerning parallel lines which is an important text in the history of mathematics. By far the most famous of his works is the *Hidāyat al-ḥikmah* which made his reputation as a major *mashshāʾī* philosopher following the revival of this school by Ṭūsī.

There are clear indications, however, that Abharī was also well versed in the teaching of Suhrawardī. Both Shahrazūrī and Ibn Kammūnah attest to this fact. Moreover, in two philosophical works of Abharī that have survived, *Muntahaʾl-afkār fī ibānat al-asrār* (The Summit of Thoughts Concerning the Clarification of Mysteries) and *Kashf al-ḥaqāʾiq fī taḥrīr al-daqāʾiq* (The Discovery of Truth

Concerning the Accurate Statement of Subtleties), there are sections which reveal Abharī's evident knowledge of *ishrāqī* teachings. In any case not all the works of Abharī, even those extant, have as yet been studied in detail in order to make his ideas fully known, even his scientific and poetic works. Meanwhile, he remains a major representative of later *mashshā'ī* thought through his exceptionally popular *Hidāyat al-ḥikmah*.

As for the commentator upon the text translated here, that is, Maybudī, he was a ninth/fifteenth-century theologian, philosopher and Sufi poet as well as an accomplished astronomer. His full name is Qāḍī Amīr Ḥusayn ibn Mu'īn al-Dīn Ḥusaynī Yazdī Maybudī and he hailed from Maybud near the city of Yazd. It is said that he studied in Shiraz and was a student of Jalāl al-Dīn Dawānī. Being a Sunni in *madhhab*, he faced severe opposition after Shah Ismā'īl imposed Twelve-Imam Shi'ism as the official state religion in Persia and most likely Maybudī was put to death in 909/1503–1504 because of his opposition to Shi'ism.

Qāḍī Maybudī has left behind a numbers of scientific works including the glosses upon the recension of the *Elements* of Euclid by Naṣīr al-Dīn Ṭūsī and the astronomical treatise of Qāḍī-zādah Rūmī, works on logic, commentary upon the *Dīwān* of poetry attributed to 'Alī ibn Abī Ṭālib and works on Sufi technical vocabulary and Sufi manners (*ādāb*). He is also the author of *Jām-i jahān-namā* (The Cup Revealing the World) which reveals his combined interest in philosophy, *'irfān* and cosmology. His most important and famous work remains, however, his commentary upon Abharī's *al-Hidāyah* known also as *Sharḥ al-hidāyat al-athiriyyah*, selections of which are included in this section.

The sections included here begin with a discussion concerning the knowledge of the Creator and continue by treating the relationship between the attribute of necessity and Divine Reality. In a highly detailed and complex set of metaphysical arguments, Abharī demonstrates that necessity is inherent in the Divine Essence and not a contingent attribute.

The theme of necessity and its relation to God's Being runs through the entire section and such concepts as reality, existence, non-existence and essential and non-essential attributes are discussed here.

S. H. Nasr

COMMENTARY UPON GUIDANCE THROUGH WISDOM

Sharḥ hidāyat al-ḥikmah

Translated for this volume by Nicholas Heer from Amīr Ḥusayn Maybudī, *Sharḥ hidāyat al-ḥikmah* (Istanbul, 1321/1903), pp. 100–107.[1]

Chapter Two
On Knowledge of the Creator and His Attributes

Section [One]: On the Proof for the Necessarily [Existent] by virtue of Its essence[2]

[1] The Necessarily [Existent] by virtue of Its essence, if considered as It is in Itself (min ḥaythu huwa huwa), *is that which does not accept non-existence* (al-ʿadam). *In proof of this* (burhānuhu)[3] *one may say that if there were not in existence an existent which was necessary by virtue of its essence, then an impossibility would result. This is because all existents would then constitute a totality* (jumlah) *made up of individuals* (āḥād) *each one of which would be contingent by virtue of its essence* (mumkin li-dhātihi). It follows that the totality would also be contingent because of its need for each of its contingent parts, since what is in need of what is contingent has all the more reason to be contingent. *Therefore it*, that is, the totality, *would need an external cause to bring it into existence* (ʿillah mūjidah khārijiyyah), that is, a cause external to the totality. *And the knowledge of this is self-evident* (badīhī), that is, necessary (*ḍarūrī*) and intuitively inferred (*fiṭrī al-qiyās*).

[2] In confirmation of this (*taqrīruhu*)[4] it may be said that the cause cannot be the totality itself, which is apparent, nor one of its parts, since the cause of the

1. Passages in italic are from the original text so as to distinguish them from the Commentary; the complete original text is appended at the end of the translation.

2. That is, that being which exists necessarily by virtue of its own essence rather than by virtue of some cause external to its essence. The adjectival phrase *wājib al-wujūd li-dhātihi* has been translated throughout as 'necessarily existent by virtue of its essence'. Similarly, the nominal phrase *al-wājib li-dhātihi* has been translated as 'the Necessarily [Existent] by virtue of Its essence', and the noun *al-wājib* has been translated as 'the Necessary [Existent]'. There are a number of words in Arabic which have the general meaning of 'essence'. To avoid confusion *dhāt* has been translated as 'essence', *māhiyyah* as 'quiddity', *ḥaqīqah* as 'reality', and *ṭabīʿah* as 'nature'.

3. The proof which follows is essentially the same as the one given by Ibn Sīnā in both *al-Najāt* and *al-Ishārāt wa'l-tanbīhāt*. See p. 235 of *al-Najāt*, and vol. III, pp. 20–28 of *al-Ishārāt wa'l-tanbīhāt*. An analysis of Ibn Sīnā's proof is given by Herbert Davidson in his *Proofs for Eternity, Creation and the Existence of God in Medieval Islamic and Jewish Philosophy*, pp. 281–310.

4. That is, that the cause must be external to the totality.

totality is also the cause of each one of its parts. The reason for this[1] is that each part is contingent and in need of a cause. If the cause of the totality (*al-majmūʿ*) were not also the cause of each of the parts, then some of them would be caused by another cause, and the first cause would not be the cause of the totality, but, on the contrary, of some of it only. From this it follows that any part which was the cause of the totality would have to be the cause of itself.[2]

[3] Here there is room for further discussion (*wa-hāhunā baḥth*), however, because the contingency of the totality does not imply its being in need of a cause which is individually one (*wāḥidah bi'l-shakhṣ*). On the contrary, it is possible for the totality to be dependent on many causes which bring the individual parts (*āḥād*) of the totality into existence, all of which causes together are the cause of the existence of the totality. It is also possible that the contingent [parts] constitute an infinite chain in which the second is the cause of the first, the third the cause of the second, and so on. Thus, the cause of the totality is that part of it which consists of all of those parts which are both causes and effects. The only [part] excluded is the [last part which is] purely an effect (*al-maʿlūl al-maḥḍ*).[3]

[4] The commentator on *al-Mawāqif*[4] said: The discussion concerns the cause which brings something into existence (*al-ʿillah al-mūjidah*) and which is independent in effectiveness (*al-ta'thīr*) and in bringing-into-existence (*al-ījād*). If what is before the last effect is a cause which brings the whole chain into existence and is truly independent in its effectiveness with respect to it, such a cause would definitely be a cause of itself.[5]

[5] It can be said in refutation of this remark (*al-kalām*)[6] that each one of the parts would then be in need of a cause external to the chain of contingents, for if it were not external then either a vicious circle (*al-dawr*) or an endless chain (*al-tasalsul*)[7] would result. Moreover, to acknowledge the need for a cause after

1. That is, the reason the cause of the totality cannot be one of the parts of the totality.

2. In other words, if one part of the totality were the cause of the remaining parts of the totality, that part would not be the cause of the totality but only of the remaining parts. For that part to be the cause of the totality it would also have to be the cause of itself in addition to being the cause of the other parts. But if it were the cause of itself it would be necessarily existent rather than contingent. Since all the parts of the totality are by definition contingent, the cause of the totality, being necessarily existent, could not be one of its parts but, on the contrary, would have to be external to it.

3. Since, unlike all the other parts, it is not also a cause.

4. That is, al-Sayyid al-Sharīf ʿAlī ibn Muḥammad al-Jurjānī (d. 816/1413), the author of a commentary on the *Kitāb al-Mawāqif* of ʿAḍud al-Dīn ʿAbd al-Raḥmān ibn Aḥmad al-Ījī. See Brockelmann, *Geschichte*, II, 269, Supplement II, 289. His son, Muḥammad, wrote a commentary on *Hidāyat al-ḥikmah* entitled *Ḥall al-hidāyah*. See Āghā Buzurg, *al-Dharīʿah*, VII, 77.

5. And therefore necessarily existent contrary to what had been assumed.

6. That is, that it is possible for the totality to be dependent on many causes as proposed in paragraph 3.

7. That is, infinite regress.

observing that something is contingent is [an inference that is] intuitive. It should be apparent to you that this [refutation] is not pertinent to the argument.[1]

[6] *Moreover, an existent which was external to all contingents would be necessary by virtue of its essence. Thus, the existence of what is necessarily existent* (wājib al-wujūd) *follows from the assumption of its non-existence,*[2] *and that is absurd. Therefore, its non-existence is impossible, and its existence is necessary.*

Section [Two]: On [the proof] that the Necessary Existent's existence is the same as Its reality (ḥaqīqah).

[1] The grades of existents in existence (*marātib al-mawjūdāt fi'l-mawjūdiyyah*) are, according to logical division (*al-taqsīm al-ʿaqlī*), three: The lowest grade is what exists by virtue of another (*al-mawjūd bi'l-ghayr*), that is, what is brought into existence by something other than itself. Such an existent has an essence (*dhāt*) and an existence which is different from its essence, as well as a bringer-into-existence (*mūjid*) which is different from both. If the essence of such an existent is considered without consideration of its bringer-into-existence, it is possible in fact (*fī nafs al-amr*)[3] for its existence to be separated from its essence, and without doubt it is

1. According to ʿAbd al-Ḥakīm, one of the glossators of al-Maybudī's text, the reason it is not pertinent is because it requires proofs for the impossibility of both the vicious circle and the endless chain, and al-Abharī's intent was to prove the existence of the Necessary Existent without relying on such proofs. See the margin of p. 167 of the Tehran lithograph edition of 1331.

2. As stated in paragraph 1 above.

3. The literal meaning of *fī nafs al-amr* is 'in the matter itself' or 'in the thing itself'. Things can be said to exist in the external world of time and space, *fi'l-khārij*, in the mind, *fi'l-dhihn*, or in the thing itself, *fī nafs al-amr*, that is, in fact. In the introduction to his commentary al-Maybudī makes the following statement: 'The meaning of a thing's being existent in the matter itself is that it is existent in itself. 'Matter' (*al-amr*) is the same as 'thing' (*al-shay'*). The upshot of this is that its existence is not dependent on anyone's supposition (*farḍ*) or consideration (*iʿtibār*). For example, the connection between the rising of the sun and the existence of daylight is [something that is] realized in itself regardless of whether or not anyone exists to suppose it, and regardless of whether or not anyone does suppose it. [Existence in] the thing itself (*nafs al-amr*) is more inclusive (*a'amm*) than [existence in] the external world (*al-khārij*), for every existent in the external world exists in the thing itself, with no universal converse being possible (*bi-lā ʿaks kullī*). Existence in the thing itself is also more inclusive than [existence in] the mind, but in only a certain respect, for it is possible to conceive of false propositions (*kawādhib*), such as the evenness of the number five, which can exist in the mind but not in the thing itself. Such propositions are called hypothetical mental [propositions] (*dhihnī farḍī*). The evenness of the number four, on the other hand, exists in both the thing itself as well as in the mind, and such propositions are called real mental [propositions] (*dhihnī ḥaqīqī*).' (See p. 5 of the Istanbul printing of 1321, p. 5 also in the Istanbul printing of 1325, and p. 10 in the Tehran lithograph of 1331.) In summary one may say that all things that exist in the external world also exist in the thing itself, that is, in fact. Some things that exist in the mind, such as real concepts and true propositions and theories, also exist in fact as well as in the mind. Imaginary concepts and false propositions, however, exist only in the mind and never in fact. Further discussion of this subject may be found in al-Aḥmadnagarī, *Dastūr al-ʿulamā'*, III, 370–372 (under *al-mawjūd*), and al-Taḥānawī, *Kashshāf*, pp. 1403–1404 (under *nafs al-amr*), and pp. 1456–1461 (under *al-wujūd*).

also possible to conceive (*al-taṣawwur*) of its existence as being separated from its essence, for both the conceiving and the thing conceived (*al-mutaṣawwar*) are possible. Such is the status of contingent quiddities (*al-māhiyyāt al-mumkinah*), as is well known.

[2] The middle grade is what exists by virtue of its essence (*al-mawjūd bi'l-dhāt*) with an existence which is other than its essence, that is, an existent whose essence completely necessitates its existence, such that it is impossible for its existence to be separated from its essence. Such an existent has an essence, and an existence which is different from its essence. Moreover, in view of its essence, it is impossible for its existence to be separated from its essence. Nevertheless, it is possible to conceive of this separation and, although the thing conceived is absurd, its conception is possible. This is the status of the Necessary Existent according to the position of the vast majority of the theologians (*jumhūr al-mutakallimīn*).[1]

[3] The highest grade is what exists by virtue of its essence with an existence that is identical with it, that is, an existent whose existence is identical with its essence. Such an existent does not have an existence that differs from its essence, nor is it possible to conceive of the separation of its existence from it. Indeed, the separation and the conception of separation are both impossible. Such is the status of the Necessary Existent according to the position of the philosophers (*al-ḥukamā'*).

[4] If you desire further elucidation of what we have set forth, you may seek clarification of this matter in the following example. The grades of a luminous object (*al-muḍī'*) insofar as it is luminous are also three. The first is what is luminous by virtue of another (*al-muḍī' bi'l-ghayr*), that is, what receives its luminosity (*ḍaw'*) from something else, like the surface of the earth which is illumined when it faces the sun. In this case there is a luminous object, a luminosity which is different from that object, and a third thing which produces the luminosity.

[5] The second grade is what is luminous by virtue of its essence (*al-muḍī' bi'l-dhāt*) through a luminosity that is other than it, that is, something whose essence necessitates its luminosity in such a way that it cannot fail to appear. This is like the body of the sun on the assumption that it necessitates its luminosity, for this luminous object has an essence and a luminosity that is different from it.

[6] The third grade is what is luminous by virtue of its essence through a luminosity that is identical with it, like the luminosity of the sun, for it is luminous by virtue of its essence, rather than by virtue of a luminosity additional to its essence. This is the most exalted and most potent luminous object conceivable.

[7] Should it be asked: How can luminosity be described as being luminous, since the meaning of what is luminous, as initially understood, is something in which luminosity subsists? We should answer: That is the meaning with which the

1. For the position of the theologians see, for example, al-Taftāzānī, *Sharḥ al-maqāṣid*, I, 48–50, and al-Jurjānī, *Sharḥ al-mawāqif*, II, 156–169.

common people are familiar and for which the word luminous was coined in the [Arabic] language. Our discussion is not concerned with that meaning, however. When we say that luminosity is luminous by virtue of its essence (*al-ḍaw' muḍī' bi-dhātihi*) we do not mean by that that another luminosity subsists in it and that it becomes luminous by virtue of that luminosity. On the contrary what we mean by that is that what can be attributed both to something which is luminous by virtue of another and to something which is luminous by virtue of its own essence, although by means of a luminosity that is other than its essence, namely, visibility (*al-ẓuhūr*) to the eyes due to the luminosity, can also be attributed to luminosity [as it is] in itself in accordance with its own essence rather than through something additional to its essence. Indeed, visibility in the case of luminosity is stronger and closer to perfection, for luminosity is visible in its essence with no [trace of] invisibility (*khafā'*) at all. Luminosity, moreover, also makes visible what is other than itself in accordance with the capacity of that other [to become visible].

[8] *This is because if Its existence were additional to Its reality (*ḥaqīqah), *it would be inherent* ('āriḍ) *in it.*[1] It has been said that this is because of the impossibility of Its division (*al-juz'iyyah*) since such division would imply composition (*tarkīb*) in the essence of the Necessary Existent.[2] This calls for further discussion, however, for the composition which is impossible in the Necessary Existent is external composition, since it implies being in need in the external world, and that, in turn, implies contingency. As for mental composition with respect to the Necessary Existent, we do not admit its impossibility, because such composition does not imply being in need in the external world, but only in the mind, and being in need in the mind does not imply contingency, since the contingent is what is in need of what is other than itself for its external existence.

[9] *And if it were inherent in it, [Its] existence, as it is in itself* (min ḥayth huwa huwa), *would be in need of something other than itself*, that is, in need of what it inheres in (al-ma'rūḍ).[3] *It would then be contingent by virtue of its essence and dependent upon a cause* ('illah). *It would therefore require an effector* (mu'aththir), *and if that effector were identical with the reality [of the Necessary Existent], that effector would have to exist before [its own] existence, since the cause which brings a thing into existence must precede its effect in existence.* Indeed, as long as the intellect (*al-'aql*) is not cognizant that a thing exists, it is impossible for it to be cognizant of it as a source (*mabda'*) and bestower (*mufīd*) of existence. *And thus that thing would have to exist before itself, and that is absurd. If, on the other hand, the effector*

1. al-Abharī's argument in this and the following paragraph is similar to the argument given by Ibn Sīnā in several of his works. See *al-Shifā', al-Ilāhiyyāt*, pp. 344–347; *al-Ishārāt wa'l-tanbīhāt*, III, 30–40; *Dānishnāmah, Ilāhiyyāt*, pp. 76–77 (Morewedge trans. pp. 55–56); and *al-Risālah al-'arshiyyah*, p. 4 (Arberry trans. pp. 27–28).

2. That is, the essence of the Necessary Existent would be composed of a reality and of a separate existence which inhered in the reality as an accident.

3. Namely, the reality of the Necessary Existent.

*were something other than the quiddity (*māhiyyah*) [of the Necessary Existent], then the Necessary Existent by virtue of Its essence would be in need of what is other than Itself for Its existence, and that is impossible.*

[10] The verifiers (*al-muḥaqqiqūn*)[1] said: 'Existence, while identical with the Necessary Existent, nevertheless has expanded over the forms (*hayākil*) of existents and has become manifest in them. Thus there is nothing at all that is without it. Indeed, it is their reality (*ḥaqīqah*) and identity (*'ayn*), for they have been distinguished from each other and made multiple through qualifications and individuations that exist only in the mind (*taqayyudāt wa-ta'ayyunāt i'tibāriyyah*).'

*Section [Three]: On [the proof] that [Its] necessity of existence (*wujūb al-wujūd)[2] *as well as Its Individuation (*ta'ayyun) *are identical with Its essence.*

[1] Should it be asked:[3] 'How can the attribute of a thing be conceived as being identical with its reality when both the attribute (*al-ṣifah*) and what it qualifies (*al-mawṣūf*) testify to their being different from each other?' I should answer: The meaning of their saying that the attributes of the Necessary Existent are identical with Its essence is that 'what results from the essence of the Necessary Existent [alone] is what [in other cases] results from an essence and an attribute combined.'

[2] To explain how the Necessary Existent can be identical with [Its] knowledge (*'ilm*) and power (*qudrah*) they said: 'Your own essence [for example] is not sufficient to reveal (*inkishāf*) things and make them apparent (*ẓuhūr*) to you, for in order for things to be revealed and made apparent to you, you must have the attribute of knowledge subsisting in you. It is different in the case of the essence of the Necessary Existent, however, for It is not in need of an attribute subsisting in It in order for things to be revealed and made apparent to It. On the contrary all concepts (*mafhūmāt*) are revealed to It by reason of Its essence [alone], and in this regard Its essence is the reality of knowledge (*ḥaqīqat al-'ilm*). Such is also the case with respect to the power [of the Necessary Existent], for Its essence is effective in itself (*mu'aththirah bi-dhātihā*) rather than by means of an attribute additional to it, as is the case with our own essences. When regarded in this way the essence of the Necessary Existent is the reality of power (*ḥaqīqat al-qudrah*), and accordingly

---

1. According to Mīr Hāshim, one of the glossators of al-Maybudī's commentary, these are the Sufis. See the Tehran lithograph edition of 1331, p. 169. The passage which follows is quoted from al-Jurjānī's *Ḥāshiyat sharḥ al-tajrīd,* fol. 63b, and represents the doctrine of the *waḥdat al-wujūd,* or unity of existence, school of Sufism founded by Muḥyī al-Dīn ibn 'Arabī (d. 638/1240). See Brockelmann, *Geschichte,* I, 571, Supplement I, 790. Another passage from the same work is quoted in section 6, paragraphs 5–6.

2. That is, the necessity of the existence of the Necessary Existent.

3. Most of this paragraph and the next are quoted from al-Jurjānī's *Sharḥ al-mawāqif,* VIII, 47.

the essence and attributes of the Necessary Existent are really (*fi'l-ḥaqīqah*) united, although they differ from each other in accordance with the manner in which they are regarded and understood (*bi'l-i'tibār wa'l-mafhūm*). Upon investigation, this [unity of essence and attributes] is based on (*marji'uhu*) the denial of the Necessary Existent's attributes along with [the affirmation of] the occurrence (*ḥuṣūl*) of their effects and fruits by virtue of Its essence alone.'

[3] *As for the first*[1] *it is because the necessity of existence, if it were additional to Its reality, would be an effect of Its essence* (ma'lūl li-dhātihi), in accordance with what was said above.[2] *As long as the existence of a cause is not necessary*, its existence is not possible, and consequently *it is impossible for its effect to exist. And since that necessity [which is under consideration] is necessity by virtue of its essence* (al-wujūb bi'l-dhāt), *that necessity of existence by virtue of the essence would,* necessarily, *exist before itself, and that is absurd.*

[4] *As for the second*[3] *it is because Its individuation, if it were additional to Its reality, would be an effect of Its essence, and as long as a cause is not individuated it does not exist and so cannot bring into existence its effect. Therefore Its individuation would be existence* (ḥāṣil) *before itself, and that is absurd.*

Section [Four]: On [the proof] for the oneness (tawḥīd) *of the Necessary Existent.*[4]

[1] If we suppose two necessarily existent beings (mawjūdayn wājibay al-wujūd), *both would have necessity of existence* (wujūb al-wujūd) *in common but would differ with respect to something else. That which served to distinguish them from each other would either be the entire reality* (ḥaqīqah) *or not be [the entire reality]. The first [alternative] is impossible because if the distinction were with respect to the entire reality, then necessity of existence, because it is common to both, would have to be external to the reality of both. That is impossible because, as we have explained,*[5] *necessity of existence is identical to the reality of the Necessary Existent.*

[2] I say: Further discussion is called for here, because the meaning of their assertion that necessity of existence is identical with the reality of the Necessary Existent is that the effect of the attribute of necessity of existence (*athār ṣifat wujūb al-wujūd*) becomes manifest from that very reality, not that that reality is identical with that attribute.[6] Therefore, what is meant by two necessarily existent beings having neces-

1. That is, the necessity of Its existence.

2. In paragraphs 8 and 9 of section 2, which deal with the question of whether existence is additional to the essence of the Necessary Existent.

3. That is, Its individuation.

4. The argument that follows is similar to the argument of Ibn Sīnā in *al-Shifā', al-Ilāhiyyāt*, pp. 43, 349–354; *Dānishnāmah, Ilāhiyyāt*, pp. 75–76 (Morewedge trans. pp. 54–55); and *al-Risālah al-'arshiyyah*, p. 3 (Arberry trans. pp. 25–26); and *al-Najāt*, pp. 230–231.

5. In section 3, paragraph 2 above.

6. See the quotation from al-Jurjānī in section 3, paragraphs 1 and 2.

sity of existence in common is merely that the effect of the attribute of necessity [of existence] becomes manifest from each of them. Thus there is no inconsistency (*munāfāh*) between their having necessity of existence in common and their being distinguished from each other with respect to the entire reality.

[3] *The second [alternative] is also impossible, because each one of them would then be composed of what they had in common and what served to distinguish them from one another, and, since everything that is composed is in need of something other than itself,* that is, its two parts, *each would therefore be contingent by virtue of its essence, and that is contrary* (hādhā khulf) *[to what was assumed].* Here there is also room for discussion, since it was previously mentioned[1] that the composition which implies contingency is external composition (*al-tarkīb al-khārijī*) not mental (*al-dhihnī*) [composition]. It has been objected: Why is it not possible for the distinction [between the two] to be made by means of an accidental entity (*amr ʿāriḍ*) rather than by a constituent (*muqawwim*) [of the essence], so that composition would not be implied [in the essence]? The reply has been that that requires that the individuation [of the Necessary Existent] be accidental, and that is contrary to what has been established by demonstration.[2] I say: It is possible to amend (*tawjīh*) the author's argument[3] so that that [objection] cannot be directed against it by saying: If what served to distinguish them from one another were not the entire reality, then it would either be a part of the reality or an accident of it. In either case each of the two [necessary existents] would have to be composed. In the first case they would be composed of genus (*jins*) and difference (*faṣl*), and in the second of reality (*ḥaqīqah*) and individuation (*taʿayyun*).

[4] One might argue that what we have shown to the effect that the individuation of the Necessary Existent is identical with Its reality[4] is sufficient to prove Its unity, because whenever individuation is identical with a quiddity (*māhiyyah*), the species (*nawʿ*) of that quiddity is necessarily restricted to a [single] individual (*shakhṣ*). I should reply: This calls for further discussion (*fīhi naẓar*), because what is intended by this proof is to show that the Necessary Existent is a single reality (*ḥaqīqah wāḥdah*) whose individuation is identical with it. From what has been mentioned previously, however, that proof is not conclusive (*thābit*) [for this purpose] because of the possibility of there being [a number of] different necessarily existent realities each one of which has an individuation identical with it. It is therefore necessary to provide a [separate] proof for the unity [of the Necessary Existent].

1. In section 2, paragraph 8.
2. Namely, that the individuation of the Necessary Existent is identical with Its essence. See section 3, paragraph 4 above.
3. As given at the beginning of this paragraph.
4. In section 3, paragraph 4.

Section [Five] On [the Proof] that the Necessarily [Existent] by virtue of Its essence is necessary in all of Its aspects (jihāt), that is, It has no anticipated state not yet actualized (*ḥālah muntaẓarah ghayr ḥāṣilah*).[1]

[1] *This is because Its essence* (dhāt) *is sufficient with respect to the attributes it possesses, and It is therefore necessary in all of Its aspects. We say that Its essence is sufficient with respect to the attributes It possesses only because, were it not sufficient, then some of Its attributes would be [derived] from another being and the presence,* that is, existence, *of that other being would be a cause* ('illah) *in general* (fi'l-jumlah) *of that attribute's existence, and its absence,* that is, its non-existence, *would be a cause of the attribute's non-existence. If such were the case, Its essence, considered as it is in itself* (min ḥayth hiya hiya), and unconditioned by the presence or absence of that other being, *would not be necessarily existent.*

[2] *This is because [if It were] necessarily existent, it would be so either with the existence (wujūd) of that attribute or with its non-existence* ('adam). *If It were necessarily existent with the existence of that attribute, its existence,* that is, the existence of the attribute, *would not be because of the presence of another being,*[2] because the attribute's existence would [already] be established in the essence of the Necessary [Existent] as it is in itself without consideration of the presence of another being. *If, on the other hand, It were necessarily existent with the non-existence of that attribute, the non-existence of the attribute would not be because of the absence of another being,*[3] because the attribute's non-existence would [already] be established in the essence of the Necessary [Existent] as it is in itself without consideration of the absence of another being. Here there is room for further discussion (*hāhunā baḥth*), however, since the non-existence of something does not follow simply from its not being taken into consideration.

[3] *Thus, if it,* that is, the essence of the Necessary [Existent], *were not necessarily existent unconditionally* (bi-lā sharṭ),[4] *then the Necessarily [Existent] by virtue of Its essence would not be necessarily [existent] by virtue of Its essence, and that is absurd.* This [argument] can be refuted, however, by [applying it to] the relations [of the Necessary Existent], since it is applicable to such relations also, even though the essence of the Necessary [Existent] is not sufficient to bring them into existence, for they depend necessarily on matters which are separate and distinct from Its essence.

[4] It has been said that the best way of proving this point is to say: Everything which is possible (*mumkin*) for the Necessary [Existent] in the way of attributes is

1. Ibn Sīnā's arguments for this proposition may be found in *Dānishnāmah, Ilāhiyyāt,* p. 76 (Morewedge trans. pp. 55–56); *al-Najāt,* pp. 228–229 and *al-Risālah al-ʿarshiyyah,* p. 5 (Arberry trans. pp. 28–29).

2. Contrary to what was stated in paragraph 1 above.

3. Again, contrary to what was stated in paragraph 1 above.

4. As stated in the last sentence in paragraph 1 above.

necessitated by Its essence (*yūjibuhu dhātuhu*). Everything which is necessitated by Its essence is necessarily actualized (*wājib al-ḥuṣūl*).[1] As for the major premise, it is obvious. As for the minor premise, it is true because if it were not, then the necessity of existence of some of the attributes would be by virtue of something other than the essence. And if that other were necessary by virtue of its essence, what is necessarily existent would be more than one.

[5] On the other hand, if that other were contingent, either it would be necessitated by the essence, in which case the essence would be the necessitator of those attributes we had assumed it did not necessitate, since the necessitator of a necessitator is also a necessitator, or that other would not be [necessitated by the essence], in which case it would be necessitated by some second necessitator (*mūjib thānī*), and the argument would be transferred to it. Either the chain of necessitators would regress to infinity, or else it would end with a necessitator necessitated by the essence, and that would be in contradiction to what had been assumed. The gist of this (*al-ḥāṣil*) is that if the essence did not necessitate all of the attributes, then one of these impossibilities would result: either the multiplicity of the Necessary [Existent] (*taʿaddud al-wājib*),[2] or an infinite regress (*al-tasalsul*), or the contradiction of what had been assumed (*khilāf al-mafrūḍ*).[3] Therefore the essence [of the Necessary Existent] is the necessitator of all Its attributes, and the question is proven. I say: There is room here for further discussion, for if this were the case, then every contingent would exist from eternity (*qadīman*) regardless of whether it was an attribute of the Necessary [Existent] or not.

Section [Six]: On [the proof] that the Necessarily [Existent] by virtue of Its essence does not share Its Existence with contingents.

That is, absolute existence (*al-wujūd al-muṭlaq*) is not a specific nature (*ṭabīʿah nawʿiyyah*) both for an existence which is identical with the Necessary [Existent] as well as for the existences of contingent beings (*wujūdāt al-mumkināt*).[4] On the contrary absolute existence is predicated accidentally (*qawlan ʿaraḍīyan*) of contingents by analogy (*bi'l-tashkīk*).[5]

[1] *This is because if It shared Its existence with contingents in the way mentioned, then absolute existence as it is in itself would be either necessarily independent* (al-

1. And therefore, everything which is possible for the Necessary [Existent] is necessarily actualized.

2. As shown above in paragraph 4.

3. As shown above in the previous sentence.

4. That is, absolute existence is not a class which includes both the existence of the Necessary Existent as well as the individual existences of contingent beings.

5. Rather than univocally.

tajarrud) *of quiddities,*[1] *or necessarily not independent (al-lā-tajarrud) [of quiddities],*[2] *or neither the one or the other, and all three are impossible.*

[2] *If it were necessarily independent, then the existence[s] of all contingents would have to be independent of, rather than inherent in, quiddities,* because what is required by a specific nature (*muqtaḍā al-ṭabīʿah al-nawʿiyyah*) does not differ [from one instance of the species to another]. *This*[3] *is absurd because we can conceive of a seven-sided figure* (al-musabbaʿ)[4] *while doubting its external existence.*[5] It would be appropriate to drop this restriction [to external existence] since the discussion is concerned with absolute existence, which includes both mental (*dhihnī*) and external (*khārijī*) existence. *Thus if its existence were the same as its reality* (ḥaqīqah) *or a part of it,*[6] *then a single thing would at the same time* (fī ḥālah wāḥidah) *be both known and unknown,*[7] *and that is impossible.*

[3] It would be more appropriate to say: because we can conceive of a seven-sided figure and be unaware of its existence. Thus if its existence were the same as its reality or a part of it, then a single thing would at the same time be both known and unknown. Or one could say: because we can conceive of a seven-sided figure while doubting its existence. Thus if its existence were the same as its reality, doubt would not be possible, since it is evident (*bayyin*) that a thing can [always] be predicated of itself. The case would be similar if existence were an essential attribute (*dhātī*) of its reality, because it is evident that an essential attribute can [always] be predicated of that [reality] of which it is an essential attribute. You are aware, of course, that all of this can only be the case if the quiddity is conceived in its true essence (*bi'l-kunh*).

[4] *If, on the other hand, absolute existence were necessarily not independent [of quiddities], then the existence of the Creator* (wujūd al-Bārī') *would not be independent* (mujarrad) *[of a quiddity] which is absurd. If it were neither necessarily independent nor necessarily not independent, then it would be possible for it to be either one or the other, but by virtue of a cause. In that case the Necessary Existent would be in need of what is other than Itself for Its independence, and Its Essence* (dhāt) *would not be sufficient [in causing] what It has in the way of attributes. That is absurd.* This is what people are currently saying on this topic.

---

1. Like the existence of the Necessary Existent, whose existence does not inhere in Its reality or quiddity but is the same as Its reality.

2. Like the existences of contingent beings, whose existences inhere in quiddities.

3. That is, that the existences of all contingents would have to be independent of quiddities.

4. According to the commentary of Ṣadr al-Dīn Shīrāzī what is meant is a solid figure enclosed by seven equal plane surfaces (*al-jism al-muḥāṭ bi-sabʿat suṭūḥ mutasāwiyah*), i.e., a heptahedron. See p. 300 of his *Sharḥ hidāyat al-ḥikmah.*

5. And we can therefore infer that its existence inheres in its quiddity and is not independent of it.

6. That is, independent rather than inherent in its reality.

7. That is, if the quiddity of the seven-sided figure were the same as its existence, and the quiddity were known, but its existence were unknown, then a single thing (the quiddity and its existence) would be both known and unknown.

[5] One of the verifiers (*ba'ḍ al-muḥaqqiqīn*) has said:[1] 'Every concept (*mafhūm*) which is other than existence, as, for example, the concept "humanity", does not exist at all in fact (*fī nafs al-amr*)[2] as long as existence has not been conjoined with it in some way. Moreover, as long as the mind has not observed that existence has been conjoined with it, it cannot make the judgment that it exists. Thus every concept other than existence is in need of what is other than itself, namely, existence, in order to exist in fact. And everything which is in need of what is other than itself in order to exist is contingent, for there is no meaning to contingent except that which is in need of what is other than itself in order to exist. Thus, every concept which is other than existence is contingent, and nothing that is contingent is necessary. It follows that no concepts which are other than existence are necessary.

[6] 'It has been demonstrated, moreover, that the Necessary [Existent] exists. It cannot but be identical with that existence that exists by virtue of its own essence rather than by virtue of something that is other than its essence. Moreover, since it is necessary that the Necessary [Existent] be a real and self-subsistent particular (*juz'ī ḥaqīqī qā'im bi-dhātihi*) and that Its individuation (*ta'ayyun*) be by virtue of Its essence not by virtue of something additional to Its essence, it is necessary that existence also be like that, since existence is identical with the Necessary Existent. Therefore, existence is not a universal concept (*mafhūm kullī*) comprising individuals (*afrād*). On the contrary, it is in itself (*fī ḥadd dhātihi*) a real particular with no possibility of becoming multiple or of being divided. It is self-subsistent and free (*munazzah*) from being inherent in what is other than it. Therefore, the Necessary [Existent] is Absolute Existence, that is, existence free (*mu'arrā*) of any limitation (*taqyīd*) by, or conjunction (*inḍimām*) with, what is other than It.

[7] 'On the basis of foregoing, one cannot conceive of existence as inhering in contingent quiddities (*al-māhiyyah al-mumkinah*). What is meant by a contingent quiddity's being existent is merely that is has a special relation (*nisbah makhṣūṣah*) to the Presence of the Self-Subsistent Existence (*ḥaḍrat al-wujud al-qā'im bi-dhātihi*). This relation has different aspects and various modes whose quiddities are difficult to detect. Thus what exists (*al-mawjūd*) is universal (*kullī*) even though existence (*al-wujūd*) is particular and real (*juz'ī ḥaqīqī*).' A certain learned man said: We used to hear him say that this was the doctrine of the verifying philosophers (*al-ḥukamā' al-muḥaqqiqīn*), the earlier ones as well as the later.'

---

1. This and the following two paragraphs are quoted from al-Sayyid al-Sharīf al-Jurjānī's *Ḥāshiyat sharḥ al-tajrīd*, fols. 62b–63a. Like the passage quoted previously from al-Jurjānī in section 2, paragraph 10, this passage represents the doctrine of the *waḥdat al-wujūd* school of Sufism. The passage is quoted in a number of other works as well. See, for example, al-Qūshjī, *Sharḥ al-tajrīd*, p. 61; Rāghib Bāshā, *al-Lum'ah*, pp. 11–12; al-Aḥmadnagarī, *Dastūr al-'ulamā'*, III, 443–444 (under *al-wujūd*).

2. See note 3 of p. 271 above.

Appendix

Translation of al-Abharī's Original Text

Chapter Two

On Knowledge of the Creator (*al-Ṣāni'*) and His Attributes

Section [One] On the Proof (*ithbāt*) for the Necessarily [Existent] by Virtue of Its Essence (*al-wājib li-dhātihi*). The Necessarily [Existent] by virtue of Its essence, if considered as It is in Itself (*min ḥaythu huwa huwa*), is that which does not accept non-existence (*al-ʿadam*). In proof of this (*burhānuhu*) one may say that if there were not in existence an existent which was necessary by virtue of its essence, then an impossibility would result. This is because all existents would then constitute a totality (*jumlah*) made up of individuals (*āḥād*) each one of which would be contingent by virtue of its essence (*mumkin li-dhātihi*). Therefore it would need an external cause to bring it into existence (*ʿillah mūjidah khārijiyyah*). And the knowledge of this is self-evident (*badīhī*). Moreover, an existent which was external to all contingents would be necessary by virtue of its essence. Thus, the existence of what is necessarily existent (*wājib al-wujūd*) follows from the assumption of its non-existence, and that is absurd.

Section [Two] On [the Proof] that the Necessary Existent's Existence is the Same as Its Reality (*ḥaqīqah*). This is because if Its existence were additional to Its reality (*ḥaqīqah*), it would be inherent (*ʿāriḍ*) in it. And if it were inherent in it, [Its] existence, as it is in itself (*min ḥayth huwa huwa*), would be in need of something other than itself. It would then be contingent by virtue of its essence and dependent upon a cause (*ʿillah*). It would therefore require an effector (*mu'aththir*), and if that effector were identical with the reality [of the Necessary Existent], that effector would have to exist before [its own] existence, since the cause which brings a thing into existence must precede its effect in existence. And thus that thing would have to exist before itself, and that is absurd. If, on the other hand, the effector were something other than the quiddity (*māhiyyah*) [of the Necessary Existent], then the Necessary Existent by virtue of Its essence would be in need of what is other than Itself for Its existence, and that is impossible.

Section [Three] On [the Proof] that [Its] Necessity of Existence (*wujūb al-wujūd*) as well as Its Individuation (*taʿayyun*) are Identical with Its Essence. As for the first it is because the necessity of existent, if it were additional to Its reality, would be an effect of Its essence (*maʿlūl li dhātihi*). As long as the existence of a cause is not necessary, it is impossible for its effect to exist. And since that necessity [which is under consideration] is necessity by virtue of the essence (*al-wujūb bi'l-dhāt*), that necessity of existence by virtue of the essence would exist before itself, and that is absurd. As for the second it is because Its individuation, if it were additional to Its reality, would be an effect of Its essence, and as long as a cause is not individuated it does not exist and so cannot bring into existence its effect. Therefore Its individuation would be existent (*ḥāṣil*) before itself, and that is absurd.

Section [Four] on [the Proof] for the Oneness (*tawḥīd*) of the Necessary Existent. If we suppose two necessarily existent beings (*mawjūdayn wājibay al-wujūd*), both would have necessity of existence (*wujūb al-wujūd*) in common but would differ with respect to something else. That which served to distinguish them from each other would either be the entire reality (*ḥaqīqah*) or not be [the entire reality]. The first [alternative] is impossible because if the distinction were with respect to the entire reality, then necessity of existence would have to be external to the reality of both. That is impossible because, as we have explained, necessity of existence is identical to the reality of the Necessary Existent.

The second [alternative] is also impossible, because each one of them would then be composed of what they had in common and what served to distinguish them from one another, and, since everything that is composed is in need of something other than itself, each would therefore be contingent by virtue of its essence, and that is contrary (*hādhā khulf*) [to what is assumed].

Section [Five] On [the Proof] that the Necessarily [Existent] by Virtue of Its Essence is Necessary in All of Its Aspects (*jihāt*). This is because Its Essence (*dhāt*) is sufficient with respect to the attribute it possesses, and It is therefore necessary in all of Its aspects. We say that Its essence is sufficient with respect to the attributes It possesses only because, were it not sufficient, then some of Its attribute would be [derived] from another being and the presence of that other being would be a cause (*ʿillah*) in general (*fi'l-jumlah*) of that attribute's existence, and its absence would be a cause of the attribute's non-existence. If such were the case, Its Essence, considered as it is in Itself (*min ḥayth hiya hiya*) would not be necessarily existent.

This is because [if It were] necessarily existent, it would be so either with the existence (*wujūd*) of that attribute of with its non-existence (*ʿadam*). If It were necessarily existent with the existence of that attribute, its existence would not be because of the presence of another being. If, on the other hand, It were necessarily existent with the non-existence of that attribute, the non-existence of the attribute would not be because of the absence of another being. Thus, if it were not necessarily existent unconditionally (*bi-lā sharṭ*), then the Necessarily [Existent] by virtue of Its essence would not be necessarily [existent] by virtue of Its essence, and that is absurd.

Section [Six] on [the Proof] that the Necessarily [Existent] by Virtue of Its Essence does not Share Its Existence with Contingents. This is because if It shared Its existence with contingents, then existence as it is in itself would be either necessarily independent (*al-tajarrud*) or necessarily not independent (*al-lā-tajarrud*) [of quiddities], or neither the one or the other, and all three are impossible. If it were necessarily independent, then the existence[s] of all contingents would have to be independent of, rather than inherent in, quiddities. This is absurd because we can conceive of a seven-sided figure (*al-musabbaʿ*) while doubting its external existence. Thus if its existence were the same as its reality (*ḥaqīqah*) or a part of it, then a single thing would at the same time (*fī ḥālah wāḥidah*) be both known and unknown, and that is impossible.

If, on the other hand, absolute existence were necessarily not independent [of quiddities], then the existence of the Creator (*wujūd al-Bāriʾ*) would not be independent (*mujarrad*) [of a quiddity], which is absurd. If it were neither necessarily independent nor necessarily not independent, then it would be possible for it to be either one or the other, but by virtue of a cause. In that case the Necessary Existent would be in need of what is other than Itself for Its independence, and Its essence (*dhāt*) would not be sufficient [in causing] what It has in the way of attributes. That is absurd.

5

Quṭb al-Dīn Rāzī

Abū Ja'far Muḥammad ibn Muḥammad Rāzī Būyahī known also as Quṭb al-Dīn Rāzī was born in the village of Varāmīn near Tehran. The date of his birth is not known but he died in Damascus in 776/1374. Virtually no record remains of the life of this major and prolific figure, who was recognized both as a philosopher and as a logician. His commentaries on the texts of *al-Shamsiyyah* and *al-Maṭāli'* were the reason for his fame as a logician and his major work, *al-Muḥākamāt*, in which he discusses the perspectives of Nasīr al-Dīn Ṭūsī and Imam Fakhr Rāzī, gained him recognition as a philosopher.

What we do know about him is mostly based on brief references made to him by a few biographers. Tāj Subkī in his work *Ṭabaqāt al-shāfi'iyyah* describes him as 'a learned master in intellectual sciences whose fame had spread to distant lands. He arrived in Damascus in 763/1361; we found him to be a leader in logic and philosophy and knowledgeable in *tafsīr* (Qu'rānic interpretation), rhetoric and grammar and intelligence was exuding from him.' Suyūṭī in *Ṭabaqāt al-Najāt* said, 'he was one of the leaders of the intellectual sciences who had learned from 'Aḍudī and others.' Muḥammad ibn Makkī, known as *al-Shahīd al-awwal* (the First Martyr), also confirmed these accounts and after he met with Quṭb al-Dīn Rāzī he said, 'he was a vast sea of knowledge who would not dry up … undoubtedly he was an Imamī Shi'a and I heard him assert that he was a Shi'a and his attachment to the household of the Prophet is clear.' The same author tells us that he was the special student of 'Allāmah Ḥillī. Among his other teachers were 'Aḍud al-Dīn Ījī, who was a theologian. It is therefore plausible that Quṭb al-Dīn had studied *kalām* with him.

Among his works we can mention his commentary on a text on logic by Kātibī-yi Qazwīnī, entitled *Sharḥ shamsiyyah*. His other works include *Sharḥ al-maṭāli'*, *Sharḥ al-ḥāwī*, *Sharḥ al-ishārāt* of Ibn Sīnā, *Baḥr al-ṣadaf* which is a commentary on *tafsīr*, *Tuḥfat al-ashrāf*, his major work on philosophy *al-Muḥākamāt*, *Sharḥ qawā'id al-aḥkām*, a commentary on 'Allāmah Ḥillī's work on jurisprudence and a treatise entitled *Taṣawwur wa'l-taṣdīq*, perhaps named after Ṭūsī's famous work of the same title.

In this chapter, we have included a section of Rāzī's *Taṣawwur wa'l-taṣdīq* (Conception and Judgment). This text is primarily on epistemology, in which the author discusses how conceptions are formed in the mind and investigates the affirmative and negative nature of the propositions that address the content of the mind. Referring to Ibn Sīnā as 'the Shaykh', Rāzī begins a series of enquiries about propositions and what Ibn Sīnā and Ṭūsī have said in that regard. Knowledge, certainty, proof and verifiability are among the themes that run through the entire treatise. Rāzī concluded this treatise by affirming that Ibn Sīnā's views in this regard were valid and authoritative.

M. Aminrazavi

CONCEPTION AND JUDGMENT

al-Taṣawwur wa'l-taṣdīq

Translated for this volume by Majid Fakhry from Quṭb al-Dīn Rāzī, *Risālat al-Taṣawwur wa'l-taṣdīq*, ed. Mahdī Sharī'atī (Qum, 1416/1995), pp. 92–128.

In the Name of God, the Merciful, the Compassionate

Preface

This is an epistle, seeking to elucidate the meaning of 'conception' (*taṣawwur*) and 'assent' (*taṣdīq*)[1] and to give their definitions, which I have written for some of my friends, trusting in the Almighty Source of Truth and Veracity.

Chapter 1
Basis of the Distinction between Conception and Assent

You should know that knowledge (*'ilm*), which is the basis of the division into conception and assent, consists in that renewed knowledge, which is not reducible to mere presence, as is the case with the knowledge of the Almighty Creator, the knowledge of abstract entities in themselves and our own knowledge of ourselves. Otherwise, knowledge could not consist exclusively in conception and assent; since conception consists in the form of the object existing in the mind, while assent presupposes that conception. Knowledge of presence[2] does not consist in conceiving a certain form.

In fact, renewed knowledge of things which are absent can only be achieved by conceiving their forms. For, if nothing new arises in us in consequence of something else disappearing, the stated, knowledge and what precedes it would be identical, which is absurd.

Now, if something disappears, then what disappears upon our knowledge of *this* is clearly other than that which disappears upon our knowledge of *that*; otherwise our knowledge of the one would be the same as our knowledge of the other. It follows that there are in us an infinite number of things equivalent to our knowledge of infinite objects, such as figures or consecutive numbers. Those things existing in us would then be simultaneous and consecutive. Otherwise, the larger number,

1. The Aristotelian terms 'conception' and 'judgment' are replaced in Islamic philosophy by 'conception' and 'assent'. The Arabic equivalent of judgment, *ḥukm*, is sometimes used in the sense of assent.

2. *al-'Ilm al-ḥuḍūrī*, or intuitive knowledge.

for instance, would not presuppose the smaller, since the existence of the smaller necessitates the non-existence of the larger. Thus, if the non-existence of one and two and the cause of their non-existence exist actually in us, then the non-existence of infinite numbers would exist in us also. However, the falsity of this proposition has been shown in philosophy.[1]

It is clear from the above that knowledge is a matter of acquisition, rather than nullification; and since knowledge as a matter of acquisition, rather than nullification, is a matter which we find in ourselves, it follows that it does not call for a proof.

Moreover, what is given upon the knowledge of one of two objects of knowledge is other than that which is given upon the knowledge of another object of knowledge, preceding it. It follows that there must exist in the mind something corresponding to the object known, which is knowledge thereof rather than of something else. This is the meaning of saying that the form of the thing is in the mind.

It is also necessary that that knowledge be more general than being corresponding to what is in the object itself or not, affirmative or not. It would then include all varieties of conception and assent. For in logic, universal and comprehensive notions are sought, as well as the five arts.[2]

Chapter 2
On Conception

Conception has been interpreted in a variety of way. One is that it consists in the form of the object existing in the mind. In that sense, it is equivalent to knowledge as such. The other is that it consists in the form of the object existing in the mind only, which admits of two interpretations. One is the existence of the form of the object, with reference to the absence of assent; the other is the existence of the form of the object without reference to judgment. This interpretation is more general than the former; because it entails that it[3] can co-exist with judgment, which is more specific than the other interpretation, which entails that it cannot co-exist with judgment.

Chapter 3
On Assent

Assent has been interpreted in a variety of ways. The first, which is attributed to the philosophers, is that it consists in judgment, which has been interpreted in three ways. The first is that it consists in one thing affecting the other, affirmatively

1. Meaning philosophical writings.

2. Or five divisions of Aristotelian logic, *Isagoge*, or (Introduction), *Interpretation, Prior Analytics, Posterior Analytics* and *Sophistica*.

3. That is, conception.

or negatively. The second is that it is a form of relation, rather than attachment, whereas knowledge is a passion.[1] The third is that it consists in the soul conceiving that the relation exists or does not exist.

The second interpretation (of assent) is that it consists in the sum-total of our conceptions of what is judged, what it is judged with, the relation and the judgment itself.[2] This is the view of the Imam (Fakhr al-Dīn Rāzī).

The third interpretation is that it consists in a conception accompanied by a judgment. Conception would then be a form of assent, provided it is accompanied by judgment. This is the view of the author of *Maṭāliʿ al-anwār* (The Rising of the Lights)[3] and others. He may have intended to give the view of al-Imam (Fakhr al-Dīn).

The fourth is that it consists in the soul's assent to the intent of the proposition and consenting to it. This is other than saying that the intent of the proposition exists in the soul, but rather something else concurrent with it, which is the form of consenting to it; namely, that the notion which exists in the soul corresponds to what the thing is in reality. This consent is more general than correspondence to what the thing is in itself or not. For belief in correspondence does not necessarily mean that the thing believed actually corresponds to what the thing is in itself.

Chapter 4
What the Shaykh[4] Held in *al-Mūjaz al-kabīr* (The Great Summary)

This (last) interpretation accords with what the Shaykh held. For, he states in *al-Mūjaz al-kabīr*, in the first chapter of the third treatise on demonstration, literally that knowledge is of two types: one is assent, the other is conception. Conception consists in that the meaning of the term arises in the soul, which differs from the fact that there arises with it in the soul the meaning of a proposition which the soul assents to. Rather, when the meaning of a proposition is grasped by the soul, this entails that it is either an object of doubt, affirmation or denial. In all three cases, conception would have already taken place in the form of the meaning existing in the soul. As for doubt and denial, they are not objects of assent. Affirmation, which is a synonym of assent, differs from the fact that the meaning of the proposition is grasped by the soul; it is something else concurrent with it and consisting in the form of consenting to it. For, the meaning which arises in the soul corresponds to what the thing is in itself, so that the meaning of the grasped proposition, insofar as it is conceived in the soul, is not the same as the meaning of an intelligible proposition, but rather another occurring in the soul.

1. That is, the first is active, the other is passive.
2. Cf. footnote 1, p. 97 of the text.
3. Or Sirāj al-Dīn Abū Bakr al-Urmawī (d. 682/1283).
4. Ibn Sīnā.

From the words of the Shaykh (i.e. Ibn Sīnā), it is clear that conception denotes the grasping of the meaning of the expression by the soul unconditionally, whether that meaning is simple or composite; regardless of whether that composite is a proposition, a command, a prohibition, an admonition, a relation, a judgment or something else.

A proposition is more general than the fact of its being acceptable or unacceptable. An acceptable proposition is one which is the object of assent, and assent has another meaning conjoined to the meaning of the proposition and consisting in the soul's concurrence with the meaning of the proposition which is assented to, affirmed or accepted. By consent is meant that the meaning which is grasped by the soul conforms with what the thing is in reality. This is more general than the fact that that meaning conforms with reality itself or not. For, the soul's consent to a meaning, regarded as corresponding to reality as such does not entail that it actually corresponds with reality as such; correspondence being one thing and consenting to correspondence being something else. Thus, assent in this sense does not conflict with sophistry or other arts.

Everybody agrees that a proposition is a statement whose utterer may be told: 'You have said the truth, or you have lied.' Now, truth and falsity may be predicated of a proposition, when the relation is part of it, otherwise they are not. It follows that assent is not the same thing as judgment, as recent scholars have contended, ascribing that to the (ancient) philosophers. Assent is then a form of consenting to the relation,[1] and thus the term assent is applied to judgment figuratively.

This is how the reality of conception and assent should be understood, so that the doubts raised in their regard may be rebutted.

Chapter 5
The Shaykh's Words in *al-Shifā'*[2]

The proof of what we said regarding assent is this statement of the Shaykh (Ibn Sīnā) in *al-Shifā'*, in the third chapter of the First Article of the First Part of the general statement of the Introduction to Logic: 'A thing is known in two ways; the first is to be merely conceived; so that, if it happens to have a name which is uttered, its meaning is represented in the mind, regardless of truth or falsity; just as we say "man" or "do that". For, once you have grasped the meaning of what you have been told, you would have conceived it.

'The Second is for conception to be accompanied by assent. Thus, if, for instance, someone says to you: "Every white colour is an accident", you will not have a conception of the meaning of this statement only, but you will assent to it as well. However, if you doubt that this is the case, you would have still conceived what is said; since

1. Between subject and predicate.
2. *al-Shifā'*, or *The Book of Healing*, is Ibn Sīnā's most famous and comprehensive work.

you cannot doubt what you do not conceive or understand; but you have not assented to it yet. Thus, every assent is accompanied by a conception; but the converse is not true. Conception in this sense entails that the form of this composition[1] and what is composed, such as whiteness and accident, arise in the mind. Assent, on the other hand, consists in the fact that the relation of this form to the things themselves, as conforming to them, has arisen in the mind; while denial is the opposite of this.'[2]

Chapter 6
al-Abharī's Words on the Subject of Clarifying Thoughts

You should know that the eminent Athīr al-Dīn Abharī has stated in the preface of this book, *Classifying Thoughts*,[3] that knowledge is the act of grasping the form of the thing by the mind. It consists either of conception, such as conceiving the meaning of the word 'man', or conception accompanied by assent; as happens when we conceive the meaning of the statement 'man is an animal', and then assent to it. Thus, conception consists in the concept of both terms, together with their composition, arising in the mind; whereas assent consists in the conformity of the form of this composition with the things themselves arising in the mind.[4]

I say his (al-Abharī's) interpretation of assent corresponds fully to the Shaykh's (Ibn Sīnā's) interpretation. For, he (Ibn Sīnā) says that the occurrence of both terms, together with their composition—that is the meaning of the proposition in the mind, is called conception; whereas assent consists in the form of this conformity with the things themselves occurring in the mind. This corresponds to the interpretation of consenting to the meaning of the proposition as given by the Shaykh. It corresponds to his words: 'Then we assented to it'; that is, consented to it. He was criticized by the 'Master of all Scholars', Khwājah Naṣīr al-Millah wa'l-Dīn.[5] God have mercy on him. In commenting on *al-Tanzīl*,[6] he says: as for his statement, 'then we assented to it', he must mean by it the same as his interpretation of the form of this composition in the mind as conforming with the things themselves. Then, the meaning of his words, '[then we assented to it', would be that the form of this composition has arisen in our mind; but what is understood by his statement],[7] our conceiving the meaning of the words, 'man is an animal', is identical with the occurrence of this composite in our mind. Thus, the meaning of his statement, if we conceive the meaning of our statement, 'Man is an animal, then assent to it', is

1. Of subject and predicate.
2. Cf. Ibn Sīnā, *al-Shifā'*, 1, Introduction, 17.
3. The full title of this book by al-Abharī (d. *c.* 663/1264) is *Ta'dīl al-mi'yār fī tanzīl al-afkār.*
4. Cf. al-Abharī, *Ta'dīl al-mi'yār*, pp. 139f.
5. That is, Naṣīr al-Dīn Ṭūsī.
6. i.e. al-Abharī's book.
7. The statement in brackets is not found in the original text of *al-Tanzīl.*

the same as saying that when we grasp the form of the composite which consists of the forms of the two terms and their composition, then the form of that composition is grasped by us. However, the form of this composite cannot occur except subsequently to its parts which make up the form of that composition, and the occurrence of the form of this composition following the occurrence of the form of that composite is redundant, which is absurd.

I say: part of the composite consists in the form of that composition absolutely, rather than the conformity of the form of this composition to things themselves, which is the meaning of consenting to it. The meaning of the statement, 'then we assented to it', consists in the conformity of the form of that composition to things themselves, which is more specific than the form of that composition absolutely and this is not redundant.

Then, he[1] says that assuming this to be correct, the occurrence of the form of that composition in the mind would be a form of conception; whereas the occurrence of the composition itself, rather than its form, would be a form of assent.

I say: The occurrence of the composition itself is an act of attribution or judgment; but judgment cannot be regarded as assent, because it is *active*, whereas assent, which is knowledge, is simply *passive*. The occurrence of the form of composition in the mind, in conformity with the things themselves, is equivalent to assent, insofar as it is consent or approval of what is assented to, even if it is considered a form of conception, insofar as it occurs in the mind. This will be followed by added clarification.

Then, he[2] adds: If it is said that by his words 'then we assented to it', he intended that 'we have judged it to be true', in the sense in which assent is understood linguistically, rather than conventionally; our response would be that the judgment of truth is a secondary form of assent, while we are talking here about primary assent. Moreover, it is necessary that the judgment which we repudiate not be regarded an assent. All this is contrary to what he holds.

We further comment that the intent of his words 'then we believed' is simply: we have consented to its truth and affirmed it. Therefore, it is not a secondary mode of assent, since it is not a judgment of truthfulness, but rather a primary assent.

As for his statement, 'the judgment which we repudiate cannot be a form of assent', that is true, because the proposition accompanied by repudiation cannot be assented to and so assent cannot attach to it, as we reported in reference to the Shaykh (Ibn Sīnā). It is also possible that the same proposition may be understood by three different persons to mean assent, doubt or repudiation.

He then states that it is said by his words is meant 'then we assented to it'; that is, then we judged thereby. We say, although this may be true, it conflicts nevertheless with his own interpretation of assent, as well as that of others; because assent

1. Ṭūsī.
2. Ṭūsī.

is a series of conceptions accompanied by judgment, although here he meant by it assent only.

Moreover, by its intent is not meant, 'We then judged it to be such', but rather the intent is what we have said repeatedly; namely, interpreting assent as conceptions accompanied by judgment. He did not mean by it simply judgment, but rather affirming the composition, as we have seen. That would not be incompatible with his interpretation, but rather that of others.

He then says: I would also comment on his[1] reference to the conformity (of the conception) to the things themselves that the provision of conformity may be taken into account where the interpretation of truthfulness is concerned, but not the interpretation of assent in this sense. For assent in this sense may not be accompanied by conformity, or conformity may not be taken into account with respect to it.

He is free to adhere to this view in contradiction to anyone else. Then, he would be obliged to comply with his convention, when he uses it; but the fact is that he has divided assent into intuitive and acquired. He also added that the disagreement among reasonable people bears on the acquisitive part. However, it is impossible that all that reasonable people have disagreed upon should be conformable. Therefore, some forms of assent are not conformable, according to him.

Moreover, he has divided propositions, in the first part of the Fifth Article of this book, into what affects the soul by means of a matter of assent and what affects it by means of a matter of non-assent. He then included conjectural, deceptive and conclusive propositions in the first part. Accordingly, he has included in the category of assent that which is not conformable, as well as that which is not considered as liable to conformity. From this, it appears that he did abide by the above convention.[2]

I say that there is no doubt that truth consists in that your predicating one thing of another, affirmatively or negatively, is in conformity with reality. Assent consists in admitting the conformity, but admitting conformity with respect to some judgment does not entail necessarily that that judgment is conformable, as was mentioned. How? The philosophers in interpreting vision, for instance, are of two opinions: one is that vision is caused by the rays' emanation; the other is that vision is a matter of impression.

Now, admission, consent or assent with respect to each opinion is a fact, although the fact in itself cannot be more than one. It follows that admitting conformity in a given judgment does not entail that that judgment is conformable. Therefore, all modes of assent are conformable with respect to consent or admission, even though some of them may not be conformable to what the thing is in itself.

---

1. al-Abharī's.
2. Namely, the division into what affects the soul as a matter of assent and what does not.

Now, conjectural, deceptive and necessary propositions fall into the category of assent in this sense and we should not diverge from convention.

Then, he says: 'If it is said that assent, which is one of the two divisions of knowledge, must be conformable or else it is not knowledge', having himself divided knowledge into conception and assent and nothing else; I would say, 'Knowledge is also applied to what is not certain, such as dialectic and the like. Therefore, what is an object of assent does not have to be conformable'.

For me, this is true. For, there is no doubt that the term 'knowledge' is applied to what is not certain, and therefore what is an object of assent need not conform to reality. However, having interpreted assent as the admission of conformity, regardless of whether it is conformity to reality or not, he[1] is not open to this proviso and this objection does not affect his position.

Then he said: 'Regarding everything which ought to conform, it is not necessary that conformity should be taken into account in the process of interpreting it. For, there is a difference between what the meaning of conformity implies and what attaches to it. This is similar to our saying: "Animal is divisible into rational and non-rational", followed by our interpreting the rational alone, rather than the rational animal, as a body which is capable of thinking. This would be false because body does not enter into the concept of rational. That is why it is applied in a sense to immaterial entities which are not bodily; although rational animal can only refer to what is bodily. Rational in this sense denotes, then, bodily by necessity, not by implication. The same is true of assent insofar as it entails conformity attaching to it, not in being knowledge.'

I say: Conformity which is taken in the interpretation of assent is other than that conformity which attaches to the thing itself. For, the first is part of assent by way of implication; whereas the latter is extraneous to it and attaches to it only in certain cases. Thus, in interpreting it,[2] the first type of conformity should be taken into account, rather than the second. However, the example he gives is sound and does not affect his position adversely.

He then says: 'If the concept of conformity is taken into account in relation to scientific assent, it should also be taken into account in relation to conception, which is its counterpart. Taking it into account in relation to one of the two disjunctives[3] is an aberration'.

I say: He is not referring here to conformity in relation to scientific assent, but rather conformity in relation to the concept of assent absolutely. Assent in this sense attaches to all conceptions or some of them regardless of whether the conception in question consists of a single term or a proposition. That is why it has been said that conception is never independent of assent.

1. al-Abharī.
2. i.e. assent.
3. Assent and conception.

In that respect, knowledge is divisible into conception independent of assent and conception attended by assent. All the sciences consist of conceptions only; although assent attaches to some of them, but not to the others. Moreover, assent, insofar as it occurs in the mind, is equivalent to conception, but insofar as it refers to the object assented to, is a form of assent. Were the acknowledgement of conformity with respect to the thing itself as conceived, that conception would not be a form of pure conception, but conception attended by assent. Further, clarification of this point will follow.

He then said: 'Conformity cannot be taken into account in the case of naïve conception; otherwise it will not be naïve. For, we say that conception is divisible into: 1) real, preceded by the knowledge of the existence of the conceived object, in such a way that its conformity with the existing entity is presupposed; otherwise it would be a conception of something other than that conceived object, which is a form of ignorance, or 2) what is not real, and is not preceded by the existence of the object conceived or its non-existence. This is a form of nominal conception, which should rather be affiliated to verbal cognitions.

It is clear that conformity should be taken into account in scientific conception, which is the counterpart of scientific assent. But if this is taken into account in connection with the interpretation he has given, then there would be no difference between conception and assent, except in the case of the conception of the object and the concept of composition itself, regardless of whether they are both considered in connection with conformity or not.

I say: what he means by assent is not scientific assent or that of which the particular conception he mentioned is the counterpart; but rather something more general. If this is the case, we would argue that conception consists in the fact that the meaning of the term is grasped by the mind, regardless of whether (the term) is simple or composite, in conformity or not. Thus, conformity or non-conformity should not be taken into account therein. It is not the counterpart of assent, but an object of assent. Therefore, taking conformity into account in interpreting such an object in another sense does not justify taking it into account where the object is concerned. Even if assent in this sense were to involve all kinds of conceptions, such conceptions would not become forms of assent, but rather objects of assent. The difference between the object and what it applies to, that is between conception and assent, will always be there. God is the guide!

You should also know that applying the terms predicate and object is a matter of latitude. For the truth is that conception is the primary knowledge and assent is not possible except in the wake of conception.

The proof that assent is not identical with judgment and is not something ensuing on consent is that if we say 'the world has a beginning' and 'the whole is greater than the part', predication and assertion of the relationship is perceived in both propositions. The perception of this predication requires no acquisitive knowledge, because predication and judgment are acts of the soul, whose actions depend on its choice. Thus, if you choose to conceive the two terms (of the proposition), you would predicate one or the other; otherwise not.

If this is granted, then the first assent is acquired, the second is intuitive. Now, predication is not acquired, therefore assent is something other than predication and consent occurs in the second proposition without intermediary, while in the first it does not occur unless a middle term has occurred.

Assent is thus other than judgment in the sense of predication, and is other than the object or the subject of judgment, which are the components of the judgment. It is also other than the sum-total of the judgment, its object or its subject; as well as judgment in the sense of the relation of the object to the subject of the judgment. For, conceiving the relation between the two depends on the soul's choice.

The statements of some modern scholars show that assent is not the same as judgment. For, they state that judgment is the act of predicating one thing or another, either positively or negatively. They have also stated that acquired assent is that kind of assent in which the conception of the two terms of a proposition is not sufficient for affirming predication.

Moreover, there is no doubt that affirming predication is other than that predication which is judgment, and other than affirming the relationship which is judgment, and other than affirming the relationship which is judgment, according to a modern view. Affirmation in fact is assent; that is, consenting, affirming and confessing the truth of what is assented to.

The Shaykh (Ibn Sīnā) has said in the above-mentioned chapter of *al-Mūjaz al-kabīr* (The Great Summary) that assent depends on two things: the first is conception of what is assented to; that is, what is required in it; the second conceiving that which is known to be certain and assenting to it.

Now, nothing in predication or relation depends on that. Therefore, it has been established that assent is other than judgment, according to both interpretations; and conceiving the object and subject of judgment is the pre-condition of assent and not part of it.

On this basis, it is permissible to divide knowledge into conception only and conception accompanied by assent, as the Shaykh has distinguished the two in *al-Ishārāt* (Remarks and Admonitions). Knowledge of one thing may therefore be a matter of conception, some of whose parts differ from other parts by virtue of an accident attaching to it, which is assent, or its non-attaching to it. Assent, too, insofar as it is grasped by the mind, will be a form of conception and insofar as it attaches to another will be a form of assent. Knowledge may also be divided into conception and assent, as he (Ibn Sīnā) has done in *al-Mūjaz al-kabīr* (The Great Summary). Thus, some cognitions are either forms of conception, which comprise what is grasped by the mind, whether it is composite or simple; while other (cognitions) are forms of assent; that is the recognition of conceptions within the soul and consenting to them, even though consent, insofar as it arises in the mind, is a form of conception. No objection or doubt can be raised against this double division.

That is what may be said about assent according to this interpretation.[1]

Chapter 7
An Account of What has been Said about Assent, according to the First Interpretation

What has been said about assent, insofar as it is regarded as judgment will now be given.

Al-Shaykh al-Suhrawardī[2] states in *al-Muṭāraḥāt* (The Exchanges) that 'defining assent as judging one thing as being another is not sound. For, this applies to assent with regard to categorical (propositions), but does not apply to assent regarding conditional (propositions). One should rather adhere in explaining this matter to what we have mentioned in *al-Talwīḥāt* (Book of Allusions)'. Here, he states that knowledge is either a form of conception, or the grasping of the form of the thing by the mind, or a form of assent; namely, the act of judging of conceptions, negatively or affirmatively, so as to comprise assent in the case of conditional (propositions).

He has also stated in *al-Muṭāraḥāt* that there is a difference between proposition and assent, insofar as proposition is a discursive statement, which is either verbal or mental; whereas assent is a rational judgment which is not verbal. Assent in fact is identical with judgment, except that judgment is not fulfilled except by means of conceptions.

He also stated in *al-Muṭāraḥāt*: 'As for dividing knowledge into conception and assent, that may be permissible in elementary books, because it is a matter which is not susceptible of scrutiny. The most comprehensive division is the one given by Shaykh Abū 'Alī,[3] in some places, that knowledge is either conception only, or conception accompanied by assent. What they both have in common is conception, while to one is added assent, which is judgment'.

Now, every term applied to two things, one of which is distinguishable by virtue of what is proper to it, is rather applied by virtue of what is common to the two. Now, since it has been said in the process of division that knowledge is either this or that, it follows that division is not possible unless the term is used in one sense. For, a common term cannot be divided, except in accordance with what was stated earlier. It is as though he took the term 'knowledge' in this context as equivalent to conception, which he then divided into simple or accompanied by assent.

1. i.e. the fourth given by al-Abharī.
2. Shihāb al-Dīn al-Suhrawardī, known as Shaykh al-Ishrāq (d. 587/1191)
3. Ibn Sīnā.

Moreover, assent is a form of judgment, which is the act of affirming a relationship or denying it. Now, grasping the meaning of a certain act is not the same as that act itself; that is, grasping is not the same as that act. Thus, our grasping that act, which is the same as judgment, consists in conceiving that act, namely, judgment. The above-mentioned knowledge is thus reducible to conception.

Moreover, conception may bear on external matters or on mental judgments, which are forms of assent. Therefore, our various forms of knowledge are reducible to conceptions, even when they happen sometimes to consist of conceptions of judgments or forms of assent, which are mental acts of affirming or denial.[1]

I say: His[2] statement, in interpreting judgment as a form of affirming the relation (of two terms), is similar to the notion of affirming, consenting or recognizing. The commentator[3] of *al-Talwīḥāt* (The Allusions), in explaining these words, states that when the form of the thing is in the mind, it is either accompanied by a judgment or not. In both cases, that condition is called conception, whereas judgment, considered insofar as it is in the mind, is a form of conception also, the property of its being a judgment is called assent.

Conception, then, is the act of grasping the thing by the mind, without reference to judgment. For, if it is determined by the absence of judgment, as claimed by some modern scholars, who hold that what is grasped by the mind and is unaccompanied by judgment is conception, but if accompanied by judgment is assent. Thus, they make assent dependent on conception in accordance with the view of those who identify assent with judgment, as is proposed in *al-Talwīḥāt* (Allusions), in the manner of ancient philosophers. Nor would it be part of assent, as those who regard it as the sum-total of three conceptions, the object, the subject and the act of judgment assert. This is the view of the Imam.[4] However, all scholars are agreed that assent requires conceptions, but the converse is not true.

For, if judgment is presupposed as a correlative, then conception would require assent, as assent requires it, and then the converse would follow in the process of each presupposing the other, as such, and this is something they have all rejected.

It follows that presupposing the concurrence of judgment or its non-concurrence does not correspond to the view of the majority; but rather, the view that does not conflict with their account of conception and assent is what is mentioned in *al-Talwīḥāt*. As for conception, it is just as I have shown; but as for assent, it follows from their consensus that failure to assent to primary propositions might depend on their obscure conceptions of their terms. Thus, were assent other than judgment, pure and simple, and was a matter of the three above-mentioned conceptions, then it would not be intuitive, unless those conceptions were intuitive.

1. Cf. Suhrawardī, *Muṭāraḥāt*, p. 56.
2. Suhrawardī's.
3. Ibn Kammūnah (d. 683/1284).
4. Fakhr al-Dīn Rāzī.

This is contrary to what they conceded with respect to primary propositions, despite the fact that some of them; I mean the Imam, have contradicted themselves in some places.

If this is granted, then it follows that knowledge is of two types: 1) One is conception, which consists in the mind grasping the form of the thing; as when a term denoting the thing and then is uttered, its meaning is perceived by the mind. This is independent of whether it is expressed in a single term, such as 'man', or a compound, such as 'rational animal' or 'the world is contingent or possible', just as you have learned that judgment, as grasped by the mind is an object of conception. In fact, it is a form of assent, precisely because it is judgment; but it cannot be grasped by the mind, unless the object and subject of judgment are grasped, too. Thus, that object of conception is a proposition assented to, whereby it is the object and subject of judgment at the same time, as in the above-mentioned example.

2) The other is assent, which consists in the judgment that the thing is conceived with respect to its being or non-being, on the one hand, or the existence of a state pertaining to it, on the other. This is in general a form of judging a certain conception negatively or positively, as the example given in *al-Talwīḥāt* shows. That includes both categorical and conditional modes of assent. This is more appropriate than the claim of some scholars that assent consists in judging of two things that one is identical or not identical with the other. For, this is true of categorical, but not conditional (propositions), and therefore does not cover all types of assent.

This is all that can be said about assent, according to the first interpretation. However, his[1] statement that 'then the claim that assent presupposes conception… and is part of assent' should be reconsidered; because it is not excluded that the opposition of part and whole may entail that one is implied in the other, as one and may imply each other. What is rather excluded is the claim that both are true of the same thing in the same respect.

This is true, because it is impossible that the same thing may be both a single or compound mode of understanding. The examples illustrating this point are numerous, such as five, which is odd, implies two, which is even, or a compound term, which implies a single one. Similarly, it is not excluded that the condition and the conditioned are regarded as opposites; rather than their truth in reference to the same entity.

You should know the import of his statement, 'Then that conceived object is an assertory proposition of which and by which judgment may be made, as in the aforementioned example'; namely, that the world is contingent. For, once the meaning of an assertory proposition is conceived, which amounts to conceiving the object, the subject and the act of judgment, then the relation between the two

---

1. Suhrawardī, in *Ḥikmat al-ishrāq*.

extreme terms will be grasped. This relation in fact depends on the choice of the conceiver, relationship being his own action and his action depending on his choice. However, on this assumption no acquired assent is left.

Whoever interprets assent as a form of consent will not be faced with this problem. For, he may posit a relationship, but still doubt that this relationship is to be acknowledged or not. Then, he would acquire that admission by recourse to conjunctive premises.

Therefore, he who investigates assent ought to probe the meaning of consent and that of judgment. If he finds that both are the same, then assent is the same as judgment. This will actually follow if judgment is interpreted as the recognition of relation, not relation itself; but if judgment is interpreted as relationship, then the difference is obvious, as was stated above.

As for those who assert that assent is the same as judgment, and then interpret judgment as the relation between the object and the subject of judgment, rather than the predication of the relation, in order to escape the charge that relationship is an action, whereas assent is a passion, insofar as it is a form of knowledge; it should be asserted that their claim is vacuous. For, you have already learned that relation, insofar as it is grasped by the soul, is equivalent to conception; but insofar as it is specifically regarded as judgment, is equivalent to assent.

Some[1] have described the difference between judgment and assent as follows. Assent is an act of *passion,* because it is part of the renewed knowledge and is in fact an impression of the knower; whereas judgment consists in asserting a positive or negative relation, which is an *action.* For assertion is an action of the knower. Therefore, one cannot be equated with the other, and thus calling judgment a form of assent is purely figurative.

The proof of this is that, since understanding consists in the presence of the object known to the knower, then the presence which leads him to recognize that a positive relation exists or does not exist, amounts to assent; and what is present to him then is the object of assent, whereas asserting the relation or denying it is equivalent to judgment. As for the presence which accompanies the (understanding), it is the same as we said above. If, however, something else is present or the sense of occurrence and non-occurrence is understood as something else, then it is conception, and the present object is the conceived object. Therefore, assent is not independent of judgment, but is the same as it.

The proof of their divergence is the view of all the modern scholars, who assert that understanding, accompanied by judgment, is equivalent to assent. For, what accompanies a thing is other than that thing, which is identical with the view of al-Khwājah (Ṭūsī) in his commentary on *al-Ishārāt,*[2] where he states that the object of assent is what is present in it as a concurrent thereof and signifying it. For, what

1. Namely, Quṭb al-Dīn al-Shīrāzī (d. 710/1310), colleague of Ṭūsī.
2. Of Ibn Sīnā.

is concurrent with a thing is other than that thing, but it is because assent and judgment are inseparable that one is called by the name of the other figuratively, as in the 'flowing of the drain.'

I say: the words of the moderns prove that they[1] are different, but the words of the Khwājah (Ṭūsī) does not; for he states in his commentary on *al-Ishārāt* that judgment is the same as assent and whatever is subject to judgment is assented to. This is followed by these words: 'that this is how the reality of conception and assent should be understood, so that problems raised might be rebuffed'. Similarly, were assent equivalent to understanding accompanied by judgment, then:

(1) Judgment would be other than assent, while it is identical with it or part of it;

(2) Assent, moreover, would be acquired. For, were absolute understanding dependent on reflection, then the understanding accompanying it would be dependent on it, as the part on the whole;

(3) And then each assent would consist of three assents, since it is accompanied by three acts of understanding;

(4) Also, it would then be possible to grasp assent by recourse to explicative statements, although it is not grasped except by reference to reality.

The first point is countered by what you have learned regarding the necessary association of judgment and the act of understanding accompanying the judgment, rather than being identical with it or part of it.

The second point is countered by the statement that acquired assent is that which requires acquisition in the process of affirming the relation or denying it. For, whatever is such that its conceptions are acquired will not need it[2] in that respect, but rather from the standpoint of the necessary conception.

The third point is countered by asserting that assent is a mode of presence, whereby the relation is shown to be present or not present. The presence of each of the three modes of understanding is not that way.

The fourth point is countered by asserting that the assent which cannot be grasped, except by recourse to proof, is assent in the sense of judgment; I mean, either asserting the relation or denying it. As for that assent which denotes qualified presence, it can only be grasped by recourse to a discursive proof.

It cannot be said that the first question is not well-stated, because if he[3] means by assent judgment, then we do not grant that it is a passive property. If, on the other hand, he means by it judgment accompanied by the conception of both extreme terms, then we do not grant that judgment applies to it. However, if it is said that assent is equivalent to judgment, as an active property, then it will not be possible to classify knowledge according to it. For, we say that assent must be passive assertion,

1. Conception and assent.
2. The assent.
3. Ṭūsī.

because it is part of knowledge, and then it will not be equivalent to judgment, which is an active assertion.

I say: It is clear from the words of this eminent scholar[1] that assent and judgment are different, but correlative. According to the interpretation which we derived from the Shaykh (Ibn Sīnā), assent is more specific than judgment. For the existence of assent requires the existence of judgment, but the converse is not generally true. On this interpretation, the above objections do not arise.

Chapter 8
How One Can Counter Assent, According to the Second Interpretation

As for those who state that assent is the sum-total of the object, the subject and the act of judgment, they may be rebutted by stating that judgment may be accompanied by doubt, denial, or affirmation. But, it is impossible that assent may be accompanied by doubt or denial.

Some subtle scholars have urged against it the objection that the Imam (Rāzī) has stated that conception is the act of grasping the form of the thing only, adding that conception is a part of assent; because assent is the sum-total of the three conceptions.[2] But, he has also stated that judgment applies to the object and the subject of the judgment and therefore is part of the assent, which is the object of judgment.

I say: The form embedded in the mind is the object known, rather than knowledge itself and its emergence is equivalent to knowledge. Thus, the parts of assent, identified with knowledge, are not the same as the object known, but rather knowledge itself.

If this is granted, we conclude that the parts of assent, according to this view, consist in the conception of the object and the subject of judgment; I mean, their being grasped by reason, and conceiving the judgment binding them. Thus, the form of the object of judgment and the notion of the subject of judgment, which are known together, are the two conditions of the existence of assent and judgment alike. And it does not follow from their statement that judgment consists of the object and the subject of judgment which necessarily entail that they are the two parts of assent.

Chapter 9
Comment on Assent, According to the Third Interpretation

The author of *al-Matāliʿ* has stated in *Kitāb al-Bayān* (The Book of Clarification) that conception is the act of understanding the thing as such, regardless of whether

1. Suhrawardī.
2. Namely, the object, the subject and the act of judgment.

it is the object or subject of judgment, positively or negatively. What is considered simultaneously with both of them is assent. Thus, if we say, for instance, that man is an animal or is a not a brute, we would understand first the meaning of man, animal, and brute and then that he is or it is not such. We, then, assert that he is an animal or is not a brute. The first act of understanding is actually conception, and together with the judgment that it is such or not such is assent.

I say: The words of this eminent scholar show that assent is different from judgment, because assent is conception attended by judgment. He may also mean that the sum-total of conception and judgment amount to assent, as the Imam (Rāzī) also held.

It is said that certain objections may be raised against this view on the first interpretation.

One is that were assent equivalent to conception attended by judgment, then judgment would be external to it, but it is actually identical with it or is its part.

Secondly, assent is acquired when its conceptions are acquired, due to the fact that, if absolute understanding depends on reflection, then attendant understanding would depend on it, too, since it depends on its parts.

Thirdly, then every assent would amount to three assent, due to the occurrence of three concurrent understandings.

Fourthly, then assent could be achieved by means of discursive speech; whereas it is only achieved by means of proof.

(We may respond) to the first objection by saying that judgment is the precondition of conception turning into assent, rather than assent itself or its parts.

(We may respond) to the second objection by saying that acquired assent is that conception which requires acquisition, so as to posit the relation, or its opposite, among its parts. However, assent, whose conceptions are acquired, will not be needed in that respect, but only with respect to that conception which is its part or its accessory.

(We may respond) to the third objection by saying that assent is that which is accompanied by judgment, originally and without intermediaries, and thus is the sum-total of all three conceptions. As for its being attended by each, that is the result of its being attended by all (three); so that not each one of them would be an assent. For, a precondition of assent is that judgment should accompany it first, and accompany its parts by means of the whole, subsequently.

(We may respond) to the fourth objection by saying that what is grasped by means of discursive speech is conception, in which judgment is not taken into account, rather than that in which judgment is taken into account. Nor does it follow that from grasping the first by means of discursive speech, the second is grasped, too.

The author of *al-Qisṭās*[1] (The Balance) has stated that, whether the relation is grasped by reason or not grasped, not in the sense of conceiving the act of grasping or not grasping it, then that is part of the act of conception, but not in the sense that the positive relation exists or does not exist—for that is part of the process of conception, but rather in the sense that the positive relation exists or does not exist. That act is equivalent to assent, which is identical with judgment.

I say: Having admitted that assent is a matter of reason grasping that the relation exists with respect to the thing itself or does not exist—which is the meaning of consent or belief, then it is indifferent whether he calls it judgment or something else.

Chapter 10
Conclusion

This is the sum of what has been said with respect to conception and assent. The truth is what we have reported on the authority of the Shaykh (Ibn Sīnā). For, whatever is grasped by the mind is either the forms of certain entities, consent, admission or belief, that those forms are in conformity with what the mind grasps. The first is conception, the second is assent. Consent, as perceived by the mind, is conception too, but insofar as it is consent to something else, it is equivalent to assent. No object can be raised against this view.

Moreover, what confirms the statement of all scholars that assent is a form of consent or belief is their statement in the context of acquired assent, that 'this proposition is well-known in point of conception, but unknown in point of assent'.[2] There is doubt that, prior to reasoning,[3] the proposition coexists with its parts; I mean, the subject, the predicate, and the relation between the two; but after the reasoning only consent to the fact that the relation exists remains; that is, that it is in conformity with the thing itself.

1. M. Ibn Ashraf al-Samarqandī (d. *c.* 710/1310).
2. The authors of this statement are not given.
3. Or syllogism, Arabic *qiyās*.

PART III

Philosophical Sufism

Introduction

The period primarily under consideration in this volume, namely from the seventh/thirteenth to the tenth/sixteenth century, is one in which philosophical Sufism was to undergo an unparalleled flowering in Persia as in many other Islamic lands. The seventh/thirteenth century was witness to a remarkable revival of Sufism itself, the appearance of numerous saints and seers and the writing of seminal works which have acted as basic sources and a watershed for all later Sufism. One need only recall the names of such colossal figures as Ibn ʿArabī, Abu'l-Ḥasan al-Shādhilī, Najm al-Dīn Kubrā, Jalāl al-Dīn Rūmī, Ṣadr al-Dīn Qūnawī and many others who together completely transformed the spiritual and intellectual landscape of the Islamic world. From the point of view of spirituality this period is like a return to the beginning of the Islamic revelation and is witness to a providential revivification of Sufism that was to mark in many ways the life of Islamic society over the nearly eight centuries of Islamic history that followed.

From one point of view nearly all of the major spiritual currents of this period starting in the seventh/thirteenth century have a philosophical dimension, including the teachings of Rūmī, although he was openly opposed to the *falāsifah*. In fact because of the philosophical dimension of the *Mathnawī*, it came to be studied in later centuries by some of the philosophers themselves and as famous a philosophical figure as Ḥājjī Mullā Hādī Sabziwārī, with whom we shall deal in the next volume, wrote a commentary on it. What has been mentioned about Rūmī could also be said *mutatis mutandis* of the celestial poetry of Ḥāfiẓ and other masters of Sufi poetry. But for this *Anthology* we have limited our scope somewhat by concentrating for the most part on doctrinal expositions of Sufism, associated with the school of Ibn ʿArabī, which have a distinctly doctrinal and openly philosophical character and which can be properly called philosophical mysticism in its Islamic setting.

The earlier phase of philosophical Sufism, preceding Ibn ʿArabī and associated with the two Ghazzālīs and ʿAyn al-Quḍāt Hamadānī, has been included to clarify the role of these Persian figures in the earlier expression of this philosophy. Of course the line of separation of such writings from the works of a Rūmī still remains thin but for those familiar with Sufism in its relation to philosophy, it is clear why such a distinction can be made. As to why it was made in this volume, it was again because of the question of space. If we had decided to include works of Sufi poets such as ʿAṭṭār, Saʿdī, Rūmī and Ḥāfiẓ with an explanation of their metaphysical, cosmological, philosophical, psychological and ethical significance, we would have needed to add another volume to this already vast *Anthology*. Not wanting to do so caused us to use a narrower gauge and select works with direct philosophical import and of a doctrinal nature while remaining aware that there is an ocean of philosophical significance, if philosophy be understood in its Platonic and Pythagorean sense, in numerous writings of this period in Persia, as elsewhere, including works of Najm al-Dīn Kubrā, his disciple Najm al-Dīn Rāzī, ʿAlāʾ al-Dawlah Simnānī and so many other illustrious masters of Sufism. The study of the phenomenology of colours in the School of Najm al-Dīn Kubrā by Henry Corbin is sufficient proof of the philosophical significance of other schools of Sufism such as the Central Asian which, for reasons already mentioned, have been left out of this volume.

Having limited ourselves to the definition given above and being concerned with Persia and not elsewhere in this *Anthology*, we have begun this part on philosophical Sufism somewhat earlier in the sixth/twelfth century with the two Ghazzālīs and have terminated the volume with the famous 'Seal of Poets', ʿAbd al-Raḥmān Jāmī, who was also a master of gnosis of the School of Ibn ʿArabī. The writings selected for this section demonstrate the remarkable richness of the tradition of philosophical Sufism or *maʿrifah*/*ʿirfān* expressed in a more systematic manner rather than through allusions and indications that were characteristic of masters of old such as Junayd. The subjects treated in this section are centred around pure metaphysics and knowledge of God but they also include the discussion of knowledge itself and its modes, Being and the chain of existents, the structure of the cosmos and the human soul and the correspondence between the microcosm and macrocosm, the gnostic meaning of love and many other issues of the deepest significance for the understanding of who we are, where we are and where we are going.

We have dealt with Abū Ḥāmid Muḥammad Ghazzālī in the last volume, but there we were concerned with his role as an Ashʿarite theologian with a philosophical bent although he was an opponent of *mashshāʾī* philosophy. But Ghazzālī was also a Sufi and in fact one of the major figures in the long tradition of Sufism. His works in this domain include the most influential Islamic work on ethics, namely, *Iḥyāʾ ʿulūm al-dīn* (The Revivification of the Sciences of Religion). They are not, however, limited to ethics. Even in the *Iḥyāʾ* in the book on knowledge, Ghazzālī wrote with remarkable mastery of gnosis and doctrinal Sufism or what we have called philosophical Sufism. Furthermore, in the latter part of his life, he composed a number of more esoteric treatises meant for his advanced students on principial knowledge and wisdom based on the gnostic understanding of the meaning of intellect and revelation. Such works mark the beginning of what we have called philosophical and doctrinal Sufism which was to flower fully with Ibn ʿArabī a century and a half after Ghazzālī.

The younger brother of Abū Ḥāmid, Aḥmad Ghazzālī is one of the poles of Sufism and represents a current of Sufism distinct from that of Ibn ʿArabī and his school. If Aḥmad Ghazzālī is included here, it is because through his masterpiece *Sawāniḥ al-ʿushshāq* (Auspices of Divine Lovers) he forged a genre of Persian prose that was to have a long history in the tradition of Persian Sufism and created a whole school of philosophical Sufism very different from that of Ibn ʿArabī, Qūnawī and their students, but one which also sometimes intermingled with certain currents of the school of Shaykh al-Akbar. Aḥmad Ghazzālī did not speak of intellect but of love but this was love impregnated with gnosis and unitive knowledge. He expressed a whole metaphysics and not only the metaphysics of love and he did so in a distinct language which elevated Persian prose to a new height for the expression of metaphysics and mystical philosophy. He is also significant in that he provided the language with which many later Persian gnostics were to express Ibn ʿArabian metaphysics, bringing these two district traditions together. The *Sawāniḥ* of Aḥmad Ghazzālī has its sequels in the *Lamaʿāt* (Divine Flashes) of Fakhr al-Dīn ʿIrāqī and the *Ashiʿʿāt al-lamaʿāt* (Rays of Divine Flashes), a commentary on ʿIrāqī's work by ʿAbd al-Raḥmān Jāmī. Now, both ʿIrāqī and Jāmī were thoroughly acquainted with the school of Ibn ʿArabī and were among its most important representatives in Persia. Aḥmad Ghazzālī's *Sawāniḥ* is, therefore, not only important in itself as a masterpiece of Sufi prose with profound philosophical significance but also as a seminal text in a tradition of works on Sufi metaphysics written in the language of love used even by those deeply immersed in gnosis in general and the doctrinal Sufism of the Ibn ʿArabian School in particular.

Aḥmad Ghazzālī influenced deeply ʿAyn al-Quḍāt Hamadānī, whose short life curtailed the intellectual and spiritual influence of one of the most remarkable figures of Sufism. Although put to death at an early age, ʿAyn al-Quḍāt nevertheless wrote a few works which mark him as a major figure in philosophical Sufism preceding Ibn ʿArabī. His *Tamhīdāt* (Dispositions) in many ways follows the *Sawāniḥ* and also reveals his familiarity with both Islamic philosophy and *kalām*. His *Zubdat al-ḥaqāʾiq* (The Best of Truths) is perhaps even more philosophical and deals in depth with such issues as the intellect, movement and being. As for his letters, they reveal his intimate familiarity not only with Sufism, but also with the whole of the Islamic intellectual tradition before him. His discussion of Ghazzālī and Ibn Sīnā included in this volume are proofs of this assertion. Altogether, ʿAyn al-Quḍāt is one of the remarkable figures of Islamic thought and belongs not only to any history of Sufism, but also to any serious history of Islamic philosophy. One can speculate what would have happened if his life had not been terminated in the prime of his youth. He would have probably laid an even more extensive foundation for philosophical and doctrinal Sufism before Ibn ʿArabī although his approach differed in many ways from that of the Andalusian master.

Between the establishment of the School of Ibn ʿArabī and the tenth/sixteenth century which marks the end of the historical period under consideration in this volume, a vast corpus of works appeared in Persia in both Persian and Arabic dealing with the teachings of this School. These works range from technical commentaries upon the bible of gnosis, the *Fuṣūṣ al-ḥikam*, by such figures as ʿAbd al-Razzāq Kāshānī, Tāj al-Dīn Khwārazmī, and Bābā Rukn al-Dīn Shīrāzī to poetry of the highest quality of which some, such as the poems of ʿIrāqī, Shabistarī and Jāmī are among the peaks of Persian Sufi poetry. This school also produced many outstanding Persian works of Sufi prose with a highly philosophical content such as *al-Insān al-kāmil* (Universal Man) of ʿAzīz al-Dīn Nasafī and a number of works by Saʿd al-Dīn Ḥamūyah. Even the works of ʿAlāʾ al-Dawlah Simnānī, who opposed certain theses of the Ibn ʿArabian School, were nevertheless deeply affected by this school whose influence is easy to detect everywhere because of both distinct doctrines and a particular technical vocabulary. Altogether the influence of the School of Ibn ʿArabī upon both the intellectual and spiritual life of Persia was immense. Nearly one hundred of the 120 or so commentaries written on the *Fuṣūṣ* were written by those who belonged to the Persian cultural sphere. There is also the influence of authors of Persian origin living in other zones of Islamic culture to consider as far as the school of Ibn ʿArabī is concerned. One need only cite ʿAbd al-Karīm al-Jīlī, who lived for some time in Yemen and who wrote one of the most influential systematizations of the teachings of Ibn ʿArabī, *Kitāb al-Insān al-kāmil* (The Book of the Universal Man) written in Arabic and pre-dating the Persian text of Nasafī.

In any case out of this vast ocean we have chosen five authors, all major figures, who also represent various dimensions and aspects of the doctrines of Ibn ʿArabī as 'systematized' philosophical Sufism. We have started with the *Nuṣūṣ* (The Texts), an important work of Ṣadr al-Dīn Qūnawī (Qunyawī) which is a systematization in summary form of Ibn ʿArabian metaphysics. Ṣadr al-Dīn Qūnawī, the premier student and step-son of Ibn ʿArabī, was more familiar than his master with *falsafah* and presented Ibn ʿArabī's teachings in a more philosophical and systematic fashion than did Ibn ʿArabī himself. It was mostly through his eyes that the eastern lands of Islam viewed Ibn ʿArabī during later centuries.

The introduction of Ibn ʿArabian teachings into Persia did not only influence those Sufi circles which on the formal plane were associated with Sunnism, but also Twelver Shiʿism. Considering the future destiny of Persia with the establishment of Shiʿism as the official state religion by the Safavids in the tenth/sixteenth century, the meeting between Shiʿi theology and gnosis and Ibn ʿArabian gnosis during the period of concern to this volume appears as providential and is in any case of great intellectual import. The central figure in whom this conjunction took place perhaps for the first time was Sayyid Ḥaydar Āmulī, at once a Shiʿi theologian and gnostic and an avid follower of the teachings of Ibn ʿArabī. Besides writing a commentary upon the *Fuṣūṣ*, he wrote important treatises on various metaphysical subjects such as Being. His masterpiece, however, of which selections appear below, is the *Jāmiʿ al-asrār* (The Sum of Secrets) which is a *summa* of Shiʿi gnosis in Ibn ʿArabian dress and at the same time Ibn ʿArabian gnosis in a Shiʿi version. This text remains seminal for the understating of the later integration into Shiʿism of Ibn ʿArabian gnosis and the continuity of the life of the School of Ibn ʿArabī in Shiʿi Persia. Just during the past several decades there have appeared a number of commentaries and glosses on the *Fuṣūṣ* in Persia by such figures as Fāḍil-i Tūnī, Ayatollah Khomeini, Sayyid Jalāl al-Dīn Āshtiyānī, and Ḥasan Ḥasan-Zādah Āmulī bearing witness to the living character of this tradition. At the same time all of those works point to the importance of the synthesis achieved between Ibn ʿArabian and Shiʿi gnosis by Sayyid Ḥaydar Āmulī.

Another figure of major importance in the tradition of Ibn ʿArabian gnosis, who preceded the Safavid period and also influenced many of the significant figures of that period, is Ibn Turkah Iṣfahānī. Well versed in *falsafah,* including the schools of *ishrāq* and *kalām* as well as *ʿirfān*, he sought to synthesize various Islamic intellectual perspectives into a unity as was to be done later by Mullā Ṣadrā. Ibn Turkah was also associated with the school of the Ḥurūfīs, which was an esoteric school especially interested in the symbolism of letters and words in relation to their numerical equivalents as in Kabbalistic *gematria.* Ibn Turkah wrote many notable works in Persian and Arabic, but his most influential opus is *Tamhīd al-qawāʿid* (Establishing the Principles), which remains to this day one of the most popular texts for the teaching of *ʿirfān.* In fact notable studies and commentaries continue to be written on it, such as the recent voluminous study by Jawād Āmulī. The work of Ibn Turkah is a prime example of a systematic and philosophical treatment of doctrinal Sufism and therefore concerns exactly what we have called here 'philosophical Sufism'.

Among the most remarkable literary works of the Persian language is the *Gulshan-i rāz* (The Secret Garden of Divine Mystery) by Maḥmūd Shabistarī. Written during a short period as a response to a set of questions sent to him by a Sufi master from Khurāsān, the poem explains the principles of *ʿirfān* in the most beautiful poetic dress conceivable, in a poetry that is truly inspired. Many later masters have written commentaries upon this sublime peak of Persian Sufi poetry including an Ismaili author. But the most famous and most widely read is by a later Sufi teacher, Shams al-Dīn Lāhījī. His long commentary is among the masterpieces of Persian Sufi prose devoted to *ʿirfān* and is therefore read and studied widely to this day in Persia. Were the whole of this long work be translated into English, it would provide an unparalleled source for the study of philosophical Sufism combined with extensive literary references as well as quotations from the Qurʾān and *ḥadīth.*

ʿAbd al-Raḥmān Jāmī who died at the end of the ninth/fifteenth century within the period under consideration in this volume, was at once a great poet in the line of Niẓāmī, Rūmī and Ḥāfiẓ, and also a master of the School of Ibn ʿArabī. He wrote several commentaries and summaries of Ibn ʿArabī especially the *Fuṣūṣ* and himself authored treatises on gnosis which became very popular, especially the *Lawāʾiḥ* (Gleams), a short treatise in Persian of high literary quality whose reputation spread as far as China and which became one of the first Islamic treatises to be translated into Chinese. Jāmī was equally popular in India and in Persia itself was considered the seal of classical poets. Jāmī was not only a great Sufi poet and biographer of the Sufis, but he was also a major metaphysician. His treatise on Being, translated below, reveals his mastery of this central subject of Islamic philosophy as well as his acquaintance with the views espoused by followers of *falsafah* and *kalām* on this subject.

The selections chosen for this section on philosophical Sufism do not do full justice to the very rich and diverse forms of intellectual activity in this domain. But we hope that those we have presented below will at least convey something of the profundity and diversity of this type of philosophical activity in Persia between the seventh/thirteenth and the tenth/sixteenth centuries. A knowledge of this school along with those concerned in the earlier sections and their interactions with each other, especially in the School of Shiraz, will it make possible to understand the sudden flowering of the School of Isfahan in the tenth/sixteenth century and in fact to comprehend better the historical roots of later intellectual and philosophical currents in Persia down to the present day.

S. H. Nasr

1

Abū Ḥāmid Muḥammad Ghazzālī

In Volume Three of this *Anthology* we included a section on Ghazzālī where part of his theological thought was discussed. In this volume, the focus is upon Ghazzālī's philosophical Sufism.

Abū Ḥāmid Muḥammad Ghazzālī Ṭūsī is perhaps the most influential figure in the annals of Islamic intellectual thought. This great jurist, philosopher, Qur'ānic commentator, theologian, logician and Sufi is considered by some scholars to be the greatest figure in Islam after the period of the 'rightly-guided caliphs'. Ghazzālī was a 'one-man university' given such titles as 'Proof of Islam' (*ḥujjat al-islām*), the 'Renewer of Religion' (*mujaddid*), and the 'Ornament of Faith' (*zayn al-dīn*).

Ghazzālī was born in Ṭūs in Khurāsān in 450/1058. His father, a textile weaver, was not literate but he had Sufi tendencies. On his deathbed, Ghazzālī's father left the guardianship of his children to Imam Aḥmad Rādkānī, a family friend known for his piety and participation in Sufism.

Abū Ḥāmid Ghazzālī studied with a number of masters in Ṭūs, Jurjān, and especially Nayshāpūr, in the province of Khurāsān, which at the time was one of the major centres of learning in the Islamic world. His most famous teacher was Imam al-Ḥaramayn Abu'l Ma'ālī Juwaynī, a well-known Ash'arite theologian. Abū Ḥāmid was in his mid-thirties when he was invited by the famous Seljuq wazir Khwājah Niẓām al-Mulk to come to the Niẓāmiyyah of Baghdad, the most prestigious centre of learning in the Islamic world at that time, to teach Shāfi'ī law.

Abū Ḥāmid, who had already established himself as a major scholar, accepted the invitation and in 484/1091 went to Baghdad where he taught for four years. But having gained much success and fame in the Abbasid capital, he experienced his famous doubt over the epistemological foundations of religious principles. This came about as a result of studying philosophy, which he thought was based on reason, the solid intellectual ground for which he was seeking. His failure to find certainty through the discursive philosophy of the Peripatetics strengthened his sense of doubt, which had subsided temporarily. The result was bewilderment and yet another attempt to find certainty, this time outside the realm of law and philosophy. For Ghazzālī intellectual honesty demanded that he should not live in a state of hypocrisy, so he relinquished his position, bade farewell to his family and began a spiritual journey in search of certitude (*yaqīn*). From 488/1095 to 498/1104 he lived the life of a hermit, wandering throughout the Islamic world. We know that during this period he went to Mecca, Jerusalem, and Damascus, among other places. He embraced Sufism and dedicated himself to spiritual practices, meditation, invocation and prayer.

Sufism became the means through which he was delivered from doubt. Later he composed a book titled *Munqidh min al-ḍalāl* (Deliverance from Error) in which he outlined his intellectual and spiritual autobiography. His Sufi practices had lifted the veil from his heart and through them he achieved certitude with regard to the realities of the spiritual world.

Afterwards he returned to his native land and taught for a year at the Niẓāmiyyah of Nayshāpūr, but he left that city and spent the last six years of his life in his birthplace, Ṭūs. It was there that he trained a number of his highly gifted students and wrote his final works. He died in 505/1111 and is buried in Ṭūs within a few miles of Firdawsī, the legendary poet who has been called 'the Homer of Persia'.

The life of Ghazzālī is essential to the understanding of his intellectual perspective. In the Islamic sciences, especially in the Sunni world but also in Shiʿism, he has influenced three main areas: law, theology, and Sufism. He was a doctor of law who became the foremost authority in Shāfiʿī jurisprudence; a theologian whose views were shaken by Avicennan philosophy, against which he wrote extensively; and a Sufi who regained his certitude through the path of Sufism. It is for this reason that he is read to this day by students of Islamic law, theology, philosophy, and Sufism. As discussed in Volume Three of this *Anthology*, theologically Ghazzālī opened a new chapter in Ashʿarite *kalām,* usually called philosophical theology. Ghazzālī's defence of Sufism, deemed by many Sunni jurists before him to be heretical, went a long way in bringing acceptance to the esoteric interpretation of Islam among formal Sunni circles of learning and brought about a rapprochement between the exoteric and esoteric dimensions of Islam.

As evidenced by his works, Ghazzālī was a great synthesizer. He wrote perhaps the most important work in Islam on ethics, titled the *Iḥyāʾ ʿulūm al-dīn* (The Revivification of the Sciences of Religion), and he himself offered a synopsis of the treatise in exquisite Persian prose entitled *Kīmīyā-yi saʿādat* (The Alchemy of Happiness). In the realm of the esoteric teachings of Sufism he composed *al-Risālat al-laduniyyah* (The Wisdom from God) as well a commentary on the Light verse of the Qurʾān, called *Mishkāt al-anwār* (The Niche of Lights), a work that influenced Suhrawardī. Mullā Ṣadrā wrote an important commentary upon the same verse that was heavily influenced by Ghazzālī.

Ghazzālī's attempt to establish a balance between the exoteric and the esoteric is evidenced in a number of his works. In one of his most famous treatises, *al-Iqtiṣād fi'l-i'tiqād* (The Just Mean in Belief), the very use of the word *iqtiṣād* in the title implies balance between the inward and the outward.

Even though Ghazzālī is known for his opposition to the Peripatetics, his *Maqāṣid al-falāsifah* (The Purposes of the Philosophers) is itself an excellent summary of *mashshā'ī* philosophy. Furthermore, a number of his works such as the *Book of Knowledge* of the *Iḥyā'* contain discussions that pertain to Sufi metaphysics and epistemology and are of considerable philosophical importance, having influenced many later thinkers. Among his other writings, which discuss ethics and eschatology, one can mention his Qur'ānic commentaries. Ghazzālī wrote three works on logic: *Maḥakk al-naẓar* (Touchstone of Speculation), *Mi'yār al-'ilm* (The Criterion of Knowledge), and *al-Qisṭās al-mustaqīm* (The Straight Balance). The latter contains a criticism of the Ismailis, and he also wrote another work, *al-Faḍā'iḥ al-bāṭiniyyah*, specifically devoted to a critique of Ismailism. These three works deal with the principles of logic. Of interest in them is the terminology Ghazzālī uses, which is based not only on Aristotelian logic but also on the Qur'ān. Asserting that the origin of logic is divine revelation, and that even the Greeks learned their logic from what God had revealed, he was the first Muslim philosopher to extract the laws of logic and its vocabulary from the Qur'ān. Such prophets as Abraham and Moses, he argued, had come to know the principles of logic through revelation, and this accounts for the logical nature of the principles of religion itself.

There has been much debate in recent years as to whether Ghazzālī was actually anti-philosophical, or whether he was merely trying to demonstrate the limits of discursive thought. A complete discussion of this question goes beyond the scope of this introduction, but in any event historically the major philosophical contribution of Ghazzālī lies in his criticism of Peripatetic philosophy. Ghazzālī first offered a synopsis of Ibn Sīnā's views in the work titled *Maqāṣid al-falāsifah* (The Purposes of the Philosophers). This work, which is practically an Arabic translation of Ibn Sīnā's Persian work *Dānishnāma-yi 'alā'ī* (The Book of Science Dedicated to 'Alā' al-Dawlah), became, paradoxically, a favourite source for the learning of Islamic philosophy. It was through the Latin translation of this work that Ghazzālī came to be known as Algazel in the West, a philosopher ranking with Ibn Sīnā, not as an adversary to him. Having prepared the ground in this work, Ghazzālī proceeded to write his *magnum opus* in the criticism of *mashshā'ī* philosophy, entitled *Tahāfut al-falāsifah* (The Incoherence of the Philosophers), to which Ibn Rushd was to respond in his *Tahāfut al-tahāfut* (The Incoherence of the Incoherence).

There has been much discussion as to whether or not it was this work of Ghazzālī that played a major role in curtailing the power of rationalism in the Islamic world. However, such a perspective becomes reductive when one takes the complexity of Islamic thought at the time into consideration. The Islamic world at the time of Ghazzālī was too large and too intellectually rich and diverse for a single volume to have such a devastating effect on rationalistic philosophy, not to mention Ibn

Rushd's decisive success in certain circles in destroying the possible side effects of *Tahāfut al-falāsifah*. Ghazzālī's deconstructionism may have been more influential in indirectly preparing the ground for the appearance of schools of thought as such as the School of *ishrāq* associated with Suhrawardī. Among theologians (*mutakallimūn*), Ghazzālī began a distinct theological *genre*, usually called *tahāfut* literature, generally marked by an anti-philosophical spirit.

There were others who were inspired to write works associated with the concept *tahāfut*, among whom are Quṭb al-Dīn Rāwandī (sixth/twelfth century), ʿAlāʾ al-Dīn Ṭūsī (ninth/fifteenth century) and Khwājah-Zādah Muṣliḥ al-Dīn ibn Yūsuf (ninth/fifteenth century). Among other works inspired by Ghazzālī's *Tahāfut*, are *Muṣāraʿāt al-falāsifah* (Wrestlings with the Philosophers) of Muḥammad ʿAbd al-Karīm Shahrastānī and *Taʿjīz al-falāsifah* (The Impotence of the Philosophers) of Imam Fakhr al-Dīn Rāzī, both written during the century following Ghazzālī.

Even though Ghazzālī may not have been the most outstanding philosopher of Persia, he was the most influential thinker in the history of the country's Islamic intellectual thought, if not in the Islamic world. His contributions to the development of Shāfiʿī jurisprudence, Ashʿarite *kalām*, *tafsīr*, ethics and Sufism are extremely significant. Even though his writings curtailed interest in philosophy in Persia for a limited period, his most important role was important since it created a change of direction and paved the intellectual path for a number of other philosophical schools of thought which came to fruition after him.

The first section of this chapter is from Ghazzālī's *Mishkāt al-anwār* (The Niche of Lights) followed by *al-Risālat al-laduniyyah* (The Wisdom from God), and finally *Thalāth rasāʾil fiʾl-maʿrifah* (Three Treatises on Knowledge). Together, they provide a comprehensive picture of Ghazzālī's views on philosophical Sufism. In the *Mishkāt al-anwār* (The Niche of Lights) he uses the Neoplatonic scheme of emanation to explain the hierarchy of lights. Within this context, traditional concepts that are prevalent in gnosis, such as knowledge of God, refinement of character, and the problem of unity and multiplicity are discussed.

The second section, *al-Risālat al-laduniyyah* (The Wisdom from God), begins with a brief discussion concerning different worlds, e.g. manifest, hidden, and angelic, and continues with an examination of the divisions of the soul. This treatise also addresses different types of knowledge such as intellectual, religious, and Sufi, as well as various methodologies for acquiring knowledge.

In the *Thalāth rasāʾil fiʾl-maʿrifah* (Three Treatises on Knowledge), presented in the third section, we find a discussion on the relationship between soul, heart, spirit, and intellect. Throughout this section different types of intellects, their faculties, and their relationship with revelation are discussed.

M. Aminrazavi

THE NICHE OF LIGHTS

Mishkāt al-anwār

Reprinted from Abū Ḥāmid Muḥammad Ghazzālī, *Mishkāt al-anwār*, tr. David Buchman as *The Niche of Lights* (Provo, UT, 1998), pp. 1–24.

In the Name of God, the Compassionate, the Merciful

[Author's Introduction]

My Lord, Thou hast blessed, so increase by Thy bounty!

(1) Praise belongs to God, Effuser of Lights, Opener of Eyes, Unveiler of Mysteries, Lifter of Coverings. And blessings be upon Muḥammad, light of lights, master of the devotees, beloved of the All-Compeller, bringer of good news from the All-Forgiver, warner on behalf of the Overwhelming, tamer of the unbelievers, disgracer of the wicked. And blessings be upon his family and companions—the good, the pure, the chosen.

(2) Now to begin: You asked me, O noble brother—may God lead you to search for the greatest felicity, train you to ascend to the highest summit, anoint your insight with the light of Reality, and cleanse all other than the Real from your innermost centre—that I unfold for you the mysteries of the divine lights, along with an interpretation of the apparent meanings of those recited verses and narrated reports that allude to the divine lights, like His words, 'God is the light of the heavens and the earth' [24:35]; and [that I explain] the sense of His comparing this with the niche, the glass, the lamp, the olive, and the tree; and likewise the saying of the Prophet: 'God has seventy veils of light and darkness; were He to lift them, the august glories of His face would burn up everyone whose eyesight perceived Him.'[1]

(3) With your question you have climbed a difficult slope, one before whose upper regions the eyes of the observers fall back. You have knocked at a locked door that is not to be opened except for the firmly rooted possessors of knowledge. What is more, not every mystery is to be unveiled and divulged, and not every truth is to be presented and disclosed. Indeed, 'the breasts of the free are the graves of the mysteries.'[2] One of the gnostics has said, 'To divulge the mystery of Lordship is unbelief.'[3] Indeed, the Master of the First and the Last [the Prophet] said, 'There is a kind of knowledge like the guise of the hidden; none knows it except the knowers of God.

1. Muslim Nayshābūrī, *Ṣaḥīḥ Muslim*, vol. 1, p. 111.
2. A proverb attributed to Sufis.
3. This saying with different wording is ascribed to Sahl b. ʿAbd Allāh Tustarī.

When they speak of it, none denies it except those who are arrogantly deluded about God.'[1] And when the people of arrogant delusion become many, it becomes necessary to preserve the coverings upon the face of the mysteries. But I see you as one whose breast has been opened up[2] by God through light and whose innermost consciousness has been kept free of the darknesses of delusion. Hence, in this discipline I will not be niggardly toward you in alluding to sparks and flashes or giving symbols of realities and subtleties, for the fear in holding back knowledge from those worthy of it is not less than that in disseminating it to those not worthy of it.

> He who bestows knowledge on the ignorant wastes it,
> And he who withholds it from the worthy has done them wrong.[3]

(4) So be satisfied with abridged allusions and brief hints, since the verification of this discussion would call for laying down principles and explaining details which my present moment does not allow, nor do my concern and thought turn toward such things. The keys of hearts are in God's hand; He opens hearts when He wills, as He wills, and how He wills. The only thing opening up at this moment is three chapters.

The First Chapter
Clarifying that the Real Light is God and that the Name 'Light' for Everything Else is Sheer Metaphor, Without Reality

(1) This is clarified through coming to know the meaning of the word 'light' in the first sense of the term, following the view of the common people; then in the second sense, following the view of the elect; then in the third sense, following the view of the elect of the elect. You will then come to know the degrees and realities of the mentioned lights that are ascribed to the elect of the elect. It will be unveiled to you, when the degrees of these lights become manifest, that God is the highest and furthest light, and, when their realities become unveiled, that He is the real, true light—He alone, without any partner in that.

(2) Regarding the first sense of the word, for the common people, 'light' alludes to manifestation. Manifestation is a relative affair, since without doubt a thing may be manifest to one person while remaining non-manifest to another; hence, a thing is relatively manifest and relatively non-manifest. Its manifestation is unquestionably ascribed to the faculties of perception. The strongest and most obvious of these, in the view of the common people, are the senses, among which is the sense of sight.

---

1. Fakhr al-Dīn Rāzī, *al-Tafsīr al-kabīr*, vol. 2, p. 5.
2. He is alluding to v. 22 of *Sūrat al-zumar*.
3. This is a famous poem by Muḥammad b. Idrīs al-Shāfiʿī.

(3) In relation to visual sensation, things are of three kinds: first are those which cannot be seen in themselves, such as dark bodies. Second are those which can be seen in themselves but by which other things cannot be seen, such as bright bodies or stars and glowing coals that are not aflame. Third are those which can be seen in themselves and by which other things can be seen, such as the sun, the moon, a lamp, and a flaming fire. 'Light' is a name that belongs to this third kind.

(4) Sometimes the name 'light' is applied to that which flows forth from these bodies onto the manifest dimensions of dense bodies. Then it is said, 'The earth is illuminated,' 'The light of the sun has fallen on the earth,' and 'The light of the lamp has fallen on the wall and the clothing.' Sometimes the name 'light' is applied to these same radiant bodies, since they are also lit up in themselves.

(5) In sum, 'light' consists of that which is seen in itself and through which other things are seen, such as the sun. This is its definition and reality in the first sense.

A fine point

(6) The mystery and spirit of light is manifestation to perception. Perception is conditional upon the existence of light and also upon the existence of the seeing eye. For light is that which is manifest and makes manifest; but for the blind, lights are neither manifest nor do they make things manifest. Hence, the seeing spirit and the existence of manifest light are equivalent in that they are inescapable supports for perception. What is more, the seeing spirit is superior to the manifest light, since it perceives and through it perception takes place. As for light, it neither perceives nor does perception take place through it; rather, when it is there, perception takes place. Therefore, it is more appropriate that the name 'light' be given to the seeing light than to the seen light.

(7) People apply the name 'light' to the light of the seeing eye. They say that the light of the bat's eyesight is weak, the light of the nearsighted man's eyesight is weak, the blind man lacks the light of eyesight, and the colour black gathers and strengthens the light of eyesight. [They say that] the divine wisdom singled out the colour black for the eyelids and made them surround the eye in order to gather the brightness of the eye. As for the colour white, it disperses the eye's brightness and weakens its light to such a degree that persistent looking at radiant whiteness, or at the light of the sun, dazzles and effaces the light of the eye, just as the weak becomes effaced next to the strong.[1]

(8) Thus, you have come to know that the seeing spirit is called light, and why it is called light, and why this name is to be preferred. This is the second sense of the term, the sense followed by the elect.

1. Ghazzālī uses the term 'light of the eye' to describe the eye's power to see.

A fine point

(9) Know that eyesight's light is branded with many kinds of imperfection: it sees other things while not seeing itself. It does not see what is far away from it. It does not see what is behind a veil. It sees manifest things, but not non-manifest ones. It sees some of the existent things, but not all of them. It sees the finite things, but not that which is infinite. And it commits many errors in seeing: it sees the large as small, the far as near, the motionless as moving, and the moving as motionless. These seven imperfections are never separate from the outward eye. If there is an eye to be found among the eyes, free of all these imperfections, tell me whether or not it is more worthy of the name 'light'!

(10) Know also that the heart of the human being has an eye whose qualities of perfection are precisely this [lack of the seven imperfections]. It is this eye that is sometimes called the rational faculty, sometimes the spirit, and sometimes the human soul. However, put aside these expressions; because when they become many, they make the person of weak insight imagine many meanings. What we mean by this eye is that meaning whereby the rational person is distinguished from suckling infants, animals, and madmen. Therefore, let us call it the 'rational faculty', in keeping with the technical terms of most people. Therefore, we say:

(11) The rational faculty is more worthy to be named light than the outward eye, because its measure is lifted beyond the seven imperfections, which are: [First,] that the eye cannot see itself, while the rational faculty perceives other things and its own attributes. Since it perceives itself as knowing and powerful, it perceives its knowledge of itself, it perceives its knowledge of its knowledge of itself, and so on *ad infinitum*. This is a characteristic that is inconceivable in that which perceives through bodily instruments. And behind this lies a mystery that would take too long to explain.

(12) The second imperfection is that the eye does not see what is far from it and what is extremely close to it, while near and far are equal for the rational faculty. In a glance it ascends to the highest heavens, and with a look it descends down into the confines of the earths. Indeed, when the realities have been ascertained, it will be unveiled that the rational faculty is so pure that the meanings of near and far that are assigned to bodily things cannot revolve in the regions of its holiness. The rational faculty is a sample of the light of God; and a sample does not lack a certain resemblance, though it never climbs to the peak of equality. Perhaps this discussion has moved you to fathom the mystery of the Prophet's words, 'Verily, God created Adam upon 'His own form.'[1] But to enter into this discussion now is inappropriate.

(13) The third imperfection is that the eye does not perceive what lies behind veils, while the rational faculty moves freely around the throne [of God, around

1. This is a sound *ḥadīth* (see Wensinck, *Concordance*, 2:71).

His] footstool, [around] that which lies behind the veils of the heavens, and around the higher plenum and the most exalted dominion [of God]. In the same way, it moves freely around its own specific world and nearby kingdom—that is, its own body. Or rather, no realities whatsoever are veiled from the rational faculty. As for the veiling undergone by the rational faculty when it does become veiled, this is the rational faculty's veiling itself due to certain attributes that are associated with it. In a similar way, the eye becomes veiled from itself when the eyelids are closed. You will come to know about this in chapter three of this book.

(14) The fourth imperfection is that the eye perceives the manifest dimension and surface of things, not their non-manifest dimension. Or rather, [it perceives] their frames and forms, not their realities. But the rational faculty penetrates non-manifest dimensions and mysteries of things, perceiving their realities and their spirits. It searches out their secondary cause, their deeper cause, their ultimate end, and the wisdom [in their existence]. [It discovers] what a thing was created from, how it was created, why it was created, and how many meanings were involved in its being brought together and compounded. [It finds out] on what level of existence a thing has come to dwell, what its relationship is with its Creator, and what its relationship is with the rest of His creatures. It makes many more discoveries which to explain would take too long, so we will cut this short.

(15) The fifth imperfection is that the eye sees only some existent things, since it fails to see the objects of the rational faculty and [also] many of the objects of sensation. It does not perceive sounds, odours, flavours, heat, cold, and the perceptual faculties—namely, the faculties of hearing, seeing, smelling, and tasting. Nor, moreover, [does it perceive] the inner attributes of the soul, such as joy, happiness, grief, sadness, pain, pleasure, passionate love, appetite, power, desire, knowledge, and so forth. These existent things cannot be enumerated or counted. Hence, the eye has a narrow domain and an abridged channel. It cannot pass beyond the world of colours and shapes, which are the most base of existent things. After all, bodies, at root, are the most base of existent things.

(16) All existent things are the domain of the rational faculty, since it perceives those things which we have listed and an even greater number which we have not. Hence, the rational faculty moves freely over all things and passes an indisputable and truthful judgment upon them. Inward mysteries are apparent to it, and hidden meanings are disclosed to it. How can the outward eye vie with it and seek to keep up with it in worthiness for the name 'light'?

(17) No, the eye is light in relation to other things, but it is darkness in relation to the rational faculty. Or rather, the eye is one of the rational faculty's spies. It has been entrusted with the most base of the rational faculty's storehouses—the storehouse of the world of colours and shapes—in order that the eye may take news of this world up to the rational faculty's presence. Thereupon, the rational faculty decides about these reports in virtue of what its piercing view and penetrating

judgment demand. The five senses are the rational faculty's spies, and besides these it has spies in the non-manifest dimension: imagination, fantasy, reflection, recollection, and memory. Beyond these spies are servants and soldiers who are subject to the rational faculty in its own world. The rational faculty subjugates them and has free disposal over them just as a king subjugates his vassals, or even more intensely. To explain this would take too long, and I have mentioned this in one of the books of the *Iḥyā'*, *'Ajā'ib al-qalb* [The Wonders of the Heart].[1]

(18) The sixth imperfection is that the eye does not see what is infinite, since it sees the attributes of bodies, and bodies can only be conceived of as finite. But the rational faculty perceives objects of knowledge, and it is inconceivable that objects of knowledge be finite. Certainly, when the rational faculty observes differentiated knowledge, then what is actually present with it can only be infinite. But it has the potential to perceive what is infinite. However, to explain this would take too long. If you desire an example of this, take it from things that are obvious: The rational faculty perceives numbers, and numbers are infinite. Or rather, it perceives the multiples of the numbers two, three, and so on, and no one can conceive of an end to these. It perceives the different types of relationships that exist among numbers, and an end to these is also inconceivable. Finally, it perceives its own knowledge of something, the knowledge of its knowledge of that thing, and its knowledge of its knowledge of its knowledge. Hence, in this single instance the rational faculty's potential is infinite.

(19) The seventh imperfection is that the eye sees large things as small. Hence, it sees the sun as having the size of a shield and the stars in the form of dinars scattered upon a blue carpet. The rational faculty, however, perceives the stars and the sun as many times larger than the earth. The eye sees the stars as though they were motionless, [sees] shadows as motionless in front of it, and [sees] a boy as motionless during his growth. But the rational faculty perceives that the boy is in motion through his perpetual growth and increase, that the shadow is perpetually moving, and that the stars move many miles at each instant. Thus the Prophet said to Gabriel, 'Does the sun move?' He answered, 'No—Yes!' The Prophet then said, 'How is that?' Gabriel replied, 'From the time I said "No" to the time I said "Yes", it moved a journey of five hundred years.'[2]

(20) Eyesight commits many sorts of errors, while the rational faculty is free of them. You may say, 'We see the people of the rational faculty committing errors in their consideration'. But you should know that these people have imaginings, fantasies, and beliefs and that they suppose that the properties of these are the same as those of the rational faculty. Hence, the errors are attributable to these things.

1. See Ghazzālī, *Iḥyā'*, 3:7–74. A partial English translation of *A Book Setting Forth the Wonders of the Heart* is provided in Appendix V of Ghazzālī, *Freedom and Fulfilment*, pp. 363–382.

2. This *ḥadīth* is not found in Wensinck's *Concordance* and is not listed in the *ḥadīth* index of Ghazzālī's *Iḥyā'*.

We explained all this in the books *Mi'yār al-'ilm* (The Standard of Knowledge) and *Maḥakk al-naẓar* (The Touchstone of Consideration).

(21) As for the rational faculty, once it disengages itself from the coverings of fantasy and imagination, it is inconceivable that it can commit an error. On the contrary, it will see things as they are in themselves. However, for the rational faculty to achieve disengagement is extremely difficult. Its disengagement from the pull of these things only becomes perfected after death, when the wrappings are lifted, the mysteries are disclosed, and everyone meets face to face the good or evil that he has sent forward.[1] He witnesses a book that 'leaves nothing behind, great or small, but it has numbered it' [Qur'ān 18:49]. At that time it is said, 'Therefore, We have removed from thee thy covering, so thine eyesight today is piercing' [Qur'ān 50:22]. This covering is the covering of imagination, fantasy, and other things. At this time those deluded by their fantasies, their corrupt beliefs, and their unreal imaginations say, 'Our Lord, we have seen and heard; now return us, that we may do good works, for we have sure faith' [Qur'ān 32:12].

(22) You have come to know through this discussion that the eye is more worthy of the name 'light' than the well-known light. Further, you have come to know that the rational faculty is more worthy of the name 'light' than the eye. Indeed, there is such a difference between the two that it is correct to say that the rational faculty is more worthy—or, rather, that the rational faculty in truth deserves the name alone.

A fine point

(23) Know that although rational faculties see, but the objects that are seen are not with them in the same manner. On the contrary, some of [the objects] are with them as if they were actually present, such as self-evident knowledge. For example, the rational faculty knows that a single thing cannot be both eternal and created, or both existent and non-existent; that a single statement cannot be both true and false; that when a judgment about a thing has been made, the same judgment can be made for similar things; and that when a more specific thing exists, the more general must exist. Thus, if blackness exists, colour must exist, and if man exists, animals must exist. But the rational faculty does not see the contrary of this as necessary, since the existence of blackness does not necessarily follow from the existence of colour, nor the existence of man from the existence of animals. There are also other self-evident statements pertaining to necessary, possible, and impossible things.

(24) There are other objects of sight which, when submitted to the rational faculty, do not always join with it. Or rather, it must be shaken, and fire must be kindled within it; it must take notice of them by having them called to its attention.

1. This is in reference to Qur'ān 3:30: 'The day every soul shall find what it has done of good brought forward, and what it has done of evil.'

This is the case with affairs that pertain to rational consideration. However, nothing other than speech of wisdom can bring things to its attention; for when the light of wisdom radiates, the rational faculty comes to see in actuality, after having been able to see only potentially.

(25) The greatest wisdom is the speech of God. Among [those things that] He has spoken is the Qur'ān specifically. For the eye of the rational faculty, the Qur'ān's verses take the place that is occupied by the sun's light for the outward eye, since seeing occurs through it. Hence, it is appropriate for the Qur'ān to be named 'light', just as the light of the sun is named 'light'. The Qur'ān is like the light of the sun, while the rational faculty is like the light of the eye. In this way, we should understand the meaning of His words, 'Therefore, have faith in God and His messenger and in the light which We have sent down' [Qur'ān 64:8] and His Words, 'A proof has now come to you from your Lord. We have sent it down to you as a clear light' [Qur'ān 4:174].

A supplement to this fine point

(26) You have learned from this discussion that the eye is of two types: outward and inward. The outward eye derives from the world of sensation and visibility, while the inward eye derives from another world—namely, the angelic realm.[1] Each of these two eyes has a sun and a light through which sight in these worlds is perfected. One of the two suns is outward, while the other is inward. The outward sun belongs to the visible world; it is the sun perceived by the senses. The other belongs to the world of angelic realm; it is the Qur'ān and the revealed books of God.

(27) When this has been unveiled to you with complete unveiling, then the first door of the world of the angelic realm will have been opened to you. In this world there are wonders in relation to which the visible world will be disdained. If a person does not travel to this world, then, while incapacity makes him sit in the lowlands of the visible world, he remains a beast deprived of the specific characteristic of humanity. Or rather, he is more astray than a beast, since the beast does not have the good fortune [of being able] to ascend with the wings of flight to this world [of the angelic realm]. That is why God says, 'They are like cattle—nay, rather, they are further astray' [Qur'ān 7:179].

(28) Know also that the visible world in relation to the world of the angelic realm is like the shell in relation to the kernel, the form and the body in relation to the spirit, darkness in relation to light, and the low in relation to the high. That is why the world of the angelic realm is called the 'high world', the 'spiritual world', and the 'luminous world', while standing opposite to it is the low, the corporeal, and the dark world. And do not suppose that by the 'high world' we mean the heavens,

1. The term 'angelic realm' (*malakūt*) is derived from the Qur'ān (6:75; 7:185; 23:88; 36–83).

since they are 'high' and 'above' only in respect to the visible and sensible world, and the beasts share in perceiving them.

(29) As for the servant, the door to the world of the angelic realm will not open for him and he will not assume its treats unless, in relation to him, the earth changes to other than the earth, and the heavens [to other than the heavens].[1] Then everything that enters into the senses and imagination will become his earth, and this includes the heavens; and whatever stands beyond the senses will be his heaven. This is the first ascent for every traveller who has begun his journey to the proximity of the Lordly Presence.

(30) The human being has been reduced to the lowest of the low.[2] From there he climbs to the highest world. As for the angels, they are part of the world of the angelic realm; they devote themselves to the Presence of the Holy, and from there they oversee the lowest world. It is for this reason that the Prophet said, 'Verily, God created the creatures in darkness, and then He cast upon them of His light.'[3] He also said, 'God has angels who are better informed of people's deeds than people themselves.'[4]

(31) When the ascent of the prophets reaches its farthest point, when they look down from there upon the low, and when they gaze from top to bottom, they become informed of the hearts of the servants and gaze upon a certain amount of the sciences of the unseen. For when someone is in the world of the angelic realm, he is with God, 'and with Him are the keys to the unseen' [Qur'ān 6:59]. In other words, from God the secondary causes of existent things descend into the visible world, while the visible world is one of the effects of the world of the angelic realm. The visible world comes forth from the world of the angelic realm just as the shadow comes forth from the thing that throws it, the fruit comes forth from the tree, and the effect comes forth from the secondary cause. The keys to knowledge of effects are found only in their secondary causes. Hence, the visible world is a similitude of the world of the angelic realm—as will be mentioned in the clarification of the niche, the lamp, and the tree. This is because the effect cannot fail to parallel its secondary cause or to have some kind of resemblance with it, whether near or far. But this needs deep investigation. He who gains knowledge of the innermost reality of this discussion will easily have unveiled for himself the realities of the similitudes of the Qur'ān.

---

1. An allusion to Qur'ān 14:48: 'Upon the day the earth shall be changed to other than the earth, and the heavens, and they sally forth unto God, the One, the Overwhelming.'

2. This is an allusion to Qur'ān, 95:4–5: 'We indeed created man in the fairest stature, then We reduced him to the lowest of the low.'

3. This is a variation of a sound *ḥadīth* (see Tirmidhī, *Īmān* 18 and Aḥmad 2:176) that reads, 'God created His creatures in darkness, then cast upon them of His light.'

4. This *ḥadīth* is neither mentioned in Wensinck's *Concordance* nor listed in the *ḥadīth* index of Ghazzālī's *Iḥyā'*.

A fine point that goes back to the reality of light

(32) We say: That which sees itself and others is more worthy of the name 'light'. So if it be something that also allows other things to see, while seeing itself and others, then it is [even] more worthy of the name 'light' than that which has no effect at all on others. Or rather, it is more appropriate that it should be called a 'light-giving lamp', since it pours forth its light upon other things. This characteristic is found in the holy prophetic spirit, because it is through this spirit that many types of knowledge are poured forth upon creatures. Hence, we understand the meaning of God's naming Muḥammad a 'light-giving lamp' [Qur'ān 33:46]. All the prophets are lamps, and so are the *'ulamā'*, but the disparity between them is beyond reckoning.

A fine point

(33) If it is proper to call that from which the light of vision comes a 'light-giving lamp', then it is appropriate to allude to that by which the lamp itself is kindled as fire. Hence, these earthly lamps originally become kindled only from the high lights. As for the holy prophetic spirit, 'its oil well-nigh would shine, even if no fire touched it', but it only becomes 'light upon light' [Qur'ān 24:35] when touched by fire.

(34) It is appropriate that the place from which the earthly spirits are kindled be [called] the high divine spirit that has been described by 'Alī and Ibn 'Abbās—God be pleased with them—both of whom said, 'God has an angel who has seventy thousand faces; in every face are seventy thousand tongues, through all of which he glorifies God.' It is this angel who stands before all the other angels, for it is said that the day of resurrection is 'the day when the Spirit and the angels stand in ranks' [Qur'ān 78:38]. When this Spirit is viewed in respect to the fact that the earthly lamps are kindled from it, then the only similitude that this Spirit can have 'fire'. And one can only become intimate with this fire 'on the side of the Mount' [Qur'ān 28:29].[1]

A fine point

(35) If the heavenly lights from which the earthly lights become kindled have a hierarchy such that one light kindles another, then the light nearest to the First Source is more worthy of the name 'light' because it is highest in level. The way to perceive a similitude of this hierarchy in the visible world is to suppose that moonlight enters through a window of a house, falls upon a mirror attached to a wall, is reflected from the mirror to an opposite wall, and turns from that wall to the earth so as to illuminate it. You know that the light on the earth comes from that on the wall, the light on the wall from that on the mirror, the light on the mirror from that in the

1. This is in reference to the Qur'ānic version of Moses' encounter with God through the burning bush on Mount Sinai.

moon, and the light in the moon from the light in the sun, since light shines from the sun onto the moon. These four lights are ranked in levels such that some are higher and more perfect than others. Each one has a 'known station'[1] and a specific degree which it does not overstep.

(36) Know that it has been unveiled to the possessors of insights that the lights of the angelic realm are likewise only to be found in a hierarchy, and that the light 'brought near'[2] is the one that is closest to the Furthest Light. Hence, it is not unlikely that the level of Isrāfīl (Raphael) is above that of Gabriel; that among the angels is one who is the most near because of the nearness of his degree to the Lordly Presence, which is the source of all lights; that among the angels is the furthest; and that between these two are so many degrees that they cannot be counted. The only thing known about these degrees of light is that there are many of them and that their hierarchy derives from their stations and ranks. They are just as they themselves describe, since they have said, 'We are those ranged in ranks; we are they that give glory' [Qur'ān 37:165–66].[3]

A fine point

(37) Since you have recognized that lights have a hierarchy, know also that this hierarchy does not continue on to infinity. Rather, it climbs to the First Source, which is light in itself and by itself and to which no light comes from any other. From this light all the lights shine forth, according to the hierarchy. Consider now if the name 'light' is more appropriate and worthy for that which is illuminated and borrows its light from another, or for that which is luminous in itself and which bestows light upon everything else. It seems to me that the truth of this is not hidden from you. Thus, it is verified that the name 'light' is more appropriate for the Furthest, Highest Light, beyond which there is no light and from which light descends to others.

A reality

(38) Or rather, I say—without trepidation—that the name 'light' for things other than the First Light is a sheer metaphor, since everything other than that Light, when viewed in itself, has no light of its own in respect to its own self. On the contrary, its luminosity is borrowed from another, and this borrowed luminosity is not supported by itself, but rather by another. To attribute a borrowed thing

1. This is an allusion to Qur'ān 37:164–66: 'None of us is there, but has a known station, we are those ranged in ranks, we are they that give glory.'

2. 'Those brought near to God' (*al-muqarrabūn*) is a title that the Qur'ān (4:172) gives to the angels.

3. For a discussion of the role and meaning of angels in Islamic cosmology, see Sachiko Murata, 'Angels', in *Islamic Spirituality Foundations*, ed. S. H. Nasr (New York, 1987).

to the one who has borrowed it is sheer metaphor. Do you think that someone who borrows clothing, a horse, a blanket, and a saddle, and who rides the horse when the lender let him do so and [only] to the extent that he allows is truly rich, or [just] metaphorically so? Is the lender rich or the borrower? It is obvious! In himself the borrower is poor, just as he always was. The only one who is rich is the lender, from whom come loans and gifts and to whom things are returned and taken back.

(39) So the Real Light is He in whose hand is 'the creation and the command' [Qur'ān 7:54] and from whom illumination comes in the first place and by whom it is preserved in the second place. No one is a partner with Him in the reality of this name, nor in being worthy for it, unless He should name him by it and show him kindness by naming him so, like a master who shows kindness to his slave by giving him property and then calling him a master. When the reality is unveiled to the slave, he knows that he himself and his property belong only to his master, who, of course, has no partner whatsoever in any of this.

A reality

(40) Now that you recognize that light goes back to manifestation, to making manifest, and to its various levels, you should know that there is no darkness more intense than the concealment of non-existence. For something dark is called 'dark' because sight cannot reach it, so it does not become an existent thing for the observer, even thought it exists in itself. How can that which does not exist for others or for itself not be worthy of being the utmost degree of darkness while it stands opposite to existence, which is light? After all, something that is not manifest in itself, does not become manifest to others.

(41) Existence can be classified into the existence that a thing possesses in itself and that which it possesses from another. When a thing has existence from another, its existence is borrowed and has no support in itself. When the thing is viewed in itself and with respect to itself, it is pure non-existence. It only exists inasmuch as it is ascribed to another. This is not a true existence, just as you came to know in the example of the borrowing of clothing and wealth. Hence the Real Existent is God, just as the Real Light is He.

The reality of realities

(42) From here the gnostics climb from the lowlands of metaphor to the highlands of reality, and they perfect their ascent. Then they see—witnessing with their own eyes—that there is none in existence save God and that 'Everything is perishing except His face' [Qur'ān 28:88]. [It is] not that each thing is perishing at one time or at other times, but that it is perishing from eternity without beginning to eternity

without end. It can only be so conceived since, when the essence of anything other than He is considered in respect of its own essence, it is sheer non-existence. But when it is viewed in respect of its own essence, it is sheer non-existence. But when it is viewed in respect of the 'face' to which existence flows forth from the First, the Real, then it is seen as existing not in itself but through the face adjacent to its Giver of Existence. Hence, the only existent is the Face of God.

(43) Each thing has two faces: a face toward itself, and a face toward its Lord. Viewed in terms of the face of itself, it is non-existent; but viewed in terms of the face of God, it exists. Hence, nothing exists but God and His face: 'Everything is perishing except His face' from eternity without beginning to eternity without end.

(44) The gnostics do not need the day of resurrection to hear the Fashioner proclaim, 'Whose is the Kingdom today? God's, the One, the Overwhelming' [Qur'ān 40:16]. Rather, this proclamation never leaves their hearing. They do not understand the saying 'God is most great' to mean that He is greater than other things. God forbid! After all, there is nothing in existence along with Him that He could be greater than. Or rather, nothing in existence along with Him that He could be greater than. Or rather, nothing other than He possesses the level of 'with-ness';[1] everything possesses the level of following. Indeed, everything other than God exists only with respect to the face adjacent to Him. The only existent thing is His Face. It is absurd to say that God is greater than His Face. Rather, the meaning of 'God is most great' is to say that God is too great for any relation or comparison. He is too great for anyone other than He—whether it be a prophet or an angel—to perceive the innermost meaning of His magnificence. Rather, none knows God with innermost knowledge save God. Or rather, every object of knowledge enters the power and mastery of the gnostic only after a fashion. Otherwise, that would contradict God's majesty and magnificence. This can be verified, as we mentioned in the book *al-Maqṣad al-asnā fī sharḥ maʿānī asmāʾ Allāh al-ḥusnā* (The Highest Goal in the Meanings of God's most Beautiful Names).[2]

An allusion

(45) The gnostics, after having ascended to the heaven of reality, agree that they see nothing in existence save the One, the Real. Some of them possess this state as a cognitive gnosis. Others, however, attain this through a state of tasting. Plurality is totally banished from them, and they become immersed in sheer singularity. Their rational faculties become so satiated that in this state they are, as it were, stunned.

1. *Maʿiyyah,* literally 'with-ness,' is a term derived from Qur'ān 57:4: 'He is with you wherever you are.'

2. For an English translation of this book, see al-Ghazzālī, *The Ninety-Nine Beautiful Names of God,* tr. D. Burrell and N. Daher (Cambridge, 1993).

No room remains in them for the remembrance of any other than God, nor the remembrance of themselves. Nothing is with them but God. They become intoxicated with such an intoxication that the ruling authority of their rational faculty is overthrown. Hence, one of them says, 'I am the Real!' another, 'Glory be to me, how great is my station!' and still another, 'There is nothing in my robe but God!'[1]

(46) The speech of lovers in the state of intoxication should be concealed and not spread about. When this intoxication subsides, the ruling authority of the rational faculty—which is God's balance in His earth—is given back to them. They come to know that what they experienced was not the reality of unification[2] but that it was similar to unification. It was like the words of the lover during a state of extreme passionate love:

I am He whom I love,
  and He whom I love is I![3]

(47) It is not unlikely that a person could look into a mirror in an unexpected place and not see the mirror at all. He supposes that the form he sees is the mirror's form and that it is united with the mirror. Likewise, he could see the wine in a glass and suppose that the wine is the glass's colour. When the situation becomes familiar to him and his foot becomes firmly established within it, he asks for forgiveness from God and says:

The glass is clear, the wine is clear,
  the two are similar, the affair confused,
As if there is wine and no glass,
  or glass and no wine.[4]

There is a difference between saying 'The wine is the cup' and 'It is *as if* the wine is the cup.'

(48) When this state gets the upper hand, it is called 'extinction' in relation to the one who possesses it. Or, rather, it is called 'extinction from extinction', since the possessor of the state is extinct from himself and from his own extinction. For, he is conscious neither of himself in that state, nor of his own unconsciousness of himself. If he were conscious of his own unconsciousness, then he would [still]

1. These are famous ecstatic utterances, the first by Manṣūr Ḥallāj (d. 922) and the next two by Bāyazīd Basṭāmī (d. 875). See Ernst, *Words of Ecstasy*, p. 3, p. 11, and *passim*.

2. 'Unification' implies the uniting of two things and is normally condemned as a heresy in Islamic thought when it is used to explain the unity of God and His creation. See Chittick and Wilson's discussion of 'unificationism' in Fakhruddīn 'Irāqī, *Divine Flashes*, tr. and ed. William C. Chittick and Peter Lamborn Wilson (New York, 1982), pp. 145–146.

3. The 'lover' here is Ḥallāj, and this is one-half of a line of a famous poem by him.

4. This oft-quoted poem is by Ṣāḥib ibn 'Abbād (d. 995). See 'Iraqī, *Divine Flashes*, 82.

be conscious of himself. In relation to the one immersed in it, this state is called 'unification', according to the language of metaphor, or is called 'declaring God's unity,' according to the language of reality. And behind these realities there are also mysteries, but it would take too long to delve into them.

Conclusion

(49) Perhaps you desire to know the manner in which God's light is ascribed to the heavens and the earth—or, rather, the manner in which God is the light of the heavens and the earth in His own essence. It is not appropriate to keep this knowledge hidden from you, since you already know that God is light, and there is no light other than He, and that He is the totality of lights and the Universal Light. This is because the word 'light' is an expression for that through which and by which things are unveiled; in a higher sense, in a still higher sense, it is that through which, for which, and by which things are unveiled. Then, in the true sense, light is that through which, for which, and by which things are unveiled and beyond which there is no light from which this light could be kindled and take replenishment. Rather, it possesses light in itself, from itself, and for itself, not from another. Moreover, you know that only the First Light has these qualities.

(50) In addition, you know that the heavens and the earth are filled with light from the two levels of light; that is, the light ascribed to eyesight and [the light ascribed] to insight; or, in other words, [light ascribed] to the senses and to the rational faculty. As for the light ascribed to eyesight, that [light] is the stars, the sun, and the moon that we see in the heavens, and their rays that are deployed over everything on the earth that we see. Through [this light] the diverse colours become manifest, especially in springtime. This light is also deployed over every situation of the animals, minerals, and all types of existent things. Were it not for these rays, colours would have no manifestation—or, rather, no existence; and all shapes and measures that become manifest to the senses are perceived by the function of colours. The perception of colours is inconceivable without these rays.

(51) As for the suprasensory, rational lights, the higher world is filled with them; they are the substances of the angels. The lower world is also filled with them; they are animal life and human life. Through the low, human light, the proper order of the world of lowness becomes manifest, just as through the angelic light the proper order of the world of highness becomes manifest. This is what God means by His words: 'He configured you from the earth and has given you to live therein' [Qur'ān 11:61]. He also said, 'He will surely make you vicegerent in the earth' [Qur'ān 24:55]. Again, He said, 'And He has appointed you to be vicegerents in the earth' [Qur'ān 27:62]. And He said, 'I am setting in the earth a vicegerent' [Qur'ān 2:30].

(52) Once you have come to know this, you will know that the world in its entirety is filled with both manifest, visual lights and non-manifest, rational lights.

Then you will know the following: The low lights flow forth from one another just as light flows forth from a lamp. The lamp is the holy prophetic spirit. The holy prophetic spirits are kindled from the high spirits, just as a lamp is kindled from a light. Some of the high things kindle each other, and their hierarchy is a hierarchy of stations. Then all of them climb to the Light of lights, their Origin, their First Source. This is God alone, who has no partner. All other lights are borrowed. The only true light is His. Everything is His light—or, rather, He is everything. Or, rather, nothing possesses 'ipseity' other than He, except in a metaphorical sense. Therefore, there is no light except His light.

(53) Other lights are lights derived from the light that is adjacent to Him, not from His own Essence. Thus, the face of every possessor of a face is toward Him and turned in His direction. 'Whithersoever you turn, there is the face of God' [Qur'ān 2:115]. Hence, there is no god but He. For, 'god' is an expression for that toward which a face turns through worship and becoming godlike. Here I mean the faces of the hearts, since they are lights. Indeed, just as there is no god but He, so also there is no he but He, because 'he' is an expression for whatever may be pointed to, and there is no pointing to anything but Him. Or, rather, whenever you point to something, in reality you are pointing to Him. If you do not know this, that is because you are heedless of 'the Reality of realities' that we mentioned.

(54) One does not point to the light of the sun but, rather, to the sun. In the obvious sense of this example, everything in existence is related to God just as light is related to the sun. Therefore, 'There is no god but God' is the declaration of God's unity of the common people, while 'There is no he but He' is the declaration of God's unity of the elect, since this declaration of God's unity is more complete, more specific, more comprehensive, more worthy, and more precise. It is more able to make its possessor enter into sheer singularity and utter oneness.

(55) The final end of the creatures' ascent is the kingdom of singularity. Beyond it, there is no place to climb. Climbing is inconceivable without plurality, since climbing is a sort of relation that demands something away from which one climbs and something toward which one climbs. But when plurality disappears, oneness is actualized, relationships are nullified, and allusions are swept away. There remains neither high or low, nor descending and ascending. Climbing is impossible, so ascent is impossible. Hence, there is no highness beyond the highest, no plurality alongside oneness, and no ascent when plurality is negated. If there is a change of state, it is through descent to the heaven of this world[1]—that is, through viewing the low from the high, since the highest, though it has a lower, does not have a higher.

1. The descent to the heaven of this world is mentioned in a well-known *ḥadīth*, the text of which is as follows: Our Lord descends to the heaven of this world every night and says, 'Is there any supplicant? Is there anyone asking for forgiveness?' This *ḥadīth* is provided with minor variations in Muslim, *Muṣāriʿīn*, 17, and Aḥmad 2:433 and 3:34.

(56) This is the ultimate of goals and the final end of everything searched for. He who knows it knows it, and he who denies it is ignorant of it. It belongs to the 'kind of knowledge which is like the guise of the hidden; none knows it except those who know God. When they speak of it, none denies it except those who are arrogantly deluded about God.'[1]

(57) It is not unlikely that the *'ulamā'* will say that 'the descent to the heaven of this world' is the descent of an angel, for the *'ulamā'* come up with even more unlikely ideas. For example, one of them says that the person who is drowned in singularity also has a descent to the heaven of this world—namely, his descent to employ his senses or move his limbs. This is alluded to in God's words: 'I become the hearing by which he hears, the seeing by which he sees, and the tongue by which he speaks.'[2] When He is his hearing, his sight, and his tongue, then He alone hears, sees, and speaks. This is alluded to in His words: 'I was sick and you did not visit me,'[3] and so on to the end of the narration. Hence, the movements of this person who has realized God's unity come from the heaven of this world. His sensations, like hearing and seeing, come from a higher heaven, and his rational faculty is above that. He climbs from the heaven of the rational faculty to the utmost degree of the ascent of the creatures. The kingdom of singularity completes the seven levels. Then he sits upon the throne of oneness and from it governs the affair of the levels of his heavens.[4]

(58) It may happen that an observer considering this person will apply the words, 'God created Adam upon the form of the All-Merciful', unless he considers carefully and comes to know that this saying has an interpretation, like the words 'I am the Real!' and 'Glory be to Me!' Or rather, it is like God's words, to Moses, 'I was sick and you did not visit Me', and His words, 'I am his hearing, his seeing, and

---

1. Ghazzālī has already cited this as a *ḥadīth*.

2. This is a part of a sound *ḥadīth* (see Bukhārī, *Riqāq*, 38). A variation of this *ḥadīth* reads as follows: 'I love nothing that draws My servant near to Me more than [I love] what I have made obligatory for him. My servant never ceases drawing near to Me through supererogatory works until I love him. Then when I love him, I am his hearing through which he hears, his sight through which he sees, his hand through which he grasps, and his foot through which he walks.' This translation is from Murata, *Tao of Islam*, 253.

3. The first part of the complete *ḥadīth* found in Muslim, *Birr*, 43. is as follows: On the Day of Resurrection God will say, 'O son of Adam, I was ill and you did not visit Me'. He will reply, 'How should I visit Thee, when Thou art Lord of the worlds?' He will reply, 'Did you not know that my servant so-and-so was ill, but you did not visit him? Did you not know that had you visited him, you would have found Me with him?' This translation is from William C. Chittick, *The Sufi Path of Knowledge: Ibn al-'Arabī's Metaphysics of Imagination* (Albany, NY, 1989), 392 n. 33.

4. Allusion to four Qur'ānic verses: 'Surely your Lord is God, who created the heavens and the earth in six days, and then sat Himself upon the Throne, governing the affair' (10:3); 'He governs the affair from heaven and earth' (32:5); and also 10:31 and 13:2. Thus, according to Ghazzālī's interpretation (*ta'wīl*) of this verse, the perfected seeker governs the levels of his own inner world just as God governs the heavens and the earth—or, rather, his governing himself in this state of singularity is identical with God governing himself.

his tongue.' I think I will hold back from clarification, because I see that you are incapable of bearing anything greater than this.

Some encouragement

(59) Perhaps your aspiration does not rise high enough for these words, but rather falls short below their summit. So take for yourself words that are nearer to your understanding and more suitable to your weakness.

(60) Know that you can come to know the meaning of the fact that God is the light of the heavens and the earth in relation to manifest, visual light. For example, when you see the lights and greenness of springtime in the brightness of day, you do not doubt that you see colours. But you may suppose that you do not see anything along with colours, since you say, 'I see nothing with greenness other than greenness.' A group of people have insisted on this, since they suppose that light has no meaning and that there is nothing along with colours except colours. Hence, they deny the existence of light, even though it is the most manifest of things. How could it not be? For through it things become manifest. It is light which is seen in itself and through which other things are seen, as we said earlier.

(61) When the sun sets, when lamps are put away, and when shadows fall, the deniers perceive a self-evident distinction between the locus of the shadow and the place of brightness. Hence, they confess that light is a meaning beyond colours that is perceived along with colours. It is as if the intensity of light's disclosure prevents it from being perceived and the intensity of its manifestation keeps it hidden. Manifestation may be the cause of concealedness. When a thing passes its own limit, it reverts to its opposite.

(62) Now that you have recognized this, you should know that the masters of insight never see a thing without seeing God along with it. One of them might add to this and say, 'I never see a thing without seeing God before it.'[1] This is because one of them may see things through God, while another may see the things and see Him through the things. Allusion to the first is made by His words, 'Suffices it not as to thy Lord, that He is witness over everything?' [Qur'ān 41:53]. Allusion to the second is made with His words, 'We will show them Our signs in the horizons' [Qur'ān 41:53]. The first is a possessor of witnessing, while the second is a possessor of conclusions that he draws about Him. The first is the degree of the righteous,[2] while the second is the degree of those firmly rooted in knowledge. There is nothing after these two except the degree of those who are heedless and veiled.

---

1. According to Ibn 'Arabī (d. 1240), this saying belongs to the Prophet's relative through marriage and first political and religious successor—the first of the four 'rightly guided' caliphs—Abū Bakr (d. 634). See Chittick, *Sufi Path of Knowledge*, 102, 178, 215, 348.

2. Because of Abū Bakr's piety during the Prophet's lifetime, he acquired the surname al-Ṣiddīq, 'the Righteous.'

(63) Now that you have recognized this, you should know that just as everything becomes manifest to eyesight through outward light, so also everything becomes manifest to inward insight through God. God is with everything and not separate from it. Then He makes everything manifest. In the same way, light is with all things, and through it they become manifest. But here a difference remains: It is conceivable that outward light may disappear through the setting of the sun. It becomes veiled so that shadow appears. As for the divine light through which everything becomes manifest, its disappearance is inconceivable. Or, rather, it is impossible for it to change, so it remains perpetually with the things.

(64) Thus, the way of drawing conclusions about God through separation is cut off. If we suppose that God's light were to disappear, then the heavens and the earth would be destroyed. Because of this separation, something would be perceived that would force one to recognize that it makes things manifest. But since all things are exactly the same in testifying to the oneness of their Creator, differences disappear and the way becomes hidden.

(65) The obvious way to reach knowledge of things is through opposites. But when something neither changes nor has opposites, all states are alike in giving witness to it. Hence, it is not unreasonable that God's light be hidden, that its concealedness derive from the intensity of its disclosure, and his hiddenness stems from the radiance of its brightness. So glory be to Him who is hidden from creatures through the intensity of His manifestation and veiled from them because of the radiance of His Light!

(66) It may be that some people will fall short of understanding the innermost meaning of these words. Hence, they will understand our words, 'God is with everything, just as light is with the things', to mean that He is in each place—high exalted and holy is He from being ascribed to place! Probably the best way not to stir up such imaginings is to say that He is before everything, that He is above everything, and that He makes everything manifest. This is what we mean by our saying that 'He is with everything'. Moreover, it is not hidden from you that the manifester is above and before everything made manifest, although it is with everything in a certain respect. However, [the manifester] is with [everything] in one respect and before it in another respect, so you should not suppose that this is a contradiction. Take an example from sensory objects, which lie at your level of knowledge: Consider how the movement of a hand is both with the movement of its shadow and before it. He whose breast cannot embrace knowledge of this should abandon this type of science. There are men for every science, and 'the way is eased for each person to that for which he was created'.[1]

1. This is a sound *ḥadīth*. See Chittick, *Faith and Practice,* 213, which lists Bukhārī, *Tafsīr*, *Sūrah*, 92, 93; Bukhārī, *Adab*, 120; Bukhārī, *Qadar*, 4; Bukhārī, *Tawḥīd*, 54; and Muslim, *Qadar*, 6–8.

THE WISDOM FROM GOD

al-Risālat al-laduniyyah

Reprinted from Abū Ḥāmid Muḥammad Ghazzālī, 'al-Risālat al-laduniyyah', tr. Margaret Smith in *JRAS* 2 (1938), pp. 188–200; and 3 (1938), pp. 353–360.

Treatise concerning Knowledge from on High

Praise be to God, Who hath adorned the hearts of His chosen servants with the light of Saintship, and hath nurtured their spirits with all loving kindness and, with the key of knowledge, hath opened the door of Unification (*tawḥīd*), to the gnostics among the wise.[1] I pray for the blessing of God upon our Lord Muḥammad, the lord of the Muslims, who summoned men to the true faith and carried out its obligations, who guided the community in the right road; and upon his family, who dwell in the ancestry of protection.

Know that one of my friends related of a certain theologian that he denied the esoteric knowledge, upon which the elect of the Sufis rely, and to which the followers of the Mystic Way trace back their origin. For they declare that knowledge from on high is greater and more reliable than the types of knowledge acquired and obtained by study. My friend declared that the aforesaid person asserted: 'I am unable to conceive of the knowledge of the Sufis and I do not suppose that anyone in the world speaks of true knowledge as the result of reflection and deliberation apart from study and acquisition.' Then I said: 'He does not seem to have investigated the different methods of attainment, nor to know the power of the human soul and its qualities, and its capacity for receiving impressions of the Invisible and for attaining to knowledge of the Divine World.'[2]

---

1. Cf. al-Hujwīrī, 'Real unification consists in asserting the unity of a thing and in having a perfect knowledge of its unity … I declare that Unification is a mystery revealed by God to His servants and that it cannot be expressed in language at all.' *Kashf al-maḥjūb* (tr. R. A. Nicholson), pp. 278 ff. Cf. also *Rawḍat al-ṭālibīn*, p. 153.

2. Cf. *Iḥyā'*, iv, p. 216 (ll. 7 ff.): 'Know that there are worlds through which you must pass, the material, visible world is the first … and this stage may be passed without difficulty. The second is the Divine World and it is beyond me, and when you have passed beyond me, you have arrived at its stations. It contains extensive deserts and wide expanses and lofty mountains and fathomless seas, and I know not how you will be saved therein. The third is the Celestial World … which is like a ship moving between the land and the water and it has not the constant motion of the water, nor has it the complete immobility of the land and its stability, and everyone who walks on the land walks in the world of *mulk* and *shahādah*, and when he is strong enough to sail on a ship he is like one who walks in the world of *jabarūt* and when he reaches the stage of being able to walk on the water without a ship, he walks in the world of *malakūt*, without sinking. When you are not able to walk upon the water, then depart, for you have passed beyond the land, and have left the ship behind, and there remains before you only the limpid water.' Cf. also *Mishkāt al-anwār*, pp.

Then my friend said: 'Yes, that man declares that knowledge consists only of jurisprudence, that interpretation of the Qur'ān and scholastic theology are sufficient, and that there is no knowledge beyond them; and these sciences are acquired only by submitting to instruction and by thorough knowledge.' I replied: 'Yes, and how is the science of interpretation to be learned? For the Qur'ān is an ocean comprehending all things, and not all that it signifies, nor the full truth of its interpretation, are to be found in those literary works which are in general circulation, but the interpretation thereof goes beyond what that claimant knows.' My friend said: 'That man knows only those commentaries which are well known and spoken about, attributed to Qushayrī and Tha'labī and Māwardī and others.' I said: 'He has strayed a long way from the straight road (which leads to) the truth, for Sulamī, in the *Tafsīr*,[1] made a collection of the statements of those who attained to something like certainty (i.e. the Sufis), and these statements are not mentioned in other commentaries. That man who reckons that knowledge consists only of jurisprudence, scholastic theology, and a commentary which is well known, apparently does not know the different branches of knowledge, their distinctions and classes, their true significance, their outward expression, or their inward meaning. But it is not unusual for one ignorant of a thing to deny that thing, and that claimant has not tasted the draught of spirituality nor attained to knowledge from on high, so how can he acknowledge that? I am not satisfied with his acknowledgment of it, in pretending to know or guessing at what, in fact, he did not know.'

Then that friend said: 'I wish that you would mention some of the classes of the sciences, prove that the knowledge which you claim (i.e. inspired knowledge) is valid, attribute it to yourself and maintain your assertion of it.'

I replied: 'This which you seek to have explained is exceedingly difficult, but I will show its antecedents, as far as I can, and in accordance with the time at my disposal and what occurs to my mind. I do not want to prolong the discussion, for the best discourse is that which is brief and shows the way.' I have asked God for His favour and help, and I have mentioned the request of my good friend, in regard to this officious proceeding on my part.

Chapter I

Know that knowledge (*'ilm*) is the representation of the reality of things in the rational tranquillized soul (*al-nafs al-muṭma'innah*),[2] along with their modes and

122 ff., and A. J. Wensinck, *The Relation between al-Ghazālī's Cosmology and his Mysticism*.

1. *Kitāb Ḥaqā'iq al-tafsīr.*

2. Cf. 'Abd al-Razzāq's definition of (*al-nafs al-muṭma'innah*) 'that of which the spiritual illumination has been perfected so that it has been stripped of its vices and has replaced them by virtues and it has turned its face towards the heart (i.e. the highest self), following it in ascending towards the Invisible World, having been cleansed from all defilement, being assiduous in devotion, dwelling in the highest of abodes, so that its Lord may address it face to face.' For (*al-nafs*

their quantities and their substances and their essences, if they are simple (i.e. uncompound). And the knower is the one who comprehends and perceives and apprehends, and that which is known is the essence (*dhāt*) of the thing, the knowledge of which is engraved upon the soul. The nobility of the knowledge is in accordance with the nobility of the thing known, and the rank of the knower corresponds to the rank of the knowledge. There is no doubt that the most excellent of things known, and the most glorious, and the highest of them, and the most honoured, is God the Maker, the Creator, the Truth, the One. For knowledge of Him, which is knowledge of the Unity, is the most excellent branch of knowledge, the most glorious and the most perfect, and this knowledge is necessary; it must be acquired by all rational beings, as the Lawgiver (upon whom be blessing) said: 'The search for knowledge is an obligation upon every Muslim.' He also said (may God bless him): 'Seek knowledge even in China', and he who possesses this knowledge is the most honourable of those who know. For this reason God distinguished such men by giving them the highest rank, saying: 'God bears witness that there is no God but He and (so also do) the angels and men endued with knowledge.'[1] Those who have absolute knowledge of the Unity are the prophets, and after them the theologians, who are the heirs of the prophets.

But this knowledge, though it is excellent in essence and perfect in itself, does not do away with the other types of knowledge; indeed, it is not attained except by means of many antecedents, and those antecedents cannot be ordered aright except through various sciences, such as the science of the heavenly bodies and the spheres, and the science dealing with the things that God has made. The other branches of knowledge are derived from the knowledge of Unity and we shall classify them in their place.

Know that knowledge is excellent in itself, without consideration of the thing known, so that even the knowledge of sorcery is excellent in itself, even though it be futile. That is because knowledge is the contrary of ignorance, and ignorance is one of the accompaniments of darkness, and darkness belongs to the sphere of immobility, and immobility is near to non-existence, and what is false and misleading is to be classed with this. For the sphere of knowledge is the sphere of what is existent, and existence is better than non-existence, for guidance and truth and activity and light are all linked up with existence. Since existence is better than non-existence, then knowledge is more excellent than ignorance, for ignorance is like blindness and darkness, and knowledge is like sight and light and 'the blind

---

al-nāṭiqah) cf. Plotinus, *Ennead*, v, 9, 7, and *Theology of Aristotle*, 6, 120 ff., and also Ghazzālī, *al-Maʿārif al-ʿaqliyyah*, fols. 8*a*, 11*b*, and *Rasāʾil Ikhwān al-Ṣafāʾ*, 'Rational souls rejoice in knowledge and understanding. When the rational soul has awakened from the sleep of neglect, the eye of insight is opened for her and she beholds her teacher and recognizes her Maker and therewith yearns for her Creator.' iii, 270, 271.

1. Qur'ān 3:18.

man shall not be held equal to him who sees, nor darkness to light.'[1] God made this manifest when He said: 'Shall those who have knowledge and those who have it not, be held equal?'[2] Then, since knowledge is better than ignorance and ignorance is one of the accompaniments of the body and knowledge is one of the attributes of the soul, the soul is more honourable than the body.

Now knowledge has many divisions, which we shall enumerate in another chapter; and for the one who knows there are numerous paths in the search for knowledge, which we shall mention elsewhere. And now, after you have realized the excellence of knowledge, all that you need to do is to attain to understanding of the soul, which is the tablet of knowledge, and its abode and place of habitation. That is because the body is not an abode for knowledge, for bodies are limited and will not contain the many branches of knowledge; indeed, they can receive only impressions and inscriptions, but the soul is able to receive all types of knowledge without prevention or hindrance or fatigue or cessation, and we will explain briefly what the soul is.

Chapter II
Concerning the Soul and the Human Spirit

Know that God Most High created man from two different things, one of them the body, which is dark, gross, subject to generation and corruption, composite, made up of parts, earthly, whose nature cannot be complete except by means of something else,[3] and that other is the soul, which is substantial, simple,[4] enlightened, comprehending, acting, moving, giving completion to instruments and bodies.[5] For God Most High compounded the flesh of elements and nutriment, grew it with particles of blood, laid down a rule for it, arranged its affairs, and appointed its limits. Then the substance of the soul was made manifest by His command, the One, the Perfect, the Most Excellent, the Benefactor. Now by the 'soul,' I do not mean the faculty which seeks nutrition, nor the faculty which motivates lust and anger, nor the faculty which resides in the heart, producing life, which issues sensation and movement from the heart to all the organs, for this faculty is called the animal spirit, and feeling and movement and lust and anger are among its 'troops.' And that faculty which seeks for nutrition, which resides in the liver, for the disposal of food, is called the natural spirit, and the digestion and secretion are among its attributes; and the power of imagination and of procreation and growing and the rest of the natural powers are all of them servants to the flesh, and the flesh

1. Qur'ān 35:19–20.
2. Qur'ān 39:29.
3. Cf. Plotinus, *Ennead,* iv, 7, 1; *Theology of Aristotle,* 160 ff.
4. Cf. *Ennead,* iv, 8, 8, and *Theology of Aristotle,* 41.
5. Ibid, 42.

is the servant of the animal spirit, because it receives its powers from it and acts in accordance with its instigation.

But by the soul I mean only that perfect personal substance which is concerned solely with remembrance and recollection and reflection and discernment and deliberation.[1] It is receptive to all types of knowledge and does not weary of perceiving forms which are abstracted from matter. This substance is the ruler of the spirits (i.e. those aforementioned) and the controller of the faculties, and all serve it and comply with its command. Now the rational soul, by which I mean this substance, has a special name with every group of people: the philosophers call this substance 'the rational soul', the Qur'ān calls it 'the soul at rest' and the 'spirit which is of the command (*amr*) of God',[2] and the Sufis call it the 'spirit' (*rūḥ*) and sometimes the 'heart' (*qalb*) but though the names differ the meaning is one; it does not differ. In our opinion the 'heart' and the 'spirit' and the 'soul at rest' are all names for the rational soul, and the rational soul is the living substance which lives and acts and comprehends, and when we use the term 'spirit' unconditionally, or 'heart', we mean by it only this substance.[3] But the Sufis call the animal spirit 'soul' (i.e. the lower self, *nafs*) and it is stated in the prophetic tradition that: 'The greatest of your enemies is your *nafs*.' And the Lawgiver also used the term *nafs* absolutely and, indeed, strengthened it by putting it in the construct case, for he said: 'Your *nafs* which is between your two sides',[4] and he indicated by this term only the force of sensual desire and passion, for they are both aroused by the heart which rests between the two sides.

So when you have realized the distinction between the (different) names, then know that those who have investigated the matter express this delicate substance in different ways, and they hold different views concerning it. For the scholastic theologians reckon the soul to be a body and state that it is a subtle body, corresponding to this gross body. They hold that there is no difference between the spirit and the flesh except in respect of subtlety and grossness. Then certain of them reckon the spirit as an accident, and some of the physicians incline towards this view. Certain of them consider the blood to be a spirit—and all of them were content to limit their consideration to what they were able to conceive of, and they did not go as far as the third division.

Know that the three divisions are the body, the accident, and the simple substance. For the animal spirit is a subtle body, like a lamp, which has been kindled and placed in the glass-vessel of the heart, by which I mean (here) that cone-shaped object which is located inside the chest, and the life is the light of the lamp and the blood is its oil; feeling and movement are its flames, and lust is its heat, and passion

1. Cf. *Theol. of Aris.*, 43.
2. Qur'ān 17:85.
3. Cf. *Iḥyā'*, iv, 23. 'By the heart I mean the inner self which belongs to the world of *amr*.'
4. Fakhr al-Dīn Rāzī; *al-Tafsīr al-kabīr*, vol. 28, p. 83.

is its smoke; and the force seeking sustenance (i.e. appetite), which is situated in the liver, is its servant and guard and protector, and this spirit is found in all the animals, for it is shared by the cattle and other beasts and man, and it is a body and the impressions it receives are accidents. Now this spirit does not follow the right road to knowledge and does not know the path which the creature should take, nor what is due to the Creator. It is only a servant, a captive which dies with the death of the body. If the oil[1] is in excess, that lamp is extinguished by excess of heat, and if it is lacking (the lamp) is extinguished by excessive cold, and its extinction is the cause of the death of the body. Neither the Word of the Creator, praise be to Him, nor the duties imposed by the legislator (i.e. the Prophet) are (meant) for this spirit, for the brutes and the rest of the animal creation are without duties imposed, and to them the ordinances of the Law are not addressed. Man is laid under obligations and addressed because of another meaning (i.e. attached to the term 'spirit') found only in himself, which is additional and applicable especially to him. And that meaning signifies the rational soul and the spirit at rest, and this spirit is not a body nor an accident, for it (proceeded) at the command of God Most High, as He said: 'Say, the spirit (proceedeth) at the command of my Lord,'[2] and He said also: 'O soul at rest, return unto thy Lord, well-pleased, well-pleasing.'[3]

Now the command[4] of the Creator Most High is not a body nor an accident, but a Divine faculty like the First Intellect [5] and the Tablet and the Pen,[6] and they are simple substances, free from materiality; indeed, they are incorporeal splendours, intellectual, without sensibility. Now the spirit and the heart, in our use of the term, is derived from those substances,[7] and is not susceptible of corruption and does not disappear nor pass into nothingness nor die, but is separated from the body and expects to return to it on the Day of Resurrection. That was declared to be the case in the *Shāriʿ* and was authenticated in those sciences which are established by categorical proofs. So it is plainly proved that the rational spirit is not a body or an accident; indeed, it is an abiding, eternal substance, and [it is] incorruptible. So we have no need to recapitulate the proofs and add to the evidence, because they are well established and have been recorded. Let him who wishes to verify them consult the books suitable for that purpose.

---

1. The Cairo text reads 'blood'.
2. Qur'ān 17:85.
3. Qur'ān 89:27–30.
4. On the world of *amr* cf. *Iḥyā'*, iv, 23.
5. Cf. *Theol. of Aristotle*, 39, and Plotinus, 'The Intellectual-Principle … the offspring of God … For here is contained all that is immortal; nothing here but is Divine Mind; all is God.' *Ennead*, v, 1, 4, ff.
6. 'The Pen is that which God created to enable the hearts of men to be inscribed with knowledge.' *Iḥyā'*, iii, 14. Identified with the First Intellect in *al-Maʿārifah al-ʿaqliyyah*, fol. 21*b*.
7. Cf. Plotinus, 'Sprung from the Intellectual-Principle, Soul is intellective … its substantial existence comes from the Intellectual-Principle,' *Ennead*, v, 1, 3.

But our method is not to bring forward proofs, but to rely upon unveiling, and we trust in witnessing through faith and the fact that God related the spirit sometimes to Himself, sometimes to His command, and sometimes to His glory, for He said: 'I breathed into him of My Spirit,'[1] and He said also: 'And We breathed into him of Our Spirit.' Now God Most High is too glorious to attach unto Himself a body or an accident, because of their lowliness, their liability to change, and their swift dissolution and corruption. But the Lawgiver (God's blessing upon him) said: 'The spirits are like troops assembled,'[2] and he said: 'The spirits of the martyrs are in the crops of green birds.'[3] Now the accident does not subsist after the substance has passed away, because it does not subsist in itself. For the body is subject to dissolution as it was subject to being compounded of matter and form, which is set forth in the books. And from these verses and traditions and intellectual proofs, we have come to know that the spirit is a simple substance, and perfect, having life in itself. From it is derived what makes the body[4] sound or what corrupts it, for the natural and the animal spirits and all the bodily powers are all among its troops. We have learned, too, that this substance receives the images of things known[5] and (understands) the real meaning of existent things, without being concerned with their actual selves or corporeal forms. For the rational soul is capable of knowing the real meaning of humanity without seeing a human being, as it is acquainted with the angels and demons, but has no need to see their forms, since the senses of most human beings do not attain to them.

Moreover, certain of the Sufis maintain that the heart possesses an organ of sight like the body, and outward things are seen with the outward eye, and inward realities with the eye of the mind. For the Apostle of God (may God bless him) said: 'Every servant has two eyes in his heart,' and they are eyes by which he perceives the Invisible, and when God wishes well to one of His servants He opens the eyes of his heart so that he may see what is hidden from his outward sight.[6] Now this spirit does not die with the death of the body, for God Most Holy summons it to His door and says: 'Return unto thy Lord': it is only separated from, and discards, the body. The bodily and the natural powers cease to function and their activity is halted, and that halt is called Death.

---

1. Qur'ān 15:29, and 38:72.
2. Bukhārī; *al-Ṣaḥīḥ*, vol. 4, p. 104
3. Ibn Kathīr; *Tafsīr*, vol. 1, p. 203.
4. For 'body' the Cairo edition reads 'religion'.
5. Cf. Plotinus, v, 3, 3.
6. Cf. *Iḥyā'*, iii, 15. 'The inward eye is the eye of the soul, which is subtle, perceptive, and it is like the rider and the body like the horse, and the blindness of the rider is more harmful to him than the blindness of the horse.' Cf. also iv, 430. 'The Invisible Divine World is not seen with the outward eye, but only with another eye, which was created in the heart of every man, but man has veiled it by his lusts and worldly pre-occupations and he has ceased to see with it.' Cf. also *Rawḍat al-ṭālibīn*, p. 164.

The people of wayfaring, namely the Sufis, depend upon the spirit and the heart, more than they depend upon the corporeal form. Now since the spirit (proceeded) from the command of the Most High Creator, it is like a stranger in the body and it will look towards its Source[1] and unto Him it will return. Therefore it will obtain more benefit from its Source than it will from the bodily form, when it is strong and is not defiled by the defilements of human nature. When you have come to know that the spirit is a simple substance, and you have learned that the flesh must have a habitation and is an accident, for it subsists only through the substance, then know that this substance does not abide in any place, nor dwell in a habitation, and the body is not the habitation of the spirit, nor the abode of the heart, but the body is the instrument of the spirit, the implement of the heart, and the vehicle of the soul. The spirit is not attached to the particles of the body, nor detached from it, but it concerns itself with the body, is beneficial to it, and generous towards it.

Now the first manifestation of its light is on the brain, because the brain is its special place of manifestation. It takes a guard for itself from its forefront, from the midst of it a prime minister and controller, from the back part of it a treasury, a treasurer, and a guardian, and from all parts of it infantry and cavalry. From the animal spirit (it takes for itself) a servant, from the natural spirit a sergeant, from the body it takes a vehicle, and from this world a sphere of action. From life it obtains goods and wealth, from activity merchandise, and from knowledge profit. The next world provides it with a destination and place of return and the Canon Law with a way and a road. The headstrong soul (*al-nafs al-ammārah*) gives it a guard and a leader, and the reproachful soul (*al-nafs al-lawwāmah*) an admonisher.[2] The senses are its spies and allies, and from religion it takes a coat of mail, while the reason serves it as instructor, and the sensibility as pupil, and the Lord, glory be to Him, is behind all these, on the watch.[3]

The soul then, being such as this, with this equipment, does not advance towards this gross body and is not essentially attached to it, but brings it benefit, while itself facing towards its Creator, and its Creator commands it to obtain profit, to the appointed end. So then the spirit, during this journey (i.e. through this life), is concerned only with the search for knowledge, because knowledge will be its adornment in the world to come, for 'wealth and children are the ornament of life in this world.'[4] As the eye is concerned with the sight of visible things, the hearing is assiduous in listening to sounds, the tongue is alert to form words, as the animal spirit seeks the delights of passion, and the natural spirit loves the pleasures of eating and drinking, (so also) the spirit at rest, by which I mean the heart, seeks only knowledge and is not satisfied except with it. It learns throughout its life,

1. Cf. Plotinus, vi, 8, 'The soul's movement will be about its Source'.
2. Qur'ān 75:2.
3. Qur'ān 85:20.
4. Qur'ān 18:46.

and takes pleasure in knowledge all its days, until the time of its separation, and if it welcomes anything other than knowledge, it is concerned with it only in the interests of the body, not out of desire for the body itself and the love of its origin. Then, when you have come to know the states of the spirit and have realized that it is immortal, and understand its love for knowledge and passionate desire for it, you ought to consider the different types of knowledge, for they are many, and we will enumerate them briefly.

Chapter III
On the Different Types of Knowledge and its Divisions

Know that Knowledge can be divided into two types, one being religious knowledge (*shar'ī*) and the other intellectual (*'aqlī*), and most of the branches of religious knowledge are intellectual in the opinion of him who knows them, and most of the branches of intellectual knowledge belong to the religious code, in the opinion of him who understands them. 'And he, to whom God does not commit light, has no light.'[1]

1. The first type of Knowledge, which is religious knowledge, is divided into two classes, (a) one of them is concerned with fundamental principles (*uṣūl*), and it is the knowledge of Unity, and this knowledge is concerned with the Essence of God Most High, and His eternal attributes and His creative attributes and His essential attributes, which are set forth in the Divine Names, as mentioned. It is concerned also with the states of the Prophets, the Imams after them, and the Companions. It deals, further, with the states of death and life and with the states of the Resurrection, the Summons, the Assembly, the Judgment, and the Vision of God Most High. Those who concern themselves with this type of knowledge have recourse first to the verses of the Qur'ān, which is the Word of God Most High, then to the traditions of the Apostle (may God bless him), then to intellectual proofs and syllogistic demonstration; and they took the premises of argumentation, syllogistic and eristic, and what belongs to them both, from the philosophers, and they placed most terms in other than their (right) place. In their expressions, they use such phrases as substance, accident, direction, consideration, demonstration, and argument and the meaning of each of these terms differs with each group, so that by 'substance' the philosophers mean one thing, the Sufis mean another, and the theologians something else, and so on. But it is not the purpose of this treatise to verify the meaning of the terms according to the opinions of each group and we will not enter upon it.

Now these people are specialists in the discussion of fundamental principles and the knowledge of Unity, and their title is the *Mutakallimūn*, for the name of *kalām*

1. Qur'ān 24:40.

has become known in connection with the knowledge of Unity. Included also in the knowledge of fundamental principles is interpretation, for the Qur'ān is one of the greatest of things, the most eloquent and most precious. It contains many obscure and difficult passages, which not every mind can comprehend, only that one to whom God has granted understanding of His Word. The Prophet, God bless him, has said: 'There is not a verse of the Qur'ān but has a literal sense and an allegorical sense, and its allegorical sense includes another allegorical meaning up to seven allegorical meanings'[1] and in one account, 'up to nine'. The Prophet said also: 'Every word of the Qur'ān has a moral sense (*ḥadd*) and every moral sense has also a mystical sense (*maṭla*ʿ).'[2] Now in the Qur'ān, God has given information about all types of knowledge, both what is manifest of existent things and what is hidden, what is small among them and what is great, what is perceptible and what is intelligible among them. There is an allusion to this in the Word of God, where it is stated: 'There is neither a green thing nor a dry, but it is (set forth) in a clear book.'[3] And God said also: 'Let them meditate on His verses and let men of understanding remember.'[4]

Since the subject-matter of the Qur'ān is the greatest of subjects, what commentator has done justice to it? Or what theologian has fulfilled his responsibility to it? Each one of the commentators enters upon the explanation of it in accordance with his ability, and embarks upon the exposition of it according to the capacity of his mind, and in accordance with the amount of his knowledge. For all of them said—and they spoke truly—that knowledge of the Qur'ān gives an indication of the knowledge of fundamental principles and what is derived from them, and from religious and intellectual knowledge. Now the commentator ought to consider the Qur'ān from the point of view of the language and from the point of view of metaphor and from the point of view of the composition of the vocables also from the point of view of the particulars of the grammar and of the usage of the Arabs and of the subject-matter of the philosophers and of the doctrine of the Sufis, so that his interpretation comes near to the truth of things. But if he confines himself to one point of view and is content in his exposition with one science, he has not fulfilled his duty of explaining it fully and he finds himself opposed by the evidence of faith and the establishment of the proof.

Included also in the knowledge of fundamentals is the knowledge of the traditions, for the Prophet (God bless him) was the most eloquent of Arabs and foreigners, and was a teacher to whom revelation was made by God Most High, and his intelligence encompassed all things, high and low. Beneath every one of his words, yea, every utterance of his, are to be found seas of mysteries and treasuries of hints. Therefore, the knowledge of his traditions and the understanding of his sayings is a

1. Majlisī, *Biḥār al-anwār*, vol. 8, p. 455.
2. Cf. *Kitāb al-Arbaʿīn*, 48, and L. Massignon, *La Passion d'al-Ḥallāj* (Paris, 1922), p. 704.
3. Qur'ān 6:59.
4. Qur'ān 38:29.

great matter and an important thing. No one is able to have a thorough knowledge of the Prophet's teaching, except by training himself to imitation of the Lawgiver, and removing distortion from his heart through the straightening effect of the law of the Prophet (God bless him).

So he who wishes to discuss the interpretation of the Qur'ān and the elucidation of the Traditions and to discuss rightly, must first gain a knowledge of the language, secure a thorough mastery of the science of grammar, and be well-grounded in the different conjugations. For knowledge of the language is a ladder and a staircase to all the sciences, and for him who does not know the language there is no way to the study of the sciences, for he who wishes to ascend to a roof must first set up a staircase, and after that he can ascend. Now knowledge of the language is an important means and a great staircase, and he who seeks for knowledge cannot dispense with a good command of the language, for knowledge of the language is the most fundamental thing. Knowledge of the language begins with the understanding of the particles, which are represented by the separate words, and after that comes understanding of the verbs, such as the trilateral, the quadrilateral, and others. It is also incumbent upon the philologist that he should investigate the poetry of the Arabs and the worthiest and the most perfect of it is the poetry of the *Jāhiliyyah,* for it provides a means of discipline for the mind and refreshment for the soul. Then, after the study of that poetry and the particles and the names, it is necessary to acquire a knowledge of grammar, for in the knowledge of the language it takes the place of the lever balance for gold and silver, and logic for the science of philosophy, and prosody for poetry, and the yardstick for clothes, and the measure for grain; for in anything which is not weighed in a balance excess and deficiency is not clear. Now the knowledge of the language is a means to a knowledge of interpretation and of the traditions, the knowledge of the Qur'ān and the traditions is a guide to the knowledge of the Unity, and the knowledge of the Unity is that by which alone the souls of God's servants find salvation, thus there is no deliverance from the fear of the Resurrection except thereby. This, then, is an analysis of the knowledge of fundamental principles.

(b) The second class of religious knowledge is the knowledge of what is derived (i.e. from these principles), because knowledge is either theoretical or practical and the knowledge of fundamental principles is theoretical and the knowledge of their consequences is practical, and this practical knowledge includes three obligations:

(i) The first is what is due to God, and it consists of the essentials of religious devotion, such as purification, prayer, almsgiving, the pilgrimage, the Holy War, and devotional readings; also the observance of feast days and the Friday prayers, and what is additional to these in the way of works of supererogation and obligatory duties.

(ii) The second is what is due to one's fellow-servants, and it includes all kinds of customary usages and takes two directions:

(a) One of them includes transactions, such as buying and selling, and partnership and compensatory gifts, the lending of money and the borrowing of it, retaliation, and all kinds of blood-wit.

(b) The second of them is contractual obligation, such as marriage, divorce, manumission, servitude, the law of inheritance, and what is involved in these.

The term 'jurisprudence' applies to these two obligations, and jurisprudence is a noble science, profitable, universal in application, necessary; men cannot do without it because of the universal necessity for it.

(iii) The third obligation is what is due to the self, and it is the knowledge of moral qualities. Now moral qualities are either blameworthy and ought to be rejected and abandoned, or they are praiseworthy and ought to be acquired, and the self should be adorned with them. What is blameworthy among qualities and what is praiseworthy of them is made plain in the Word of God Most High and in the traditions of the Prophet (God bless him). He who assumed a single one of them entered Paradise.

2. As for the second type of knowledge, which is intellectual knowledge, it is a knowledge which is difficult and intricate, including what is wrong and what is right, and it is divided into three classes.

(i) The first class, which is the beginning, comprises the science of mathematics and logic. As for mathematics, it includes arithmetic and is concerned with numbers and geometry, which is the science of dimensions and figures, and astronomy, by which I mean the science of the heavenly bodies, the stars, the regions of the earth, and what is connected therewith. From it is derived the science of astrology and the determination of the times of births and horoscopes. From mathematics is derived also the art of music, which is concerned with the relation of chords.

As for logic, it is concerned with definition and description in regard to things which are apprehended by the imagination, and it investigates things from the point of view of analogy and proof, in respect of the exact sciences. For logic follows this method, beginning with the simple terms, then proceeding to the compound terms, then to propositions, then to the syllogism, then to the moods of the syllogism, then to the search for the proof, which is the end of logic.

(ii) The second class, which is in the middle, is natural science, and the natural scientist is concerned with the universe and the component parts of the world, the substances, and the accidents, with motion and rest, and the states of the heavens, and action and reaction. This science gives rise to the investigation of the states of the different classes of existent things, and the types of selves, the humours, the number of the senses, and the way in which they perceive sensible things. Then it leads to the consideration of the science of medicine, which is the science of bodies, infirmities, medicines, remedies, and what belongs to them. Among its branches, also, are the science of meteorology and the science of mineralogy, the recognition of the properties of things. It also extends to the science of alchemy, which is the treatment of ores that are ailing (i.e. base metals) in the interior of mines.

(iii) The third class, which is the highest, is the investigation of existence, then its division into self-existent (necessary) and the contingent, then the consideration of the Creator and His Essence and all His Attributes and actions, His command and His ordinance and His decree, and His appointment of the manifestation of existent things. In addition to that it includes the consideration of the celestial beings and simple substances, the incorporeal intelligences, and the perfected souls. Then comes consideration of the states of the angels and the demons, and this extends to the knowledge of prophecy, the matter of miracles (*muʿjazāt*), the conditions of thaumaturgic gifts (*karāmāt*), the consideration of the souls in bliss, the state of sleep and being awake, and the stations of dreaming. From it is derived the science of talismans and enchantments and what belongs to them. Now these sciences have divisions and accidents and degrees: for a clear explanation it would be necessity to give extensive proofs, but brevity is more fitting.

Chapter IV
The Knowledge of the Sufis

Know that intellectual knowledge is simple in itself, but it gives rise to a composite knowledge, which includes all the states of the two simple types of knowledge. That composite knowledge is the knowledge of the Sufis and the Way to the attainment of their mystic states. For they have a special science of a plain Way of life, which combines the two types of knowledge. This science includes knowledge of the mystic state and the spiritual condition (*waqt*),[1] audition, ecstasy, longing, intoxication, sobriety, affirmation, effacement, poverty, the passing away of self (*fanāʾ*), saintship and discipleship and (the position of) the Shaykh and the disciple, and what is involved in their states, together with spiritual illumination,[2] endowments, and stations, and we will speak of these three types of knowledge in a special book, if God will. But now it is our intention only to enumerate the sciences and their different classes in this treatise, and we have limited it and have enumerated them briefly, in order to summarize. So let him who desires more than this and a full exposition of these sciences, betake himself to reading the books (which deal with them). Since the discourse setting forth the enumeration of the classes of sciences is ended, know for a certainty that each one of these arts and each one of these sciences demands a number of conditions in order that it may be impressed upon the souls of those who seek it, and after the enumeration of the sciences you must know the methods of study, for there are specific methods of acquiring knowledge, and we will analyse them.

1. For a discussion of *waqt* cf. Hujwīrī, *Kashf al-maḥjūb*, pp. 367–370.
2. Cf. Hujwīrī, *Kashf al-maḥjūb*, p. 384.

THREE TREATISES ON KNOWLEDGE

Thalāth rasāʾil fiʾl-maʿrifah

Translated for this volume by Alma Giese from Abū Ḥāmid Muḥammad Ghazzālī, *Thalāth rasāʾil fiʾl-maʿrifah*, ed. Maḥmūd Ḥamdī Zaqzūq (Cairo, 1979), pp. 15–22; 31–53; 77–95.

First Treatise, *Risālah fī bayān maʿrifat Allāh*

You have asked me—and may God give you success—about a matter which is doubtful to you, and that is: The mind of none of us can encompass with its knowledge the corporeal and the spiritual things—even if a person had understanding and knowledge in abundance—and it does not realize itself in him as it [really] is. So how can it be permitted to anyone to claim knowledge of God as He is in His qualities? For who [ever] claims this puts to God, Most High, a limit and an end, because his knowledge puts a limit to His Essence. Now, everything that encompasses a thing is its beginning and its end, seen from its outside and from its inside. But God Most High has spoken: *He is the First and the Last* [57:3].

The answer is: It is necessary before any other thing that one understand that nobody knows God Most High truly but God Most High Himself, and nobody can encompass the true nature of His majesty except Him. One should not consider this improbable, for I say: Except for the king himself nobody really knows the king, and except for the prophet himself, nobody really knows the prophet. Also, except for the learned one nobody really knows the learned one. I would even say: When the student has not reached the rank of the teacher in the sciences he does not really know the teacher. And when he has reached his rank in the sciences he has a knowledge that is different from the knowledge of his teacher. For he knows first what his teacher has taught him and he understands this himself. Then, he knows the teacher in relation to himself. And he thus knows that he encompasses the knowable things which he himself encompasses. I would even say that it cannot be imagined that the state of him who has sexual intercourse at the fulfilment of his desire can really be known by somebody else, because the perfect knowledge of this state comes about through experience and awareness. The nature of this fulfilment cannot be imagined before it has been attributed to him. The utmost that can be imagined of it is to believe in the truth of an established fact, the true nature of which is truly not known to him.

Now how can man aspire to truly know God, Most High, when he does not truly know his own soul? For, he knows his own soul—in most of his states—by its actions and its characteristics, without grasping its nature. Nay, if the human being wants to reach a full understanding of the ant or the bedbug in the completeness of all its facts and its characteristics, he will be unable to do so. The utmost would be that he perceives with his eyes its form, its colour and the construction of its body parts, and their difference in exterior matters. Concerning the species-establishing differences by which the bedbug per se is different from the ant per se so that from their difference derives the difference of their shape and their qualities, one is not able to do that.

Now if you were to imagine that God Most High had someone comparable and similar [to Himself]—He is high above this—then it would be possible to say: The comparable one has true knowledge of Him through comparison with his own soul; he first knows it and then compares it to the essence of the other, just as one learned person knows another like him by comparing [him] to his own soul.

I say: The human being has different stages: First his being an embryo, then a small child, and then a discriminating being; after that he is in full possession of his mental faculties and then [he is] one of the saints of God Most High. The embryo does not understand its own state and it cannot possibly have true knowledge of the child. The child does not know the discriminating being, and the discriminating being—in the state of conscious perception—does not know the one who is in full possession of his mental faculties. The intelligent person who, with the contemplation of the intellect, grasps the intelligible can only understand the visionary saint by way of inference. The saint does not know the Prophet—for the state of prophethood is beyond the state of sainthood. The prophet does not know the angel like the angel knows himself, and the angel does not know God Most High like God Most High knows His own Self. These are hierarchically organized perfections, and he who is veiled from each one of these ranks falls short of grasping its innermost essence.

Yes, at times man has a proof establishing the truth of his origin. When you have recognized this you should also know that the utmost knowledge of human beings is their knowing that this wondrous, well-ordered, organized world has need of a living, powerful and knowing ruler who is not like the world and whom the world does not resemble. So, creation for him indicates proof of something from which creation originates. This is knowledge of His act, not knowledge of His Essence.

It indicates proof for life, knowledge and power, and this is knowledge of the qualities, not of the true nature. Neither is it knowledge of the true state of the qualities, but rather [knowledge] of a kind of comparison: If the human being were not described as having knowledge, life and power, it would not be possible for him to understand through evidence the existence of the origin of these matters.

And likewise it (i.e. creation) indicates that origination, corporeality, accidentality, and other such [qualities] are unthinkable regarding Him. This amounts to a knowledge of negating things concerning Him, not a knowledge of the true nature of His Essence.

Mankind's knowledge of God Most High, can be reduced to these three approaches, even if men differ in the grades of illumination, the path of knowledge, and the amount of the knowable things. All this is based on the knowledge of the need of the world for One who performs all that, not on the comprehension of the innermost truth of His Essence.

Then, after the acquisition of these types of knowledge, when the knower goes even deeper, it will become clear to him—in a manner that would take too long to relate—that it is impossible for mankind to gain insight into the knowledge of the true nature of His Essence.[1] This is the utmost degree of those who know, and at this they say: 'The inability to reach understanding is itself understanding'. For, inasmuch as man perceives that the inability to reach the nature of His majesty is inevitable, he reaches that which is the utmost of his perfection, for that is the ultimate perfection of man.

If, then, the knowledgeable one would say: 'I do not know him', he would tell the truth in one way, and if he were to say: 'I know Him', he would also, in a way, tell the truth. An analogy to him is he to whom a well-formed handwriting is shown and he is asked: 'Do you know the one who wrote it?' He is existent, living, able, knowing, endowed with hearing and seeing—because the art of writing cannot be completed without these qualities—and he is neither mineral nor plant nor beast. He then says: 'I do know him'. He could also say: 'Although I recognize all of this, I do not know him'.

Therefore, the one who is knowledgeable has two states: In one of them he says: 'I do not know God, Most High', and in the other he says: 'I do not know anything but God'. He speaks the truth in both cases. Concerning the first state (it means) he does not know[2] the essence per se although the inclination of his heart is towards it, so nothing but perplexity befalls him that weighs heavily on him. That is when he says: 'I do not know Him'.

In the second state he looks upon His acts insofar as they are His acts. He then sees nothing else in the existing things but God—mighty and great is He—and His acts, and with that he says: 'I do not know anything other than God Most High. There is nothing in the earth except for Him and He is everything if one thinks about it. For he who does not look anywhere but to the sun and its lights that are spread through the world, and whose heart beholds the things that are illuminated by it, not insofar as they are minerals or beasts [but as illuminated things]—with him it is as if he sees nothing but the sun. In such a state the knowledgeable one experiences expansion through divine lights that come upon him, that have shone upon him from the things of the world. The other state is the state of contraction. That is why the master of the envoys and the lord of those who know—may God's blessings and His peace be upon him—has said: '*Meditate on God's creation, but do not meditate on His Essence.*'

This is a *ḥadīth* on which thoughtful men have much reflected. But the one who knows cannot exhaust the oceans of knowledge from which God has poured it out

1. I prefer to read *maʿrifat kunh dhātih* instead of *kunh maʿrifat dhātih.*
2. I read *lā yaʿrifu khuṣūṣ al-dhāt* instead of *lā khuṣūṣ al-dhāt.*

over him, even if he were given a life like the life of Noah—peace be upon him. All of the knowledge of those who know is, in relation to the knowledge of God Most High, less than a drop in relation to the oceans of the world, and what it (i.e. the drop) is in relation to them (i.e. the oceans) is the most extreme proportion.

Now, this much of an answer is sufficient to clear up the doubt, for it (i.e. the doubt) is based on [the assumption] that man is intent on [mentally] encompassing God [Most High] and on that many assertions as to the absurdity [of this opinion] can be built.[1] The presupposition in positing [this question] is false. If that is recognized, the claim of absurdity is repelled.

Second Treatise, *Risālah fi'l-maʿrifah*

You should know that knowledge [*maʿrifah*] is of two kinds: The knowledge of one's duty [*maʿrifat al-ḥaqq*] and the knowledge of the essential truth [*maʿrifat al-ḥaqīqah*]. Knowledge of one's duty is flight from the soul, and this flight is the means for salvation and deliverance[2] from the tribulation of the soul. For he who listens to his soul and desists from fleeing it is deceived. Now, fleeing from it is hardly possible without first knowing its manifest and hidden properties. Knowledge of the essential truth [however] is dwelling with God Most High. But this dwelling with God cannot happen without first knowing His essential and non-essential attributes [*ṣifātuhu'l-dhātiyyah wa'l-maʿnawiyyah*].

The characteristics of the soul and its place in the body:

Know that the jurisprudent, if he had an exact knowledge of the acts of obedience [to God] and did not live by them, or if he had an exact knowledge of the acts of sin and did not abstain from them and not cleanse his soul from them, if he had an exact knowledge of the praiseworthy character traits and did not possess them—he would be deceived, since God Most High has spoken: *He is indeed successful who causeth it to grow* [91:9]; He does not say: 'He is indeed successful, who has knowledge.'

If someone says: 'What is the real meaning of the soul?' one would reply: The soul is a fine substance lodged in this [human] frame, and it is the place of the blameworthy defective character traits, such as: derogation and oppression, anger and malice, desire for the Muslims' possessions and help for the hypocrites. And so spoke the Most High: *Verily, the hypocrites will be in the lowest depth of hell* [4:145[3]]

1. I read *(wa)-yubnā ʿalayh al-istibʿādāt,* which is an emendation of *ybny (?) ʿalayh al-istiʿādāt,* which the editor has left out in the printed edition, because it does not make sense to him.

2. Following the editor's suggestion, I read *sabab li'l-najāt wa'l-khalāṣ* instead of … *min al-khalāṣ*.

3. The remaining part of the verse is: *and you will find none to help them.*

Similarly, the spirit is a fine substance[1] lodged in this frame [of the body]; it is the locus of praiseworthy character traits, and if (man) is characterized by it, he will be at rest from tribulation.[2]

Now, if it is said: What are its attributes?—the answer is: It is commanding evil, is false and ungrateful, is an infidel who gives associates to God—as God Most High has spoken: *But as for him who has feared his Lord's high rank, and has restrained his soul from lust—verily, paradise is his dwelling* [79:40–41]. Its actions are such that it aims for the cutting off of the heads of Muslims—as is told by this story: A governor tried hard to make a pious man take over a certain public function for him—but he refused. So the governor said to him: 'You either start with this job and this activity, or I shall cut off your head!' Thereupon the pious man said: 'If I take over this function, then my soul will cut off my head. Now that *you* cut off my head is easier for me, than that my soul cut it off once I started on this'.

If someone says: Does the soul have a form? The answer is: Yes, indeed! Its head is haughtiness, its eyes are vanity, its mouth is envy and its tongue is mendacity, its ears are forgetfulness, its chest is spite, its belly lust, its hands are crime and theft, its feet are expectation, and heedlessness is its heart and its spirit; it has neither knowledge nor understanding,[3] selling, as it does, paradise and its bliss and access to it for a momentary passion in the abode of transience. And, it does not die and vanish by being fought against; it only retreats and hides, while still being your enemy. And where is your hostility towards your soul which is between your two sides[4]—and your parting from it by fighting it, so that through the fight it withdraws [from you]?[5] Therefore, it is present[6] [with you again] as soon as you neglect the fight [against it]. So, one is never safe from its evil. Hence, all that veils man from God Most High is the soul, and it is the soul that distracts him—as God Most High has spoken: *Verily, the soul commands the evil* [12:53].

1. I prefer to read *al-rūḥ laṭīfah* (parallel to *al-nafs al-laṭīfah*) instead of *al-rūḥ al-laṭīfah*.

2. The editor quotes here in a footnote a passage from al-Ghazzālī's *Iḥyā' 'ulūm al-dīn*, of which the following is a translation: The third word: the soul. This is also being shared by several meanings, two of which are connected with our goal. One of them is that with which is meant the general concept of the power of anger and lust in the human being, and as such it is used predominantly among the Sufis, because by 'soul' they mean the general seat of the blameworthy character traits of the human being. They say: It is absolutely necessary to fight against the soul and to break it. There is a hint to this in the words of him on whom be peace: *Your greatest enemy is your soul which is between your two sides.*—The second meaning: It is a fine substance which is the human being in his true form, and it is the self of the human being and his essence. It is, however, described in different ways according to its different states … So, the soul in the first meaning is blameworthy and the object of blame, but in the second meaning it is praiseworthy.

3. The word knowledge (*'ilm*) has been added by the editor.

4. This refers to the *ḥadīth*: Your greatest enemy is your soul which is between your two sides.

5. I read *fa-taghība* instead of *wa-taghību* which seems to make more sense.

6. The editor adds *ḥuḍūr*.

Now, should someone say: What is the soul's place in the [human] frame? The answer would be: The soul has different parts: one of its parts is in the eye and gazes with treachery, another one of its parts is in the ear and listens to what does not please God, still another one of its parts is in the tongue and talks libel and slander, calumny, lie, and mischief. As God Most High has spoken: *Mischief is worse than killing* [2:191], and about libel God Most High has spoken: *And spy not, nor backbite one another* [49:12], and about lying: *And there awaits them a painful chastisement for that they have cried lies* [2:10].[1] Another one of the soul's parts is in the hand and commands stealing. God Most High spoke: *As for the thief, both male and female, cut off their hands* [5:38]. There is one part of the soul in the foot that commands it to walk towards all sins. God Most High has spoken: *Because of their sins they were drowned, then made to enter a Fire* [71:25]. Another one of its parts is in the belly, and from it passion is engendered. God Most High has spoken: *Lo! You come with lust unto men instead of women!*[7:81] Still another part of the soul is in the heart, and from it comes forth heedlessness. There is no hair on the body in which there is not a part of the soul.

Should someone say: What is the difference between the whims of the soul and the whisperings of the devil? The answer would be: The soul calls for its worldly share, i.e. what it has an interest in, the good life[2] and the wish to have something, to have rank, good fortune, and glory. But the devil calls man with his whisperings to something that amounts to rebellion. The devil disappears when God is mentioned. The soul, however, does not disappear [at this], because it is like a mordacious dog. It does, however, have no stability in the state of illumination [*kashf*] and witnessing [*shuhūd*] [of God]. But when man becomes distracted from his witnessing of God the soul returns to him, and it is like the harmful snake of the *wādī*: when you think that you have killed it; if you then were to touch it, it would harm you with its poison.

If someone would say: 'What is the sign of him who aims at disciplining his soul?' the answer would be: that he has no demands, for demanding is the main characteristic of the soul,[3] that he does not change through roughness and rebuke,[4] and is not taken by friendly reception and praise, that he does not get mixed up with jealousy, and that no covering[5] comes over the eye nor a fine veil. This means that he sees things in their [true] meaning without additions to the measures of things; he is not ruled by anger, and he does not make mistakes in his perception. The following occurs in the prayers: 'O God, show us the truth as it really is and

1. A. J. Arberry's translation.

2. With a change of diacritics and the addition of a letter one could read *buḥbūḥah*, which makes more sense than *najwā*. See also the rather helpless footnote of the editor.

3. The editor quotes the following Sufi saying: Sufism means 'that one is not possessed by anything and does not possess anything.'

4. The editor quotes another Sufi saying: The Sufi is not troubled (lit.: not rendered turbid) by anything, but everything is made pure by him.

5. I read *saḥāt* for *sakhā'* and *wa-lā* for *wa-lahā*.

grant us the gift of adhering to it. Show us futility as it really is and grant us the gift of keeping away from it.'

Now, you should know that the soul has three [stages]: God Most High mentions in His book the commanding [*ammārah*], the blaming [*lawwāmah*], and the peaceful [*muṭma'innah*] soul. I say:[1] The commanding [soul] consists in deception, violence, vanity, self-sufficiency, and consorting.[2] That is, it loves [all] this.[3] The blaming [soul] is the heart [*qalb*], and the [soul] at peace is the spirit [*rūḥ*]. It is also said that the commanding [soul] is the evil-doing soul, that the blaming [soul] is the moderate soul,[4] and that the [soul] at peace is the preceding soul.[5]

A wise saying: Seek not the companionship of him who has a hundred praiseworthy qualities, but also has one blameworthy quality, namely ignorance of his soul/self. Rather seek the companionship of him who has a hundred blameworthy qualities, but also one praiseworthy quality which is knowledge of his soul/self. For he who knows his soul/self knows his Lord.

If someone would say: With what can it be compared? the answer would be: In envy it is like Satan, because he was the first one who was envious of Adam. In haughtiness it is like the Pharaoh. In its excessive eating it is like a child and in its lust like a donkey. In its decoration it is like a woman and in its excessive laughter and bad manners it resembles the drunk and the shameless. While living in comfort, it rebels against the order of God Most High, and it implores God at the time of misfortune. It is not content with little and cannot be satisfied with abundance. It talks about things that do not concern him [its master].

A wise saying: It is a sign of the repentants [*tā'ibūn*] that they have left behind the sins; to leave behind the world is the sign of the ascetics [*zāhidūn*], and to leave behind the soul is the sign of those endowed with knowledge [*'ārifūn*]. Man cannot draw near to the love of God Most High, save through enmity toward the soul. Do not associate with the world save by renunciation, do not associate with the soul save by opposition, nor associate with the devil save by enmity. Do not associate with the people save by sincere admonition, and do not associate with God save by being in accordance with His decree.

---

1. I follow the author's emendation. The text says: *He (i.e. God) said.*

2. *'Ishrah* in Arabic does not normally have a negative meaning. It may thus be a slip of the pen (for *qaswah,* 'cruelty'?).

3. I prefer to reject the emendation of the editor, proposing instead to read *tuḥibbuhā* for *tuḥibbuhu* in the Ms.

4. To clarify this, the editor quotes from al-Ghazzālī's *Iḥyā',* where he says that the soul, when it is not yet in a state of complete peace, but is opposing and resisting the passions is called the blaming soul, because it blames its possessor when he falls short of obedience toward God.

5. This tripartition 'is found as early as the Qur'ānic commentary by Ja'far al-Ṣādiq. He holds that the *nafs* is peculiar to the *ẓālim,* "tyrant", the *qalb* to the *muqtaṣid,* "moderate", and the *rūḥ* to the *sābiq,* "preceding one, winner"; the *ẓālim* loves God for his own sake, the *muqtaṣid* loves Him for Himself, and the *sābiq* annihilates his own will in God's will'. Annemarie Schimmel, *Mystical Dimensions of Islam* (Chapel Hill, NC, 1975), p. 191.

You should know that your soul is your prison: when you are with it you are in prison and in distress, but when you get away [from it] you fall into comfortable rest. And man will not be freed from it save by steadfastness [*istiqāmah*]. Shaykh ʿAbd Allāh[1] has said: 'Be truthful with God and fair with men, repressive with the soul and humble with the scholars, subservient with the shaykhs and generous with the mendicant dervishes, tender with the children and silent with the ignorant.

Divine attributes and the different levels of knowing God

If someone would say: The attributes of the Creator—great is His glory—can be divided into how many parts?, the answer would be: into two parts: the essential quality [*dhātiyyah*] and the non-essential [*maʿnawiyyah*] quality. The essential quality is one which, if we were to assume its absence, would necessitate the absence of the essence, and [the essential attribute] cannot inhere [in the essence] because of its (i.e. the essence's) absence. If one were to imagine the existence of the essence together with the essential quality's absence it would be necessary to change its genus, such as its subsisting in itself and its being of necessary existence. The non-essential quality has two kinds: one of them is that which requires an eternal attribute and accident, for instance, when we say: He is powerful and knowing, willing and living, hearing and seeing, everlasting[2] and speaking, because this means power, knowledge, will, life, hearing, seeing, speech, everlastingness and praise;[3] the second is that which requires a necessary temporal accident, as we say about his qualities: He is the Creator, the Provider, the Life and the Death-giver, and whatever else makes necessary one of His actions.

If someone now would say: Does God have more than these eight qualities? the answer would be: Certainly not, because, if we were to assume that there would be another quality in addition to the eight qualities, this would necessarily be either a quality of praise and perfection or a quality of deficiency and blame. If it were a quality of praise and perfection, then its non-existence at a certain point would be a deficiency. The Creator Most High is [always] described in qualities of perfection in every respect. If it is a quality of blame and deficiency, its non-existence would be necessary. Because these two possibilities are invalid, it is established that it is not permissible to describe Him with other qualities in addition to the eight qualities.

If someone would say: What is the most specific description of God? the answer would be: God is most specifically described by His power of creation [*ikhtirāʿ*] and bringing forth anew [*ibdāʿ*]; nobody else can share this with him. Who confirms that in this He has a partner, confirms that God has a partner, and therefore has established two gods for the unicity of God Most High. Thereby, he has deserved the Fire,

1. ʿAbd Allāh al-Anṣārī?
2. This does not fit in with the other attributes.
3. I agree with the editor who says that there is no place here for this attribute.

and God will never show His mercy to him unless he renounces two gods. Through God we have protection from sin.

If someone should say: What is the station [*maqām*] of those who are truthful? the answer would be: the greatest rank [*martabah*] of men, the highest degree [*manzil*] among them is [their] knowledge of God. Now, as to this knowledge, there are three kinds of men: [first] the one who has knowledge of the essence of God, and this is the station of the prophets, the messengers, and the most excellent of the truthful and the saints. The lord in this is the Messenger of God—may God bless him and give him peace. God Most High has spoken: *So know that there is no deity save (the one) God* [47:19], and he, on whom may be blessings and peace, has said: *I am among you the one who is most knowledgeable about God, and among you the most fearful of God.* Next, the knowledge of God's qualities is the station of the select among the believers, according to the words of Him who is Most High: *Will they not then ponder on the Qur'ān?* [4:82] [Finally,] the knowledge of the acts[1] of God Most High is the station of the broad mass of the believers, according to the words of the Most High: *Will they not regard the camels, how they are created?* [88:17]

Knowledge of the essence of God Most High occasions awe [*hayba*] and glorification [*taʿẓīm*]. Awe is the exaltation of God the Real through diminution of man; glorification is to hold in high honour [God] the Real through debasement of man. So, one should abstain from the glorification and exaltation of anything other than Him so that anything else but Him falls away from the mystery of exaltation and honouring,[2] and nothing is glorified next to Him, nothing originated is looked at and nothing created is turned to, except [as] it is left aside and subsumed under the categories of knowledge of His Attributes, so that one is safe[3] from anthropomorphism [*tashbīh*].

It is said: Knowledge is oblivion of what is besides Him, and God is above all anthropomorphizations. Did you not see how God Most High described His messenger when He said: *The eye turned not aside nor yet was over bold* [53:17].

Knowledge of God's qualities occasions tranquillity [*sukūn*] with God, and fear [*khawf*] of God Most High, striving for safety from the Fire through the mercy of God Most High. Tranquillity with God, hope [*rajā'*] towards God, [complete] trust [*tawakkul*] in God, and the other stations which His servants have, are in accordance with the revelation of the attributes in their innermost hearts. He, on whom may be blessings and peace, has said: *Serve God as if you can see Him, for if you cannot see Him, He can see you.* This is the station of those who have knowledge of the essence of God and the attributes of God which are subsistent in Him.

Knowledge of the acts of God Most High occasions reliance on the worship of

1. I have added *afʿāl* here, because this is the third category as taken up again on the next page of the text.
2. I read *wa-ʿan al-iʿzāz* instead of *wa-iʿzāz*.
3. I read *fa-yuslam* instead of just *yuslam*.

God Most High—God Most High has spoken: *And serve thy lord until the inevitable cometh unto thee* [15:99] i.e. striving for rewards from God, fleeing from God's punishment and spending [everything] on God's path. God Most High has spoken: *Who forsake their beds and cry unto their Lord in fear and hope and spend of what We have bestowed on them* [32:16].

The true nature of knowledge, the sign of the truly knowledgeable and the conditions for the knowledge of God

If someone said: What is the true nature of knowledge? the answer would be: Vision of the Real, while one has lost vision of that which is other than Him until all of the kingdom of God Most High is, in his vision, smaller than a mustard seed.[1] Now, this cannot be borne by the hearts of those who are heedless. A poet has said:[2]

The lover[3] strives for his Beloved's contentment
   and the hearts of the knowers wish to meet Him.
Forever he looks at Him with his hearts' eye
   and the heart knows its Lord and sees Him.
Content is the lover[4] with the Beloved by His nearness
   without regard for men, and nothing he wants that is other than He.

Abū Yazīd, may God have mercy on him, said: Verily, in the night there are God's folk who pass their time in longing for Him. He recited:

You planted the seed of love into my heart
   and it will not be consoled until the day of meeting.
There is not ever someone more miserable than the lover
   although he finds passion sweet of taste.
And he weeps when He is far, out of yearning for Him
   and he weeps when He is near, from fear of separation.
You have taken possession of my heart continuously
   and my yearning increases while love becomes apparent.
He gave me a draught to drink which has enlivened my heart
   with the cup of desire from the ocean of love.
So, my passion is growing—and passion does increase

1. In agreement with the editor I leave out the second *fī janb ru'yat Allāh taʿālā,* because it does not seem to make sense.

2. The editor has made significant changes in the text of the poem, because of metrical defects.

3. I read *muḥibb* instead of the editor's *ḥabīb*, which also fits in metrically.

4. See preceding note.

my patience is lost and the ecstasy of love becomes apparent.
My heart, O my heart, O my heart!
as if you were thirsty in every *wādī*.[1]
And if it were not for God who protects those who know Him
the knowers would be thirsty in every *wādī*.

If someone would say: What is the sign of him who has knowledge? the answer would be: The signs of him who has knowledge are that he looks at the world with the eye of example-taking and at the hereafter with the eye of expectation, at the soul with the eye of contempt and at obedience with the eye of excuse, at knowledge with the eye of welcoming and at God with the eye of being proud [of God].

Abu'l-Qāsim al-Kharrāzī al-Maghribī said: 'The one who has knowledge is satisfied with everything until he reaches God, and when he has reached Him he is satisfied with God without anything else—and people are in need of him'.

Rābiʿah al-ʿAdawiyyah—may God be content with her—said: 'He who has knowledge asks God for his heart as a gift, and He gives it to him. Then, when he owns the heart he gives it to his Lord, so that in His grasp it is preserved and in His veil it is concealed from all creatures'.

Dhū'l-Nūn al-Miṣrī—may God have mercy on him—said: 'For those who have knowledge it is necessary to renounce all sins out of shame for His glory and out of fear for His punishment'.

And one of them [i.e. the mystics] said: 'The sun of those who have knowledge is brighter than the sun of the day and more brilliant, for the sun of the day is eclipsed at times, but the suns of the heart are not eclipsed ever;[2] they have light in every form. The sun of the day sets with the night, but not so the sun of the hearts'. About this he has recited:

The sun of the day disappears by night
the sun of the hearts does not set in us.

Problem: Man does not truly know his Lord until he knows three things: Firstly: that he knows the world by its transience; secondly, that he knows the soul by its faultiness. Who knows the world by its transience occupies himself with the warning [example it presents], and his sign is that he turns away from it. The one who knows the outcome (i.e. the Hereafter) by its permanence occupies himself with worship, and his sign is that he has a longing for it. Who knows the soul by its faultiness occupies himself with servitude, and his sign is that he abandons his rank.

When man now knows these things as we have mentioned them, then he has

1. Compare Qur'ān 26:225; *Hast thou not seen how they stray in every valley.*
2. I prefer to read the ms.'s *tankasif* instead of the editor's *yankasif.*

true knowledge of his Lord, and his sign is rejection of the soul, the world and[1] the outcome.

If someone would say: What is the difference between worship [*ʿibādah*] and servitude [*ʿubūdiyyah*]? the answer would be: Worship is the affirmation of obedience and servitude is the absence of the consideration of sincere devotion in obedience.

The soul and the world as veils

You should know that all that veils man from God Most High is the soul. Now, the soul [consists of] four things: feasting and people, fortune and rank. Whoever leaves behind people and feasting to him has been given wisdom and nearness to God. And whoever leaves behind fortune and rank, to him have been given contentment and vision [of God].

A man who [was] with al-Junayd—may God's mercy be upon him—said: 'The veil that separates man from God consists of three things: the soul, people, and the world'. Thereupon Junayd—may God be pleased with him—said: 'This is the veil for the common people but the veil of the elect consists of three things: consideration of obedience, consideration of the reward for obedience, and consideration of high esteem'.[2]

The reality of the world is [its being] the first part of life which is followed by death and annihilation. None of the created things will remain. He who seeks it is like the dung beetle that falls in love with excrement. For the devout and the worshippers it is like prison, and the devout and the worshippers cannot be restful in it. It has no permanence, no stability, and no weight. Its beginning is permanence and its end is annihilation. But the Hereafter is the everlasting life which does not cease to be, nor does it become extinct. God Most High has spoken: *That which ye have, wasteth away and that which God hath remaineth.*[3]

You should know that Paradise is of two kinds: the postponed [*muʾajjalah*] paradise and the immediate [*muʿajjalah*] paradise. The postponed paradise is reward and felicity, and the immediate paradise is the sweetness of service, the abundance of worship and religious exercises, abandonment of the world in all its active ways, and abandonment of things except for God Most High.

Snippet: You should know that vision is of two kinds: the postponed vision and the immediate vision. The postponed vision is gazing at God Most High in Paradise in the state of address. The immediate vision is contemplating [*shuhūd*] and witnessing [*mushāhadah*].

1. Here, I leave out the editor's insertion *al-iqbāl ʿalā*.

2. This could be translated as: *consideration of (God's) honour (of him),* i.e. being able to perform supernatural feats, the miracles of the saints.

3. Qurʾān 16:96.

Snippet: You should know that what is service for people in active life is sanctification for those who have knowledge. If someone asks: 'What is the difference between the two?' the answer is: service is movement of the body according to the command [of God] and with security [for others].[1] Sanctification is stillness of the heart in the presence of the command through the security. The command concerns service and the security [for others] [results] from the security [with God].[2] Service leads to the Hereafter and sanctification leads to the vision of the Lord.[3] Service is like merchandise, [while] sanctification leading to vision[4] is like the saleability of the merchandise. Since, for each merchandise for which there are no sales, there is no value. Likewise, if with it (i.e. service) there is no sanctification, no use can be drawn from it.

Aspiration, will, and desire

'Man of aspiration' [means] that he is travelling on his path; 'man of volition' [means] he is halting on his path or seemingly so. Others say: The man of aspiration is reaching his goal, the man of volition is travelling on the path, and the man of desire is falling on the path. It is also said: The man of aspiration is free from the shackle of the intermediaries and the veil, the man of volition is free from the veil and tied with the shackle of intermediaries, and the man of desire is tied with the shackle of the veil and the intermediaries. Junayd—may God have mercy on him—has said: 'The man of aspiration is a male, the man of volition is a hermaphrodite, and the man of desire is a female'. It is also said: Aspiration is in the innermost centre, will is in the heart and desire is in the soul.

Self-deprivation and self-isolation

You should know that self-deprivation is for the commonalty and self-isolation is for the elect. Self-deprivation means an outward depriving oneself[5] of things, an inward depriving oneself of [hoped-for profits],[6] and the substitution [of this world] for the next. Its meaning is: One should not look for the world as a goal. Self-isolation is the withdrawal from one's states and acts until one's only wish is God Most High. It is said: Self-deprivation is your separation from everything that is not He and self-isolation is your being withdrawn from seeing that which is not He.

1. According to a *ḥadīth* 'the person of faith is he before whom people feel secure (*amn*) with their possessions and themselves', as quoted in William C. Chittick, *The Sufi Path of Knowledge* (Albany, NY, 1989), p. 194.

2. This is a literal translation with my additions. The text seems to be corrupt.

3. Here, the text has: 'He said', which can be left out.

4. Text corrupt, I propose the admittedly radical emendation *al-muwaṣṣilatu ilā* for *ka-rāḥimīn wa-*.

5. I read *al-tajarrud* instead of *al-mujarrad.*

6. I adopt the editor's emendation *al-aʿrāḍ* instead of *al-amrāḍ.*

It is also said: Self-deprivation is taking leave of passion, and self-isolation is divorce from passion. And they say: Self-deprivation is leaving aside the world because of the Hereafter and self-isolation is leaving aside the Hereafter because of the Lord. Also, it is said: Self-deprivation is the elimination of reliance from existence, and self-isolation is the reliance in all things on the godhead which will bring about everything aimed at.

The spiritual struggle, the unveiling and the witnessing

You should know that the spiritual struggle [*mujāhadah*] is the manifestation of exertion and strength in the arena of exertion. Unveiling [*mukāshafah*] is the lifting up of the uncertainty from the heart in the arena of knowledge. Witnessing [*mushāhadah*] is the presence of the innermost secret with the Real in the place of seclusion in the Dominion.

It is said: The spiritual struggle is fire with fire, the unveiling is light with light, and the witnessing is light upon light. It is also said: Witnessing is of three kinds: the witnessing of the adepts, that is, the vision of the heart; the witnessing of the sincere devotees and that is the heart being in seclusion veraciously with the Truth. God Most High has spoken: *Is not the time ripe for the hearts of those who believe to submit to God's reminder* [57:16]. This is the seclusion of the heart from everything but the Lord, His command and that which is sent down from the Real. The witnessing of those who have knowledge is the legitimate vision in everything, as the Seclusionists say about the seclusions, meaning, however, that he (i.e. the knower) sees in the created things the signs of His omnipotence, as the poet says:

And in everything there is a sign of Him that points to Him being the One.

Third Treatise, Knowledge of the Soul and God, this World and the Hereafter (*Risālah fī maʿrifat al-nafs*)

You should know that the structure of Islam rests on four things: knowledge of the soul, and knowledge of God Most High, knowledge of this world and knowledge of the hereafter.

As to the first principle, it is necessary for every human being to know his soul. Because when he does not know his soul, there is no way by which he could know God Most High. For knowledge of the soul is the key to knowledge of God Most High. The Messenger of God—may God bless him and give him peace—has said: *Whosoever knows his soul thereby knows his Lord.* And in the books of the preceding prophets [it is said]: *Oh Man, know thy soul that you may know thy Lord.* In the Gospels [it is said]: *Be not like those who forget their souls, and so forget God*—may

He be praised! God said in what He, indeed, sent down to His Messenger: *Who would find the religion of Abraham distasteful except one who is ignorant of his soul* [2:130], meaning [one] 'who does not know it.' And God Most High has spoken: *We shall show them Our portents on the horizon and within themselves until it will be manifest unto them that it is the Truth* [41:53].

The human being: body and heart and their relation to each other

You should know that the human being is created from two things: the body and the heart.

Concerning the body; God Most High created it composed of skin and flesh, sinews and veins, of blood, bones, and marrow. God Most High has spoken: *And He created you by (diverse) stages* [71:14]. In every one of its parts there is a wondrous meaning and thousands of sinews, bones, and veins and other parts. Each one of them has a shape and a form that is different from the other and none of them has been created if not for a designed purpose. The eye is composed of ten different layers. If one of them[1] were defective, vision would be defective. They have composed volumes about the functions of these layers.

The liver was created so that the foods of different kinds can get to it from the stomach. Then it makes them into one single kind, this is the substance of blood, so that it can serve as nourishment for the seven [organs]. Now, when the blood cooks in the liver a sediment is generated in the lower part, and that is the black bile. In its upper part yellow water [is generated] and that is the yellow bile. The blood itself is of fine substance, without firmness.

Then the spleen was created to draw the black bile from it (i.e., the blood) to itself, and the gallbladder was created to draw the yellow bile from it. The kidneys were created to draw the water from the blood so that it would get firmness. The blood then gets to the veins, then to the organs. Should damage come to the gallbladder, however, the yellow bile would stay in the blood, and from it would be generated jaundice, fever, and other yellow bile-related illnesses. If damage should befall the spleen, the black bile would stay in the blood and from it would be generated epilepsy, blindness, and other black bile-related illnesses. If damage would befall the kidneys, the water would stay in the blood, and from it would be generated dropsy. And so every one of the outer and inner parts is created for a specific use, and if it were not for that part the order of the body would be disturbed. This summary cannot possibly give the multiplicity of those functions.

Rather there are in the body of one single human being, despite all the smallness of its stature, equivalents of that which is in the heavens and the earth. The bones

1. I translate the variant given in the footnote which makes sense. The main text says 'all of them'.

are equivalents of the mountains, the veins [are equivalents] of the rivers, the hairs are like the plants, the brain like the heaven, and the senses are like the stars. In it are likenesses of all the craftsmen in the world. The force which digests the food in the stomach is like the cook, the one who sends the pure food to the liver and the dregs to the thick intestines is like the [oil or juice] presser, the force that makes the food into the colour of the blood is like the dyer, the one that changes the blood into the colour of the milk in the breasts and makes it a drop in the testicles is like the bleacher, the force that draws from the liver nourishment to every single part of the organs and sends the water to the bladder is like the cupbearer, the force that discharges the dregs to the outside is like the street-sweeper, and the one that eliminates harm and illness is like the righteous leader.

God Most High has granted every human being the things that he needs as a necessary means for his viability, like the heart, the liver, the brain and the fundamentals of living beings. He has also granted things that he (i.e. the human being) needs, although they do not belong to the absolute necessities of his life, like hand and foot, eye and tongue. And He has granted him things to make his beauty perfect, like the blackness of the hair, the redness of the lips, the curves of the eyebrows, and things like that.

Now, it is necessary for every Muslim to contemplate those wonders of the craftsmanship of God Most High in his body which I have made clear, and [it is necessary] that he firmly believes that God Most High is powerful, that there is no weakness in His power, and that He is the Knowing One in whose knowledge there is no shortcoming; that the Most High is wise and in His wisdom there is no feebleness nor shortcoming and so on for the other qualities of perfection. So, he who contemplates the wonders of a poem in well-balanced words and meaning, or the writing of a scholar skilled in the sciences, or the artefact of a skilled craftsman, and he perceives its wonders and its intricacies—the powers of poet, writer, and craftsman[1] become overwhelmingly grand in his heart. Likewise, he who contemplates the wonders of the craftsmanship of God Most High in his body and his heart will firmly believe that the power of God Most High, His knowledge and His Wisdom, His Loving-kindness and His Mercy are perfect and inexhaustible, that the one who has the power of creating something like this from despised water[2] most certainly has the power of reviving him after death, that he [should] occupy himself after gratefulness for Him, the Most High, with not rebelling against him by the faculties of these limbs, as Junayd—May God have mercy on him—has said: *Gratefulness is not rebelling against God Most High for His blessings,* that he occupy himself with the performance of what is made incumbent upon him, because that belongs to thankfulness. God Most High has spoken: *Give thanks, O House of David! Few of*

1. I omit *al-ʿālim,* because it upsets the group of three.

2. See Qur'ān 32:8; *He made his seed from a draught of despised fluid,* and 77:20; *Did we not create you from a base fluid.*

my bondsmen are thankful [34:13]. He [should] consider that, if one of the kings of the world were to send his slave to him to serve him all his life, while God Most High has sent to his inward and outward self several thousand craftsmen that they should serve him all of his life, but he does not thank Him.

All of this is about the knowledge of the body.

As for the heart; it is the soul and essence of the human being. It is that which knows God Most High, and is God's close friend when it is free of the mean qualities and adorned with the praiseworthy qualities. But it is an enemy to God Most High when it is sullied with the impurities of non-belief and [the] acts of disobedience and [when it is] characterized by the evil qualities of trickery, deception, and hypocrisy. Now, the body follows it in all of this. The heart is a spiritual thing that cannot be grasped by the senses. It is, however, created and originated.

It has an advantage over the body of two kinds: One is with regard to knowledge, and the second with regard to capability.

Concerning the first, God Most High has given man the capacity to understand all the sciences—the sciences of the religious laws and religion, geometry and arithmetic, medicine and astrology, and the different kinds of crafts and trades. He can encompass all these spheres of knowledge, nay, the whole world is in him as the tiny grain in the desert of the Banū Isrāʾīl, and he travels in his mind from the highest to the lowest, and from East to West in a single moment. He knows the measurement of the heavens and the earth and the measure of all the stars. With ingenious devices he pulls the large fish[1] out of the depth of the sea, makes the birds fall out of the sky, and he makes subservient even the animals that have strength like the elephant, the camel, and the horse.

Concerning its superiority with regard to its capacity, it is such that the heart belongs to the category of the angelic substance. So, just as the world of bodies is subservient to the angels by the decree of God Most High, they make the rain fall and let loose the winds, they give the different kinds of living beings their form in the womb and to the plants in the belly of the earth and on the outside of it, and each one of its different classes is entrusted with one kind of these things, just like that does the heart have the power with which it makes subservient to itself some of the bodies.

The special world for every human being is his body, and this body is subservient to his heart, like the subservience of the rain to the angel[2] who is charged with letting it fall, like the subservience of death to the angel of death, and the subservience of the winds that are let loose to the angel who is entrusted with them. Whenever the heart commands the hands, the feet, and the fingers to move, they move, and if it commands them to be still, they are still. If anger emerges in the heart the veins will swell in every part of the body, and if desire for sexual intercourse emerges a

1. Arabic: *ḥītān* (pl. of *ḥūt*). This could also mean 'the whales'.
2. 'Angel', *malak*, is missing in the Arabic text.

wind from the heart will blow to the site of the sexual organs; if [the human being] wants to eat food the gland which is underneath the tongue will start to set free the water gradually until the food is moistened and he can swallow the food—and other things like this, which are not hidden from anybody whether he be clever or stupid.

Character and character traits

You should know that every deed of a human being—be it good or bad—even if it is small, creates different effects in his heart. These effects are being presented to him in his book on the Day of Resurrection; and these effects are called character.

The heart of the believer corresponds to a polished mirror. Blameworthy character traits such as envy, gloating, haughtiness and aggressiveness, ruse, deception, treachery and dissimulation, conceitedness, hypocrisy, grudge, and whatever resembles them correspond to the smoke and the murkiness that falls upon the mirror, blackens it, and makes it concealed from God Most High in the hereafter—and God save us from that!

The good character traits such as contentment, bashfulness and patience, noble-mindedness, knowledge, learning and reason, wisdom, righteousness, and the likes of them correspond to light that falls upon the mirror and removes the darknesses of disobedience and the badness of the ugly character traits. The Messenger of God, may God bless him and grant him peace, hints at this with his words. *Let the bad be followed by the good,—it will then wipe it out.*

The hearts will assemble on the Day of Resurrection either polished and illuminated or blackened and sullied, and no one but the one who brings to God a blameless heart will be saved.

Among the polished and illuminated hearts are some that are more polished and more illuminated than others. Sometimes one of the hearts of the faithful is [very] strong and the strength of its light reaches the point that, if its awe-inspiring appearance would fall upon a lion, he would follow it. And if he devotes his zeal to a sick person, this person would be healed instantly. If he would happen to think about a man who was far away from him, whom he would wish to come near to him, there would emerge inside of that man movement and determination and he would then rise and go to him. And if it would be his intention that the heavens should rain, the rain would fall—and likewise with other miracles of the saints.

Just as the illuminated hearts are different [from each other] so do the blackened hearts differ [from each other in] degree; some are more blackened and more evil than others.

Sometimes the badness of the heart of a hypocrite or an unbeliever is [very] strong and he looks, for instance, at a beautiful creature with the eye of envy and that creature perishes instantly. This is affliction by the evil eye, and this does certainly exist. The Messenger of God—may God bless him and grant him peace—has said: *The evil eye is a reality.* He also said: The *evil eye brings a man into the grave and the camel into the cooking pot.* Some sorcery is of this category, that is, the category of the malignancy of the heart. Now if I were to explain its way, then this would be teaching sorcery on my part, about which one is not allowed to speak clearly.

Of praiseworthy and blameworthy character traits there are many, but in spite of their large number they can be reduced to four categories:

(1) The character traits of the hoofed animals: abundance of food and abundance of copulation.
(2) The character traits of the predatory animals: like causing pain and injury to the Muslims.
(3) The character traits of the devils: like temptation, trickery, and deception.
(4) The character traits of the angels: like faith, knowledge, intellect, self-control, righteousness, and fear of God.

Now man has been charged with disciplining the pig of greed and voracity, the wolf of injury and killing and the devil of trickery and deception, and to put them under the administration of reason and self-control until he has reached permanent bliss and attains the praiseworthy character traits. If he would not discipline them, but submit to them he would attain the blameworthy character traits which are the source to this man in a dream or in a wakefulness he would see himself standing in front of the pig or the wolf or the devil, submitting to them, obeying them, nay, prostrating and humiliating himself in front of them. And this is so, not because the pig, the wolf, and the devil are blameworthy as to their appearance and their form, but through the qualities they have in themselves namely injury, voracity, and deception.

In the tradition it is said: There are among the angels such as have the forms of the hoofed animals, those that have the form of the wild animals, and those that have the form of the birds. All angels however, are exempt from the blameworthy character traits like unbelief and hypocrisy, aggressiveness, malice, deception, temptation, and so forth. They are exclusively given to the praiseworthy character traits like faith, knowledge, sincerity, and the like. If now the hoofed animals, the wild animals, and the devil were blameworthy because of their form and appearance then those angels would be blameworthy in the eyes of God Most High, but this is not so. However, those who are dominated in this world by inflicting injury and damage to the believers, they will be gathered on the Day of Resurrection in the form of a wolf, a dog, or a snake. Those who are dominated in this world by voracity and desire for mean deeds, they will be gathered in the form of the pig. Those, who are dominated in this world by trickery and deception, they will be gathered in the form of the devil. Those, however, who were dominated in this world by learning and knowledge, by intellect and righteousness, they will be gathered in the form of an angel near to God.

If someone would say: Since the characteristics of the animals of prey and the hoofed animals, the devil, and the angels come together in man, how do you know that the original state [of man] is that of the angels, and that the others are accidental? How do you know that it is demanded of him to acquire the character traits of the angels rather than any of the others?

I would say: The human being is truly the most noble and the most preferred of all living being and the devils—there is no doubt about it. God Most High has spoken: *Verily We have honoured the children of Adam* up to where He spoke: *and have preferred them above many of those whom We created with a marked preferment.*[1]

Now if his preference and nobility were in [matters of] food and drink, then the camel and the elephant would be more entitled to be preferred and honoured than he, because they both eat much more and have bigger bellies. If it were for the frequency of copulation, then the sparrow would be preferable and more in favour than he, because the lowliest of the sparrows copulates more than he. And if it were for causing pain and damage the lion would preferable to him. If it were for trickery, ruses and deception, the devil would be preferable to him. But it is not so.

However, God Most High has granted him like what He has granted the other creatures and more than that, which is, sincerity, and similar praiseworthy qualities. So he knows that his superiority, his high rank, and his noble status lie in this, not in that which he shares with the other living beings. For, when two things are alike in a special characteristic and one of them is singled out by the advantage of an additional characteristic then one knows that it has been created for the special distinction with which it has been favoured. For instance, the horse is similar to the donkey in its capacity to carry burdens, but it is especially characterized by galloping in battles fighting the infidels, so one knows that it has been created for running in battles, fighting the infidels. The Messenger of God—May God bless him and grant him peace—hinted at this when he said: *The good is tied into the forelock of the horse.* Now when the horse becomes too weak to run [in battles] and is not too weak to carry burdens, then it has left the horse character and has been brought down to the level of the donkey and that is its ruin and its downfall. And so all men share something with the hoofed animals, but are distinguished by learning and knowledge, reason and modesty, and similar things in which the other living beings do not participate. So you should know that he (i.e. man) is honoured and has excellence because he is special in these [qualities] and not in those that he shares with the hoofed animals, the animals of prey, and the devils. But who straightaway bans the praiseworthy character traits and takes on as characteristics trickery and deception, he has left the level of humanity and stepped down to the

1. Qur'ān 17:70. The text in between reads: *We carry them on the land and the sea and have made provision of good things for them ...*

abodes of the devils. So it is also with the other qualities. From all we have said has come about knowledge of the soul and knowledge of God Most High.[1]

The world and man's place in it

As to the third principle, which is knowledge of the world, you should know that this world and the Hereafter[2] are two expressions of your two conditions: what is[3] before death—and this is that which is nearer and closer—is called the world (*al-dunyā*) which is the feminine of 'nearer' (*adnā*), just as *al-ʿulyā* is the feminine of *al-aʿlā* (highest)—and what is after death is called the hereafter.

The world is one of the way-stations of those who travel to God Most High, a market place erected in the desert on the path of those who travel the road of religion for them to buy from it provisions for the journey towards God Most High.

Man, in his beginning, was created in imperfection, but he has the disposition that enables him to attain perfection and to become worthy of the proximity of the Divine Presence and seeing God Most High. This is his paradise and the highest degree of his bliss. For this he was created and with this he has been charged. But the vision of God Most High is not possible for him as long as his eyes are not opened, and his eyes are not opened as long as knowledge of God most High has not come to him. Knowledge of God does not come to him as long as he does not know the wonders of the handiwork of God Most High, and the knowledge of the wonders of the handiwork of God Most High does not come to him save by the senses. It is not possible for the senses to exist in this mould that is made of water and dust. So, there is an urgent need for the world of water and dust that he takes provisions from it, and two things are necessary for him.

One is that with which he protects his heart from the causes of its ruin and with which he can attain nourishment for the heart.

The second one is that with which he protects his body from destructive influences and with which he attains nourishment for the body.

The heart's nourishment is knowledge of God Most High and love of Him. The reason for its ruin is that man becomes absorbed in loving something else rather than God Most High.

One should care for the body because of the heart, for it is for the heart what the camel is for the pilgrim on the road of pilgrimage, to bring him to the Kaʿba and to make easier for him the hardships of the journey. So, for the pilgrim it is necessary to care for the camel according to its needs. If, however, he kept himself occupied with it in a way that exceeds the extent of its needs until, one day, the caravan moves on and he stays behind, busy with the care of his camel, he would

1. These are the first two principles mentioned in the beginning of the text.
2. I omit *knowledge* in front of *this world and the hereafter*, because it is not logical.
3. Read *fa-mā* instead of *fī mā*.

be one looking after his camel not one on a pilgrimage. And so the human being, when he busies himself with the care for his body and neglects the care for his heart, is deprived of his bliss.

The needs of the body

What the body needs in this world are three things: Food for eating, clothes for covering up, and an abode to ward off from his body damage from heat and cold. All this [is] according to necessity, so that if he ate more than his body's limit, this would become a reason for his ruin, and he would be responsible for it.

If he would put on many clothes their weight would be heavy for him to carry and he would be harmed by them. And if he would have more of an abode than necessity requires, he would be harmed by the care for it—contrary to the nourishment of the heart which is knowledge of God Most High and the love of Him, for the more it gets increased the better it becomes.

God Most High has in His benevolence given desire power over the human being, so that he may desire for whatever is necessary for him in terms of food, housing, and clothing. [This is] so that his body which is his mount may not perish. Now desire has not been created for staying within a limit, so God Most High created reason to keep it from exceeding its limits. Then God Most High sent down the religious prescriptions of Islam onto the tongue of the messengers—Blessings and peace may be upon them—to make clear the limits.

However, desire was laid down in the body before reason because of [the] necessity of the minor for it, and he was charged with the religious prescriptions after reason was put into him. So desire settled down in the body and took possession of it before reason and religious law, and then rebelled against those two. But they admonish and remind him of what the food, the clothes and the abode was really for, so that he would not forget the nourishment for the heart, which is the provision in his Hereafter.[1]

Since the body needed food, clothing, and housing, it needed farming in the attainment of food, weaving in the attainment of clothing, and building in the attainment of housing. Then it found need for branches of these crafts like cotton ginning and spinning, which fulfil the needs of the weaver, and like sewing which completes the clothing after the weaving. All of this needed instruments made of wood, iron and other materials, and from this came forth the other handicrafts like smith-craft and carpentry.

Every one of those professionally engaged people was in need of support of his companions because of his incapability to master all the crafts. So they needed a society in one place, so that the tailor could sew the cloth of the weaver for a price,

1. I prefer to read *fī ākhiratihī* instead of *fī ākhirihi.*

and the weaver could weave the yarn of the spinner for a price, that the builder could build a house for the tailor and the weaver for a price. And so came forth between them the human relations which lead to dispute and controversy. Now there arose the necessity for three other crafts: these are governance, dispensation of justice and jurisprudence, by which are made known the laws of mediation between people.

Man's craving for the world

Many are the distractions of the world, and the human being occupies himself with it with his heart and his body, by loving it, as far as the heart is concerned, and by possessing it, as far as the body is concerned. Now through the love of it are engendered in his heart destructive qualities like greed, stinginess and envy, enmity, malice, estrangement and the like. So people are going astray from their souls, something comes between them and their hearts, and they forget that the basic needs are three, and these are: food, clothing and housing. These three are there because of the body, and the body is there because of the heart, and the heart is there for attaining knowledge of God Most High. So they forget their souls and their Creator, and they become like the pilgrim who forgets the Kaʿba, forgets the journey towards it, and occupies himself all his life with looking after the camel. The Messenger of God—May God bless him and give him peace—hints at this with his words: *Beware of the world, for it is more bewitching than Hārūt and Mārūt.*[1]

1. See also Qur'ān 2:102.

2

Aḥmad Ghazzālī

Aḥmad Ghazzālī is the younger brother of the legendary Abū Ḥāmid Ghazzālī whose fame has historically over-shadowed the significance of Aḥmad's contributions. He was born sometime between 451–454/1059–1062 in the village of Tābirān near the town of Ṭūs in Khurāsān and died sometime between 517–520/1123–1126 in Qazwīn.

His father, a textile weaver, was not literate but had Sufi tendencies. On his death-bed Aḥmad's father left the guardianship of his children to Imam Aḥmad Rādkānī, a family friend known for his piety and Sufism. Little is known about the nature of Aḥmad's early studies but what is known is that he studied under the direction of Rādkānī in his youth. Aḥmad studied Islamic jurisprudence in Ṭūs and practised austere forms of Sufism under the supervision of Shaykh Abū Bakr Nassāj. His ascetic practices and hermit-like lifestyle became legendary to those who knew him. In fact he became one of the most famous Sufis of his time and is considered as the pole (*quṭb*) of many Sufi orders.

According to the tradition of many Muslim authorities, Aḥmad Ghazzālī journeyed to Baghdad where he taught at the Niẓāmiyyah university as a replacement for his brother Abū Ḥāmid between the years 488–498/1095–1104. He continued his journey afterwards to the cities of Tabriz, Marāghah, Hamadān and Isfahan. He finally travelled to the city of Qazwīn near Tehran where he lived from 515/1121 until his death in 520/1126.

Among those who were influenced by Aḥmad Ghazzālī were, first and foremost, his older brother Abū Ḥāmid Muḥammad Ghazzālī. Recent studies clearly indicate that, especially in the domain of Sufism, this influence has been underestimated. Among Aḥmad's other notable students and followers are: ʿAbd Allāh ibn Muḥammad Miyānijī Hamadānī also known as ʿAyn al-Quḍāt Hamadānī, Sanāʾī Ghaznawī, the great poet and gnostic, Abu'l-Faḍl Ṣāʾin ibn ʿAbd Allāh Ṣūfī Baghdādī who is one of the revered Sufi masters of the Niʿmatullāhī order, Shaykh ʿAbd al-Wāḥid Āmidī, Shaykh Rūzbihān Kabīr who was from Fārs province in Iran but is buried in Egypt, and Abu'l-Qāsim 'Umar ibn Muḥammad known as Ibn al-Bizrī Jazarī, a Shāfi'ī jurist. The list is a testament to the fact that Aḥmad Ghazzālī was one of those Sufi masters who was also proficient in Islamic law. Finally, one can name among his disciples 'Abd Allāh Suhrawardī, who is the founder of the Suhrawardiyyah Sufi order, and 'Alī ibn Māzandarānī who was a Shi'i authority in the transmitted sciences.

The opponents of Aḥmad Ghazzālī have criticized him severely for having advocated a controversial Sufi practice known as '*shāhid bāzī*' in which focusing on earthly beauty becomes a reminder of Divine Beauty. Many Sufis are known to have reflected upon the beauty of the face of youth as a locus of manifestation of Divine Beauty, a practice that provoked criticism from many exoteric jurists. Aḥmad Ghazzālī also had a particular love for *samā'*, the Sufi practice of music and sacred dance. This practice too was deemed deviant by some of the exoteric jurists such as Yūsuf Hamadānī, Ibn Jawzī Ḥanbalī, Ibn Ṭāhir Muqaddasī Qayṣarānī and Ibn Ḥājar. Aḥmad Ghazzālī appears to have been a very wealthy man. Such figures as Ṣadr al-Dīn Qūnawī and Aḥmad Rāzī among others admonished him for lecturing on the virtues of poverty and asceticism while his wealth was known to those who knew him. Finally, among the controversial aspects of Aḥmad Ghazzālī one should mention his commentary on Lucifer, or Iblīs. While Iblīs, in Islam, is considered to be a fallen angel, there is a literary genre that offers an esoteric interpretation of this. Aḥmad Ghazzālī also offered such an interpretation in which he considers Iblīs to be the true lover of God since he rejected loving anyone else but God. This interpretation, in addition to the previously mentioned practices, made Ghazzālī a somewhat controversial figure and perhaps it was for the above reasons that he remained a relatively neglected figure in comparison with his brother.

There have also been many who have defended him. The Seljuk kings, in particular, Sulṭān Malik Shāh and his son Sulṭān Sanjar were among the devotees of Aḥmad. Also to the list of his admirers can be added his own brother Abū Ḥāmid who spoke highly of Aḥmad's faith, as well as 'Ayn al-Quḍāt Hamadānī, Ibn Athīr, Ibn Khallakān, Sayyid Muḥammad Nūrbakhsh and, above all, Rūmī.

Aḥmad Ghazzālī's legendary piety and fame as a Sufi master became the basis for some to attribute to him the ability to perform miracles. These miracles which included having visions at will of the Prophet Muḥammad and the ability to read other people's minds have been mentioned by some of his admirers such as Ibn Kathīr, Ibn Mustawfī Arbalī and 'Ayn al-Quḍāt Hamadānī.

Tracing the spiritual genealogy of Sufi masters and their respective orders has always been an integral part of the Sufi tradition. There are a number of Sufi masters and Sufi orders which have been identified with Aḥmad Ghazzālī in one way or another. Among them we can mention the Ni'matullāhiyyah, Ṣafī 'Alī Shāhiyyah, Dhahabiyyah, Kubrawiyyah, Suhrawardiyyah and even Mawlawiyyah also known as Mevlevi whose grand-master was Rūmī himself.

In this chapter we have included a section from the *Sawāniḥ al-ʿushshāq* (Auspices of Divine Lovers), a masterpiece of Persian prose that is essentially a gnostic interpretation of love not as a mode of feeling but as a mode of knowledge. Ghazzālī offers a detailed and highly esoteric interpretation of the concept of lover, love and the beloved and the relationship between them and analogizes this triune reality to the epistemic relation between the knower, known and knowledge. Such Sufi concepts as separation and unity, stages and types of love and the role of will power in this complex relationship are among the topics discussed here.

M. Aminrazavi

AUSPICES OF DIVINE LOVERS

Sawāniḥ al-ʿushshāq

Translated for this volume by Joseph Lumbard from Aḥmad Ghazzālī, *Sawāniḥ al-ʿushshāq*, selections.[1]

7

Love comes and goes, it has increase, decrease and perfection, and the lover has states within it. In the beginning he may deny it, then he may submit to it. Then he may be disgraced and again take to the path of denial. These states change according to the moment and the individual; sometimes love increases and the lover denies it, sometimes love decreases and the one who possesses it denies the decrease. For love must open the castle of the lover to have a house for itself within, so that the lover becomes tame and surrenders.

> I said to the heart, 'Do not tell the secret to the companion!
> Beware! Tell no more of love's tale.'
>
> The heart said to me, 'Don't say this again.
> Expose your body to affliction and say no more.'

8

(1) The special character of man is this, is it not enough that he was beloved before being a lover? This is no small virtue. 'He loves them'[2] brought down so much

1. There are many printed editions of the *Sawāniḥ*. The four most reliable editions are: *Sawāniḥ*, ed. Aḥmad Mujāhid, in *Majmūʿa-yi āthār-i fārsī-yi Aḥmad Ghazzālī*, pp. 89–173; *Sawāniḥ*, ed. Naṣrullāh Pourjavady (Tehran, 1359 Sh./1980); *Sawāniḥ*, in *Ganjīna-yi ʿirfān*, ed. Ḥāmid Rabbānī (Tehran, 1973); *Sawāniḥ*, ed. Helmut Ritter (Tehran, 1368 Sh./1989). The edition by Pourjavady is based upon that of Ritter and supplemented by additional manuscripts which predate those upon which Ritter relied. Though five editions were published between those of Ritter and Pourjavady, none surpassed Ritter's. The edition of Pourjavady can in some ways be seen as a supplement to Ritter's, as he admittedly builds upon Ritter's extant apparatus. Mujāhid's edition has a critical apparatus adopted in part from other editions. It is, however, nowhere near the quality of Ritter's apparatus. Rabbānī's edition does not provide an apparatus, but in several instances Rabbānī provides readings which make more sense than those of Pourjavady or Ritter. For this translation I will therefore rely upon the editions of Pourjavady, Ritter and Rabbānī. In re-rendering the *Sawāniḥ* into English, I am deeply indebted to Naṣrullāh Pourjavady for his previous English translation; *Sawāniḥ: Inspirations from the World of Pure Spirits, The Oldest Sufi Treatise on Love* (London, 1986).

2. This is a reference to the famous Qurʾānic verse, 'He loves them and they love Him' (5:54). Aḥmad Ghazzālī sees this as an expression of the beginning of all human love through a pact with

sustenance for that beggar before his arrival that he continues to partake of it for eternity upon eternity, yet it remains.

(2) O noble lad, the sustenance which is sent down in pre-temporality, how can it be received fully except in post-temporality? No, rather contingency can only receive the sustenance which eternity placed in pre-temporality completely in post-temporality.

(3) O noble lad, pre-temporality has reached here, post-temporality can never reach an end. The sustenance that descends will never reach complete exhaustion. If you gain insight into the secret of your moment, know that the 'two bows-length'[1] of pre-temporality and post-temporality are your heart and your moment.[2]

9

(1) The secret of this—that love never shows the whole of its face to anyone—is that it is the bird of pre-temporality. What has come here is the traveller of post-temporality. Here it does not show its face to the vision of contingent beings, for not every house deserves to be a nest for it, as it has always had a nest in the abode of the magnificence of pre-temporality.[3] Now and then it flies with pre-temporality and hides behind the veil of the curtain of its majesty and greatness. It has never shown the face of beauty completely to the vision of knowledge and will never reveal it.

---

the Divine. He explains this love-pact by referring to the Qur'ānic story of man's pre-temporal covenant with God made while all of mankind was still in Adam's loins. As the Qur'ān states: And when thy Lord took from the Children of Adam, from their loins, their seed, and made them testify touching themselves, 'Am I not your Lord?' They said, 'Yes, we testify'—lest You should say on the Day of Resurrection, 'As for us, we were heedless of this' (7:172).

The day of this covenant is known in the Persian Sufi tradition as *rūz-i alast* (the day of 'Am I not [your Lord]'). It is understood by Aḥmad Ghazzālī and others as a covenant fashioned in love and through love. When God said to man 'Am I not your Lord' this was His love for them. When man responded by saying 'yes' (*balā*) this was his love for God. From this perspective, only through God's making him beloved did man become a lover, and all of man's love and striving for God originates from God's pre-temporal love for man. Man's love for God is thus the self-same love which God has for man. Although man's love finds expression in the temporal order, its origin is pre-temporal and its goal is post-temporal.

1. This is a reference to the famous night journey and ascension of the Prophet Muḥammad, wherein he is said to have been 'two-bows-length' from God; 'He was two bows-length or nearer. Then God revealed to him what He revealed' (53:9–10). For Ghazzālī, the two bows represent the arc of spiritual descent from pre-temporality and the arc of spiritual ascent to post-temporality. Together they comprise the entire circle of existence. Pre-temporality is the point from which the arc of descent begins and post-temporality is the point to which the arc of ascent returns. As one descends into the corporeal world, one actualizes various modes of manifestation, but in order for these to be integrated and unified one must return upon the path of ascent.

2. To say that the path of descent from pre-temporality and the path of ascent to post-temporality are the spiritual wayfarer's heart and moment is to say that one's true nature is determined by where one stands in the process of spiritual reintegration.

3. i.e. the pure human heart.

(2) Because of this secret, if for a moment one sees the locus of its trust,[1] it would be the moment at which he is liberated from the attachments and obstacles of 'mundaneness' and released from the imagination of knowledge, the calculation of fantasy, the philosophy of imagination and the espionage of the senses.

Bring what draws the hearts of the friends together;
Like a whale draw sorrow from my heart with one breath.

When I draw the sword of wine from the sheath of the goblet,
  time must suffer from me;
Bring the son of the Magian and give it to the old Magian.

For Rustam is carried only by Rustam's Raksh;[2]
For those two are both from 'thereness', not 'hereness'.

10

Love is its own bird and its own nest, its own essence and its own attribute, its own wing and its own wind, its own arc and its own flight, its own hunter and its own game, its own direction and what is directed there, its own seeker and its own goal. It is its own beginning and its own end, its own king and its own subject, its own sword and its own sheath. It is garden as well as tree, branch as well as fruit, nest as well as bird.

In the sorrow of love we are our own consoler;
We are frenzied and bewildered by our own affair,

Enamoured by our own fortune,
Ourselves the hunters, ourselves the game.

11

Beauty is one thing and belovedness is another. The glance of beauty is one thing and the coquetry of belovedness is another. The coquetry of beauty has no face toward another and has no connection with what is outside. But as for the coquetry of belovedness, amorous gestures, flirting, and coquetry, that is a reality which

1. i.e. realizes the moment of belovedness on the day of the pre-temporal covenant—*rūz-i alast*. See note 1 above.

2. Rustam is a character in Firdawsī's *Shāh-nāmah* who was of such power and stature that only his steed Rakhsh could carry him.

derives its support from the lover, without him they will find no way. There is no doubt that the beloved is here dependent upon the lover.

A Story:

There was a king with whom the stove-tender of the public bath fell in love, and the vizier informed the king. The king wanted to punish him. But the vizier said, 'You are known for justice. It is not proper that you punish him for love and a deed in which there is no choice. Punishing him for what is beyond his will is far from just.'

It so happened that the king's route passed by the stove of that poor man, who would sit in that place everyday waiting until the king would pass by. The king when reaching that point would join the glance of belovedness to the glance of beauty and the vizier noticed this. Until one day the king came and the stove-tender was not sitting there. The king had assumed the glance of belovedness; that glance of belovedness required the glimpse of the need of love. When he was not there the king was left naked, for he did not find the place of acceptance. Anger overtook the king. The vizier was shrewd and perceived what had happened. He bowed down and said, 'I said that punishing him would have no meaning, for no harm came from him. Now we know for ourselves that his need has to be answered.'

(2) O noble lad, the glance of belovedness in beauty is like salt in the pot in order that the perfection of charm (*milāḥat*) be connected to the perfection of beauty.

O noble lad, what would you say if it was said to the king that he is free of you and has taken up with another and become his lover? I do not know if any jealousy would arise from within him or not.

O friend, do what you like but do not be the companion of another.
For then there will no longer be anything left for me.

(3) Love is the connecting band; it has an attachment to both sides. If its relation to the side of the lover becomes sound a connection is necessary from both sides, for it itself is the prelude to oneness.

12

The secret of the face of everything is the point of His connection and a sign hidden in creation, and beauty is the brand of creation. The secret of the face is that which faces love. So long as one does not see that secret, he will never see the sign of creation and beauty. That face is the beauty of 'and the face of your Lord remains'

Other than Him there is no face, for 'all that dwells upon the earth will perish'.[1] And that face is naught, as you know.

13

(1) The eye of beauty looks away from its own beauty, for it cannot find the perfection of its own beauty except in the mirror of the love of the lover. In this way beauty must have a lover so that the beloved can take nourishment from its own beauty in the mirror of love and the seeking of the lover. This is a great secret and the secret of many secrets.

My increasing in drunkenness from her face was not without cause;
There was wine, the cup and no rival to joy.

Forgive me if you say it was you;
It was she who was searching, for I sought nothing.

(2) So the lover himself is closer to the beauty of the beloved than the beloved, for the beloved takes nourishment through the intermediary of the lover from her own beauty and loveliness. Thus the lover is more a self than the self of the beloved. That is why the beloved becomes jealous of the lover because of his vision of the beloved. Regarding this reality it has been said:

O Lord, take justice for me from Alexander's soul,
For he has made a mirror in which You behold Yourself.

(3) Here where the lover becomes more the beloved than the beloved, the wonders of the attachments of connection are prepared as a condition for the non-attachment of the lover with himself. Love's connection will reach to the place where the lover claims that he himself is the beloved: 'I am the Real'[2] and 'Glory be to me'[3] are this point. And if he is in the very state of banishment, separation and unwantedness, he imagines that he has no place and that he himself is the beloved.

There is so much coyness in my head from your love
That I mistakenly think you are a lover for me.

---

1. Qur'ān 55:26. Beauty is the means whereby the lover witnesses the manifestation of Absolute Love in the delimited form of the beloved. The beauty of each thing is called by Ghazzālī 'the brand of creation'. This beauty is the secret face which faces Absolute Love and by virtue of which all things truly exist. For if they did not have a face turned towards the absolute, there would be no way for them to derive their existence from it.
2. A famous saying of Manṣūr Ḥallāj (d. 309/922).
3. A famous saying of Bāyazīd Basṭāmī (d. 261/875).

Either union with you pitches a tent by my door,
Or I have lost my head in complete error.

14

The beloved said to the lover: 'Come! Become me! For if I become you, then the beloved will be in need, the lover will increase and need and necessity will become greater. Yet when you become me the beloved will increase, all will be beloved not lover, all will be coyness not need, all will be finding not necessity, all will be wealth not poverty, all will be remedy not helplessness.'

15

(1) This affair will reach a place where he will become jealous of himself and jealous of his own eye. Regarding this reality they have said:

O friend, I do not take you to be the friend himself.
Being envious of you, I take not the vision of myself as a friend.

I am sad not because I am not with you in my quarter,
I am sad because I am not with you in the same skin.

(2) And this point will sometimes reach a place where if one day the beloved becomes more beautiful, the lover will become distressed and angry. So long as one has not tasted this meaning it is difficult to understand.

16

(1) In reality love is affliction. Intimacy and comfort in it are strange and borrowed, since separation in love is really duality and union is really one. The rest is all the imagination of union, not the reality of union. Regarding this it is said:

Love is affliction. I am the one who does not withdraw from affliction.
When love is asleep, I stir up evil.

My friends told me to withdraw from affliction.
Affliction is the heart, how can I withdraw from the heart.

The tree of love grows from within the heart.
When it needs water, I pour it from the eyes.

Although love is pleasant, and unpleasant is love's sorrow,
I am happy when I mix the two together.

17

(1) Since love is affliction, its nourishment in knowledge is from the persecution which the beloved performs. There where there is no knowledge, love itself is the reality of its nourishment from oneness.

(2) Until there is proof for love and until a connection [between the lover and the beloved] is the necessity of the moment, a conflict chosen by the friend is more desired than ten reconciliations.

(3) The beggar of love is combined from rebuke and conflict, so that the heart will take to guarding its breaths, for it cannot disregard anything. Until at last it eats regret and bites his hand because of the regret of separation and strikes the top of regret with the hand of remorse.

When I was in union with my idol,
I was always in strife and conflict with her.

When distance came I was content with imagination;
O wheel! Punish me well for my interloping.

Thus it is among conflict, strife, peace, reconciliation, coquetry and glancing that this discourse will be established.[1]

18

(1) To be self through one's own self is one thing, and to be self through one's own beloved is another. To be self through one's own self is the unripeness of the beginning of love. When on the path of ripening he is self and arrives from self, then he has reached beyond her. Then he will reach beyond the self with her and beyond her.

(2) Here is where annihilation becomes the *qiblah* of subsistence, the pilgrim begins to circumambulate the holy Ka'ba, and like a moth connects to annihilation from the frontier of subsistence.[2] This is not contained in knowledge except

1. i.e. the discussion of spiritual wayfaring is a discussion of these states, until one reaches union which is beyond all spiritual states.

2. *Fanā'* (annihilation) and *baqā'* (subsistence) are considered by many to be the final two stages of the spiritual path. As Sachiko Murata observes: 'Annihilation designates the purification of the self and the elimination of the constricting limitations of ignorance and forgetfulness; or the transformation of blameworthy character traits into praiseworthy character traits. It is usually paired with 'subsistence' (*baqā'*), which is the actualization of the Divine Attributes in whose image the human being was created.' *Chinese Gleams of Sufi Light* (Albany, 2000), p. 56.

through allegory. Perhaps these verses which I composed in my youth indicate this reality:

So long as the world-revealing cup is in my hand,[1]
Out of wisdom, the highest wheel is subservient to me.

So long as the Kaʿba of non-being is the *qiblah* of my being,
The most sober man of the world is intoxicated with me.

(3) 'This is my Lord',[2] 'I am the Real', and 'Glory be to me' are all the chameleon of this colouration (*talwīn*) and are far from stability (*tamkīn*).[3]

19

(1) So long as he is his own self through himself, he is subject to the edicts of separation and union, receiving and rejecting, expansion (*basṭ*) and contraction (*qabḍ*), and sorrow and joy, and he is captive of the moment. When the moment overcomes him he must follow the edict of the moment's colour, whatever edict the moment has. The moment paints the lover according to its colour and edict and he will belong to the moment. But in the path of annihilation from self, these edicts are wiped out and these opposites are removed, because its origin transcends cause and desire.

(2) When the lover comes back from it (love) to his self his way to self is from it and through it. Since his way to self is from it and through it, these edicts do not apply to him. What would the edicts of separation and union do here? When would acceptance and rejection entangle him? When would expansion and contraction and sorrow and joy go around the court of his empire?[4] As these verses say:

We sought the foundation of the universe and the origin of the world.
And passed easily beyond cause and caused.

---

1. The 'world-revealing cup' (*jām-i jahān namā*) is a legendary possession of the pre-Islamic Persian king Jamshīd. It came to be used by Sufis as a symbol for the heart of the gnostic-lover which, purified of ignorance and forgetfulness, is able to behold all things as they truly are.

2. Qur'ān 6:76–8. This is a reference to the story of Abraham who said of a star, then of the moon and then of the sun 'This is my Lord', then denied each as it set until he affirmed pure monotheism.

3. The degree of stability (*tamkīn*) is considered by many Sufis to be the highest degree of spiritual realization. Here the lover has transcended the degree of colouration (*talwīn*) of moving from state to state in the lover-beloved duality and is now in the stability (*tamkīn*) of love wherein nothing but pure love remains.

4. This paragraph refers to the state beyond the first paragraph. The first is seeing the images of the beloved on the surface of the ocean of love. The second is being completely immersed in the ocean, beyond all forms and imaginations.

And that black light which is beyond the point of *lā*,
Beyond this too we passed, neither this nor that remained.[1]

(3) Here he is the master of the moment.[2] When he descends to the sky of the world he will overcome the moment, the moment will not overcome him, and he will be free from the moment.

(4) Yes, his being is to her and from her.[3] Perhaps this is the separation of this state, and his annihilation is from her and in her. They call this 'hiding in the essence of *illa*.'[4] Sometimes they call it being a hair in the beloved's tress. As has been said:

I have suffered so much cruelty from your tress,
That I have become a hair from those two curved tresses.

What wonder from this then if I stay together with you?
What does one hair add or remove from your tress?

---

1. These verses are most likely by Abu'l-Ḥasan al-Bustī (d. *c.* 485/1092). They have circulated widely in Persian Sufi literature. Aḥmad Ghazzālī's foremost disciple, 'Ayn al-Quḍāt Hamadānī cites them twice in the *Tamhīdāt*, ed. 'Afīf 'Usayrān (Tehran, 1962), p. 119 and p. 249, and is the first to attribute them to Bustī; Rashīd al-Dīn Maybudī cites them twice in *Kashf al-asrār*, ed. 'Alī Aṣghar Ḥikmat (Tehran, 1381 Sh./2002), vol. 1, p. 114 and vol. 2, p. 249; they are also transmitted by 'Abd ar-Raḥmān Jāmī in *Nafaḥāt al-'uns*, ed. Maḥmūd 'Ābidī (Tehran, 1380 Sh./2001) p. 413.

The point of the *lā* referred to in the third verse is where the *lām* and *alif* are joined in the *lā* of the first testimony of faith (*shahādah*)—*lā ilāha illa'Llāh*—No god, but God. Aḥmad Ghazzālī sees this *lā* as the word of ultimate negation (*nafy*) in which attachment to everything save God is obliterated. The point of the *lā* is the very essence of negation, for were it not for that point, the *alif* and *lām* would not be joined. It is thus the archetype of spiritual *fanā'* (annihilation) beyond separation and union. The black light is then an allusion to the station of *baqā'* (subsistence) in which one abides with the Divine alone, beyond all the edicts of separation and union, expansion and contraction, sorrow and happiness. But once in the black light of subsistence, he is the master of the moment, for the edicts of colouration cannot bear the effulgence of the black light. Regarding this experience no discursive knowledge can be obtained, for it is beyond all distinctions and can only be perceived or tasted in the trans-personal depth of one's pre-temporal being, i.e. in the heart.

2. Before Aḥmad Ghazzālī, Sufis had termed the accomplished spiritual wayfarer as a 'son of the moment (*ibn al-waqt*).' He turns this diction on its head to say that 'the son of the moment' is still subject to colouration (*talwīn*) but in spiritual stability (*tamkīn*) he becomes 'the master of the moment.'

3. i.e. to the beloved and through the beloved—but in fact through and to love vis-à-vis the beloved.

4. This refers to the 'but' of the first testimony of faith, 'No god but God'—*lā ilāha illa'Llāh*. This means that the spiritual wayfarer has reached a point where he abandons all the hidden inner idols for the true worship of the One God.

20

(1) When this reality becomes known, affliction and oppression are her castle-crashing mangonel for removing your you-ness from you until you become her.

(2) When an arrow has been shot from the bow of the will of the beloved at your you-ness suppose it to be an arrow of oppression or kindness, for the conversation is about defect or not—the arrow must have a direction or target, and its target must be the *qiblah* of the moment. Until she has turned her entirety to you, how can she shoot? And when the shooting is at you specifically it will no doubt require an account from you. How can these many links not be sufficient, when one of them itself is enough? Here is where it has been said:

Draw one arrow from your quiver to shoot it.
Then place it in your strong bow.

If you want a target, here is my heart.
From you a violent shot, from me a joyful sigh.

21

(1) The beginning of love is this, that the seed of beauty is planted in the ground of the heart's seclusion by the hand of witnessing. Its nurture is from the shining of observation (*naẓar*), but it is not one colour. The planting of the seed and its picking must be one. Regarding this they have said:

The origin of all loverness is from vision;
When the eye sees, then the affair begins.

How many birds fall into the snare of covetousness?
In coveting light the moth falls into the flame.

(2) Love's reality is a conjunction between two hearts. But the lover's love for the beloved is one thing, and the beloved's love for the lover is another. The love of the lover is real and the love of the beloved is the image of the reflection of lover's love in her mirror.

(3) Since there has been conjunction in witnessing, the lover's love requires helplessness, baseness, suffering, wretchedness and submission in all affairs, and the beloved's love requires hubris, august and sublime.

Because of the beauty and the majesty of our beloved,
We are not suitable for her, she is suitable for us.

(4) However, I do not know which is the lover and which the beloved. This is a great mystery, because it is possible that the beloved's allure comes first, then [comes] accomplishment of this. But here the realities are opposite: 'And you do not will unless God wills.'[1] 'He loves them' is before 'they love him'[2]—no doubt. Bāyazīd [Basṭāmī] said, 'For a long time I imagined that I desired Him. He Himself first desired me.'[3]

22

(1) Although in the beginning the beloved's friends are friends and his enemies are enemies, when the affair reaches perfection it is opposite and jealousy appears. The lover would not want anyone to look at her:

I cannot watch the wind blow upon you,
Nor can I see anyone in the world look upon you.

A piece of dust which the soul of your foot has graced,
Your servant will envy.

(2) From this turn the affair will reach a place where her friend becomes an enemy and her enemy becomes a friend, so long as no injury comes to him. Then this affair reaches a place where the lover is jealous of her name, let alone of her. He does not want to hear her name from anybody. He does not want anyone to see her beauty, which is the locus of the heart's consideration. He does not want anyone to hear her name, which is the locus of his consolation. It would seem that she is the *qiblah* of love, and he does not want anyone to reach there.

1. Qur'ān, 81:19.
2. Qur'ān, 5:57. See n. 1.
3. Bāyazīd Basṭāmī (d. 261/875). This is a famous Persian saying, similar versions of which are attributed to Basṭāmī in Farīḍ ad-Dīn 'Aṭṭār's *Tadhkirat al-awliyā'*, ed. R. A. Nicholson, (London and Leiden, 1905–1907), p. 168 and p. 255, which was, however, written over one century after the *Sawāniḥ*. A similar Arabic saying is attributed to Basṭāmī in Abū Nu'aym Iṣfahānī's *Ḥilyat al-awliyā' wa ṭabaqāt al-aṣfiyā'*, ed. Muṣṭafā 'Abd al-Qādir 'Aṭā' (Beirut, 1997), vol. 10, p. 34: 'At the outset I erred in four things: I imagined that I remembered Him, that I knew Him, that I loved Him and that I sought Him. When I reached the end, I saw that His remembrance preceded my remembrance, that His knowledge preceded my knowledge, that His love was before my love, and that His seeking me came first so that I would seek Him.'

23

(1) So long as love is in the beginning, wherever he sees a likeness of this affair he brings it to the beloved. Majnūn had not eaten food for some days when a deer fell in his trap. He was kind to it and set it free. [They asked him why did you do that?] He said, 'There was something resembling Laylā in it.' Cruelty is not fair.

(2) But this is still the very beginning of love. When love reaches perfection, we believe perfection belongs to the beloved and finds no likeness to her among what is other than her, and cannot find [such likeness]. His intimacy with others is cut off, except from that which has an attachment with her, like the dog of her quarter, the dust of her way, and what is like unto that.

(3) When it reaches greater perfection, this consolation also withdraws, for consolation in love is deficiency—and his ecstasy increases. And every yearning from which union can take something away, that is something diseased and defective. Union must be the kindling for the fire of desire, so that it increases. This is that step where the lover believes the beloved is perfection and seeks unification, and whatever is outside of this will never satiate him. And he sees a crowd because of his own existence. As has been said:

In your love my singleness is intense.
In describing you my ability is impotence.

24

(1) In the beginning there is shouting, crying out, and lamentation, for love has not yet taken the entire dominion (*wilāyat*). When the affair reaches perfection and it has taken control, the situation is complete, and the lamentation [of the lover] is replaced by [his] leanness and [his] observation [of the beloved]; for impurity has been replaced by purity. As the poet said:

In the beginning when I was new to love,
My neighbour had no rest from my cries.

Now that my pain has increased, the cries have decreased.
When fire consumes all, smoke decreases.

25

When the lover sees the beloved, agitation arises within him, because his being is borrowed and has a face toward the *qiblah* of non-being. His existence becomes agitated in ecstasy, until he sits with the reality of the affair. Yet there is still not complete maturity. When he becomes completely mature, he becomes absent to himself in the encounter; for when the lover becomes mature in love and love has opened his true nature, then when the vanguard of union appears, his existence will leave in accordance with the measure of his maturity in the affair.

A Story:

It has been transmitted that the people of Majnūn's tribe gathered together and said to Laylā's family, 'This man will be destroyed because of love. What harm is there in giving him permission to see Laylā once?' They said, 'On our part there is no stinginess regarding this, but Majnūn himself does not have the fortitude to see her.' They brought Majnūn and drew back the door of Laylā's tent. Laylā's shadow had not yet appeared when Majnūn, it must be said, became unconscious. They said, 'We said that he did not have the capacity to see her.' Here is where the lover has an affair with the dust of her quarter.[1]

> If separation does not grant me audience with your union,
> I will have an affair with the dust of your quarter.

[This is] because he is able to eat nourishment from her in the being of knowledge. But he cannot eat nourishment from the reality of union, since [there] his he-ness does not remain.[2]

26

(1) The flight of the beloved from the lover is because union is no small affair. Just as the lover must surrender in order to not be him[self], so too the beloved must surrender in order for the lover to be her lover. So long as she does not consume him completely within herself and does not consider him to be part of herself, and so long as she does not accept him completely, she will flee from him. For although he does not know this reality outwardly, his heart and soul know the

---

1. The dust of her quarter is here the knowledge of the Beloved which pertains to the realm of Divine Oneness (*wāḥidiyyah*) but not yet to the realm of unseen of the unseen or *ghayb al-ghuyūb*.

2. The fullness of love which is realized in 'union' is beyond and discursive knowledge, it can only be 'tasted.' Aḥmad Ghazzālī maintains that even the Prophet Muḥammad was incapable of 'knowledge' of the Divine Essence or the unseen of the unseen: Whenever the Messenger of God was carried to the ocean of knowledge it would flow forth, but when he was cast into the ocean of gnosis he said, 'I do not realize, I only worship (*lā adrī innamā aʿbudu*).' Aḥmad Ghazzālī, *Majālis-i Aḥmad Ghazzālī*, ed. with Persian translation by Aḥmad Mujāhid (Tehran, 1385 Sh./1998), p. 61.

whale of love, which is in the inner nature of the lover,[1] what he extracts from it and what is sent to it.

(2) Then this unification is of many kinds: sometimes it is the sword and this is the sheath, sometimes the opposite. Sometimes there is no way to account for it.

27

(1) From this reality it becomes known that if separation is through the choice of the beloved, it is because she is not content with one lover. And if it is through the choice of the lover then it is because he has not yet completely entrusted his dominion (*wilāyat*) and has not been fully tamed by love.

(2) And it may be that surrender and contentment come from both sides, but separation is the edict of the moment and the blow of fortune, for many affairs lie outside their choice, save an affair outside of which there is nothing.

28

(1) Separation is beyond union to some degree; for so long as there is no union there is no separation, since separation is itself a kind of connection. In reality union is separation from self, just as in reality separation is union to self, except in imperfect love where the lover has still not reached complete maturity.

2) The fault which the lover commits under the domination (*qahr*) of love is that he seeks separation from himself through his own destruction, for union is bound to it. It may also be that his failure to find is due to the oppression of his affair or the predominance of zeal.

29

(1) As long as love is in the beginning, in separation there is nourishment from imagination and that is the vision of knowledge, observing a form which has been represented within mind. But when the affair reaches perfection and that form enters the heart, neither knowledge nor imagination can eat nourishment from it. Because what is perceived through the imagination is same as the locus of imagination. So long as love has not taken hold completely something of the lover remains, so that he brings a report about it back with the externality of knowledge in order to be informed. But when it takes over the realm completely, nothing remains of the lover to give a report in order to eat nourishment from it.

(2) Furthermore, when it comes inside, the externality of knowledge cannot find

1. This is an allusion to the fact that the full reality of love is always deep within the lover—it is in fact his very reality—though he must travel through the veils of loverness and belovedness to discover it.

the coinage of the interior of the secret's curtain. Then there is finding, but there is no report from finding, for all is the essence of the affair. Perhaps 'the incapacity to realize perception is perception'[1] is an allusion to something of this nature.

30

(1) The lover is not an external existence, so as to always have a report from himself. This external existence is an observer, sometimes the coinage of the moment may show a face to him within and sometimes it may not. Sometimes his own coinage may present itself to him, sometimes it may not. The inner worlds cannot be realized so easily. This is not so easy because there are screens, veils, treasures and wonders there. In this station there is no capacity to explain that.

31

(1) If one sees in his sleep, that is because he has a face towards himself. His whole body has become the eye, and the whole eye has become the face and been brought to the beloved, or to her form; for it has been imprinted on his being.

(2) Here there is a great secret, it is that whatever is the lover is inherent to the love of the beloved and nearness and farness do not veil her; for the hand of nearness and farness does not reach her skirt. Seeking that point is one thing, seeking the outward is another.

(3) Now, when he sees in sleep that is because he has seen something on the face of the heart and sends the awareness toward knowledge in order to bring out a report from within the veils.

32

(1) The lover is duplicitous with creation, with himself and with the beloved. His duplicity with creation and with himself is of the kind where he is pleased with a lie he himself has told, although he knows he is lying. The reason is that when the mind accepts the event of union, the presence of the beloved becomes established within–in the imaginal [realm]–and his mind sees a share of union. So at that moment he eats nourishment from her.

(2) So long as he is still himself, he is not free of hypocrisy and he still fears blame. When he has become tame, he has no fear and has been saved from every kind of hypocrisy.

(3) The hypocrisy with the beloved is that the light of the lover shines within him and the outward hides [love] to the extent that for a while he hides love from

1. A famous Arabic saying attributed to Abū Bakr al-Ṣiddīq (d. 13/634), a close companion of the Prophet Muḥammad and the first Sunni caliph.

the beloved, and while hiding from her loves her. But when the defect withdraws and surrender comes, the light of love also shines upon his face; for his whole being has been lost in her. In this state is found the magnificence of oneness. What place is there for reticence?

33

(1) The royal court of love is the balcony of the spirit, for in pre-eternity the brand of 'Am I not your lord'[1] had put its mark there. If the curtains become transparent, it will also shine from within the veils.

2) Here there is a great secret, for the love of this court comes outside from within and the love of man comes inside from without. But it is apparent that it can only go so far. Its end reaches the pericardium (*shaghāf*). Regarding that state of Zulaykhā the Qur'ān revealed, 'he has affected her so that the love of him has entered beneath the pericardium of her heart' (*qad shaghafahā ḥubban*).[2] The pericardium is a cover, an externality of the heart, the heart is in the middle of the realm and the descent of the illumination of love reaches to it.

(3) If the veils withdraw completely, the soul will also come to the affair. But a lifetime is required in this affair in order for the soul to come to the path of love. The free scope of the world, creation, passions and language is in the curtains of the heart's externality. It is rare that it reaches the heart, and the heart itself never reaches love.

34

(1) The beginning of love is such that the lover wants the beloved for his own sake. This person is a lover of himself through the intermediary of the beloved, but he does not know that he wants to use her on the path of his own will. As the poet said:

> I said, 'You become an idol which is a homeland for the spirit.'
> She said, 'Speak not of the soul if you are not a Shaman.'
>
> I said, 'How much you beat me with the sword of argument!'
> She said, 'You are still a lover of yourself.'

---

1. Qur'ān 7:172. See n. 1.

2. Qur'ān 12:30. This is a reference to the famous story of Joseph and Zulaykhā, which is often used as a symbol of the transformative power of true love. Zulaykhā had desired Joseph, but Joseph chose chastity over fornication. She thus plotted to have him imprisoned. Later Sufi commentators expand upon this to say that after Joseph was released Zulaykhā came to love him with a pure love though this dimension of the story is not found in the Qur'ān.

(2) When the perfection of love shines its smallest portion is that he wants himself for her, and in pleasing her he gives his soul gleefully. Love is this, all else is delirium and deficiency.

35

Love is a man-eater. It eats man and leaves nothing. When it eats man, it is the master of the dominion (*wilāyat*) and the edict belongs to it. If beauty shines upon perfection, love also eats the otherness of the beloved, but this happens so much later.

36

(1) The beloved never became familiar with the lover, and at that moment that he considers himself closer to her and her closer to him she is farther because the kingdom is hers and 'the king has no friend.' The reality of familiarity pertains to having the same level, and this is impossible between the lover and the beloved, because the lover is all the earth of baseness and the beloved is all the sky of greatness and grandeur. If there is familiarity it would be by the edict of the breath and the moment, and this would be borrowed.

> I endured sorrow equal in weight to heaven and earth,
> Neither I become satiated nor loved other.
>
> A gazelle, for example, may become accustomed to people.
> You will not, though I did a thousand tricks.

(2) When will the magnificence of the beloved and the baseness of the lover come together? When will the grace of the one sought and the need of the seeker come together? She is this one's cure and this one is her helpless one. The patient needs medicine. Medicine has no need for the patient; for the patient dwindles from not attaining medicine, whereas the medicine need not regard the patient. As has been said:

> What can the lover do who has no heart ?
> What can the indigent one do who has no provisions?
>
> The nobility of your Beauty is not due to my bazaar.
> What loss to the idol if it has no idol worshipper?

37

The reality of love rides nothing but the mount of the spirit. But the heart is the locus of its attributes and it itself is glorious through the veils of its glory. What does anyone know of its essence and attributes? Not a single one of its subtle points shows its face to the eye of knowledge. For it is not possible that anything more than an explanation or a sign be given from the surface of the heart's tablet. But in the imaginal world, in order to reveal its face, sometimes love may have a sign concretely and sometimes it may not.

38

(1) Sometimes the sign is through the tress, sometimes through the cheek, sometimes the mole and sometimes stature, sometimes the eye and sometimes the eyebrow, sometimes a wink, sometimes the giggle of the beloved and sometimes through rebuke.

(2) Each of these realities has a sign from the quest of the lover's spirit. That which has the sign of love upon the eye of the beloved, its nourishment is from observation of the beloved and is further from deficiencies, for it is the precious pearl of the heart and spirit. Love which makes a sign with the eye of the beloved in the world of imagination is an indication of the quest of the spirit and the heart and is far from bodily deficiencies. And if it is with the eyebrow [that it makes a sign] it is a quest from his spirit. But the vanguard of bewilderment stands before that quest, because the eyebrow is apportioned to the eye.

(3) In this way, each one of these signs on the path of the perspicacity of love makes clear a quest pertaining to the spirit, the body, deficiency or fault; for love has a sign in each of the interior curtains and these realities are its signs on the curtain of imagination. Thus its sign makes clear the level of love.

39

(1) When the reality of love appears, the lover becomes the nourishment for the beloved. The beloved does not become the nourishment for the lover because the lover can be contained in the compass of the beloved, but the beloved cannot be contained in the compass of the lover. The lover can become one hair in the tress of the beloved, but the whole of the lover cannot bear one hair of the beloved and can give it no refuge.

(2) The nourishment of the moth that becomes the lover of fire is distant from illumination. The vanguard of the illumination welcomes him and invites him, and he flies toward love with the wings of his aspiration (*himmat*) in the air of his quest. But he must have many wings in order to reach fire. When he reaches fire he has

no course. The course of fire is within him. Nor does he have any nourishment, the fire has nourishment. And this is a great secret. For one moment he becomes his own beloved. This is his perfection. And all of his flying and circumambulating were for this one moment. When shall this be? Before this we have explained that the reality of union is this. One hour the attribute of 'being fire' welcomes him and soon sends him out through the door of 'being ash.' There must be so much provision that he reaches love. His being and attributes are themselves the provision of the path. 'You have wasted your life building the inward, where is annihilation in witnessing oneness (*tawḥīd*)?'[1] is this.

(3) Of all that the lover can have there is nothing that can become the instrument of union. The beloved can have the instrument of union. This is also a great secret, for union is the level of the beloved and her right. It is separation which is the level of the lover and his right. Thus the existence of the lover is the instrument of separation and the existence of the beloved is the instrument of union.

Love itself, in its essence, is far from these attachments and defects; for love has no attributes from union and separation. These are the attributes of the lover and the beloved. Thus union is the level of the glory and greatness of the beloved and separation is the level of the baseness and poverty of the lover. Therefore, the beloved can possess the instrument of union and the lover that of separation and the existence of the lover is one of the provisions of separation.

In your love my singleness is a crowd.

One whose existence is a crowd and a provision of separation, from where will he obtain the provision of union?

(4) The ground of union becomes non-being and the ground of separation becomes being; so long as the witness of annihilation associates, union is union. When he returns the reality of separation cast its shadow and the possibility of union withdraws, for the lover cannot possess the provision of union because that is the function of the beloved.

A Story

It has been transmitted that one day Sultan Maḥmūd[2] was sitting in his court. A man came and had a plate of salt in his hand. He came to the middle of the assembly of Maḥmūd's court and cried out, 'Who will buy salt?' Maḥmūd had never seen that and ordered that they arrest him. When he was alone, he summoned him and said, 'What insolence is this that you commit? And what kind of place is Maḥmūd's palace for crying out to sell salt?'

1. This is a famous saying of Manṣūr Ḥallāj, *al-Risālah al-qushayriyyah fī 'ilm al-taṣawwuf*, ed. Ma'rūf Zarīq and 'Alī 'Abd al-Ḥamīd Balṭājī (Beirut, 1413/1993), p. 165.

2. Sultan Maḥmūd of Ghazna (389/999–421/1030).

He said: 'O noble lad, our affair is with Ayāz,[1] salt is but a pretext.'

Maḥmūd said, 'O beggar, who are you that you can put your hand in a bowl with Maḥmūd? I who have eight hundred elephants, a worldwide kingdom and realm, and you do not have a night's worth of bread!'

He said, 'Don't speak so long, for this that you own and possess is the provision of union, not the provision of love. The provision of love is a roasted heart,[2] and my heart is perfectly so–this is a condition for the affair. No Maḥmūd, rather my heart is empty, therefore there is no place for eight hundred elephants in it. Accounting and managing many realms is not the affair. I have an empty heart burning with the love of Ayāz. O Maḥmūd do you know what the secret of this salt is? That in the pot of your love must be the salt of disengaging and abasement, for you're so dominating. Know that verse of the highest assembly, 'And we glorify in praise of You and call You Holy.'[3] He said to six hundred peacock feathers, 'You need the disengaging which is the condition of this affair, but when that happens, you will not be what you are now. You do not have the provision for that so as to separate yourselves.'

O Maḥmūd, all this that you possess is the provision of union, and love has no attribute from union. When the moment of union comes, Ayāz himself has the provision of union completely. O Maḥmūd, are these eight hundred elephants and the entire realm of China and India worth anything without Ayāz, or can they stand in the place of one hair from his tress?'

Maḥmūd said, 'No.'

He said, 'Is being with him in the dung-room of a public bath-house or in a dark room like being in the garden of Eden, and the state of perfect union?'

Maḥmūd said, 'It is.'

He said, 'Then all this that you possess is not even the provision of union, for only the beloved can have the provision of union, not the lover.' This is perfect beauty, and the cheek, the mole and the tress. And those are the signs of beauty.

(5) From here you know that love has no attribute from union or from separation, and nothing is known to the lover about the provision of union, nor can it be known. The provision of union is the existence of the beloved and the provision of separation is the existence of the lover, and love has no need for either. If the joy of the moment assists, this existence becomes the sacrifice for that existence. This is perfect union.

---

1. Ayāz b. Uymāq Abū Najm (d. 449/1059) is known as the perfect loyal servant and was therefore beloved to Sultan Maḥmūd. Here he is used as a symbol of the beloved just as Laylā was used as a symbol in the story of Laylā and Majnūn. Both of these love legends have been used by Sufis as models of the pure and chaste love for the beloved. It is important that for the Sufis the beloved can be either male or female, what matters is the essence of love which is beyond all duality.

2. Here Ghazzālī is playing on the term which he has previously used for maturity (*pukhtagī*) which literally means 'cooked'. 'A broiled heart' would thus be even more immersed in love.

3. Qur'ān 2:30.

A perfect love and a beautiful heart-render,
The heart full of speech and the tongue mute.

Where has there been a state rarer than this?
I thirst, and before me flows pure water.

40

(1) As regards the reality of the affair, the beloved gains no profit from the lover, nor loss. But as regards the manner (*sunnah*) of love's generosity, love binds the lover to the beloved. Through the connection of love, the lover becomes the locus of the beloved's observation in every state.

(2) Here is where separation through the choice of the beloved is more union than union through the choice of the lover. Because in the beloved's choosing separation, the lover becomes the locus of observation for the heart of the beloved and choice and her desire. And on the path of her lover's choosing union, there is not any observation from the beloved, and she has no concern for him. This is a great level in gnosis. But no one can understand this perfectly. Thus the beloved's observation of the lover is a scale in measuring the degrees and attributes of love, in perfection, increase and decrease.

41

(1) Whatever is glory, magnificence, self-sufficiency and greatness in the share of love becomes the attributes of the beloved, and whatever is baseness, weakness, wretchedness, poverty, need and helplessness is the share of the lover. Thus the nourishment of love is the attributes of the lover, for love is the master of the lover's fortune–whatever fortune may bring. And this changes according to the moment.

2) However, these attributes of the beloved do not become manifest except through the manifestation of their opposites in the lover–so long as the poverty of this is not, her self-sufficiency does not appear. Likewise, all the attributes are suitable for her because of this.

42

When it is like this the lover and beloved are opposites. Thus they are not together except on condition of sacrifice and annihilation. Regarding this it has been said:

When the green-beloved saw my face yellow,
She said, 'No longer hope for my union.

'Because you have become our opposite in vision,
You have the colour of autumn and we the colour of spring.'

43

(1) The beloved itself is the beloved in every state, thus self-sufficiency is her attribute. And the lover is the lover in every state, thus poverty is his attribute. The lover always needs the beloved, thus poverty is always his attribute. And the beloved needs nothing, for she always has herself. Therefore, self-sufficiency is her attribute.

Every night, out of sorrow for you, my tears are blood,
And from separation with you, there is a nightly assault in my heart.

You are with yourself O Beloved, from that you are joyful.
You are never without yourself, how do you know what night is like?

You always steal hearts, you are excused.
You have never experienced sorrow, you are excused.

I have spent a thousand nights in blood without you.
You have never spent a night without yourself, you are excused.

(2) And if this error comes to you, that it may be that the lover is the master and the beloved is the servant, such that in union she is next to the lover, that is a grave error. For the reality of love puts the necklace of the sultanate on the neck of the beloved and takes off the ring of servitude.

(3) The beloved can never be a possession. This is why those who speak of poverty lose the heart and spirit and put religion, the world and fortune in the middle.[1] They do anything and withdraw from everything. They also do not fear [for] their heads and put their foot on the two worlds. But when the affair reaches the point of love, they never put the beloved in the middle and are not able to do so. Because it is only a possession which can be put in the middle, not the possessor. The beloved is a possessor.

(4) The hand of freedom never reaches the edge of love and loverness. Just as all bonds are released there–I mean in the freedom of poverty–all openings are bound here–I mean in the bondage of love.

(5) When these realities become known, then perhaps the magnificence of love will appear so that the lover loses his own profit (*sūd*) [in order] to withdraw from deficiencies and is saved from profit and loss.

1. i.e., risk everything.

44

If it were possible for the lover to eat nourishment from the beloved, it would only be in the compass of the heart. But since loverness is being without a heart, when will this reality be? So where will the heartless one eat? She steals his heart and she sends nourishment, but he still has not eaten and she takes it back. We say nourishment is from the beloved and this is far, far away. I do not want that nourishment which is from imagining through words heard and beauty seen, for that is not union. That is not on this page. Those who look at the sun are many and the world is illuminated by its light. But in reality people have no nourishment from it. So do not be in error.

45

(1) Love is such that oppression from the beloved in the union of love becomes increase and kindling for the fire of love; for the nourishment of love is from oppression. Thus love increases. So long as he is in union it is of this attribute. But in separation the oppression of the beloved would help and be the cause of consolation–so long as he is in the door of choice and something from him is observing the affair.

(2) But when he becomes completely and perfectly tame before love and the sultanate of love has taken complete control, how will increase and decrease have a way there?[1]

> I do not flee from the friend because of a hundred and one afflictions.
> This is a condition for me in love if I hold fast.

1. i.e. there is no increase and decrease when one has gone beyond the beloved into love itself.

3

ʿAyn al-Quḍāt Hamadānī

ʿAbd Allāh ibn Muḥammad ibn ʿAlī Miyānijī Hamadānī, also referred to as Abu'l-Maʿālī, and known primarily as ʿAyn al-Quḍāt Hamadānī, was one of the most eminent masters of philosophical Sufism. He was born in 492/1098 in the city of Hamadān in the western part of Persia. ʿAyn al-Quḍāt's intellectual acumen and esoteric assertions angered some of the exoteric jurists to the extent that they declared him an apostate and called for his execution. He was hanged in Hamadān in the year 525/1130.

There is very little information about the early education of this ill-fated Sufi master. We know that he was highly influenced by both Abū Ḥāmid Ghazzālī and his younger brother Aḥmad Ghazzālī, with whom ʿAyn al-Quḍāt corresponded and whom he embraced as his Sufi teacher. While Aḥmad Ghazzālī remains the most influential figure in the life of ʿAyn al-Quḍāt, there were others such as Shaykh Barakat Hamadānī. ʿAyn al-Quḍāt may have attended Hamadānī's Sufi sessions for nearly seven years, during which time he studied the esoteric meaning of the Qur'ān. Among his teachers was Abū ʿAbd Allāh Ḥamūyah ibn ʿUthmān, a Sufi master whom ʿAyn al-Quḍāt ranked with the Ghazzālī brothers. Finally, it is said that he had benefited from meeting both ʿUmār Khayyām, the erudite scientist and philosopher, and Bābā Ṭāhir ʿUryān, the Sufi poet. Neither of these affiliations, however, is certain.

ʿAyn al-Quḍāt belongs to a Sufi school of thought often referred to as '*madhhab-i ʿishq*' (path of love), a tradition with which many eminent figures such as Aḥmad Ghazzālī, ʿAṭṭār, Rūmī, and Ḥāfiẓ have also been affiliated. What distinguishes ʿAyn al-Quḍāt from so many other Sufi masters belonging to this school is the centrality of love combined with philosophical interest in all aspects of his teachings. Omid Safi, the translator of this chapter, says "ʿAyn al-Quḍāt and Aḥmad Ghazzālī are bards of this new *madhhab-i ʿishq*.'

ʿAyn al-Quḍāt's epistemology, which is based fundamentally on the Qur'ān and the sayings of the Prophet Muḥammad, makes full use of the notion of love. For ʿAyn al-Quḍāt, mystical knowledge comes directly from the Divine Presence that permeates the Qur'ān and the very being of the Prophet Muḥammad. For him there are men of an exoteric nature whom he classifies as 'appearance-seers' and those of an esoteric nature, whom he calls 'inward-seekers'. The 'appearance-seers' lack the faculty of spiritual perception (*baṣīrat*) which transcends discursive thought. 'Ayn al-Quḍāt's spiritual hermeneutics (*ta'wīl*) argue that the reality of the Prophet Muḥammad can only be fully understood through the faculty of spiritual perception. The concept of Muḥammad as light, and as the very first principle of creation is a well-known Sufi and Shi'i understanding of the inner reality of the Prophet Muḥammad. In his *Tamhīdāt*, 'Ayn al-Quḍāt offers an explanation of Muḥammad's cyclical journey which starts with his departure from God into creation and ends with his return to God.

'Ayn al-Quḍāt extends his esoteric interpretations to certain theological problems such as the uncreated nature of the Qur'ān. What differentiates his version from that of many Muslim theologians who had previously talked about the Qur'ān as uncreated Divine Speech is that he discusses this doctrine in relation to the layers of meaning in the Qur'ān.

In this chapter, we have included a section of the *Tamhīdāt* (Dispositions) and *Nāma-hā* (Letters) of 'Ayn al-Quḍāt. While most of 'Ayn al-Quḍāt's works are no longer extant, his *magnum opus, Tamhīdāt*, which is a major text of Islamic mystical philosophy, and which can be regarded as a forerunner to Ibn 'Arabī, is extant. The *Tamhīdāt* is an example of a beautiful work of philosophical Sufism in Persian prose, interspersed now and then by lines of poetry. In his *Tamhīdāt,* 'Ayn al-Quḍāt continues the central themes his master Aḥmad Ghazzālī had discussed on 'radical love' in his Persian work the *Sawāniḥ*. The two texts, *Tamhīdāt* and *Sawāniḥ*, should therefore be treated as a complementary set of gnostic works. *Tamhīdāt*, one may argue, is an extensive commentary on the *Sawāniḥ* of Hamadānī's spiritual guide, and its literary style is similar to that of Sa'dī's *Gulistān*. 'Ayn al-Quḍāt frequently interpolates verses from the Qur'ān and traditions of the Prophet Muḥammad often followed by brief Arabic passages.

The *Tamhīdāt* is made up of ten chapters with the final chapter, the longest of the book, consisting of one hundred pages. The chapters are:

1. The Difference between acquired knowledge and knowledge obtained directly from the Divine Presence.
2. Conditions incumbent upon one who is a seeker on the path of God.
3. Humanity has been created in three primordial forms.
4. Know thyself so that you may know God.
5. Exposition of the five pillars of Islam.
6. Reality and spiritual states of radical love.
7. Reality of the spirit and the heart.
8. Secrets of the Qur'ān and the wisdom behind the creation of the human being.

9. Elucidation of the reality of faith and infidelity.
10. The reality and root of heaven and earth are to be found in the light of Muḥammad and Satan (Iblīs).

ʿAyn al-Quḍāt's emphasis on rejecting the idols of intellectual convention allows him a genuine dialogue with philosophers, jurists, theologians, and even Sufis belonging to other schools of thought. The following passage appearing in the ninth chapter of the *Tamhīdāt* indicates how ʿAyn al-Quḍāt establishes such a dialogue, 'O friend, if you saw what the Christians see in Jesus, you too would become Christian. If you saw what the Jews see in Moses, you too would become a Jew. Indeed, if you saw in idols what the idol-worshippers see, you too would become an idol-worshipper.'[1]

Tamhīdāt remains a major text of philosophical Sufism in Persian, one in which the notion of a love-based approach to the human-Divine relationship and radical love constitute the central theme. From a historical perspective, *Tamhīdāt* also provides us with detailed information about Sufis whose names and sayings would not have been otherwise known to us.

In the first part of this chapter we have included a extract from *Tamhīdāt* in which ʿAyn al-Quḍāt opens with a discussion of the differences between acquired knowledge and Divine knowledge and goes on to explain the different types of knowledge and the role of a spiritual teacher in leading the novice to the right one. This section ends with two short remarks. In the first, ʿAyn al-Quḍāt tells us how he was 'saved from falling' by studying the works of Abū Ḥāmid Ghazzālī and in the second he ironically supports Ibn Sīnā's views on the eternity of the world against Ghazzālī's creation *ex-nihilo*. The distinctions between two epistemic modes of cognition, acquired knowledge and knowledge by presence, are then discussed. The Sufis saw knowledge from on high (*ʿilm ladunī*) as the knowledge that is bestowed by God. ʿAyn al-Quḍāt advocates a certain type of philosophy and theology whereby knowledge is a fluid as opposed to a crystallized entity, remaining in a continuous state of flux with its quality perpetually shifting. He offers a number of interesting narrative techniques to allude to the dynamic quality of knowledge and the undoing of rigid categories. In offering classifications of knowledge, he often changes them to allow room for other types of knowledge.

ʿAyn al-Quḍāt's *Letters*, of which a short portion appears in the second part of this chapter, offers an esoteric interpretation of some Qur'ānic verses and the role of the Prophet Muḥammad as the ultimate spiritual guide.

M. Aminrazavi

1. ʿAyn al-Quḍāt, *Tamhīdāt* (Tehran, 1994), p. 285.

DISPOSITIONS

Tamhīdāt

Translated for this volume by Omid Safi from ʿAyn al-Quḍāt Hamadānī, *Tamhīdāt*, ed. ʿAfīf ʿUṣayrān (Tehran, 1373 Sh./1994), pp. 1–19.

In the Name of God, Most Gracious, Most Merciful

We seek aid from Him. *Praise be to God, the Lord of all the Worlds* [1:2]. *The Afterlife is (best) for those are in awe of God* [7:128] [1] *[Let there be] no hostility except to those who oppress.*[2] Blessing and Peace upon the best of His creation Muḥammad, and upon the entirety of his pure and good family, and upon his companions, the pleasure of God Almighty upon them.

A group of friends requested that some words be collected for their sake, in order to benefit the world. Their plea was granted. This treatise, *Essence of Spiritual Realities in Unveiling the Subtleties*, was completed in ten *tamhīds*[3] so that the readers might derive benefit from it.

The Difference between Acquired Knowledge and Divine Knowledge[4]

Know this: In addressing Muṣṭafā [Prophet Muḥammad], Peace and Blessing of God upon him, regarding those who see only the external appearances and not the inner meanings, and those who seek only the outward manifestations and neglect the inward realities, the Qurʾān states: *And you see them looking at you, but they do not perceive* [7:198].

O Precious one, I say this: Have you not read this verse in the Qurʾān: *Indeed there has come to you from God a Light and a clear Book*? [5.15] Have you not heard

1. I translate the term *taqwā* not merely as 'piety', but more as a type of God-consciousness rooted in the experience of *mysterium tremendum* of God, a term we borrow from Rudolph Otto.

2. In Qurʾānic discourse, the term *ẓālim* has the connotation of those who have committed a double tyranny: oppression of others, and oppression of their own true selves. It is important to point out that etymologically the term is related to that for darkness (*ẓulamāt*). Those who oppress others and themselves are in darkness, as it were, whereas those who live in God-consciousness are brought into the light (*nūr*).

3. In a characteristic hermeneutic move, ʿAyn al-Quḍāt plays with etymological meaning in order to move from the external to the inner meanings and towards the very soul of the spiritual seeker. The word '*tamhīdāt*' comes from the root (*ma ha da*), which means to arrange, prepare, lay out in an even fashion. Therefore one possible meaning is an easy to follow outline of spiritual life which has been laid out by God, and the second meaning is the preparation of the soul of the spiritual seeker.

4 In many Sufi interpretations, *ʿilm-i ladunī*, literally 'knowledge from Us' [i.e. from God], is taken to mean Divinely bestowed knowledge, the expression itself is taken from Qurʾān 18:65.

of it? Muḥammad is called *light*! The Qur'ān, which is the Word of God, is also called *light*, '*follow the light which has been sent down with him*' [7:157].

When you look at the Qur'ān, you only see black letters on a white page. Know that the paper and the pen and the lines are not light. Then which is *that* 'Qur'ān, the uncreated Speech of God'?[1]

People saw from Muḥammad only an appearance, a body, and a person. God manifested Muḥammad to the onlookers as a human in the creature condition, as in '*And Say: Verily I am a human being like you, except that an inspiration has come to me*.' [41:18] Therefore, in this station of understanding: *They said: 'what sort of a messenger is this, who eats food, and walks through the marketplace?'* [25:7].

But in reality, God manifested Muḥammad to the people of insight and spiritual reality, who saw his reality with heart and soul.

Some of them said: 'O God, Place us among the community of Muḥammad.'

Some of them said: 'O God, do not withhold from us the companionship of Muḥammad.' Another group said: 'O God, sustain us through the intercession of Muḥammad.'

If in this ecstasy, and in this station of sainthood, they called Muḥammad human or consider him merely human, they would become infidels. Consider this: *And they say: 'Shall a mere human guide us?', so they committed infidelity* [64:6]. This continued until Muḥammad elucidated the matter by saying: 'I am not like any of you'.

The reality of the Qur'ān, which is a sacred attribute of God[2] is conjoined and attached to the hearts of the prophets and people of sanctity. This group lives through that reality. That reality of the Qur'ān is not in the book, yet you seek it in the book. 'What is between the two covers is the Word of God'. But the seekers of the Qur'ān have been shown in the book that: 'The Qur'ān has an external level of meaning, and an internal one. The internal one itself has interior levels, up to seven.' He said: 'Every verse from the Qur'ān has an outward, and after every outward there is an inward up to seven inward levels.'

I do realize that some have comprehended the outward exposition, but who is it that knows the inward expositions? Who has seen it? And in another place he said: 'The Qur'ān was sent in seven types, each one unequivocal and appropriate.' When the bride of the beauty of Qur'ān manifests herself to the people of Qur'ān, they see through seven forms, each form with complete clarity.

It is no doubt from this understanding that he said: 'The people of the Qur'ān are the people of God and His elite'. That when the reader arrives at the book, '*And*

1. In Ash'arī thought, the theological school adopted by 'Ayn al-Quḍāt, the Qur'ān was considered to be uncreated. The Mu'tazilīs rejected this perspective, insisting on a created Qur'ān.

2. In Ash'arī theology, there are five Divine Attributes par excellence. The Qur'ān as *Kalām Allāh*, the Word of God, is one of them.

with him is the Mother of the Book' [13:9[1]], he has arrived at the inner meanings of the Qur'ān. The beauty of the light of the Qur'ān will so efface him from himself that neither the Qur'ān remains nor the reader, nor the book: all will be read, and all will be written.

But the real intention is that you will know this: there is another reality other than this creaturely aspect in humanity. Other than this outward form, there is another inward, spiritual meaning. Other than this body, there is another soul and another kernel. Other than this world, there is another world.

For us, there is another world other than this
There is a place apart from heaven and hell.
The noble one lives through another soul
and that pure jewel is from another mine.
The capital of love is revelry and roguishness:
Frequent recitation of Qur'ān and asceticism
are from another world.
They tell us: this is another sign
Since other than this language, there is another language!

The verse *There is none of us, except that he has a place appointed* [37:164] has elucidated and expounded on all of this. *And God has graced some of you above others in sustenance* [16:71] has provided the pretext for this. *Those messengers We have graced some above others* [2:253] has made it evident. *And above every one with knowledge there is another with [more] knowledge* [12:76[2]] has made it manifest.

What is all this? And what does it mean? *No one knows its esoteric interpretation except for God and those who are firmly rooted in knowledge.* And what is this esoteric interpretation that only God and those firmly grounded in knowledge know?[3] Recite: *Here are the self-evident signs, in the hearts of those bestowed with knowledge* [29:49].

Where are they to seek this heart? *And as for he whom God has opened his heart to Islam, he is illuminated through a light from his Lord. So woe be to those whose hearts are hardened* [39:22].

Where are they to search for such a light? *Verily in this is a remembrance for anyone who has a heart* [50:37].

Those who are lost in the way have lost sight of this, whereas those who have

1. The verse in full provides the context of 'Ayn al-Quḍāt's point: 'And God effaces whom He wishes; and establishes [whom He desires]: and with him is the Mother of the Book.'

2. Some recent translations wish to remove the gradation of this verse by reading it as a contrast between human and Divine knowledge: 'For over all endued with knowledge there is One, the All-Knowing'; see A. Yusuf Ali, 572.

3. A variant reading: 'Who is the one firmly rooted in knowledge?'

achieved guidance see this as evident. It was for this reason that Muṣṭafa [Prophet Muḥammad], peace and blessings of God be upon him, said: 'Verily there is a concealed body of knowledge. None of the scholars know of it except those who know by God; so when they speak of it, no one renounces them except those who are heedless of God.'

Knowledge comes in three types: one type is the knowledge for the descendants of Adam, the second type is the knowledge for the angels, and a third type is the knowledge for the created beings and creatures. But the fourth is the knowledge that belongs to God Almighty, The Sacred. This is what is called a Secret and Treasured knowledge. So no one knows this secret knowledge other than the one who knows God. Have you ever known who is the one who knows God? I don't know if you have.

As the Prophet said, 'Seek knowledge even if it is in China'. So you ought to go to China and beyond China, then you will find the scholars of my community who are like the prophets of the children of Israel.

Which path should one follow? The path of action. I am not speaking of the action of the body, but of the action of the heart. It is known that he said: 'On one who acts on his knowledge, God will bestow a new knowledge'.[1]

Take heed: 'Speak to people at the level of their intellect' is perfect advice. So in these pages some words will be said that are not intended for you, O precious one, but rather for other lovers of God who are not present at the time of writing. They too have a share, so do not think that all of this is intended for you.

Whoever hears something that is not in his station or appropriate to the level of his comprehension will not comprehend it. O precious one, do you ponder that the Noble Qur'ān is addressing one group? Or a hundred clans? Or a hundred thousand? Rather, every verse and every word is simultaneously addressing one individual while it is intended for another person—even another world!

And that which was written in these pages, every line is conveys a different station and state. Every word has a different purpose. Every word has a different audience. Each seeker is addressed differently. That which is said to Zayd is not that which is said to ʿAmru. Bakr, for example, does not see what Khālid does.

O precious one, you ponder that Abū Jahl heard *praise be to God, the Lord of all worlds*? [1:2] Or that the verse was intended for him? All that he hears from the Qur'ān is *Say: O you infidels* [109:1] this alone was his share. However, *praise be to God* [1:2] was the share of Muḥammad, and Muḥammad heard it.

If you do not believe this, listen to ʿUmar Khaṭṭāb, who said: 'Muṣṭafa, peace and blessings of God be upon him, would say words to Abū Bakr that sometimes I would hear and I would understand. Sometimes I would hear them, and I would not understand. Sometimes I would neither hear nor understand them.'

What do you say about this? Did Muḥammad withhold something from ʿUmar?

---

1. Literally: 'Whoever acts based on what he knows; God will bestow on him a knowledge that he doesn't know'.

No, God forbid! Not at all! Muḥammad did not withhold from 'Umar. However, a young child who is suckling is kept away from roast lamb and sweets, since his stomach cannot bear them. Then, when he reaches the age of maturity, he can eat them, since those food and drinks will not harm him.

'Abd Allāh ibn 'Abbās says: 'If I were to explain the verse *Verily your Lord is God, who created the Heavens and the Earth in seven days and then established Himself upon the Throne,* [10:3] the Companions of Prophet, may God be pleased with them, would cast stones at me.' Abū Hurayrah, may God be pleased with him, said: 'If I were to expound upon this verse *God is He who created seven Heavens and on Earth a similar number. Through the midst of them His Command descends* [65:12] people would call me an infidel.'

'Abd Allāh ibn 'Abbās says: One night I stayed awake till the daybreak with 'Alī ibn Abī Ṭālib may God honour his countenance. He was expounding on the *Bā* of *Bism-i Allāh*, I saw my own self as a jar before an immense ocean. How much can you get from an ocean? Until you reside in the ocean, whatever you find has a measure and a limit. How can a sailor limit and describe the ocean? What can he get from it? ... But what does the land creature know of the ocean? *Mischief has appeared on land and sea* [30.41]. Whatever has been learned through people is of land, and whatever is learned through *God The Gracious who has taught the Qur'ān* [55.1] is of ocean and oceanic. The ocean has no end: *and they grasp nothing of His knowledge* [2:255].

O precious one, what do you apprehend? A small mention of the Prophetic tradition *The Believer is the mirror of the believer* is apropos here. Whoever does not know something and wants to know it has two options: One is to refer to his own heart in meditation and contemplation. Then, through his heart, he will attain to his own self. Muṣṭafā [Prophet Muḥammad], peace and blessings of God be upon him, said:

Consult your heart [for a verdict], even if a fool is delivering that opinion. He said whatever comes up, its verification has to be legislated through the sincerity of the heart.

If the heart grants an opinion (*fatwā*), it is the command of God: do it! If it does not give an opinion, leave the whole endeavour and adopt avoidance of the task since *The angel has a little influence and Satan has a little.* Whatever opinion the heart issues is from God, and whatever it rejects is from Satan. There is a portion of these influences in everybody, from the people of belief and Islam.

Our affairs are difficult since our jurist is the *nafs al-ammārah*, the ego-self which commands to evil: *Verily the ego-self commands to evil* [12:53]. A person who refers matters to his heart lives in awe of God, and is felicitous. Whoever judges matters according to his ego-self is wretched, and in loss.

[There is also a second way of obtaining spiritual answers.] If a person does not have this spiritual skill and aptitude to know through the mediation of his own heart, let him seek the heart of another who has this skill: *Ask the people of Divine Remembrance if you do not know* [21:16], so that another person's heart will become your mirror.

O friend, there are two types of heart. One type is facing God's Pen, and it is inscribed upon, as in *God has inscribed faith upon their hearts* [12:53]. God's Right Hand is doing the writing. When he refers to his own heart something that he does not know, he will know for this reason that God inscribes the answer upon his heart. Then he will know.

The second type of heart is still immature, and a raw one cannot face God's pen. When he asks what he does not know from one whose heart is a mirror and a tablet before the Divine Pen, he will know. He will then realize what it is to see God in the mirror of a spiritual guide's soul. A spiritual guide sees himself in the mirror of the disciple's soul, whereas a disciple sees God in the spiritual guide's soul.

Here is an analogy of everything that I have said: a group of patients arise and go to a physician, seeking their cure. The physician gives different prescriptions to them for the sake of ameliorating their ailments. If someone said that this difference in prescriptions is due to the physician's ignorance, he has spoken incorrectly. The ignorant one is the one who said the above, since the difference in the prescription is due to the difference in the causes of the ailments. There are multiple causes, and to prescribe as if all causes are the same is a severe ignorance and error. Those who know what is being said know.

Now do you think that the cause of the ailments confronting religion and Islam is [so simple as to be] homogenous? *Islam is established upon five pillars* has given specific prescriptions: these five-fold prescriptions are the cure and medicine of all believers. However, the interior affair and the heart's path have easy cure.

Therefore every initiate needs a spiritual guide who will be a skilled physician of the heart to cure the disciple, and to order a different cure for each different malady. Those who have abandoned the cure and the [wisdom of the] physician, it is as well that they immerse themselves in the ailment, *since and if God had found in them any good, He would have indeed made them hear* [8:23].

Therefore when the skilled physician comes across one who has set out on the spiritual path, joining with the spiritual teachers, may God sanctify their spirits, becomes an obligation upon the seeker. Based on this, it is said: 'Who does not have a spiritual teacher, does not have a religion'.

The spiritual teacher also has an obligation: accepting the vicegerency (*khilāfah*), and training the disciples is the obligation of the path. If you want a more complete description, hear it from God Almighty who said *He is the One who put for you vicegerents on Earth, and raised some of you degrees above others* [6:165]. And in another place He has elucidated the meaning of inward vicegerency: *He will surely put them as vicegerents on Earth, as He put others before them* [24:55].

The secrets of one's heart
  cannot be conveyed to another.
One cannot shun the condition of one's own heart
  One cannot turn the realm of Law upside down.
A human being cannot leave his own self
One cannot exchange glances
  with those who are veiled in the faith.
But one cannot wander unto His alley
  with one's own self.

Take heed: The condition of creatureliness is like a lock on the hearts, and the shackle of ignorance is on the thoughts. This is the meaning of *And do they not contemplate upon the Qur'ān, or are their hearts locked up?* [47:24]. When the illumination[1] of the victory and help that comes from God Almighty appears, as in *When comes the help of God and the Victory* [110:1], this lock is removed from the heart. *We shall show them our signs in the farthest horizons and within their own souls* [41:53] becomes manifest, and the plant of *God has planted for you on Earth* is harvested. He emerges out of his own selfhood, and sees the Angelic realm and Dominion. He becomes the Dominion and the lord of Dominion. Due to *And thus we showed the power of the heavens and Earth to Abraham* [6:75], he emerges out of his own selfhood.

Jesus, peace be upon him, thus reported of this occurrence:[2] 'Whoever is not born again will not reach the Kingdom of Heaven'. That is, whoever comes from the realm of the mother's womb, will see this earthly world; and whoever comes out of his own self will see that heavenly world. This is the spiritual meaning of 'Their bodies are in the world, and their hearts are in the hereafter'. The mirror of *he knows the secret in the Heavens and on Earth* becomes the book of his moment. *He who knows his own self* will manifest itself to him, and *so knows his Lord* tells the tale of his spiritual moment. He will have surpassed *the day the Earth changes* and arrives at *to other than Earth* [14:48]. He sees *I saw my Lord with my heart* and will taste *I spend a night with my Lord, he feeds me and gives drink*. He will hear *He conveyed the inspiration to His servant that which he conveyed* [53:10].

O precious one, if you want the beauty of these secrets to become manifest unto you, cease from custom-worship (*'ādat-parastī*) since custom-worshipping is idol-worship. Don't you see what the slander of this people does: *We found our fathers following a certain religion, and we will certainly follow in their footsteps* [43:23].

---

1. I have translated *futūḥ* as 'illumination' rather than 'Opening', following the translation of Ibn 'Arabī's well-known work *al-Futūḥāt al-Makiyyah*, which is often rendered: 'The Meccan Illuminations'.

2. *Wāqi'ah* can also mean a spiritual vision: Sajjādī, *Iṣṭilāḥāt wa ta'bīrāt-i 'irfānī*, 779, reports that *wāqi'ah* can refer to a spiritual vision of the Unseen Realm.

Forget whatever you have heard from creatures! *The worst instrument of a man is his allegation.* Ignore everything you have heard, since *The slanderer does not enter paradise.* And whatever he shows you treat as if unseen, since *spy not on each other* [49:12]. Explore any difficult points you encounter only through the language of the heart, and be patient until you arrive at *and if they had been patient until you could come out to them, it would be best for them* [49:5]. Accept the advice of Khiḍr, *ask me no questions about anything until I myself speak to you concerning it* [18:70].

When the moment comes, God will manifest Himself: Soon will I show you my signs, then you will not ask Me to hasten! [21:37]. And ask for Him to come quickly since *God will perchance bring about thereafter some new situation* [65:1]. If you go, you will get there, and you will see. You will never get there unless you go. *Have they not travelled on the Earth and seen?* [40:82]. Is God's Earth not expansive? Then travel about therein [4:97] is a command to journey and travel. If you go, you will see the wonders of the world in every abode: *whoever travels for the sake of Allah will find on Earth many a spacious refuge* [4:100]. In every abode you will be given advice, as in: *and give advice since the advice benefits the believers* [51:55].

You only know these verses as analogies: *The analogy of the Garden which is promised to the God-fearing* [13:35]. They will deliver you to a place where obstacles and mountains will be like coloured wool: *And the mountains shall be like carded wool* [101:5]. They will manifest to you *verily Gog and Magog spread mischief on Earth.* [18:94]. Do you know which attributes these correspond to in the body of the human being? So know that the Dajjāl is the condition of the *nafs al-ammārah. The most inimical of your adversaries is your ego-self which is your inside.*

Then *there is a kind of attraction, coming from God, which is equivalent to the acts [of worship] of humanity and Jinn* will emerge and will cause you to die and make you annihilated, as in *Whoever desires to look upon the dead walking on Earth, let him look at Ibn Abī Quḥāfah.* Then you become alive: *or he who was dead, and we then brought him to life* [6:122]. When you become subsistent, you will be told what to do and what must be done: *And those who struggle in Us We shall guide them to Our paths* [29:69]. Then they will put you in the bush of love, where you will be told: *and struggle in God as is worthy of His struggle* [22:78] until the fire makes you burnt. When you are burnt then you become light, as in *light upon light, God guides to his light whomever he wills* [24:35]. Your light is all false, and His light is Truth and Reality. When His Light hastens forth, your light is vanished and becomes null. All of you will be His Light: *Thus does God (by parables) show forth Truth and falseness;*[1] *verily We cast truth upon falseness, and truth shall triumph over falseness.*

And if you cannot recognize any of God's signs, then *and he is illuminated through a light from his Lord* [39:22] says that the affair is such and such. If you desire the affair, keep to the affair; if not, you will be occupied with own affairs. Have

1. First three words are from Qur'ān 13:17.

you not heard of Dhū'l-Nūn Miṣrī who said: 'If you are able to perform sacrifices of the Spirit, then do it; and if not then do not mock the Sufi path'. If you have the intention that with the first step, you sacrifice your life, then make preparations for it. And if you cannot, then what benefit will the mockery of Sufis and Sufi allegory and formalities bring to you? Khwājah Abū ʿAlī Sarakhsī has stated these lines in discussion, and it is appropriate to state them [to elucidate] the meaning of the statement of Dhu'l-Nūn:

O my soul, enter into this affair with me if you are a friend
If not, go in peace that you are just starting.
If you are not my fellow-traveller on this path,
then leave, go on your own path!
Wellness for you, and I will hang my head in shame
Trust me to him in the abode of the intoxicated ones.
Do not give me unto the sorrow of this realm
I need some wine for intoxication
I am so fed up with this cleverness and consciousness!

I told you that although you are addressed, another is intended to hear this discourse and benefit from it. One who is absent now will grasp this. Have you not heard from that saint who said: 'For thirty years I have been having discourse with God the Exalted, and people think that I am speaking with them!' O precious one, forgive!

What does the idle-talker judge from Hamadān [ʿAyn al-Quḍāt], have to do with these discourses of secrets? The speaker doesn't even know what he is saying! What can the listener apprehend of what he is hearing!

Over an extended period of time, I wrote many letters to Qāḍī Imam Saʿd al-Dīn Baghdādī and Khwājah Imam 'Izz al-Dīn and Imam Ḍiyā' al-Dīn and Khwājah Kāmil al-Dawlat wa'l-Dīn that came to many volumes. As of this very hour, it has been a long time since I have had an intention to write, and the writing had dwindled and was ended. That intention which I had had at past times I did not have now. Since for a while the heart of this enamoured soul used to listen to the tongue, since the tongue was the speaker and the heart the listener. At that time I had the intention and resolution to write, but now it has been some time that my tongue listens to my heart. Now the heart is speaker and the tongue the listener. And for some time, this wretched soul has had some awesome moments and spiritual states.

But our Master [Muḥammad]—peace and blessings of God be upon him—in every instant and every moment had both of the spiritual states that have been spoken of. *And he does not speak of his own desires, verily it is no less than an inspiration sent down to him* [53:3–4] describes this spiritual meaning.

When he wanted his tongue to listen to the heart, he would say: 'Soothe our hearts O Bilāl'; Give us an hour from the selfness of ourselves with reality. And when he wanted to make his heart to be the listener of his tongue, he would say: 'Speak to me, O little red-faced one [an affectionate diminutive referring to 'Ā'ishah]', O 'Ā'ishah give me an hour from reality with yourself, and bring me with yourself to benefit those of the worlds. Thus he indicates: *I was sent to perfect the most noble of behaviours.*

This has passed. The desired meaning was that the exalted precious one, you, had posed some questions to me. To answer them I took a commandment to my own essence and reality. My reality and essence took the commandment to my heart. My heart took the commandment to the soul of Muṣṭafā, Muḥammad, Peace be upon him. The spirit of Muṣṭafā, Muḥammad, received a commandment from God the Exalted. [God provided the answer.] My heart received a commandment from the soul of Muṣṭafā, peace be upon him. My reality received a commandment from my heart. My tongue received a reality from my essence and reality.

So whatever you read and hear in the writings and dictations of this wretched soul, you have not heard from my tongue, but from my heart; nay, even from the spirit of Muṣṭafā you have heard. And whatever you have heard from the spirit of Muṣṭafā, peace be upon him, you have heard from God, since *he does not speak of his own desires, verily it is no less than an inspiration sent down to him* [53:3–4].

In other words, *whoever obeys the Messenger has obeyed God* [4:80]. Of the same [spiritual] meaning is *whoever makes an allegiance with you has made an allegiance with God, the Hand of God is on top of their hands* [48:10]. The source of all this is *and they ask you about the Spirit. Say the Spirit is on the command of my Lord* [17:85]. O precious one, *verily in their stories are instructions for those possessed of understanding* [12:111] has given a permission and an audacity to speak and to manifest the encounter of the Spiritual teachers with the disciples: *And all the stories that we relate to you from the messengers we do so to validate your heart* [11:120]. He said: 'We recite unto you the stories of prophets and messengers and what we seek from this is the tranquillity and ease of your heart'.

Since the spiritual state came as I had said, I too will speak as it comes: From that which they give to me I put the essence of it on the table-cloth of writing, but one cannot oversee its organization. But the travelling wayfarer, even though he is changeable and keeps changing, will at some point stop and settle down. Speaking will become a veil on his path, but whether he speaks or not, what danger there is! Still, he cannot bring the organization, the prose, or the expression into a more beautiful form. This is the portion of the elite: silence. 'Whoever knows God, his tongue becomes weary' tells the same spiritual meaning. This discourse is not the same thing as realization and Wisdom. But the elite of the elite have arrived at the reality of their own being, and God will not abandon them to themselves apart from

Him. And if He does let them be to themselves for some time, it is limited. In any case he will not stay in a place long enough to describe his own spiritual states.

He has an immense spiritual station! If he comes upon a commandment from God, he'll give a discourse to the spiritual folk for the sake of guidance and serving as a model of emulation by the disciples. However, he will not be able to oversee the organization of this discourse.

But the root of the discourse is very strong and accurate; but not everyone will understand. That is because it is cloaked in an expression whose comprehension is not in everyone's eye. In this station is 'He who knows God his tongue is extended.' When I see myself absent, that which I say is involuntary; if at times He gives me the choice, He Himself has written it: *and God has full control over his affair*, that is, the affair of his servants: *He does what He wills and He orders what He desires* [14:22] And God is the guide.

THE LETTERS

Nāma-hā

Translated for this volume by Omid Safi from ʿAyn al-Quḍāt Hamadānī, *Nāma-hā,* ed., ʿAlī-Naqī Munzawī and ʿAfīf ʿUṣayrān (Tehran, 1969), vols. 1 and 2, pp. 487–488.

The example of those who have plunged themselves into *kalām* is like those whose ailment was not getting better through permissible medicines. Given the exigent circumstances, it is therefore permissible to cure them with forbidden medicines. In Islamic Law, drinking wine is forbidden. However, if there is a patient regarding whom physicians says that he can only be cured through drinking wine—and that if he does not drink it he will die—certainly the consensus of all religious scholars would be that drinking wine is permissible for him. In fact, if he does not drink it, he is being disobedient… . Likewise, it is not permissible for anyone to study *kalām*, except through necessity.

In the age of the Prophet, peace and blessings upon him, no one occupied themselves with *kalām*. Neither did anyone do so in the age of the Companions, may God be pleased with them. It was after them that the heretically innovative sects came into being. The Prophet, peace and blessings upon him, said: 'Whatever comes after me which is not traced to me is heretical innovation, and going astray. Avoid it.'

Therefore, plunging into *kalām* is only permissible for two groups, and forbidden to all else. One is a firmly rooted scholar, who is walking on firm ground in terms of religion. When he sees that innovators are in positions of authority, and that one cannot refute their discourse except through *kalām*, then it is permissible for him to learn enough *kalām* to offer a response to these enemies.

The other person [who should be permitted to study *kalām*] is one whose belief in God and the Messenger is weakened due to the heretical teachings he has heard, which have influenced his heart. If the discourse of the preachers does not cure him, and the religious scholars say that he can study enough *kalām* to know that the innovator's discourse is all false, then it is permissible for him to do so.

Apart from these two, if someone studies *kalām* and seeks to offer his own esoteric and allegorical interpretation, this person is a heretical innovator, and one who seeks to cause strife.

4

Ṣadr al-Dīn Qūnawī

Abu'l-Ma'ālī Ṣadr al-Dīn Muḥammad ibn Isḥāq Qūnawī (also written as Qunyawī) was born in 605/1207 in Anatolia where he also had his earliest schooling. Little is known of his family background except that his father died when he was a young boy and his mother married Ibn 'Arabī when Ṣadr al-Dīn was twelve or thirteen years old. From that time on he was with his stepfather nearly all the time, travelling with him to Aleppo and Damascus where he stayed with the master until the latter's death in 638/1241. During this period Ibn 'Arabī did leave Ṣadr al-Dīn for a period in the hands of Awḥad al-Dīn Kirmānī for training and it is said that Ṣadr al-Dīn used to state, 'I drank milk from the breasts of two mothers' (referring to Ibn 'Arabī and Awḥad al-Dīn Kirmānī). It was also during this period probably between 620/1223 and 635/1237 that Ṣadr al-Dīn went to some Persian cities such as Shiraz. Even during the life of Ibn 'Arabī, Ṣadr al-Dīn apparently held important sessions for students to whom he taught the former's doctrines.

After the death of Ibn 'Arabī, Ṣadr al-Dīn began to travel. He performed the *Ḥajj* and then set out for Egypt in 638/1245–46 where he held long discussions with Ibn Sab'īn. It is also said that he met Shaykh Abu'l-Ḥaṣan al-Shādhilī during this journey but this assertion has not been historically verified. In any case, Ṣadr al-Dīn returned to Quniyah (Konya) where he spent the last part of his life and where he died in 673/1272. His mausoleum remains to this day a famous site in that city. It was in this city that he trained most of his well-known students and where he wrote his major works. Ṣadr al-Dīn was a contemporary and close friend of Mawlānā Jalāl al-Dīn Rūmī, who also lived in Konya, and it was he who performed the prayer for the dead before the body of Mawlānā.

Ṣadr al-Dīn is the most important interpreter and disseminator of the teachings of Ibn 'Arabī. His writings are mostly philosophical exposition of the highly inspirational works of Ibn 'Arabī. While the master's work is replete with illuminations and spiritual visions like a series of bolts of lightning, his pupil and stepson Qūnawī casts continuous light upon the truths he expounded. 'Abd al-Raḥmān Jāmī said of

Ṣadr al-Dīn 'It is impossible to understand Ibn ʿArabī's teachings concerning the Oneness of Being in a manner consistent with both intelligence and the Sacred Law without studying al-Qūnawī's works'.[1] It was Ṣadr al-Dīn who more than any other figure, transformed the doctrines of Ibn ʿArabī into what we call here philosophical Sufism without in any way betraying the nature of Sufi gnosis or reducing it simply to a 'harmless' mental philosophy devoid of spiritual and practical significance. As Ibn ʿArabī was known by the followers of his School and even the general public as 'al-Shaykh al-Akbar', the Supreme Master, so did Qūnawī come to be known as 'al-Shaykh al-Kabīr', or the Grand Master.

Ṣadr al-Dīn trained a number of students whose role was crucial in the spread of Ibn ʿArabian mystical theology (*ʿirfān*). Among the most important of them one can mention:

1. Saʿd al-Dīn Farghānī, the author of *Mashāriq al-darārī al-zahar* (Orients of Radiant Stars). This is a Persian commentary upon Ibn al-Fāriḍ's Arabic poem *Naẓm al-sulūk* (Poem of the Way) written as a summary of Qūnawī's lectures on the poem. Qūnawī' himself wrote an approving foreword to the book. Farghānī subsequently rewrote his commentary in Arabic, adding a great deal to it. Both the Persian and the Arabic texts, especially their introduction, were highly esteemed in the later tradition.
2. Mu'ayyid al-Dīn Jandī, another major figure of this School who was the author of a very influential commentary upon the *Fuṣūṣ* as well as the Persian *Nafḥat al-rūḥ* (The Breath of the Spirit) which discusses practices associated with the teachings of Ibn ʿArabī.
3. Fakhr al-Dīn 'Irāqī (or ʿArāqī) one of the greatest Persian mystical poets, whose *Lamaʿāt* (Divine Flashes), which is a masterpiece of Persian *ʿirfānī* prose, was inspired by the lectures of Ṣadr al-Dīn on the *Fuṣūṣ*.
4. Abū Bakr ʿAlī al-Malāṭī al-Sīwāsī is significant as the person through whom the initiatory chain issuing from Qūnawī reached later generation of Sufis.

Such later Persian thinkers, mystics and poets as Shams al-Dīn Maghribī, ʿAbd al-Razzāq Kāshānī, Shāh Niʿmat Allāh Walī, Maḥmūd Shabistarī and ʿAbd al-Raḥmān Jāmī along with numerous figures of the centuries that followed, some of whom will be treated in the next volume of this *Anthology*, from Mullā Ṣadrā to Āqā Muḥammad Riḍā Qumsha'ī, owe their knowledge of Ibn ʿArabī to a large extent to Ṣadr al-Dīn's works and those of his immediate students.

As for Ṣadr al-Dīn Qūnawī's works, they were written in both Arabic and Persian and include some two dozen texts of which perhaps the most significant and influential but not the only pertinent writings are the following:

1. From the *Nafaḥāt al-uns*, ed. M. Tawḥīdīpūr (Tehran, 1336 Sh./1957) p. 556.

1. *Miftāḥ al-ghayb* (The Key to the Unseen). This is the most widely read and influential work of Ṣadr al-Dīn, one that is still a textbook on *ʿirfān* in Persia. It is a systematic treatment of both the metaphysical and cosmological teachings of Ibn ʿArabī. This text is usually studied with the commentary of the Ottoman gnostic and religious scholar and authority Shams al-Dīn Muḥammad Fanārī entitled *Miṣbāḥ al-uns* (The Lamp of Familiarity).
2. *Tafsīr al-fātiḥah* (Commentary upon the 'Opening' [chapter of Qurʾān]). One of the most profound commentaries ever written on the *Sūrat al-fātiḥah*, this work deals with the three 'books', namely, the Qurʾān, the cosmos and man and their relations with each other and to God.
3. Correspondence with Naṣīr al-Dīn Ṭūsī. This very significant series of exchanges between two of the colossal figures of Islamic thought during the seventh/thirteenth century, deals with both similarities and differences between Ibn ʿArabian *ʿirfān* and *mashshāʾī* philosophy.
4. *al-Nafaḥāt al-ilāhiyyah* (Breaths of Divine Inspiration). This is a long work that deals mostly with mystical states rather than pure metaphysics.
5. *al-Nuṣūṣ* (The Texts). This is a masterly summary of Ibn ʿArabian metaphysics in the form of a synoptic commentary upon and summary of the *Fuṣūṣ*.

Considering the immense influence of the *Nuṣūṣ* upon later Islamic thought in general and philosophical Sufism in particular, we have decided to include a translation of part of this text in this section. Unfortunately shortage of space did not allow for the translation of other works, especially his *Miftāḥ*. This is regrettable considering the wide influence of this work of Ṣadr al-Dīn upon later *ʿirfān*. In any case one must be at least aware of the continuing influence of this work during later centuries in the Persian world among gnostics, philosophers and even some poets.

In this chapter, about one half of the text of *al-Nuṣūṣ* (The Texts) is presented in the English language for the first time. It begins with a discussion concerning knowledge, its modalities and its relationship to existence, unity and plurality and the Real. The chapter continues by examining stations of knowledge and the degrees of knowing, different levels of knowing God and the Real as Being. Identifying the Real as Being which is also the conclusion of this treatise is at the heart of Qūnawī's argument throughout this work.

S. H. Nasr

THE TEXTS

al-Nuṣūṣ

Translated for this volume by William C. Chittick from Ṣadr al-Dīn Qūnawī, *al-Nuṣūṣ*.[1]

The Keys to the *Fuṣūṣ*

Praise belongs to God, who, by means of the resting-places of aspiration, clarified the levels and degrees of certainty, which are knowledge, eye, and truth; who, by stilling the disquiet of the seekers upon arrival at the utmost wish of their souls, elucidated the disparity of their degrees in the way-stations of knowing Him and being near to Him; and who, from among His creatures, set apart an elect by not giving them any goal among all His worlds and all the Presences of His names and attributes other than His Essence. Rather, He made the utmost aim of their aspirations the most eminent objects of His Essential knowledge and the highest objects of His desire, so the object of their desire and their furthest wish is what He

1. I have used the edition of the text established by Sayyid Jalāl al-Dīn Āshtiyānī, which includes notes by the early twentieth-century scholar Āqā Mīrzā Hāshim Ashkawarī (d. 1332/1953). However, the edition has many minor errors, which I have tried to correct by collating it with two good manuscripts from the Süleymaniye Library in Istanbul, copies of which were kindly supplied by the Muhyiddin Ibn ʿArabi Society in Oxford. These are Şehid ʿAlī Pāshā 1351, copied in 690, sixteen years after Qūnawī's death; and Ayasofya 1724, copied in 813. Neither is without copyist errors, and a critical edition of the text will certainly need to take into account other manuscripts (of which there are well over thirty in the Süleymaniye alone). Significant discrepancies between the Āshtiyānī edition and the two manuscripts have been indicated in the notes.

In translating the treatise, I have refrained as much as possible from adding explanatory material, even though this is perhaps the densest work of a notoriously difficult author. I have tried to be consistent in rendering technical terminology, so I have usually limited myself to one mention of the original Arabic term (typically in *maṣdar* form).

Qūnawī pays much less attention than Ibn ʿArabī to the images and symbols implicit in Qur'ānic Arabic. He tends rather to employ words in keeping with the abstract, technical meanings that had been given to them in the sciences. Although I have tried to translate the text using the same terminology that I have employed elsewhere in translating Ibn ʿArabī, I have often opted instead for a more abstract, philosophical-sounding word. To cite but one example, Ibn ʿArabī commonly speaks of the '*athar*' or 'trace' of a divine name, a word that carries the same sort of significance as Qur'ānic 'sign' (*āyah*). But Qūnawī uses the word in a more abstract manner, and I render it as 'influence'.

The word *wujūd* is central to Qūnawī's vocabulary, and indeed, in this treatise we see some of the first instances of the expression *waḥdat al-wujūd*, always associated in the later tradition with Ibn ʿArabī's name (though he did not use it). Qūnawī is fully aware of the broad range of meanings embraced by the word *wujūd*, including being, existence, finding, awareness, and consciousness. To choose one English term over another leads to an unwarranted specification of the word's meaning, so I have left it untranslated. As for the adjective *wujūdī*, I translate it as 'of *wujūd*' rather than, e.g., 'ontological', which may or may not be appropriate in a given context.

desires through His Essence for His Essence with regard to the highest modalities of His original, first tasks and the most elevated of His entifications. Hence, He is identical with their knowledge, eye, and truth of certainty, in all the levels of His Essential Knowledge, which is connected first to Him and then to the objects of His knowledge, while they *qua* they are effaced in Him, though their ruling remains and pervades all His existents and His Presences.

And God bless him who realized Him in respect of the most perfect witnessing and the most complete, eminent, and inclusive knowledge while having perpetual presence with Him in all of his homesteads, states, levels, and configurations—our master Muḥammad; and the purified among his community and his brethren, those who possess the most complete inheritance of his knowledges, states, and stations along with the realization of the results of their own exclusive shares that distinguish them from him; through these become distinct the specificities of the intermediaries, the fruits of the following, and the rulings of the interrelations. May that blessing be continuous in ruling and perpetual in ripening throughout the perpetuity of time in respect of His universal reality and the forms of its differentiated rulings, which are called 'His years, His months, His days, and His hours'.

[1] An Eminent Text, the First of the Texts that Must be Offered

Know that it is not correct, in respect of the Real's Essential Nondelimitation [*iṭlāq dhātī*], for Him to be ruled by any ruling [*ḥukm*], to be recognized by any description [*waṣf*], or to have any relation [*nisbah*] whatsoever ascribed to Him—whether oneness [*waḥdah*], the necessity [*wujūb*] of *wujūd*, originatingness [*mabda'iyyah*], the demand of existence-giving [*ījād*], the emergence of an influence [*athar*], or the connection [*ta'alluq*] of His knowledge to Himself or to anything other than Himself.

For, all of this demands entification [*ta'ayyun*][1] and delimitation [*taqayyud*], but there is no doubt that the intellection [*ta'aqqul*] of an entification demands being preceded by nonentification [*lā ta'ayyun*], and everything that we mentioned precludes nondelimitation. Or rather, the condition [*sharṭ*] of conceiving [*taṣawwur*] of the Real's nondelimitation is that it be intellected in the meaning of a

1. Use of *ta'ayyun* as a specific technical term apparently begins with Qūnawī. Ibn 'Arabī uses the word on occasion, but not in a technical sense. From Qūnawī onward, it is a standard expression among Ibn 'Arabī's followers. When translated as 'determination', as it often is, its connection with the word *'ayn*, one of the most important technical terms of this school of thought is obscured. *Ta'ayyun* means basically 'to become an *'ayn*' or 'to take on the characteristics of an *'ayn*'. *'Ayn* means 'entity', that is, a 'thing' (*shay'*) as distinct from other things. The 'First Entification' is Real *Wujūd* inasmuch as It discloses Itself in characteristics and attributes that allow us to understand and conceptualize It as an entity distinct from that which is absolutely nondelimited and nondistinct, i.e., the Essence (*al-Dhāt*).

negatory [*salbī*] description, not that it be a nondelimitation whose opposite [*ḍidd*] is delimitation. On the contrary, it is nondelimited by both the oneness and the manyness [*kathrah*] that are known, as well as by *restriction* [*ḥaṣr*] in nondelimitation or delimitation, in comprehending [*jamʿ*] all that, or in being incomparable [*tanazzuh*] with it. In respect to Him, all of that is correct while He is incomparable with it all, so ascribing all of it and anything else to Him is equal to negating it from Him. Neither is more appropriate than the other.

Once this has been elucidated, then it is known that oneness, originatingness, influencing [*taʾthīr*], the existentiating act [*al-fiʿl al-ījādī*], and so on may correctly be ascribed to the Real from the standpoint [*iʿtibār*] of entification.

The first of the intellected entifications is the Essential Relation of Knowledge [*al-nisbah al-ʿilmiyyah al-dhātiyyah*] from the standpoint of its being distinct [*tamayyuz*] from the Essence, but through a relative [*nisbī*], not a true, distinction. By means of the Essential Relation of Knowledge are intellected the oneness of the Real, the necessity of His *wujūd*, and His originatingness; especially in the respect that [1] His knowledge of Himself is through Himself, and His very knowledge of Himself is a cause [*sabab*] of His knowledge of everything; [2] the 'things' [*ashyāʾ*] consist of the entifications of His universal [*kullī*] and differentiated [*tafṣīlī*] intellections; [3] the 'quiddities' [*māhiyyāt*] consist of the intellections; and [4] these intellections are configured [*intishāʾ*] one from another—not in the sense that they arrive newly [*ḥudūth*] in the Real's intellection (exalted is God beyond what is improper for Him!); rather, the intellection of some is posterior in level [*mutaʾakhkhirat al-rutbah*] to others. All are endless [*abadī*] and beginningless [*azalī*] intellections in an identical manner. They are intellected in knowledge, which becomes connected to them in accordance with what their realities [*ḥaqāʾiq*] demand.

The demand [*muqtaḍā*] of their realities is of two sorts: The first is that they are intellected inasmuch as their manyness is effaced [*istihlāk*] in the Oneness of the Real. This is the intellection of the differentiated [*mufaṣṣal*] within the undifferentiated [*mujmal*], like the intelligent knower who witnesses in one kernel, with the eye of knowledge, all the branches, leaves, and fruit that it contains potentially and, in each individual fruit, the like of what was in the first kernel, and so on ad infinitum.

The other sort is the intellection of the rulings [*aḥkām*] of oneness in one group [*jumlah*] after another such that each group is intellected through the quiddities that it comprises. These are the forms of the multiple, plural intellections of the One *Wujūd*. This is the reverse of the effacement mentioned first, for that consisted of the effacement of manyness in oneness, and this consists of the effacement of oneness in manyness. So, let this be known!

[2] The Second Text

Know that the Real, in respect of His nondelimitation and His encompassment [*iḥāṭah*], is not named by any name, nor is any ruling ascribed to Him, nor does He become designated by any description or impression [*rasm*]. The relation of demand [*iqtiḍā'*] is not more appropriate for Him than the relation of not demanding, for the demand that is thereby intellected or negated is an entified ruling and a delimited description.

You should also know that although demand is Essential, it has three levels:

Its ruling in respect of the first level is that its entification does not depend [*tawaqquf*] upon any condition [*sharṭ*], nor is there any reason [*mūjib*] that is the cause [*sabab*] of its entification.

Its ruling in respect of the second level is that its entification depends only on one condition.

Its ruling in respect of the third level is that the manifestation of its rulings depends upon conditions, causes, and intermediaries.

So, the ruling of the first demand is the Essential Effusion [*al-fayḍ al-dhātī*], not for any reason. No receptacle [*qābil*] or preparedness [*istiʿdād*] is intellected as its counterpart [*muqābil*].

The ruling of the second demand depends upon one condition of *wujūd* alone, and that condition of *wujūd* is the First Intellect, which is the intermediary between the Real and those contingent things [*mumkināt*] whose *wujūd* has been ordained [*taqdīr*] until the Day of Resurrection.

As for the ruling of the demand in respect of the third level, the manifestation of its influence [*athar*] and ruling depends upon many conditions, such as the rest of the existents [*mawjūdāt*].

I do not mean by this that we have three demands, diverse in their realities. Rather, there is one demand with three levels. In respect of each of the three levels, an influence or some influences become manifest and entified. So understand!

[3] Among the Divine Texts

Know that plurality [*taʿaddud*] is ascribed to the unitary, Essential Knowledge in respect of its connection [*taʿalluq*] to the known things [*maʿlūmāt*]. Perception [*idrāk*] of them is realized only in respect of its entifications and connections. Its connection to each known thing follows the known thing as that thing is in itself—whether the known thing be simple or compound, temporal [*zamānī*] or locational [*makānī*], nontemporal or nonlocational, temporary [*muwaqqat*] in reception [*qabūl*] and finite [*mutanāhī*] in ruling and description, or nontemporary and infinite in what we have mentioned. So know this!

Also, one of the branches of the mentioned texts is that the ruling of any ruler [*ḥākim*] concerning any ruled thing [*maḥkūm ʿalayh*] follows the state [*ḥāl*] of the ruler at the moment [*waqt*] of ruling; and, it follows the state of the ruled thing in the state of the ruler's ruling.

If the ruled thing is such that it undergoes transition [*tanaqqul*] in states, then the rulings of what rules over it will be varied [*tanawwuʿ*] in each state, and the ruler will differ in keeping with its becoming clothed [*talabbus*] by those states. If, however, the ruled thing is such that it stays fixed [*thābit*] in one manner, then the ruling of what rules over it will be fixed in keeping with the first connection designated by the ruling and the demand of the ruler.

There remains the situation according to the state of the ruler. Is the demand of the ruler's essence (transformation [*taqallub*] in states? Or, is the demand of its essence)[1] that it be fixed, and that the states undergo transformation over it?

So, the ruling of the ruler will follow in accordance with one of the two affairs that *restricts* the levels of the ruling of every ruler and every ruled thing, since no ruling of any ruler and no ruled thing is outside what I mentioned.[2]

[4] Among the Texts

Knowledge follows *wujūd*, in the sense that, wherever there is *wujūd*, there will be knowledge, without disjoining [*infikāk*].

The disparity of knowledge accords with the disparity of the quiddity's complete [*tāmm*] or defective [*nāqiṣ*] reception of *wujūd*. So, when something receives *wujūd* in a more complete manner, knowledge will be more complete. Knowledge will be defective in the measure of the defective reception and the domination [*ghalabah*] of the rulings of contingency [*imkān*] over the rulings of necessity [*wujūb*], in contrast to what we mentioned first. So know this!

[5] Among the Realized Texts

I have hinted at something of this in one place in my books in the midst of and in the language of something else. Nonetheless, I have set this book apart for the

1. Missing in the two manuscripts.

2. Ashkawarī says in his notes that the purport of this Text is to explain the four possible types of ruling in terms of ruler and ruled. In the first type, both ruler and ruled are fixed, as in the case of the Real, who is the subject and object of His own knowledge. In the second, neither ruler nor ruled is fixed, such as the wayfarer who undergoes transformations as he passes over the stations on the path to God. In the third, the ruler is fixed but not the ruled, such as *wujūd*, which rules over its entifications, because the Real determines the creatures. The fourth type is the opposite, such as the entifications, which rule over *wujūd* and determine the way it becomes manifest, since they are fixed in the First Entification (the fact of their being known to God in Himself).

mention of texts derived from tastings [*adhwāq*] specific to the elect station of perfection [*khuṣūṣ maqām al-kamāl*], leaving aside its common tongue [*lisān ʿumūm*], namely, the delimited tastings gained by the masters of specific stations; at root, these latter depend upon the Presence [*ḥaḍrah*] of one of the divine names or attributes, which is the source and headspring of that specific tasting.

So, it is incumbent upon me to single out and distinguish what pertains specifically to the tasting of the most perfect and the most comprehensive station and [to show] the correctness of affirming it and its congruence [*muṭābaqah*] with what God knows in the highest, most complete, and most perfect degrees of His knowledge of the affair that is being spoken of, without stipulating its correctness and affirmation in relation or ascription [*iḍāfah*], or in one station rather than another station, or from the standpoint of a state or a moment to the exclusion of other states and moments or what was mentioned.

So we say, having offered this introduction clarifying the text that we intend to elucidate: When man perceives [*idrāk*] any known thing with his theory [*naẓar*], his unveiling [*kashf*], his senses [*ḥiss*], or his imagination [*khayāl*], together or individually, and when his theory or his unveiling of that affair—or his perception of it through the senses or imagination—does not reach as far as the perception of what lies beyond it after having recognized its essentialities [*dhātiyyāt*] and universal requisites [*lawāzim kulliyyah*], then he has not perceived the thing with right perception nor recognized it with right recognition [*maʿrifah*].

It makes no difference whether his perception and recognition are connected to the cosmos in respect of its meanings [*maʿānī*] and spirits [*arwāḥ*], or in respect of its forms [*ṣuwar*] and accidents [*aʿrāḍ*]; or if his recognition is connected to the Real.

When the true state of affairs is unveiled for him along with the form of the entification of every known thing in the Real's knowledge, he will find the affair to be so. This is because, as long as his recognition of the Real does not reach as far as His nondelimitation and the utter, true oneness of His Essence—which is not designated by any name, description, ruling, or impression, nor apprehended [*inẓibāṭ*] by any witnessing [*shuhūd*] or intellection, nor restricted by any designated affair—he will not know that 'There is no target beyond God,'[1] that encompassing Him in knowledge and witnessing [*shuhūd*] is absurd [*muḥāl*], and that beyond the Nondelimited *Wujūd* of the Real there is nothing but imaginary non-existence [*al-ʿadam al-mutawahham*].

There is, nonetheless, another path to the recognition of the impossibility of knowing God as He knows Himself that is even higher, more complete, and more

1. A well-known *ḥadīth* that is not found, however, in Wensinck's *Concordance*.

unveiled. We have recognized it through tasting and witnessing—by the praise and favour of God the exalted—but it is among the things whose clarification and recording is forbidden. Its utmost clarification is the mentioned hint. So be it.

Tasting, the recognition gained by its possessor, and witnessing—inasmuch as the tasting and station depend upon the presence of one of the divine names, which is the *qiblah* of the possessor of that station and the furthest limit [*ghāyah*] of his recognition of the Real—are an utmost limit [*nihāyah*], especially from the standpoint that demands the name to be the same as the Named [*al-musammā*], as we have elucidated in various places in our discourse. But these are relative furthest limits, for the origins and furthest limits are waymarks of the relative perfections.

The situation in respect of true perfection is otherwise. God alludes to this in His words to the most perfect of His servants, 'Surely at thy Lord is the endpoint' [53:42]. He placed in this verse a hidden subtlety, and that is the fact that He did not say, 'Surely at thy Lord is thy endpoint.' Rather, He pointed out to him that his furthest limit in unqualified Lordship [*muṭlaq al-rubūbiyyah*] is the furthest limit that is the furthest of all furthest limits. After that, there is nothing but the differentiations of the degrees in most-perfectness [*akmaliyyah*], which do not come to a halt at any boundary or furthest limit.

The Prophet alluded to what we have mentioned in one of his intimate prayers, for he said, 'I seek refuge in Thy good pleasure from Thy anger and in Thy pardon from Thy punishment and I seek refuge in Thee from Thee. I do not enumerate Thy laudation. Thou art as Thou hast lauded Thyself.' In other words, 'I do not reach everything that is in Thee.' Thus he pointed out the impossibility of encompassment, and he combined with it giving knowledge of his having reached the furthest of the furthest limits in his recognition of the Real. This is like a commentary on the mentioned verse, that is, His words, 'Surely at thy Lord is the endpoint.'

In the prophetic *ḥadīth*s there are many pointers that allude to what we have mentioned. Those who explore them after waking up to and understanding what I have mentioned will find them lucid and resplendent.

Now we say: The afore-mentioned station and tasting has tongues that translate it in diverse styles. Among its tongues in the Qurʾān in respect of naming is 'the Ramparts' [*al-aʿrāf*], concerning which He gave news that its 'men recognize each by its mark' [7:46]. This is one of the characteristics of gazing over all sides by reaching the point of recognizing things to the furthest limit, which makes it necessary to raise up one's gaze to what is beyond them.

Its tongue and name in the station of prophethood is 'place of cognizance' [*muṭṭalaʿ*]. Thus the Prophet said concerning the Mother of the Qurʾān, or rather, concerning the mystery of each of the Qurʾān's verses, that it has 'a manifest sense, a non-manifest sense, a limit, and a place of cognizance, up to seven non-manifest senses.' According to another version, 'up to seventy non-manifest senses.' I have informed about this in *Tafsīr al-fātiḥah*, so one can look for it there.[1]

Its name and tongue in the terminology of the Folk of God is 'halting place' [*mawqif*], which is the endpoint of every station and which gazes over the coming station.

Its name and tongue in the tasting of the station of perfection relative to every two stations is 'the isthmus [*barzakh*] that comprehends the two', and, relative specifically to the station of perfection, 'the isthmus of isthmuses'.

[6] An Eminent Text, Difficult of Access

'The Unseen of the Real's He-ness' [*ghayb huwiyyat al-ḥaqq*] is an allusion to His nondelimitation from the standpoint of nonentification and His true oneness that erases all standpoints.

The 'names, attributes, relations, and ascriptions' consist of the Real's intellection and perception of Himself in respect of His entification. This entificational intellection and perception follow the mentioned nondelimitation, but, relative to the Real's entification within the intellection of any intellecter in any self-disclosure [*tajallī*], it is a nondelimited entification; it is the vastest entification and is witnessed by the Perfect [*kummal*]. This is the Essential Self-Disclosure that has the station of the highest *tawḥīd*.

The 'originatingness' of the Real follows this entification. The originatingness is the source of the standpoints and the headspring of the relations and ascriptions that become manifest in *wujūd* while staying non-manifest in the courtyard of intellections and minds [*adhhān*].

What is said to be 'a Nondelimited, One, Necessary *Wujūd*' consists of the entification of *wujūd* in the Essential, divine relation of knowledge. In respect of this relation, Realizers call the Real 'the Origin' [*mabda'*], not in respect of any other relation. So understand and ponder this, for I have inserted in this text the root of the roots of the divine knowledges. And God is the right-guider.

[7] A Text

When any traveller [*sālik*] travels on a path whose furthest limit is the Real on condition of his winning from Him some sort of felicity [*sa'ādah*], that traveller is the possessor of a *mi'rāj* and his travelling is an ascent [*'urūj*]. So understand!

---

1. *Tafsīr al-fātiḥah* is the same as *I'jāz al-bayān fī tafsīr umm al-Qur'ān* (Dā'irat'l-Ma'ārif al-'Uthmāniyya, Hyderabad-Deccan, 2nd edition, 1949). Also published by 'Abd al-Qādir Aḥmad 'Aṭā' as *al-Tafsīr al-ṣūfī li'l-Qur'ān* (Cairo, 1969). For the passage Qūnawī refers to here, see *I'jāz*, pp. 262–263; *al-Tafsīr*, pp. 377–378.

[8] An Eminent, Universal Text, Containing Resplendent Mysteries

Know that whenever something is described as influencing [*ta'thīr*] one thing or some things, the application of this description to it will not be completely true so long as it does not influence the reality of the thing inasmuch as it is it, without the intellection of the inclusion of another limitation [*qayd*] or some outside condition—whatever it may be—within the reality described as exerting the influence.

I only mention these limitations because of the influences that are ascribed to things in respect of their levels, or in respect of standpoints that are requisites of their realities; and because of what has also become widespread among the folk of theoretical intellect and most of the folk of tastings; namely, that when something is described by mirrorness [*mir'ātiyyah*], whether its mirrorness be supraformal [*ma'nawī*] or sensory [*ḥissī*], its mirror has an influence on what is reflected within it, because it gives the form of the reflected thing back to it, and the form of the reflected thing becomes manifest within it according to it.

This is correct in a certain way, but not in an unqualified sense. It would be correct for the mirror to influence the reflected thing only if it influenced its reality per se. This, however, does not happen. One affirms the mirror's influence on the reflected thing only in respect of the perception of those who do not know the reality of the reflected thing and who perceive it only in the mirror. The mirror, however, is not a locus for the reality of the reflected thing, but rather a locus for the disclosure of its image and some of its manifestations. Manifestation is a relation that is ascribed to the reflected thing in respect of the reflection of its form in the mirror; it is not the very reality of the reflected thing.

By my words 'some of its manifestations' I mean to point out that the essential, exclusive self-disclosures [*al-tajalliyyāt al-dhātiyyah al-ikhtiṣāsiyyah*] are not within a locus of manifestation [*maẓhar*] or a mirror, nor do they accord with some level. For, when someone perceives the Real in respect of these self-disclosures, he has witnessed the Reality as It is outside the mirror, not according to a locus of manifestation or a level, as we said—not a name, an attribute, a designated state, or anything else. It is he who knows by tasting that the mirror has no influence on the Reality. Our Shaykh the leader used to name these self-disclosures 'the Essential, lightning-like [*barqī*] self-disclosures'.[1] In those days I did not know the reason for this nomenclature, nor what the Shaykh meant by it.

These Essential, lightning-like self-disclosures occur for no one except those who are completely detached [*farāgh*] from all descriptions, states, and rulings—both those pertaining to necessity and [divine] names and those pertaining to contingency. This detachment is a nondelimited detachment that does not

1. For a few references to these lightning-like self-disclosures in Ibn 'Arabī's writings, see Chittick, *Imaginal Worlds* (Albany, NY, 1994), pp. 81–82.

differ from the nondelimitation of the Real except that it lingers no more than one breath [*nafas*], which is why it is likened to lightning. The reason for its lack of continuity [*dawām*] is the ruling of the all-comprehensiveness [*jamʿiyyah*] of the human reality. Just as this all-comprehensiveness does not demand its continuity, so also, if human all-comprehensiveness did not entail this description—namely, the detachment and nondelimitation that attract these self-disclosures—then human all-comprehensiveness would not be an all-comprehensiveness that fully embraces every description, state, and ruling. So, the ruling of all-comprehensiveness affirms it and negates its continuity.

I found, when God granted me this self-disclosure, that it had wonderful rulings in my inward and my outward. Among them was that, although it did not stay for two breaths, it left in the locus [*maḥall*] descriptions and sciences that no one but God can calculate. I came to know in the night that I wrote down this Arriver [*wārid*][1] that he who does not taste this locus of witnessing [*mashhad*] is not a Muḥammadan inheritor [*wārith Muḥammadī*]; he does not know the secret of his words, 'I have a moment when no one embraces me other than my Lord'; nor the secret of his words, 'God was, and nothing was with Him'; nor the secret of God's words, 'Our command is but one, like a glance of the eyesight' [54:50]. Nor does he know the secret of the fact that existence-giving does not originate in any existent time.

In the same way, when someone tastes this locus of witnessing, having already known that the fixed entities [*al-aʿyān al-thābitah*] are the realities of the existents; that they are not made [*ghayr majʿūl*]; that the reality of the Real is incomparable with making [*jaʿl*] and influencing; and that there is no third thing other than the Real and the entities; then he will necessarily know—if indeed he has what we have mentioned—that nothing influences anything, that the things influence themselves, and that what are named influencing 'causes' [*ʿilal*] and 'occasions' [*asbāb*] are conditions for the manifestation of things in themselves. It is not that one reality influences another reality.

So also he should know the situation in 'assistance' [*madad*]. There is nothing that assists anything else. Rather, assistance reaches the manifest side of something from its non-manifest side, and this is made manifest by the luminous self-disclosure of *wujūd* [*al-tajallī al-nūrī al-wujūdī*]. But making manifest does not take place by influencing the reality of what is made manifest. So, the relations influence each other, in the sense that some of them are the cause of the configuration of the ruling of others and of their manifestation in the reality that is their source.

Among the things that come to be known by the taster of this self-disclosure is that the fixed entities, in respect of being mirrors, have no influence on the divine

1. In the technical language of Sufism, an 'Arriver' is an influx of knowledge by way of unveiling. See the translation of Ibn ʿArabī's chapter on the Arriver from the *Futūḥāt* in Chittick, *The Self-Disclosure of God* (Albany, NY, 1998), pp. 148–150.

self-disclosure of *wujūd* except in respect of the manifestation of the plurality latent in that self-disclosure. So, this is an influence in the relation of manifestation and a condition of making manifest. The Real, however, transcends being influenced by other than Himself, and the realities of the engendered things [*al-kā'ināt*] transcend being influenced in respect of their realities, for, from this standpoint, they are—in the tasting of the Perfect—the same as the Tasks [*shu'ūn*][1] of the Real, so it is not permissible that others should influence them. Hence, in the respect that it is a mirror, a mirror has no influence on the reality of what is reflected within it, because of the explanation already given.

So, understand this text and ponder it, for I have inserted within it precious sciences and mysteries whose measure cannot be measured by any but God. This is the certain truth and the clear text. Even though something you hear that opposes it may be correct, it is relatively correct. This is the explicit truth within which there is nothing dubious. And God is the right-guider, the guide.

[9] Among the Universal Texts

These are texts that I mentioned in the book *Miftāḥ ghayb al-jam' wa tafṣīlihi* and in other books.[2] I composed them without mixing in the words of anyone else, for that is not my custom, because God has preserved me from that—with His high, unadulterated gifts, He has delivered me from any need for low, outside borrowings. But I have specified this book for mentioning the texts, so it is also necessary to mention those texts here.

So, I say: Among them is that inasmuch as something is the cause of the *wujūd* of manyness [*kathra*] and many [*kathīr*], it is impossible for it in that respect to become entified through manifestation, nor will it appear to a gazer [*nāẓir*] except in something gazed upon [*manẓūr*].

Among them: Nothing that is opposed to [*muḍāddah*] or different from [*mubāyanah*] a thing emerges [*ṣudūr*] or results from it, despite the diversity of the sorts and kinds of results [*thamar*]—the supraformal [*ma'nawī*], spiritual [*rūḥānī*], imaginal [*mithālī*], imaginary [*khayālī*],[3] sensory [*ḥissī*], and natural [*ṭabī'ī*]. This holds generally for anything that is called 'a place of emergence' [*maṣdar*] or 'a result-yielding root' [*aṣl muthmir*] for a thing or things. However, it has this description from the standpoint of intellecting it inasmuch as

1. This term derives from the Qur'ānic verse, 'Each day He is upon some task' (55:29) which Ibn 'Arabī interprets in terms of the day of the 'He-ness' or the Essence, which is the present moment, and the fact that there is no repetition in divine self-disclosure. See Chittick, *The Sufi Path of Knowledge* (Albany, NY, 1989), pp. 98–99.

2. Compare Qūnawī, *Miftāḥ al-ghayb*, text in Fanārī, *Miṣbāḥ al-uns*, edited by Muḥammad Khwājawī (Tehran, 1374 Sh./1995), pp. 13–14.

3. Şehid Ali Paşa 1351 lacks the word 'imaginary', and Ayasofya 1724 lacks both it and 'imaginal'.

it is it, and, from another, hidden standpoint, of which only rare Realizers gain cognizance.

When it is thought that something happens counter to what we mentioned, that will only be so because of and in accordance with a condition or conditions, external to the essence of the thing, and in accordance with the guise [*hay'a*] that is intellected because of the coming together—I mean the coming together of the reality that is described by emergence and result-yielding and the external conditions and standpoints along with the rulings of the level within which the coming together becomes entified.

'Each works similar to its way' [17:84]. Nothing results in or makes manifest anything that is the same or completely similar to it, because that would require that *wujūd* had come about and become manifest twice in one reality and in one level in one way and mode. This would be to gain what is already there [*taḥṣīl al-ḥāṣil*], which is absurd; it would be empty of benefit and would pertain to the useless [*'abath*], but the Wise, Knowing, Real Actor transcends useless acts. Hence, the roots must be different from their results. Moreover, the contingent things are infinite, and effusion from the Real, who is the Root of roots, is one. So, in the view of him who knows what I have mentioned, there is no repetition in *wujūd*. So understand!

This is why the Realizers have said, 'God does not disclose Himself twice in one form to one individual, nor to two individuals in a form.' On the contrary, there must be a separating factor and a difference in one or more ways, as I pointed out earlier. So understand! And God is the right-guider.

[10] An Eminent Text

Know that, given that it is not possible to ascribe any attribute or name to the Real in respect of His nondelimitation, or to apply to Him any ruling, whether negatory or affirmative, it is thus known that attributes, names, and rulings are not applied or ascribed to Him except in respect of the entifications.

Once it is clear that every manyness in *wujūd* and intellection must be preceded by oneness, then it becomes necessary that the entifications—in respect of which names, attributes, and rulings are ascribed to the Real—be preceded by an entification that is the origin and source of all the entifications, in the sense that nothing lies beyond it save unmixed nondelimitation; this is a negatory affair that requires the negation of descriptions, rulings, entifications, and standpoints from the core [*kunh*] of His Essence as well as the lack of delimitation or restriction by any description, name, entification, or anything else that we have enumerated or mentioned in summary fashion.

Now, unimpaired intellects, even if they lack sound unveiling, may take the standpoint of the ensuing attributes and names. If they are unable to intellect any names or attributes beyond what they conceptualize [*taṣawwur*] and if their intellective perceptions reach only that, then, in relation to them, these are 'the names of the Essence'. In the stage of the theoretical intellect and the state of this veil [*ḥijāb*], they will draw conclusions about these realities from the inclusiveness [*shumūl*] of their ruling, from the fact that the other names and attributes are subordinate [*tabaʿiyyah*] to them, and from the fact that what comes after them becomes entified depending upon them.

So, the Essential [*dhātī*] and name-related [*asmāʾī*] divine gifts [*ʿaṭāʾ*] are known from this rule, in the sense that every gift and good [*khayr*] that reaches creation from the Real will be either an Essential or a name-related gift, or it will combine the Essence and the names.

There is no way to reckon the Essential gifts. Their entifications are not restrained or restricted by number.

As for the name-related gifts ascribed both to the Essence and the names, either their relation to the Presence of the Essence will be stronger and more complete than their relation to the Presence of the names and attributes, or the contrary. If their relation to the names and attributes dominates over their relation to the Essence, then they may be reckoned, either with difficulty or ease, according to the domination [*ghalabah*] and the being dominated over [*maghlūbiyyah*] that occur in this case. But here there is a great secret that cannot be divulged.

If the result of domination and being dominated over is that the relation of the gifts to the Presence of the Essence is strong, this will have no reckoning, because the Essential gifts and whatever has a strong relation to them emerge and are received only because of an Essential correspondence [*munāsaba*]. There is no reason for them other than this correspondence.

Whoever does not recognize this principle does not know the reality of His words, 'He gives provision to whomsoever He will without reckoning' [2:212], or the secret of His words, 'This is Our gift, to bestow or withhold without reckoning' [38:39], or the like of that, mentioned repeatedly in the Exalted Book and also in the prophetic *ḥadīth*s, such as his words, 'Surely from my community seventy thousand will enter paradise without reckoning, and with every thousand, seventy thousand.' These are the possessors of the name-related gifts. Their relation to the Presence of the Essence, however, is stronger than their relation to the Presence of the names and attributes. This is why they follow the possessors of the Essential correspondence and share with them in their states. So know that!

Now that we have mentioned the sorts and the rulings of gifts, let us mention the sorts of their recipients [*qābilūn*]. For, in their taking, they have classes that become numerous according to the requests of their preparedness, state, level, spirit, constitutional [*mizājī*] nature, or accidental [*ʿaraḍī*] nature. It is these that are expressed by the tongue of the receiving seeker.

In short, the highest level of the recipients in receiving what reaches them from the effusion and gifts of the Real is the vision of the Real's face in the conditions and causes named 'the intermediaries' [*wasā'iṭ*] and 'the chain of [cosmic] order' [*silsilat al-tartīb*]. The taker knows and witnesses that the causative intermediaries are nothing but the entifications of the Real in the divine and engendered [*kawnī*] levels in all the diversity of their kinds. In other words, there is nothing between the received effusion of the Real and the recipient except the very entification of the effusion through the delimited receptivity. There is no inclusion of a ruling of contingency [*ḥukm imkānī*] that would be demanded and made necessary by the influence of the effusion's passing over the levels of the intermediaries and by its becoming coloured [*inṣibāgh*] by the rulings of their contingencies. It is seen that the effusion is one of the self-disclosures of the Real's Nonmanifest, for the pluralities (and entifications)[1] joined with it are among the rulings of the name Manifest in respect of the fact that the Real's Manifest is a locus of disclosure for His Nonmanifest. So, the rulings of manifestation pluralize the nondelimited oneness of non-manifestation. It is these rulings that are named 'recipients', and they are the forms of the Tasks, nothing else. So understand. 'And God speaks the truth, and He guides whomsoever He will to a straight path' [35:41].

[11] A Resplendent Text and Universal Rule Providing Knowledge of the Divine Compliance and Response, and His Withholding the Two

Know that the complete, explicit scale [*mīzān*] and the taste-derived, sound demonstration [*burhān*] in recognizing when the servant is among those who obey their Lord and when he will quickly be given the divine response [*ijāba*] in exactly what he asks, without substitution or delay, is sound recognition and perfect compliance [*muṭāwaʿa*]. When someone's recognition of the Real is sounder and his conception of the Real is sounder, then the response to him will be quicker in exactly what he requests. When someone is more complete in watching over [*murāqaba*] the commandments of the Real and in undertaking them with perfect compliance, then the Real's compliance with him will also be more complete than His compliance with other servants. This is why the state of the great ones among the Folk of God demands that most of their supplications receive a response—because of the perfection of compliance and the soundness of recognizing God and conceiving of God. God alludes to this with His words, 'Supplicate Me and I will respond to you' [40:60].

When someone lacks sound recognition by way of witnessing, he is not the supplicant of the Real to whom He guarantees a response with His words, 'Supplicate Me and I will respond to you'. For he turns his attention only to the form

1. Not found in the two manuscripts.

individuated [*mushakhkhaṣ*] in his mind [*dhihn*] and resulting from his theory [*naẓar*] and imagination [*khayāl*], or from the imagination and theory of someone else, or from what all this has given him. This is why someone of this sort is deprived of being given a response with exactly what he asked for, or there is a delay in it—I mean, in the response. When someone like this receives a response, its cause is the mystery of the divine withness [*maʿiyyah*], which demands that nothing be empty of the Real; or it is the complete concentration [*jamʿiyyah*] that is gained by the distressed [*muḍṭarr*], who are promised a response when they supplicate in distress,[1] and the preparedness they have gained from that—that is, the distress.

The state of someone who has this description is different from the state of the possessor of sound conception and realized recognition, for the latter calls the Real to presence [*istiḥḍār*] and turns his attention [*tawajjuh*] toward Him with a realized calling to presence and turning of attention. Even if he does not have this in every respect, it is enough that he has conceived of the Real and called Him to presence in his attention only in some levels and in respect of some names and attributes. This is the state of the intermediate Folk of God, whereas the just-mentioned state is the state of the veiled.

As for the Perfect [*kummal*] and the Solitaries [*afrād*],[2] their attention to the Real follows the Essential self-disclosure that they have, and their realization of the station of perfection depends on having attained it. For them it results in a complete recognition that comprehends the modalities [*haythiyyāt*] of all the names, attributes, levels, and standpoints along with a sound conception of the Real in respect of His already mentioned Essential self-disclosure gained by them through the most complete witnessing. This is why the response is not delayed for them.

Also, the Perfect and those Solitaries whom God wills are the folk of cognizance of the Guarded Tablet, or rather, of the station of the Pen, or rather, of the Presence of the Divine Knowledge. Hence they are aware of what has been ordained to come to be, because of foreknowledge [*sabq al-ʿilm*] of its inescapable occurrence. So, they do not ask for something absurd, something whose *wujūd* has not been ordained. Their aspirations are not incited to seek [*ṭalab*] or desire [*irādah*] that.

I only say 'desire that' because there are those upon whose desire the occurrence of things depends, even if they do not supplicate or ask the Real for it to come about. I witnessed that from our Shaykh—may God sanctify his mystery—for many years in uncountable affairs. He reported to me that he saw

1. The reference here is to Qur'ān 27:62: 'He answers the distressed one when he supplicates Him, and He removes the evil.'

2. In Ibn ʿArabī's teachings a Solitary is a perfect human being who stands at the same level but outside the scope of the Pole (*quṭb*); the latter governs the unseen world of sanctity. See Chittick, *Sufi Path of Knowledge*, p. 413, n. 23.

the Prophet in one of his visions[1] and that he gave him good news and said to him, 'God is quicker to respond to you than you are to supplicate Him'. This station is above the station of receiving response to supplications and is one of the specificities of perfect compliance.

The station of perfect compliance is above the station of compliance, for the station of compliance is specific to what was alluded to—namely undertaking to observe commandments, following everything that pleases the Real, and performing His rights [*ḥuqūq*] in the measure of ability. The Prophet alluded to it when he replied to his uncle Abū Ṭālib, who said to him, 'How quickly your Lord hastens to do what you want, O Muḥammad!', when he had seen the quickness of the Real's response to him in what he would ask from Him. According to another version, he said to him, 'How your Lord obeys you!'

The Prophet said to him, 'And you, O Uncle—if you obey Him, He will obey you.'

This station, which we said is above that, goes back to the perfection of the servant's fulfilling what the Real desires from him in respect of his reality through the first, universal desire, which is connected to the achievement of the Perfection of Disclosure and Discovery [*kamāl al-jalā' wa'l-istijlā'*].[2] This is the reason for giving existence to the cosmos and Perfect Man, who is precisely God's Intended Entity [*'ayn maqṣūdah*]. Everything else is intended by way of subordination to him and because of him. For, when there is something without which the sought thing [*maṭlūb*] cannot be reached, that also is sought. This is what I mean by my words, 'by way of subordination'.

Perfect Man alone is desired for himself because he is a complete locus of disclosure [*majlā*] for the Real. Through him the Real becomes manifest in respect of His Essence and all His names, attributes, rulings, and standpoints as He knows Himself through Himself in Himself; and through everything comprised by His names, His Attributes, and all the rulings and standpoints that I alluded to, and the realities of the things known by Him [*ma'lūmāt*], which are the entities of the things He engenders—without any alteration by reason of defective reception, or a deficient mirrorness that would demand that [Perfect Man] reflect something that becomes manifest other than as it is in itself.

When someone is of this sort, he has no desire distinct from the Real's desire. Rather, he is the mirror of His Lord's desire and His other attributes. Thus his

1. 'Vision' translates *wāqi'ah*, which means befaller, happening, event, occurrence. In the Sufi vocabulary it denotes a true vision, typically seen during wakefulness. The word is derived from the Qur'ānic verse, 'When the Befaller befalls, no one will deny its befalling' (56:1).

2. By this expression Qūnawī is referring to the full actualization of God's goal in the creation of the universe as announced in the famous *ḥadīth qudsī*, 'I was a hidden treasure and I desired to be known, so I created the creatures that I might be known.' For more on Qūnawī's teachings here, see Chittick and Peter Lamborn Wilson, *Fakhruddīn 'Irāqī: Divine Flashes* (New York, 1982), the discussion of 'the perfection of distinct-manifestation and distinct-vision', pp. 23 ff.

supplication is effaced in his desire, which does not differ from his Lord's desire. So, what he desires occurs, just as He says: 'Doer of what He desires' [85:16].

If someone who has reached the realization of what we mentioned supplicates, he will be supplicating with the tongues and levels of all the inhabitants of the cosmos, because he is a mirror of them all. In the same way, when he leaves aside supplication, he leaves it aside only in respect of being the Real's locus of disclosure from the standpoint of that face among his two faces that is adjacent to the Divine Side.[1] He does not differ from Him in respect of His being 'doer of what He desires.' No one can aim at any target or climb to any level or station beyond this station.

Below him is the one who turns his attention toward the Real with complete recognition and sound conception, the one intended by the address, 'Supplicate Me and I will respond to you'—and the Real's report is truthful. This has become easy for the servant alluded to, so the result is inescapable, that is, the response, in contrast to the other turners of attention whose characteristics were mentioned.

So know this! You will attain exalted mysteries and wonderful sciences to which thoughts and imaginings do not climb, nor do fingers inscribe them with pens. And God is the right-guider.

[12] An Eminent Text

Know that the highest degree of knowledge of a thing—whatever thing it may be, in relation to whatever knower it be, and whether the thing known be one or more things—is gained only through unification [*ittiḥād*] with the known thing and the knower's being no different [*mughāyarah*] from it; for, what causes ignorance of something and prevents perfect perception of it is nothing other than the domination of the ruling through which the two are distinct [*imtiyāz*]. This is a supraformal distance [*buʿd maʿnawī*]. Distance, in whatever respect, prevents perfect perception of the distant thing.

The disparate degrees of knowledge of the thing are in the measure of the disparate domination of the ruling that unifies the knower with the known thing. True nearness eliminates the separation that is true distance, which was alluded to as the rulings through which difference and distinction come to be.

When you witness this affair and taste it with realized unveiling, you will know that the Real has perfect knowledge of things only because He discovers [*istijlāʾ*] them in Himself while their manyness and otherness are effaced in His oneness. For, when something is within something else—whether the locus be supraformal or formal—it will only come to be and become manifest in accordance with that within which it is entified and manifest. This is why we say that the Real knows

1. On the two 'faces' (*wajh*) of all things, one directed at the Real and the other at creation, see Chittick, *Self-Disclosure*, pp. 135 ff.

Himself through Himself and He knows the things in Himself through His very knowledge of Himself.

Divine reports have come that 'God was, and nothing was with Him', thus negating the otherness of things relative to the oneness that is their unseen[1] locus and affirming the firstness of the Real in respect of the oneness. Through the distinction of the manyness of the things that are intellected in the second place and latent [*kāmin*] before that in oneness, and through the fact that in actuality oneness comprehends [*jamʿ*] the things, the perfection that was first concealed in oneness becomes manifest. Thereby the door is opened to the Perfection of Disclosure and Discovery, which is the true sought object. Thereby become manifest the rulings of oneness in manyness, and of manyness in oneness.

Oneness makes manyness one [*waḥḥadat al-kathrah*], for it becomes the common measure [*qadr mushtarik*] among the many things, which are distinct from each other by essence; hence it joins [*tawṣīl*] their separations [*fuṣūl*], because by essence it comprehends, as we mentioned. And the many things [*mutakaththirāt*] pluralize [*taʿdīd*] the One in respect of the entifications, which are the cause of the variation of the One's manifestation in colour [*ṣibgh*] and colours and [the cause] of the diverse qualities [*kayfiyyāt*] that demand the diversity of the preparednesses of the many things that receive the One Self-Disclosure. Thereby is renewed recognition of the kinds of manifestations and their requisite rulings, which consist of some influencing others by holding together and taking apart, outwardly and inwardly, high and low, temporarily and not temporarily, correspondingly and not correspondingly—all that by means of the conjunction [*ittiṣāl*] that they have through the unitary self-disclosure of *wujūd* that comprehends them all, as was mentioned.

So knowledge, bliss [*naʿīm*], and felicity in all their diverse kinds accord only with the correspondence [*munāsabah*]; and ignorance, chastisement, and wretchedness accord with the strength of the rulings of difference [*mubāyanah*] and distinction. As for the intermixing [*imtizāj*] of those rulings through which there is unification and of those rulings through which there is distinction, its governing authority [*salṭanah*] has no end.

The source of each group of rulings through a sort of correspondence, the place to which they refer in respect of ascription, and that to which they are traced back [*mustanad*] is named 'the level'. So understand!

When I started to write this text, it was said to me in my inwardness while I was writing: In respect of oneness, the root of the rulings ascribed to oneness and to the One Real and called 'the rulings of necessity' is one ruling, and that is the reality

1. Reading *ghaybī*, in keeping with Şehid ʿAlī Pāşā 1351 and an alternative reading offered in the printed edition. Both the latter and Ayasofya 1724 have *ʿaynī*, in which case the meaning would be not 'unseen', but 'in entity'. This could mean 'as fixed entities' (i.e., invisible objects of divine knowledge) or 'in their state of being existent entities' (i.e., as present in the universe).

of the 'decree' [*qaḍā'*]. The measures [*maqādīr*] of the influence of the pluralities of the known things belong to the one ruling. The One *Wujūd* becomes manifest by reason of these pluralities, first by being influenced, and second by influencing these pluralized things through returning their influences to them. So know this, and ponder the wonderful thing that I have pointed out! You will attain exalted knowledge. And God is the right-guider.

5

Sayyid Ḥaydar Āmulī

The most important figure in the integration of the teachings of Ibn ʿArabī into the Shiʿi intellectual world was Sayyid Ḥaydar Āmulī. He was born in Māzandarān in 720/1320 to a distinguished family and it was there that he received his earliest education, as we learn from two autobiographical accounts which he has left us at the beginning of his major Qur'ānic commentary *al-Muḥīṭ al-aʿẓam* (The Supreme Ocean) and *Naṣṣ al-nuṣūṣ* (The Text of Texts). We also learn that he went to Khurāsān and Isfahan to pursue advanced studies, returning aged twenty-five to Āmul where he became an important public and political figure. He even rose to the position of wazir to the Bāwandid king Fakhr al-Dawlah, enjoying every possible success in worldly life. But he had a religious conversion and a new yearning for God. So he left everything behind, departing from Āmul with a simple cloak on his back.

He went to Isfahan in 750/1349–50 with the aim of making the *Ḥajj* and stayed for a while in the city frequenting only Sufi circles and becoming the disciple of a Sufi master by the name of Nūr al-Dīn Ṭihrānī. Then in 751 Āmulī set out for Iraq and from there to Mecca and Medina where he was planning to remain. However, for health reasons he returned to the holy Shiʿi cities of Iraq where he passed the rest of his life. There he spent some time studying with a number of Shiʿi authorities especially Fakhr al-Muḥaqqiqīn, the son of ʿAllāmah Ḥillī and a student of Naṣīr al-Dīn Ṭūsī and Dabīrān-i Kātibī. Āmulī himself became a leading theological figure of Shiʿism in Iraq. He never returned to Persia and it was in Iraq that he died some time after 787/1385. His life was, therefore, clearly divided into a Persian and an Iraqi period.

Some thirty-four works were written by Āmulī in Arabic and Persian and three or four others are attributed to him though their attribution is not certain. Most of his writings are, however, lost. The major theme of his works is to demonstrate that in their essential reality Sufism and Shiʿism are the same. He also provided a Shiʿi version of Ibn ʿArabian doctrines. Therefore, while praising Ibn ʿArabī, the Shaykh al-Akbar, in the highest terms, he differed from him in the identification of the universal Muḥammadan 'seals of sanctity' *(khātam al-walāyah/wilāyah)*. Ibn 'Arabī considered Jesus to be the universal and himself the Muḥammadan 'seal of sanctity', whereas Āmulī believed these two functions to have belonged to 'Alī ibn Abī Ṭālib and the Mahdī respectively. Otherwise, on the discussion of *wujūd*, theophany, universal man and other major *'irfānī* doctrines, he followed Ibn 'Arabī closely.

Āmulī's works include such titles as *Amthalat al-tawḥīd* (Examples of Unity) which is a response to the *Lama'āt* (Divine Flashes) of 'Irāqī; *Talkhīṣ iṣṭilāḥāt al-ṣūfiyyah* (Summary of the Technical Vocabulary of the Sufis) which is a new rendition of the famous work of 'Abd al-Razzāq Kāshānī of the same title; *al-'Ilm wa taḥqīquhu* (Knowledge and its Realization) on the meaning of *'ilm* according to the theologians, philosophers and Sufis; and *Risālat al-nafs fī ma'rifat al-rabb* (Treatise of the Soul Concerning Knowledge of the Lord). The most important surviving works of Āmulī, however, are as follows:

1. *al-Risālah fī ma'rifat al-wujūd* (Treatise on the Knowledge of Being). Written in 768/1367, this treatise is supposed to be a summary of a much larger work whose manuscript has not as yet been located, but the extant treatise is itself a major philosophical text dealing in depth with the philosophical question of *wujūd* which is, however, treated in an *'irfānī* fashion distinct from the ontology of both Ibn Sīnā and Ibn Rushd.
2. *al-Muḥīṭ al-a'ẓam* (The Greatest Ocean), a Qur'ānic commentary in seven volumes completed in 777/1375–76. This great *'irfānī* commentary is a major work in its genre comparable to the esoteric commentaries of Rūzbahān Baqlī, 'Abd al-Razzāq Kāshānī Maybudī and Najm al-Dīn Kubrā. Āmulī states that this book, like the *Fuṣūṣ* of Ibn 'Arabī, was not a creation from him but was received as a creation from on high upon him.
3. *Naṣṣ al-nuṣūṣ* (The Text of Texts). Completed in Baghdad in 782/1380–81, this treatise is a notable commentary upon the *Fuṣūṣ* of Ibn 'Arabī. In this work there is lavish praise for Ibn 'Arabī along with the Prophet and the Shi'i Imams. Āmulī also uses diagrams, for which he had a propensity, to complement his written words. As Corbin has said, Āmulī had the gift of 'diagrammatic art' which was meant not only to aid the memory but to be a support for—in Corbin's words—'*ars interiotativa*' or '*ars meditativa*'.[1]

In this chapter we have included a major section of Āmulī's most important work, *Jāmi' al-asrār* (The Sum of Secrets). The work begins with an exegesis of the concept of 'Unity' and continues by discussing some of the manifestations of Divine Unity and the process of 'Divine Self-disclosure.' The relationship between

1. Henry Corbin, *En Islam iranien* (Paris, 1972), vol. 3, p. 178.

existence, reality and human faculties are discussed next, both discursively and also based on what has been transmitted by Sufi masters and gnostics. Āmulī then turns to the subject of the essential unity of religions and offers a discourse on the harmony between reason and revelation. This treatise ends with a brief discussion of what Āmulī calls 'Islam: its various levels'.

S. H. Nasr

THE SUM OF SECRETS AND THE SOURCE OF LIGHTS[1]

Jāmiʿ al-asrār wa manbaʿ al-anwār

Translated for this volume by Latimah-Parvin Peerwani from Sayyid Ḥaydar Āmulī, *Kitāb Jāmiʿ al-asrār wa manbaʿ al-anwār,* critical edition of the Arabic text in *La Philosophie shiʿite*, ed. with French introduction by Henry Corbin and Arabic introduction by Osman Yahya (Tehran-Paris, 1969), pp. 210–228, 327–338, 685–691.

Ontology

The Unity of Being: *tawḥīd*

Etymologically and technically [the term] *tawḥīd* consists of 'many things becoming one thing', or 'to make many things into one thing'. It could be cognitive (*'ilmī*), practical, or the gathering together of both, which is superior to the former two. That which is cognitive is, for instance, many kinds subsumed under one species, or many species subsumed under one genus, or many genera subsumed under one reality. I mean, for instance, many classes of men and individual men subsumed under one absolute species of man; or species of animals subsumed under one absolute genus of animal; the animal [species] subsumed under one reality of the universal body or the simple [or non-composite] body; many bodies subsumed under one reality of the substance; and many substances subsumed under one pure, sheer Being called the Absolute [Being].[2]

As for the practical [*tawḥīd*], it is, for instance, many pharmacological drugs [combined] to make one paste; many names subsumed under one name; many

1. Content in square brackets is from the translator.

2. The central thesis of Āmulī's metaphysical thought which dominates his entire *Jāmiʿ al-asrār* and this section is his metaphysics of Being or Existence (*wujūd*) which is an integration of Ibn ʿArabī's metaphysics of 'Being' with Shiʿi theosophy. Being, according to him, is the sole, absolute, all-comprehensive Reality that permeates the whole universe. The phenomenal forms, or 'essences', are nothing but the internal modifications under which the absolute Reality reveals itself in the empirical dimension of human experience. Such a vision of Reality and the experience of Being, according to him, are obtainable as an actual experience only by a mode of cognition called by him by various terms, such as *kashf* (unveiling), *shuhūd* (witnessing), *dhawq* (tasting) etc. He who obtains such a vision of Reality in its double aspects is called 'a man of two eyes'. He is a man who with his one eye 'sees' the divine Unity, while with his other eye he 'sees' the Multiplicity, i.e., the world of phenomenal things or essences. Simultaneously he 'witnesses' that these two are ultimately one and the same thing, i.e., the phenomenal forms are the self-determinations of the Reality which flows or runs through all of them. This metaphysical view of Reality is unlike the Peripatetic view which is akin to the level of popular thinking or common-sense view of Reality according to which the Absolute Reality is separated from the phenomenal forms which are viewed as determined essences separated from the Reality.

parts of minerals and plants [combined] to make one form and one nourishment; many names subsumed under one name; four elements subsumed under one nature or one body, etc. These examples, though remote from [our] object, which in itself is something simple and nonmaterial (*mujarrad*), that is, the Absolute Being, non-determined, and non-compound, whereas those varieties are compound things, and one cannot compare the simple with the compound thing, this is a subtle point. [Our] object of inquiry here is not with respect to its Essence only, so that it makes [the above criterion] requisite, but it is [to consider] it from the point of its self-manifestation (*ẓuhūr*), in the loci of manifestation (*maẓāhir*). Since that is the case, there is no problem in presenting [those analogies], because they are not remote from [our object sought], for in the compound as well as in the simple there is none but He, as you have learned, and will learn, God willing. *Those similitudes, We coin them for the people, but no one understands them save those who have knowledge* [29:43].

Another similitude: The similitude of Existence [or Being] and its self-manifestation in the forms of loci of manifestation is precisely the same as the similitude of ink and its manifestation in the forms of letters [of a script]. Just as the manifestation of ink in the form of letters does not detract its pure oneness and the oneness of its reality, in the same way the self-manifestation of Existence in the forms of existents does not detract from its pure oneness and the oneness of its reality. If you have comprehended this, [then know that the] real oneness [is witnessed] in these two forms, the form of ink and letters, or Existence and existents, is understood by paying no attention to the multiple forms of their loci of manifestation, i.e., halting at witnessing the reality of each one of the two. I mean the oneness in the form of ink and letters may be [witnessed] by ignoring the forms of all the letters, their demarcations and multiplicity. This is witnessing the reality of the ink per se, because the existence of the letters is something mentally posited (*iʿitibārī*); in reality they have no existence [of their own] externally, for in truth it is only the ink which has existence externally. So is *tawḥīd* with regard to Existence and existents. It is witnessed by not paying attention to the forms of all existents, their entifications, and multiplicity. This is witnessing the Existence per se because the existence of the existents is something mentally posited; they have no existence [of their own] externally, for in reality the existent externally is only the Existence named the Absolute Reality (*al-Ḥaqq*).

The knower (*ʿārif*) of the former only witnesses the ink in reality because of his knowledge that the existence of all the letters are existent by [the ink], and without it they are non-existent. There is nothing in the letters but [the ink], for the letters are nothing but it. Likewise, the knower of the latter [i.e., the Existence] only witnesses in reality the Existence because of his knowledge that the existence of all the existents is through existence alone, without existence they are non-existent. Nay, in the existence [there is none] but existence. By [such a witnessing] the knower [of this reality] is 'the maker of [many things] into one', [both] cognitively and intuitively (*'aynan*), in reality and metaphorically. This was the object of discussing *tawḥīd* in this station. God is All-knowing of what is right. In the similarity of the ink and the letters with regard to the Existence and its loci of manifestation, there are many secrets. But this is not the place [to explain] them. We have alluded to it in [our] *Muntakhab al-ta'wīl*[1] in detail. Here we have indicated some of it.

If this is realized, then know once again that the two things exist externally, and, according to knowledgeable people, they are confined to the necessary and contingent. Their becoming one reality in the form of these two aspects—that is, the cognitive and practical—would be if the inquirer considers first the reality of everything by returning it inductively to its root from which that thing has issued until he reaches the sheer, pure Existence that is pure and subsists by Itself, so that externally there is none but It. I mean, it is necessary for the inquirer to consider every thing other than the Necessary (Being), until he knows Its reality and he knows that the existence in each of the existents is something relative to a thing and not a reality because it is additional to its quiddity; additional to it from the Absolute Existence which is not related to other than It. That is because if the Absolute (Being) is related to that which is other than It, It comes forth from Its absoluteness. Also, other than the Absolute Being is the sheer non-existence, so the Existence [or Being] is not related to the non-existence. Hence if one negates existence from the quiddity of the existents, one by one he will reach the Existence from which it is not possible to negate Its existence from Its quiddity. That is because the existence of the Necessary [Being] is Its quiddity itself, which is precisely the same as Its reality, so it is not possible to negate it, for the possibility of its negation is the possibility of negating the existence of every existent other than It. And the possibility of negating every existent is impossible, for that would necessitate the transformation of the reality of existence into the reality of non-existence, and that is impossible. So the negation of Its existence [that is, of the Necessary Being] from Its quiddity is impossible. Since it is not possible to negate Its existence from Its quiddity, but it is possible to negate from that which is other than It, then from his consideration, that is, from the consideration of that inquirer, there is none but the One Existence that is self-subsistent, and not related to other than Itself. Therefore, his cognitive consideration would be a maker of the reality of two existences as one existence. This in brief is the intention behind the cognitive *tawḥīd*.

Detailed [explanation]: It is incumbent to consider the reality of every existent and its existence, until it is known from which aspect it is a creature and from which aspect it is the Absolute (*al-ḥaqq*). For every existent is Absolute in one aspect and creature in another. I mean, [it is] the Absolute Reality with regard to Its reality, Its

1. This work is in manuscript form and not yet published.

essence and Its existence, and creature with regard to its determination (*taʿayyun*), individuality, and limitation. When one considers the reality of things and their essences in this regard, that is, the consideration of the knowledge of its reality, he comes to know that all return to one essence, and that is the Absolute Being, or Reality, which is the merging of ascription and relation [in Its essence]. The ascription and relation disappear at the manifestation of the [Absolute], and the Object of relation and the related [are perceived] united in existence. He sees the Absolute as self-subsisting, and the creatures annihilated in It pre-eternally and post-eternally without being stopped by the time and location. [This is] as His saying: *Everything is annihilated except His Face* [28:88].

If he considers the determination of every existent and its individuality, also considering the knowledge of its reality, he comes to know that the determinations and individualities, though mentally posited entities additional to the reality of the things and their quiddities, are not disappearing as such. But, as a matter of fact, it cannot be otherwise. So he comes to know that all of that is annihilated in itself, subsisting by Its Existence, as His saying: *All that dwells upon the earth is undergoing annihilation, and there subsists the Face of thy Lord, possessor of majesty and honour* [55:26–27]. By [this knowledge] he becomes a knower of the Absolute and creatures, a knower of both. This is the final goal of the cognitive oneness, as well as differentiation. Its simpler explanation will follow, God willing.

Practical *tawḥīd*: It is obtaining all of it [mentioned above] through 'witnessing' and intuition, not by knowledge and explication. I mean this knowledge is attained by a person through 'tasting' (*dhawq*), 'witnessing', 'unveiling', and 'intuition' (*muʿāyanah*); not through explication and demonstration (*burhān*). As the Prophet, may God's blessing and peace be upon him and upon his progeny, said, 'You shall see your Lord just as you see the moon on the night when it is full.'[1] Here 'seeing', according to the general understanding of the verifiers (*muḥaqqiqūn*), means complete [intellectual] unveiling and nothing else. There is no doubt that it is so, because the witnessing of the Absolute and the things through [intellectual] unveiling is clearer and more evident than witnessing the full moon by the [sensible] vision and sense, because the senses are subject to error, whereas the unveiling by its possessor is beyond that. However, the similitudes coined from the objects of senses are for the people who rely upon the [external] senses because they do not understand other than those. If there is someone who is higher than them [in knowledge and understanding] he would understand [more] from those [concrete similitudes] and other than them as degrees [of divine Speech] which are unlimited. These are the peculiarities of the Speech (*kalām*) of God, the speech of His messengers and His friends (*awliyāʾ*), that is, the share of each one is according to his measure [knowledge and understanding].

1. This *ḥadīth* is found in many versions. The closest to that mentioned here is Bukhārī, *Ṣaḥīḥ*, *Kitāb al-Tawḥīd*, p. 532.

In reality, He [the Exalted] has alluded to this witnessing by His saying, *We will show them our signs upon the horizons and in their souls, until it is clear to them that He is the Reality. Is it not enough that thy Lord is witness over every thing? Are they still in doubt about the encounter with their Lord? Does not He encompass everything?* [41:53–54]. The preceding [means], He says: I will anoint their insight by the light of My guidance and success (*tawfīq*) by which they will witness Me in My loci of manifestation of horizons and souls, a witnessing which is an unveiling and concrete, by that it would become clear to them that in the existence, whether in the horizons or in the souls, there are only the traces (*āthār*) of My Names, My Attributes, My loci of manifestation and My perfections. Thus they will realize that I am the First, I am the Last, I am the Exterior, I am the Interior, and that other than Me nothing has existence, be it mental or extra-mental.

Affirming this meaning by the way of astonishment and sarcasm, He said: *Is it not enough that thy Lord is witness over every thing?* So that they know through verification that *He is the witness over every thing*, i.e., they verify witnessing Him in every thing, a witnessing [which is] intuitive and through unveiling. He also said, *Are they still in doubt about the encounter with their Lord? Doesn't He encompass every thing?* Meaning those worshippers are in doubt about the encounter with their Lord in spite of this obvious witnessing of His loci of manifestation in the horizons and in their souls. Now which encounter is greater than this? *Does not He encompass every thing?* That is: Does not He encompass every thing by [His] Essence and Existence? Is it possible to witness the encompassed without the existence of its Encompasser? That is: Is it possible to witness the Exterior without the existence of His loci of manifestation? *This is the eternal religion, but most people know not* [12:40]. Meaning, this is the unveiling and clear witnessing (*bayān*), which is the real oneness (*tawḥīd*) and primordial religion (*al-dīn al-ḥanīf*), *but most people*, due to their ignorance and blindness, *know not that. Surely in that there is a reminder for the one who has a heart, or will give an ear while he is a witness* [50:37], like the prophets, the friends [of God] and the most perfect [men]. Because this witnessing, that is, witnessing the Absolute in the creation and the creation in the Absolute without any one of the two veiling the other, is the greatest witnessing and the ultimate goal [of the wayfarers]. This is their witnessing and the witnessing of those of their kind from among the most perfect [mystics] and the [spiritual] Poles. May God the Exalted give us the provision to attain it!

The possessor of this witnessing is called by the group [of gnostics] the 'possessor of reason' (*dhu'l-'aql*) and the 'possessor of intuition' (*dhu'l-'ayn*), having both reason and intuition together. They also allude to it in their saying that 'the possessor of reason' is one who sees the creation as exterior (*ẓāhir*) and the Absolute as interior (*bāṭin*). The Absolute becomes the mirror for the creation before him, because the mirror by its exterior form veils itself in itself, [i.e.,] the Absolute is veiled by the limited. Whereas the possessor of intuition is the one who sees the Absolute as exterior and the creation as interior, so the creation becomes the mirror of the Absolute for the self-manifestation of the Reality before him and the concealment (*ikhtifāʾ*) of the creation in form in It. But the possessor of reason and intuition is the one who sees the Reality in the creation and the creation in the Reality, neither of the two veils the other. Rather, he sees One Existence identical to the Reality in one respect, and the creation in another respect. He is not veiled by the multiplicity from witnessing the 'Face' of the One Unique, nor does the multiplicity become an obstacle [for him] in witnessing the multiple loci of manifestation of the oneness of the Essence that self-discloses (*tajallī*) Itself in them; nor does the oneness of the 'Face' of the Reality veil him from witnessing its self-disclosure in its multiple receptacles of self-disclosure (*majālī*). The perfect Shaykh Muḥyī al-Dīn ibn ʿArabī,[1] may God sanctify the core of his heart (*sirr*), alludes to these three levels in his verses:

Thus in the creation see the Reality Itself,
  if you are a possessor of intuition,
And in the Reality you see the creation itself,
  if you are a possessor of reason.
But if you are a possessor of both intuition and reason,
  then you see nothing therein but the Essence of one thing in it by form.[2]

The second aspect: He would know that the existential oneness [or unity] is witnessing the existence of the Reality from the respect of being Absolute and determined, Non-differentiated and differentiated, and the two aspects gathered together as such that the witnessing of the one does not veil the other. That is because if he stops at one of the two, he becomes veiled from the other and exits from the cycle of oneness. For anyone who witnesses His Existence and His Essence from the aspect of He *qua* He, transcended from all the limitations (*al-quyūd*), independent of all mental positing, and as Absolute and Non-differentiated, says: 'There is none in existence except He', because other than Him is absolute non-existence and sheer nothing. But by that he is veiled by Being and Essence from the Names and Attributes and their differentiated and non-differentiated perfections in their loci of manifestations. So he limits [Him] by the limits of absoluteness and non-differentiation and is pleased by half gnosis.

1. Cf. Toshihiko Izutsu's analysis of the metaphysics of Being in his *Concept and Reality of Existence* (Tokyo, 1971) pp. 35–55, in which he discusses briefly but substantially Āmulī's metaphysics of Being among others.

2. Ibn ʿArabī, Muḥyī al-Dīn, *al-Futūḥāt al-makkiyyah* (Beirut, n.d.) vol. 3, p. 290. The last word of these verses in Āmulī's text reads *shakl* (form) whereas in *al-Futūḥāt* it reads *fiʿl* (act). The latter seems to make more sense in the context of Ibn ʿArabī's metaphysics of being, so we have replaced 'form' by 'act'.

So also he who witnesses Him in every locus of manifestation from His Names, His Attributes, and His Acts, and says: 'this is the locus of the manifestation of [His] gentleness', 'this is the locus of manifestation of [His] severity', 'this is the locus of manifestation of [His] majesty', and does not witness Him disengaged from them, that is, from these loci of manifestation, that no distinction between the Manifest and the locus of manifestation, between the Essence and Attributes is attained by him, and he determines Him by that and differentiates Him in His loci of manifestation, and says, 'He is all, and there is none in existence but Him', he is also veiled by the loci of manifestation and the loci of theophany. He limits [Him] by differentiation and determination, and is pleased by the other half of gnosis.

If he combines the two and witnesses Him as Absolute (*muṭlaq*) and determined (*muqayyad*), Undifferentiated (*mujmal*) and differentiated (*mufaṣṣal*), that is, Absolute in determined and determined in Absolute, Undifferentiated in differentiated and differentiated in Undifferentiated, and neither of the two veils him from the other, he becomes a gnostic, perfect and perfecter; a witnesser who witnesses with clear intuition and 'taste' (*dhawq*) that there is none in existence but God (the Exalted), His Names, and His Attributes. He comes to know by verification that all is He, that all is by Him, from Him, and [returns] to Him. Then he recites correctly His words by the tongue of [his spiritual] state: *He is the First, He is the Last, He is the Exterior, He is the Interior, and He is the All-Knowing of everything* [57:3]. He becomes cognizant with certainty about the meaning of His words: *God is the Light of the heavens and the earth, the similitude of His Light is that of a lamp in a niche, the lamp is in a glass, the glass is like a glittering star kindled from a blessed tree, an olive that is neither of the East nor of the West* [24:35]. May God give us provision to arrive at this station by Muḥammad and his noble progeny.

In other words, this (station) is of witnessing the Absolute from the respect of one and many, gathering and differentiation, and the combination of the two. If he were to witness one Being bereft of all multiplicities of Names and Acts, then he witnesses Him as He is at the level of His Essence. At the level of His Essence, He is qualified by all perfections pre-eternally and post-eternally. One of His perfections is His manifestation in the forms of all existents and their meanings (*maʿānī*), pre-eternally and post-eternally. By that (particular witnessing), He becomes veiled by His Essence from His perfections, and by His Being from His specifications. If he witnesses One Being multiplied by these multiplications, determined by these determinations, he will not obtain the difference between multiplicity and unity, and distinction between differentiation and gathering [of the Being]. In this case he will not witness what He is from the aspect of oneness and gathering, because at the level of His Essence He transcends multiplicity and determinations absolutely. I mean, [He transcends] external and mental (determinations of existence). Rather, all that is from His perfections of Names and Attributes refer to His Essence at the second degree of the level of Being.[1] The possessor of this particular witnessing also becomes veiled from His Essence by His perfections of Names, and from His Being by His specifications of Attributes. This is like the former [state], and is not praiseworthy.

If he combines the two degrees as such that one does not veil the other, I mean, the unity is not veiled by the multiplicity, and gathering by discrimination, he becomes unifier, gnostic, perfect, the possessor of discrimination (*al-furqān*) specific to Moses and Jesus, peace be upon them, and of the (linking, *al-Qur'ān*) specific to Muḥammad, may the benediction of God be upon him and his progeny. For *al-furqān* is discriminated knowledge specific to Moses and Jesus, peace be upon them, and *al-Qur'ān* is the sum of knowledge together with discriminated knowledge specific to Muḥammad, peace be upon him. For *Qur'ān* etymologically means 'linking'. We have already explained that in detail in our treatise titled *Muntakhab al-ta'wīl.*

Its explanation according to the measure of this station: He the Exalted said: *If you are God-fearing he will give you discrimination* (*furqān*) [8:29], that is, if you are God-fearing and cautious in my gnosis and worship from the manifest polytheism and hidden polytheism, then I will make you the possessor of discrimination. That is, I will gift you and grant you knowledge which discriminates between real and false; a consideration which integrates the creation and the Reality, with a perfect discrimination between the One who manifests and the object of manifestation such that you witness Me as Exterior in precisely the Interior and Interior in precisely the Exterior, the First in precisely the Last and as the Last in precisely the First. So it is in regard to the degrees of unity and multiplicity, discrimination and gathering etc. from the divine degrees which are the higher degrees of witnessing by the prophets and friends [of God], peace be upon them. The God-fearing has levels, the lowest being cautious of illicit, and the highest being absolutely cautious of witnessing other [than God] called polytheism, be it manifest or hidden. [This cautiousness] necessitates obtaining the knowledge of 'discrimination' and 'integration', and leads to the real Muḥammadan unity *tawḥīd*, mentioned earlier.

To this kind of *tawḥīd*, the great master Muḥyī al-Dīn ibn 'Arabī, may God sanctify his secret heart (*sirr*), says in his words: 'Beware of Gathering and Differentiation! The first one inherits heresy (*al-zandaqah*) and deviation (*al-ilḥād*), the second one inherits the non-operation of the Absolute Agent. You should safeguard both. The gatherer of the two is a real man of unification, and he is called [the possessor of the station] of "gathering of gathering", and the gatherer of all. He has [attained] the highest degree and ultimate goal.'

---

1. What he intends here is that Being has various forms of Its self-unfolding. This is a metaphysical system of Ibn 'Arabī by which Āmulī and other metaphysicians of Islam were influenced according to which the same Reality is given a number of degrees or stages in accordance with the various degrees of its Self-unfolding or Self-manifestation. Izutsu, pp. 48–55.

This distinction and gathering [or unifying] are from the second distinction and gathering which is witnessing the subsistence of the creation by the Reality, the vision of unity in multiplicity and multiplicity in unity without its possessor being veiled from one by the other. It is not the first (distinction and gathering) which is the Absolute being veiled by the creation, and the subsistence of the creational descriptions in their state. It is also said concerning it: The gathering without distinction is heresy, and distinction without gathering is making ineffectual (the gathering), and gathering together with distinction is *tawḥīd*. This is not hidden from its Folk, but it is an admonition for some seekers.

Who grasps my saying, his perception will not dim,
Nor may one grasp it save he be endowed with perception.
Whether you assert unity or distinction, the Self is unique,
As also the Many that are and yet are not.[1]

Since this is verified that the intention behind the gathering of gathering is the unification of distinction after the gathering, then know that the station of gathering is an exalted station, and there is no station and no degree higher than it, and no ascent of any one of the prophets and friends [of God], peace be upon them, higher than this level. That is because this degree is the end, and above the end there cannot be any end, otherwise the end will have an end. This is the intention behind the praiseworthy station *or nearer* [53:9], 'the spiritual ascent (*al-miʿrāj al-maʿnawī*)', 'the real arrival' (*al-wuṣūl al-ḥaqīqī*) [in the Divine presence] etc. from the indications [given in some sayings of the realized ones]. It is said concerning it, 'There is no village beyond ʿAbbadān'. The Commander of the faithful [ʿAlī ibn Abī Ṭālib], peace be upon him, alluding to this [station] said in his saying: 'Even if the veil is removed completely [from the Absolute], my certitude [in the Absolute] will not increase.'[2] Concerning this state the great master [Ibn ʿArabī] said in his *Fuṣūṣ*, 'If you have experienced this [in the spirit] you have experienced as much as is possible for a created being, so do not seek nor weary yourself in any attempt to proceed higher than this, for there is nothing higher, nor is there beyond the point you have reached aught except the pure un-manifested [Absolute].'[3] Further in regard to this [station] he said: 'Though this be [the eternal truth] of the matter, none knows it [directly] save certain

1. Ibn ʿArabī, *Fuṣūṣ al-ḥikam*, ed. ʿAfīfī (Beirut, 1946), p. 79, translated into English by R. W. J. Austin as *The Bezels of Wisdom* (Lahore, 1999), p. 88.

2. This famous saying is attributed to ʿAlī ibn Abī Ṭālib; cf. Jalāl al-Dīn Rūmī, *Discourses of Rūmī*, trans. A. J. Arberry (London, 1975), p. 40, whereas some other classical Sufi texts such as al-Sarrāj, Abū Naṣr's *Kitāb al-Lumaʿ*, ed. R. A. Nicholson (Gibb Memorial Series, no. 22. Leiden, 1914) p. 70, Abū Ṭālib al-Makkī's *Quṭb al-qulūb*, (Cairo, 1381/1961) vol. 2, p. 205, attribute it to ʿĀmir ibn ʿAbd Qays, one of the eight early Muslim ascetics.

3. *Op.cit.*, p. 62; trans. Austin, p. 65.

among the elite of the friends [of God]. Should you meet one who possesses such knowledge you may have complete confidence in him, for he is a rare gem among the elite of the Folk.'[1] *Praise belongs to God, who guided us unto this; had God not guided us, we had surely never been guided* [7:41].

Know that the similitude of Absolute Existence or the Reality, may He be exalted, is like a limitless ocean, while the determined things and existents are like innumerable waves and rivers. Just as the waves and the rivers are nothing other than the unfolding of the sea according to the forms of its perfections which it possesses *qua* water as well as its peculiarities which it possesses *qua* sea, so are the existents and determined things nothing other than the unfolding of the Absolute under the forms of its essential perfections as well as its peculiarities belonging to Its Names.

Further, the waves and the rivers are *not* the sea in one respect, while in another respect they are not other than it. In fact, the waves and rivers are different from the sea [only] in respect of their being entified and determined. But they are not different from it in respect to [their] reality and essence which is pure water, because from this aspect they are identical to it. So are the existents and determined things, because although they are different from the Absolute in being entified and determined, they are not different from it in respect to their essence and reality which is existence. So from the [latter] respect they are identical to It. Some verses already mentioned have been said in this context:[2]

The sea is sea as it was from eternity,
  but the contingent things are its waves and rivers.
Do not let the forms which it resembles veil you from the One,
  that takes form within them for these are [Its] veils.

Its explanation in detail: The sea, when it is entified by the form of the wave, is called a wave, when entified by the form of the river it is called a river, and when entified by the form of the brook it is called a brook. In the same way it is called rain, snow, ice, etc. when it is entified by those forms. However, in reality, there is absolutely nothing but the sea or water, because the wave, river, brook, etc. are merely the linguistic names indicating the sea. In truth [the sea in its unconditioned reality] bears no name or description. Nay, the word 'sea' is its name from sheer linguistic convention.

Exactly the same is true [of Existence]. If the Existence or the Reality is determined by a determination, it is named by it. Its first [determination] is called the

1. Ibid., p. 66; trans. Austin, p. 69.

2. Āmulī has mentioned these verses in his *Jāmiʿ al-asrār*, 161, with his metaphysical commentary which is not different from his commentary mentioned here. These verses are attributed to Ibn ʿArabī according to O. A. Yahya; for reference, *Kitāb Jāmiʿ al-asrār*, 806.

Intellect, the next one the Soul, then the spheres, then the Body, then the natures, then the 'off-springs' [i.e., the three kingdoms, mineral, plant and animal], etc. However in reality, there is neither the Intellect nor the Soul nor the sphere, because these are the linguistic names indicating the Reality or the Existence [entified by those forms]. In truth, It bears no name or description [in Its un-entified reality], as mentioned earlier when discussing Its attribute.

Nay, the word 'Reality' (*ḥaqq*) or 'Existence' (*wujūd*) is its name from the linguistic convention according to His saying: *Those whom you worship beside Him are but names which you have named, you and your fathers. God has revealed no sanction for them. The decision rests with God only, Who has commanded you that you worship none save Him. That is the eternal religion, but most men know not* [12:40]. By God! Again by God! Even if there had not been any other verse in the Book of God except this, it would have been a sufficient demonstration [from the divine guidance] for the elimination of multiplicity and affirming [His] *tawḥīd* called the 'eternal religion', *but most men know not* due to their ignorance and blindness.

Ḥaydar Āmulī's commentary on ʿAlī ibn Abī Ṭālib's saying on *tawḥīd*

One of the conversations [of Imam ʿAlī ibn Abī Ṭālib] not mentioned in the *Nahj* [*al-balāghah*], but [one which] is quite famous is the one which is addressed to Kumayl ibn Ziyād, may God be pleased with him. It starts with [Kumayl] questioning him:

'What is Reality (*al-ḥaqīqah*)?'

'What hast thou to do with Reality?'

'Am I not your confidant?'

'Yes! But whatever overflows from me will sprinkle on you.'

'Can someone like thee frustrate the one who quests [for something] from him?'

'Reality is the unveiling of the splendours of Divine Majesty to which no allusion is possible.'

'Tell me more.'

'It is the obliteration of conjectures when the Object of knowledge becomes evident.'

'Tell me more.'

'The curtain is rent by the triumph of the [spiritual] secret (*sirr*).'

'Tell me more.'

'The [essential] Unitude (*aḥadiyyah*) attracts him to Unity (*tawḥīd*) by [its] attribute.'

'Tell me more.'

'A light has shone since the dawn of pre-eternity. It flashes its traces (*āthār*) on the temples of Unity.

'Tell me more.'

'Extinguish the lamp, the morning has come.'[1]

This conversation [of the Imam] has been given many meanings in the commentaries. The essence of this [conversation] in brief is that [the Imam] is alluding to the Self-manifestation (*ẓuhūr*) of the Exalted in the forms of loci of manifestation (*maẓāhir*), and their non-existence [in themselves] along with their existence (*thubūtuhā*) [through Him].

[The Imam] said: '[Reality] is the unveiling of the splendours of Divine Majesty to which no allusion is possible.'

This [statement] alludes to the removal of the [veil of] multiple names after the [veil of] creaturely multiplicity, interpreted as the loci of manifestation, has been removed. [To this unveiling], neither the rational nor the sensory allusion is possible. This is a beautiful secret which indicates the divine Encompassment and [its] absoluteness, for the absolute Encompassment is not subject to allusion at all, because that is not possible. Nay, it is absolutely impossible.

[The Imam] subjected the splendours of Divine Majesty under [the splendours of] Divine Beauty. This is because the [splendours of] Divine Majesty are specific to the divine names and qualities, whereas the [splendours of] Divine Beauty are specific to the Divine Essence (*dhāt*) only. [The pair are also called by the names and qualities of] severity (*qāhariyyah*) and gentleness (*laṭīfah*) as you have already learned. In either case, it is more appropriate that the splendours of Divine Majesty be prior to the splendours of Divine Beauty because the unveiling of the splendours of Divine Beauty is only possible after the [unveiling] of the splendours of Divine Majesty. This is the spiritual travel (*sulūk*) from multiplicity to Unity, from the creation to Reality. This [interpretation] is very much agreeable to the majority [of gnostics].

[The Imam] said: 'It is the elimination of all the conjectures when the Object of knowledge becomes evident.'

This [statement] also alludes to the removal of the loci of manifestation (*maẓāhir*) and witnessing in them the Manifest (*al-ẓāhir*) in reality. For when the spiritual traveller witnesses the effacement of the fantasies which are other than [the Reality] called the [estimative] creations, and are nothing but the empty fantasy imprint[s] that have become firmly settled and deeply rooted in him due to the domination of [his] estimative faculty (*quwwat al-wahm*), with the Devil (*shayṭān*, i.e., fantasy) over him when he (witnesses) their total lifting from him, then the Object of his knowledge which is the Absolute, the Exalted, becomes

1. This is a well-known Shi'i *ḥadīth* known as *ḥadīth 'alawī* which has been the subject of many commentaries by Shi'i and Sunni gnostics. Cf. J. Āshtiyānī's introduction to the commentary on this *ḥadīth* by 'Abd Allāh Zunūzī, *Anwār-i jaliyyah*, ed. with introduction by J. Āshtiyānī (Tehran, 1976). This is yet another commentary on this *ḥadīth* by Āmulī, which is based on the metaphysics of Being (*wujūd*). Its essential unification and phenomenal dispersion can be understood by the supporting evidence in the form of Qur'ānic verses, sayings of the Prophet, sayings of the Shi'i Imams, and remarks of the Sufi masters (*mashāyikh*).

clear of estimative doubts and suspicions. He becomes completely liberated from [this] veil. By this I mean the horizon of his heart and spirit becomes clear of the clouds of creational multiplicity as the sky becomes clear when the clouds disappear. Then the Absolute manifests among them as the manifestation of the sun after the dispersion of the clouds in the sky. He witnesses the Reality as clearly as he witnesses the full moon according to the saying of the Prophet, upon him and his progeny be peace and salutation, 'You will see your Lord just as you see the moon on the night when it is full.'[1]

[The Imam] said, 'The curtain is rent by the triumph of the [spiritual] secret (*sirr*).'

This [statement] has two meanings: One, when this secret overpowers him, it is impossible for his spirit to hold its secret like [the state of Manṣūr] al-Ḥallāj[2] and the others. Nay, he does not mind expressing it. It is quite possible that it is expressed involuntarily by him like the actions of the intoxicated in the external form. Alluding to [such a state, the Imam] said: 'But whatever overflows from me will sprinkle on you.' The other meaning is, when this secret overpowers him he does not pay attention to the veils which are the loci of [His] manifestation. Rather, he only witnesses in them the Manifest. At this stage [of the spiritual wayfaring, the traveller] only desires to remove the veils from the face of the Beloved and tear them completely, that is, to take them off and lift them from him. The latter meaning is more related to the subject that we are in the process of affirming than the former.

And what [the Imam] said next, 'the [essential] Unitude attracts him to Unity by [its] attribute', proves our point. For he says: the essential Unitude (*al-aḥadiyyah al-dhātiyyah*), which is not subject to multiplicity, attracts him to unadulterated Unity and pure Oneness, which is the Divine Presence of gathering and the station of the annihilation of the lover in the Beloved. Its explanation will soon follow. Once [the spiritual traveller] crosses this station, then he commences [his travel] in the attribute of His Self-manifestation and differentiations (*tafāṣīl*). This is the station of 'dispersion' (*farq*) [experienced] after [the station] of 'gathering (*jamʿ*).'

[The Imam] said, 'A light has shone since the dawn of pre-eternity. It flashes its effects on the temples of Unity.'

That means that the Absolute, called Reality (*ḥaqīqah*), is the Light which illuminates, i.e., it manifests from the direction of the dawn of pre-eternity, [and] it is the Absolute [Divine] Essence. 'It flashes on the temples of Unity', i.e., it manifests on all the loci of manifestation of existence by Its traces, acts, perfections, and particular traits. These are the reports about the self-manifestation of the Divine Essence in the loci of Names and Attributes in pre-eternity and post-eternity, witnessing the

1. Cf. op.cit., p. 441, note 1.

2. al-Ḥusayn ibn Manṣūr al-Ḥallāj, the famous Sufi who was executed in 309/922. The indication here is to his ecstatic saying: 'I am the Reality' (*ana'l-ḥaqq*) famous among the Sufis.

[Divine] Oneness in multiple forms, witnessing the [Divine] Gathering (*jamʿ*) in the very differentiations [of forms] and the existence of differentiations [of forms] in the [Divine] Gathering itself, as mentioned earlier. This is the highest spiritual station. There is no [higher] witnessing beyond this [witnessing] which is expressed [by Imam ʿAlī] in his saying, 'Even if the veil is removed completely [from the Absolute], my certitude [in the Absolute] will not increase.'[1] The others [in this station] have said, 'There is no other village beyond ʿAbbādān.'

This is precisely the reason, when [Kumayl] desired more explanation about this [level, the Imam] said, 'Extinguish the lamp, the morning has come.' That means: extinguish the lamp of rational inquiry (*ʿaql*) and verbal questioning [about this level] at the rising of the dawn of spiritual unveiling and witnessing the 'Face' of Reality in it. That is because the spiritual unveiling is not dependent on rational thought and its perception, just as the dawn does not need the lamp and its irradiation [for its illumination]. For a concrete proof requires no further explanation [according to the proverb], 'There is no information better than personal observation.'

If you say: these words are strange, unusual, and contrary [to our common experience]; we do not understand their meaning, nor do we find a way to comprehend them; speak to us in a simpler way, or in the form of similitude nearer to our mind, so that we understand it and obtain from it our goal and aim, because we only witness this [concrete] world and these different, contradictory multiplicities which are [always] in a state of flux and extinction; we only know that they are not Reality and are the creatures, but you say they are Reality, and in existence there is only the Exalted Reality, and all that [you see] is [Its] loci of manifestation; you say that between It and Its loci of manifestation there is no difference in reality; this matter is too difficult [to comprehend] and [this kind of] speech is too subtle [to understand] so we do not know its meaning; we can only differentiate between these multiplicities and the Absolute the Exalted by the way already expressed by us. [Between what you say and what we say] there is a wide gulf.

I say: This matter [concerning Reality and Its multiple loci of manifestation] is very simple. Its perception is very easy and its meaning is absolutely clear. It has been mentioned repeatedly [but you have not comprehended it] because you are sunk deep in the darkness of [your] nature (*ṭabīʿah*) and lowest human levels. Nay, [you are sunk] in the lowest degree of [unthinking] conformism (*taqlīd*) and that is the greatest of all the veils [between you and the Absolute]. In fact, in relation to those people who understand this meaning, you are like a fetus confined to the prison of the womb in comparison to a discriminative child, a discriminative child in comparison to an intelligent person, an intelligent person in comparison to an *ʿālim* [a scholar of religious learning], an *ʿālim* in comparison to a gnostic (*ʿārif*), a

1. Ibn ʿArabī, *Fuṣūṣ al-ḥikam*, 79. *The Bezels of Wisdom*, 88.

gnostic in comparison to a perfect friend [of God] (*walī*), or a *walī* in comparison to the prophet. There is a great difference among these degrees. That is why He, the Exalted, said, *Lo! herein verily is a reminder for men of understanding* [39:20].

But even the followers of shells (*arbāb al-qushūr*), i.e., the externalists (*ahl al-ẓāhir*) and rationalists (*ahl al-ʿuqūl*), do not crave [to know the above matter], because in relation to the prophets, the friends [of God], and the perfect men who are the kernel of the kernels, they are like the shell in relation to the kernel. Anyhow, we will start once again to explain to you [this matter], nay we will repeat it several times in the best possible way with more deft similitudes, and will endeavour to make you understand this [matter].

We say: Know that if you are convinced that there is only one Existence, and it is Absolute, not determined, and that determined things are related to It, then you have learned that determined things have no real existence [of their own] because their existence is a connective relation. It consists of the relation of the Absolute to the determined, (that is, this relative) has no external reality [of its own].

You have also learned that the Absolute is determined (by being entified, but) in another respect, the determined is Absolute along with having the determination of relation; that in the external world there is nothing but the Absolute [Existence]. For if you drop [Its] relation by connection to all the existents, you will find the Existence in its unadulterated Unity and pure Absoluteness, and you will find the determined is existent through the Absolute [Existence], and non-existent without It. This is the meaning of their [i.e., the Sufis'] saying, '*Tawḥīd* means the elimination of all relations.'

Its identical similitude, that is, the similitude of that Absolute with the determined, and its Existentiality with its non-existentiality, is like the sun with shadows. They are existent through it at its manifestation and at its occultation. For shadows do not have existence except through the sun. If the sun were not to be, the shadows would not have existence, although when the sun manifests by itself then shadows do not have existence, because their existence is through the sun. They become invisible by its orb and rays, for when it manifests by its orb and rays, the shadows are annihilated, and following that their existence disappears. When (the sun) is concealed from them by its essence and orb, its trace becomes manifest and its existence subsists. Thus it becomes a shadow entified by the sun as shadowy existence.

So in reality only the sun and its trace have existence and the shadows are only in name and concept. The names and concept are privations; they do not have external existence. So is the existence of all existent things in relation to the Absolute. When the Absolute manifests by Its existence, there does not remain existence for the creatures. That is because the existence of the creatures, as discussed earlier, is only a relative, mentally posited existence, and the relative and mentally posited are not existent externally.

So the real existence is only for the Absolute. This is the meaning of His words:

Everything is annihilated except His Face [28:88]; I mean everything related to Him is annihilated in itself except His Essence, for that is abiding and eternal. *To Him belongs the property* [28:88], that is, to Him belong the real eternal subsistence, *and to Him you shall be returned* [28:88], that is, to Him will return these existents after the removal of the relativities. According to the understanding [of the Folk of God], 'Face' is the (divine) Essence. Hence, according to this appraisal, *everything is annihilated except His Face* and *wherever you turn, there is the Face of God* [2:109]. That is why He said: *Everyone upon it is undergoing annihilation, and there subsists the Face of the Lord, possessor of majesty and generous giving* [55:26–27]. By 'upon it', it is meant the reality of Being by which the existents subsist. The exegesis of these two verses has been given repeatedly. The truth is, these two verses after His sayings, *God is the Light of the heavens and the earth* [24:35], and *We shall show them Our signs upon the horizons and in their souls until it is clear to them that He is the Reality* [41:53] are some of the greatest verses of the Qur'ān, and most eminent in the context of *tawḥīd* and its reality. *Those likenesses We coin them for the people, but no one understands them save those who have knowledge* [29:43].

If you say: This example is not in accordance with your claim. For you said the shadows do not exist except after the absence of the sun from them. Further, you said the creatures do not exist except by the existence of Reality. Nay, you said the creatures are Reality according to some consideration and they are creatures according to another consideration. But the shadows are not like that. For a shadow is not the sun in any respect. To this I say: One aspect is enough in the example [to prove the point] and that is, the shadows do not have existence except by the sun, and its concealment from them is by its orb and essence. So are the creatures (in relation to Reality). For the creatures do not have existence except by the Reality, and Its concealment from them is in essence and reality. Just as the concealment of the sun consists of the subsistence of the shadow in itself and by its determination, and its presence consists of the annihilation of the shadow and its non-existence, likewise the concealment of Reality consists of the subsistence of the creatures in themselves and by their limitation, and Its presence consists of their annihilation and non-existence.

Explanation of *sharīʿah*, *ṭarīqah* and *ḥaqīqah*

Know that *sharīʿah* (the law) is the name for the rules of the divine path. It consists of roots and branches; permissions and resolutions; [actions considered] good and excellent. As for the *ṭarīqah* (spiritual path), it is the way of maximum precaution, the path of the best and surest [action]. Thus any path that leads man to the best and surest [way] in speech or action, and to [the actualization of] an attribute or [the experience of] a [spiritual] state (*ḥāl*) is called *ṭarīqah*. As for the *ḥaqīqah* (reality and truth), it is the affirmation of the [existence] of a thing either through unveiling, or intuition, or through [experiencing] a [spiritual] state or consciousness (*wijdān*). That is why it is said, [the meaning of] *sharīʿah* is that you worship Him, of *ṭarīqah* that you attain His Presence, and of *ḥaqīqah* that you witness Him.[1]

Furthermore, it has been said that *sharīʿah* means that His command makes you subsist; *ṭarīqah* means that you subsist by His command, and *ḥaqīqah* that you subsist by Him. The complete meaning [of *sharīʿah*, *ṭarīqah* and *ḥaqīqah*] is testified in the conversation of the Prophet, upon him and his progeny be peace and benediction, with Ḥārith ibn Mālik al-Anṣārī. The Prophet asked him, 'O Ḥārith, how are you this morning?' He answered, 'I have become a true believer.' He, on him be peace, said, 'For every belief there is a reality, so what is the reality of your belief?' He replied, 'I saw the people of the Garden visiting each other and the people of the Fire howling at each other; I saw distinctly the Throne of my Lord.' He, on him be peace, said, 'You have spoken correctly, so adhere to it.'[2]

Now, his faith in the unseen was truly *sharīʿah*, his seeing the Garden and the Fire through unveiling and ecstasy was *ḥaqīqah*; his renunciation [of pleasure] in the world, his night vigils [for worship], and his thirst [for God] were his *ṭarīqah*. The religion (*sharʿ*) is inclusive of all these [levels]. It is like the complete almond nut which consists of the oil, the kernel, and the shell. The almond as a whole is like the *sharīʿah*, the kernel is like the *ṭarīqah*, and the oil like the *ḥaqīqah*. The same is also said for the prayer (*ṣalāh*): the *ṣalāh* is service [to God], coming closer [to God], and arrival [in His Presence]. 'The service' corresponds to the *sharīʿah*, 'coming closer' to Him is the *ṭarīqah*, and the 'union' (*al-waṣlah*, [with the Divine]) to the *ḥaqīqah*. The name *ṣalāh* is inclusive of all these [levels]. God has said about this unveiling in the aforementioned degrees in His Book, *Nay, if you had known the knowledge of certitude, then you would have seen the hellfire. Then you would have seen it with the vision of certitude* [102:5–7]; and *Lo! This is real certitude* [56:95]. The first [degree] corresponds to the *sharīʿah*, the second to the *ṭarīqah*, and the third to the *ḥaqīqah*.

Further, know that *sharīʿah* is an expression for affirming in the heart the veracity of the acts of the prophets and acting according to them; *ṭarīqah* is an expression for the realization of their acts and character-traits by action and performing what is worthy of them; and *ḥaqīqah* is witnessing their states by 'taste' and by being described by them because he [i.e., Prophet Muḥammad] is a good model according to His saying, *You have a good model in the Messenger of God* [33:21]. They cannot be actualized but

1. The dominant idea in this section is Āmulī's concept of practical spirituality, that is, the three levels of Divine Revelation *shariʿah, ṭariqah, ḥaqiqah*. He maintains that the Divine Revelation constitutes the above three levels, like a walnut which contains the outer shell, the kernel and the oil.

2. This is a famous *ḥadīth* attributed to the Prophet which alludes to the 'eye of certainty' (*ʿayn al-yaqīn*) possessed by Ḥāritha ibn Malik al-Anṣārī who had the knowledge of 'seeing' the hidden things of Paradise and its inhabitants, etc. It is recorded by Kulaynī in *Uṣul al-kāfī*, (Beirut, 1401/1980) vol. 2, p. 54, and also by al-Suyūṭī, in *Jāmiʿ al-aḥādith*, ed. A. ʿAbd al-Jawād, and A. Aḥmad Ṣiqar (Damascus, n.d), vol. 7, pp. 62, 339.

through them, that is, through observing these degrees [of Revelation] as they really are. Indeed a 'good model' is an expression for the one who undertakes to fulfil the requirements of all the dimensions of his Revelation which is inclusive of the *sharīʿah, ṭarīqah* and *ḥaqīqah*.[1] [The Prophet], on him and his progeny be peace and benediction, said, 'The *sharīʿah* is my words, *ṭarīqah* my actions, *ḥaqīqah* my states, gnosis (*maʿrifah*) my capital, reason the root of my religion, love my foundation, yearning (*shawq*) my mount, fear my companion, knowledge my weapon, forbearance my friend, trust my cloak, contentment my treasure, truthfulness my way-station, certitude my refuge, poverty my honour, for by it I attained an honour above the rest of the prophets and messengers.' Therefore, whoso desires to make his prophet his foundation as it is requisite then it is necessary that he should be described by all these qualities or some of them according to the measure of his preparedness, and never refuse to acknowledge anyone who is described by these qualities. That is because the source of all [the revelations] is one reality which is the prophetic Revelation and the Divine Law, although the [particular] divine laws differ.

In reality these levels are the requisites of the other levels which correspond to their principle. The *sharīʿah,* in reality, is the requisite of the messenger-ship; the *ṭarīqah* is the requisite of the prophethood; and the *ḥaqīqah* is the requisite of friendship [with God, *wilāyah*]. Messenger-ship consists of conveying what the individual obtained from prophet-hood, such as the laws, administration, cultivation through ethics, and teaching by wisdom. This is precisely the *sharīʿah*. The prophet-hood consists of expressing what one obtains from *wilāyah* (friendship with God), such as cognizance of the gnosis of the essence of the Real, His names, attributes, acts and properties for His worship so that they are attributed by His Attributes, and obtain the character-traits [which reflect] His character-traits. This is precisely the *ṭarīqah*. The *wilāyah* consists of witnessing pre-eternally and post-eternally His Essence, Attributes, and Acts in the loci of manifestation of His perfection, and in the receptacles of (His) Self-disclosures in His entifications. This is precisely the *ḥaqīqah*. All [three] refer to one reality which is the reality of man described by them, or to one individual such as the foremost in greatness among the messengers, for they are likewise.

The intention behind divine Revelation (*al-sharʿ al-ilāhī*), and prophetic enactment is one reality inclusive of all these degrees, that is, *sharīʿah*, *ṭarīqah*, and *ḥaqīqah*. These names are applied to them as synonyms and as different expressions [of the same reality].

The similitudes of that in other than this form are plenty. For instance, the names 'intellect', 'knowledge', and 'light' apply to one reality which is the reality of

1. It should be noted that Ḥaydar Āmulī does not interpret *sharīʿah* as only the legal code of Islam but the totality of the Divine Message. This view was also maintained by early Muslim thinkers, cf. Wilfred Cantwell Smith, 'Islamic Law: *Sharīʿah and Sharʿ*', in *On Understanding Islam* (New York, 1981), pp. 87–110.

man as macrocosm. As it is recorded in some reports, 'The first thing that God the Exalted created was the intellect',[1] and 'the first thing that God created was my light';[2] and the names such as 'the centre of the heart' (*al-fu'ād*), 'the heart' (*al-qalb*), and 'the breast' (*al-ṣadr*) also point to the one reality (which is the reality of) man as microcosm as [is indicated by] the saying of the Exalted: *His heart* (fu'ād) *lies not about what he saw* [53:11]; and *It was brought down by the Faithful Spirit upon thy heart* (qalb) [26:193–194], and *Did We not expand thy breast* (ṣadr) [94:1], and in addition to these are the proofs and similitudes recorded in this context.

That is why among the prophets and the friends [of God], peace be upon them, no contradiction has occurred in the general foundation and the real root [of religion]. This [understanding] is the pillar of religion and principle of Islam. As He, the Exalted, said: *He has laid down for you as religion that which He charged Noah with, and that We have revealed to thee [O Muḥammad], and that We charged Abraham with, and Moses, and Jesus: Perform the religion, and scatter not regarding it* [42:13]; and His saying: *The same did Abraham enjoin upon his sons, and also Jacob, [saying]: O my sons! God has chosen for you the religion; see that you die not except you are surrendered* (muslimūn*) [unto Him]* [2:132]; and, *this is My straight path, so follow it, and follow not diverse paths, lest they scatter you from its road* [6:153], and then His saying which is the sum of all, *this is the eternal religion, but most people know not* [12:40], that is, they do not know that observing the three pillars (i.e., *sharīʿah, ṭarīqah,* and *ḥaqīqah*) and fulfilling the requirements of each is the 'eternal religion' and the 'straight path'. The cause of [people not observing the three pillars completely] is nothing but their ignorance and distance from the Real, and their expulsion from His threshold.

If it is understood that there has never been any contradiction among the prophets and the friends [of God], on them be peace, regarding the general matters and roots of the Religion, though there has been contradiction in the particular [divine] laws and formal acts, then it is requisite to know that the differences in quality and quantity of a thing do not indicate any difference in their essence and reality. It is also (necessary to) know that the reality [or the essence] of the Divine Revelation has been the same in all ages and locations; indeed it is untouched by contention and difference, though there has been variation in rules and laws according to [different] levels [of understanding of people], and [different types] of individuals.[3]

---

1. Cf. *Uṣul al-kāfī*, by Kulaynī, vol. 1, *Kitāb al-ʿAql wa'l-jahl*, no.1.

2. Cf. *Aḥādīth-i mathnawī*, by Badiʿ al-Zamān Furūzānfar (Tehran, 1955), no. 342.

3. The essential unity of diverse revealed religions has been maintained by many Muslim metaphysicians and mystics, cf. Abū Ḥātim al-Rāzī (Ismaili thinker, d.*c.* 322/933–934), *Aʿlām al-nubuwwah*, ed. with introduction by Ṣalāh al-Ṣāwī and Ghulāmriḍā Aʿwānī, English preface by S. H. Nasr (Tehran, 1977); and our article, 'Abū Ḥātim al-Rāzī on the Essential Unity of Religions', in *Beacon of Knowledge: Essays in Honor of Seyyed Hossein* Nasr, ed. M. H. Faghfoory (Louisville, 2003), pp. 269–287; William C. Chittick, *Imaginal Worlds: Ibn al-ʿArabī and the Problem of Religious Diversity* (Albany, 1994), part III, pp. 123–176.

6

Ibn Turkah Iṣfahānī

ʿAlī ibn Muḥammad ibn Afḍal al-Dīn Muḥammad Turkah Khujandī, called Ṣāʾin al-Dīn, and usually known as Ibn Turkah Iṣfahānī, marks a turning-point in the history of Islamic thought as far as integrating various schools of Islamic thought and preparing the ground for the appearance of Mullā Ṣadrā's *al-ḥikmah al-mutaʿāliyah* (the transcendent theosophy/philosophy) is concerned. Ṣāʾin al-Dīn was born in Isfahan in 764/1362–63 into a famous family of scholars who were of Turkman origin and hailed originally from Khujand. He received his earliest education in Isfahan and was a young man when Tamerlane conquered the city and killed many of its inhabitants. Ṣāʾin al-Dīn and other members of his family were exiled to Samarqand. For the next fifteen years he studied and travelled in various regions including the Hijaz, Syria and Egypt and was in Iraq when Tamerlane died. He then returned to Isfahan but his life was entangled with the political upheavals of his day. He was imprisoned for a time but also met favour with some of Tamerlane's descendants, eventually becoming chief judge (*qāḍi*) of Yazd. He also travelled extensively in various parts of Persia and especially Khurāsān. He was even tried in Herat by his opponents because of his esoteric writings. It was in Herat that he died in 835/1432 or 836/1433.

Many have discussed the question of whether Ibn Turkah was Sunni or Shiʿi. There is no doubt that he was made a judge among Sunni Muslims by rulers who were Ḥanafī, but also that he showed great love and respect for the Family of the Prophet (*ahl al-bayt*). It is not, therefore, possible to answer this question with certainty. But there is no doubt that he was deeply drawn to Sufism and was an authority of the Ḥurūfī School, founded in its nascent form by Mughīrah in Iraq in the early Islamic centuries, and based on the esoteric significance and symbolism of the letters and words of the Qurʾān, similar to the Kabbalah in Judaism. Ibn Turkah also had much influence on later Ḥurūfīs whose concern for the symbolism of letters and the science of *jafr* was shared by certain schools of Sufism, Twelver Shiʿism and Ismailism. In one of his treatises on the significance of the cleaving of the moon (*shaqq al-qamar*), he mentions the views of seven schools of thought, that is, the jurisprudents, the Peripatetics, the Illuminationists, the Sufis, the followers of Ibn ʿArabī, the Ḥurūfīs and Shiʿi scholars. He then seeks to interpret these views within a grand synthesis.

More particularly, Ibn Turkah was well versed in *kalām*, both Sunni and Shiʿi, philosophy, both Peripatetic and Illuminationist, and various schools of Sufism especially the *ʿirfān* of the school of Ibn ʿArabī. He is remembered in later Islamic history not so much for his *ḥurūfī* views, but for the synthesis he sought to achieve between the various schools of philosophy, *ʿirfān* and *kalām*, preparing the ground perhaps more than any other single figure for Mīr Dāmād and, especially, Mullā Ṣadrā.

If we count his writings individually, there are over fifty-five works in Arabic and Persian that we know to have been authored by Ibn Turkah. They deal with philosophy, *ʿirfān,* esoteric commentary upon the Qurʾān and *ḥadīth,* the science of letters, the symbolic science of numbers, and general religious and theological subjects. There are also a number of commentaries by him upon important works of Sufism including poetry and prose by such masters as Ibn al-Fāriḍ, ʿIraqī, Shabistarī and Ibn ʿArabī. In the latter category Ibn Turkah's extensive commentary upon the *Fuṣūṣ al-ḥikam* is of particular importance, covering the whole of the original text. Most of these works have as yet to be printed and made available to the general public.

Among Ibn Turkah's writings by far the most famous and popular is the *Tamhīd al-qawāʿid* (Establishing the Principles) which has remained among the four or five most often used texts for the teaching of *ʿirfān* over the centuries in Persia. Many commentaries have been written upon it, the latest being a major work by the contemporary master of *falsafah* and *ʿirfān* in Qum, Jawād Āmulī. This work of Ibn Turkah is a commentary upon a treatise entitled *Qawāʿid al-tawḥīd* (Principles of Unity) written by one of Ṣāʾin al-Dīn's ancestors, Abū Ḥāmid Muḥammad Iṣfahānī, who was first a Peripatetic philosopher but then turned to Sufism. Abū Ḥāmid is the author of some other known works including *al-Ḥikmah al-munīʿah* (Precious Wisdom), *al-Ḥikmah al-rāshidiyyah* (Guiding Wisdom) and a Persian commentary upon Ibn al-Fāriḍ's famous poem rhyming in *tāʾ*, *al-Tāʾiyyah*. The *Qawāʿid al-tawḥīd* is a masterly treatise on the doctrines of gnosis centred on the principle of Unity. It served as the basis for a commentary by Ṣāʾin al-Dīn that was soon recognized as one of the best works explaining *ʿirfān* by a master who was also deeply versed in theology and philosophy.

For a long time the correctly-edited text *Tamhīd al-qawāʿid* was not available although it has been commented upon by such Qajar masters as Āqā Muḥammad Riḍā Qumshaʾī and his student, Mīrzā Maḥmūd Qummī. During the first half of the fourteenth/twentieth century one of the outstanding masters of *ʿirfān* of the day, Mīrzā Aḥmad Āshtiyānī, who was also a saintly figure, corrected the text in his own hand. It was this text that served as the basis for the edition that Sayyid Jalāl al-Dīn Āshtiyānī published in 1976 and which has served for the translation that follows. In a sense this text contains in itself two centuries of the history of *ʿirfān* in Persia.

The influence of Ibn Turkah, and especially his *Tamhīd al-qawāʿid,* on later centuries was very notable. Mullā Ṣadrā, and through him his students, were deeply influenced by Ibn Turkah as were a number of major figures of the Qajar period. Today the work continues to be taught in many circles in Persia and the teachings of Ibn Turkah continue to be influential in Persia as part and parcel of the living tradition of *ʿirfān.*

In this chapter a section of Ibn Turkah's *Tamhīd al-qawāʿid* (Establishing the Principles) has been included. This important, but outside Persia still unappreciated philosopher, begins the treatise by attempting to elucidate the laws of *tawḥīd* (unity) and offers a classification of the different ways of knowing, e.g. reasoning, reflecting, inspiration, etc. Ibn Turkah, applying Plato's doctrine of participation to existence argues that existence participates in both meaning and concepts and continues by discussing different types of intelligibles, the necessity of existence and its relation to existents.

S. H. Nasr

ESTABLISHING THE PRINCIPLES

Tamhīd al-qawāʿid

Translated for this volume by Joseph Lumbard based upon two semi-critical editions of Ibn Turkah Iṣfahānī, *Kitāb Tamhīd al-qawā'id fi sharḥ qawāʿid al-tawḥīd*, ed. Jalāl al-Dīn Āshtiyānī (Qum, 1381 Sh./2002); ed. Ḥasanzādih Āmulī (Qum, 1381 Sh./2002).[1]

Praise be to God who made the places obscured by the shadows of His magnificence, loci in which are disclosed the lights of His beauty, differentiating what is undifferentiated among the inherent properties (*aḥkām*);[2] who made the forms of His Self-disclosures (*tajalliyāt*)[3] places in which the suns of realities arise, completing what is universal among the blessings. So they became, for both His servants who receive His loving-kindness and for those opposed to Him who are distant from Him, the loci wherein the stars of the Gnostic sciences (*maʿārif*) arise and in which the foremost gifts (*ʿawārif*) set,[4] granting the desires that the tongue of preparedness[5] expresses.

Glory be to Him for a non-manifest whose hiddenness has no cause other than the extremeness of manifestation through the illuminations of His tribunes and what the manifestation of lights, through coverings, necessitates from among the flashes of luminiscences. Magnificent is His task (*sha'n*),[6] which is manifest without a cause[7] for its becoming manifest, and without its being (*kawn*) penetrating into

1. Major discrepancies between the editions will be noted in the footnotes.

2. The *aḥkām* or 'ruling properties' refer to the determining principles through which all manifestations of the created order or cosmos come into existence. This process of manifestation is referred to as the differentiating of what is undifferentiated because the ruling properties are differentiated in the cosmos but are manifest in an undifferentiated mode in the highest of the heavenly spheres.

3. From the perspective of Ibn Turkah, following from the teachings of Ibn ʿArabī, all existent things are Self-disclosures of the Divine Itself, Who manifests Himself in the world, but still remains utterly beyond it. See William Chittick, *The Self-Disclosure of God* (Albany, NY, 1998).

4. Āshtiyānī's footnote explains: 'That is rising in relation to the receivers of loving-kindness and setting in relation to the people of opposition' (p. 161).

5. The idea of preparedness is closely related to that of self-disclosure. The extent to which anything receives God's self-disclosure is pre-determined by its 'preparedness'. This pertains to one's knowledge of God, but moreover, to one's ontological status.

6. The use of the word task is derived from the Qur'ānic verse, 'Every day He is upon a task' (55:29). As Sachiko Murata explains: 'These 'tasks' of God are the things or realities or entities considered as specific activities of the 'Reality of realities'—God inasmuch as he embraces all realities and entities without exception.... In the broadest sense 'tasks' designate everything in God that gives rise to the multiple things of the universe.' *Chinese Gleams of Sufi Light* (Albany, NY, 2000), p. 120.

7. Here I have followed the Āshtiyānī edition which reads '*lā ʿillata*' (p. 162). The Āmulī edition reads '*li ahlihī*' (to His people) (p. 6).

the non-manifest aspects of His veils and the duskiness of darkness that follows necessarily upon it.

A non-manifest which is hardly hidden,
And a manifest which is hardly apparent.[1]

Prayers and blessings upon Muḥammad, the locus from which every good is dispersed, that which opens every opening and seals every closing. He is the radiant light that is not corrupted by the blemishes of shadows and the obfuscations of clouds.

Do not cast the shadow of otherness in his sun,
For it is sun, it is shadow, it is shade.

Prayers and blessings also upon his family and companions, the niche that comprises every variagation and the lamp that gathers every shadow.

To proceed: As for the issue of attesting to unity (*tawḥīd*) according to what the witnessers verify and following what the verifiers[2] witness from the highest unveiling and from clear viewing (*ʿiyān*), it—the moment at which those with intellects perceive—is among that to which the torchbearers of proofs and demonstrations[3] do not lead, except those whom God supports with a light from Him, whom He grants success with His guidance to it, from among those who attain the two degrees of intellectual demonstration and sapiential witnessing, those who succeed on the paths of exalted knowledge and sound unveiling, whom God has delivered from the constrictions of rhetorical and demonstrative introductory matters to the realms of the unveiling inrushes (*al-wāridah al-kashfiyyah*) and the proclamations of observation through the beauty of following the prophets—God's blessings and peace upon them all. The prophets are the connections to the subtle bonds of realities (*raqāʾiq*

1. This appears as verse in the Āmulī edition (p. 6) and as prose in the Āshtiyānī edition (p. 162).

2. *Muḥaqqiqūn* (verifiers) is a term taken from early Sufi texts. Ibn ʿArabi identifies the verifiers as those who have attained to unveiling (*kashf*) and are able to see things as they are in themselves (*kamā hiya*). He did not often refer to himself and those of his ilk as Sufis, but preferred the term *muḥaqiqqūn*: 'I mean by "our companions" those who possess hearts, witnessings and unveilings, not the worshippers or ascetics, and not all Sufis, save those among them who are the people of truths and verification (*taḥqīq*).' *al-Futūḥāt al-Makiyyah*, n.e. (Cairo, 1911; repr. Beirut, n.d.), vol. 1, p. 261.

3. i.e. Theologians and philosophers.

al-ḥaqā'iq),[1] from the entity of gathering (*'ayn al-jam'*)[2] to the locus of differentiation, and intermediaries for the descent of realities from the heaven of holiness to the station of descending, especially he among them who consoles—*a fair example*[3]—the first of them in existence and rank, the last of them sent in time, Muḥammad; he who is the ultimate objective of objectives, whose exalted traditions are the spring of perfections and the source of happiness—the best of blessings and most beautiful greetings upon him and his family.

Thus you see that when his noble people try to verify the realities of *tawḥīd* they reconcile the intellectual demonstration and the transmitted scriptures to an extent which could not be greater, as they obliterate the ambiguities of some of the philosophers who fail to make what sound vision bestows upon them coincide with what descends upon them from the pure text.[4] Likewise, in the rest of the real sciences and the Gnostic certainties they have clarified the places where they err and displayed the matters upon which they stumble through that by which the place of obscurity is made clear and the small star is distinguished from the sun. All of that is a ray from intelligence encompassing a pitch-dark night.

Our time[5] has born witness to its utmost perfection.[6] The family tree of its advance has ripened and the time for harvesting its fruits has arrived, and the mask has been removed from seclusions of its virgins with what illuminates the pages of its days from the traces found in the heavenly descended books and the exalted unveiling gospels. By my life! You will find that what the great ones only attained to after years of training their souls with severe exhausting exercises by day and night has become a conversational tidbit for the elite and the masses. That

---

1. The *raqā'iq* (sing. *raqīqah*) are the subtle forms of existence that connect different levels of existence. They are 'ladders' by which forms in the lower world are connected to their likenesses (*mithāl*) in the higher worlds. To perceive them is to see things as they are, for one sees the manner in which things are connected to their higher origins. For a further explanation of *raqā'iq* see William Chittick, *The Sufi Path of Knowledge* (Albany, NY, 1989), p. 406, n.6.

2. The 'entity of gathering' (*'ayn al-jam'*) refers to the first stage of God's Self-disclosure, which is identical to the last stage of return to Him. The first stage is represented by the name *Allāh*, which is the 'gathering name' (*al-ism al-jāmi'*) in which all other divine names and created realities are 'gathered'. In the Divine Essence all things are present in a completely undifferentiated mode of existence prior to their deployment in the lower levels of manifestation and differentiation. The level of gathering is the first level that is discernibly different.

3. 'A fair example' (*uswat*^{un} *ḥasanat*^{un}) is a term appearing three times in the Qur'ān: 33:21, 60:4 and 60:6. In the second and third instances it refers to 'Abraham and those with him' (60:4). But in Islamic texts it is almost always used in reference to 33:21 which refers to the Prophet Muḥammad: 'There is for you in the Messenger of God a fair example for those who hope for God and the last day and remember God much.'

4. i.e. the Noble Qur'ān.

5. Ḥasanzādih Āmulī observes that the meaning of 'our time' is the Islamic era as a whole, not the time of Ibn Turkah himself (p. 9, n. 3).

6. i.e. The combination of intellectual demonstrations and transmitted scriptures.

the dissemination of which was divulged through the spilling of the blood of great men has become as well-known as the afternoon sun.

To summarize, what is not possible for one who seeks perfection is to traverse the stages of his journey without removing the two sandals.[1] Nor can anyone turn round its axis except by folding in both feet—rather, by stripping off the two powers. Its secrets are heard from their straps and the abundance of its intricacies are gleaned from the subtle bonds (*raqā'iq*) of their warp and weft by gleaning the intangibles of its realities from the nets of their perceiving. So with the two faculties of sense-intuition (*wahm*)[2] and intellect (*ʿaql*) and the ordering of what they perceive through the auspices of these moments and times, the person of understanding arrives at it and stumbles upon it. He arrives at the most magnificent of certainties and stumbles upon the first of all that is self-evident.

How much is all that appears in the two fields,
While the sign and affair are clearer than fire upon a minaret.

What was desired by the ancient sages (*ḥukamā'*)—who are from the group of the pure, the prophets and saints—according to revelation, and Hermes, called Idris [in the language of revelation], and Pythagoras, called Seth, and the Divine Plato—was none but this. But the later ones among the companions of the First Teacher (Aristotle)—I mean the peripatetics—when they limited the path of examination and the seeking of true wisdom to sheer proof and mere research, the veils of dark ambiguities formed from the rules of disputation upon which they established their methodologies prevented them from realizing that which is the truth in that magnificent affair.[3] Those among them who claim the benefit of verification or delineation make one wonder. They only come with the addition of obstacles and criticism. Then through the process of gradual deterioration their writings become a collection of darknesses, one upon the other. So, none but a few escaped from their desolation: 'And God did not oppress them, but they oppressed themselves' (16:38).

As for the treatise composed by my master and grandfather, Abū Ḥāmid Muḥammad al-Iṣfahānī, who is known as 'Turkah', it includes certain demonstrations and the luminous proofs regarding the origin of *tawḥīd* in conformity with what the

1. The sandals here representing the life of this world and the next. The reference is taken from Qur'ān 20:2, when God tells Moses to remove his sandals because he is 'in the Holy Valley (*al-wādī al-muqaddas*)'.

2. *Wahm* (sense-intuition) refers to the third of four modes of perceiving: *ḥiss* (sense-perception), *khayāl* (imagination), *wahm* and *ʿaql* (intellect). *Ḥiss* perceives particular things in the outside world through the sense organs, *khayāl* perceives particulars internally, *wahm* perceives universals in the form of particulars, and *ʿaql* perceives universals themselves. So here Ibn Turkah is referring to the two modes of perceiving universals.

3. i.e. The questions of *tawḥīd*.

verifiers claim. The author has done his utmost to obliterate these doubts with the subtleties of his clarification and taken great pains to tame these damages with the power of his exposition (*tibyān*), to the extent that no spoiling blemish regarding what is true among these certainties will remain for one with the slightest training in intellectual matters. But due to the depth of his penetration into sapiential matters (*ḥikamiyyāt*) and the extent of his involvement with the sciences of demonstration, the understanding of most of those who infer (*al-mustafīdīn*) are cut off from the goals of his noble objectives, and the perceptions of the rest who seek guidance are barred from the springs of his august lessons. So during my sessions with some of those among the sincere brothers who share in investigation, I tried to remove the mask of brevity from the faces of the secluded maidens of these expressions with the clearest explanation (*bayān*) and to spread its exalted benefits and fulfil its wonts, alluding to most of the principles of the people of unveiling (*ahl al-kashf*) and the sources of their rulings, indicating the complications of these researches and the universality of their objectives, preserving the terms and expressions which circulate among them, attentive to what is considered appropriate among their technical terms and metaphors, cautious of understanding the opposite of what is sought. This led to striking upon examination of iniquity, and after its completion was named *The Book Facilitating Explanation of the Treatise: The Laws of* Tawḥīd.

[The author of *The Laws of* Tawḥīd], Abū Ḥāmid Muḥammad al-Iṣfahānī, said 'Praise be to His vicegerent and blessings upon His Prophet Muḥammad and his family. Verily, establishing the problem of *tawḥīd* in the manner of the gnostics (*al-ʿārifūn*) the manner, to which the verifiers allude, is among the most recondite problems to which the thoughts of the speculative remonstrating scholars do not reach. Nor do the minds of the eminent researchers among the speculators perceive it.'

I say: know that the context in which this treatise is here begun comprises the issue of what necessarily comes first as regards writing and composing and also includes what indicates the objectives of this treatise, summarizing what is required for teaching and appraising (*tafhīm*). That is because the discussion is based upon two issues.

First: The affirmation of the oneness and necessity of Absolute Existence and the limitation of what merits praise among the universal attributes in it (existence). His saying: 'Praise to His vicegerent' is an allusion to that.

Second: The affirmation that the Absolute Reality, although all existents are loci for its manifestation, in all of its degrees it is a oneness, the whole of which is only manifest in the real human species, who verify the aforementioned degrees through tasting and witnessing. Among them is one who is distinguished as the loci of manifestation and reflection [of the Divine qualities] by virtue of sealing and completion—peace and blessings upon him and his family. His saying 'Blessings upon him' is an allusion to that.

Then his saying, '... in the manner of the gnostics' is an allusion to the later Muḥammadan saints—may God be content with them—who openly divulge it and disclose it by composing and reciting poetry and prose, who demonstrate is affirmation through reason and revelation for those who are perceptive. And his saying, 'the manner to which the verifiers allude' is an allusion to those who came before, such as the prophets—the Mercy of God upon them—and their pupils, the saints among the Hermeticists and the ancient philosophers (*al-ḥukamā' al-qudamā'*) who do not aim for it in the majority of their expressions except in a manner of hinting and intimation, following in every era what the perceptions of its people dictate, descending to the level of their understanding, and only indicating it through an intimation in which there is a form of covering and concealing, so that all of their words are universally beneficial for both the elite and the commons.

His saying, 'the speculative remonstrating scholars' is likely intended to the theologians, just as his saying, 'the eminent researchers' is directed toward a group among the peripatetic philosophers.

Abū Ḥāmid Muḥammad al-Iṣfahānī said: 'Most of them claim that certainty regarding it [*tawḥīd*] indicates consolidation of a bad temperament in the objects of the soul faculties [resulting] from deviation of the sound corporeal matters and the black bile overpowering the primary noble organs, since certainty in the baselessness (*buṭlān*) of all intellectual, sensorial, primal, and natural properties follows the performance of onerous endeavours and practices that arise from the whispers of the imagination (*al-khayāl*) not possible for anyone except through the appearance of that initial cause (*al-sabab al-ḥādīth*) and testing it against what we have mentioned regarding the unseemly illness.'

I say: Know that it is the custom of the author—as is known from the examination of the rest of his books—to first determine, upon establishing the areas of investigation, the argument of the adversary, according to what it demonstrates about him with the firmest examination, and to strive to establish its rules (*qawā'id*) and erect its intricacies as much as possible. Then he undertakes to examine the sources of its doubts and ambiguities and determine the components of its obscurities. So he wanted to follow his customary practice in this treatise. Therefore, he began it with that by which the adversary could demonstrate the depravity (*fasād*) of their path for reaching the unveiling they seek and their gnostic sapiential sciences—named the path of purification and withdrawal (*takhliyah*). That is because he is here in the position of conveying the perspective regarding the path of demonstration, so he must introduce it in accordance with the rest of the researches and sayings.

His clarification is that certainty in the realness of this issue [*tawḥīd*] indicates that the temperaments (*amzijah*) of the soul faculties, upon which perceivings depend, has deviated from its origin, rather bad temperament (*mizāj*) has been consolidated within them, and that which requires treatment persists. If it is not treated then when one is completely certain of it, the root cause and the path by which one arrives at that certainty is the defectiveness (*ikhtilāl*) of the perceiving faculties. And there is no doubt that every path which is an expression of the defectiveness of the perceiving faculties is but a path to ignorance and deficiency, to say nothing of its reaching the sciences of certainty and the real perfections.

Were you to say, 'How is it possible to demonstrate through certain knowledge—which is from the soul qualities—despite the deviation of the objects of the soul-faculties' temperaments—which are from the body qualities?'

We say that it is from demonstration through the affirmation of what is caused by verification of the cause—now known as proof (*burhān*) by the people of speculation (*ahl al-naẓr*).

The clarification of causality is apparent, for the defectiveness of the objects of the soul faculties—I mean the organs for the mental thought instruments which are for the insight (*al-baṣīrah*) that discerns and judges things as they are through the parts of the eye and the stages of the faculty of vision—is the cause of the defectiveness of the perceptions of these objects, just as the defectiveness of a part of the eye necessitates defectiveness of its perceptions. That is because each perceiving that is through the intermediation of one of the bodily instruments is no doubt through the judgment of a hidden subtle bond (*raqīqah khafiyyah*)[1] and the intermediary of an adjoining correlation (*munāsabah*)[2] between the nature of that instrument and the mode of perceiving. If not, then what other instrument would be suited for it?

Then it is necessary that the deviation of the temperament of this instrument from its balanced reality require the baselessness of the judgment of something when that thing is absent. Thus, due to its remoteness from the correlation (*munāsabah*)[3] there occurs defectiveness and corruption in the perceiving. So whenever the temperament deviates, the perceptions necessarily deviate from their true sound origin (*aṣlihā al-qawīm*) and their straight way, especially when that deviation is consolidated and persistent.

Let it not be said that this only occurs if the issue is one of the forms and partial meanings that the soul perceives through the intermediary of the bodily faculties and the instruments pertaining to matter. If they are from the universals that the

1. In place of 'hidden subtle bond' Āshtiyānī's edition reads 'through the subtle bond of reality' (*raqīqat-i ḥaqīqatin*) (p. 201).

2. *Munāsabah* (correlation) is sometimes synonymous with *raqīqah* (subtle bond). That appears to be the case here. See Ibn ʿArabī, *al-Futūḥāt al-Makiyyah,* vol. 3, p. 260.

3. In Islamic metaphysics *taʿayyun* (entification) refers to the manifestation (*ẓuhūr*) of a thing as a Self-disclosure (*tajallī*) of the Divine. Entification is simply that by which one thing is differentiated from another and thus fully its own self or entity. The term seems to have been coined by Ibn ʿArabī and then made a technical philosophical term by his foremost disciple, Ṣadr al-Dīn Qūnawī (d. 1274). The entifications are the different levels of manifestation or 'Self-disclosure' that make up the created order from the first self-determination of the Divine Essence (the Essence itself being beyond entification) to the pebbles on the sea shore.

soul intelligizes without the intermediation of anything from the instruments, then how could this demonstration be complete?

That is because we say, by way of concession that this issue [*tawḥīd*] is among the universals, we do not concede that all universals are only intelligized by the soul without the intermediation of the instruments. For among the universals are those things that it intelligizes through the instruments by extracting them from the particularities and deleting the distinctive characteristics; and it is called a universality after multiplicity. And if we conceded that—but we do concede that this demonstration applies only to the soul's perceiving this matter—rather, it is only through consideration of what is required by the raising of what is witnessed and what is first. Therefore, he demonstrated this by saying, 'since certainty in the futility of all intellectual [sensual, primal, and natural properties]...' The explanation of that is that certainty in the baselessness of the issue of *tawḥīd* is certainty in the baselessness of all kinds of certainties from what is intellectually proven, what is analogous to that, the sensible [properties] derived from direct witnessing, the primal [properties] which are what pertains to immediate awareness (*wijdān*). And that, according to their claim that the judgment of the mutual distinction of the quiddities (*māhiyyāt*) and the mutual difference of the entifications (*taʿayyunāt*)—in accordance with that follows necessarily from these introductory matters—negates the judging of this issue when raised to (*rāfiʿah ilā*) the judgments of separation and distinction.

Then the appearance of the marks of illness—when preceded by engaging in their causes—requires sound intuition (*ḥads*) and a mind directed to the level of that unseemly illness [to treat it]. Therefore, he preceded that demonstration by saying, 'follows the performance of onerous endeavours and practices', which is an expression for sleeplessness and hunger, the two detachers that are necessary for the black bile to rule over the fundamental noble mental organs that are the support for the rest of the intellectual perceiving and the fundamental origin for the form[1] that determines the reality pertaining to the human species.

Abū Ḥāmid Muḥammad al-Iṣfahānī said: 'But the affair is quite different from what they suppose, rather it is the opposite of what they imagine.'

I say: That is because what they demonstrated regarding *tawḥīd*, which is based upon the bad temperaments of the objects of the soul faculties, is only an indication of the healthiness of these temperaments and their soundness. For the perceiving of the perceptive faculties and the sensory organs, when it follows the thing itself and their judgement of things as they are, simply indicates the soundness of the temperaments of the faculties' objects. Because the issuing of actions from the objects is free of deficiency it is only an indication of their healthiness. So

1. Here the term 'form' (*ṣūrah*) is used in the philosophical sense wherein it denoted the eternal reality of a thing, or the 'intelligible reality' of a thing that can be perceived by the actualized human intellect.

the matter is as it is in the aforementioned demonstration: '... quite different from what they suppose, rather it is the opposite of what they imagine.' Since what they claim to be the indication of the bad temperament of the object of the percvings of those who are fully certain of this issue (i.e. *tawḥīd*) is in fact the indication of the consolidation of the bad temperament of the objects of the perceiving of those who have failed to attain the degree of certitude.

That is because every faculty and foundation—be it natural, animal or of the soul—when it fulfils the objective particular to it, then falls short of it, this objective, in following from it, is only that at the level of a bad temperament which is accidental to it and deviates from its origin (*aṣl*). For were that temperament and its nature left free of obstacles, it would be drawn to its completeness, then its objective would follow upon it. And there is no doubt that the objective of the perceiving soul faculties is only to perceive things as they are. So when this objective falls short of it that is due to the level of bad temperament. It is thus apparent that the matter of bad temperament arising is the opposite of what they imagine.

Were you to say: 'The claim that the issue of *tawḥīd* is as mentioned from all the perceivings which are of things as they are and that the intended objective of the soul faculties is the first issue and the subject of debate, then how is the demonstration regarding it sound according to their way?'

We would say: These matters are presented in accord with the subject at hand in order to prove them according to the position appropriate to it in the course of writing what is customary for them in affirming matters pertaining to speculation.

Abū Ḥāmid Muḥammad al-Iṣfahānī said: 'I wanted to write a treatise in which I clarify reality of the way (*madhhab*) of the gnostics and the falsity of those who cast lies and accusations [against them]. I further wanted this treatise to contain the quintessence of what has come to me through inspiration (*ḥads*) regarding this affair, and to comprise the cream of cream of what I have concluded by reflecting upon this issue. We decided to establish this affair in the way of the speculative [philosophers] and to follow the way of debate with the accusers, and to affirm it with strong arguments by which to refute the accusation of the deniers and intensify the desire of the seekers.

'O God, place us among the victorious who are saved, not among the lost who are rejected. O brothers of attaining (*taḥṣīl*), race to attaining the real perfection and the everlasting subsistence before the inevitable annihilation and the everlasting extinction overcomes you. Hasten in your lives before natural death hastens you on. Seek aid from Him in all affairs and rely upon Him if you are believers.'

I say: Know that it is the habit of the author to support all the realities pertaining to taste and unveiling upon intuition in accordance with the method of the people of speculation, despite disparities in expressions (*'ibārāt*). For them there is no equivalent to thought (*fikr*) other than intuition, as will be verified later. The remainder of what is mentioned here is clear.

Then he addresses the exhortation to 'the brothers of attaining', that is those among the people of speculation who have insight due to the proximity of their preparedness to avail themselves of the sapiential gnostic sciences and their receptivity to the effusion of the real perfections by advancing from imaginal forms and partial sensations to intellectual meanings (*al-maʿānī al-ʿaqliyyah*) and universal gnosis (*al-maʿārif al-kuliyyah*), and being free from the noose of established customs which lead one to mistake the rulings pertaining to illusional particularities for universal realities, based upon the intellect and its receptivity to speculations and allusions in the place of receiving certainties and intelligibles. But due to their inability to attain real perfection—because of their confining the species of perfection to the summoning of partial conventions that are inscribed in the bodily instruments and the corporeal faculties enfolded within their objects—upon the extinction of the elemental configuration,[1] that development does not fully benefit them. And their seeking to have real perfection follow immediately upon eternal subsistence in the text is an allusion to this.

Concerning the Participation of Existence in both Meaning[2] and Notion[3]

Abū Ḥāmid Muḥammad al-Iṣfahānī said: 'Know that existence is comprised entirely of particular existences, not according to the expression, but according to the meaning (*maʿnā*), as we have made clear in our other books.'

I say: Insofar as the reality of existence is self-evident in what-ness (*halliyyah*) and in what-is-itness (*māhiyyah*),[4] as has been clarified previously, it begins in its ruling properties (*aḥkām*) and precedes participation because it is closer to

1. A 'configuration' (*nash'ah*) refers to a world (*ʿālam*) or one of the various cosmic realms. Here 'the elemental configuration' refers to the lowest world, that of the four elements.

2. The word *maʿnā* is here translated as 'meaning', but its meaning is far more nuanced. As William Chittick writes: 'It designates not abstract, mental notions, or ideas in the modern sense, but rather concrete, spiritual realities that exist independently of the mental faculties in the realm of the First Intellect. The term is used more or less synonymously with reality (*ḥaqīqah*), quiddity (*māhiyyah*), and fixed entity (*ʿayn thābit*). It is thus a synonym for form (*ṣūrah*) in the philosophical sense, but not in the Sufi sense. In philosophical usage … form is contrasted with matter (*māddah*). The forms are the *maʿqūlāt*, the 'intelligibles' or eternal realities that come to be known when the intellect is actualized. In the Sufi usage, meaning is a thing's reality with God or the First Intellect, whereas form is the thing's outward appearance. Thus 'meanings' in the Sufi sense are the same as 'forms' in the philosophical sense'. Mullā Ṣadrā, *The Elixir of the Gnostics*, translated, introduced and annotated by William Chittick (Provo, UT, 2003), p. 101, n. 15.

3. This section heading is not part of the original text, but is added by Āshtiyānī (p. 205). I have followed him in this because it marks a natural break within the original text.

4. We have translated *māhiyyah* throughout as 'quiddity', but have here translated in the literal sense as 'what-is-it-ness' to bring out the correlation with '*halliyyah*' or 'whatness', a rarely used Arabic word deriving from the interrogative particle '*hal*' which has no direct translation in English, but turns a statement of fact into a question when placed at the beginning of an Arabic sentence.

the ruling properties as regards the reality and as regards the point to which all other properties and issues sought in this treaties, such as existence and oneness, return.

So although the evidentness of the reality necessitates the evidentness of its participation, nonetheless, the author has here reported in various insightful manners, all of which increase one's insight, that the concept of existence is known immediately. If it does not participate among all existents, the absence of everything entirely would not be made necessary of its being absent from the entirety. Rather that is false, because we know necessarily that everything that does not have the notion of being immediately known is completely negated.

It should not be said that what is clarified in the rest of his books is only the participation of the meaning (*maʿnā*) of existence according to the technical vocabulary of the Peripatetics, because his discussion with the Peripatetics in these books is according to their methods. Therefore that clarification (*bayān*) does not necessitate the participation of existence in accordance with the meaning which concerns us here when we clarify the difference between the two meanings, according to the two technical usages.

We say that what the author is claiming regarding the two meanings of existence is none other than the real [meaning] which the seekers of truth (*muḥaqqiqūn*) claim, not the conceptual [meaning], as is the opinion of some later [philosophers]. After the clarification of the decrepitude and defectiveness that this opinion comprises and apprising [one] of the destruction of principles and the absence of order that results there from, it has been affirmed, in other than what is found in his book, that the meaning of existence with which we are dealing is the real meaning. That is made clear in those matters which the one who reflects does not hesitate to recognize if he comes upon the principles of their craft and knows them, with certainty and resolute verification of what is true, from plunging into that deep research, as he says in his book *al-Iʿtimād* (The Reliance) after completing the replies to what the Master of Illumination [Shihāb al-Dīn Suhrawardī] and others posed regarding the conceptuality of existence (*iʿtibāriyyat al-wujūd*).

If you know this, then we say: If what this eminent author intended by what he mentioned is that the verification in the entities (*aʿyān*) has no verification in the entities added to itself then it is true, but that does not require that it itself be a conceptual thing. But if by that he intended that its reality is only necessitated by something among the conceptual notions (*al-mafhūm al-iʿtibārī*), and from the joining of the two affairs there results a conceptual thing, we are not opposed to that. But that does not require that existence itself be a conceptual thing. If by that he intended the self-same verification from the intelligible concepts (*al-iʿtibārāt al-ʿaqliyyah*), then it is clear that this is not so, because each one of the quiddities existing in an entity is a verification and an entified verification itself would be among those things which are real, because there is no doubt that that through which the real thing abides and by which it is verified must be real. And if the two are the same quiddity, then that verification is either the very quiddities themselves or a part of them due to its participating among them all. So it is not simply a conceptual thing.

Furthermore, if entified existence does not have a reality in the entities, then the quiddities realized in the entities would be realized, in their entity, in the mind. Then the realizing in the mind would be better suited to be conceptual and there would be no opposition between mental and external quiddities, except through conceptualization (*iʿtibār*), and if existence were sheer intelligible meanings that would require either the negation of things being instaured [with existence] or that quiddities be instaured [with existence]. In addition, when we realize verification in entities, it is impossible that that verification not be verified in the entities. So it is verified in the entities.

It might be said: 'Were that sound, then it would be sound to say that it is impossible for the existence of an occurrence non-existent at present to exist, for it would exist and would not be non-existent at present.'

We say: We do not submit to the futility of what you have concluded, since existence does not admit non-existence, just as it (non-existence) does not admit existence. Rather, what admits non-existence is the quiddity. But it only becomes non-existent through the cessation of its association with existence. The truth is that just as external existence (*al-wujūd al-ʿaynī*) is immediately apparent, so too, its verification in entities is known immediately. But doubt regarding things like this may arise, not because of obscurity and inscrutability, but because of the intensity of clarity and disclosure.

Know that if the intelligent one who is aware of the principles of the craft (philosophy) encompasses all the subjects that I have presented here, then perhaps the truth of this matter will shine upon him. As for the explanation of the claim regarding what is witnessed through strong intuition (*al-ḥads al-qawiy*) and clear proof, that is in our book entitled The Invincible Wisdom (*al-Ḥikmah al-munīʿah*). He also mentioned in a section of The Guiding Wisdom (*al-Ḥikmah al-rashīdiyyah*): 'So if you make entified existence like the rest of the negations and additions, then we will make all of the remaining notions follow their course, rather they are more properly put among the tribe of conceptual things (*al-iʿtibārāt*).[1] Then we make existence itself a real source for all that is other than it among the entities.'[2]

Regarding another issue from The Guiding Wisdom, Abū Ḥāmid Muḥammad al-Iṣfahānī said: 'There is no doubt that the qualification of the quiddities by entified existence in the entities requires that existence occur in those entities,

1. The Āmulī reads *iʿtibāriyyāt* (p. 53). *Iʿtibārāt* is printed in the Āshtiyānī edition, though *iʿtibāriyyāt* is noted as an alternative (p. 207).

2. Both Āshtiyānī and Āmulī agree that this is a citation from The Guiding Wisdom, but do not give an exact citation. The work appears to be unavailable at present.

in opposition to that reality of which is this existence itself or its necessary concomitant. Perhaps the pure[1] have doubts regarding this matter, not due to its hidden-ness and abstruseness, rather because of the intensity of its manifestation….' These were his words.

Upon the removal of the mask from these faces from which the lights of verification arise one has no doubts that what shines upon him regarding the meaning (*maʿnā*) of existence is distinct from the opinions of the later philosophers, especially among the Peripatetics among them.

It should not be said: 'How is that, when we have seen him follow in their tracks in the clarification of their objectives and the ordering of their proofs? Then he began declaring some false and following others.'

That only occurs with the coordination of technical vocabulary and the agreement between the two customs. Because we claim that his illumination is in accord with what the onlooker attains to after condescending to participate in their customary discourse, following the principles of their craft[2] and improving upon it and verifying it to the greatest possible extent, then sifting what is indispensable from the various types of deficiency and derangement, supported by demonstrations around which the blemishes of illusions do not circle. Among those things by which the investigation is distinguished from the clothes of systematization is that the controversy regarding this [outer] form is confined to expression only and that the meaning (*maʿnā*) which the philosophers claim to consider is what the author has clarified as being real in the aforementioned ways. So that what they claim is real among the quiddities, he claims is real through relations and concepts. So they do not specify the word 'existence', in all of its degrees and divisions, as being from one of the two existences [entified or conceptual] and apply it universally to existences as being entified. They are far removed from what the verifiers maintain regarding generality (*ʿumūm*) and particularity (*khuṣūṣ*) in accordance with what I have indicated in the introduction.[3] As for what the author claims according to what is known from the scrutiny of his words, existence is particular only without being general.[4] When this is established, then his discussion with them is through,

1. Text reads *azkiyā'* (those who are pure), though *adhkiyā'* (those who are intelligent) may be the proper reading.

2. Both editions read '*ṣaḥibihim*' (their companions) but note that *ṣināʿatihim* is in an alternative manuscript. I have chosen the alternative.

3. Āshtiyānī notes: 'For the existence of things in the manner of the real oneness which is the level of unicity (*al-aḥadiyyah*) is existence according to the verifier, not the philosopher. And its existence in the manner of multiplicity and the heedlessness (*ghaflah*) of oneness is existence according to the philosopher, not the verifier. So the point of agreement is the existence of things through external existences which pertain to themselves.'

4. Āshtiyānī notes: 'In accordance with the claim that the quiddities are modes of existences; for all that is existence according to the philosopher is existence according to the verifier, not the opposite.'

This sentence in the text is very poorly edited and makes little sense in the printed edition.

as is his deducing in accord with them. Because what is established for the general is no doubt established for the particular.

Regarding the Necessity of Existence[1]

Abū Ḥāmid Muḥammad al-Iṣfahānī said: 'It is clear that its reality, insofar as it is itself, does not admit non-existence into its own essence, due to the impossibility of any two opposites being qualified by the other, and the impossibility of a nature being transformed into another nature. And when non-existence is impossible in its essence, it [itself] is necessary in its essence.'

I say: After the affirmation of participation of the meaning (*ma'nā*) of existence, he commences with the clarification of its necessity, which is one of the objectives [of philosophy]. The affirmation of that is that the reality of existence, insofar as it is it [self], does not admit non-existence in its essence. This results in the reality of existence being necessary in its essence. As for the greater, it is apparent. As for the lesser, that is because if the reality of existence admits non-existence in its essence then it is possible for it to be qualified by it, and if it is possible for it to be qualified by it then it is not necessary that it be impossible. But the latter is false, as it is deemed necessary that it be inconceivable. That is because what is qualified would then not be in need of remaining in its reality upon its being qualified by non-existence from the start. And if it were remaining [in that state] it would be necessary that one of the two contraries be qualified by the other. If it did not remain [in that state] the transformation of the nature of existence into the nature of on-existence would be necessary, and both of these are clearly impossible.

This is what suffices the author for the affirmation of the necessity of existence, since a little suffices one who is perspicacious and much does not suffice the ignoramus. But it is possible to affirm it in many ways. We will undertake some of them as enlightenment for those who reflectively observe (*al-nāẓirīn*) and to arouse the desire of the insightful among them.

First: Absolute Existence is a simple uncaused existent. All that which is like this, is necessary in its essence. As for its being existent, that is because if it were non-existent it would be necessary that something be qualified by its contrary, and what is qualified abides through its qualifier, and something does not abide with what negates it. As for its being simple, that is because if its components are existent, existence would then have to precede itself. If they were non-existent, its non-existence would be necessary. As for its being uncaused, that is because if it were not so it would be necessary for a thing to precede itself, as necessarily follows from the fact that the existence of the cause must precede what is caused. As for a

This is the closest approximation I could make.

1. This heading does not appear to part of the original text, though it does appear in both critical editions. Āmulī adds 'and this is the second issue' to the heading (p. 55).

clarification that all that for which these properties are established is necessary in itself, that is evident.

Second: If it were not necessary, it would be possible or impossible, following necessarily from the classification of notions (*mafhūmāt*) under the three categories, [possible, impossible and necessary]. The first [category] is inconceivable since the possible thing does not admit both existence and non-existence in its essence, and something does not admit both itself and its contradiction. The second [category] is also inconceivable, since what is impossible is non-existent and existence is existent, as has previously been explained, and because its impossibility requires the negation of existences, as follows necessarily from the necessity of the qualification of the particular by that by which the absolute general (*al-ʿāmm al-muṭlaq*) is qualified. Some of the later [philosophers] have undertaken to reply to this. Among them are those who chose the second alternative and made the meaning of the qualification of something by existence that if it occurs to the mind it is qualified by existence. Just as external things are qualified by necessity and possibility, although neither has external ipseity, so too, existence would have no external ipseity. For that they rely solely upon the explanation of the eminent Naṣīr al-Dīn Ṭūsī (d. 672/1274) that it is among the secondary intelligibles;[1] and you have learned what defects lie in this. Alas for this eminent one, was he not content with the particulars of the issues to the exclusion what was transmitted from the great masters of unveiling and the prominent guiding Imams, because it is among the convincing [arguments]. How did he convince himself regarding this important issue with transmission from some of the eminent reflectors, clinging to what he acquired from sheer conjecture and being content with it.

Among them there are also those who choose the first alternative, exaggerating what it implies to the extent that if absolute existence took on non-conditionality (*lā bi-sharṭ shay'*)—I mean the universal nature—it would not be a single thing, but multiple things, since absolute existence verifies the existence of the necessary and the possibilities.[2] So some of absolute existence would be necessary and of some

1. Secondary intelligibles are notions which have no corresponding existent in the external world. They are divided into logical secondary intelligibles and philosophical secondary intelligibles. The latter is what the author is here addressing. For philosophical secondary intelligibles the occurrence is in the mind, but the qualification is derived from a real existent. Ibn Turkah is arguing against those who believe that existence is merely a philosophical secondary intelligible, because quiddity precedes existence ontologically and existence is therefore a notion derived from quiddity.

2. For later Islamic philosophers, existents are of three different kinds: negatively conditioned (*bi-sharṭ lā shay'*), non-conditioned (*lā bi-sharṭ shay'*), and conditioned by something (*bi-sharṭ shay'*). Absolute Existence must be negatively conditioned is a second stage of existence which is intermediate between absolute existence and relative, conditioned existence. This intermediate stage is referred to as 'unfolded existence' wherein the absolute existence begins the process of unfolding itself in different delineated manifestations, but is still absolute existence. Ibn Turkah is here criticizing those who misunderstand the level of unfolded existence, seeing it as a form of

it would be a particular possibility. It is not hidden to anyone who has the least experience with their ways that this multiplicity is only conceived for what this nature verifies among individual things. And as for the very reality of that notion which is the universal nature, it has no multiplicity and no plurality.

Third: Existence is existent, as has been previously demonstrated.[1] If it were not necessary, it would be possible, for its cause is inevitably existent, so it is either itself of a division among its divisions. [But] all of these require that something precede itself.

They have sometimes also responded to this by claiming that its cause is but a division among its divisions, and that something to the fact that the cause must be preceded by existence and that the impossible precedence in each of their estimations is absurd. Sometimes they have replied that absolute existence is not a single thing such that it would have a single cause. Rather the necessary is an absolute existent and all of the possibilities are an absolute existent, so the cause of every absolute existent is another absolute existent, until one arrives at an absolute existent with no mover beyond it.

You know the deficiencies in this. I have only related the account of their argument in order that the sagacious one may be aware that so long as the intellect is in its sound mode (*fi ṭarzihi al-salīm*), free of conventional judgements and customary considerations, the clarifications of proofs will not benefit it, nor will theoretical demonstration bring it to certainty. So what is going on with these eminent [philosophers]? Despite their plunging into the affair of disputation and the great extent to which they follow the path of researching and theorizing, you see them failing to rely upon the clear truth, in spite of their proofs pursuing this course; and they ride the mount of possibility and guessing.

Fourth: Existence is existent, its existence is itself and all that is such is necessary in its essence. As for its being existent, that is in what has preceded. As for its existence being itself, that is because if not for that, it would either be a part of it or outside of it. The first leads to existence being composed [of parts], and the falsity of this has been explained. The second necessitates the implausible chain of infinite regression.

Fifth: The existent is a thing which has existence; and is what has existence too general to be the entity of existence or other than it, in opposition to the nature of existence? So the thing is confirmed in itself because what cannot be eliminated from the essence does not influence what is outside of it—and that for which existence is affirmed without the intermediary of another thing, that is necessary.

---

existence which is conditioned by something and thereby posing multiplicity in the absolute itself. For a fuller explanation see Toshiko Izutsu, *The Fundamental Structure of Sabzawarī's Metaphysics*, chapter 7, 'The structure of the Reality of Existence.'

1. i.e. from the argument that if it were non-existent it would need to be qualified by something through opposition to it and the thing qualified abides with the qualification and something does not abide with its negation.

7

Maḥmūd Shabistarī and Shams al-Dīn Lāhījī

The commentary of Lāhījī upon the *Gulshan-i rāz* of Maḥmūd Shabistarī is one of the most important texts of philosophical Sufism in the Persian language while the *Gulshan-i rāz* (The Secret Garden of Divine Mystery) itself is a supreme masterpiece of Persian Sufi poetry. In introducing this section an account must be given, needless to say, of both Shabistarī and Lāhījī. The *Gulshan-i rāz* was written in a period of a few days by Maḥmūd Shabistarī in response to a number of questions sent to him by the Khurāsānī Sufi master Amīr Ḥusayn Hirawī, who was a *khalīfah* of the celebrated Suhrawardiyyah Shaykh Bahā' al-Dīn Zakariyyā' of Multan. The *Gulshan-i rāz*, consisting of about a thousand verses, soon became extremely famous and has remained to this day one of the most widely read and oft-quoted of Sufi poems because it combines heavenly-inspired beauty with remarkable clarity and simplicity while discussing the most important elements of *ʿirfān*. Yet, despite the exceptional fame of this work, little is known about the life of its author.

What we know about Saʿd al-Dīn Maḥmūd ibn Amīn al-Dīn ʿAbd al-Karīm Shabistarī is that he was born in a town near Tabriz by the name of Shabistar. He studied in that area, and travelled in various Islamic countries such as Egypt, Arabia and Anatolia. He underwent Sufi training with at least two known masters of Azarbaijan, Shaykh Amīn al-Dīn and Shaykh Bahā' al-Dīn. He was famous as both a Sufi and a religious scholar and died in Shabistar where his tomb is to be found to this day. It is believed that he was born in 687/1288 and, according to most scholars of later centuries, died in 720/1320–1321 at the age of thirty-three. Some recent scholars, basing themselves mostly on a work by Ḥāfiẓ Ḥusayn Karbalā'ī Tabrīzī entitled *Rawḍāt al-jinān* (The Garden of Paradise), one of the earliest works to mention Shabistarī, believe, however, that the poet died some twenty years later in 740/1339–1340. Shabistarī also wrote a few other works, among the most important being *Ḥaqq al-yaqīn* (The Truth of Certainty) and *Mir'āt al-muḥaqqiqīn* (Mirror of the Verifiers).

It is known that Shabistarī was a Sunni in *madhhab* and an Ashʿarite in *kalām*. But above all else he was a Sufi deeply influenced by the teachings of the School of Ibn ʿArabī. Much of the *Gulshan-i rāz* is pure metaphysics in Persian poetic form, sometimes one or two lines summarizing a whole treatise of the Shaykh al-Akbar. In his *Saʿādat-nāmah* (The Treatise on Happiness), Maḥmūd Shabistarī writes that he studied the *Futūḥāt* and the *Fuṣūṣ* of Ibn ʿArabī thoroughly, but that despite this deep attraction to his works and command of his teachings, felt a certain unease when reading them. His master explained to him that this unease came from a dark element of his own soul but reflected in Ibn ʿArabī's writings. In any case along with ʿIrāqī, Shams al-Dīn Lāhījī and Jāmī, Shabistarī is the greatest Sufi poet of the Persian language associated with the gnosis and philosophical Sufism of the School of Ibn ʿArabī. As for his *Gulshan-i rāz*, it is a unique work of the Persian language in combining poetry of celestial inspiration with the lucid exposition of the most profound metaphysical teachings.

Precisely because of its clarity and its synthesizing nature, the *Gulshan-i rāz* became the subject of numerous commentaries over the ages, from those of Kamāl al-Dīn Ḥusayn Ardibīlī, Shāh Dāʿī ila'Llāh, Niẓām al-Dīn Maḥmūd Ḥusaynī and Qādī Mīr Ḥusayn Yazdī, to the *Mishwāq* (Incitement to Yearning) of Mullā Muḥsin Fayḍ Kāshānī, which is a commentary on a number of symbols used in the *Gulshan*, to Muḥammad Iqbāl's 'new' *Gulshan-i rāz*. Besides Iqbāl, other commentators were formally Sufis belonging to various schools of *taṣawwuf*, but one can also count an Ismaili commentator among them.

The most important commentary is, however, that of Shams al-Dīn Muḥammad ibn Yaḥyā Lāhījī entitled *Mafātīḥ al-iʿjāz fī sharḥ gulshan-i rāz* (Keys of Wonder in the Commentary upon the *Gulshan-i rāz*) written in 877/1473. This long work of over 800 pages in its current edition is based entirely on Ibn ʿArabian terminology and provides a complete cycle of *ʿirfān* written in clear Persian and embellished with poems of many other Sufis especially Rūmī and Maghribī. It is certainly among the most complete and thorough texts of philosophical Sufism in the Persian language.

Little is known about the life of Lāhījī except that he was the foremost *khalīfah* of the famous Sufi master Sayyid Muḥammad Nūrbakhsh and belonged to the Nūrbakhshiyyah Order. He entered the order in 849/1445 and served his master for sixteen years. It is also known that he enjoyed great fame as a major Sufi master during his own lifetime, died in Shiraz in 912/1506–1507 and is buried in that city near the Shāh Dāʿī Gate. He was visited by such famous philosophers as Dawānī, Ghiyāth al-Dīn Manṣūr Dashtakī and Qāḍī Maybudī, all of whom held him in utmost respect. It is said that Lāhījī always wore black and that when Shah Ismāʿīl visited him and asked why he did so, Lāhījī announced that he was in mourning throughout the year for the death of Imam Ḥusayn. There was, however, a more esoteric reason. In his commentary Lāhījī speaks of the meaning of black light which Shabistarī mentions and identifies with the state of realization of Reality beyond all manifestation and differentiation. It is said that Lāhījī identified himself with that station and therefore wore black.

Besides this commentary, Lāhījī composed a *mathnawī* entitled *Asrār al-shuhūd* (Mysteries of Contemplation) and a *dīwān* of poetry in which he used the pen-name Asīrī. But his most important work is without doubt the commentary upon the *Gulshan-i rāz*, a selection of which appears below.

S. H. Nasr

COMMENTARY ON THE SECRET GARDEN OF DIVINE MYSTERY

Sharḥ gulshan-i rāz

Translated for this volume by Mohammad H. Faghfoory from Shams al-Dīn Muḥammad Lāhījī Gīlānī, *Sharḥ gulshan-i rāz*, ed. with an introduction by ʿAlī Qulī Maḥmudī Bakhtyārī (Tehran, 1381 Sh./2002), pp. 69–104.

It is generally held among the seekers of truth that the first obligation of those obedient to God who reach the age of adolescence is knowledge of God (*maʿrifat Allāh*), which is the foundation of all realized knowledge and religious beliefs. In relation to this, the obligation of all the mandatory rites and religious duties becomes secondary. With regard to the particulars, the paths to acquire Divine knowledge are countless, [for it has been said that] the roads toward God are as numerous as the number of God's creatures. In respect to the universals, however, there are two ways toward this end. One is through rational arguments (*istidlāl*), and the second through intuition and unveiling (*kashf*), as has been discussed previously.

The way of rational argument is to seek proof of the Creator from the created. The way of unveiling is for the created to remove the veils of [Divine] beauty. Both of these paths rely on the intellect and contemplation, for intellection and contemplation are ways of journeying from the manifest to the non-manifest, from the form to the meaning. Therefore, the contemplative man first questions his own intellect and says, 'I am perplexed with regard to my own intellect'. One of the first difficulties that arises is that I am bewildered about the nature of my own intellect and cannot properly comprehend what is called 'intellection' in the terminology of the seekers of truth. He [Shabistarī] states that knowing the nature of intellection is an obligation because it is necessary for the knowledge of God.

Poem:
Knowledge is the foundation of knowing God,
It is like the sight for the eye of the heart.
On the path of knowing God, you will never be on the right course,
Until you know yourself well.

Since real knowledge of God, that is to say becoming connected to the Real Origin, is attainable only through a vertical journey toward Him, and because the dominance of the contingent rules of multiplicities prevent seeing the beauty of the One Necessary Being, [Shabistarī] alludes to the special journey upon which knowledge of God depends.

Poem:
You asked, 'Tell me what is intellection?
For I have remained perplexed about its meaning'.
Since you asked this question repeatedly [I shall answer] so that the eager
Seeker is encouraged and devotes his total attention to the answer.

[Shabistarī] says:
Intellection is a journey from falsehood to Truth.
It is to see in the particular the Absolute Universal.

Falsehood stands in opposition to the truth. Truth is of two categories: the real (*ḥaqīqī*) and that which is relational to it (*iḍāfī*), and so is false. The Real Truth is the Being of the One Absolute Being who stands opposite to non-existence. Therefore, the real false is non-existence, 'Be aware that all things except God are false'.

Relative falsehood is that which is real only in relation to something lower than itself. For example, honey is useful and real only in relation to moist and cold natures, and harmful and false in relation to hot and dry natures. The skin of melon and rice and the straw of wheat are false in relation to man because they are not edible, but they are real and useful in relation to animals, and so forth.

The relatively real and relatively false are both categories of the real Truth, for they are under the category of existence and not outside of it. By the true and false of this group we mean 'real true' and 'real false'. The meaning of this poem is that intellection, according to this group, is the wayfarer's journey toward unveiling multiplicities and entifications, which are in reality non-existence in relation to the Truth, that is to say, in relation to the Absolute Unity of Being which is the Real Truth. This journey consists of the wayfarer reaching the station of the annihilation in God (*fanā' fi'Llāh*), and the disappearance of all particles of engendered things in the rays of the light of the unity of His Essence like a drop in the ocean.

Poem:
Travel on this path in such a manner
  that duality disappears.
And if duality still remains,
It will begin to disappear
As you proceed on the path.
You shall not become Him, but if you try,
You will reach a station where your 'I-ness' will disappear.

The second stanza of the [previous] poem, which asserts, 'It is to see in the particulars the Absolute Universal', is an allusion to [attaining] utmost perfection in knowing God (*maʿrifah*), which is finding subsistence in God (*baqāʾ biʾLlāh*). There is no station above this station. There are differences among stations of those who have reached union [with God], because often entification and individuation prevent witnessing true Unity. He says that in the terminology of the people of the path [i.e. Sufis], intellection, which is the means of acquiring God's knowledge, refers to the path on which the wayfarer finds that his own individuality and all other individualities are immersed in the ocean of Divine Unity. After annihilation and return to his original nothingness, he [a Sufi] would find subsistence in God (*baqāʾ biʾLlāh*). Hence he will see all visible and invisible things and those phenomena which are the locus of the manifestation of a single Truth that is manifested in different forms and in different places. He would see the single Truth manifested in all contingent things.

Poem:
For the sake of those who have discernment,
The One God made the six directions
The locus of manifestation of His signs of power.
That is why the Noble Being told us,
'Wherever you turn, there is His Face.'
If I drink water in a pitcher to quench my thirst,
I am witnessing the Truth hidden in the water.

With discernment and a truth-seeking eye, the wayfarer will become free of the pain of otherness (*ghayriyyah*) and see the Absolute Truth in every single entity that is in fact part of the totality of Truth. If one looks with discernment [one will realize that] all entifications are the very same Absolute which is entified. In reality, entification is a contingent being that has not been actualized in the external world, and other than the Absolute Being there is no reality. This station is the utmost degree of witnessing by those who have attained perfection.

Since he [the Shaykh] has presented the description of intellection in the terminology of the people of vision and witness, he also alludes to the way of the people of opinion and rational argument and says: 'And to Allah belongs the East and the West, so wherever to turn you shall see Allah's Countenance. Verily Allah is All-Encompassing and All-Knowing' (Qur'ān 2:115). *Philosophers who have reflected on this, have confirmed it.*

A philosopher (*ḥakīm*) is a person who knows through rational argument and acts on the basis of that knowledge. According to truth-seeking people, one is not called a philosopher (*ḥakīm*) merely on the basis of one's knowledge of things. [The meaning of the poem is that] the wise who have contemplated and commentated on the meaning of intellection, have defined it as follows:

Poem:
When a hypothesis appears in one's heart,
First it is called recollection.

It means whenever a form from among forms appears in the soul, it finds its way to the heart. According to the definition of people it is the rational soul that differentiates among meanings. Before discussing the notion of intellectual conception, by which we mean knowledge, there is a form that appears first in the mind called recollection (*tadhakkur*). When a philosopher wants to prove an unknown through rational argument and reason, he must first gather desired principles and precepts so that he can demonstrate the known principles from the unknown. Therefore, whenever he conceptualizes the preliminary information that he knows [whether its principles are known or unknown] he is recollecting or being reminded (*tadhakkur*). This is because he had forgotten [the truth] and now he has remembered it, for there is a thirst to know the unknown. That is to say, understanding that which is known and perceived in general terms has to reach the heart, but because of physical impurities and obstacles one forgets what he has perceived but may remember with full concentration and removal of obstacles. Those things become known because of the removal of the obstacles. As some philosophers have stated, although in the beginning he knew the principles of things, he had forgotten them because he did not pay attention to them. When he pays attention to remembering them, he is thus reminded of them. [However], merely remembering those principles is not enough to learn them. Further consideration and contemplation are needed.

Poem:
When you recollect something during contemplation,
In common usage it is called taking heed (*ʿibrat*).

The above lines state that when one comes across the principles one seeks, one should think about the quality of the known and the unknown. If what one seeks is conceptual (*taṣawwurī*), how should its universal or particular aspects, or genus (*jins*) and specific differentia (*faṣl*), be arranged and prioritized so that it can lead toward knowing that which is sought? And if the unknown is a conceptual judgment (*taṣdīq*), how should the hierarchical order of the two initial concepts be in the general (*iqtirānī*) and exceptional (*istithnāʾī*) analogy to lead toward the desired result?

As for the second part of the poem, it tells us that the philosophical term for the concept that was just mentioned, according to his interpretation, is *ʿibrat*, which derives from *ʿubūr*, meaning 'transition'. That is why bridges built over rivers and passages are called *maʿbar*, which means 'the place of transition', because people use them to pass from one point to another. At this point a philosopher has gone past conceptualizing preliminary precepts, and in a special way has attained that which he was seeking. That is why it is called *ʿibrat*, because conceptualizing precepts in such a manner leads to the desired results, as he said:

Poem:
A hypothesis upon which one reflects
Is called intellection by the people of reason.
When conceptualization is accompanied by contemplation, as described,
By the people of intellect who are masters of rational discourse,
    and know things according to the laws of intellect,
This is called intellection (*tafakkur*).

Now Shabistarī describes intellection according to the definition of the people of intellect and says:

Poem:
Through hierarchical order of known hypotheses,
The unknown is proved and becomes known.

Since intellect is defined as the hierarchical order (*tartīb*) of known principles that lead to the discovery of the unknown, know that the view of the people of knowledge is that meditation and intellection require finding the unknown through that which is known. Undoubtedly, it is not possible to find every unknown just through every known, and therefore it is necessary to find each unknown through the known that corresponds to it. In addition, there is no doubt that acquiring a particular unknown from what is known is not possible in every sense that one may desire; rather, it requires a particular order (*tartīb*) of those known things, which are contingent on whether they are in relation to a concept (*taṣawwur*) or a judgment (*taṣdīq*), as was mentioned previously.

The known consist of those known subjects that are the basis (*mabādī*) of the objective that is sought. From that particular hierarchical order, the proof of the unknown becomes known, in other words, the proof of the unknown objective becomes known. For example, the reality of a human being is an unknown hypothesis composed of two parts, that of an animal and a rational faculty, in a special hierarchical order that prioritizes the universal over the particular. The creation of the world, a conceptual unknown, is composed of the concept of a changing world and the concept of a created universal that undergoes change. This is how the particular hierarchical order, that is the priority of the major premise over minor premise, and the necessity of the minor and the universality of major and the like are understood, that is to say, how the conclusion becomes known and proved.

Know that a conceptual hypotheses (*majhūl-i taṣawwurī*) is derived from a concept and a conceptual judgment (*majhūl-i taṣdīqī*) is derived from concepts. However, no one has presented an explanation why *taṣawwur* cannot be derived from *taṣdīq* and vice-versa. Therefore, it is possible that it could also happen. Here, his statement that the proof of the unknown becomes known could be an allusion to the fact that it could be possible for it to happen. Although proving a concept among the seekers of truth is defined as knowledge based upon a hypothetical subject that is predicated upon the relationship between the two, among the possessors of intuition, in fact, *taṣdīq* is taken to denote its literal meaning, not a logical concept. Since during the formation of the unknown concepts, the known concepts must be prioritized and their hierarchies determined, the two must meet in the middle so that they would lead to the proof of the concept that is desired. As he said:

Poem:
The major premise is like a father,
Followed by the minor premise, which is like a mother.
O brother! Know that the result is like a child.

In predicative propositions, the minor and major premises and in conditional propositions (*qaḍāyā-yi sharṭiyyah*), the two premises that are technically one after the other, are like a man (father) and a woman (mother) who marry each other, and a child is born out of their marriage. Shabistarī expressed this in philosophical terminology and said that the details of such a disposition need to observe certain rules:

Poem:
But such an order in its details,
Is in need of following certain rules.

The above discourse advocates contemplation in the style of philosophers, and says that the way people of intellect obtain knowledge requires them to ascertain the rules. These rules are universal and correspond to all their particulars and components in order to be applicable to them. Here, by 'rule' we mean the science of logic whose rules are universal and explain the order of existents of the known in a manner that would lead to the discovery of the hypothetical or conceptual unknown. However, attaining real certainty, which is peace of heart and liberation from the anxiety of doubt, is not possible except through witnessing and examining that which corresponds to *ʿayn al-yaqīn* and *ḥaqq al-yaqīn* (The Truth of Certainty). As he said:

Poem:
If all those efforts are not accompanied by God's help,
Indeed it would be nothing but sheer emulation.

If the special order and the rules of logic, argumentation, and proofs are not accompanied by Divine Guidance, which includes also spiritual preparedness and inner purity, and if the heart is not illuminated by Divine Light, nothing will be accomplished except pure imitation and repetition.

Poem:
That imitating man is like a handicapped person;
Although he possesses reason and sound argument,
The depth of his argument and form of presentation
Distance him from discernment and sound judgment.

Since multiplicity and unity are contradictory, it is hardly possible for man to attain Divine knowledge by merely relying on the hierarchical order of premises (*muqaddamāt*). As he points out:

The road is long and tedious, abandon that.
Like Moses cast thy staff aside for a while.

Philosophers and theologians unanimously agree that understanding the reality of things by way of rational argumentation and reason alone is most difficult. Acquiring knowledge of God's Attributes and Essence is impossible, as it has been said: 'The reality of God's Attributes and Essence is hidden from the understanding of reason.' Whenever we perceive a conceptual judgment (*taṣdīqī*) and seek to understand it in the most perfect manner, our mind must be directed toward that which it knows so that it can pass from one object of knowledge to another in an undifferentiated manner until it can find its desired object of knowledge. Our mind already knows those knowables as principles (*mabādī*), but the mind must put the principles in a special order that leads it toward the unknown which it is looking for. Obviously that special order requires paying attention to that which is sought, detaching the mind from ties and attachments and directing the mind toward the intelligibles (*maʿqūlāt*).

In spite of all this, that which is related to the [Divine] Essence must be appropriately differentiated from that which is concerned with Attributes. Otherwise, truths will remain hidden. That is why he [Shabistarī] said: 'That journey is long and tedious, abandon it.' For after endless troubles, the ultimate result is that understanding the reality of things can only be attained through attributes and characteristics of things. Acquiring Divine knowledge, exalted is He, is a spiritual journey to His immanent, negative Attributes, and this kind of knowledge (*maʿrifah*) will not be free of doubts and can be understood through illusive imaginations. Gaining perfect knowledge about things is thus impossible by this method. Acquiring true knowledge will not be possible except through purification and illumination of the heart. Purification is contingent upon the negation of all that is other than God, for as long as a pungent substance is not cleansed from the heart with the water of invocation, the inscription of real *ṭawḥīd* will not be engraved upon it. The way of reason that is based on proving something on the basis of logical demonstration (*burhān*) is the opposite of the way of purification. For a man of discursive orientation, reason is the explanation and elaboration of the reasoned, whereas for the gnostic, reason is a veil for the reasoned. Therefore, the more reasons one presents, the more hidden the object of inquiry becomes. Indeed the utmost perfection of *ṭawḥīd* is negation of otherness, as it has been said: 'The perfect form of *ṭawḥīd* is negation of attributes from it.' That which is a rational argumentation for a scholar is intuitively demonstrated for a gnostic (*'ārif*); that which is the veil of the Face of the Veiled is the mirror of the beauty of the Beloved held before the people of vision and discovery.

Poem:
The perfection of the man on the path of certainty is that
He will see God in whatever he sees.

As for the second part of the poem which says, 'Like Moses cast thy staff aside for a while', the staff represents rational argumentation (*istidlālī*). The correspondence between these two is very obvious, for just as the blind man relies on his staff to walk, those whose hearts are not illuminated with the 'staff' of unveiling, and cannot see true unity with a spiritual eye, walk on the path of gnosis (*ma'rifah*) with the help of the 'staff' of rational argumentation.

Poem:
The abode of our intellect and reflection is the realm of [Divine] Attributes.
Divine Essence is far superior to knowledge and gnosis.
His Light is enough to be the guide of the caravan,
Nobody who follows the Truth will ever get lost.
One should know the command and creation only from God,
[Do you know anyone] who came to know of God through this or that person?

In other words, as long as Moses was saying, 'The Lord of Heaven and Earth', the Pharaoh did not believe him and kept saying, 'Verily your prophet whom God sent to you is mad.' When [God] commanded [Moses] to 'cast away thy staff', the light of unity appeared from behind the veil of that which was visible and destroyed all the illusions and imaginary realities that the Pharaoh had accumulated, for 'It swallowed up whatever they [sorcerers] had brought forth' (Qur'ān 7:117). Therefore, the seeker of God must totally abandon the way of rational argument and pay attention to the Real Originator. With the guidance of a perfect spiritual guide he must purify his heart from the dust of strangers so that the beauty of the True Beloved will be shown in that mirror. Whatever other people have heard will then become visible to him.

Poem:
Because it was made possible for me to see [the Face of the Beloved],
Today, I am not a hostage to the Day of Judgment.

Dhaʿlab Yamānī once asked His Holiness Ḥaẓrat ʿAlī, 'Did you see your Lord?' ʿAlī replied, 'Would I worship that which I do not see?' and added, 'I saw Him, then I recognized Him, then I worshipped Him. I would not worship a lord which I do not see.' As the Qurʾān says: 'Whoever hopes to meet his Lord, he must do righteous deeds and must worship his Lord and not assign a partner unto his Lord' (Qurʾān 18:110).

Poem:
I [am the one] who can see the Beauty of the Friend eye to eye,
I do not need any description of His Face.
The eye that is weak in its sight,
Is blind during the day like a bat.

Since the path that leads to the Friend is the path of lovers who are the people of purity, and because these people go toward the path of Divine Unity through unveiling and witnessing, he [Shabistarī] said:

Poem:
Come to the abode of peace where suddenly,
A bush will tell you 'Verily I am God.'

In the above poem, the abode of peace consists of purifying the heart in a manner that makes it worthy of God's theophany, for witnessing the Beauty of the Possessor of Majesty is not possible through the aforementioned path. The bush is the reality of humanity that is the locus of the manifestation of Divine Attributes and Essence. This meaning is taken from the verse of the Qurʾān where God says: 'When [Moses] reached [the bush] he was called from the right side of the valley in the blessed field from the bush: O Moses verily I am God, the Lord of this world and the next.'

In other words, from the abode of peace that is the goal of the path of purification of the heart and adornment of the soul comes Divine emanation and opening, especially for the people of witness and unveiling. In the blessed field, where the realm of the Perfect Man lies, one seeks what one seeks. In the world of multiplicities there is no realm more blessed than that where a special bush alludes to its own perfection, which is the reality of the bush, and says to Moses, 'verily I am the nurturer of the people of this world and the next.'

Poem:
I[ness] and we[ness] are the veils of the path,
When we [ness] disappears, we are not 'we'.

In this poem the Shaykh calls the aspiring wayfarer on the path and advises him to follow the path of purification and cleanse the mirror of the heart from the dust of strangers so that by virtue of the dominance of the theophany of the One, and unity of the symbol and the symbolized, with the ear of his heart he will hear the call of *'Verily I am Allāh'* and with the truth-seeing eye he will see and know himself and God.

When a gnostic reaches the utmost degree of witnessing and unveiling of [the truth] without the disturbance of illusions by impurities, he sees in all things the Beauty of the Unity of the Absolute One, as he said:

Poem:
For the truth-seeking man for whom unity is in witnessing,
The first glance is to the light of Being.

A seeker of truth is that Perfect Man for whom the reality of things have been disclosed and revealed as they are. This station is only attainable for the person who has reached the station of Divine Witnessing and who, with the eye of vision, has seen that the reality of all things is, in fact, the Truth. Other than the One Absolute Being no other being exists. The existence of other things is nothing more than pure attribution.

Poem:
The eye that sees the Truth cannot see anything other than the Truth,
The falsity lies only in the eyes of those without vision.

What is meant by unity (*waḥdah*) is Unity of the Truth as it is manifested by Itself in the realm of multiplicities, for it has illuminated the created order with the light of existence. It is the witnessing of the vision of the Truth by the Truth. In other words, the Perfect Man has traversed the illusive stations of multiplicities of forms and meanings and has reached the station of witnessing Divine Unity (*tawḥīd*) with the truth-seeing eye, and he who possesses the eye of the Truth sees the Truth in all forms of existing things. Since he sees himself and all created things as subsisting in God, inevitably 'otherness' and 'duality' are removed from his sight. Therefore, whatever he sees is seen by the Truth and known by the Truth. In seeing all things he first sees the light of the Being of the Absolute One. He who witnesses in this way is like a person who has two pairs of eyes by which he sees God manifested and the created world as non-manifested. Creation for him is the mirror of the Truth in which the Truth is manifested and creation veiled, as the mirror itself is hidden by the face.

Poem:
In the theophany of that Essence,
Existence manifested Itself to my eye.
So whatever I see, I see in His vision.

Poem:
Whatever I look at, I see Thy Face.
That is because only Thou comest before my sight.

In some manuscripts the first part of the poem 'The seeker of truth for whom Unity is in witnessing' is recorded as 'The seeker of Truth who has witnessed Divine Unity'. In this case it means that the seeker of Truth is the one who has attained divine knowledge through witnessing and unveiling, and not by way of reason and rational argumentation. This is because for a gnostic, the Truth consists of the Absolute Being. The Shaykh [Shabistarī] considers the Absolute Being and Truth as synonymous. He says:

The heart that witnessed the light and purity of Divine Knowledge,
In whatever he saw, he saw God first.

This indicates that the one who grasps the reality of things in the creation of human beings, which is the essence of the forms of engendered things, possesses a heart that is illuminated with purity and the light of knowledge (*maʿrifah*). The heart is the locus of the manifestation of the Divine Station (*sha'n*) and the essence of human beings. As Maghribī said:

You are that Treasure which became hidden
From the sight of the two worlds in the ruins of the heart.

A gnostic is a person whom Divine Presence has elevated to the station of witnessing His Attributes and Essence. This station comes by way of attaining certain states and through the unveiling [of Truth], which descends upon such a person not merely by virtue of his knowledge, for it has been said that knowledge is like an eye for such a person and *maʿrifah* is the state of being a gnostic. A heart that is adorned with this perfection sees God first in whatever he sees. This is the station of *dhu'l-ʿaynayn,* that is to say, where one possesses two [a pair of] eyes.

As was mentioned before, [such a person] sees God as manifest and creation as non-manifest. The most visible thing in creation is God, who is the Truth, because He is manifest by Himself whereas other things are manifested through Him. Do you not see that, for example, if an object is seen from a far distance, its existence is perceived first? However, sometimes it happens that because the distance is too far, it is not clear whether it is an object, or a bear, or something else. But under all circumstances it is perceived by the reality of its existence. Otherwise it does not exist, because other than that form everything is non-existent. That is why the seeker of truth says, 'God is perceived and creation is intelligible'.

Poem:
Thy Face is manifest in the universe but is hidden in essence.
If It is hidden, then what is manifest in the universe?
The universe has become the locus of manifestation of Thy Goodness and Beauty,
O my Beloved, tell me where the locus of manifestation and the soul of the Universe is?

In the previous poem, [the Shaykh] says that the first glance is upon the light of Being. In the above poem he adds, 'Whatever he saw, he first saw God in it'. To clarify, according to this group who seeks the Truth, God is the One Being that is manifested in a [specific] form in each place. Since the witnessing of the people of vision varies according to their dispositions in different times, in his description of Divine Names each person has informed us from another station. One says, 'I saw nothing unless I saw God before it'.

Poem:
By God, in whatever we set our sight,
We did not see other than God.

We explained this station before. Another person says, 'I saw nothing unless I saw God after it'. Since Reality is hidden and veiled by certain accidents and entifications, the seeker first sees the veil and then witnesses the Truth.

Poem:
Beyond this veil I have a Beloved,
The beauty of Her face is worthy of being veiled.
The whole universe is like a curtain filled by many forms,
And all things are designed over that curtain.
This veil separated me from Thee,
This is what a veil does by nature.

No! No! There is never separation between us,
Never would this veil separate Thee from me.

The person who possesses this station is called 'possessor of intellect' and sees creation as manifest and God as non-manifest and hidden. For him God is the mirror of creation, and like the hiding of the Absolute in the relative, the mirror itself appears hidden in that station. This station is the opposite of the previous one (Possessor of Eye) which we described. Another person said, 'I saw nothing unless I saw God in it'. Similar to the contingent archetypal entities that are reflected in their manifestations, the cup and the bowl are realities in which wine has been contained.

Poem:
Are these bowls that are illuminated with wine,
Or suns that are covered by clouds?

Poem:
From the purity of the wine and the subtlety of the cup,
The colour of the wine became mixed and transformed.
As though all is cup, and wine is not,
Or all is wine, and cup is not.

Still somebody else utters, 'I saw nothing unless I saw God with it'. For according to the law of union, the symbol and the symbolized, and the lover and the Beloved, do not possess existence outside of each other, although the intellect makes such a distinction between the two and regards the reality of each one as independent and different from the other.

Poem:
If you can differentiate the lover from the Beloved,
You shall see with certainty that—
The king and the beggar are companions of each other.

The one who reaches this station is called 'the possessor of intellect and eye' and sees God in creation and creation in God, and by witnessing one, he is not veiled from the other. Rather, from one perspective he sees the One Being as God, and from another as a created world. By seeing the multiplicity of the locus of manifestation, he is not veiled from witnessing the One.

Poem:
This universe is—
But the scene of theophany of the Friend's Countenance.

What is the manifestation of the universe, but all is He?
Although in appearance the universe is the locus of His manifestation,
If you look with discernment,
Both the symbol and the symbolized is He.
In reality, there is no existent other than the Beloved,
Reflection of everything else is your illusive imagination.
The Friend Himself is the mirror of His Face,
In the reflection of the mirror where is any other than the Friend?

Since for the people of vision attaining that which is sought through intellection is contingent upon detachment of the mind from inhibiting preoccupations, the Shaykh asserts:

Proper intellection is based on detachment,
And the Light of Divine providence.

Those people who reach what they seek through reason and rational argumentation believe that reasoning has a special kind of hierarchical order. It necessitates contemplating that which is sought and detaching the mind from intelligibles so that the desired result is achieved. For the people of the *ṭarīqah* (spiritual journey), who are the people of spiritual unveiling and witnessing, intellection, which consists of journeying toward God, (*sayr ila'Llāh*), journeying in God (*sayr fi'Llāh*), and journeying with God (*sayr bi'Llāh*), is contingent upon detachment from the outward (*tajrīd-i ẓāhir*) and keeping the inward alone with God (*tafrīd-i bāṭin*). In other words, intellection among the people of the *ṭarīqah* is the abandonment of preoccupation with wealth, property, position and ambition in the realm of the manifest world. It is abandoning and detaching oneself and turning away from all that distracts one from remembrance of the Friend.[1]

Know that the Necessary Being is the One whose Being is necessitated by His Essence. Possible being is that whose existence is not necessitated by its essence. In order for possible being to exist it is in need of another thing that is its cause for existence. For philosophers, possible being (caused) by the Necessary Being is a possibility. That is why he [Shabistarī] said: 'They try to prove the Necessary Being by means of contingent being.'

Since in this approach rationalist philosophers equate existence and non-existence in regards to the essence of the contingent [beings], they treat them as equals. Neither side of this equation has preference over the other except by means of its opposite. For a theologian, the reason for contingent beings is that the Cause wanted a created order. Contingent beings are made to exist by a Cause through emanation

1. Several pages of the text have been omitted due to the repetition of the content.

(*ṣudūr*) from non-existence to existence. That is how creation came to be. Some believe that the reason for contingency is the need to have created beings with specific conditions and orientations. In other words, philosophers and perhaps followers of reason have argued from the existence of the contingent to prove the existence of the Necessary Being in an absolute way. They say that the contingent being, precisely because of its contingency and createdness, is in need of a cause (creator). If that creator is a Necessary Being it proves their argument. If it is another contingent being, then again precisely because of its contingency it is in need of another cause, which in relation to it would be Necessary Being. So here rationalists become perplexed. Now, if this contingent being is the same as the first one, because rationalists try to prove the Necessary Being through contingent being, they will fall into the trap of a vicious circular argument (*dawr*). If it is a different one that leads to the Necessary Being or to infinite possibilities, they shall fall into the trap of infinite regression (*tasalsul*). Therefore, since they try to prove the Necessary Being through contingent beings, they become perplexed in knowing the Essence of the Necessary Being. What is caused becomes the effect of the Cause and the essence and attributes are all the effects [of the Cause]. Inevitably, there must be something of the Cause in the effect, and consequently, in the preliminary principles of reasoning one must include what results from them. Since the essence of contingent beings for rationalist philosophers is in every aspect different from the Essence of the Necessary Being, the Cause could not contain anything of the effect. For as long as something does not exist in a person, it inevitably follows that he cannot imagine that thing or convey it to someone else, and that is why he becomes perplexed and lost.

Poem:
This long distance will become very short for you,
If you are present in His Sacred Presence.
What your soul is seeking is just before you,
Look at it, and do not be afraid of it.
For fear would push you further from Him,
The Friend should not be associated with other than the Friend.

If there is no inherent connection between a cause and its effect, as rationalist philosophers believe, then intellectual arguments cannot provide the perfect knowledge that would lead to the knowledge of certainty. That is why the Shaykh said:

Sometimes they are trapped in a vicious circle of circular arguments (*dawr*).
Other times they become prisoners of infinite regression (*tasalsul*).

Dawr, or circuitous argument, means basing an argument on something upon which there is no stopping. *Tasalsul*, or infinite regression, is when a contingent being causes another existence that is its effect, and supports that effect by another cause that is the effect of the first cause and so on ad infinitum. In such an argument, since the possibility of the equality of existence and non-existence is present, in order for one to have preference over the other, the contingent needs a cause. If the cause is the Necessary Being, the argument of the advocate is proved, and if the cause is contingent, the possibility exists that the very same contingent cause is the first hypothesis. If another contingent being is the first cause, the argument becomes circular. However, if the first possibility is contingent upon the second possibility, and the second on the first, then it becomes circular regression. This is the problem with circular arguments and infinite regressions. Regardless of what they postulate regarding the cause, the argument becomes circular.

Poem:
Circulatory argument is false, and infinite regression impossible.
Therefore, He is the Beginning, and the final destination is the Friend.

Since the necessity of infinite regression is required for the hierarchy of the existing infinite affairs, the Shaykh said:

When the intellect contemplated His Being,
Its feet became entangled in infinite regression;

That is to say, when the intellect of the [rationalist] philosopher reflects on existence or that which exists in the external world where one possibility is contingent on another, and another upon another and the like to infinity, infinite regression wraps itself around the feet of the philosopher. In accordance with the dictum, 'And your Lord ordained that you do not worship anyone except Him' (Qur'ān, 17:24) he inevitably comes to believe that there is only one Necessary Being, for otherwise one of these two false things, that is, circulatory argument or infinite regression, becomes necessary. Therefore, it becomes clear [for rationalists] that there must be one Necessary Being. However, true knowledge (*maʿrifah*) of reality is not attained by the rationalist because such knowledge is not acquired through demonstrations and proofs, but by negating that which is other than Him. The more philosophers try to prove Necessary Being, the more distant they become from Divine Unity.

Whoever wants to know God through existent beings is ignorant of the Truth, and whoever tries to know things through Him is a gnostic (*ʿārif*). When the Prophet (Peace be Upon Him) was asked, 'How did you come to know God?' He said, 'I came to know all things through God.'

Poem:
O man of excessive claims, free yourself of knowledge,
Abandon your self so that Divine Mercy will descend upon you.
Intelligence is the antidote of failure and need,
Abandon intelligence and be content with simplicity.

8

ʿAbd al-Raḥmān Jāmī

ʿAbd al-Raḥmān, later known as Jāmī, was born in 817/1414 in the village of Kharjird near Jām, a city in the eastern province of Khurāsān. He lived in Jām until he was about fourteen and then moved to Herat. His mother's family had immigrated from Isfahan to Khurāsān while his father, Niẓām al-Dīn Aḥmad Dashtī, was a prominent member of his community with close connection to the Sufi masters in the region. We know little of his family life except that, apparently in his late forties, he married the granddaughter of his Sufi master, Saʿd al-Dīn Kāshgharī, and had four children. Three of them died, however, affecting him profoundly. The child who did survive, Ḍiyāʾ al-Dīn, was so special to Jāmī that he composed two books of a didactic nature for him, *Bahāristān* (The Book of Spring) and *al-Fawāʾid al-ḍiyāʾiyyah* (Benefits of Luminosity). It was after the birth of this son that Jāmī's sadness lifted and he composed *Nafaḥāt al-uns min ḥaḍarāt al-quds* (Breaths of Intimacy from the Realms of the Sacred).

Among the Sufi masters in whose circles Jāmī was raised were Bahāʾ al-Dīn ʿUmar Abardihī, Fakhr al-Dīn Luristānī and the grand master of the Naqshbandiyyah Sufi order, Khwājah Muḥammad Pārsā. It may have been these early contacts that account for Jāmī's later interest in the Naqshbandiyyah which he joined.

Jāmī, who later on also came to be known as ʿImād al-Dīn (pillar of faith) and Nūr al-Dīn (light of faith), studied Arabic grammar with his father until he was about fourteen when the family moved to Herat in today's Afghanistan. It was there that, despite his youth, he studied with some of the masters of his time such as Mawlānā Junayd Uṣūlī, with whom he read the *Miftāḥ al-ʿulūm* of Sakkākī and *Muṭawwal* of Taftāzānī with its commentary. He also studied with Muḥammad Jājarmī and Khwājah ʿAlī Samarqandī who was the distinguished pupil of Mīr Sayyid Sharīf Jurjānī. Following the completion of his religious studies with the above-mentioned teachers, Jāmī, who was now in his early twenties, went to Samarqand. There he met with Qāḍīzādah Rūmī with whom he studied mathematics and astronomy. Jāmī's genius was immediately recognized by Rūmī.

Jāmī, who may have experienced a failed love, had a dream in which a Sufi master by the name of Saʿd al-Dīn Kāshgharī from Herat addressed his earthly love and his difficulties. He decided to return to Herat where he spent time with Kāshgharī who became his Sufi teacher, and under Kāshgharī's supervision he practised austere forms of asceticism. A few years after the death of Kāshgharī in 860/1455, Jāmī met ʿUbayd Allāh Aḥrār, another Sufi master from the Naqshbandī order who became more of a spiritual companion for him. It was Shaykh Aḥrār who instructed Jāmī to abandon research and scholarship and devote himself entirely to practical wisdom and the purification of his soul. While Jāmī resided and taught in Herat, he travelled to Samarqand frequently to meet with the Sufi masters of the Naqshbandī order.

It was during these years that Jāmī wrote some of his most important works on philosophical Sufism, such as *Naqd al-nuṣūṣ fī sharḥ naqsh al-fuṣūṣ* (Critique of Texts on the Commentary of the Impact of [Ibn ʿArabi's] *Fuṣūṣ al-ḥikam*). Jāmī was also well versed in the Sufi literary genre and profoundly influenced by Rūmī's Sufi poetry, while being fully immersed in the philosophical gnosis of the School of Ibn ʿArabī. In fact, it appears that after 876/1471, he became increasingly influenced by Ibn ʿArabī and his vast corpus of writings. His work *Ashiʿʿat al-lamaʿāt* (The Flashes of Light), his commentary upon the *Lamaʿāt* of Fakhr al-Dīn ʿIrāqī and his own *Lawāʾiḥ* (Gleams) are clear indications of his preoccupation with the teachings of the Andalusian master.

Following the invasion of Herat by Sultan Ḥusayn Mīrzā, who had heard of Jāmī's rank as a scholar, Jāmī was invited to stay at the court where he received the attention and prominence he had deserved. Jāmī decided to make his pilgrimage to Mecca with a large number of companions. His journey, which took him through Nayshapūr, Sabzawār, Basṭām, Hamadān and Iraq, is significant in that during this journey he met with a number of learned scholars and Shiʿi gnostics, especially in Baghdad. While in Hamadān, Jāmī was given royal treatment by Manūchihr Shah, and later when he was in Baghdad he wrote the *Lawāʾiḥ* and dedicated it to the king. Jāmī, who had encountered much hostility from various Shiʿi communities in Baghdad and Najaf, returned to Tabriz where he met with Sayyid Aḥmad Lālih, a scholar of Ibn ʿArabī. Despite the insistence of Uzun Ḥasan, the Amir of Tabriz, that Jāmī stay there permanently, he did not agree and returned to Khurāsān. Jāmī's status as a courtier, however, increased when Amīr ʿAlīshīr Nawāʾī, the chamberlain, became his devotee and was initiated into the Naqshbandī Sufi order by him.

In 884/1479, Jāmī went to Samarqand for the third time to see Khwājah ʿUbayd Allāh Aḥrār. There the two men discussed Ibn ʿArabī's *al-Futūḥāt al-Makkiyyah* (Meccan Revelations). It was following his return to Herat that Jāmī produced a number of major works beginning with his collection of poems *Fātiḥat al-shabāb* (The Beginning of Youth), his second collection of poems *Wāsiṭat al-ʿiqd* (The Focal Point of Union), *Shawāhid al-nubuwwah* (Witnesses to Prophecy) and a poetic rendition of *Salāmān wa Absāl* which he dedicated to Sultan Āq-quyunlū. In the next two years, his poetic and intellectual genius brought to fruition such major works as *Ashi‘‘at al-lama‘āt* (The Flashes of Light), *Arba‘īn* (The Forty) and *Tuḥfat al-aḥrār* (Deliverance from Perplexity). In 886/1481, the Ottoman sultan Bāyazīd II invited Jāmī to visit him. Jāmī initially accepted but on his arrival in Hamadān he heard that plague had spread in the area and returned home. He composed *al-Durrah al-fākhirah* (The Precious Pearl), a comparative work on the ideas of theologians, philosophers and Sufis, regarding the meaning of existence and its related subjects, and dedicated it to the sultan.

Jāmī, who from 887/1482 to the end of his life remained in Herat, devoted himself to teaching and managing the affairs of Langar-khānah Nurā, a Sufi centre. Most of Jāmī's mystical poetry was written in the later period of his life. Two years after he completed his last work of poetry, ironically titled *Khātimat al-ḥayāt* (The End of Life), he died on a Friday during the month of Muḥarram 898/1492. It needs to be mentioned that besides being a major authority on gnosis and philosophical Sufism, Jāmī is considered to be one of the greatest poets of the Persian language with many famous lyrical poems and romances.

In this chapter we have included a section of Jāmī's *al-Durrah al-fākhirah* (The Precious Pearl). Jāmī himself describes this work in the introduction saying:

> This is a treatise dealing with the verification of the doctrine of the Sufis, the theologians and the early philosophers, and with the establishment of their beliefs concerning the existence of the Necessary Being in Himself, the realities of His Names and Attributes, the manner in which multiplicity emanates from His Unity without any impairment to the perfection of His sanctity and glory, and other subsequent inquiries prompted by thought and reason.

In treating these topics, Jāmī touches on a variety of other related subjects such as causality, and unity and multiplicity, and makes frequent references to major thinkers and schools. This treatise is important not only because of the nature of the philosophical arguments it presents, but also from a historical perspective.

M. Aminrazavi

THE PRECIOUS PEARL

al-Durrah al-fākhirah

Reprinted from Jāmī, *al-Durrah al-fākhirah*, together with his glosses and the commentary of ʿAbd al-Ghafūr Lārī, tr. Nicholas Heer as *The Precious Pearl* (Albany, NY, 1979), pp. 33–72.

In the Name of God, the Merciful, the Compassionate

1. Praise be to God, Who became manifest (*tajallā*) through His Essence (*bi-dhātihi*) to His Essence (*li-dhātihi*), so that the manifestations (*majālī*) of His Essence and of His Attributes became individuated (*taʿayyana*) in His inner knowledge, the effects (*āthār*) of these manifestations being then reflected upon His outward aspect (*ẓāhir*) from within (*al-bāṭin*), such that unity (*al-waḥdah*) became multiplicity (*kathrah*), as you see and behold. May God's blessing and peace be upon him through whom this multiplicity reverted to its original unity, and upon his family and companions, who have inherited of this virtue a large portion.

2. *To Proceed,* this is a treatise dealing with the verification of the doctrines of the Sufis, the theologians, and the early philosophers, and with the establishment of their beliefs concerning the existence of the Necessary Existent in Himself (*al-wājib li-dhātihi*), the realities (*ḥaqāʾiq*)[1] of His names and attributes, the manner in which multiplicity emanates from His unity without any impairment (*naqṣ*) to the perfection of His sanctity and glory, and other subsequent inquiries (*mabāḥith*) prompted by thought (*al-fikr*) and reason (*al-naẓar*). It is hoped that God will permit every unbiased seeker to benefit from this treatise and that He will protect it from every unthinking bigot, for He is sufficient for me and an excellent guardian.

3. *Preface.* Know that there is in existence a necessary existent (*wājib*), for otherwise that which exists (*al-mawjūd*) would be restricted to contingent being (*al-mumkin*), and consequently nothing would exist at all. This is because contingent being, even though multiple (*mutaʿaddid*), is not self-sufficient (*lā yastaqill*) with respect to its existence, as is obvious, nor with respect to bringing another into existence, since the stage of bringing-into-existence (*martabat al-ījād*) is consequent to that of existence.[2] Thus, if there is neither existence nor bringing-into-existence, there can be nothing that exists, either through itself or through another. Thus the existence of the Necessary Existent (*al-wājib*) is proven.

---

1. *Ḥaqīqah* is the term used for a quiddity (*māhiyyah*) which has external existence. See al-Jurjānī, *al-Taʿrīfāt,* under *al-māhiyyah*; Aḥmadnagarī, *Dastūr al-ʿulamāʾ*, III, 192, under *al-māhiyyah,* and III, 283, under *al-maʿnā.*

2. For this premise, see, for example, Jurjānī, *Sharḥ al-mawāqif,* II, 140–141. Jāmī's argument here appears to be taken from *Sharḥ al-mawāqif,* VIII, 12.

4. The apparent position (*madhhab*) of both Shaykh Abu'l-Ḥasan al-Ash'arī[1] and Shaykh Abu'l-Ḥusayn al-Baṣrī[2] of the Mu'tazilites is that the existence of the Necessary Existent (*al-wājib*) indeed the existence of everything, is identical with its essence (*dhāt*) both in the mind (*dhihnan*) and externally (*khārijan*). This implies that existence is common (*ishtirāk*) to proper existences (*al-wujūdāt al-khāṣṣah*)[3] in name only (*lafẓan*) rather than in meaning (*ma'nan*), and this is obviously false, because, as has been explained elsewhere in works dealing with this subject, belief concerning [the existence of] something in an absolute sense endures even though belief as to its particular characteristic (*khuṣūṣiyyah*) ceases, and because [existence] is subject to division in meaning (*al-taqsīm al-ma'nawī*).[4] Some people, therefore, did not interpret their position literally, but claimed that what they meant by identity (*al-'ayniyyah*) was indistinguishability in the external world, that is, that there is not in the external world something which is the quiddity (*al-māhiyyah*) and something else subsisting in it (*qā'im bihā*) externally which is existence, as one who follows their proofs understands.

5. The majority of the theologians (*jumhūr al-mutakallimīn*) took the position that existence is a single concept (*mafhūm wāḥid*) common to all existences, and that this single concept becomes multiple and is divided into portions (*ḥiṣṣah*) through its attribution to things (*al-ashyā'*), as, for example, the whiteness of this snow [as distinguished from the whiteness of] that snow. The existences of things are these portions, and these portions along with that concept (*al-mafhūm*) intrinsic to them (*al-dākhil fīhā*) are external (*khārijah*) to the essences of things and only mentally superadded to them (*zā'idah 'alayhā*) in the view of their verifiers (*muḥaqqiqīhim*),[5] and both mentally and externally in the view of others.

6. The gist (*ḥāṣil*) of the position of the philosophers[6] is that existence is a single concept common to all [proper] existences. These [proper] existences, however, are dissimilar realities which are multiple in themselves not merely through the accident of attribution (*'āriḍ al-iḍāfah*), for in that case they would be similar to each other (*mutamāthilah*) and agree in reality, though not through

---

1. See Fuat Sezgin, *Geschichte des arabsichen*, 602. *Schriftums*, I, 602.

2. See Sezgin, *Geschicte*, I, 627.

3. *al-Wujūdāt al-khāṣṣah* are the existence of particular individual things. See Amélie Marie Goichon, *Lexique de la langue philosophique d'Ibn Sīnā*, 419; and Ibn Sīnā, *al-Shifā', al-Ilāhiyyāt*, 31.

4. That is, it can be divided, for example, into necessary and contingent existence and the latter can be further divided into substantial and accidental existence. See Aḥamadnagarī, *Dastūr al-'ulamā'*, I, 333, under *al-taqsīm*. For this and other arguments that existence is common in meaning to proper existences, see Taftāzānī, *Sharḥ al-maqāṣid*, I, 46; and Jurjānī, *Sharḥ al-mawāqif*, II, 112–127.

5. The *muḥaqqiq* is the scholar who establishes a thesis by using proofs (*dalā'il*). See Jurjānī, *al-Ta'rīfāt*, under *al-taḥqīq*; al-Aḥmadnagarī, *Dastūr al-'ulamā'*, III, 228, under *al-muḥaqqiq;* al-Tahānawī, *Kashshshāf*, 336, under *al-taḥqīq*.

6. This paragraph is derived almost entirely from Taftāzānī, *Sharḥ al-maqāṣid*, I, 53–54.

specific differences (*al-fuṣūl*), for in that case Absolute Existence (*al-wujūd al-muṭlaq*) would be their genus (*jins*). On the contrary, existence is an accident concomitant with them (*ʿāriḍ lāzim lahā*) like the light of the sun and the light of a lamp. Although both the sun and lamp differ in reality (*al-ḥaqīqah*) and in concomitants (*al-lawāzim*), they, nevertheless, have in common the accident of light. Similar to this are the whiteness of snow and the whiteness of ivory, or quantity and quality, which have in common accidentality (*al-ʿaraḍiyyah*), or even substance and accident, which have contingency (*al-imkān*) and existence in common. However, since each [proper] existence does not have its own name, as is the case with the divisions of contingent being (*aqsām al-mumkin*) or the divisions of accident (*aqsām al-ʿaraḍ*), it was imagined that the multiplicity (*takaththur*) of existences and their division into portions was due entirely to their attribution to the quiddities which are their substrata, like the whiteness of this snow and [the whiteness] of that, or the light of this lamp and [the light] of that. Such, however, is not the case. On the contrary, they are different and dissimilar realities subsumed under this concept which inheres [in them] but is external to them. When one considers that this concept becomes multiple and is divided into portions through its attribution to quiddities, then [one realizes] that these portions also are external to those existences with dissimilar realities (*al-wujūdāt al-mukhtalifat al-ḥaqāʾiq*).

7. Three things are thus [involved]: the concept of existence (*mafhūm al-wujūd*), its portions individuated through its attribution to quiddities, and the proper existences with dissimilar realities (*al-wujūdāt al-khāṣṣah al-mukhtalifat al-ḥaqāʾiq*). The concept of existence is essential (*dhātī*) and intrinsic to (*dākhil fī*) its portions, but both are external to (*khārij ʿan*) proper existences. Proper existence is identical with the essence in the case of the Necessary Existent (*al-wājib*), but superadded (*zāʾid*) and external (*khārij*) in the case of everything else.

8. *Ramification.* If you have understood this, we say further:[1] Just as it is possible for this general concept (*al-mafhūm al-ʿāmm*) to be superadded to Necessary Existence (*al-Wujūd al-Wājib*) and to contingent proper existences, on the assumption that the latter are dissimilar realities, it is also possible for it to be superadded to a single absolute and existent reality (*ḥaqīqah wāḥidah muṭlaqah mawjūdah*) which is the reality of Necessary Existence (*ḥaqīqat al-Wūjud al-Wājib*) as is the position taken by the Sufis who hold the doctrine of the unity of existence (*waḥdat al-wujūd*). This superadded concept would then be a mental entity (*amr iʿtibārī*)[2]

1. This paragraph is identical with paragraph 10 of Jāmī's *Risālah fi'l-wujūd.* See 'Jāmī's 'Treatise on Existence', in Parviz Morewedge, ed., *Islamic Philosophical Theology* (Albany, NY, 1979), pp. 223–256.

2. That is, an entity that exists only in the mind of the person considering it and during the time he is considering it. See Jurjānī, *al-Taʿrīfāt,* under *al-amr al-iʿtibārī;* Aḥmadnagarī, *Dastūr al-ʿulamāʾ,* I, 187, under *al-amr al-iʿtibārī,* and III, 193, under *al-māhiyyah;* al-Tahānawī, *Kashshāf,* p. 72, under *al-umūr al-iʿtibāriyyah.* Izutzu and Mohaghegh in their edition of Hādī Sabziwārī's *Sharḥ ghurar al-farāʾid* translate *iʿtibārī* as mentally posited. See pp. 65–66, 71 of Izutsu's English

existing only in the intellect (*al-ʿaql*), and its substratum (*maʿrūḍ*) would be an external and real existent (*mawjūd ḥaqīqī khārijī*) which is the reality of existence.

9. Furthermore,[1] that existence is predicated by analogy (*al-tashkīk al-wāqiʿ fīhi*) does not indicate that it is an accident with respect to its singulars (*afrād*), for no proof has been adduced to show that it is impossible for quiddities and essential attributes (*al-dhātiyyāt*) to differ by analogousness (*bi'l-tashkīk*).[2] The strongest argument they have mentioned is that if a quiddity or an essential attribute differs in its particulars (*al-juz'iyyāt*), then neither the quiddity nor the essential attribute is one. This [argument], however, is refuted (*manqūḍ*)[3] by the

---

introduction, 'The Fundamental Structure of Sabzawārī's Metaphysics'.

1. This paragraph is apparently derived from Qūshjī, *Sharḥ al-tajrīd*, 10; and Jurjānī, *Ḥāshiyat sharḥ al-tajrīd*, fols. 17a–17b.

2. Concepts which differ in their particulars with respect to superiority (*awlawiyyah*) or lack of it, priority (*taqaddum*) or posteriority (*ta'ahkhur*), or strength (*shiddah*) or weakness (*ḍaʿf*) were said to be predicated analogically (*bi'l-tashkīk*) or their particulars rather than univocally. See Quṭb al-Dīn Rāzī, *Taḥrīr al-qawāʿid al-manṭiqiyyah*, I, 210–213; and Jurjānī, *al-Taʿrīfāt*, under *al-tashkīk*. It was commonly argued that since essential concepts did not differ in their particulars, only accidental concepts could be predicated analogically. See Naṣīr al-Dīn Ṭūsī, *Sharḥ al-ishārāt*, 203; and Quṭb al-Dīn Rāzī, *al-Muḥākamāt*, 281.

3. According to works on the art of disputation (*ādāb al-baḥth*) such as Ījī's *Ādāb al-baḥth*, Ṭāshkubrāzādah's *Ādāb al-baḥth wa'l-munāẓarah*, and Sāchuqlīzādah's *al-Risālah al-waladiyyah*, objection to a thesis may take one of the following three forms:

1. *Manʿ*, or denial (also called *naqḍ tafṣīlī*, or particular refutation), in which the objector denies one of the premises in the defender's proof of his thesis.

2. *Muʿāraḍah*, or opposition, in which the objector offers a proof for a proposition incompatible with the defender's thesis.

3. *Naqḍ*, or refutation (also known as *naqḍ ijmālī*, or general refutation), in which the objector finds fault with the proof as a whole. He does this by showing either 1) that its conclusion leads to an impossibility, such as a circle or an endless chain, or 2) that the same proof can be used to demonstrate a proposition known to be false.

The present case is an example of this second type of *naqḍ*. The defender has argued as follows:

All quiddities (essential attributes) are one.
No things which differ in their particulars are one.
Therefore, no things which differ in their particular are quiddities (essential attributes).

The objector can apply this same proof to accidents and argue as follows:

All accidents are one.
No things which differ in their particulars are one.
Therefore, no things which differ in their particulars are accidents.

This conclusion contradicts what is known about accidents, namely, that they do, in fact, differ in their particulars. Consequently one of the premises of the proof must be false. Since the truth of the major premise is admitted by both defender and objector, the minor premise, namely that no things which differ in their particulars are one, must be false. Since the defender's proof also contains this premise, his proof is thereby shown to be defective.

In his *al-Risālah al-waladiyyah*, 125–127, Sāchuqlīzādah gives a similar example of this type of

case of the accident. Also, a difference in completeness or incompleteness in the same quiddity, such as a cubit or two cubits of measure does not imply a difference in the quiddity itself.

10. Al-Shaykh Ṣadr al-Dīn al-Qūnawī said in his *al-Risālah al-hādiyah:*[1] If a reality differs 'by being more powerful (*aqwā*), prior (*aqdam*), stronger (*ashadd*), or superior (*awlā*) in something, all of that is due, in the opinion of the verifier (*al-muḥaqqiq*), to its manifestation (*al-ẓuhūr*) rather than to any multiplicity (*ta'addud*) occurring in the reality [itself] which is becoming manifest. [This is so] regardless of whether that reality is one of knowledge, of [real] existence, or of something else. There is, thus, a recipient (*qābil*) predisposed for the manifestation (*ẓuhūr*) of the reality such that the reality is more complete in its manifestation in one recipient than it is in its manifestation in another, even though the reality [itself] is one in all [recipients]. The inequality (*al-mufāḍalah*) and dissimilarity (*al-tafāwut*) occurs between its manifestations in accordance with the command causing its manifestation (*al-amr al-muẓhir*) and requiring an individuation[2] in some other matter. There is, thus, no multiplicity (*ta'addud*) in the reality as such, nor is there any division (*tajziyah*) or partition (*tab'īḍ*). What has been said to the

---

naqḍ. The defender, a philosopher, gives the following proof for the eternity of the world:

All things that are effects of an eternal being are eternal.
The world is an effect of an eternal being.
Therefore, the world is eternal.

The objector, applying the same proof to daily events, then argues:

All things that are effects of an eternal being are eternal.
Daily events are effects of an eternal being.
Therefore, daily events are eternal.

This conclusion is obviously false, and, since the truth of the minor premise is not in dispute, the major premise, which is the same in both proofs, must be false.

1. See MS Wetzstein II 1806, fol. 57b; MS Vat Arab. 1453, fol. 38a–38b. *Al-Risālah al-hādiyah* was written in answer to the *Risālah* of Naṣīr al-Dīn Ṭūsī which in turn was written in answer to the questions put to Ṭūsī by Qūnawī in his *Risālat al-mufṣiḥah*. The passage quoted here is in answer to Ṭūsī's argument that since existence is predicated analogically rather than univocally it cannot be a single reality but is, on the contrary, many different realities. Concepts which are also predicated analogically, according to Ṭūsī, are light and knowledge. If light were a single reality, all types of light would be equally brilliant and would cause the cessation of night blindness. In fact, however, only sunlight is brilliant enough to do this. Likewise if knowledge were a single reality, human and divine knowledge would be the same, and human knowledge would cause the existence of the thing known just as God's knowledge does. See Naṣīr al-Dīn Ṭūsī, *Risālat*, MS Wetzstein II 1806, fol. 36a–36b; MS Warner Or. 1133, fols. 26a–27a; MS Vat. Arab. 1453, fol. 17a–17b.

2. All the manuscripts of *al-Durrah al-fākhirah* as well as the two manuscripts available of *al-Risālah al-hādiyah* read *ta'ayyunuhu*, whereas *ta'ayyunuhā*, with *hā* referring to the feminine *ḥaqīqah*, would be expected.

effect that if light and knowledge necessitated [respectively] the cessation of night-blindness (*al-ʿashā*) and the existence of something known, then every light and knowledge would do the same, is true, as long as one does not mean by this that there is any difference in the reality.'

11. Moreover, the basis (*mustanad*) of the position taken by the Sufis is mystical revelation and insight (*al-kashf wa'l-aʿyān*) rather than reason and demonstration (*al-naẓar wa'l-burhān*). For indeed, since they have turned towards God in complete spiritual nudity (*al-taʿriyah al-kāmilah*) by wholly emptying their hearts of all worldly attachments (*al-taʿalluqāt al-kawniyyah*) and the rules of rational thought (*al-qawānīn al-ʿilmiyyah*), and by unifying the will (*tawaḥḥud al-ʿazīmah*), persisting in concentration (*dawām al-jamʿiyyah*), and preserving along this path without slackening, interruption of thought (*taqsīm khāṭir*) or dissolution of will (*tashattut al-ʿazīmah*), God has granted to them a revealing light (*nūr kāshif*) to show them things as they really are.[1] This light appears within at the appearance of a level beyond the level of the intellect (*ṭawr warāʾ ṭawr al-ʿaql*). Do not think the existence of that improbable, for beyond the intellect are many levels whose number is hardly known except by God.

12. The relation of the intellect to this light is the same as the relation of the estimation (*al-wahm*) to the intellect. And just as it is possible for the intellect to judge something to be true which cannot be apprehended by the estimation, such as the existence of a being (*mawjūd*), for example, which is neither within the world nor outside it,[2] so also can that revealing light judge to be true certain things which cannot be apprehended by the intellect, such as the existence of an all-encompassing and absolute reality (*ḥaqīqah muṭlaqah muḥīṭah*) unlimited by any determination (*taqayyud*) and unrestricted by any individuation (*taʿayyun*), although the existence of such a reality is not [a proposition] of this sort, for many of the philosophers and theologians have taken the position that natural universals (*al-kullī al-ṭabīʿī*)[3] exist in the external world. Moreover, all those who have

---

1. The preceding part of this paragraph has been summarized from pages 21 and 34 of Qūnawī's *Iʿjāz al-bayān*. The remaining sentences of the paragraph are quoted from ʿAyn al-Quḍāt al-Hamadānī, *Zubdat al-ḥaqāʾiq*, 26–27.

2. On the false judgments of the estimation, see Ibn Sīnā, *al-Shifāʾ*, *al-Manṭiq*, *al-Burhān*, 64–65; also Jurjānī, *Sharḥ al-mawāqif*, II, 41–42; Kātibī, *al-Risālah al-shamsiyyah*, 28 of Arabic text, 35 of translation; and Quṭb al-Dīn Rāzī, *Taḥrīr al-qawāʿid al-manṭiqiyyah*, II, 248–249.

Judgments of the estimation (*al-wahmiyyāt*) made, however, with respect to sensibles (*al-maḥsūsāt*) were considered to be true and were sometimes included among the premises on which demonstration was based. See Jurjānī, *Sharḥ al-mawāqif*, II, 41–42; and Taftāzānī, *Sharḥ al-risālah al-shamsiyyah*, 185.

3. The natural universal (*al-kullī al-ṭabīʿī*) was usually defined as the nature (*al-ṭabīʿah*) or quiddity (*al-māhiyyah*) as it is in itself (*min ḥaythu hiya hiya*), absolute and unconditioned by anything (*lā bi-sharṭ shayʾ*), whether universality, particularity, existence, non-existence, or anything else. It was distinguished from two other universals, the mental universal (*al-kullī al-ʿaqlī*), which is the nature insofar as it is a universal, that is, the nature conditioned by universality (*bi-sharṭ*

undertaken to prove the impossibility [of this proposition] have used premises which are not free from suspicion of being defective. The intention here, however, is merely to eliminate from this position (*al-masʾalah*) any logical impossibility along with the usual reasons for thinking it improbable, not to establish it with proofs and demonstrations. Indeed, those who have studied this proposition, either to verify or support it or to invalidate or impair it, have been able to produce only insufficient proofs and demonstrations of it or to point out uncertainties (*shukūk*) and raise weak and unfounded objections (*shubah*) against it.

13. One of the proofs for the impossibility of the [external] existence of natural universals is that given by al-Muḥaqqiq al-Ṭūsī in his *Risālah* written in answer to the questions asked him by al-Shaykh Ṣadr al-Dīn al-Qūnawī.[1] He argues that 'a concrete thing (*al-shayʾ al-ʿaynī*) does not subsist in (*lā yaqaʿ ʿalā*) numerous things, because if it were in each of those things, it would not be one concrete thing (*shayʾ bi-ʿaynihi*) but rather [many] things. Alternatively, if it were in the whole [of them] insofar as [they are] a whole (*min ḥaythu huwa kull*), the whole constituting in this respect a single thing, then it would not subsist in [numerous] things. If, on the other hand, it were in the whole in the sense of being divided among its units (*āḥād*), then there would be in each unit only a part of that thing. Thus, if it is neither in the units nor in the whole, it does not subsist in them.'

14. Al-Mawlā al-ʿAllāmah Shams al-Dīn al-Fanārī answered him in his commentary on *Miftāḥ al-ghayb*.[2] Choosing the first alternative (*al-shiqq al-awwal*)[3] [for refutation] he said: 'The meaning of the realization (*taḥaqquq*) of a universal reality (*al-ḥaqīqah al-kulliyah*) in its individuals (*afrād*) is its realization at one time qualified by this determination (*al-taʿayyun*) and at another by that individuation. This does not necessitate its being many things, just as the transformation

---

lā-shayʾ), and the logical universal (*al-kullī al-manṭiqī*), which is the concept of universality itself. See Ibn Sīnā, *al-Shifāʾ, al-Manṭiq, al-Madkhal*, 65–72; al-Kātibī, *al-Risālah al-shamsiyyah*, 6 of the Arabic text, 11 of the English translation; Quṭb al-Dīn Rāzī, *Taḥrīr al-qawāʿid al-manṭiqiyyah*, I, 289–292; and *Lawāmiʿ al-asrār*, 53–54.

In general the position of the philosophers was that natural universals existed externally, whereas that of the theologians was that they existed only in the mind. For the position of the philosophers, see Ibn Sīnā, *al-Shifāʾ, al-Ilāhiyyāt*, 202–212; Sufis, *Sharḥ al-ishārāt*, 192–193; al-Kātibī, *al-Risālah al-shamsiyyah*, 6 of the Arabic text, 11 of the English translation; al-Urmawī, *Maṭāliʿ al-anwār*, 53. For that of the theologians, see Quṭb al-Dīn Rāzī, *Risālah taḥqīq al-kulliyyāt;* and *lawāmiʿ al asrār*, 53–56; Taftāzānī, *Sharḥ al-risālah al-shamsiyyah*, 46–47; and Jurjanı, *Ḥāshiyah ʿalā sharḥ al-maṭāliʿ*, 134–138. A summary of the objections which can be raised against the position of the philosophers on this question is given in Kāshif al-Ghiṭāʾ, *Naqd al-ārāʾ al-manṭiqiyyah*, 195–207.

1. This is the *Risālat* written in answer to the questions contained in al-Qūnawī's *al-Risālah al-mufṣiḥah*. See MS Wetzstein II 1806, fol. 39a–39b; MS Warner Or. 1133. fols. 30b–31a; and MS Vat. Arab. 1453, fol. 20a.

2. See al-Fanārī, *Miṣbāḥ al-uns*, 35.

3. That is, if the universal subsisted in each one of a number of things, it would not be one concrete thing but many things.

(*taḥawwul*) of a single individual into different (*mukhtalifah*) or even completely distinct (*mutabāyinah*)[1] states does not necessitate its being [many] individuals.' He then said: 'Should you say: How can what is one in essence (*al-wāḥid bi'l-dhāt*) be described by contrary qualities (*al-awṣāf al-mutaḍāddah*) like easternness and westernness, or knowledge or ignorance, and so forth? I should answer: You think this improbable because you make universals analogous to particulars and the invisible world (*al-ghā'ib*) analogous to the visible world (*al-shāhid*). There is no proof for the impossibility of this with respect to universals.'

15. Another [proof] is that of Mawlā Quṭb al-Dīn Rāzī,[2] which states that numerous realities such as genus, difference, and species, are all realized in one singular (*fard*). If they existed [externally], however, predication between them would be impossible because of the impossibility of predication between multiple [external] existents (*mawjūdāt muta'addidah*).

16. 'Allāmah Fanārī[3] answered him saying that 'it is possible for numerous related realities (*ḥaqā'iq mutanāsibah*) to exist through a single existence which includes them as such, just as fatherhood subsists in the sum total of the parts of the father as a whole.' The lack of multiple existences (*'adam al-wujūdāt al-muta'addidah*) does not imply the lack of existence absolutely. Indeed they explicitly state that the creation (*ja'l*) of the genus, the difference, and the species is one.[4]

17. As for the proofs for the existence of natural universals in general, they are not such as to be useful [in proving] this thesis (*al-maṭlūb*) to the point of certainty but only to the point of probability, although they are mentioned in the well-known works [dealing with this subject] together with the objections raised against them. We have, therefore, avoided taking up these proofs and shall concern ourselves only with what serves to prove this thesis itself.

18. We say, therefore, that there is no doubt that the Source of Existents (*Mabda' al-mawjūdāt*) exists, and that his source can be either the reality of existence

---

1. Two universals are said to be *mutabāyin* if neither of them is true of what the other is true of. For example, no horse is a human and no human is a horse. They are said to be *mutasāwī* (coextensive) if each is true of what the other is true of. For example, every human is rational and every rational being is human. Finally one universal can be more general (*'āmm*) or more specific (*akhaṣṣ*) than the other. For example, all humans are animals but not all animals are humans. See Kātibī, *al-Risālah al-shamsiyyah*, 6 of the Arabic text, 11 of the English translation; Quṭb al-Dīn Rāzī, *Taḥrīr al-qawā'id al-manṭiqiyyah,* I, 294–298; al-Aḥmadnagarī, *Dastūr al-'ulamā',* I, 270, under *al-tabāyun*, I, 291, under *al-tasāwī*.

2. Jāmī is still quoting here from al-Fanārī's *Miṣbāḥ al-uns,* 35. For Rāzī's arguments against the existence of natural universals, see his *Lawāmi' al-asrār,* 54–56; and his *Risālat taḥqīq al-kulliyyāt,* MS Warner Or. 958 (21), especially fols. 68b-69a.

3. See his *Miṣbāḥ al-uns,* 35.

4. That is, that the genus and the difference are created through the creation of the individual of the species and not through separate creations. All three therefore exist through the one existence of the individual. In commenting on this sentence Muḥammad Ma'ṣūm refers to Naṣīr al-Dīn Ṭūsī's *Tajrīd al-'aqā'id* and the commentaries on it. See *al-Farīdah al-nādirah,* fol. 66b; as well as Ḥillī, *Kashf al-murād,* 45; and al-Qūshjī, *Sharḥ al-tajrīd,* 108.

(*ḥaqīqat al-wujūd*) or something else. It cannot, however, be something else, since everything except existence is in need of another, namely existence, in order to exist, and to be in need is inconsistent with necessary existence (*al-wujūb*). Therefore, this source must be the reality of existence. Moreover, if it is absolute (*muṭlaq*), then the thesis (*al-maṭlūb*) is proven. If, on the other hand, it is individuated (*muta'ayyin*), then it is impossible for its individuation to be intrinsic to it (*dākhil fīhi*), for otherwise the Necessary Existent is a simple entity which is existence, and that its individuation is an attribute inhering [in it].

19. Should you ask: Why is it not possible for its individuation to be identical with it? I should answer: If by individuation you mean that through which it is individuated, then it is possible for it to be identical with it. However, this does not harm our position, because if that through which it is individuated is its essence, then it cannot in itself be individuated, otherwise an endless chain would result. On the other hand, if what is meant is the individuation (*al-tashakhkhuṣ*) itself, then this cannot be identical with its essence, because it is one of the second intelligibles (*al-ma'qūlāt al-thāniyah*),[1] to which nothing corresponds in the external world.

20. It is evident to anyone familiar with the doctrines promulgated in their books that what is related of their revelations (*mukāshafāt*) and visions (*mushāhadāt*) attests only to the affirmation of the existence of an absolute essence (*dhāt muṭlaqah*) encompassing the intellectual and concrete planes (*al-marātib al-'aqliyyah wa'l-'ayniyyah*) and expanding over both mental and external existents, but having no individuation which prevents it from appearing in other individuations whether divine or created. Thus, it is not impossible to affirm of it an individuation which is consistent with (*yujāmi'*) all individuations and is not inconsistent with (*lā yunāfī*) any of them, which is identical with its essence and not superadded to it either in the mind or externally, and which the intellect, should it conceive of it in a certain individuation, would be unable to imagine as being common (*mushtarak*) to many in the same way that universals are common to their particulars, but would be able to conceive of as being transformed into or as appearing in numerous forms (*al-ṣuwar al-kathīrah*) and infinite manifestations (*al-maẓāhir al-ghayr al-mutanāhiyah*), both cognitively and concretely (*'ilman wa-'aynan*) and in the invisible world as well as the visible (*ghayban wa-shahādatan*), in accordance with various relations (*al-nisab al-mukhtalifah*) and different aspects (*al-i'tibārāt al-mutaghāyirah*).[2]

---

1. Second intelligibles or second intentions are universals which can only be predicated of other universals as they exist in the mind. First intelligibles, on the other hand, are universals which can be predicated of individuals existing outside the mind. For example, the universal concept human is a first intelligible which can be predicated of each individual human existing in the external world. The universal concept species, however, can only be predicated of other universal concepts, such as human, as they exist in the mind. It is therefore a second intelligible with no individuals existing outside the mind. See Aḥmadnagarī, *Dastūr al-'ulamā'*, III, 290, under *al-ma'qūlāt al-thāniyah;* and Taftāzānī, *Sharḥ al-maqāṣid,* I, 56.

2. According to Jāmī, God's Names and Attributes are relations (*nisab*), aspects (*i'tibārāt*), or

21. Consider this by analogy with the rational soul (*al-nafs al-nāṭiqah*), which pervades the parts of the body and their external senses and internal faculties (*quwāhā al-bāṭinah*); or even better (*bal*) by analogy with the perfectional rational soul (*al-nafs al-nāṭiqah al-kamāliyyah*), which, if realized (*taḥaqqaqat*) as a manifestation of the comprehensive Name (*maẓhariyyat al-ism al-jāmiʿ*),[1] is spiritualized (*kān al-tarawḥunna*)[2] of some of its concomitant realities (*ḥaqāʾiqihā al-lāzimah*) and appears in numerous forms without determination (*taqayyud*) or limitation (*inḥiṣār*), all of which can be predicated of it and of each other because of the unity of its individual essence (*ʿayn*) just as it becomes many because of the variation of its forms.

22. For this reason it was said of Idrīs that he was Ilyās sent to Baalbek,[3] not in the sense that his individual essence (*al-ʿayn*) shed the Idrīsid form (*al-ṣūrat al-idrīsiyyah*) and put on the Ilyāsid form, since this would be a profession of metempsychosis (*al-tanāsukh*), but rather in the sense that the ipseity (*huwiyyah*)[4] of Idrīs, while subsisting in his individual existence (*inniyyah*)[5] and form (*ṣūrah*) in

---

attributions (*iḍāfāt*) connecting His Essence with the objects of His knowledge, will, power, etc. See paras. 28, 29 (and 39) and glosses 22 (and 33) as well as Larī's commentary on para. 28.

1. *al-Ism al-jāmiʿ*, also known as *al-ism al-aʿẓam*, is a term for the Name *Allāh*, since this name is said to comprehend all of God's Names and Attributes. See *Sharḥ al-durrah al-fākhirah*, fol. 105a; Ḥusaynābādī, *al-Risālah al-qudsiyyah*, fol. 102b; Kāshānī, *Iṣṭilāḥāt*, 89, under *al-ism al-aʿẓam;* and Jurjānī, *al-Taʿrīfāt*, under *al-ism al-aʿẓam*.

2. *al-Tarawḥun* is apparently derived from *rūḥānī*. In *Sharḥ al-durrah al-fākhirah*, *al-tarawḥun* is defined as sanctification and shedding or casting off [of bodily attributes] (*al-taqaddus wa'l-insilākh*). See fol. 105a. See also Dozy, *Supplément*, I, 568, under *rawḥana*. Jāmī also uses this term in his commentary on the 22nd *faṣṣ* of Ibn ʿArabī's *Fuṣūṣ al-ḥikam*. See his *Sharḥ fuṣūṣ al-ḥikam*, II, 266.

3. Idrīs and Ilyās are each mentioned twice in the Qur'ān without, however, being identified with each other. See Qur'ān 19:56 and 21:85 for Idrīs and 6: 85 and 37:123–130 for Ilyās. For their identity with each other and other pertinent information, see A. J. Wensinck, 'Idrīs' and 'Ilyās' in Gibb, *Shorter Encyclopedia of Islam*, 158–159, 164–165; as well as Ṭabarī, *Jāmiʿ al-bayān*, VII, 172; XVI, 72; XVII, 58, XXIII, 60; and Ibn ʿArabī, *Fuṣūṣ al-ḥikam*, I, 181; II, 257.

4. *Huwiyyah*, which has been translated here as ipseity, is commonly defined as the particular reality (*al-ḥaqīqah al-juzʾiyyah*) or particular quiddity (*al-māhiyyah al-juzʾiyyah*), that is, the individuated quiddity as opposed to the universal quiddity. The word is sometimes used, however, to mean existence. See Jurjānī, *al-Taʿrīfāt*, under *al-māhiyyah;* Aḥmadnagarī, *Dastūr al-ʿulamā'*, III, 283, under *al-maʿnā*, and III, 478, under *al-huwiyyah*. For the origin of the word, see Fārābī, *Kitāb al-Ḥurūf*, 112–113.

5. *Inniyyah (anniyyah, āniyyah)* is translated here as individual existence in accordance with the definition given by Kāshānī in his *Iṣṭilāḥāt al-ṣūfiyyah*, 91. Almost identical definitions are given by Jurjānī, *al-Taʿrīfāt*, under *al-āniyyah*, and Aḥmadnagarī, *Dastūr al-ʿulamā'*, I, 197. Much has been written on the origin and meaning of this term. See, for example, Simon van den Bergh, 'Annīyah' in *The Encyclopedia of Islam*, New Edition, I, 513–514; Fārābī, *Kitāb al-Ḥurūf*, 61, *Kitāb al-Alfāẓ*, 45; Soheil M. Afnan, *Philosophical Lexicon*, 12–13; Goichon, *Lexique*, 9–12; Richard M. Frank, 'The Origin of the Arabic Philosophical Term *Annīyah*', in *Cahiers de Byrsa* 6 (1956): 181–201; and Marie-Thérèse d'Alverny, 'Anniyya-Anitas' in *Mélanges offerts à Étienne Gilson* (Paris-Toronto 1959), 59–91.

the fourth heaven, nevertheless appeared and became individuated (*taʿayyanat*) in the individual existence of Ilyās, who remains to this time. Thus the ipseity of Idrīs with respect to his individual essence (*al-ʿayn*) and reality (*al-ḥaqīqah*) is one, but with respect to formal individuation (*al-taʿayyun al-ṣūrī*) is two. In like manner Jibra'īl, Mīkā'īl, and 'Izrā'īl appear at one and the same time in 100,000 places in different forms, all of which subsist in them.

23. Similar to this are the spirits of the perfect (*arwāḥ al-kummal*). For example, it is related of Qaḍīb al-Bān al-Mawṣilī[1] that he was seen at one and the same time in numerous gatherings, in each of which he was occupied with a different matter. And since the estimations (*awhām*) of those immersed in time and place could not understand this account, they received it with opposition and resistance and judged it false and erroneous. Those, on the other hand, who had been granted success in escaping from this predicament (*al-maḍīq*), seeing him exalted above time and place, realized that the relation of all times and places to him was one and the same; and they thus believed it possible for him to appear in every time and every place, for any matter he wished, and in any form he desired.

24. *Analogy.* If a single particular form (*ṣūrah wāḥidah juz'iyyah*) is impressed (*inṭabaʿat*) in many mirrors which differ with respect to being large or small, long or short, flat, convex or concave, and so forth, then there can be no doubt that this form multiplies (*yatakaththar*) in accordance with the multiplicity of the mirrors, and that its impressions differ in accordance with the differences in the mirrors. Furthermore, this multiplicity [of impressions] does not impair the unity of the [original] form, nor does the appearance [of the form] in any one of these mirrors preclude it from appearing in the others. The True One (*al-Wāḥid al-Ḥaqq*), 'and God's is the loftiest likeness',[2] is thus analogous to the many mirrors with their differing predispositions (*istiʿdādāt*). God appears in each and every individual essence (*ʿayn*) in accordance with that essence, without any multiplicity (*takaththur*) or change (*taghayyur*) occurring in His holy Essence. Moreover, His appearing in accordance with the characteristics (*aḥkām*) of any one of these individual essences does not prevent Him from appearing also in accordance with the characteristics of the others, as you have learned from the foregoing analogy.

25. *On His Unity* (*waḥdah*). Inasmuch as the Necessary Existent (*al-Wājib*), in the opinion of the majority of theologians, is a reality (*ḥaqīqah*) existing through a proper existence, they all found it necessary, in order to prove His unicity

1. An associate of 'Abd al-Qādir Jīlānī, he died in 570 AH. See Jāmī, *Nafaḥāt al-uns*, 524–525 of Tehran edition; al-Tādhifī, *Qalā'id al-jawāhir*, pp. 118–120; al-Munāwī, *al-Kawākib al-durriyyah*, fol. 207a–207b; and particularly al-Nabhānī, *Jāmiʿ karāmāt al-awliyā'*, II, 23–31, which reproduces the *fatwā* of al-Suyūṭī entitled *al-Munjalī fī taṭawwur al-walī* (Brockelmann, *Geschicte*, II, 201, Supplement, II, 188, 195) on the question of whether a *walī* can be in two places at once.

2. Qur'ān, 16:60. The translation of this as well as the other Qur'ānic citations appearing in the texts is based on that of Mohammed Marmaduke Pickthall in *The Meaning of the Glorious Koran* (New York, 1953).

(*waḥdāniyyah*) and deny a partner to Him, to make use of proofs and demonstrations, which they have provided in their works. The Sufis who profess the unity of existence (*waḥdat al-wujūd*), however, since it was evident to them that the reality of the Necessary Existent (*ḥaqīqat al-Wājib*) is absolute existence (*al-wujūd al-muṭlaq*), did not find it necessary to put forward a proof for the assertion of His unity and the denial of a partner to Him. In fact, it is impossible to imagine in Him any duality (*ithnayniyyah*) and multiplicity (*taʿaddud*) without considering individuation (*taʿayyun*) and determination (*taqayyud*) to be in Him also. For everything multiple, whether seen, imagined or apprehended, is either an existent (*al-mawjūd*) or attributive existence (*al-wujūd al-iḍāfī*)[1] not absolute [existence] (*al-muṭlaq*), since its opposite is non-existence (*al-ʿadam*), which is nothing.[2]

26. Furthermore, the True Existence (*al-Wujūd al-Ḥaqq*) possesses a unity (*waḥdah*) which is not superadded to His Essence, but is rather His being considered as He is in Himself (*min ḥaythu huwa huwa*), for when considered in this way (*bi-hādhā'l-iʿtibār*) His unity is not an attribute (*naʿt*) of the One (*al-Wāḥid*), but is rather identical with Him. This is what the verifiers (*al-muḥaqqiqīn*) mean by essential oneness (*al-aḥadiyyah al-dhātiyyah*), from which are derived the unity (*al-waḥdah*) and the multiplicity (*al-kathrah*) which are familiar to all (*al-jumhūr*), namely numerical unity and multiplicity. Moreover, if it is considered as being devoid of all aspects (*al-iʿtibārāt*), it is called oneness (*aḥadiyyah*), but if considered as being qualified by them, it is called singleness (*wāḥidiyyah*).[3]

27. *On His Attributes in General.* The Ashʿarites took the position[4] that God has eternal and existent attributes superadded to His Essence. He is, thus, knowing through knowledge, powerful through power, willing through will, and so forth. The philosophers, on the other hand, took the position that His Attributes are identical with His Essence, not in the sense that there is an essence which has an attribute and that the two are in reality united, but rather in the sense that what results from (*yatarattab ʿalā*) His essence is what [in other cases] results from an essence and attribute together. For example, your own essence is not sufficient to reveal things to you but requires for this the attribute of knowledge which subsists in you. God's Essence is altogether different, for, in order that things be revealed and made apparent in Him, God does not need an attribute subsisting in Him. Indeed, all concepts (*al-mafhūmāt*) are revealed to Him through His essence, so that, in this respect, His Essence is the reality of knowledge. It is the same in the

---

1. That is, existence attributed to quiddities. According to Fanārī, *al-wujūd al-iḍāfī* is another way of expressing the concept of *al-mawjūdiyyah*, or being existent. See his *Miṣbāḥ al-uns*, 53.

2. This last sentence is quoted from Fanārī, *Miṣbāḥ al-uns*, 121.

3. For further clarification of the distinction between *aḥadiyyah* and *wāḥidiyyah*, see al-Tahānawī, *Kashshāf*, 1463, under *al-aḥadiyyah*, and 1467, under *al-wāḥidiyyah*; Reynold A. Nicholson, *Studies in Islamic Mysticism*, 94–97; Jāmī, *Lawāʾiḥ*, Flash XVII, 16 of English translation, fols. 11a–11b of Persian text; Qayṣarī, *Maṭlaʿ khuṣūṣ al-kilam*, 11.

4. For the source of this paragraph, see Jurjānī, *Sharḥ al-mawāqif*, VIII, 44–45, 47.

case of His power, for His Essence is effective (*mu'aththirah*) in itself rather than through an attribute superadded to it, as in the case of our own essences. Thus, in this respect, His Essence is power, and consequently His Essence and Attributes are in reality united, although they differ from each other with respect to aspect (*al-i'tibār*) and concept (*al-mafhūm*).

28. As for the Sufis, they took the position that God's Attributes were identical with His Essence with respect to existence (*bi-ḥasab al-wujūd*) but other than it with respect to intellection (*al-ta'aqqul*). Shaykh [Muḥyī al-Dīn ibn 'Arabī] said: 'Some denied His Attributes, although the intuition (*dhawq*) of the prophets and saints testifies to the contrary; others affirmed them and judged them to be completely different from His Essence. This is complete unbelief and pure polytheism.

29. Someone, may God sanctify his soul, said:[1] 'Whoever affirms [God's] Essence but does not affirm [His] Attributes is an ignorant innovator (*mubtadi'*), and whoever affirms Attributes which are entirely different from [His] Essence is an unbelieving dualist (*thanawī kāfir*) as well as ignorant.' He also said: 'Our essences are imperfect (*nāqiṣah*) and are only perfected by attributes, God's Essence, however, is perfect (*kāmilah*) and in no way is in need of anything, for everything which is in need of something in any way is imperfect, and imperfection does not befit the Necessary Existent. His Essence is sufficient for everything and with respect to everything. It is, thus, knowledge with respect to objects of knowledge (*al-ma'lūmāt*), power with respect to objects of will (*al-murādāt*). It is one and has no duality (*ithnayniyyah*) in it whatsoever.'

30. *On His Knowledge.* All are in agreement in affirming His knowledge except a small and insignificant group of early philosophers. Since the theologians affirmed attributes superadded to His Essence, they found no difficulty with respect to the connection (*ta'alluq*) of His knowledge with things outside His Essence by means of forms (*ṣuwar*) corresponding to those things and superadded to Him.

31. Since the philosophers, on the other hand, did not affirm the Attributes, their doctrine was confused on this question. The gist (*ḥāṣil*) of what Shaykh [Ibn Sīnā] said in *al-Ishārāt*[2] was: 'Since the First (*al-Awwal*) apprehends ('*aqala*) His essence by means of His Essence and because His Essence is the cause ('*illah*) of multiplicity (*al-kathrah*), it follows that He apprehends multiplicity because of His apprehension of His Essence by means of His Essence. Thus, his apprehension of multiplicity is a concomitant (*lāzim*) effected by Him (*ma'lūl lahu*), and the forms of multiplicity, which are the objects of His apprehension (*ma'qūlāt*), are also His effects (*ma'lūlāt*) and His concomitants ranked in the order of effects and therefore posterior to (*muta'akhkhirah 'an*) the reality of His Essence as an effect is posterior to its cause. His Essence is not constituted (*mutaqawwimah*) by them or by anything

1. 'Ayn al-Quḍāt al-Hamadānī in his *Zubdat al-ḥaqā'iq*, 40, 42.
2. The quotation, which extends through para. 36, is actually from Naṣīr al-Dīn Ṭūsī, *Sharḥ al-ishārāt, namaṭ* 7, 329–331.

else. It is one, and the multiplicity of concomitants (*al-lawāzim*) and effects (*al-ma'lūlāt*) is not inconsistent with the unity of their cause (*'illah*), of which they are the concomitants, regardless of whether these concomitants are established (*mutaqarrirah*) in the cause itself or distinct (*mubāyinah*) from it. Therefore, the establishment (*taqarrur*) of caused multiplicity (*al-kathrah al-ma'lūlah*) in the Essence of the Self-Subsistent One, who is prior to them with respect to causality (*al-'illiyyah*) and existence, does not necessitate His being multiple. The gist of this is that the Necessary Existent is one, and His unity does not cease on account of the multiplicity of the forms established in Him.'

32. To this the learned commentator [Naṣīr al-Dīn Ṭūsī][1] objected: 'There is no doubt that to acknowledge the establishment of concomitants of the First in His Essence is to acknowledge that a single thing can be both an agent (*fā'il*) and a recipient (*qābil*) at the same time, that the First is qualified by Attributes that are neither relative (*iḍāfiyyah*) nor negative (*salbiyyah*), that He is a substratum (*maḥall*) for His multiple and contingent effects, may He be high exalted above that, that His first effect is not distinct (*mubāyin*) from His Essence, and that He does not bring into existence (*lā yūjid*) anything which is distinct from Him through His own Essence anything but rather through the mediacy (*tawassuṭ*) of entities subsisting in Him, as well as other [propositions] which contradict the apparent positions (*madhāhib*) of the philosophers. In fact, the early philosophers who denied God's knowledge, as well as Plato, who affirmed the self-subsistence of intelligible forms (*al-ṣuwar al-ma'qūlah*), and the Peripatetics, who affirmed the union of knower (*al-'āqil*) and known (*al-ma'qūl*), took these absurd positions only in order to avoid committing themselves to such ideas as these.'

33. He then indicated what he himself believed the truth to be, saying:[2] 'Just as an apprehender in perceiving his own essence through his essence does not require a form other than the form of his own essence through which he is what he is, so also in perceiving that which emanates from his essence he does not need any form other than the form of the emanation through which the emanation is what it is. Consider your own case when you apprehend something by means of a form which you have imagined or brought to mind. This form does not emanate absolutely from you alone, but rather with a certain participation of something else. Nevertheless, you do not apprehend that thing through the form, but rather, just as you apprehend that thing through the form, so also do you apprehend the form itself through the same form without there being any doubling of forms within you. Indeed, the only things that double are your [mental] considerations (*i'tibārāt*) connected with your essence and that form only, or by way of superimposition (*al-tarakkub*). If such is your situation (*ḥāl*) with respect to what emanates from you with the participation of something besides

1. See Ṭūsī, *Sharḥ al-ishārāt*, 329.
2. See Ṭūsī, *Sharḥ al-ishārāt*, 330–331.

yourself, what, then, do you think of the situation of an apprehender (*al-ʿāqil*) with respect to what emanates solely from his own essence without the intervention (*mudākhalah*) of anything else?'

34. 'Do not think that a condition for your apprehending this form is your being a substratum (*maḥall*) for it, for you apprehend your own essence, although you are not a substratum for it. Your being a substratum for that form is merely a condition for the occurrence (*ḥuṣūl*) of that form to you, and the occurrence is, in turn, a condition for your apprehending the form. Therefore, if the form occurs to you in any way other than by inhering (*al-ḥulūl*) in you, then the apprehension (*al-taʿaqqul*) also occurs without inhering in you. It is well known that the occurrence [of the form] of a thing to its agent (*fāʿil*), insofar as it occurs to something other than itself, is not inferior to its occurrence to its recipient (*qābil*). Therefore, the essential effects (*al-maʿlūlāt al-dhātiyyah*) of the Apprehender and Agent through His Essence (*al-ʿāqil al-fāʿil li-dhātihi*) occur to Him without inhering in Him, and He apprehends them without their being inherent in Him.'

35. 'Having presented the foregoing I proceed as follows: You have learned that the First apprehends His Essence without there being any difference (*taghāyur*), with respect to existence (*fīʾl-wujūd*), between His Essence and His apprehension of His essence, except as conceived in the minds of those considering [this] (*fī iʿtībār al-muʿtabirīn*). Moreover, you have concluded (*ḥakamta*) that His apprehension of His Essence is the cause (*ʿillah*) of His apprehension of the first effect (*al-maʿlūl al-awwal*). Therefore, if you have concluded that the two causes, namely, His Essence and His apprehension of His Essence, are one thing with respect to existence without there being any difference between them, you can conclude that the two effects also, namely, the first effect and the First's apprehension of it, are, with respect to existence, one thing without there being any difference between them which would require one of them to be distinct (*mubāyin*) from the First and the other to be established (*muqarrar*) in Him. Therefore, just as you concluded that the difference between the two causes was purely mental (*iʿtibārī*), you can conclude that the difference between the two effects is also mental. The existence of the first effect is thus identical with the First's apprehension of it without there being any need for a newly effused form (*ṣūrah mustafāḍah mustaʾnafah*) to subsist in the Essence of the First, may He be exalted above that.'

36. 'Furthermore, since the intellectual substances (*al-jawāhir al-ʿaqliyyah*) apprehend those things which are not effects of theirs through the occurrence of the forms of those things in them, and since they also apprehend the Necessarily Existent First (*al-Awwal al-Wājib*), and because nothing exists which is not an effect of the Necessarily Existent First, all the forms of both universal and particular beings, exactly as they are in existence (*ʿalā mā ʿalayhiʾl-wujūd*), occur in them. The Necessarily Existent First apprehends these [intellectual] substances, together with these forms, not through other forms but rather through those identical substances

and forms. In this way [He apprehends] existence exactly as it is (*al-wujūd ʿalā mā huwa ʿalayhi*). Thus, 'not an atom's weight escapes Him'[1] nor must any of the aforementioned impossibilities be resorted to.' End of quotation from Ṭūsī.

37. One of the commentators on the *Fuṣūṣ al-ḥikam*[2] raised against him the objection that because those intellectual substances are contingent (*mumkinah*), they are therefore originated (*ḥādithah*) and preceded by essential non-existence (*al-ʿadam al-dhātī*), as well as known to the Truth (*al-Ḥaqq*) before their existence. How, then, can the First's knowledge (*ʿilm*) of them be identical with their existence? Furthermore, [such a position] nullifies divine providence (*al-ʿināyah*), which is explained by the philosophers as [God's] active and eternal knowledge (*al-ʿilm al-azalī al-fiʿlī*) connected with universals in a universal manner (*kullīyan*) and with particulars in a universal manner also and which is prior to the existence of things. Moreover, it also implies that His Essence, with respect to the most noble of His Attributes, is in need of that which is other than He and emanates from Him. The truth is that one who is fair-minded will realize that He who created (*abdaʿa*) things and brought them out of non-existence into existence, whether that non-existence was temporal (*zamānī*) or not, knew both the realities of those things and their concomitant mental and external forms (*ṣuwaruha al-lāzimah lahā al-dhihniyyah wa'l-khārijiyyah*) before He brought them into existence. Otherwise, it would have been impossible to give them existence. Thus, knowledge of them is not the same as their existence. Moreover, the doctrine that it is impossible for His Essence and His knowledge, which is identical with His essence, to be a substratum (*maḥall*) for multiple entities is valid only if they are distinct from Him, as in the opinion of those veiled from the truth (*al-maḥjūbīn ʿan al-ḥaqq*). If, on the other hand, they are identical with Him with respect to existence (*al-wujūd*) and reality (*al-ḥaqīqah*), but different from Him with respect to determination (*al-taqayyud*) and individuation (*al-taʿayyun*), then it is not impossible [for Him to be a substratum]. In reality, however, He is neither subsistent (*ḥāll*) nor is He a substratum (*maḥall*), but is, rather, a single thing appearing sometimes with the quality of being a substratum (*al-maḥalliyyah*) and at other times with the quality of being subsistent (*al-ḥālliyyah*).

38. *Further Substantiation.* If the First knows His Essence through His Essence, He is, considering that He knows and is known, both a knower (*ʿālim*) and something known (*maʿlūm*), and, insofar as He knows His Essence through His Essence and not through a form superadded to Him, He is knowledge (*ʿilm*). Three things are thus involved which are indistinguishable from each other except as considered in the mind (*bi-ḥasab al-iʿtibār*). If His Essence is considered (*uʿtubira*) as being a cause (*sabab*) for His appearing to Himself, then luminosity (*al-nūriyyah*) attaches

1. Qur'ān 34:3.

2. Dāwūd ibn Maḥmūd al-Qayṣarī. See his *Maṭlaʿ khuṣūṣ al-kilam*, 16–17, quotations from which constitute most of this paragraph.

to Him. If He is considered as being a giver of existence (*wājid*) to the object of His knowledge (*maʿlūm*) and not a depriver of it (*ghayr fāqid lahū*), as being present with it (*shāhid iyyāhū*) and not being absent from it (*ghayr ghāʾib ʿanhū*), then the relation (*nisbah*) of existence (*al-wujūd*), of presence (*al-shuhūd*), of giving existence (*al-wājidiyyah*), of receiving existence (*al-mawjūdiyyah*), of being present (*al-shāhidiyyah*), and of being the object of presence (*al-mashhūdiyyah*) is determined.[1]

39. There is no doubt that His knowledge of His Essence and of these considerations (*al-iʿtibārāt*), which are His Attributes, does not require a form superadded to Him. Neither does His knowledge of the quiddities (*māhiyyāt*) of things or their ipseities (*huwiyyāt*), for their quiddities and ipseities are nothing but His transcendent essence (*al-dhāt al-mutaʿāliyah*) clothed in these aforementioned considerations whose intellections are derived one from another (*al-muntashiʾat al-taʿaqqul baʿḍuhā ʿan baʿḍ*), collectively and individually (*jamʿan wa-furādā*) in either a universal or a particular manner (*ʿalā wajh kullī aw juzʾī*). Thus, in knowing them He does not need a superadded form (*ṣūrah zāʾidah*), and consequently there is neither act (*fiʿl*) nor receptivity (*qabūl*), nor subsistent (*ḥāll*) nor substratum (*maḥall*). Moreover, He has no need, with respect to any of His perfections, for what is other than He and emanates from Him. High may He be exalted above what the evildoers say!

40. *That His Knowledge of His Essence is the Source* (mansha') *of His Knowledge of all Other Things.* The philosophers said: the First knows things by reason of His knowledge of His Essence. This is because He knows His Essence, which is the origin (*mabdaʾ*) of the particulars of a thing (*tafāṣīl al-ashyāʾ*). He thus possesses a simple entity (*amr basīṭ*), which is the origin of His knowledge of the particulars of things, and this is His knowledge of His Essence. This is because knowledge of the cause entails knowledge of its effects regardless of whether these effects occur through an intermediary (*wāsiṭah*) or not. Thus, His knowledge of His Essence, which is the essential cause (*ʿillah dhātiyyah*) of the first effect (*al-maʿlūl al-awwal*), includes knowledge of the first effect. Then the combination [of the two] is

---

1. The meaning of the last half of this paragraph is not clear to me, and I have consequently resorted to a completely literal translation of it. Muḥammad Maʿṣūm in his commentary on *al-Durrah al-fākhirah* entitled *al-Farīdah al-nādirah*, fol. 142a, interprets *al-nūriyyah* (luminosity) to mean *ʿilm* (knowledge) and *al-shāhidiyyah* to mean *al-ʿālimiyyah* (being a knower) and *al-maʿlūmiyyah* (being an object of knowledge) respectively. If such is the case the last half of this paragraph can be interpreted as follows:

If God's Essence is the cause of His self-knowledge, that is, if He knows His Essence through His essence directly rather than through a superadded form, then He can be said to be knowledge or luminosity (*al-nūriyyah*). If he is further considered as being the cause of His own existence, that is, as being a giver of existence to His Essence which is also the object of His knowledge, and as being present to His Essence, that is, being a knower of His Essence, then He can be said to have six aspects: existence (*wujūd*), being a giver of existence (*wājidiyyah*), being a recipient of existence (*mawjūdiyyah*), knowledge (*shuhūd*), being a knower (*shāhidiyyah*), and being an object of knowledge (*mashhūdiyyah*).

a proximate cause (*ʿillah qarībah*) of the second effect (*al-maʿlūl al-thānī*), so that knowledge of it is entailed also, and so on to the last effect. Thus, His knowledge of His Essence includes the knowledge of all existents as a whole (*ijmālan*). Moreover, if what is in His knowledge is particularized (*fuṣṣila*), these existents then become differentiated from each other and particularized (*mufaṣṣalah*). His knowledge is thus like a simple entity (*amr basīṭ*) which is the origin (*mabdaʾ*) of the particulars of numerous things (*tafāṣīl umūr mutaʿaddidah*), and just as His Essence is the origin of the characteristics (*khuṣūṣiyyāt*) of things and their particulars (*tafāṣīl*), so is His knowledge of His Essence the origin of His cognitions (*al-ʿulūm*) of things and their particulars. This is analogous to what has been said to the effect that knowledge of a quiddity includes the knowledge of its parts (*ajzāʾ*) as a whole (*ijmālan*), and that such knowledge is the origin of its particulars.

41. Do not let it escape you that this doctrine implies His knowledge of particulars (*al-juzʾiyyāt*) as particulars, for particulars are caused by Him just as are universals, and He must, therefore, know them also. Although the philosophers are known for having claimed that He has no knowledge of particulars as particulars, since this would imply change (*al-taghayyur*) in His real Attributes (*ṣifātihā al-ḥaqīqiyyah*), one of the more recent philosophers (*baʿḍ al-mutaʾakhkhirīn*) has disclaimed this, saying:[1] 'The denial that His knowledge is connected with particulars is something that has been ascribed to the philosophers by those who do not understand their doctrine. How can they deny that His knowledge is connected with particulars when these emanate from Him, and when, in their opinion, He apprehends His Essence, and when their position is that knowledge of the cause necessitates knowledge of the effect? Indeed, having denied His being in space, they made the relation of all places to Him a single identical relation (*nisbah wāḥidah mutasāwiyah*), and having denied His being in time, they also made the relation to Him of all times, past, future, and present, a single relation. They maintained that just as one who knows places, although he is not himself spatial (*makānī*), knows, nevertheless, Zayd's position with respect to ʿAmr's, how each of them can be pointed out with respect to the other, and what the distance between them is, and so forth with respect to all substances of the universe (*dhawāt al-ʿālam*) and just as he does not relate any of these things to himself because he is not spatial (*makānī*), so also does one who knows times, if he is not himself temporal (*zamānī*) know at what time Zayd is born and at what time ʿAmr, how much time separates them, and so forth with respect to all events tied to [particular] times. He does not relate any of them to a [particular] time which is [then] present to him, and therefore, does not say: This has passed, this has not yet happened, and this exists now. Rather, all things which are in time are present to him and equally related to

1. Naṣīr al-Dīn Ṭūsī in his *Risālah* to Ṣadr al-Dīn al-Qūnawī, MS Warner Or. 1133, fol. 33a–33b; Wetzstein II 1806, fol. 41a–41b; MS Vat. Arab. 1453, fols. 21b–22a. The quotation extends to the end of para. 42.

him, although he knows their relationship to each other as well as the priority of some of them to the others.'

42. 'Although this [doctrine] was established among them, and they determined upon it, nevertheless the estimations (*awhām*) of those immersed in space and time were unable to understand it, and some of them consequently judged God to be spatial, and they point to a place proper to Him. Others judged Him to be temporal and say that this has passed Him and that that has not yet happened to Him. They therefore attribute to those who deny this of Him the doctrine that He does not have knowledge of temporal particulars (*al-juz'iyyāt al-zamāniyyah*), although such is not the case.'

43. The Sufis, may God sanctify their souls, say that inasmuch as the Truth (*al-ḥaqq*) necessitated (*iqtaḍā'*) everything either through His Essence or through one or more conditions (*shurūṭ*), everything is therefore one of His concomitants or a concomitant of one of His concomitants, and so forth. Consequently, the Creator (*al-Ṣāniʿ*), who is not distracted from anything by anything, the Kindly One and the Well-Informed (*al-Laṭīf al-Khabīr*), who lacks no perfection, inevitably knows His Essence as well as the concomitant of His Essence and the concomitant of His concomitant, both collectively and individually (*jamʿan wa-furādā*), as a whole and in particular (*ijmālan wa-tafṣīlan*) to an infinite degree. They also say[1] that the Truth, because of His essential absoluteness (*iṭlāqihi al-dhātī*) possesses essential coextension (*al-maʿiyyah al-dhātiyyah*)[2] with every existent thing, and that his being present (*ḥuḍūr*) with things is His knowledge of them, so that not an atom's weight escapes His knowledge on earth or in the heavens.

44. The gist of this is that He knows things in two ways. One of these is through the chain of succession [of causes and effects] (*silsilat al-tartīb*) in a manner close to that of the philosophers. The other is through his oneness (*aḥadiyyah*), which encompasses all things. It is obvious, of course, that His knowledge of things by the second way is preceded by His knowledge of them by the first way, for the first is absentational knowledge (*ʿilm ghaybī*) of them prior to their existence, and the second is presentational knowledge (*ʿilm shuhūdī*) of them during their existence. In reality, however, there are not two knowledges, but rather there attaches to the first knowledge through (*bi-wāsiṭah*) the existence of its connection (*mutaʿalliq*), that is, the thing known (*al-maʿlūm*), a relation (*nisbah*) in consideration of which we call that knowledge presence (*shuhūd*) and attendance (*ḥuḍūr*). It is not that another knowledge has originated. Should you say that this implies that His knowledge by the second way is limited to presently existing things (*al-mawjūdāt*

1. This last sentence is quoted from al-Fanārī, *Miṣbāḥ al-uns*, 60. See also Qur'ān 10:61, and 34:3.

2. The literal meaning of *maʿiyyah* is 'witness'. According to Ḥusaynābādī in his commentary, *al-Risālah al-qudsiyyah*, fol. 112b, God's coextension is not like the coextension of substances and accidents but, on the contrary, like that of the soul with the body.

al-ḥāliyyah), I should answer yes, but all existents in relation to Him are present, since [all] times are the same in relation to Him as well as present (*ḥāḍirah*) with Him, as has just been mentioned in the quotation from one of the verifiers (*baʿḍ al-muḥaqqiqīn*).[1]

45. *On His Will (al-irādah)*. Both the theologians and the philosophers agreed in asserting the doctrine that He is willing (*murīd*), although there was great difference as to what was meant by His will. In the view of the theologians from among the people of the approved way (*ahl al-sunnah*) His will is an eternal Attribute (*ṣifah qadīmah*) superadded (*zāʾidah*) to His Essence, as is the case with the rest of His real Attributes (*al-ṣifāt al-ḥaqīqiyyah*). In the opinion of the philosophers, however, it is His knowledge of the most perfect order (*al-niẓām al-akmal*), which they call providence (*ʿināyah*). Ibn Sīnā said: 'Providence is the First's all-encompassing knowledge of everything and of how everything should be, so as to be in the best order (*aḥsan al-niẓām*). Thus, the First's knowledge of the correct manner (*kayfiyyat al-ṣawāb*) for the arrangement of the existence of the whole (*tartīb wujūd al-kull*) is the fountainhead (*manbaʿ*) for the effusion (*fayaḍān*) of good (*al-khayr*) over the whole, without there arising any intention (*qaṣd*) or desire (*ṭalab*) on the part of the True First (*al-Awwal al-Ḥaqq*).[2]

46. In clarification of the two positions we can say that it is obvious that our mere knowledge of what can possibly emanate from us is not sufficient for its occurrence. On the contrary, we experience within ourselves a certain psychical state (*ḥālah nafsāniyyah*) following upon our knowledge of what it would contain of benefit (*al-maṣlaḥah*). We then need to move the members [of the body] by means of the force (*al-qūwwah*) distributed in our muscles. It is our essence (*dhāt*), then, that is the agent (*al-fāʿil*), and our muscular force that is the power (*al-qudrah*). Moreover, the conceiving (*taṣawwur*) of that thing [which is to emanate] is [our] awareness (*al-shuʿūr*) of the object of that power (*al-maqdūr*), and the knowledge of the benefit [to be derived] is [our] knowledge of the goal (*al-ghāyah*). The psychical state called inclination (*al-mayalān*) is what follows upon [our] desire (*al-shawq*) which, in turn, stems from [our] knowledge of the goal. These are all entities distinct from each other, and each one has a role (*madkhal*) in the emanation of that thing.

47. Those theologians who deny that His acts are motivated by purposes (*aghrāḍ*) affirm to Him an Essence and a power (*qudrah*) superadded to His Essence, as well as knowledge of the object of that power (*al-maqdūr*) and of the benefit [to be found] in it, also superadded to His Essence, and will (*irādah*). They ascribe a role in bringing-into-existence (*al-ījād*) to all of these with the

---

1. That is, the quotation from Ṭūsī found in paragraphs 41 and 42.

2. Jāmī's source for the first part of this paragraph is Taftāzānī, *Sharḥ al-maqāṣid*, II, 69. The rest of the paragraph including the quotation from Ibn Sīnā is derived from Jurjānī, *Sharḥ al-mawāqif*, VIII, 81. The original source of the quotation from Ibn Sīnā is his *al-Ishārāt wa'l-tanbīhāt*, Part 3, *namaṭ* 7, 729–730.

exception of the knowledge of the benefit, for it is a purpose and goal not a final cause (*'illah ghā'iyyah*).

48. The philosophers, on the other hand, affirmed of Him an Essence and a knowledge of things which is identical with His Essence. They make His Essence and His knowledge together sufficient for bringing-into-existence (*al-ījād*), because His knowledge is identical with both His power and His will and is consequently sufficient for emanation (*al-ṣudūr*). He does not posses a state similar to the psychical inclination (*al-mayalān al-nafsānī*) which humans possess. What in our case emanates from the essence together with its attributes emanates from Him through the Essence alone. This is the meaning of the union (*ittiḥād*) of Attributes with Essence. The emanation of an act from Him is not like its emanation from us, nor is it like its emanation from such things as fire and the sun which have no awareness of what emanates from them.

Select Bibliography

Abbreviations

EI2	*The Encyclopaedia of Islam*, New edition
EIR	*Encyclopaedia Iranica*
JRAS	*Journal of the Royal Asiatic Society*

Primary Sources

Āmulī, Sayyid Ḥaydar. *La Philosophie shiʿite*, ed. Henry Corbin and Osman Yahya. Paris, 1975.

— *Le Texte des textes, Commentaire des Foṣûṣ al-ḥikam d'Ibn ʿArabī*, ed. Henry Corbin and Osman Yahya. Tehran-Paris, 1975.

Bākharzī, ʿA. *Maqāmāt Jāmī*, ed. N. M. Hirawī. Tehran, 1371 Sh./1992.

Chézy, A. L. *Médjnoun et Leila: Poème traduit du persan*. Paris, 1805.

Dawānī, Jalāl al-Dīn. *Practical Philosophy of the Mohammadan People*. London, 1839.

— *Shawākil al-ḥūr fī sharḥ hayākil al-nūr*, ed. M. ʿAbdul Ḥaq and M. Y. Kokan. Madras, 1953.

Hidāyat, Riḍā Qulī Khān. *Majmaʿ al-fuṣaḥāʾ*, ed. M. Muṣaffā. Tehran, 1336 Sh./1957.

al-Ḥurr al-ʿĀmilī. *ʿAmal al-ʿāmil fī dhikr ʿulamāʾ Jabal ʿĀmil*. Tehran, 1306 Sh./1927.

Ibn Abī Uṣaybiʿah. *ʿUyūn al-anbāʾ fī ṭabaqāt al-aṭibbāʾ*, ed. August Müller. Beirut, 1965.

Ibn Khallikān. *Wafayāt al-aʿyān*, ed. I. ʿAbbās. Beirut, 1965.

Ibn Turkah, Ṣāʾin al-Dīn. *Tamhīd al-qawāʿid*, ed. S. J. Āshtiyānī. Tehran, 1976.

Jāmī, ʿAbd al-Raḥmān. *Naqd al-nuṣūṣ fī sharḥ al-fuṣūṣ*, ed. William C. Chittick. Tehran, 1977.

— *Tuḥfat al-aḥrār, Haft awrang, Khirad nāmā-yi iskandarī, al-Durrah al-fākhirah*, ed. A. Musawī Bihbahānī. Tehran, 1358 Sh./1980.

Jāmī, ʿAbd al-Raḥmān. *Ashiʿʿat al-lamaʿāt*, ed. H. Rabbānī. Tehran, 1362 Sh./1983.

Khwāndmir, Ghiyāth al-Dīn. *Ḥabīb al-siyar*, ed. J. Humāʾī. Tehran, 1333 Sh./1954.

al-Khwansārī, Muḥammad Bāqir. *Rawḍāt al-jannāt*. Tehran, 1341 Sh./1962.

al-Majlisī, M. B. *Biḥār al-anwār*, vol. 25. Tehran, 1315/1897.

Mudarris, M. A. *Rayḥanāt al-adab*. Tehran, 1954.

Nawā'ī, Amīr 'Alīshīr. *Majālis al-anfās*. Tehran, 1363/1944.

Rashīd al-Dīn Faḍl Allāh. *Jāmi' al-tawārīkh: Tārīkh-i Ghāzānī*, ed. and French tr. Etienne Marc Quatremère as *Histoire des Mongols de la Perse*. Paris, 1836.

— *Jāmi' al-tawārīkh: qismat-i Ismā'īliyān*, ed. M. T. Dānishpazhūh and M. Mudarrisī Zanjānī. Tehran, 1338 Sh./1959.

Shahrazūrī, Shams al-Dīn Muḥammad. *Nuzhat al-arwāḥ wa rawḍat al-afrāḥ fī ta'rīkh al-ḥukamā' wa'l-falāsifah*, ed. Kh. Ahmad. Haydarabad, 1976.

— *al-Shajarah al-ilāhiyyah*, ed. N. Ḥabībī. Tehran, 1383/1963.

— *Sharḥ ḥikmat al-ishrāq*, translated by H. Ziai with critical edition, English and Persian introductions, notes and indexes, as *Commentary on the Philosophy of Illumination*. Tehran, 1993; 2nd ed., 2002.

al-Shūshtarī, Qāḍī Nūr Allāh. *Majālis al-mu'minīn*. Tehran, 1268/1852.

Suhrawardī, Shihāb al-Dīn. *L'archange empourpré*, tr. Henry Corbin. Paris, 1976.

— *Opera metaphysica et mystica 1*, ed. H. Corbin, Tehran, 2001; *Opera metaphysica et mystica* 2, ed. H. Corbin, Tehran, 2001; *Opera metaphysica et mystica* 3, ed. S.H. Nasr. Tehran, 2001; *Opera metaphysica et mystica* 4, ed. N. Ḥabībī with introduction by S.H. Nasr. Tehran, 2001.

— *Ḥikmat al-ishrāq*, tr. J. Walbridge and H. Ziai as *The Philosophy of Illumination*. Provo, UT, 1999.

— *Partaw-nāmah*, ed. and tr. H. Ziai as *The Book of Radiance*. Costa Mesa, CA, 1998.

— *The Philosophical Allegories and Mystical Treatises*, ed. and tr. W. M. Thackston. Costa Mesa, CA, 1999.

al-Tafrishī, M. *Naqd al-rijāl*. Tehran, 1318/1900.

Ṭūsī, Naṣīr al-Dīn. *Sayr wa sulūk*, ed. and tr. S. J. Badakhchānī as *Contemplation and Action*. London, 1998.

— *Risālah andar qismat-i mawjūdāt*, tr. P. Morewedge as *The Metaphysics of Ṭūsī*. New York, 1992.

— *Akhlāq-i nāṣirī*, tr. G. M. Wickens as *Nasirean Ethics*. London, 1964.

al-Waṣṣāf, M. *Tajziyat al-amṣāt*, ed. J. von Hammer-Purgstall. Vienna, 1856.

Secondary Sources

Addas, Claude. *Quest for the Red Sulphur: The Life of Ibn 'Arabī*, tr. Peter Kingsley. Cambridge, 1993.

Aminrazavi, Mehdi. 'Suhrawardī', *Oxford Bibliographies Online*. http://oxfordbibliographiesonline.com

— *Suhrawardī and the School of Illumination*. London, 1993.

Anawati, Georges C. *Études de philosophie musulmane*. Paris, 1974.

— and Louis Gardet. *Introduction à la théologie musulmane*. Paris, 1948.

Bāmdād, Mahdī. *Sharḥ-i ḥāl-i rijāl-i Īrān*. Tehran, 1347–1350 Sh./1968–1971.

Barakat, Muḥammad. *Kitāb-shināsī-yi maktab-i falsafī-yi Shīrāz*. Shiraz, 2004.

Beale, Thomas W. *An Oriental Biographical Dictionary*, new rev. ed. Henry G. Keene. London, 1894.

Brockelmann, Carl. *Geschichte der arabischen Litteratur*. Leiden, 1942.

Browne, Edward G. *A Literary History of Persia*. Cambridge, 2009.

Cahen, Claude. *Introduction à l'histoire du monde musulman médiéval: VIIe-XVe siècle*. Paris, 1982.

Carra de Vaux, Bernard. *Gazali*. Paris, 1902.

— 'Les sphères célestes selon Nasir-Eddin Attusi', in P. Tannery, ed., *Recherches sur l'histoire de l'astronomie ancienne*. Paris, 1893.

Chittick, William. 'The Central Point: Qūnawī's Role in the School of Ibn 'Arabī', *Journal of the Muhyiddin Ibn 'Arabi Society*, 35 (2004), pp. 25–45.

— 'The Circle of Spiritual Ascent according to al-Qūnawī', in P. Morewedge, ed., *Neo-Platonism and Islamic Thought*. Albany, NY, 1992.

— *Faith and Practice of Islam*. Albany, NY, 1992.

— 'Ibn 'Arabī and His School', in S. H. Nasr, ed., *Islamic Spirituality: Manifestations*. New York, 1991, pp. 49–79.

— 'The Five Divine Presences: From al-Qūnawī to al-Qayṣarī', *The Muslim World*, 72 (1982), pp. 107–128.

— 'The Last Will and Testament of Ibn 'Arabī's Foremost Disciple and Some Notes on its Author', *Sophia Perennis*, 4 (1978), pp. 43–58.

— 'Mysticism vs. Philosophy in Earlier Islamic History: The al-Ṭūsī, al-Qūnawī Correspondence', *Religious Studies*, 17 (1981), pp. 87–104.

— 'Ṣadr al-Dīn Qūnawī', *EI2*, vol. 7, pp. 753–755.

— 'Ṣadr al-Dīn Qunawī on the Oneness of Being', *International Philosophical Quarterly*, 21 (1981), pp. 171–184.

Corbin, Henry. *Avicenna and the Visionary Recital*, tr. W. R. Trask. Princeton, NJ, 1958.

— *En Islam iranien: Aspects spirituels et philosophiques*. Paris, 1971–1972.

— *History of Islamic Philosophy*, tr. L. Sherrard with the assistance of Ph. Sherrard. London, 1993.

— *Spiritual Body and Celestial Earth: From Mazdean Iran to Shi'ite Iran*, tr. N. Pearson. Princeton, NJ, 1977.

— ed. *Trilogie ismaélienne*. Tehran-Paris, 1961.

Cruz Hernández, Miguel. *Historia del pensamiento en al-Andalus*. Seville, 1985.

Daftary, Farhad. *The Ismā'īlīs: Their History and Doctrines*. Cambridge, 1990; 2nd ed. 2007.

Dānishpazhūh, Muḥammad Taqī. *Fihrist-i kitābhā-yi ihdā'ī-yi Sayyid Muḥammad Mishkāt*. Tehran, 1975.

Donaldson, Dwight. M. *Studies in Muslim Ethics*. London, 1953.

Duchesne-Guillemin, Jacques. *La Religion de l'Iran ancien*. Paris, 1962.

Fakhry, Majid. *History of Islamic Philosophy*. New York, 1983.

Ḥalabī, 'Alī Aṣghar. *Tārīkh-i falsafah dar Irān wa jahān-i islāmī*. Tehran, 1373 Sh./1994.

Ha'iri Yazdi, Mehdi. *The Principles of Epistemology in Islamic Philosophy: Knowledge by Presence*. Albany, NY, 1992.

von Hammer-Purgstall, Joseph. *Geschichte der Ilchane*. Darmstadt, 1842.

Ḥikmat, 'Alī Aṣghar. *Jāmī*. Tehran, 1363 Sh./1984.

Hirawī, Najīb Māyil. *Shaykh 'Abd al-Raḥmān Jāmī*. Tehran, 1377 Sh./1998.

Horten, Max. *Die philosophischen Ansichten von Rāzī und Ṭūsī*. Bonn, 1910.

— *Die spekulative und positive Theologie des Islam nach Rāzī und ihre Kritik durch Ṭūsī*. Leipzig, 1912.

Ibrāhīmī Dīnānī, Ghulām Ḥusayn. *Shu'ā'-i andīshah wa shuhūd dar falsafa-yi Suhrawardī*. Tehran, 1364 Sh./1985.

— *Manṭiq wa ma'rifat dar naẓar-i Ghazzālī*. Tehran, 1370 Sh./1991.

Iqbāl, 'Alī. "'Allāmah Quṭb al-Dīn Shīrāzī', *Majalla-yi Armaghān*, 16 (1311 Sh./1932), pp. 659–668.

Iqbal, Muḥammad. *The Development of Metaphysics in Persia*. London, 2001.

Izutsu, Toshihiko. *The Fundamental Structure of Sabzawārī's Metaphysics*. Tehran, 1968.

Jambet, Christian. *The Act of Being: The Philosophy of Revelation in Mullā Ṣadrā*, tr. Jeff Fort. New York, 2006.

Kennedy, E. S. 'The Exact Sciences in Iran under the Saljuqs and Mongols', in *The Cambridge History of Iran*, vol. 5, *The Saljuk and Mongol Periods*, ed. John A. Boyle. Cambridge, 1968, pp. 659–679.

Lewisohn, Leonard. *Beyond Faith and Infidelity: The Sufi Poetry and Teachings of Maḥmūd Shabistarī*. London, 1995.

Madelung, Wilferd. 'Naṣīr ad-Dīn Ṭūsī's Ethics between Philosophy, Shi'ism, and Sufism', in R. G. Hovannisian, ed., *Ethics in Islam*. Malibu, CA, 1985, pp. 85–101.

Mihrīn Shūshtarī, 'Abbās. *Outlines of Islamic Culture*. Bangalore, 1938.

Mīnuwī, Mujtabā. 'Mullā Quṭb-i Shīrāzī', in Mujtabā Mīnuwī and Īraj Afshār, ed., *Yād-nāma-yi Irānī-yi Mīnurskī*. Tehran, 1348 Sh./1969.

Mīr, Muḥammad T. "'Allāmah Quṭb al-Dīn Shīrāzī', *Khirad wa-Kūshish*, 2 (1349 Sh./1969), pp. 451–465.

— *Pizishkān-i nāmī-yi pārsī*. Shiraz, 1348 Sh./1970.

— *Sharḥ-i ḥāl wa āthār-i 'Allāmah Quṭb al-Dīn Shīrāzī*. Shiraz, 1355 Sh./1977.

Mishkāt, Sayyid Muḥammad. *Introduction to* 'Durrat al-tāj li-ghurrat al-dībāj' *by Quṭb al-Dīn al-Shīrāzī*. Tehran, 1317 Sh./1938.

Moris, Zaylan. *Revelation, Intellectual Intuition and Reason in the Philosophy of Mullā Ṣadrā*. London, 2003.

Muṭahharī, Murtaḍā. *Khadamāt-i mutaqābil-i Islām wa Īrān*. Tehran, 1354 Sh./1975.

Nasr, Seyyed Hossein. 'Afḍal al-Dīn Kāshānī and the Philosophical World of Khwājah Naṣīr al-Dīn Ṭūsī', in his *The Islamic Intellectual Tradition in Persia*, Mehdi Aminrazavi, ed., London, 1996, pp. 189–204.

— *Islamic Philosophy from its Origin to the Present*. Albany, NY, 2006.

— 'Quṭb al-Dīn al-Shīrāzī', 'Suhrawardī' and 'Muḥammad ibn Muḥammad Naṣīr al-Dīn Ṭūsī', in *The Islamic Intellectual Tradition in Persia*, pp. 125–175, 207–215, 216–226.

— 'Suhrawardī: The Master of Illumination, Gnostic and Martyr', tr. W. Chittick, *Journal of the Regional Cultural Institute*, 2 (1969), p. 212ff.
— *Three Muslim Sages*. Delmar, NY, 1976.
— and Oliver Leaman, ed., *The History of Islamic Philosophy*. London, 1996.
Nātil Khānlarī, Parwīz. *Haftād sukhan: Az gush-i wa kinār-i adabiyyāt-i fārsī*. Tehran, 1369 Sh./1991.
Netton, Ian R. *Allāh Transcendent*. New York, 1989.
Ohsson, Constantin d'. *Histoire des Mongols depuis Tschingiz Khan jusqu'à Timour Bey*. The Hague, 1834.
Partaw A'ẓam, Abu'l-Qāsim. *Andīshahā-yi falsafī-yi īrānī*. Tehran, 1373 Sh./1994.
Pearson, James Douglas. *Index Islamicus, 1906–1955*. Cambridge 1958 —.
Puech, H. C. 'L'Iran et la philosophie grècque', in Henri Massé ed., *La Civilisation iranienne*. Paris, 1952, pp. 84–88.
Qūnawī, Ṣadr al-Dīn. *Reflection of the Awakened*, tr. Seyyid Hasan Askari. London, 1983.
— *Miftaḥ al-ghayb*. Tehran, 1363 Sh./1984.
Qurbānī, Abu'l-Qāsim. 'The Original Source of Quṭb al-Dīn al-Shīrāzī's Planetary Model', *Journal for the History of Arabic Science*, 3 (1979), pp. 3–18.
Rahman, Fazlur. *The Philosophy of Mullā Ṣadrā*. Albany, NY, 1976.
Rosenthal, Erwin I. J. *Political Thought in Medieval Islam*. Cambridge, 1962.
Ṣadūqī Suhā, Manūchihr. *Ḥukamā wa 'urafā-yi muta'kharīn-i Ṣadr al-muta'āllihīn*. Tehran, 1381 Sh./2002.
Sajjādī, Ja'far. *Shihāb al-Dīn Suhrawardī wa sayrī dar falsafa-yi ishrāq*. Tehran, 1984.
Sauvaget, Jean. *Introduction à l'histoire de l'Orient musulman: Éléments de bibliographie*. Paris, 1946.
Schacht, Joseph and Clifford Edmund Bosworth, ed., *The Legacy of Islam*. Oxford, 1974.
Schmidtke, Sabine. 'Recent Studies on the Philosophy of Illumination', *Dāneshnāmeh: The Bilingual Quarterly of the Shahīd Beheshtī University*, 1 (2003), pp. 101–119.
— *Theologie, Philosophie und Mystik in zwölferschiitischen Islam des 9./15. Jahrhunderts*. Leiden, 2000.
Sezgin, Fuat. *Geschichte der arabischen Schrifttums*. Leiden, 1967 —.
Sharif, Mian Muḥammad, ed. *A History of Muslim Philosophy*. Wiesbaden, 1963–66.
Ṣiddīqī, Bakhtiyār. H. 'Jalāl al-Dīn Dawwānī', in M. M. Sharif, ed., *A History of Muslim Philosophy*, Wiesbaden, 1966, vol. 2, pp. 883–888.
— 'Naṣīr al-Dīn Ṭusī', in M. M. Sharif, ed., *A History of Muslim Philosophy*, Wiesbaden, 1963, vol. 1. pp. 564–580.
Sprenger, Aloys. *The Logic of the Arabians*. Calcutta, 1854.
Stephenson, J. 'The Classification of the Sciences according to Naṣīr al-Dīn Ṭūsī', *Isis*, 5 (1923), pp. 329–338.
Storey, Charles A. *Persian Literature: A Bio-bibliographical Survey*. London, 1927; Persian trans. Y. Āriyanpūr, Tehran, 1362/1983.
Strothmann, Rudolf. *Die Zwölfer-Schī'a*. Leipzig, 1926.

Ülken, Hilmi Ziya. *La Pensée de l'Islam*. Istanbul, 1946.

Ullmann, Manfred. *Die Medizin im Islam*. Leiden–Cologne, 1970.

Walbridge, John. *The Science of Mystic Lights: Quṭb al-Dīn Shīrāzī, and the Illuminationist Tradition in Islamic Philosophy*. Cambridge, MA, 1992.

Wickens, George Michael. 'Aḵlāq-e Jalālī', *EIR*, vol. I, p. 724.

Widengren, Geo. *Die Religionen Irans*. Stuttgart, 1965.

Wiedemann, Eilard. 'Ḳuṭb al-Dīn Shīrāzī', *EI2*, vol. 5, pp. 547–548.

Wüstenfeld, Ferdinand. *Geschichte der arabischen Ärzte und Naturforscher*. Göttingen, 1840.

Ziai, Hossein. *Knowledge and Illumination*. Atlanta, GA, 1990.

— 'Mullā Ṣadrā: His Life and Works', in Nasr and Leaman, ed., *History of Islamic Philosophy*, pp. 635–642.

— 'The Source and Nature of Political Authority in Suhrawardī's Philosophy of Illumination', in Ch. Butterworth, ed., *The Political Aspects of Islamic Philosophy*. Cambridge, MA, 1992, pp. 304–344.

Index